'A major work of investigative history, an extremely valuable contribution to the all-important post-World War Two record . . . the energy and determination of her research, to say nothing of the scepticism that nurtured it, are important signs of stirring intellectual restlessness and even of a kind of incitement, which is what is needed most of all . . . [An] excellent book.' Edward W. Said, *London Review of Books*

'*Who Paid the Piper?* is painstakingly researched and jauntily written, alive to the ironies of a campaign for cultural freedom whose boundaries were circumscribed by its shadowy sponsors . . . what makes the book so readable is the gossipy and compromising detail.' *Independent on Sunday*

'Frances Stonor Saunders's book deserves to take its place as a standard work and a springboard for further investigation.' *Irish Times*

'An absorbing, distressing and, at times, uproariously funny history of this war of delusionary images, a battle for hearts and minds which was conducted by mobilising culture.' *Observer*

'*Who Paid the Piper?* is Frances Stonor Saunders's first book, and an excellent book it is, as lively and bitchy as a literary cocktail party, one might say, penetrating and based on wide research.' *Times Literary Supplement*

'A tale of dollars and dupes, magnificently told by the author with a mixture of meticulous research and high irony.' *The Scotsman*

'*Who Paid the Piper?* illuminates a dark corner of America's cultural history, drawing on an extraordinary range of interviews and recently opened documents. Frances Stonor Saunders is strong on biographical sketches and a thorough researcher.' *Independent*

Frances Stonor Saunders graduated from Oxford University in 1987. She has worked as an independent film producer, and her documentaries include the four-hour series *Hidden Hands: A Different History of Modernism*. Her short story, 'Big Things', was published in *New Writing* 7 in 1998. She lives in London.

Who Paid the Piper?

The CIA and the Cultural Cold War

FRANCES STONOR SAUNDERS

Granta Books
London

Granta Publications, 2/3 Hanover Yard, London N1 8BE

First published in Great Britain by Granta Books 1999
This edition published by Granta Books 2000

A CIP catalogue record for this book is available from the British Library.

1 3 5 7 9 10 8 6 4 2

Typeset by M Rules
Printed and bound in Great Britain by
Mackays of Chatham plc

'What fate or fortune led
Thee down into this place, ere thy last day?
Who is it that thy steps hath piloted?'
'Above there in the clear world on my way,'
I answered him, 'lost in a vale of gloom,
Before my age was full, I went astray.'

Dante's *Inferno*, Canto XV

I know that's a secret, for it's whispered every where.

William Congreve, *Love for Love*

Contents

Acknowledgements

Writing this book has been a prolonged act of vagrancy, as I have dragged my unsightly luggage chain of tatty boxes and files from place to place. For their kindness in taking me in, together with this caravan of archival loot, and offering me the chance to work undisturbed, I wish to thank Elizabeth Cartwright-Hignett, Frank Dabell, Nick Hewer, Eartha Kitt, Hermione Labron-Johnson, Claudia and Marcello Salom. To Ann Pasternak Slater and Craig Raine, I owe special gratitude for their constant support and solid faith. Through them, I met Ben Sonnenberg in New York, and for that flourishing and (on Ben's part) erudite friendship, I am indebted. Ann Pasternak Slater also helped ease my passage by writing a letter of recommendation which, but for her own generous embellishments, followed my draft with uncanny precision. Carmen Callil's support was acquired late into the writing of this book, but counts as a powerful source of inspiration on account of its sheer and unqualified confidence at a time when I had all but lost my own. Jay Weissberg was an invaluable help: as an historian of film, I have yet to meet his equal in scholarship and breadth of knowledge. Further gratitude is extended to those who became partners in a project which had its share of misadventures, but who stayed for the bumpy ride without losing their sense of humour: my editor Neil Belton, my agent Felicity Rubinstein, everyone at Granta Books, copy editor Jane Robertson, Jeremy Bugler, Tony Cash, Tony Carew, Lawrence Simanowitz, André Schiffrin at The New Press, and Melvin Wulf at Beldock, Levine & Hoffman. For their capacious friendship and extraordinarily elastic patience, I am grateful beyond words to Madonna Benjamin, Zoë Heller, Conrad Roeber, Domitilla Ruffo, Roger Thornham and Michael Wylde. But for my mother, Julia Stonor, and my brother, Alexander Stonor Saunders, life outside of this book would have run into a cul-de-sac. For their encouragement, loving support, and endless propping up, I offer them shamelessly hyperbolic thanks and the dedication of this book.

When I started researching the cultural Cold War, I had high hopes of benefiting from America's Freedom of Information Act. It is certainly the case that many previously classified government documents have been released to researchers under this Act, and recent studies of the FBI have been greatly enriched as a result. But retrieving documentation from the CIA is another matter. My initial request to them of 1992 has yet to be answered. A subsequent application was acknowledged, though I was warned that the total cost for supplying the records I had requested would be in the region of $30,000. However, as the CIA's Information and Privacy Coordinator went on to explain that the chances of my application being successfully processed were virtually nil, I had little to worry about. The Freedom of Information Act is much vaunted by British historians, who indeed face far greater challenges in researching material relating to the defence of this realm. But its application, at least as far as the CIA is concerned, is lamentable. Compensating for this is the wealth of documentation existing in private collections. Historically, successive American administrations have spread into the private sector. In the Cold War period especially, American foreign policy was shared between government departments and a kind of consortium of freelance, quasi-governmental figures and institutions. It is this balkanization, even of clandestine or covert operations, which has ensured, paradoxically, that such operations can be scrutinized. The story is there, for those willing to trawl for it, in the sea of private papers stretching across the archives of America.

Any work relying heavily on this archival material is naturally indebted to those many archivists and librarians who so expertly lead the researcher in, through, and out again of the complexities of their collections. These people provide the joists on which the house of history rests, though I hasten to add that responsibility for any structural or architectural blemishes rests entirely with the author. For their help and advice, my thanks go to the staff of the Tamiment Library in New York, the Joseph Regenstein Library in Chicago, the Dwight D. Eisenhower Library in Abilene, the National Archives in Washington, the Butler Library at Columbia University, the George Meany Center in Washington, the Harry Ransom Humanities Research Center and the Lyndon Baines Johnson Library, both in Austin, Texas, the John F. Kennedy Library in Boston, the Harry S. Truman Library in Independence. I also wish to thank the archivists at the Public Records Office in London, and at Reading University Library, and the staff of the London Library.

Many people agreed to be interviewed for this book, and suffered my repeated visits, telephone calls, faxes and letters with elegant patience. All interviewees are named in the Notes and Sources at the end. I thank them all, but in particular Diana Josselson, who was extremely generous with her time, and bestowed on this book the benefit of her sterling memory, her firm (though not uncritical) support, and photographs from her personal collection.

Introduction

> The way to carry out good propaganda is never to appear to be carrying it out at all.
>
> Richard Crossman

During the height of the Cold War, the US government committed vast resources to a secret programme of cultural propaganda in western Europe. A central feature of this programme was to advance the claim that it did not exist. It was managed, in great secrecy, by America's espionage arm, the Central Intelligence Agency. The centrepiece of this covert campaign was the Congress for Cultural Freedom, run by CIA agent Michael Josselson from 1950 till 1967. Its achievements – not least its duration – were considerable. At its peak, the Congress for Cultural Freedom had offices in thirty-five countries, employed dozens of personnel, published over twenty prestige magazines, held art exhibitions, owned a news and features service, organized high-profile international conferences, and rewarded musicians and artists with prizes and public performances. Its mission was to nudge the intelligentsia of western Europe away from its lingering fascination with Marxism and Communism towards a view more accommodating of 'the American way'.

Drawing on an extensive, highly influential network of intelligence personnel, political strategists, the corporate establishment, and the old school ties of the Ivy League universities, the incipient CIA started, from 1947, to build a 'consortium' whose double task it was to inoculate the world against the contagion of Communism, and to ease the passage of American foreign policy interests abroad. The result was a remarkably tight network of people who worked alongside the Agency to promote an idea: that the world needed a *pax Americana*, a new age of enlightenment, and it would be called The American Century.

The consortium which the CIA built up – consisting of what Henry Kissinger described as 'an aristocracy dedicated to the service of this nation on behalf of principles beyond partisanship' – was the hidden weapon in America's Cold War struggle, a weapon which, in the cultural field, had extensive fall-out. Whether they liked it or not, whether they knew it or not, there were few writers, poets, artists, historians, scientists or critics in post-war Europe whose names were not in some way linked to this covert enterprise. Unchallenged, undetected for over twenty years, America's spying establishment operated a sophisticated, substantially endowed cultural front in the West, *for* the West, in the name of freedom of expression. Defining the Cold War as a 'battle for men's minds' it stockpiled a vast arsenal of cultural weapons: journals, books, conferences, seminars, art exhibitions, concerts, awards.

Membership of this consortium included an assorted group of former radicals and leftist intellectuals whose faith in Marxism and Communism had been shattered by evidence of Stalinist totalitarianism. Emerging from the Pink Decade of the 1930s, mourned by Arthur Koestler as an 'abortive revolution of the spirit, a misfired Renaissance, a false dawn of history',[1] their disillusionment was attended by a readiness to join in a new consensus, to affirm a new order which would substitute for the spent forces of the past. The tradition of radical dissenter, where intellectuals took it upon themselves to probe myths, interrogate institutional prerogative, and disturb the complacency of power, was suspended in favour of supporting 'the American proposition'. Endorsed and subsidized by powerful institutions, this non-Communist group became as much a cartel in the intellectual life of the West as Communism had been a few years earlier (and it included many of the same people).

'There came a time . . . when, apparently, life lost the ability to arrange itself,' says Charlie Citrine, the narrator of Saul Bellow's *Humboldt's Gift*. 'It had to *be* arranged. Intellectuals took this as their job. From, say, Machiavelli's time to our own this arranging has been the one great gorgeous tantalizing misleading disastrous project. A man like Humboldt, inspired, shrewd, nutty, was brimming over with the discovery that the human enterprise, so grand and infinitely varied, had now to be managed by exceptional persons. He was an exceptional person, therefore he was an eligible candidate for power. Well, why not?'[2] Like so many Humboldts, those intellectuals who had been betrayed by the false idol of Communism now found themselves gazing at the possibility of building a new Weimar, an American Weimar. If the government – and its covert action arm, the CIA – was prepared to assist in this project, well, why not?

That former left-wingers should have come to be roped together in the same enterprise with the CIA is less implausible than it seems. There was a genuine community of interest and conviction between the Agency and those intellectuals who were hired, even if they didn't know it, to fight the cultural Cold War. The CIA's influence was not 'always, or often, reactionary and sinister',[3] wrote America's pre-eminent liberal historian, Arthur Schlesinger. 'In my experience its leadership was politically enlightened and sophisticated.'[4] This view of the CIA as a haven of liberalism acted as a powerful inducement to collaborate with it, or, if not this, at least to acquiesce to the myth that it was well motivated. And yet this perception sits uncomfortably with the CIA's reputation as a ruthlessly interventionist and frighteningly unaccountable instrument of American Cold War power. This was the organization that masterminded the overthrow of Premier Mossadegh in Iran in 1953, the ousting of the Arbenz government in Guatemala in 1954, the disastrous Bay of Pigs operation in 1961, the notorious Phoenix Program in Vietnam. It spied on tens of thousands of Americans, harassed democratically elected leaders abroad, plotted assassinations, denied these activities to Congress and, in the process, elevated the art of lying to new heights. By what strange alchemy, then, did the CIA manage to present itself to high-minded intellectuals like Arthur Schlesinger as the golden vessel of cherished liberalism?

The extent to which America's spying establishment extended its reach into the cultural affairs of its western allies, acting as unacknowledged facilitator to a broad range of creative activity, positioning intellectuals and their work like chess pieces to be played in the Great Game, remains one of the Cold War's most provocative legacies. The defence mounted by custodians of the period – which rests on the claim that the CIA's substantial financial investment came with no strings attached – has yet to be seriously challenged. Amongst intellectual circles in America and western Europe there persists a readiness to accept as true that the CIA was merely interested in extending the possibilities for free and democratic cultural expression. 'We simply helped people to say what they would have said anyway,' goes this 'blank cheque' line of defence. If the beneficiaries of CIA funds were ignorant of the fact, the argument goes, and if their behaviour was consequently unmodified, then their independence as critical thinkers could not have been affected.

But official documents relating to the cultural Cold War systematically undermine this myth of altruism. The individuals and institutions subsidized by the CIA were expected to perform as part of a broad campaign of persuasion, of a propaganda war in which 'propaganda' was defined as 'any organized effort or movement to disseminate information or a particular doctrine by means of news, special arguments or appeals designed to influence the thoughts and actions of any given group'.[5] A vital constituent of this effort was 'psychological warfare', which was defined as 'The planned use by a nation of propaganda and activities other than combat which communicate ideas and information intended to influence the opinions, attitudes, emotions and behavior of foreign groups in ways that will support the achievement of national aims.' Further, the 'most effective kind of propaganda' was defined as the kind where '*the subject moves in the direction you desire for reasons which he believes to be his own*'.[6] It is useless to dispute these definitions. They are littered across government documents, the *données* of American post-war cultural diplomacy.

Clearly, by camouflaging its investment, the CIA acted on the supposition that its blandishments would be refused if offered openly. What kind of freedom can be advanced by such deception? Freedom of any kind certainly wasn't on the agenda in the Soviet Union, where those writers and intellectuals who were not sent to the gulags were lassoed into serving the interests of the state. It was of course right to oppose such un-freedom. But with what means? Was there any real justification for assuming that the principles of western democracy couldn't be revived in post-war Europe according to some internal mechanism? Or for not assuming that democracy could be more complex than was implied by the lauding of American liberalism? To what degree was it admissible for another state to covertly intervene in the fundamental processes of organic intellectual growth, of free debate and the uninhibited flow of ideas? Did this not risk producing, instead of freedom, a kind of *ur*-freedom, where people think they are acting freely, when in fact they are bound to forces over which they have no control?

The CIA's engagement in cultural warfare raises other troubling questions. Did financial aid distort the process by which intellectuals and their ideas were advanced? Were people selected for their positions, rather than on the basis of intellectual merit? What did Arthur Koestler mean when he lampooned the 'international academic call-girl circuit' of intellectual conferences and symposia? Were reputations secured or enhanced by membership of the CIA's cultural consortium? How many of those writers and thinkers who acquired an international audience for their ideas were really second-raters, ephemeral publicists, whose works were doomed to the basements of second-hand bookstores?

In 1966, a series of articles appeared in the *New York Times* exposing a wide range of covert action undertaken by America's intelligence community. As stories of attempted *coups* and (mostly botched) political assassinations poured on to the front pages, the CIA came to be characterized as a rogue elephant, crashing through the scrubland of international politics, unimpeded by any sense of accountability. Amidst these more dramatic cloak-and-dagger exposés came details of how the American government had looked to the cultural brahmins of the West to lend intellectual weight to its actions.

The suggestion that many intellectuals had been animated by the dictates of American policy-makers rather than by independent standards of their own generated widespread disgust. The moral authority enjoyed by the intelligentsia during the height of the Cold War was now seriously undermined and frequently mocked. The 'consensocracy' was falling apart, the centre could not hold. And as it disintegrated, so the story itself became fragmented, partial, modified – sometimes egregiously – by forces on the right and left who wished to twist its peculiar truths to their own ends. Ironically, the circumstances which made possible the revelations contributed to their real significance becoming obscured. As America's obsessive anti-Communist campaign in Vietnam brought her to the brink of social collapse, and with subsequent scandals on the scale of the Pentagon Papers and Watergate, it was hard to sustain interest or outrage in the business of *Kulturkampf*, which in comparison seemed to be fluff on the side.

'History', wrote Archibald MacLeish, 'is like a badly constructed concert hall, [with] dead spots where the music can't be heard.'[7] This book attempts to record those dead spots. It seeks a different acoustic, a tune other than that played by the official virtuosi of the period. It is a secret history, insofar as it believes in the relevance of the power of personal relationships, of 'soft' linkages and collusions, and the significance of salon diplomacy and boudoir politicking. It challenges what Gore Vidal has described as 'those official fictions that have been agreed upon by all together too many too interested parties, each with his own thousand days in which to set up his own misleading pyramids and obelisks that purport to tell sun time'. Any history which sets out to interrogate these 'agreed-upon facts' must, in Tzvetan Todorov's words, become 'an act of profanity. It is not about contributing to the cult of heroes and saints. It's about coming as close as possible to the truth. It participates in what Max Weber called the "disenchantment of the world"; it exists at the other end of the spectrum from idolatry. It's about redeeming the truth for truth's sake, not retrieving images that are deemed useful for the present.'[8]

1

Exquisite Corpse

> Here is a place of disaffection
> Time before and time after
> In a dim light
>
> T. S. Eliot, 'Burnt Norton'

Europe awoke to a freezing post-war dawn. The winter of 1947 was the worst ever recorded. From January to late March, it opened a front across Germany, Italy, France and Britain, and advanced with complete lack of mercy. Snow fell in St Tropez, gale-force winds building up impenetrable drifts; ice floes drifted to the mouth of the Thames; trains carrying food supplies froze fast to the tracks; barges bringing coal into Paris became ice-bound. There, the philosopher Isaiah Berlin found himself 'terrified' by the city's coldness, 'empty and hollow and dead, like an exquisite corpse'.

Across Europe, water services, sewage disposal, and most other essential amenities collapsed; food supplies dwindled and coal reserves slumped to an all-time low as miners struggled to operate winding-gear which was frozen solid. A slight thaw was followed by a further freeze-up, locking canals and roads under a thick layer of ice. In Britain, unemployment rose by one million in two months. The government and industry stalled in the snow and ice. Life itself seemed to freeze: more than four million sheep and 30,000 cattle died.

In Berlin, Willy Brandt, the future Chancellor, saw a 'new

terror' grip the city which most symbolized the collapse of Europe. The icy cold 'attacked the people like a savage beast, driving them into their homes. But there they found no respite. The windows had no panes, they were nailed up with planks and plasterboard. The walls and ceilings were full of cracks and holes, which people covered over with paper and rags. People heated their rooms with benches from public parks . . . the old and sick froze to death in their beds by the hundreds.'[1] In an emergency measure, each German family was allotted one tree for heating. By early 1946, the Tiergarten had already been hacked down to stumps, its statues left standing in a wilderness of frozen mud; by the winter of 1947, the woods in the famous Grünewald had been razed. The snow drifts which buried the rubble of a bombed-out city could not conceal the devastating legacy of Hitler's mythomaniacal dream for Germany. Berlin, like a ruined Carthage, was a desperate, cold, haunted place – defeated, conquered, occupied.

The weather cruelly drove home the physical reality of the Cold War, carving its way into the new, post-Yalta topography of Europe, its national territories mutilated, the composition of its populations fractured. Allied occupation governments in France, Germany, Austria and Italy struggled to cope with the thirteen million people who were displaced, homeless, demobilized. The swelling ranks of Allied personnel arriving in the occupied territories exacerbated the problem. More and more people were turned out of their homes, to join those already sleeping in halls, stairways, cellars, and bomb-sites. Clarissa Churchill, as a guest of the British Control Commission in Berlin, found herself 'protected both geographically and materially from the full impact of the chaos and misery existing in the city. Waking in the warm bedroom of some Nazi's ex-home, feeling the lace-edged sheets, studying his shelf of books, even these simple experiences gave me a warning tinge of conqueror's delirium, which a short walk in the streets or a visit to an unheated German flat immediately dissipated.'[2]

These were heady days for the victors. In 1947, a carton of American cigarettes, costing fifty cents in an American base, was worth 1,800 Reichsmarks on the black market, or $180 at the legal rate of exchange. For four cartons of cigarettes, at this rate, you could hire a German orchestra for the evening. Or for twenty-four cartons, you could acquire a 1939 Mercedes-Benz. Penicillin and 'Persilscheine' (whiter than white) certificates, which cleared the holder of any Nazi connections, commanded the highest prices. With this kind of economic whammy, working-class soldiers from Idaho could live like modern tsars.

In Paris, Lieutenant-Colonel Victor Rothschild, the first British soldier to arrive on the day of liberation in his capacity as bomb-disposal expert, had reclaimed his family house on Avenue de Marigny, which had been requisitioned by the Nazis. There, he entertained the young intelligence officer Malcolm Muggeridge with vintage champagne. The family butler, who had worked on in the house under the Germans, remarked that nothing seemed to have changed. The Ritz Hotel, requisitioned by millionaire intelligence officer John Hay Whitney, received David Bruce, a Princeton friend of F. Scott Fitzgerald, who turned up with Ernest Hemingway and a private army of liberators, and put in an order for fifty martini cocktails from the manager. Hemingway who, like David Bruce, had fought in America's wartime secret service, the Office of Strategic Services, set himself and his whisky bottles up at the Ritz, and there, in an alcoholic daze, received a nervous Eric Blair (George Orwell), and the more forthright Simone de Beauvoir with her lover Jean-Paul Sartre (who drank himself to oblivion, and recorded the worst hangover of his life).

The philosopher and intelligence officer A. J. 'Freddie' Ayer, author of *Language, Truth and Logic*, became a familiar sight in Paris as he sped about in a large chauffeur-driven Bugatti, complete with army radio. Arthur Koestler and his lover Mamaine Paget 'got tight' dining with André Malraux on vodka, caviare and blinis, balyk and *soufflé sibérienne*. Also in Paris, Susan Mary Alsop, a young American diplomat's wife, hosted a series of parties in her 'lovely house full of Aubusson carpets and good American soap'. But when she stepped outside, she found that the faces were 'all hard and worn and full of suffering. There really is no food except for people who can afford the black market and not much for them. The pastry shops are empty – in the windows of teashops like

Rumplemayer's, one sees one elaborate cardboard cake or an empty box of chocolates, with a sign saying "model" and nothing else. In the windows of shops on the Faubourg St Honoré are proudly displayed one pair of shoes marked "real leather" or "model" surrounded by hideous things made of straw. Outside the Ritz I threw away a cigarette butt and a well-dressed old gentleman pounced for it.'[3]

At much the same time, the young composer Nicolas Nabokov, cousin of the novelist Vladimir, was throwing away a cigarette butt in the Soviet sector of Berlin: 'When I started back, a figure bolted out of the dark and picked up the cigarette I had thrown away.'[4] As the super-race scavenged for cigarette ends or firewood or food, the ruins of the Führer's bunker were left unmarked and barely noticed by Berliners. But on Saturdays, Americans serving with the military government would explore with torches the cellars of Hitler's ruined Reichs Chancellery, and pocket their exotic finds: Romanian pistols, thick rolls of half-burned currency, iron crosses and other decorations. One looter discovered the ladies' cloakroom and lifted some brass coat tags inscribed with the Nazi eagle and the word *Reichskanzlei*. Vogue photographer Lee Miller, who had once been Man Ray's muse, posed fully dressed in Hitler's bunker bathtub.

The fun soon wore off. Divided into four sectors, and sitting like a crow's nest in a sea of Soviet-controlled territory, Berlin had become 'the traumatic synecdoche of the Cold War.'[5] Ostensibly working together in the allied *Kommandatura* to achieve the 'denazification' and 'reorientation' of Germany, the four powers struggled against strengthening ideological winds which revealed a bleak international situation. 'I felt no animosity to the Soviets,' wrote Michael Josselson, an American officer of Estonian-Russian extraction. 'In fact I was apolitical at that time and this made it much easier for me to maintain excellent personal relationships with most of the Soviet officers I came to know.'[6] But with the imposition of 'friendly' governments in the Soviet Union's sphere of influence, the mass show trials and swelling gulags in Russia itself, this collaborative spirit was severely tested. By the winter of 1947, less than two years after American and Russian soldiers had hugged each other on the banks of the Elbe, that embrace had dissolved into a snarl. 'It was only after Soviet policies became openly aggressive, and when stories of atrocities committed in the Soviet zone of occupation became a daily occurrence . . . and when the Soviet propaganda became crudely anti-Western, that my political conscience was awakened,'[7] Josselson recorded.

The headquarters of the Office of Military Government US was known as 'OMGUS', which Germans initially took to mean 'bus' in English because it was painted on the sides of double-decker buses requisitioned by the Americans. When they were not spying on the other three powers, OMGUS officers found themselves behind desks piled high with columns of the ubiquitous *Fragebogen* which every German seeking a job was obliged to fill in, answering questions relating to nationality, religion, criminal record, education, professional qualifications, employment and military service, writings and speeches, income and assets, travel abroad and, of course, political affiliations. Screening the entire German population for even the faintest trace of 'Nazism and militarism' was a deadly, bureaucratic task – and often frustrating. Whilst a janitor could be blacklisted for having swept the corridors of the Reichs Chancellery, many of Hitler's industrialists, scientists, administrators, and even high-ranking officers, were being quietly reinstated by the allied powers in a desperate effort to keep Germany from collapsing.

For one intelligence officer, the filling out of endless forms was no way to deal with the complex legacy of the Nazi regime. Michael Josselson adopted a different approach. 'I didn't know Josselson then, but I had heard of him,' recalled the philosopher Stuart Hampshire, who at that time was working for MI6 in London. 'His reputation had spread across Europe's intelligence grapevine. He was the big fixer, the man who could get anything done. *Anything*. If you wanted to get across the Russian border, which was virtually impossible, Josselson would fix it. If you needed a symphonic orchestra, Josselson would fix it.'[8]

Speaking four languages fluently without a hint of an accent, Michael Josselson was a valuable asset in the ranks of American occupation officers. Furthermore, he knew Berlin inside out. Born in Tartu, Estonia, in 1908, the son of a Jewish timber merchant, he had arrived in Berlin for the first time in the early 1920s, swept along in the Baltic diaspora which followed the 1917 revolution. With most of his close family murdered by the Bolsheviks, return to Tartu was impossible, and he became a member of that generation of men and women whom Arthur Koestler referred to as the 'scum of the earth' – the *déracinés*, people whose lives had been broken by the twentieth century, their identity with their homelands ruptured. Josselson had attended the University of Berlin, but left before taking a degree to join the Gimbels-Saks department stores as a buyer, becoming their representative in Paris. In 1936 he emigrated to the States, and shortly thereafter became an American citizen.

Inducted into the Army in 1943, his European background made him an obvious candidate for either intelligence work or psychological warfare. He was duly assigned to the Intelligence Section of the Psychological Warfare Division (PWD) in Germany, where he joined a special seven-man interrogation team (nicknamed 'Kampfgruppe Rosenberg', after its leader Captain Albert G. Rosenberg). The team's mission was to interrogate hundreds of German prisoners every week, for the purpose of 'rapidly separating strong Nazis from non-Nazis, lies from truthful responses, voluble from tongue-tied personalities'.[9] Discharged in 1946, Josselson stayed on in Berlin with the American Military Government as Cultural Affairs Officer, then with the State Department and the US High Commission as a Public Affairs Officer. In this capacity, he was assigned to the 'screening of personnel' in the German press, radio and entertainment media, all of which were suspended 'pending the removal of Nazis'.

Assigned to the same division was Nicolas Nabokov, a White Russian émigré who had lived in Berlin before emigrating to the United States in 1933. Tall, handsome, expansive, Nabokov was a man who cultivated friendships (and wives) with great ease and charm. During the 1920s, his flat in Berlin had become a centre of émigré cultural life, an intellectual goulash of writers, scholars, artists, politicians and journalists. Amongst this cosmopolitan group of exiles was Michael Josselson. In the mid-1930s, Nabokov went to America, where he wrote what he modestly described as 'the first American ballet', *Union Pacific*, with Archibald MacLeish. He shared a small studio with Henri Cartier-Bresson in New York for a while, when neither had any money. Nabokov later wrote that 'to Cartier-Bresson the Communist movement was the bearer of history, of mankind's future . . . I shared many of [his] views, but, despite the gnawing longing for my Russian fatherland, I could not accept nor espouse the philo-Communist attitude of so many Western European and American intellectuals. I felt that they were curiously blind to the realities of Russian Communism and were only reacting to the fascist tides that were sweeping Europe in the wake of the Depression. To a certain degree I felt that the philo-Communism of the mid-thirties was a passing fad, cleverly nurtured by a mythology about the Russian Bolshevik Revolution shaped by the Soviet Agitprop Apparat.'[10]

In 1945, alongside W. H. Auden and J. K. Galbraith, Nabokov joined the Morale Division of the US Strategic Bombing Survey Unit in Germany, where he met psychological warfare personnel, and subsequently got a job in the Information Control Division, alongside his old acquaintance, Michael Josselson. As a composer, Nabokov was assigned to the music section, where he was expected to 'establish good psychological and cultural weapons with which to destroy Nazism and promote a genuine desire for a democratic Germany'.[11] His task was 'to eject the Nazis from German musical life and license those German musicians (giving them the right to exercise their profession) whom we believed to be "clean" Germans,' and to 'control the programmes of German concerts and see to it that they would not turn into nationalist manifestations.' Introducing Nabokov at a party, one American general said, 'He's hep on music and tells the Krauts how to go about it.'[12]

Josselson and Nabokov became a congenial, if unlikely, pair. Nabokov was emotionally extravagant, physically demonstrative and always late; Josselson was reserved, high-minded, scrupulous. But they did share the same language of exile, and of attachment to the new world, America, which both believed to be the only place where the future of the old world could be secured. The drama and intrigue of post-war Berlin appealed to something in both men, giving them scope to exercise their talents as operators and innovators. Together, Nabokov later wrote, they both 'did a good deal of successful Nazi-hunting and put on ice a few famous conductors, pianists, singers and a number of orchestral musicians (most of whom had well deserved it and some of whom should be there today)'.[13] Often going against the grain of official thinking, they took a pragmatic view of denazification. They refused to accept that the actions of artists under Germany's Nazi past could be treated as a phenomenon *sui generis*, with judgement meted out according to the rendering of a *Fragebogen*. 'Josselson genuinely believed that the role of intellectuals in a very difficult situation shouldn't be decided in an instant,' a colleague later explained. 'He understood that Nazism in Germany had all been a mixed grotesquerie. Americans had no idea, in general. They just waded in and pointed the finger.'[14]

In 1947, the conductor Wilhelm Furtwängler was the subject of particular opprobrium. Although he had openly defied the branding of Paul Hindemith as a 'degenerate', he later arrived at a mutually beneficial accommodation with the Nazi regime. Furtwängler, who was appointed Prussian State Councillor, as well as holding other high posts bestowed by the Nazis, continued to conduct the Berlin Philharmonic Orchestra and the Berlin State Opera throughout the Third Reich. By December 1946, a year and a half after his case had first been brought to the attention of the Allied Control Commission, the conductor was due to appear before the Tribunal for Artists assembled in Berlin. The case was heard over two days. The outcome was vague, and the tribunal sat on his file for months. Then, out of the blue, Furtwängler learned that the Allied Kommandatura had cleared him, and that he was free to conduct the Berlin Philharmonic on 25 May 1947 at the American-requisitioned Titania Palast. Amongst the papers left by Michael Josselson is a note which refers to his part in what insiders referred to as the 'jumping' of Furtwängler. 'I played a major role in sparing the great German conductor Wilhelm Furtwängler the humiliation of having to go through the denazification procedure despite the fact that he had never been a member of the Nazi Party,' Josselson wrote.[15] This manoeuvre was achieved with Nabokov's help, though years later both were vague about the details of the case. 'I wonder whether you remember when was the approximate date that Furtwängler came to East Berlin and gave a press conference there threatening to go to Moscow if *we* would not clear him at once,' Nabokov asked Josselson in 1977. 'I seem to remember that you had something to do with bringing him out of the Soviet sector (hadn't you?) to my billet. I remember General McClure's [chief of Information Control Division] gentle fury at Furtwängler's behaviour then . . .'[16]

One American official reacted angrily to the discovery that figures like Furtwängler were being 'whitewashed'. In April 1947, Newell Jenkins, Chief of Theater and Music for the American military government of Württemberg-Baden, angrily demanded an explanation for 'how it happens that so many prominent nazis in the field of musicology are still active'. As well as Furtwängler, both Herbert von Karajan and Elisabeth Schwarzkopf were soon to be cleared by allied commissions, despite their murky records. In von Karajan's case, this was virtually undisputed. He had been a party member since 1933, and never hesitated to open his concerts with the Nazi favourite 'Horst Wessel Lied'. His enemies referred to him as 'SS Colonel von Karajan'. But despite favouring the Nazi regime, he was quickly reinstated as the undisputed king of the Berlin Philharmonic, the orchestra which in the post-war years was built up as the symbolic bulwark against Soviet totalitarianism.[17]

Elisabeth Schwarzkopf had given concerts for the Waffen SS on the eastern front, starred in Goebbels' propaganda films, and was included by him on a list of artists 'blessed by God'. Her National Socialist Party membership number was 7548960. 'Should a baker stop baking bread if he doesn't like the government?' asked her half-Jewish accompanist, Peter Gellhorn (who himself had to flee Germany in the 1930s). Obviously not. Schwarzkopf was cleared by the Allied Control Commission, and her career soared. She was later made a Dame of the British Empire.

The question of how, if at all, artists should be held to account for an engagement with the politics of their time could never be resolved by a hit-and-miss denazification programme. Josselson and Nabokov were keenly aware of the limitations of such a programme, and as such their motivation in leapfrogging its procedures could be viewed as humane, even courageous. On the other hand, they were victims of a moral confusion: the need to create symbolic anti-Communist rallying points introduced an urgent – and hidden – political imperative to clear those suspected of accommodating the Nazi regime. This produced a tolerance of suspected proximity to Fascism if the subject could be put to use against Communism – someone had to wield a baton against the Soviets. Nabokov's 1977 letter to Josselson reveals that they actually had to wrest Furtwängler from the Soviets (who had approached the conductor with an offer to take over the Staatsoper Unter den Linden), whilst Furtwängler himself was playing both sides against each other. His appearance at the Titania Palast in May 1947 clearly signalled that the allies were not going to be upstaged by the Soviets in 'the battle of the orchestras'. By 1949, Furtwängler was listed amongst German artists travelling to foreign countries under American-sponsored cultural programmes. In 1951, he conducted at the reopening of the Bayreuth Festival, which had been handed back to the Wagner family, despite the official ban on Richard Wagner (for 'nationalism').

William Donovan, head of America's wartime intelligence service, once said famously, 'I'd put Stalin on the payroll if I thought it would help us defeat Hitler.'[18] In an-all-too easy reversal, it was now apparent that the Germans 'were to be our new friends, and the saviour-Russians the enemy'. This, to Arthur Miller, was 'an ignoble thing. It seemed to me in later years that this wrenching shift, this ripping off of Good and Evil labels from one nation and pasting them onto another, had done something to wither the very notion of a world even theoretically moral. If last month's friend could so quickly become this month's enemy, what depth of reality could good and evil have? The nihilism – even worse, the yawning amusement – toward the very concept of a moral imperative, which would become a hallmark of international culture, was born in these eight or ten years of realignment after Hitler's death.'[19]

Of course, there were good reasons for opposing the Soviets, who were moving in swiftly behind the cold weather front. Communists came to power in Poland in January. In Italy and

France there were rumours of Communist *coups d'état*. Soviet strategists had been quick to grasp the potential of the widespread instability of post-war Europe. With an energy and resourcefulness which showed that Stalin's regime, for all its monolithic intractability, could avail itself of an imaginative vigour unmatched by western governments, the Soviet Union deployed a battery of unconventional weapons to nudge itself into the European consciousness, and soften up opinion in its favour. A vast network of fronts was established, some new, some revived from a dormant state since the death in 1940 of Willi Munzenberg, the brain behind the Kremlin's secret pre-war campaign of persuasion. Labour unions, women's movements, youth groups, cultural institutions, the press, publishing – all were targeted.

Experts in the use of culture as a tool of political persuasion, the Soviets did much in these early years of the Cold War to establish its central paradigm as a cultural one. Lacking the economic power of the United States and, above all, still without a nuclear capability, Stalin's regime concentrated on winning 'the battle for men's minds'. America, despite a massive marshalling of the arts in the New Deal period, was a virgin in the practice of international *Kulturkampf*. As early as 1945, one intelligence officer had predicted the unconventional tactics which were now being adopted by the Soviets: 'The invention of the atomic bomb will cause a shift in the balance between "peaceful" and "warlike" methods of exerting international pressure,' he reported to the chief of the Office of Strategic Services, General Donovan. 'And we must expect a very marked increase in the importance of "peaceful" methods. Our enemies will be even freer than [ever] to propagandize, subvert, sabotage and exert . . . pressures upon us, and we ourselves shall be more willing to bear these affronts and ourselves to indulge in such methods – in our eagerness to avoid at all costs the tragedy of open war; "peaceful" techniques will become more vital in times of pre-war softening up, actual overt war, and in times of post-war manipulation.'[20]

This report shows exceptional prescience. It offers a definition of the Cold War as a psychological contest, of the manufacturing of consent by 'peaceful' methods, of the use of propaganda to erode hostile positions. And, as the opening sallies in Berlin amply demonstrated, the 'operational weapon' was to be culture. The cultural Cold War was on.

So it was that amidst the degradation an unnaturally elaborate cultural life was dragged to its feet by the occupying powers as they vied with each other to score propaganda points. As early as 1945, 'when the stench of human bodies still hung about the ruins', the Russians had staged a brilliant opening for the State Opera with a performance of Gluck's *Orpheus*, in the beautifully lit, red plush Admiralspalast. Stocky, pomaded Russian colonels grinned smugly at American military personnel as they listened together to performances of *Eugène Onegin*, or to an explicitly anti-Fascist interpretation of *Rigoletto*, the music punctuated by the tinkle of medals.[21]

One of Josselson's first assignments was to retrieve the thousands of costumes belonging to the former German State Opera (the Deutsches Opernhaus Company, the only serious rival to the Russian State Opera), which had been safely stored by the Nazis at the bottom of a salt mine located outside Berlin in the US zone of occupation. On a dismal, rainy day Josselson set off with Nabokov to retrieve the costumes. On their way back to Berlin, Josselson's jeep, which preceded Nabokov's requisitioned Mercedes, hit a Soviet road block at full speed. Josselson, unconscious and suffering from multiple cuts and bruising, was taken to a Russian military hospital, where Soviet women medical officers stitched him together again. When he was well enough, he was retrieved back to his billet in the American zone, which he shared with an aspiring actor called Peter van Eyck. But for the care of his Soviet doctors, Josselson might not have survived to become the Diaghilev of America's counter-Soviet cultural propaganda campaign. The Soviets had saved the man who was, for the next two decades, to do most to undermine their attempts at cultural hegemony.

In 1947, the Russians fired another salvo when they opened up a 'House of Culture' on the Unter den Linden. The initiative dazzled a British cultural affairs officer, who reported enviously that the institute 'surpasses anything the other allies have done and puts our poor little effort right in the shade . . . It is most luxuriously appointed – good furniture, much of it antique, carpets in every room, a brilliance of lights, almost overheated and everything newly painted . . . the Russians have simply requisitioned all they wanted . . . there is a bar and smoking room . . . which looks most inviting and almost Ritzy with its soft carpets and chandeliers . . . [This is a] grandiose cultural institute which will reach the broad masses and do much to counteract the generally accepted idea here that the Russians are uncivilized. This latest venture is depressing as far as we are concerned — our contribution is so small – one information centre and a few reading rooms which have had to be closed down because of lack of coal! . . . We should be spurred on by this latest Russian entry into the Kulturkampf to answer with an equally bold scheme for putting over British achievements here in Berlin.'[22]

Whilst the British lacked the coal to heat a reading room, the Americans were emboldened to return fire at the Soviets by opening the Amerika-Häuser. Set up as 'outposts of American culture', these institutes offered respite from the bitter weather in comfortably furnished reading rooms, and gave film showings, music recitals, talks and art exhibits, all with 'overwhelming emphasis on America'. In a speech entitled 'Out of the Rubble', the Director of Education and Cultural Relations emphasized to Amerika-Häuser personnel the epic nature of their task: 'Few people ever have been privileged to be a part of a more important or more challenging mission, or one more replete with pitfalls than you who have been chosen to aid in the intellectual, moral, spiritual and cultural reorientation of a defeated, conquered and occupied Germany.' But he noted that 'in spite of the great contribution which has been made by America in the cultural field, it is not generally known even to Germany or the rest of the world. Our culture is regarded as materialistic and frequently one will hear the comment, "We have the skill, the brains, and you have the money."'[23]

Thanks largely to Russian propaganda, America was widely regarded as culturally barren, a nation of gum-chewing, Chevy-driving, Dupont-sheathed philistines, and the Amerika-Häuser did much to reverse this negative stereotype. 'One thing is absolutely certain,' wrote one enthusiastic Amerika-Häuser administrator, 'the printed material brought here from the

United States . . . makes a deep and profound impression upon those circles in Germany which for generations have thought of America as culturally backward and who have condemned the whole for the faults of a few parts.' Old clichés based on an historic 'presupposition about American cultural retardation' had been eroded by the 'good books' programme, and those same circles who had upheld these slurs were now reported to be 'quietly and deeply impressed'.[24]

Some clichés were harder to dispel. When one Amerika-Haus lecturer offered a view of the 'present-day position of the Negro in America', he was met with questions 'some of which were not inspired by good will'. The lecturer 'dealt vigorously with the questioners, who may or may not have been communists'. Fortunately for the organizers, the talk was followed 'by songs performed by a colored quintet. The Negroes continued to sing long after official closing time and . . . the spirit of the occasion seemed so congenial that it was decided to invite this Negro group for a repeat performance.'[25] The problem of race relations in America was much exploited by Soviet propaganda, and left many Europeans uneasy about America's ability to practise the democracy she now claimed to be offering the world. It was therefore reasoned that the exporting of African-Americans to perform in Europe would dispel such damaging perceptions. An American military government report of March 1947 revealed plans 'to have top-rank American negro vocalists give concerts in Germany . . . Marian Anderson or Dorothy Maynor appearances before German audiences would be of great importance.'[26] The promotion of black artists was to become an urgent priority for American cultural Cold Warriors.

The American response to the Soviet cultural offensive now began to gather pace. The full arsenal of contemporary American achievement was shipped to Europe and showcased in Berlin. Fresh new opera talent was imported from America's most noble academies: the Juilliard, the Curtis, the Eastman, the Peabody. The military government took control of eighteen German symphony orchestras, and almost as many opera companies. With many native composers banned, the market for American composers was exponentially increased – and exploited. Samuel Barber, Leonard Bernstein, Elliott Carter,

Aaron Copland, George Gershwin, Gian Carlo Menotti, Virgil Thomson – these and many other American composers premièred their work in Europe under government auspices.

In consultation with American academics, playwrights and directors, a massive theatre programme was also launched. Plays by Lillian Hellman, Eugene O'Neill, Thornton Wilder, Tennessee Williams, William Saroyan, Clifford Odets and John Steinbeck were offered to enthusiastic audiences huddled in freezing theatres where icicles hung menacingly from the ceiling. Following Schiller's principle of theatre as 'moralische Anstalt', where men can see presented the basic principles of life, the American authorities devised a hit list of desirable moral lessons. Thus, under 'Liberty and Democracy' came Ibsen's *Peer Gynt*, Shaw's *The Devil's Disciple*, and Robert Sherwood's *Abe Lincoln in Illinois*. 'Power of Faith' was expressed in the drama of Faust, Goethe, Strindberg, Shaw. 'Equality of Man' was the message to be extracted from Maxim Gorki's *Lower Depths* and Franz Grillparzer's *Medea*. Under 'War and Peace' came Aristophanes' *Lysistrata*, R. C. Sherriff's *Journey's End*, Thornton Wilder's *Skin of our Teeth*, and John Hersey's *A Bell for Adano*. 'Corruption and Justice' was deemed to be the theme of *Hamlet*, Gogol's *Revisor*, Beaumarchais's *Figaro's Wedding*, and most of Ibsen's *œuvre*. And so on, through 'Crime Does Not Pay', 'Morals, Taste and Manners', 'Pursuit of Happiness', to the darker imperative of 'Exposure of Nazism'. Deemed inappropriate 'for the present mental and psychological status of Germans' were 'all plays that accept the blind mastery of fate that unescapably [sic] leads to destruction and self-destruction, as the Greek classics.' Also blacklisted were *Julius Caesar* and *Coriolanus* ('glorifications of dictatorship'); Prinz von Homburg and Kleist (for 'chauvinism'); Tolstoy's *Living Corpse* ('Righteous criticism of society runs to asocial ends'); all Hamsun plays ('plain Nazi ideology'), and all plays by anybody else who 'readily shifted to the service of Nazism'.[27]

Mindful of Disraeli's injunction that 'A book may be as great a thing as a battle', a vast books programme was launched, aimed primarily at 'projecting the American story before the German reader in the most effective manner possible'. Appealing to commercial publishers, the occupation government ensured a constant flow of 'general books' which were deemed 'more acceptable than government-sponsored publications, because they do not have the taint of propaganda'.[28] But propaganda they were certainly intended to be. Translations commissioned by the Psychological Warfare Division of American Military Government alone ran to hundreds of titles, ranging from Howard Fast's *Citizen Tom Paine* to Arthur M. Schlesinger Jr's *The New Deal in Action*, to the Museum of Modern Art's *Built in the USA*. There were also German editions of books 'suitable for children at their most impressionable age', such as Nathaniel Hawthorne's *Wonder Tales*, Mark Twain's *A Connecticut Yankee in King Arthur's Court*, and Laura Ingalls Wilder's *Little Town on the Prairie*.

The post-war reputations in Germany (and the other occupied territories) of many Americans were significantly helped by these publishing programmes. And America's cultural cachet soared with distribution of works by Louisa May Alcott, Pearl Buck, Jacques Barzun, James Burnham, Willa Cather, Norman Cousins, William Faulkner, Ellen Glasgow, Ernest Hemingway, F. O. Matthiessen, Reinhold Niebuhr, Carl Sandburg, James Thurber, Edith Wharton and Thomas Wolfe.

European authors were also promoted as part of an explicitly 'anti-Communist program'. Suitable texts were 'whatever critiques of Soviet foreign policy and of Communism as a form of government we find to be objective, convincingly written, and timely'.[29] Meeting these criteria were André Gide's account of his disillusioning experiences in Russia, *Return from the Soviet Union*; Arthur Koestler's *Darkness at Noon* and *The Yogi and the Commissar*; and *Bread and Wine* by Ignazio Silone. For Koestler and Silone, this was the first of many appearances under the wing of the American government. Approval for publication was withheld for some books. One early casualty was John Foster Dulles's by now anachronistic *Russia and America: Pacific Neighbours*.

In art, Mrs Moholy-Nagy appeared before German audiences to talk about the work of her late husband, László, and the new and exciting direction taken by the 'New Bauhaus' in Chicago. Her lecture, wrote one sympathetic journalist, 'was a very informative contribution to the incomplete conception we have of American culture and art'.[30] This conception was further enhanced by an exhibition of 'Non-Objective paintings' from the Guggenheim Museum. This was the first appearance under government sponsorship of the New York School, otherwise known as Abstract Expressionism. Lest the new be thought too shocking, audiences were nursed with lectures on 'Fundamental Thoughts on Modern Art' which used comfortably familiar medieval paintings to introduce 'the abstract possibilities of artistic expression'.

With the memory of the *Entartekunst* exhibitions and the subsequent exodus of so many artists to America still painfully fresh, the impression now was of a European culture broken up by the high tides of Fascism, and washed up on the shores of the new Byzantium – America. Audiences who had experienced the mass rallies of Nuremberg were reportedly awed by one lecturer who 'told of immense symphonic concerts in the open air at night attended by audiences equalling in numbers those which usually only attend special sport events in our stadiums'.[31]

Not all efforts were of the highest calibre. The launch of the German edition of Ellery Queen's *Mystery Magazine* left people like Michael Josselson stone cold. And not everyone was convinced that the Yale Glee Club was the best vehicle for proving beyond all doubt 'the tremendous importance of the arts in the curriculum of the universities as an antidote against collectivism'.[32] Even the Darmstadt School got off to a shaky start. A bold initiative of the American military government, the 'Darmstadt Holiday Courses for New Music' nearly ended in a riot after disagreement about radical new music spilled over into open hostility. One official evaluation concluded: 'It was generally conceded that much of this music was worthless and had better been left unplayed. The over-emphasis on twelve-tone music was regretted. One critic described the concerts as "The Triumph of Dilettantism" . . . The French students remained aloof from the others and acted in a snobbish way [and] their teacher, Leibowitz, represents and admits as valid only the most radical kind of music and is openly disdainful of any other. His attitude is aped by his students. It was generally felt that next year's [course] must follow a different, more catholic pattern.'[33] Darmstadt, of course, was to become the citadel of progressive experimentation in music within a few years.

But all the symphony concerts and plays and exhibitions could not hide the one stark truth of that long, harsh winter of 1947: Europe was going broke. A rampant black market, civil unrest and a series of crippling strikes (largely orchestrated by Communist trades unions) produced levels of degradation and privation equal to anything experienced during the darkest moments of the war. In Germany, money had lost its value, medicine and clothes were impossible to obtain, whole families were living in underground bunkers with no water or light, and young girls and boys offered sex to American GIs in exchange for a bar of chocolate.

On 5 June 1947, General George Catlett Marshall, the US Army's wartime Chief of Staff, and now Truman's Secretary of State, announced a plan to deal with the 'great crisis'. Delivered at the 296th Harvard Commencement, which was attended by atomic physicist Robert Oppenheimer, D-Day commander General Omar Bradley, and T. S. Eliot (all of whom, like Marshall, were receiving honorary degrees), Marshall's ten-minute address marked a catalytic moment in the fate of post-war Europe. Warning that 'the whole world [and] . . . the way of life we have known is literally in the balance', he called upon the New World to step into the breach with a crash programme of financial credits and large-scale material assistance, and thus prevent the collapse of the Old World. 'There is widespread instability. There are concerted efforts to change the whole face of Europe as we know it, contrary to the interests of free mankind and free civilization,' Marshall declared. 'Left to their own resources there will be no escape from economic distress so intense, social discontents so violent, and political confusion so widespread that the historic base of Western civilization, of which we are by belief and inheritance an integral part, will take on a new form in the image of the tyranny that we fought to destroy in Germany.'[34]

As he spoke these words, General Marshall surveyed the faces of students gathered in the spring sunshine and he saw, like John Crowe Ransom before him, 'the youngling bachelors of Harvard/Lit like torches, and scrambling to disperse/Like aimless firebrands pitiful to slake.'[35] It was no coincidence that he had decided to deliver his speech here, rather than on some formal government podium. For these were the men assigned to realize America's 'manifest destiny', the elite charged with organizing the world around values which the Communist darkness threatened to obscure. The fulfilment of the Marshall Plan, as it became known, was their inheritance.

Marshall's address was designed to reinforce President Truman's ideological call-to-arms of a few months earlier, which had been immediately enshrined as the Truman Doctrine. Addressing Congress in March 1947 on the situation in Greece, where a Communist takeover threatened, Truman had appealed in apocalyptic language for a new age of American intervention: 'At the present moment in world history nearly every nation must choose between alternative ways of life,' he declared. 'The choice is too often not a free one. One way of life is based upon the will of the majority . . . The second . . . is based upon the will of a minority forcibly imposed upon the majority. It relies upon terror and oppression, a controlled press and radio, fixed elections and the suppression of personal freedoms. I believe that it must be the policy of the U.S. to support free peoples who are resisting attempted subjection by armed minorities or by outside pressure. I believe that we must assist free peoples to work out their own destinies in their own way.'[36]

After Truman's speech, Secretary of State Dean Acheson told Congressmen: 'We had arrived at a situation unparalleled since ancient times. Not since Rome and Carthage had there been such a polarization of power on this earth. Moreover the two great powers were divided by an unbridgeable ideological chasm.'[37] Joseph Jones, the State Department official who drafted Truman's appeal to Congress, understood the enormous impact of the President's words: '*All* barriers to bold action were indeed down,' he said. Among policy makers it was felt that 'a new chapter in world history had opened, and they were the most privileged of men, participants in a drama such as rarely occurs even in the long life of a great nation'.[38]

The heightened sense of the classical dimensions of America's post-war role evoked by Truman's address gave the rhetorical context to General Marshall's later, less conspicuously anti-Communist, speech. The combination of the two – a package of economic assistance coupled with a doctrinal imperative – delivered an unambiguous message: the future of western Europe, if western Europe was to have a future at all, must now be harnessed to a *pax Americana*.

On 17 June, the Soviet daily *Pravda* attacked Marshall's proposal as an extension of Truman's 'plan for political pressures with dollars and a programme for interference in the internal affairs of other states'.[39] Although the Soviets had been invited by Marshall to participate in his all-European recovery programme, the offer was, said George Kennan, 'disingenuous, designed to be rejected'.[40] As anticipated, they refused to be part of the plan. Their objection may have been overstated, but in essence the Soviets were right to conflate the humanitarian intentions of the plan with a less obvious political agenda. Far from envisioning cooperation with the Soviet Union, it was designed within the framework of a Cold War ethos which sought to drive a wedge between Moscow and its client regimes.[41] 'It was implicit all along that it was important that we didn't give the Communists the opportunity to stick their oar into these places,' Marshall-planner Dennis Fitzgerald later wrote. 'There was always the argument advanced that if we failed to fully appreciate the requirements of X, Y, and Z, that the Communists would take advantage of this situation to promote their interests.'[42] The plan's deputy director, Richard Bissell, supported this view: 'Even before the outbreak of the Korean War, it was well understood that the Marshall Plan was never meant to be a wholly altruistic affair. The hope was that strengthening their economies would enhance the value of the Western European countries as members of the NATO alliance, eventually enabling them to assume a defense responsibility in support of cold war efforts.'[43] Secretly, these countries were also expected to assume other responsibilities 'in support of cold war efforts', and to this end, Marshall Plan funds were soon being siphoned to boost the cultural struggle in the West.

On 5 October 1947, the Communist Information Bureau held its first meeting held in Belgrade. Formed in Moscow the previous September, the Cominform was Stalin's new operational base for political warfare, replacing the defunct Comintern. The Belgrade meeting was used to deliver an open challenge to the Truman Doctrine and the Marshall Plan, both of which were denounced as 'aggressive' ploys to satisfy 'America's aspirations to world supremacy'.[44] Andrei Zhdanov, architect of Stalin's ruthless cultural policy, told the Communists of western Europe that 'If they are prepared to take the lead of all the forces prepared to defend the cause of national honour and independence in the struggle against attempts to subjugate their countries economically and politically, then no plan for the subjugation of Europe can succeed.'[45] Just as Marshall had chosen to address the intellectual heartland of America, so Zhdanov called upon the intelligentsia of the world to rattle their pens under the banner of Communism, and hurl their ink against the American imperium. 'The Communist parties of [Europe have] achieved considerable successes in conducting work among the Intelligentsia. Proof of this is the fact that in these countries the best people of science, art, and literature belong to the Communist Party, are heading the movement of the progressive struggle among the intelligentsia and by their creative and tireless struggle, are winning more and more intellectuals to the cause of Communism.'[46]

Later that month, the Cominform's ideological storm troops were gathered at the East Berlin Writers' Congress at the Kammespiel Theatre. As the 'debate' (it was nothing of the sort, of course) wore on, a young American with a pointed beard and looking strangely like Lenin stormed the platform and grabbed the microphone. Speaking in flawless German, he held his position for thirty-five minutes, praising those writers who had had the nerve to speak up against Hitler, and exposing similarities between the Nazi regime and the new Communist police state. These were dangerous times. To disrupt the proceedings and queer the pitch of a Communist propaganda exercise was an act of either madness or courage, or both. Melvin Lasky had arrived.

Born in 1920 in the Bronx, Melvin Jonah Lasky grew up in the 'looming presence' of his Yiddish-speaking grandfather, a bearded, learned man who nourished the young Lasky with passages from the legends of the Jews. As one of the 'best and brightest' graduates of New York's City College, Lasky emerged from its seething ideological debates a staunch anti-Stalinist with a taste for intellectual – and occasionally physical – confrontation. He joined the civil service and worked as a travel guide at the Statue of Liberty, before joining the staff of Sol Levitas's anti-Stalinist magazine, the *New Leader*. Drafted into the services, he became a combat historian with US 7th Army in France and Germany, and was later demobbed in Berlin, where he became German correspondent for both the *New Leader* and *Partisan Review*.

A short, stocky man, Lasky was given to drawing his shoulder blades back and pushing out his chest, as if primed for a fight. Using his oriental-shaped eyes to produce deadly squints, he had acquired from the brusque atmosphere of City College an ill-manner which rarely deserted him. In his militant anti-Communism he was, to use an epithet he bestowed on somebody else, 'as unmovable as the rock of Gibraltar'. Lupine, grittily determined, Lasky was to become a force to reckon with as he stormed his way through the cultural campaigns of the Cold War. His explosive protest at the East German Writers' Congress earned him the title 'Father of the Cold War in Berlin'. His action even upset the American authorities, who threatened to throw him out. Appalled by the timidity of his superiors, he compared Berlin to 'what a frontier-town must have been like in the States in the middle of the 19th century – Indians on the horizon, and you've simply got to have that rifle handy or [if] not your scalp is gone. But in those days a frontier-town was full of Indian-fighters . . . . Here very few people have any guts, and if they do they usually don't know in which direction to point their rifle.'[47]

But Lasky knew the sheriff, and far from being run out of town, he was now taken under the wing of the military governor, General Lucius Clay. To him, Lasky protested that whilst the Soviet lie was travelling round the globe at lightning speed, the truth had yet to get its boots on. He made his case in a passionately argued document submitted on 7 December 1947 to Clay's office, which called for a radical shake-up in American propaganda. Referred to as 'The Melvin Lasky Proposal', this document constituted Lasky's personal blueprint for staging the cultural Cold War. 'High hopes for peace and international unity blinded us to the fact that a concerted political war against the USA was being prepared and executed, and nowhere more vigorously than in Germany,' he claimed. 'The same old anti-democratic anti-American formulas [sic] on which many European generations have been fed, and which the Nazi propaganda machine under Goebbels brought to a peak, are now being reworked. Viz., the alleged economic selfishness of the USA (Uncle Sam as Shylock); its alleged deep political reaction (a "mercenary capitalistic press," etc.); its alleged cultural waywardness (the "jazz and swing mania", radio advertisements, Hollywood "inanities", "cheese-cake and leg-art"); its alleged moral hypocrisy (the Negro question, sharecroppers, Okies); etc. etc . . . '[48]

In extraordinary language, Lasky went on to define the challenge: 'The time-honored U.S. formula of "Shed light and the people will find their own way" exaggerates the possibilities in Germany (and in Europe) for an easy conversion . . . It would be foolish to expect to wean a primitive savage away from his conviction in mysterious jungle-herbs simply by the dissemination of modern scientific medical information . . . We have not succeeded in combatting the variety of factors – political, psychological, cultural – which work against U.S. foreign policy, and in particular against the success of the Marshall Plan in Europe.' What was needed now, continued Lasky breathlessly, was an 'active' truth, a truth bold enough to 'enter the contest', not one which behaved like 'an Olympian bystander'. Make no mistake, he warned, the substance of the Cold War was '*cultural* in range. And it is here that a serious void in the American program has been most exploited by the enemies of American foreign policy . . . The void . . . is real and grave.'[49]

The 'real and grave' void to which Lasky referred was the failure 'to win the educated and cultured classes – which, in the long run, provide moral and political leadership in the community – ' to the American cause. This shortcoming, he argued, could be partly addressed by publishing a new journal, one which would 'serve both as a constructive fillip to German–European thought', and also 'as a demonstration that behind the official representatives of American democracy lies a great and progressive culture, with a richness of achievements in the arts, in literature, in philosophy, in all the aspects of culture which unite the free traditions of Europe and America.'[50]

Two days later, Lasky submitted a 'Prospectus for the "American Review"' whose purpose should be 'to support the general objectives of U.S. policy in Germany and Europe by illustrating the background of ideas, spiritual activity, literary and intellectual achievement, from which the American democracy takes its inspiration'. The review, he argued, would demonstrate that 'America and Americans have achieved mature triumphs in all the spheres of the human spirit common to both the Old and the New Worlds', and thereby constitute the first really serious effort in 'winning large sections of the German intelligentsia away from Communistic influence'.[51]

The result was *Der Monat*, a monthly magazine designed to construct an ideological bridge between German and American intellectuals and, as explicitly set forth by Lasky, to ease the passage of American foreign policy interests by supporting 'the general objectives of U.S. policy in Germany and Europe'. Set up with General Clay's backing on 1 October 1948, under Lasky's editorship, it was printed initially in Munich and airlifted into Berlin aboard the allied cargo planes on which the city depended during the blockade. Across the years, *Der Monat* was financed through 'confidential funds' of the Marshall Plan, then from the coffers of the Central Intelligence Agency, then with Ford Foundation money, and then again with CIA dollars. For its financing alone, the magazine was absolutely a product – and an exemplar of – American Cold War strategies in the cultural field.

Der Monat was a temple to the belief that an educated elite could steer the post-war world away from its own extinction. This, together with their affiliations to the American occupation government, was what united Lasky, Josselson and Nabokov. Like Jean Cocteau, who was soon to warn America, 'You will not be saved by weaponry, nor by money, but by a thinking minority, because the world is expiring, as it does not think (*pense*) anymore, but merely spends (*dépense*),'[52] they understood that the dollars of the Marshall Plan would not be enough: financial assistance had to be supplemented by a concentrated programme of cultural warfare. This curious triumvirate – Lasky the political militant, Josselson the former department store buyer, and Nabokov the composer – now stood poised at the cutting edge of what was to become, under their guidance, one of the most ambitious secret operations of the Cold War: the winning over of the western intelligentsia to the American proposition.

2

Destiny's Elect

> There's no such thing as innocence. Innocence touched with guilt is as good a deal as you can get.
>
> Mike Hammer, in Mickey Spillane's *Kiss Me, Deadly*

The American proposition had already been articulated in the Truman Doctrine and the Marshall Plan. Now, a new phase of the Cold War opened up with the creation of the Central Intelligence Agency, America's first peacetime intelligence organization. Created by the National Security Act of 26 July 1947, the Agency was originally intended to coordinate military and diplomatic intelligence. Crucially – and in extremely vague language – it was also authorized to carry out unspecified 'services of common concern' and 'such other functions and duties' as the National Security Council (created under the same Act) might direct. 'Nowhere in the 1947 Act was the CIA explicitly empowered to collect intelligence or intervene secretly in the affairs of other nations,' a government report later stated. 'But the elastic phrase "such other functions" was used by successive presidents to move the Agency into espionage, covert action, paramilitary operations, and technical intelligence collection.'[1]

The founding of the CIA marked a dramatic overhaul of the traditional paradigms of American politics. The terms under which the Agency was established institutionalized the concepts of 'the necessary lie' and 'plausible deniability' as legitimate peacetime strategies, and in the long run produced an invisible layer of government whose potential for abuse, domestically and abroad, was uninhibited by any sense of accountability.

This experience of limitless influence was exemplified by the eponymous hero of Norman Mailer's monumental *Harlot's Ghost*: 'We tap into everything,' says Harlot. 'If good crops are an instrument of foreign policy, then we are obliged to know next year's weather. That same demand comes at us everywhere we look: finance, media, labour relations, economic production, the thematic consequences of T.V. Where is the end to all that we can be legitimately interested in? . . . Nobody knows how many pipelines we have in good places – how many Pentagon Pooh-Bahs, commodores, congressmen, professors in assorted think tanks, soil erosion specialists, student leaders, diplomats, corporate lawyers, name it! They all give us input.'[2]

Owning airlines, radio stations, newspapers, insurance companies and real estate, the CIA's presence in world affairs grew so prodigiously over the decades that people began to suspect its presence behind every thicket. 'Like Dorothy Parker and the things she said, the CIA gets credit or blame both for what it does and for many things it has not even thought of doing,' one Agency man later complained.[3] Disastrous operations like the Bay of Pigs did little to improve the CIA's public image. A negative stereotype emerged of a CIA peopled by ruthless, Jesuitical, 'ugly' Americans whose view of the world was distorted by a wilderness of mirrors.

Certainly, history continues to validate this version. The Truman Doctrine and the National Security Acts which it inspired sanctioned aggressiveness and intervention abroad. But the scale of its imperial buccaneering tends to obscure some less calamitous truths about the CIA. In the beginning, its officers were animated by a sense of mission – 'to save western freedom from Communist darkness' – which one officer compared to 'the atmosphere of an order of Knights Templars'.[4] The dominant early influence was the 'aristocracy' of the eastern seaboard and the Ivy League, a *Bruderbund* of Anglophile sophisticates who found powerful justification for their actions in the traditions of the Enlightenment and the principles enshrined in the Declaration of Independence.

In this, the CIA took its character from its wartime predecessor, the Office of Strategic Services (OSS), set up in 1941 in the wake of Pearl Harbor and disbanded in September 1945 by President Truman, who said at the time that he wanted nothing to do with a peacetime 'Gestapo'. This primitive fear reflected little of the reality of OSS, which had acquired the nickname 'Oh So Social' on account of its clubby, collegiate atmosphere. Columnist Drew Pearson called it 'one of the fanciest groups of dilettante diplomats, Wall Street bankers, and amateur detectives ever seen in Washington'.[5] 'All OSS-ers carried a pack with a carbine, a few grenades, some gold coins, and a death pill,' recalled Tom Braden, who worked closely with OSS chief William 'Wild Bill' Donovan (the nickname had been earned for his exploits against Pancho Villa). 'Donovan once left his death pill in a drawer at the Dorchester Hotel and he made David Bruce send a wire from France to get the maid there to send it out. He was quite a character, Bill Donovan, a legend in his own time. He once said to me, "Braden, if you get in a tight spot, take your knife and drive it straight through his balls."'[6]

Governed by legislation which prohibited little and countenanced virtually anything, OSS-ers found themselves roving wartime Europe like latterday proconsuls. The first OSS man to reach Bucharest after the German withdrawal in autumn 1944 became a regular guest at meetings of the Romanian cabinet, and boasted to colleagues, 'Before they vote on anything, they ask me what I think . . . They pass all my laws unanimously. I never thought running a country was so easy.'[7] But running a country was precisely what most OSS-ers were brought up to do. Recruiting from the heart of America's corporate, political, academic and cultural establishment, Donovan had assembled an elite corps which hailed from America's most powerful institutions and families. Members of the Mellon family held espionage posts in Madrid, London, Geneva, Paris. Paul Mellon worked for the Special Operations Executive in London. His sister, Ailsa (once known as the world's richest woman) was married to his commanding officer, chief of OSS London, David Bruce, son of a US senator and a millionaire in his own right. J. P. Morgan's sons were both in the OSS. The families Vanderbilt, DuPont, Archbold (Standard Oil), Ryan (Equitable Life Insurance), Weil (Macy's department store), Whitney, were all represented in the ranks of Donovan's secret army.

Other OSS recruits included travel guide publisher Eugene Fodor; New York journalist Marcello Girosi, who later became the producer of Italian and American films starring Sophia Loren; Ilia Tolstoy, émigré grandson of the famous novelist, who was a member of an OSS mission to Lhasa; and Julia McWilliams Child, later a celebrity chef, who maintained OSS intelligence files at Chungking. Raymond Guest, a polo-playing socialite and cousin of Winston Churchill, cut a colourful swathe through OSS operations in France and Scandinavia. Antoine de Saint-Exupéry was a close friend and collaborator of Donovan's, as was Ernest Hemingway, whose son John was also in OSS.

Although one critic complained of the many personnel 'who seemed to be rah-rah youngsters to whom OSS was perhaps an escape from routine military service and a sort of lark',[8] there was also an assumption that each member of the higher echelons of Donovan's service 'risked his future status as a banker or trustee or highly placed politician in identifying himself with illegality and unorthodoxy'.[9] With the disbanding of OSS, many of those future bankers and trustees and politicians returned to civilian life. Allen Dulles, Donovan's brilliant deputy who had taken charge of OSS operations in Europe, went back to his law practice in New York, where he became the centre of an informal cadre of campaigners for a permanent American intelligence service. Nicknamed the 'Park Avenue Cowboys', this group included Kermit 'Kim' Roosevelt, grandson of Theodore; Tracy Barnes (who had helped Allen Dulles retrieve the famous Ciano diaries from Countess Ciano); Richard Helms and Frank Wisner, bringing gossip from Army intelligence in occupied Germany; and Royall Tyler, soon to become head of the Paris office of the World Bank.

Far from having risked their 'future status', their period in OSS enhanced their reputations and offered another network to combine with the old school tie that had brought them together in the first place. This, and their initiation into illegality and unorthodoxy, was to provide a rich resource for the

CIA. It was this historic elite, the Ivy-Leaguers who cast their influence over America's boardrooms, academic institutions, major newspapers and media, law firms and government, who now stepped forward to fill the ranks of the fledgling Agency. Many of them hailed from a concentration in Washington of a hundred or so wealthy families, known as the 'cave dwellers', who stood for the preservation of the Episcopalian and Presbyterian values that had guided their ancestors. Schooled in the principles of a robust intellect, athletic prowess, *politesse noblige*, and solid Christian ethics, they took their example from men like the Reverend Endicott Peabody, whose Groton School, run along the lines of Eton, Harrow and Winchester, was the Alma Mater of so many national leaders. Trained in the Christian virtues and the duties of privilege, they emerged believing in democracy but wary of unchecked egalitarianism. Reversing Willy Brandt's celebrated declaration, 'We are the elected of the people, not the elect,' this was the elect who had not been elected.

Those who had not served with OSS had spent the war rising through the ranks of the State Department and the Foreign Office. They orbited around figures like Charles 'Chip' Bohlen, who later became ambassador to France. During the early 1940s, his house on Dumbarton Avenue in Georgetown was an intellectual ferment at the centre of which sat George Kennan and Isaiah Berlin, who was already revered in Washington circles as 'The Prophet'. One observer described Kennan, Bohlen and Berlin as 'a homogeneous, congenial trio'. Bohlen was one of the founders of a novel branch of modern scholarship known as Kremlinology. He had lived in Russia, knew its leaders and bureaucrats, had studied its ideological literature, and could quote their classics. He had witnessed the purges and trials of the late 1930s, and the full impact of Zhdanov's 'cultural policies'. 'There are two famous "last words",' Bohlen was fond of saying. 'One is "alcohol doesn't affect me"; and the other is "I understand the Russians."' For a better understanding, he turned to Isaiah Berlin and Nicolas Nabokov, who was then working for the Justice Department. Bohlen used to refer to Nabokov as a 'psychological asset', and Nabokov returned the compliment by calling Bohlen 'my model, my source of advice'.

'These new friends had few if any illusions about "Uncle Joe",' Nabokov later wrote. 'In more ways than one, they were an anachronistic group in the Washington of those years, perhaps even in all of America. America was in a state of Sovietophilic euphoria, which none in the house on Dumbarton Avenue shared. The bulk of American public opinion had switched twice in three years in its feelings toward Russia. First it was *against* – after the partition of Poland and the "fiendish" Finnish war. Stalin in newspaper cartoons looked like a nasty mixture of a wolf and a bear. Then, as abruptly, opinion was *for* Russia: after the Nazi invasion of Russia in 1941. Stalin was suddenly beautified, represented as a knight in armour defending the Kremlin against a horde of Teutons, or reproduced from Margaret Bourke-White's slenderized and idolized profile photographs. And then, in 1943, the pro-Russian feeling was enhanced by Stalingrad. "You will see," argued trusting Americans, 'Communism will never come back to Russia the way it was. It will be a different country after the war. Didn't Stalin bring the Patriarch back from exile? And the writers and poets? And didn't Stalin re-establish officers' ranks and reinstate the historical national heroes, and even some of the tsars and saints, like Alexander Nevsky and Peter the Great?" Not so the sceptics at Dumbarton Avenue. They knew, as Kennan once said, that Stalinism is irreversible.'[10]

The Dumbarton Avenue sceptics were joined by David Bruce, Averell Harriman, John McCloy, Joseph and Stewart Alsop, Richard Bissell, Walter Lippmann, and the Bundy brothers. In long exchanges, heated by intellectual passion and alcohol, their vision of a new world order began to take shape. Internationalist, abrasive, competitive, these men had an unshakeable belief in their value system, and in their duty to offer it to others. They were the patricians of the modern age, the paladins of democracy, and saw no contradiction in that. This was the elite which ran American foreign policy and shaped legislation at home. Through think-tanks to foundations, directorates to membership of gentlemen's clubs, these mandarins were interlocked by their institutional affiliations and by a shared belief in their own superiority. Their job it was to establish and then justify the post-war *pax Americana*. And they were staunch supporters of the CIA, which was fast being staffed by their friends from school, business or the 'old show' of OSS.

The foremost articulator of the shared convictions of America's elite was George Kennan, diplomat-scholar, architect of the Marshall Plan, and as director of the State Department's Policy Planning Staff, one of the fathers of the CIA. In 1947 he advocated direct military intervention in Italy in what he saw as its imminent collapse into a civil war supported by the Communists: 'This would admittedly result in much violence and probably a military division of Italy,' he told the State Department, but 'it might well be preferable to a bloodless election victory, unopposed by ourselves, which would give the Communists the entire peninsula at one *coup* and send waves of panic to all surrounding areas.'[11] Truman, fortunately, didn't go along with this precipitate suggestion, but he did authorize covert intervention in the Italian elections instead. By July 1947, Kennan had modified his views – not about the nature of the Soviet threat, but about how to deal with it. In his famous 'X' article in the journal *Foreign Affairs*, he set forth the thesis which dominated the early years of the Cold War. Claiming that the Kremlin was committed to dominating 'every nook and cranny available . . . in the basin of world power' with its 'fanatical ideology', he proposed a policy of 'unalterable counter force', and 'firm and vigilant containment'. As part of this policy, he advocated 'the maximum development of the propaganda and political warfare techniques',[12] which, as director of the Policy Planning Staff (designed to oversee the ideological-political containment of Europe), he was perfectly placed to implement. 'The world was our oyster,' he later wrote of this office.

In a speech to the National War College in December 1947, it was Kennan who introduced the concept of 'the necessary lie' as a vital constituent of American post-war diplomacy. The Communists, he said, had won a 'strong position in Europe, so immensely superior to our own . . . through unabashed and skilful use of lies. They have fought us with unreality, with irrationalism. Can we combat this unreality successfully with rationalism, with truth, with honest, well-meant economic assistance?'[13] he asked. No, America needed to embrace a new era of covert warfare to advance her democratic objectives against Soviet deceit.

On 19 December 1947, Kennan's political philosophy acquired legal authority in a directive issued by Truman's National Security Council, NSC-4. A top-secret appendix to this directive, NSC-4A, instructed the Director of Central Intelligence to undertake 'covert psychological activities' in support of American anti-Communist policies. Startlingly opaque about what procedures should be followed for coordinating or approving such activities, this appendix was the first formal post-war authorization for clandestine operations. Superseded in June 1948 by a new – and more explicit – directive drafted by George Kennan, NSC-10/2, these were the documents which piloted American intelligence into the choppy waters of secret political warfare for decades to come.

Prepared in the tightest secrecy, these directives 'adopted an expansive conception of [America's] security requirements to include a world substantially made over in its own image.'[14] Proceeding from the premise that the Soviet Union and its satellite countries were embarked on a programme of 'vicious' covert activities to 'discredit and defeat the aims and activities of the United States and other western powers', NSC-10/2 gave the highest sanction of the government to a plethora of covert operations: 'propaganda, economic warfare, preventative direct action including sabotage, anti-sabotage, demolition and evacuation measures; subversion against hostile states including assistance to underground resistance movements, guerrillas and refugee liberation groups'.[15] All such activities, in the words of NSC-10/2, must be 'so planned and executed that any U.S. government responsibility for them is not evident to unauthorized persons, and that if uncovered the U.S. government can plausibly disclaim any responsibility for them.'[16]

NSC-10/2 established a special staff for covert operations, within the CIA but with policy and personnel under the Policy Planning Staff of the State Department (in other words, under Kennan's control). This staff was eventually called the Office of Policy Coordination (OPC), an innocuous title designed 'to ensure plausibility while revealing practically nothing of its purpose'.[17] Covert action was defined as any 'clandestine activity designed to influence foreign governments, events, organizations or persons in support of U.S. foreign policy conducted in such a way that the involvement of the U.S. government is not apparent'.[18] Virtually unlimited in scope and secrecy, OPC was without precedent in peacetime America. Here was the dirty tricks department that Allen Dulles and the Park Avenue Cowboys had been campaigning for. Emerging from their ranks to head this new operation was Frank Wisner, who was chosen from a list of candidates put forward by George Kennan.

Frank Wisner, a former Wall Street lawyer with a Mississippi twang and the unusual virtue of being a champion low hurdler at the University of Virginia, was a veteran of OSS campaigns throughout Europe, and head of its Secret Intelligence Branch. Staying on in military intelligence after the war, he was given responsibility for liaising with the Gehlen organization, the German Army intelligence unit preserved intact by the Americans to spy on Russia. Wisner was not a man to be delayed by moral arguments. As Harry Rositzke, a close colleague in OSS and later the CIA explained, 'It was a visceral business of using any bastard as long as he was anti-Communist.'[19] 'One needn't ask him to one's club,' was Allen Dulles's comment on Wisner's relationship with SS General Reinhard Gehlen.[20]

Wisner had angrily resigned from military intelligence when his superiors niggled over his request for some extra bicycles for his officers. He then joined the State Department, and from there he continued to run what was virtually his personal intelligence group, consisting of a succession of rabbit warrens hidden deep within the bureaucracy of government. It was this group which was now merged into the CIA under the Office of Policy Coordination, or OPC. Wisner's practice of hiring Nazis did not stop when he took over OPC. 'Wisner brought in a whole load of fascists after the war, some really nasty people. He could do that, because he was powerful,'[21] a CIA colleague later explained. 'He was the key to a great many things, a brilliant, compulsive man, of enormous charm, imagination, and conviction that anything, *anything* could be achieved and that he could achieve it.'[22]

Under Wisner's stewardship, OPC became the fastest growing element in the CIA. According to Edgar Applewhite, a CIA Deputy Inspector General, its staff 'arrogated to themselves total power, with no inhibiting precedent. They could do what they wanted, just as long as "higher authority", as we called the President, did not expressly forbid it. They were extremely aristocratic in their assumptions, extremely parochial about life between men and women, very romantic, and arrogant. They had a heaven-sent obligation and, God knows, what opportunity! They ate it up.'[23]

To facilitate the operations of OPC, Congress passed the Central Intelligence Agency Act of 1949, which authorized the Director of the CIA to spend funds without having to account for disbursements. Within the next few years, OPC's activities – its scope of operations, its manpower and budget – grew like a hydra. Its total personnel strength grew from 302 in 1949 to 2,812 in 1952, plus 3,142 overseas contract personnel. For the same period, its budget increased from $4.7 million to $82 million. One factor contributing to this expansion was an organizational arrangement that created an internal demand for projects. OPC activities were not programmed around a financial system, but around projects. This had important – and in the end, detrimental – internal effects: 'an individual within OPC judged his own performance, and was judged by others, on the importance and number of projects he initiated and managed. The result was competition among individuals and OPC divisions to generate the maximum number of projects.'[24]

At first, the CIA was headquartered in a series of shambolic temporary buildings, known as 'sheds', scattered around the Capitol and Washington Mall. There, in the dusty corridors, new recruits were enthralled by 'the atmosphere of wartime and the urgency of mobilization. The halls were full of earnest and worried men and women, rushing to meetings, conferring on the run, issuing crisp instructions to assistants trying to keep up with them. New people, full of enthusiasm, mingled with OSS veterans, Jedburgh colleagues with the elite of the post-war era, fresh from the Ivy League campuses in their tweed jackets, smoking pipes, and full of daring, innovative ideas, who had flocked to the Agency as the most effective place for a non-communist liberal to do battle against the communist menace.'[25]

The front line of this battle was, of course, drawn up not in Washington, but in Europe. Establishing an office at Tempelhof Air Base, half an hour outside Berlin, OPC seemed to haemorrhage its officers into Germany. Added to other CIA divisions, there were 1,400 operatives attached to the German station at this time.

One of OPC's first recruits in Germany was Michael Josselson. In his notes towards a memoir (which was never completed), Josselson wrote: 'My tour of duty . . . was coming to an end in 1948. But a return to civilian life, which for me meant going back to the world of buying for U.S. department stores, a not particularly interesting career, filled me with despair. It was at that time that an American friend who worked in intelligence introduced me to one of the chiefs of the "outfit" in Germany. There followed two or three more interviews in Washington, the filling out of an endless questionnaire, and then a very long wait while the FBI in its clumsy fashion was trying to find out whether there was anything derogatory in my life history. In the fall of 1948 my clearance came through and I joined the "outfit" as chief of its Berlin station for Covert Action (CA), as distinguished from the espionage or intelligence side (FI). Except for the "covert" aspect, this was in reality a continuation of psychological warfare, only this time directed against the Soviets and the Communists in East Germany. It was a defensive move, since the Soviets had long ago started the psychological Cold War.'[26]

Josselson's recruiter was Lawrence de Neufville, an OSS-er who had arrived in Germany with the first wave of American troops in 1944. Until early 1948, he served as a consultant with the civil administration in Berlin. He was then approached by John Baker, one of the CIA's first officers in Germany, later famously declared *persona non grata* by the Soviets 'for systematically violating the norms of behaviour for diplomatic representatives' (i.e. spying) when he was Second Secretary of the US Embassy in Moscow. 'I made no application to join CIA, or anything like that,' de Neufville later said. 'I was quite happy where I was, working on the constitution, helping to set up the Adenauer government. It was very exciting. But then one day John Baker walked into my office and said would I like to join the Agency.'[27] De Neufville accepted the offer and was assigned 'cover' working in the office of the American High Commissioner, John McCloy. His first act was to recruit Josselson, whose work in Berlin had made him something of a legend in intelligence circles.

Meanwhile, was Nicolas Nabokov aware of his friend's new job? Michael Josselson was a fiercely private man, ideally suited to the world of intelligence. When some relatives who were living in East Berlin managed to track him down in early 1949, he curtly dismissed them, telling them not to contact him again. Hurt, they assumed their 'Americanized' cousin felt they were below him now. In reality, he was concerned for their safety. For East Berliners to have a relative in the American secret service would have placed them in immediate danger. But Nabokov probably had a good idea of Josselson's new direction. There were more spies in Berlin at this time than functioning bicycles, and Nabokov had worked alongside many of them.

In fact, it appears that Nabokov was also approached to join the CIA. In 1948, he filed an application for a job in government. Not a bureaucrat by nature, it is unlikely he was interested in joining the State Department (which was scorned by many CIA recruits as 'all policy and no push-ups'), and with Allen Dulles involved in his application it can reasonably be surmised that he was trying to get a job in intelligence. But his application ran into trouble and he failed to get security clearance. His sponsor, George Kennan, deeply embarrassed, wrote advising him to withdraw his application: 'I am giving you this advice (which causes me considerable sadness and a very real concern) only because I have not been able to clarify this matter to my own satisfaction, and cannot assure you a freedom of further unpleasantness if you go ahead with the plan of working again with the Government . . . I can only say that in my opinion the entire action of the Government in this matter, taken as a whole, is ill-conceived, short-sighted, unjust, and quite inconsistent with any desire to utilize the services of sensitive, intelligent and valuable people . . . I think the Government has forfeited any right to use your advice, and if I were you I would drop the whole matter for the time being.'[28] For the moment, at least, Nabokov was left out in the cold.

And what of Melvin Lasky? Was he not an ideal candidate to join the swelling ranks of the CIA? It would later be alleged that Lasky had become an agent. This he consistently denied. Like Thaxter in *Humboldt's Gift*, the rumour 'greatly added to his mysteriousness'. His constant presence at the forefront of the CIA's cultural Cold War for the next two decades would not go unnoticed.

3

Marxists at the Waldorf

So I say, Fascism or Communism, I take the side of love, and I laugh at men's ideas.

Anaïs Nin

New York, 25 March 1949, a dank and slushy Tuesday. Outside the Waldorf Astoria hotel on Park Avenue and 50th Street, a small and desultory picket, mostly men in grey gaberdine coats, formed a slow circle on the sidewalk. Inside the hotel, the pace was frantic. Unusually for this time of year, the hotel was full, and one booking in particular was proving to be a headache.

From room 1042, a plush bridal suite on the tenth floor, the orders came thick and fast all day. A request for extra telephones to be installed was followed by a flurry of telegraph messages, dictated to the hotel's wire room; more table lamps were needed; more of everything was needed. Calls to room service issued like a constant cannonade – hamburgers, salads, steaks tartare, side orders, bottles of claret, bottles of beer, more buckets of ice, please. Not your average honeymooners.

As waiters staggered into the suite, they were met with a strange scene. Telephone cords webbed across the room, and at the end of the tangle callers were leaning animatedly into each receiver. Every available surface was occupied by a person or teetering piles of paper. The suite was heavy with cigarette smoke. Two secretaries took dictation, and an assistant worked a mimeograph machine which had been installed in the bathroom, its floor invisible beneath a mounting pile of inky paper. A perpetual flow of visitors weaved in and out of the clutter.

Amidst this ballyhoo, some members of the party looked on nervously as the waiters balanced their huge trays on the edge of the bed and hovered for tips. Who was going to pick up the tab? Sidney Hook, the philosopher from New York University who had booked the suite, seemed unconcerned about the escalating costs of the enterprise. In the bridal suite with Hook were writer Mary McCarthy and her third husband, journalist Bowden Broadwater; the novelist Elizabeth Hardwick, and her husband, the poet Robert Lowell; Nicolas Nabokov; journalist and critic Dwight Macdonald; Italian journalist and former Munzenberg ally, Nicola Chiaromonte; Arthur Schlesinger; *Partisan Review* editors William Phillips and Philip Rahv; Arnold Beichmann, a labour reporter friendly with anti-Communist union leaders; Mel Pitzele, another labour specialist; and David Dubinsky of the Ladies' Garment Workers Union. Despite his job description, Dubinsky seemed perfectly at ease in this chaotic little intellectual parliament.

Downstairs, in the Waldorf Astoria ballroom, the hotel's already stretched staff were assisting with last-minute touches to a room dressed for a conference. Flowers were being arranged around a dais which formed a crescent across the far end of the room. Microphones were checked – one two, one two. A huge banner reading 'Cultural and Scientific Conference for World Peace' was lifted across the wall behind the speakers' platform. Already, some of the thousand delegates to the conference were arriving for the inaugural reception. The demonstrators outside were picking up, heckling guests as they walked through the swing doors into the lobby. 'Softies!' they shouted, as Lillian Hellman, Clifford Odets, Leonard Bernstein, and Dashiell Hammett arrived. Special scorn was reserved for the millionaire Ivy Leaguer, Corliss Lamont, who was acting as 'sponsor' of the conference. Son of the chairman of J. P. Morgan & Co. investment bank, educated at Phillips Academy and Harvard, Lamont summoned up enough patrician reserve to ignore the insults flung at him by the angry picket.

The protest had been organized by a right-wing alliance consisting of the American Legion and a group of Catholic and patriotic societies. Its complaint was that the conference, which was sponsored by the National Council of the Arts, Sciences and Professions, was merely a 'front' for the Soviets: that the Commies were here, not, as they claimed, in the interests of goodwill and intellectual exchange between the United States and the Soviet Union, but to propagandize America. And, in effect, they were right. The conference was a Cominform initiative, a daring ploy to manipulate public opinion in America's own backyard. The Soviet party, led by A. A. Fadeyev, head of the Union of Soviet Writers, and including composer Dmitri Shostakovich, pride of their delegation, was also comfortably installed in rooms at the Waldorf. Its KGB 'nurses' and party apparatchiks could congratulate themselves on this *coup de théâtre*. The demonstrators outside had a point: the Reds weren't just under the beds, they were *in* them.

'It was big news in the press that every entrance of the Waldorf Astoria would be blocked by a line of nuns praying for the souls of the participants, who had been deranged by Satanic seduction,' wrote Arthur Miller, who had accepted an invitation to chair one of the conference's debates. 'And on the morning of the conference I actually had to step between two gentle sisters kneeling on the sidewalk as I made for the Waldorf door. Even then it was a bewildering thing to contemplate, this world of symbolic gestures and utterances.'[1]

Although they publicly dissociated themselves from the demonstration outside – 'The most dangerous thing we can do . . . is to leave the task of exposing Communist fronts to reactionaries' – Sidney Hook and the bridal suite group were here for the same reason. Former Marxists and Trotskyists, they had once spun in the same Communist orbit as the American intellectuals and artists who were, at this moment, arriving downstairs to attend the Soviet conference. Indeed, New York in the 1930s had once been described as 'the most interesting part of the Soviet Union'. But the German–Russian non-aggression pact of 1939 had produced a shock which had 'started New York City, bitter and demoralized, back from the USSR, to America'.[2] Whilst Hook and his friends had been part of this movement away from Marxist radicalism towards the political centre or right, other colleagues had yet to abandon their sympathy for Communism. 'The Stalinists were still a very powerful gang,' editor and critic Jason Epstein later claimed. 'They were like the political correctness lot now. There was good reason, therefore, to question the Stalinists' right to culture.'[3] The impressive turnout of fellow travellers at the Waldorf seemed to justify the fear of many American ideologues that Communism's seductive spell was not broken, that the Communist dream, despite Stalin's excesses, still lingered.

'For me, however, the conference was an effort to continue a good tradition that was presently menaced,' Arthur Miller later wrote. 'To be sure, the four years of our military alliance against the Axis powers were only a reprieve from a long-term hostility that had begun in 1917 with the Revolution itself and merely resumed when Hitler's armies were destroyed. But there was simply no question that without Soviet resistance Nazism would have conquered all of Europe as well as Britain, with the possibility of the U.S. being forced into a hands-off isolationism at best, or at worst an initially awkward but finally comfortable deal with fascism – or so I thought. Thus, the sharp post-war turn against the Soviets and in favour of a Germany unpurged of Nazis not only seemed ignoble but threatened another war that might indeed destroy Russia but bring down our own democracy as well.'[4]

Upstairs in the bridal suite, tempers were getting a little frayed. Ever since the decision had been taken, three weeks previously, to disrupt the conference, this inchoate group had been working relentlessly to develop an 'agitprop apparatus' of its own. The 'enemy's' preparatory activities were monitored, and the task of disrupting them was divided among the membership of a burgeoning *ad hoc* committee. An international counter-committee was named, and included Benedetto Croce, T. S. Eliot, Karl Jaspers, André Malraux, Jacques Maritain, Bertrand Russell and Igor Stravinsky. Even the Nobel Prizewinner Dr Albert Schweitzer enlisted, apparently untroubled that his name also appeared in the enemy camp as one of the 'sponsors' of the Waldorf conference. Taking advantage of their Trojan horse position within the Waldorf, the group intercepted mail addressed to the conference's organizers, and sabotaged their attempts to win over the press by doctoring official statements and releases. It issued a volley of press releases, challenging speakers and sponsors of the conference 'to identify themselves as the Communist Party members or inveterate fellow-travellers that they are'. For those whose consciences failed to be pricked, Hook and his cohorts speeded the process by publicly disclosing 'the true connections of the leaders of the Waldorf meeting'. Thus, F. O. Matthiessen's membership of a host of 'Communist-front organisations' (including the 'Sleepy Lagoon Defense Committee') was revealed in a press release. Howard Fast was listed as 'Author of propaganda novels' and Clifford Odets was exposed (in less than scientific manner) as 'Another Communist Party member according to testimony of a former staff member of the *Daily Worker*'.

As the opening ceremonies of the conference drew near, ideas about how best to subvert the proceedings differed wildly (as do later accounts of the affair). Hook, the self-appointed field marshal of the 'little anti-Communist suite', briefed his *compagnons de guerre* on how to survive a forced expulsion from the hall. Armed with umbrellas, they were to bang the floor to get attention, and then tie themselves to their chairs. Thus anchored, their removal from the hall would be delayed. If they were prevented from delivering their speeches, mimeographed copies would be distributed to reporters by Hook's sidekicks, Beichmann and Pitzele.

As it happened, these guerrilla strategies were never called into play (although, for good measure, umbrellas were banged on the floor). To their surprise, the subverters were each given two minutes to speak, though they had to wait for the first speaker, a retired Bishop from Utah, to finish his endless peroration. Mary McCarthy reserved her question for the brilliant Harvard scholar F. O. Matthiessen, author of *The American Renaissance*, who had described Ralph Waldo Emerson as an ancestor of American Communism. Did Matthiessen think Emerson would be allowed to live and write in the Soviet Union? she asked. Matthiessen conceded he would not, and then added – in what was deemed 'the non-sequitur of the year' – that Lenin wouldn't be permitted to live in the United States, either. When Dwight Macdonald asked Fadeyev why he had accepted the Politburo's critical 'suggestions' and rewritten his novel *The Young Guard*, Fadeyev replied, 'The Politburo's criticism helped my work greatly.'

Nicolas Nabokov decided to attend a panel where Shostakovich was one of the speakers. Among the musicians on the platform were people known to Nabokov, friends even. He waved to them, and they smiled nervously in response. After a typically dull and predictable session, Nabokov was finally given the floor. 'On such-and-such a date in No. X of *Pravda* appeared an unsigned article that had all the looks of an editorial. It concerned three western composers: Paul Hindemith, Arnold Schoenberg, and Igor Stravinsky. In this article, they were branded, all three of them, as "obscurantists", "decadent bourgeois formalists" and "lackeys of imperialist capitalism". The performance of their music should "therefore be prohibited in the U.S.S.R." Does Mr Shostakovich personally agree with this official view as printed in *Pravda*?'[5]

'*Provokatsya*! [Provocation!]' cried the Russian stooges, as Shostakovich received whispered instructions from his KGB 'nurse'. The composer then stood up, was handed a microphone and, his ashen face turned down to study the floorboards, murmured in Russian, 'I fully agree with the statements made in *Pravda*.'

It was an appalling episode. Rumours that Shostakovich had been ordered to attend the conference by Stalin himself had reached this New York gathering. He was the sacrificial lamb, appearing, said one observer, 'pale, slight, and sensitive looking, hunched over, tense, withdrawn, unsmiling – a tragic and heartrending figure'. Arthur Miller described him as 'small, frail, and myopic', standing 'as stiffly erect as a doll'. Any display of independent spirit on his part was a life or death matter. Nicolas Nabokov, on the other hand, was a White Russian émigré who had become an American citizen in 1939. He was safe. Nabokov was throwing punches at a man whose arms were tied behind his back.

As chairman of the arts panel at which this confrontation took place, Arthur Miller was appalled. 'It is the memory of Shostakovich that still haunts my mind when I think of that day – what a masquerade it all was! . . . God knows what he was thinking in that room, what splits ran across his spirit, what urge to cry out and what self-control to suppress his outcry lest he lend comfort to America and her new belligerence toward his country, the very one that was making his life a hell.'[6]

Thirty years later, Shostakovich's memoirs appeared in the West, giving his account of the Waldorf affair: 'I still recall with horror my first trip to the USA. I wouldn't have gone at all if it hadn't been for intense pressure from administrative figures of all ranks and colours, from Stalin down. People sometimes say it must have been an interesting trip, look at the way I'm smiling in the photographs. That was the smile of a condemned man. I felt like a dead man. I answered all the idiotic questions in a daze, and thought, When I get back it's over for me. Stalin liked leading Americans by the nose that way. He would show them a man – here he is, alive and well – and then kill him. Well, why say lead by the nose? That's too strongly put. He only fooled those who wanted to be fooled. The Americans don't give a damn about us, and in order to live and sleep soundly, they'll believe anything.'[7]

The conference continued for several days. T. S. Eliot sent a telegram opposing the conference. Another telegram came from John Dos Passos, who urged American liberals to expose Soviet tyranny so that 'with that exposure despotism will perish from its own poison'. Thomas Mann, who once commented that anti-Communism 'is the basic stupidity of the twentieth century', sent a cable in support of the conference. The 'debates' were ritualistic and deadly dull, spiced up only by the intervention of a young Norman Mailer (described by one contemporary as 'a preppy Frank Sinatra'), who surprised both sides when he accused both the Soviet Union and the United States of aggressive foreign policy programmes that minimized the chance of peaceful coexistence. 'So long as there is capitalism, there is going to be war. Until you have a decent, equitable socialism, you can't have peace,' he said, before concluding that 'All a writer can do is tell the truth as he sees it, and to keep on writing.'[8] Mailer's speech had the magic effect of uniting antagonists in a chorus of boos.

By now the picket outside had swelled to over a thousand, bristling with placards. One observer wondered how it was 'that so many noisy, tough plug-uglies are at the disposal of the extreme right'. Hook was astute enough to observe that the Communism inside the Waldorf and the kind of militant anti-Communism outside on the sidewalk were feeding off each other. His aggressive PR campaign, run by Mel Pitzele, was now beginning to bite. The newspaper magnate and paranoid anti-Communist William Randolph Hearst ordered all his editors to follow the beat of Hook's drum and denounce the 'Commie' conference and its American 'fellow travellers'.

In April, Henry Luce, owner-editor of the *Time-Life* empire, personally oversaw a two-page spread in *Life* magazine, which attacked the degradations of the Kremlin and its American 'dupes'. Featuring fifty passport-sized photographs, the piece was an *ad hominem* attack which prefigured Senator McCarthy's unofficial blacklists. Dorothy Parker, Norman Mailer, Leonard Bernstein, Lillian Hellman, Aaron Copland, Langston Hughes, Clifford Odets, Arthur Miller, Albert Einstein, Charlie Chaplin, Frank Lloyd Wright, Marlon Brando, Henry Wallace – all were accused of toying with Communism. This was the same *Life* magazine which in 1943 had devoted an entire issue to the USSR, featuring Stalin on the cover, and praising the Russian people and the Red Army.

'It was dangerous to participate in that fateful attempt to rescue the wartime alliance with the Soviet Union in the face of the mounting pressures of the Cold War, and one knew it at the time,' remembered Arthur Miller. 'The air was growing hot with belligerence . . . There was no denying the probability of retribution against the conference participants as its opening day drew near . . . And indeed, as the months passed, "Supporter of the Waldorf Conference" or "Participant" would become an important key to the subject's disloyalty . . . That a meeting of writers and artists could generate such widespread public suspicion and anger was something brand-new in the post-war world.'[9]

It certainly was dangerous. Those who were 'outed' at the Waldorf – a hotel famous for its pre-war débutante 'coming out' balls – were now the subject of FBI director J. Edgar Hoover's interest. His Federal Bureau of Investigation sent agents to cover the conference and report back on the delegates. Back at FBI headquarters, a file was opened on the young Norman Mailer. Files on Langston Hughes, Arthur Miller, F. O. Matthiessen, Lillian Hellman, Dashiell Hammett and Dorothy Parker (who was listed variously as 'an undercover Communist', 'an open Communist', and 'a Communist appeaser') had already been opened in the 1930s, but their new acts of perversion were now recorded.

In some cases, the FBI did more than monitor the Waldorf 'Communists'. Shortly after the conference, an FBI agent paid a visit to the publishing firm of Little, Brown, and told them that J. Edgar Hoover did not want to see Howard Fast's new novel, *Spartacus*, on the bookshelves.[10] Little, Brown returned the manuscript to its author, who was then rejected by seven other publishers. Alfred Knopf sent the manuscript back unopened, saying he wouldn't even look at the work of a traitor. The book finally came out in 1950, published by Howard Fast himself. The 'Stalinists' right to culture' was certainly under attack.

With coverage in *Life* magazine, the strange *pas de deux* between Communists and former Communists at the Waldorf had now become a major public spectacle. Hook congratulated himself for having choreographed the best scenes: 'We had frustrated one of the most ambitious undertakings of the Kremlin.'

Sidney Hook was born in December 1902 in New York's Williamsburg, a Brooklyn slum of unrivalled poverty in those years. This was fertile ground for Communism, to which Hook became a young adherent. Short in stature, his small face framed by round spectacles, Hook looked like a cracker-barrel sage. But he was fiercely intellectual, a cerebral brawler always ready to jump into the fight. Attracted to the muscular, bruising posturing of New Yorkist Communism, he moved easily between its various factions, from Stalinism to Trotskyism to Bukharinism. He helped prepare the first translation of Lenin's *Materialism and Empiriocriticism* for the American Communist Party. He worked for a spell in the Marx-Engels Institute in Moscow. And he published a series of articles on Marxism, the most famous of which, 'Why I Am A Communist', provoked a Hearst-led campaign to have him dismissed from New York University.

In the pattern of many New York intellectuals, Hook's faith in Communism began to weaken after a succession of betrayals: the 1936–7 treason trial of Leon Trotsky, the Nazi–Soviet Non-Aggression Pact of 1939, and a series of disastrous errors of judgement, theory and policy by Stalin. A public enemy of the Communist Party, he was denounced as a 'counter-revolutionary reptile', his supporters dismissed as 'Hookworms'. By 1942, Hook was informing on the writer and editor Malcolm Cowley to the FBI. Hook the revolutionary from Williamsburg had become Hook the darling of the conservatives.[11]

In the late afternoon of Thursday, 27 March 1949, police roped off a block on 40th Street between Fifth and Sixth Avenues. From the balcony of the aptly named Freedom House, Hook and his private army waved triumphantly at a dense crowd gathered below in Bryant Square. His 'team of promoters . . . had done a splendid publicity job', said Nabokov, who was particularly well-suited to basking in the limelight. Nabokov used this end of conference party to deliver a speech about 'the plight of composers in the Soviet Union and the tyranny of the party's Kulturapparat'. Addressing a packed audience in the hall of Freedom House, Nabokov deplored the use that was being made of Dmitri Shostakovich at the 'peace conference'. Thunderous applause. And then Nabokov saw 'a familiar face rise from the back row of the hall and come at me. It was an acquaintance of mine from Berlin who, like me, had worked for OMGUS. He congratulated me warmly: "This is a splendid affair you and your friends have organized," he said. "We should have something like this in Berlin."'[12]

The 'friend' who stepped forward was Michael Josselson. His presence at the Waldorf Astoria conference, and subsequently at the Freedom House rally, was anything but the innocent coincidence Nabokov suggests. Josselson was there at the express instructions of his boss Frank Wisner, the CIA's covert action wizard. This 'splendid affair' was being subsidized by Wisner's outfit, and Josselson was there to keep an eye on the investment. With the witting collaboration of David Dubinsky – whose presence in the bridal suite was always something of a mystery – the CIA had procured Hook's stronghold in the Waldorf (Dubinsky had threatened to have the unions close down the hotel if the management could not accommodate his intellectual friends), paid the bills (Nabokov received a large wodge of CIA dollars from Dubinsky to take back to the bridal suite), and secured wide and sympathetic press coverage.

Melvin Lasky, too, had come from Berlin to see how Hook's agitprop activities were shaping up (the two had liaised the previous year, when Hook had been in Berlin as an 'educational adviser' in the American zone). Lasky thrilled to the confrontational character of the Waldorf conference, reserving special scorn for Shostakovich. 'His timidity was extreme,' he later claimed. 'He didn't want to stand up for anything. But there are those who say, There are things that are bigger than you, Shostakovich, bigger even than your music, and you have to pay an entrance fee, whether you like it or not, in the name of a higher purpose.'[13]

Hook and his friends at the Waldorf felt they had paid their entrance fee. But most of them were not party to the hidden arrangement that had made their counteraction possible. Nicola Chiaromonte was suspicious of Hook's contacts. He warned Mary McCarthy, somewhat cryptically, to hold out against Hook and his lieutenants, whose many press releases in this hectic week had included statements explicitly supporting US foreign policy: 'What the boys and Hook do in the last analysis, is not to say they are happy about the State Department, but that finally they are prepared to yield to American raison d'Etat as against the Russians.' This, continued Chiaromonte, was 'a preordained act of conformism and a very unconstructive one, from, precisely, the democratic point of view'.[14]

This early sensitivity is very revealing, worthy of a man whose perceptions had been refined by his work as a political agent for the Munzenberg Trust. For, although Chiaromonte didn't know it yet, he had come very close to the truth. A little bit closer, and he would have discovered that it wasn't just the State Department that had taken an interest in Hook, but America's spying establishment.

Arthur Miller intuited that the Waldorf conference would

turn out to be 'a hairpin curve on the road of history'. Forty years later he wrote: 'Even now something dark and frightening shadows the memory of that meeting . . . where people sat as in a Saul Steinberg drawing, each of them with a balloon overhead containing absolutely indecipherable scribbles. There we were, a roomful of talented people and a few real geniuses, and in retrospect neither side was wholly right, neither the apologists for the Soviets nor the outraged Red-haters; to put it simply, politics is choices, and not infrequently there really aren't any to make; the chessboard allows no space for a move.'[15]

But for the CIA, the Waldorf conference represented a chance to make some new moves in the Great Game. It was a 'catalytic event', recalled CIA agent Donald Jameson. 'It was the tip-off that there was a massive campaign launched in the West on an ideological assertion of influence at a political level.' It delivered a powerful message to those in government who understood that the compelling nature of the Communist delusion was not going to be dissipated by conventional methods. 'We now understood that it was necessary to do something about it. Not in terms of suppressing these people, many of whom of course were very noble types. But rather as part of a general programme looking toward, ultimately, what we now can call the end of the Cold War.'[16]

4

Democracy's Deminform

Whenever I'm a shining Knight,
I buckle on my armour tight;
And then I look about for things,
Like Rushings-out, and Rescuings,
And Savings from the Dragon's Lair,
And fighting all the Dragons there.

A. A. Milne, 'Knight-in-Armour'

The Waldorf Astoria conference was a humiliation for its Communist backers. 'It was,' said one observer, 'a propagandist's nightmare, a fiasco that proved the last hurrah for the idea that the ideological interests of Stalinist Russia could be grafted onto progressive traditions in America.'[1] The American Communist Party was now in retreat, its membership at an all-time low, its prestige irrevocably tarnished. Just when claims of a Communist conspiracy began to take feverish grip, Stalin's strategists all but turned their back on America, and concentrated instead on extending influence and neutralizing enemies in Europe.

The Cominform's campaign to convince the thinking man of Europe that the only aggrandizement the USSR sought was one of 'peace' was seriously undermined by two crucial events in 1949. First, there was Stalin's ruthless treatment of the Yugoslav leader Marshal Tito, whose refusal to sacrifice national interests in favour of propping up Soviet hegemony in the Balkans had opened a vicious polemic between Moscow and Belgrade. Stalin had withdrawn economic and military advisers from Yugoslavia as part of a war of attrition designed to weaken this independent stance. Tito, in turn, had opened negotiations with the West to receive Marshall Plan credits to revive his crippled economy. Stalin's brutal interpretation of 'international Communism' strained the goodwill of European fellow travellers, who now rallied to Tito's defence. Secondly, Soviet calls for peaceful co-existence were further undermined by the detonation of a Russian atomic bomb in August 1949.

The British answer to the phoney claims of Soviet propaganda was belatedly taking shape. The Information Research Department (IRD), which had been set up in February 1948 by Clement Attlee's government to attack Communism, was the fastest growing section of the Foreign Office. 'We cannot hope successfully to repel Communism only by disparaging it on material grounds,' explained the IRD's architect, Foreign Secretary Ernest Bevin, 'and must add a positive appeal to Democratic and Christian principles, remembering the strength of Christian sentiment in Europe. We must put forward a rival ideology to Communism.'[2] This, indeed, was the challenge: western governments could not simply rely on denigrating the Soviet experiment, but had a duty to offer an alternative future from within a system – capitalist democracy – whose boasts often far exceeded its achievements. 'What is wrong with the world is not the strength of Communism, which Stalin and Co. have perverted into an instrument of Slavist expansion in a manner which would have shocked Lenin, but the moral and spiritual weakness of the non-Communist world,' argued the diplomat-spy Robert Bruce Lockhart.[3]

To overlook the role of the British government in manufacturing a cosy image of Stalin during the wartime alliance is to ignore one of the crucial truths of the Cold War: the alliance between the free world and Russia against the Nazis was the moment at which history itself seemed to connive in the illusion that Communism was politically decent. The problem facing the British government after the Second World War was how to set about dismantling the untruths it had systematically constructed or defended in the previous years. 'During the war, we had built up this man, though we knew he was terrible, because he was an ally,' explained Adam Watson, a junior diplomat recruited to the IRD as its second-in-command. 'Now the question was, "How do we get rid of the Good Old Uncle Joe myth built up during the war?"'[4] Many British intellectuals and writers had worked for the government in its propaganda departments during the war: now they were being called upon to disabuse the British public of those lies they had worked so inventively to protect.

The Information Research Department was, despite its innocuous title, a secret Ministry of Cold War. Drawing its budget from the secret vote (to avoid unwelcome scrutiny of any operations which might require covert or semi-covert action), its purpose 'was to produce and distribute and circulate unattributable propaganda', according to Christopher 'Monty' Woodhouse, a spy who was assigned to the department in 1953. Working on the trickle-down theory, IRD compiled 'factual' reports on all manner of subjects for distribution amongst members of the British intelligentsia, who were then expected to recycle these facts in their own work. Non-attribution was a central and distinguishing feature of this exercise, making it possible to reconcile two essentially contradictory requirements: to achieve the widest possible circulation for IRD material whilst protecting the existence of an officially sanctioned and secretly funded anti-Communist propaganda campaign about which the public knew nothing. 'It is important that in the UK, as abroad, there should not be created a public impression that the Foreign Office is organizing an anti-communist campaign,' wrote IRD's first chief, Ralph Murray. 'It would embarrass a number of persons who are prepared to lend us valuable support if they were open to the charge of receiving anti-communist briefs from some sinister body in the Foreign Office engaged in the fabrication of propaganda directed at the Soviet Union.'[5]

'If you base your work on supplying facts, it's much harder to refute than if you're supplying simply propaganda,' Adam Watson later explained. 'It's about exposing those aspects of the truth which are most useful to you.'[6] In practice, this meant that although IRD was intended to attack both 'the principles and practice of Communism, and also the inefficiency, social injustice and moral weakness of unrestrained capitalism', it was not allowed to 'attack or appear to be attacking any member of the Commonwealth or the United States'.[7] The idea that the truth could be submitted to such exigencies had long amused Noël Coward who, in his brief tenure as an intelligence officer, had delighted in over-stamping documents marked 'highly confidential' with the words 'highly truthful'.

One of IRD's most important early advisers was the Hungarian-born writer Arthur Koestler. Under his tutelage, the department realized the usefulness of accommodating those people and institutions who, in the tradition of left-wing politics, broadly perceived themselves to be in opposition to the centre of power. The purpose of such accommodation was twofold: first, to acquire a proximity to 'progressive' groups in order to monitor their activities; secondly, to dilute the impact of these groups by achieving influence from within, or by drawing its members into a parallel – and subtly less radical – forum.

Koestler himself was soon benefiting from IRD's propaganda campaigns. *Darkness at Noon*, whose depiction of Soviet cruelty had established Koestler's credentials as an anti-Communist, was circulated in Germany under its auspices. In a deal struck with Hamish Hamilton, director of the eponymous publishing house, and himself closely tied to intelligence, 50,000 copies were purchased and distributed by the Foreign Office in 1948. Ironically, at the same time, 'the French Communist Party had orders to buy up every single copy [of the book] immediately and they were all being bought up and there was no reason why it should ever stop being reprinted, so in this way K[oestler] was being enriched indefinitely from Communist Party funds.'[8]

Koestler was not only acting as a consultant for the Foreign Office's propaganda campaign. In February 1948, he had set off on a lecture tour of the United States. In March he met with William 'Wild Bill' Donovan in the General's New York townhouse on Sutton Place. Donovan, both as director of America's wartime intelligence service, and more recently, as one of the chief architects of the newly created CIA, was a core member of America's intelligence and foreign policy elite. He was a lifelong anti-Communist, keeping vigil right up to the moment of his death in 1959, when he reported spotting Russian troops marching into Manhattan across the 59th Street bridge outside his window. Koestler, formerly one of the brains behind the Soviet Union's pre-war network of front organizations (known as the 'Munzenberg Trust', after its director, Willi Munzenberg), knew better than most men living how the Soviet propaganda machine worked from the inside. Shortly before leaving for the States, Koestler had met André Malraux and Chip Bohlen, the newly appointed ambassador to France, to discuss how best to counter the Cominform's 'peace' offensive. Aboard ship whilst crossing to America, Koestler had also met, by coincidence, John Foster Dulles, brother of Allen Dulles and future Secretary of State, and the two had discussed the same problem. Now, Koestler was sitting down with William Donovan to talk about how to counter Soviet propaganda. 'Discussed need for psychological warfare,' Koestler noted in his diary, adding that Donovan possessed a 'first-rate brain'. The significance of this meeting should not be underestimated.

Arthur Koestler was born into a middle-class family in Budapest in 1905. After a Pauline conversion, he joined the Communist Party in the early 1930s. He later wrote that reading Marx and Engels had 'the intoxicating effect of a sudden liberation'. In 1932 he went to Russia and wrote a propaganda book financed by the Communist International, *Of White Nights and Red Days*. There, he fell madly in love with a clerk called Nadeshda Smirnova. He spent a week or two with her, and then denounced her to the secret police over a trifling matter. She was never heard of again. After Hitler's triumph in Germany he joined the German exiles in Paris, where he teamed up with Willi Munzenberg. In 1936 he went to Spain, probably to spy for Munzenberg. He was interned as a political prisoner, but was saved when the British government intervened following the vigorous activities of his first wife, Dorothy Ascher. By 1938 he had resigned from the Communist Party, disgusted by Stalin's mass arrests and show trials, but still believing in the attainability of the Bolshevik utopia. He stopped believing altogether when the swastika was hoisted at Moscow airport in honour of Ribbentrop's arrival to sign the Hitler–Stalin Pact and the Red Army band broke into the 'Horst Wessel Lied'. Interned in France during the war, he wrote *Darkness at Noon*, a chronicle of the abuses performed in the name of ideology, which soon became one of the most influential books of the period. On his release he made his way to England (via the French Foreign Legion) where, after yet another internment, he enlisted in the Pioneer Corps. He later joined the Ministry of Information as an anti-Nazi propagandist, work which earned him British citizenship.

His 1948 lecture tour in America was designed to disabuse the 'Babbitts of the Left'[9] of the fallacies and confusions which still dominated their thinking. He exhorted American intellectuals to abandon their juvenile radicalism and engage themselves in a mature enterprise of cooperation with the power structure: 'The task of the progressive intelligentsia of your country is to help the rest of the nation to face its enormous responsibilities. The time for sectarian quarrels in the cosy no-man's-land of abstract radicalism is past. It is time for the American radical to grow up.'[10] Thus did Koestler call for a new era of engagement, where intellectuals took it as their duty to justify the national effort, eschewing the now anachronistic privilege of distance or detachment. 'Since the writer has no way to escape, we want him to take hold of his era firmly: it is his only chance; it was made for him and he for it,' Jean-Paul Sartre was soon to declare. 'Our intention is to work together to produce certain changes in the society that surrounds us.'[11] The difference between Sartre and Koestler was not the quality of engagement, but its object. Where Sartre remained resolutely opposed to the institutions of government as mediators of truth or reason, Koestler enjoined his colleagues to help the power elite in its mission to rule.

Shortly after his meeting with Donovan in New York, Koestler travelled to Washington, where he attended a round of press conferences, luncheons, cocktails and dinner parties. Through James Burnham, an American intellectual who had made the journey from radicalism to the institutions of power with amazing speed, he was introduced to scores of State Department officials, presidential aides, journalists and trades union officials. The CIA in particular took an interest in Koestler. Here was a man who could tell them a thing or two.

The Agency had been toying with an idea for a while now: who better to fight the Communists than former Communists? In consultation with Koestler, this idea now began to take shape. The destruction of the Communist mythos, he argued, could only be achieved by mobilizing those figures on the left who were non-Communist in a campaign of persuasion. The people of whom Koestler spoke were already designated as a group – the Non-Communist Left – in State Department and intelligence circles. In what Arthur Schlesinger described as a 'quiet revolution', elements of the government had come increasingly to understand and support the ideas of those intellectuals who were disillusioned with Communism but still faithful to the ideals of socialism.

Indeed, for the CIA, the strategy of promoting the Non-Communist Left was to become 'the theoretical foundation of the Agency's political operations against Communism over the next two decades'.[12] The ideological rationale for this strategy, in which the CIA achieved a convergence, even an identity, with leftist intellectuals, was presented by Schlesinger in *The Vital Center*, one of three seminal books which appeared in 1949 (the other two being *The God That Failed*, and Orwell's *Nineteen Eighty-Four*). Schlesinger charted the decline of the left and its eventual moral paralysis in the wake of the corrupted revolution of 1917, and traced the evolution of the 'non-Communist Left' as 'the standard to rally the groups fighting to carve out an area for freedom'. It was within this group that 'the restoration of the radical nerve' would take place, leaving 'no lamp in the window for the Communists'. This new resistance, argued Schlesinger, needed 'an independent base from which to operate. It requires privacy, funds, time, newsprint, gasoline, freedom of speech, freedom of assembly, freedom from fear.'[13]

'The thesis which animated all this [mobilization of] the Non-Communist Left was one which Chip Bohlen, Isaiah Berlin, Nicolas Nabokov, Averell Harriman and George Kennan all ardently supported,' Schlesinger later recalled. 'We all felt that democratic socialism was the most effective bulwark against totalitarianism. This became an undercurrent – or even undercover – theme in American foreign policy during the period.'[14] Shortened to the initials NCL, the Non-Communist Left was a designation which soon became common usage in the bureaucratic language of Washington. 'It was almost a card carrying group,' noted one historian.[15]

This 'card carrying group' was assembled for the first time under the covers of *The God That Failed*, a collection of essays testifying to the failure of the Communist idea. The book's animating spirit was Arthur Koestler, who had returned to

London in a state of high excitement after his discussions with William Donovan and other US intelligence strategists. The subsequent history of its publication serves as a template for the contract between the Non-Communist Left and the 'dark angel' of American government. By the summer of 1948, Koestler had discussed the idea with Richard Crossman, wartime head of the German section of the Psychological Warfare Executive (PWE), a man who felt 'he could manipulate masses of people', and who had 'just the right amount of intellectual sleight-of-hand to make him a perfect professional propagandist'.[16] As a Fellow at New College alongside Isaiah Berlin (who also had contacts with the PWE during the war), Crossman was once described as 'without principles and very ambitious', someone who 'would climb over his mother's dead body to get a step higher'.[17] In his book *Plato Today* (1937), Crossman's narrator wondered whether parliamentary democracy was not in essence 'a sham, a gaily-painted hoarding behind which are kept hidden the government and the machinery of the state'. The same might be said of *The God That Failed*.

On 27 August 1948, Crossman involved another psychological warfare veteran, the American C. D. Jackson, in the project. 'I am writing to ask your advice. Cass Canfield of Harpers, and Hamish Hamilton, my publisher here, are proposing next spring to publish a book called *Lost Illusions*, for which I have taken editorial responsibility. It is to consist of a series of autobiographical sketches by prominent intellectuals, describing how they became Communists or fellow-travellers, what made them feel that Communism was the hope of the world, and what disillusioned them.'[18] C. D. Jackson's advice was that the writer Louis Fischer, a former Communist, be invited to represent America's lost illusions.

Crossman then approached Melvin Lasky, by now America's official unofficial cultural propagandist in Germany, and one of the earliest advocates of organized intellectual resistance to Communism. As Crossman received contributions for the book, he sent them immediately on to Lasky, who had them translated in the offices of *Der Monat*. According to an American High Commission Evaluation Report of 1950, 'all but one of the articles in *The God That Failed* were original contributions to *Der Monat*, or articles for which the magazine negotiated the copyright. By issue 25, *Der Monat* had completed publication of all the essays.'[19] Crossman edited the English version, which was published in 1950 by Koestler's publisher, Hamish Hamilton. Crossman's close friend from the Office of War Information, Cass Canfield (later Allen Dulles's publisher), was responsible for the American edition. With this background, *The God That Failed* was as much a product of intelligence as it was a work of the intelligentsia.

The contributors were Ignazio Silone, André Gide, Richard Wright, Arthur Koestler, Louis Fischer and Stephen Spender. 'We were not in the least interested either in swelling the flood of anti-Communist propaganda or in providing an opportunity for personal apologetics,' wrote Crossman in his introduction.[20] Yet the book achieved both these disavowed objectives. Although they collectively testified to the failure of the Marxist utopia, the essays were all deeply personal accounts, the *apologia pro politica sua* of individuals moved to express their disenchantment and sense of betrayal. A collective act of confession, the book was also a recusant statement, a rejection of Stalinism at a time when many still considered such an act heresy. It was a new book of revelations for the post-war era, and appearance in it was to act as a passport to the world of official culture for the next twenty years.

Of the six contributors to *The God That Failed*, three had worked for Willi Munzenberg. Koestler, who once said that faith was wondrous, not only capable of moving mountains 'but of making one believe that a herring is a racehorse', had been one of Munzenberg's most zealous disciples. During the 1930s, when he was as well known in America as Ed Murrow would be in the 1950s, the journalist Louis Fischer was a man whose career had also been closely shaped by his experience as a Communist working for Munzenberg. Ignazio Silone had joined the Italian Communist Party in 1921. Like Koestler's, his was a true conversion ('The party became family, school, church, barracks'), and propelled him up the ladder of the Communist International and into the arms of Munzenberg. Quietly dropping out of Party activity after 1927, Silone retained 'the ashen taste of a wasted youth'. The final break came in 1931, when the Communist Party asked him to make a public statement condemning Trotsky. He refused, and the Party expelled him as a 'clinical case'. Speaking to a group of German ex-Communists living, like him, in uneasy exile in Switzerland during the war, Silone said: 'the past, including all the wounds that it has left with us, need not be a source of weakness for us. We must not allow ourselves to be demoralized by the errors, the carelessness, the stupid things said or written. What is required from us now is a will so pure that new strength can be born from the worst of ourselves: *Etiam peccata*.'[21]

Under the covers of *The God That Failed*, these former propagandists for the Soviets were recycled, bleached of the stain of Communism, embraced by government strategists who saw in their conversion an irresistible opportunity to sabotage the Soviet propaganda machine which they had once oiled. 'The God That Failed gang' was now a nomenclature adopted by the CIA, denoting what one officer called 'that community of intellectuals who were disillusioned, who could be disillusioned, or who hadn't taken a position yet, and who could to some degree be influenced by their peers as to what choice to make'.[22]

The God That Failed was distributed by US government agencies all over Europe. In Germany, in particular, it was rigorously promoted. The Information Research Department also pushed the book. Koestler was happy. His plans for a strategically organized response to the Soviet threat were coalescing nicely. Whilst the book was rolling off the presses, he met with Melvin Lasky to discuss something more ambitious, more permanent.

If *The God That Failed* had shown that there was a warm welcome for those who wished to convert, it was also true that not everybody was ready to become a communicant at the altar of organized anti-Communism. The Cominform was quick to exploit this reticence. After the disastrous Waldorf Astoria outing, it was extra vigilant in its preparations for its next meeting, the World Congress of Peace, scheduled for April 1949 in Paris. A top-secret IRD cypher of March that year predicted, 'The technique envisaged and the organization of the Congress indicate that every attempt will be made to use it simply as a rubber-stamp for whatever the Soviet Union has in mind.'[23] The Cominform's theme, apparently, was to be that 'the U.S. and the western democracies are the war-mongers and Fascists and the Kremlin and its stooges the peace-loving democracies'. All diplomatic posts were asked to 'explore all possible action which might puncture the propaganda value of this Congress'.[24]

But the American 'cousins' in the CIA were already on to the Paris conclave. The day after the Waldorf conference had closed, Frank Wisner's side-kick Carmel Offie had asked the State Department what it intended to do about the Paris peace conference. Offie was Wisner's special assistant for labour and émigré affairs, personally overseeing the National Committee for a Free Europe, one of OPC's most important fronts, as well as other operations dealing with anti-Communist organizations in Europe. Offie dealt often with Irving Brown, the European Representative of the American Federation of Labour (AFL), whose modest title concealed a political role of huge importance in post-war Europe. Through Brown, vast sums of American tax-payers' money and Marshall Plan 'counterpart' funds were being pumped to covert operations.

Offie, a career Foreign Service officer, was by all accounts a sinister figure. Physically ugly, he taunted other men with his homosexuality by tweaking their nipples at staff meetings. He was once arrested for hanging around the public lavatories in Lafayette Park, an incident which made his CIA codename, 'Monk', laughably inappropriate. He had been tossed out of the Foreign Service after the war for using the diplomatic pouch for illegal currency transfers (he also dealt in diamonds, rubies and, on one occasion, a shipment of 300 Finnish lobsters). But he had powerful friends. Chip Bohlen and George Kennan knew him from Moscow Embassy days, and it was Bohlen who had persuaded Wisner to take him on. While working for OPC, it was said of Offie that he was the last man to see a piece of paper before it went to Wisner, and the last man to see $2 million before it disappeared.[25]

Offie and Wisner now started to plan an orchestrated response to the Paris conference, which the State Department had gloomily predicted would 'persuade [the] innocents to follow [the Kremlin's] line' and buy into 'this phony peace movement'.[26] Wisner cabled Averell Harriman of the Economic Cooperation Administration (managers of the Marshall Plan), seeking five million francs (approximately $16,000) to fund a counter-demonstration. Harriman, a great supporter of propaganda and psychological warfare, was one of the first amongst America's political mandarins to understand that Russia had declared ideological war on the West, and to think up ways of countering 'the blast of abuse which was propelled from Moscow'.[27] He was more than happy to provide Marshall Plan funds – referred to as 'candy' by Wisner – for covert operations.

Through Irving Brown, OPC contacted the French socialist David Rousset, author of several books on concentration camps (*Les Jours de Notre Mort*, *L'Univers Concentrationnaire*), and his allies at the breakaway leftist newspaper *Franc-Tireur*. Rousset agreed to allow *Franc-Tireur* to be billed as the sponsor of the CIA-inspired day of resistance.

For the Soviets, Ilya Ehrenburg and Alexander Fadeyev appeared at the main conference – 'a Cominform affair from start to finish' – together with Paul Robeson, Howard Fast, Hewlett Johnson, France's Commissioner for Atomic Energy Frédéric Joliot-Curie, the Danish writer Martin Andersen-Nexo, and the Italian Socialist Pietro Nenni. Charlie Chaplin sent a message of support. A Russian Orthodox priest blessed the conference, and Paul Robeson sang 'Ole Man River'. Picasso released his famous peace dove, which for decades to come was used as the prestige symbol of the Communist 'peace' movement. One of the conference organizers, the poet and diehard Communist Louis Aragon, had come across a lithograph of a pigeon while flicking through a folder of recent work in Picasso's studio. The pigeon had feathers like white gaiters covering its claws. Aragon thought it looked like a dove, and with Picasso's permission, it became the famous 'Dove of Peace'. It was soon to be caricatured by the CIA-backed Paix et Liberté movement as 'the dove that goes boom' ('La colombe qui fait Boum!'), in a cartoon reproduced and distributed throughout the world by American government agencies in pamphlets, handbills and posters.

Rousset's counter-conference, the International Day of Resistance to Dictatorship and War, took place on 30 April

1949, and was endorsed by messages of support from Eleanor Roosevelt, Upton Sinclair, John Dos Passos (who was on his way to becoming a staunch Republican, and already, according to Dwight Macdonald, 'neurotically scared of Russia and Communism'), Julian Huxley and Richard Crossman. Delegates arriving at the expense of OPC included Ignazio Silone, Carlo Levi, the ubiquitous Sidney Hook, author of *Studs Lonigan* James T. Farrell, Franz Borkenau and Fenner Brockway. But, despite careful planning, the day was a failure. 'Not since I was a boy thirty years ago listening to the soap-boxers on Madison Square have I heard such banalities and empty rhetoric,'[28] reported Sidney Hook. At the evening rally a group of anarchists seized the microphone and denounced the meeting, leading Hook to conclude that the lunatics had been let out of the asylum and the proceedings had been taken over by the 'psychopathic ward on the left'.

The conference also claimed America's first casualty in the *Kulturkampf* in the person of Richard Wright who was, according to Hook, 'flattered by the use which Sartre makes of him as a kind of club against American culture analogous to the use the Communists make of Robeson'.[29] Although he had contributed to *The God That Failed*, Wright was now regarded by the anti-Communist lobby as suspect, because his break with Stalinism was made 'more on personal than on political grounds', and he showed 'no understanding of its true nature'.[30] Wright was the only member of *The God That Failed* group to lose his membership of that group of apostles. For the next decade, his life and activities in Paris were monitored by the CIA and the FBI, until he died in mysterious circumstances in 1960.

Wisner and his allies in the State Department were disappointed with the Paris counter-conference. Although it attracted prominent anti-Stalinists and provoked blasts from the French Communist Party, its tone was 'too radical and neutralist'.[31] Worse, there was anti-Americanism flying on every wind. 'The French public, by and large, is shockingly ignorant of American life and culture,' Hook wrote. 'Its picture of America is a composite of impressions derived from reading the novels of social protest and revolt (Steinbeck's *Grapes of Wrath* is taken as a faithful and *representative* account), the novels of American degeneracy (Faulkner) and inanity (Sinclair Lewis), from seeing American movies, and from exposure to an incessant Communist barrage which seeps into the non-Communist press. *The informational re-education of the French public seems to me to be the most fundamental as well as most pressing task of American democratic policy in France, towards which almost nothing along effective lines has been done.*'[32]

Hook's idea that anti-Americanism could be eroded by cleansing European minds of the palsied visions of America's pre-eminent novelists seems extraordinary. In effect, what he was advocating was the purging of those expressions of American life which he judged to be in conflict with the government's 'democratic policy' abroad. This was a monumental distortion of the very principles of freedom of expression, irreconcilable with the claims of liberal democracy under whose auspices it was proposed.

But Hook was right about one thing: de-atomizing the *homme de bonne volonté* of Sartrean Paris was going to be an uphill struggle. Like Brecht, who from the comfort of his privileged life in East Germany praised Stalin as 'the justified murderer of the people', the Left Bank intelligentsia had failed to grasp that they were no longer 'truth-seekers but defenders of a beleaguered, crumbling orthodoxy'.[33] Sartre continued to extol Russia as the guardian of freedom, whilst his 'saint', Jean Genet, denied the existence of the Gulags. This, said Arthur Koestler, was the world capital of fellow travellers, of agile careerists with moderate talent like Picasso, Camus and Anouilh, who were held in awe by those many European intellectuals whom Koestler diagnosed as suffering from 'the French flu'. From Paris, Koestler quipped, the Communist Party could take over France with one phone call.

It was clear to Wisner that he had not yet found the right group to spearhead the anti-Communist campaign in France. In words which show that he was already contemplating a permanent base for this campaign, he expressed concern that 'this type of leadership for a continuing organization would result in the degeneration of the entire idea (of having a little DEMINFORM) into a nuts folly of miscellaneous goats and monkeys whose antics would completely discredit the work and statements of the serious and responsible liberals. We should have serious misgivings about supporting such a show.'[34]

Dismayed that the Soviets' propaganda armour was seemingly impregnable, a group of German intellectuals, formerly of the Munzenberg Trust, now sat down to hatch a plan. Meeting with Melvin Lasky in a Frankfurt hotel room in August 1949, Ruth Fischer and Franz Borkenau (once the official historian of the Comintern) started to sketch out their idea for a permanent structure dedicated to organized intellectual resistance. Fischer was the sister of Gerhart Eisler, a Soviet operative dubbed in 1946 'the Number One Communist in the U.S.' and convicted the following year for falsifying a visa application. Gerhart had since been promoted to run the East German propaganda bureau, and as such he would be responsible for organizing the Soviet response to Ruth's plans. Ruth had herself been a leader of the German Communist Party before her faction was expelled on order from Moscow, leading to her break with Stalin (and her brother). She now wrote about her plan to an American diplomat: 'I think we talked about this plan already during my last stay in Paris, but I have now a much more concrete approach to it. I mean, of course, the idea of organizing a big Anti-Waldorf-Astoria Congress in Berlin itself. It should be a gathering of all ex-Communists, plus a good representative group of anti-Stalinist American, English and European intellectuals, declaring its sympathy for Tito and Yugoslavia and the silent opposition in Russia and the satellite states, and giving the Politburo hell right at the gate of their own hell. All my friends agree that it would be of enormous effect and radiate to Moscow, if properly organized.'[35]

Did Michael Josselson attend the Frankfurt meeting? Certainly, he was amongst the first to hear of the plan, which he was soon to discuss with Lawrence de Neufville, who pouched the outline proposal to Carmel Offie in mid-September. 'The idea came from Lasky, Josselson and Koestler,' de Neufville later explained, 'and I got Washington to give it the support it needed. I reported it to Frank Lindsay [Wisner's deputy], and I guess he must have taken it to Wisner. We had to beg for approval. The Marshall Plan was the slush fund used everywhere by CIA at that time, so there was never any shortage of funds. The only struggle was to get approval.'[36]

What became known as 'the Josselson proposal' reached Wisner's desk in January 1950. Lasky, meanwhile, too impatient to wait for a response, had already pushed ahead with the plan, enlisting Ernst Reuter, Mayor of West Berlin, and several prominent German academics, who endorsed the idea and promised support. Together, they formed a standing committee and began issuing invitations to intellectuals of the 'free world' to come to Berlin to stand up and be counted. Lasky's freelancing, however, was not all for the good. 'As an employee of American occupation government, his activities on behalf of the Congress struck more than a few observers as proof that the U.S. government was behind the event.'[37]

OPC officers pushed ahead with Josselson's plan, producing a formal project outline with a budget of $50,000, which was approved by Wisner on 7 April. Wisner added one condition: Lasky and James Burnham, who had what might be described as a professional interest in the plan, must be kept out of sight in Berlin 'for fear their presence would only provide ammunition to Communist critics'. Josselson defended Lasky when informed of Wisner's reservations. 'No other person here, certainly no German, could have achieved such success,'[38] he cabled. Lasky by this stage was too far out to rein in. He had publicly announced himself as General Secretary of the forthcoming congress, to be called the Congress for Cultural Freedom, and it was under his and Mayor Reuter's names that invitations were issued and programmes were organized. For public relations, Lasky was joined by Arnold Beichmann, who had made such a timely appearance at the Waldorf.

In America, James Burnham and Sidney Hook were busy making arrangements for the American delegation. Both were aware of OPC's involvement (although Hook neglected to mention this in his memoirs, presumably thinking it of no consequence). Tickets for the American participants were purchased by OPC, which used 'several intermediary organizations' as travel agents. The State Department was also involved in these arrangements. Assistant Secretary of State for Public Affairs, Jesse MacKnight, was so impressed by the whole thing that he urged the CIA to sponsor the congress on a continuing basis even before the conclave in Berlin had taken place.[39] For once, such optimism was not misplaced.

5

Crusading's the Idea

> My ghosts have told me something new
> I'm marching to Korea;
> I cannot tell you what I'll do
> Crusading's the idea
> Yankee Doodle keep it up etc.
>
> Robert Lowell, 1952

Late on the night of 23 June 1950, Arthur Koestler and his wife Mamaine arrived at the Gare de l'Est to catch the night train from Paris to Frankfurt, whence they would proceed to Berlin. As they were searching for their carriage, they bumped into Jean-Paul Sartre, who was travelling on the same train, though he was destined for a different conference. Sartre, unusually, was alone, and the Koestlers were relieved that Simone de Beauvoir (whom they had nicknamed 'Castor') was not there. They shared a picnic supper together, along with a police bodyguard assigned to Koestler by the French Sûreté following death threats from the Communists (which had culminated in the Communist daily *L'Humanité* publishing a map pinpointing Verte Rive, Koestler's villa in Fontaine le Port, near Paris). Although their friendship had been increasingly strained in recent years, these ideological opponents still felt a mutual fondness for each other, and they were able to joke together as the train pulled out into the hot summer night. Sartre, along with Albert Camus, had publicly disavowed Koestler's Congress, and refused to attend. But Koestler felt sorry for Sartre, who confessed that night on the train that his friendships were evaporating under the heat of his and de Beauvoir's politics.

As Koestler was boarding his train, the American delegates were settling into transatlantic flights that would take up to twenty-four hours to make the journey to Germany. Although the Soviet blockade of Berlin had recently been lifted, the only way to reach the western sector was on military aircraft, which meant the delegates had to board C-47s at Frankfurt for the final stage of what Koestler would later refer to as an 'intellectual airlift'. Among them were James T. Farrell, Tennessee Williams, the actor Robert Montgomery, Chairman of the American Atomic Energy Commission David Lilienthal, editor of the *New Leader* Sol Levitas, Carson McCullers, the black editor of the *Pittsburgh Courier* George Schuyler, and the black journalist Max Yergan. Nobel Prize-winning genetic scientist Herman Muller brought with him a strange cargo: five thousand Drosophila fruit flies as gifts to German scientists who had lost their strains during the war.

Arthur Schlesinger Jr. and Sidney Hook travelled together from Boston, Hook apparently intoxicated by the idea of how dangerous it was going to be to go to Berlin. 'He had this fantasy about Communist attacks from all sides,' Schlesinger recalled. 'He was quite excited about it all. I think many of them were. They thought they were going to be where the action was – especially those who hadn't been in the war.'[1] After his first taste of blood at the Waldorf Astoria, Hook was chafing for a full-scale campaign. 'Give me a hundred million dollars and a thousand dedicated people,' he cried, 'and I will guarantee to generate such a wave of democratic unrest among the masses – yes, even among the soldiers – of Stalin's own empire, that all his problems for a long time to come will be internal. I can find the people.'[2] Now, flying into a city which was surrounded on all sides by the Communists, Hook fantasized that the Russians would march into the city, 'in which event every delegate would have been a prisoner of the [East German military police] in a few hours'.[3]

Nicolas Nabokov had arrived in Berlin in May to help plan the conference, together with his wife Patricia Blake, taking a charter plane run by a company called Youth Argosy, one of the 'intermediaries' used by the CIA. Chip Bohlen had urged

Nabokov to get there as early as he could, to raise the barricades on behalf of the artists who had been 'the most persistent whipping boys of both the Soviets and the Nazis'.[4] James Burnham arrived shortly after Nabokov, and together they had joined up with Josselson, Lasky, Koestler, Brown and Silone to form the conference's ruling apparat, which was headquartered in Lasky's house.

At one of the group's meetings over dinner, Silone told how during the war he had sacked anybody in his resistance movement who turned out to be a British or American intelligence agent, because he wanted to fight 'ma guerre à moi' with a clean conscience.[5] How Josselson, Burnham and Lasky digested this statement can only be imagined. For they knew what Silone presumably didn't: that he was now part of a war being run by somebody else. Silone's position neatly encapsulated the painful ironies of an age that had run roughshod over the purity of people's ideals. In the 1920s, he had run an underground network for the Soviets, and then regretted it. From 1928 to 1930 he had collaborated with Mussolini's secret service, OVRA (the circumstances behind this relationship were dire: his brother had been arrested by the Fascists, and was lingering in an Italian prison, where he was later to die). Writing to sever his relationship with his OVRA liaison in April 1930, Silone explained that he had resolved to 'eliminate from my life all that is false, duplicitous, equivocal, mysterious'.[6] In 1942, he wrote that 'The most important of our moral tasks today consists in liberating our spirits from the racket of gunfire, the trajectory of propaganda warfare and journalistic nonsense in general.'[7] In exile in Switzerland during the war, Silone had been a contact for Allen Dulles, then America's chief of espionage in Europe; in October 1944, OSS agent Serafino Romualdi was sent to the Franco-Swiss border, allegedly to deliver two planeloads of arms and ammunition to the French resistance. His real mission, 'planned outside normal channels', was to smuggle Silone into Italy. And now, in 1950, Silone had once again been drawn into a clandestine world. His defenders argue that he was ignorant of the Congress for Cultural Freedom's hidden sponsors. But his widow, Darina, recalled that he had initially been reluctant to attend, as he suspected that it was 'a U.S. State Department operation'. A few days into the conference, Koestler, who never really liked Silone, told a friend that he had always 'wondered whether basically Silone is honest or not. Now I know he is not.'[8]

Also the recipients of secret benefaction were the English delegates – Hugh Trevor-Roper, Julian Amery, A. J. Ayer, Herbert Read, Harold Davis, Christopher Hollis, Peter de Mendelssohn – whose presence in Berlin was being funded covertly by the Foreign Office, through the Information Research Department. From France came Raymond Aron, David Rousset, Rémy Roure, André Philip, Claude Mauriac, André Malraux, Jules Romains, Georges Altman; from Italy there was Ignazio Silone, Guido Piovene, Altiero Spinelli, Franco Lombardi, Muzzio Mazzochi, and Bonaventura Tecchi. By the evening of 25 June, they and most of the other 200 delegates had arrived. They were assigned accommodation in billets and hotels in the American zone and most of them, tired after the journey, turned in early that night.

They awoke the next day to the news that Communist-backed North Korean troops had crossed the 38th Parallel and launched a massive invasion of the South. As they gathered that afternoon, Monday 26 June, at the Titania Palast, for the opening ceremony of the Congress for Cultural Freedom, the Berlin Philharmonic played them in to the tenebrous strains of the Egmont overture, a propitious (and carefully selected) piece for an audience who saw themselves as participants in a darkly heroic drama.

Berlin's Mayor, Ernst Reuter (himself a former Communist who had worked closely with Lenin) asked the delegates and an audience of 4,000 to stand for a moment of silence in memory of those who had died fighting for freedom or who still languished in concentration camps. In his opening speech, he emphasized the drama of Berlin's significance: 'The word freedom, which seemed to have lost its power, has a unique significance for the person who most recognizes its value – the person who once lost it.'[9]

For the next four days, delegates moved from one panel discussion to the next, from guided tours of the Brandenberg Gate, Potsdamer Platz, and the line dividing East from West Berlin, thence to press conferences, and on to cocktail parties and specially organized concerts. The five main debates were themed around 'Science and Totalitarianism', 'Art, Artists and Freedom', 'The Citizen in a Free Society', 'The Defense of Peace and Freedom', and 'Free Culture in a Free World'. A polarization of thought over how best to oppose the Communists soon emerged, neatly encapsulated in speeches given by Arthur Koestler and Ignazio Silone. Koestler called for the formation of the western intelligentsia into a *Kampfgruppe*, a fighting squad unequivocally pledged to toppling Communism. 'Schlesinger was there, and he made a dry-as-dust, unemotional statement. After that we had Koestler who spoke from the heart, and he moved many people. It was a crusade – Koestler had changed the tone,'[10] recalled Lawrence de Neufville, who was monitoring events closely for the CIA.

The aggressive Cold Warrior tone was epitomized by James Burnham's distinction between 'good' and 'bad' atom bombs, a thesis tested on the Koestlers at dinner a month earlier. On that occasion, Burnham had explained how the USA could render Russia impotent in a day by dropping the bomb on all major Russian cities. 'He looked quite pleased at the idea,' noted Mamaine Koestler (she also noted that 'Burnham looks very sweet and gentle . . . but he is much less scrupulous about means than K[oestler]' – he also said 'he wouldn't necessarily reject torture in certain cases').[11] Using the kind of language which petrified reality, and which was one of the contributing factors of the Cold War (on both sides), Burnham now announced that he was 'against those bombs, now stored or to be stored later in Siberia or the Caucasus, which are designed for the destruction of Paris, London, Rome, Brussels, Stockholm, New York, Chicago, . . . Berlin, and of western civilisation generally . . . But I am . . . *for* those bombs made in Los Alamos, Hanford and Oak Ridge and guarded I know not where in the Rockies or American deserts, [which] for five years have defended – have been the sole defense of – the liberties of western Europe.'[12] To which André Philip replied that when atom bombs fall, 'they do not distinguish between friend or foe, enemy or freedom fighter'.

Burnham and Hook both turned their fire on those who used moral equivalence to question America's condemnation of the Soviet Union: 'Sartre and Merleau-Ponty, who refused to attend the Congress even to defend their point of view there, were quite aware of French and American injustices to Negroes when they supported the Resistance to Hitler,' clamoured Hook. 'But they can see no justice in the western defense against Communist aggression because the Negroes have not yet won equality of treatment.'[13] This equality was not far off, according to George Schuyler, who circulated a report to delegates, complete with statistics, demonstrating that the situation of blacks in America never stopped improving, and this was thanks to the capitalist system's constant ability to adapt to change. The black journalist Max Yergan endorsed Schuyler's report with a history lesson in the advancement of African-Americans since the Roosevelt era.

Burnham, who in his trajectory from socialism to the right had simply leapfrogged over the moderate centre, had no time for the spineless man of the left. 'We have allowed ourselves to be trapped and jailed by our words – this leftist bait which has proved our poison. The Communists have looted our rhetorical arsenal, and have bound us with our own slogans. The progressive man of "the non-Communist Left" is in a perpetual tremor of guilt before the true Communist. The Communist, manipulating the same rhetoric, but acting boldly and firmly, appears to the man of the non-Communist Left as himself with guts.'[14] As Burnham stood there and inveighed against the Non-Communist Left, some delegates asked themselves whether the black or white version of the world offered by the right (captured by Koestler's biblical invocation 'Let your yea be yea; and your nay, nay!') was perhaps just as threatening to liberal democracy as that offered by the far left.

Hugh Trevor-Roper was appalled by the provocative tone, set by Koestler and taken up by other speakers. 'There was very little in the way of serious discussion,' he remembered. 'It wasn't really intellectual at all in my opinion. I realized that it was a reply in the same style to [the Soviet peace conferences] – it spoke the same language. I had expected and hoped to hear the western point of view put forward and defended, on the grounds that it was a better and a more lasting alternative. But instead we had denunciations. It left such a negative impression, as if we had nothing to say except, Sock them! There was a speech by Franz Borkenau which was very violent and indeed almost hysterical. He spoke in German and I regret to say that as I listened and as I heard the baying voices of approval from the huge audiences, I felt, well, these are the same people who seven years ago were probably baying in the same way to similar German denunciations of Communism coming from Dr Goebbels in the Sports Palast. And I felt, well, what sort of people are we identifying ourselves with? That was the greatest shock to me. There was a moment during the Congress when I felt that we were being invited to summon up Beelzebub in order to defeat Satan.'[15]

Sidney Hook rallied to Koestler's defence, but had to concede that his friend could 'recite the truths of the multiplication table in a way to make some people indignant with him'. He also had the irritating habit of grinning 'like a Cheshire cat' every time he scored a rhetorical point. Silone was much more flexible, arguing that a Christian spirit of social and political reform in the West would, in and of itself, steal the fire from the God of Communism. André Philip also represented the moderate view, arguing for a middle way between Russia and America: 'Europe today is feeble after its long and painful sickness. The Americans send us penicillin to treat this illness, and the Soviets send us microbes. Naturally, any doctor would prefer a mixture of the two. But our duty as Europeans must be to deal with the microbes as soon as possible so that we no longer have need of the medicine.'[16]

To the hardliners, this espousal of 'equidistance' was nothing short of heresy. 'Neutralism was, as an idea and as a movement, sponsored by the Soviets,'[17] declared Melvin Lasky, taking up Robert Montgomery's cry that 'There is no neutral corner in Freedom's room!' Reluctant to join in this rhetorical crusade, the British delegation rallied to Talleyrand's admonishment – 'surtout pas de zèle'. 'I couldn't see why the world should be set aflame to purge the personal guilt of people like Borkenau and Koestler,'[18] concluded Hugh Trevor-Roper.

The appropriateness of political converts proselytizing the world was becoming a key question of the Berlin Congress. 'Then a Herr Grimme arose, a parson of sorts with a voice like a foghorn, to argue that all these concrete questions were basically religious,' reported Sidney Hook. 'He spoke with an eloquent emptiness and became concrete only at the end when he descended to personalities and made some contemptuous remark about Koestler being a "political convert" who now was fervently opposing what once he had fervently supported, thus showing he had never surrendered his dialectical materialism.'[19]

Koestler had already discovered the resentment of those who had never been Communists towards political converts such as himself. Repeating the arguments, Koestler wrote: 'Ex-Communists are not only tiresome Cassandras, as the anti-Nazi refugee had been; they are also fallen angels who had the bad taste to reveal that Heaven is not the place it is supposed to be. The world respects the Catholic or Communist convert, but abhors unfrocked priests of all faiths. This attitude is rationalized as a dislike of renegades. Yet the convert, too, is a renegade from his former beliefs or disbeliefs, and quite prepared to persecute those who still persist in them. He is nevertheless forgiven, for he has "*embraced*" a faith, whereas the ex-Communist or the unfrocked priest has "*lost*" a faith – and has thereby become a menace to illusion and a reminder of the abhorrent, threatening void.'[20]

The problem of the 'tiresome Cassandras' was also troubling official circles. Edward Barrett, Assistant Secretary of State for International Information, felt obliged to question the wisdom of 'current tendencies to lionize . . . ex-Communists and put them on pedestals from which to lecture all citizens who had sense enough never to become Communists in the first place. Some of us suspect the typical ex-Communist – particularly the recent ex-Communist – has great value as an informer and tipster but hardly any as a propounder of eternal verities.'[21] It was becoming increasingly apparent that the US government's embrace of the Non-Communist Left would have to be kept secret from some of its own key policy-makers.

Josselson kept out of sight, though he kept track of everything that transpired. He observed Hugh Trevor-Roper's reaction to the crusaderish tone with growing alarm. Trevor-Roper and the rest of the British element made clear their dissent whenever they got the opportunity. But this became increasingly difficult, as 'the managers' (Lasky, foremost amongst them) on the podium during the sessions carefully avoided giving the 'table thumpers' the floor. Lasky was everywhere, organizing, cajoling, drafting press releases, staging the dramatic entrance of Theodor Plievier, the German author of *Stalingrad* and former Communist who was hiding in Stuttgart. Plievier had originally recorded his message to the Congress. But on hearing the news of the invasion of Korea, he flew to Berlin, defying the danger that he might be kidnapped by the Soviets or East Germans while visiting Berlin (though the likelihood of such a calamity was reduced by the provision of a round-the-clock security watch by the Americans).

Lasky's high profile infuriated Wisner back at OPC. There was good reason to be concerned. On 24 June, the eve of the Congress, the office of Gerhart Eisler, propaganda chief of the East German Government, issued a statement tracing a fire in the Communist House of Culture in East Berlin to the coterie of 'American police spy Melvin Lasky'. Eisler's statement, which was reported in American newspapers, said the attempt to burn down the Communist club was intended as a prelude to the opening of the Congress for Cultural Freedom (which Eisler described as 'an imperialist intellectual six-day bicycle race'), but that the plot had misfired and the flames were quickly extinguished. Lasky, when asked about the incident, answered with his customary sarcasm: 'Yes, it's true. We tried to set the house on fire by dropping fireflies disguised as potato bugs from a helicopter.'[22] But Wisner was not amused, cabling instructions to Berlin that Lasky be removed from any visible connection with the Congress.

But it was to take more than the removal of Lasky to stem the rumours surrounding the Congress. Some delegates speculated about who was footing the bill. The grand scale on which the Congress was launched at a time when Europe was broke seemed to confirm the rumour that this was not quite the spontaneous, 'independent' event its organizers claimed. Lawrence de Neufville had so much money he didn't know what to do with it: 'I don't where the money came from. I never had cheques or anything, I just seemed to have the cash in Marks. We all did.'[23] This did not escape the notice of Trevor-Roper, who began to smell a rat. 'When I arrived I found the whole thing was orchestrated on so grandiose a scale . . . that I realized that . . . financially it must have been funded by some powerful government organization. So I took it for granted from the beginning that it was organized by the American government in one form or another. That seemed to me obvious from the start.'[24] Years later, the CIA's Tom Braden reflected that simple common sense was enough to find out who was behind the Congress: 'We've got to remember that when we're speaking of those years that Europe was broke. If there was a dime to be had anywhere it was probably in some criminal organization. *There wasn't any money*. So they naturally looked to the United States for money.'[25]

The conference concluded on 29 June with a dramatic speech from Arthur Koestler, who cried triumphantly to a rally of 15,000 gathered under a blistering sun at the Funkturm Sporthalle, 'Friends, freedom has seized the offensive!' He then read out the Freedom Manifesto, a fourteen-point declaration which was offered as a new constitution for cultural freedom. Drafted by Koestler after an all-night session at Lasky's base at the Hotel am Steinplatz in Charlottenberg, the manifesto was 'pushed through by him, Burnham, Brown, Hook and Lasky by forceful offensive tactics, so that virtually no opposition was encountered,' according to Mamaine Koestler.[26] But one article of the declaration which expressed intolerance of Marxist ideas was vigorously contested by the British contingent, who demanded that the offending reference be excised. Essentially, the British were objecting to the assumption that guided the more militant anti-Communists at the conference – just as it did many American foreign policy-makers – that the writings of Marx and Lenin were less 'political philosophy than the field manual of Soviet strategy'.

After incorporating the British amendments, the manifesto was adopted as the moral and philosophical cornerstone of the Congress for Cultural Freedom. Addressed to 'all men who are determined to regain those liberties which they have lost and to preserve and extend those which they enjoy', the document stated: 'We hold it to be self-evident that intellectual freedom is one of the inalienable rights of man . . . Such freedom is defined first and foremost by his right to hold and express his own opinions, and particularly opinions which differ from those of his rulers. Deprived of the right to say "no," man becomes a slave.'[27] It declared freedom and peace to be 'inseparable', and warned that 'Peace can only be maintained if each government submits to the control and inspection of its acts by the people whom it governs.' Other points stressed that a prerequisite of freedom was 'the toleration of divergent opinions. The principle of toleration does not logically permit the practice of intolerance.' No one 'race, nation, class or religion can claim the sole right to represent the idea of freedom, nor the right to deny freedom to other groups or creeds in the name of any ultimate ideal or lofty aim whatsoever. We hold that the historical contribution of any society is to be judged by the extent and quality of the freedom which its members actually enjoy.' The manifesto went on to denounce the restrictions on freedom imposed by totalitarian states, whose 'means of enforcement far surpasses that of all the previous tyrannies in the history of mankind'. 'Indifference or neutrality in the face of such a challenge,' it continued, 'amounts to a betrayal of mankind and to the abdication of the free mind.' It expressed a commitment to 'The defence of existing freedoms, the reconquest of lost freedoms,' and (at Hugh Trevor-Roper's insistence) to 'the creation of new freedoms . . . [to] new and constructive answers to the problems of our time'.[28]

Here indeed was a manifesto to read from the barricades. Koestler, a modern-day Robespierre (though his two American bodyguards hovered close by), thrilled to the occasion. This was the framework for judging the commitment of individuals and institutions to total freedom of expression, to the uninhibited flow of ideas and opinions. If Communists and Fascists alike had systematically violated the principle of *habeas corpus*, here was a pledge to resist any attack on the principle of *habeas animam*. This document was a litmus test for liberty. By it, the Congress for Cultural Freedom itself would stand or fall.

As the conference closed, its Washington sponsors began celebrating. Wisner offered his 'heartiest congratulations' to all those involved. He in turn was congratulated by his political patrons. Defense Department representative General John Magruder praised it as 'a subtle covert operation carried out on the highest intellectual level . . . unconventional warfare at its best'. President Truman himself was reported to be 'very well pleased'. American occupation officials in Germany sensed it had given 'a palpable boost to morale of West Berlin, but believed its most important effect would ultimately be felt by western intellectuals who had been politically adrift since 1945'. The Congress for Cultural Freedom, one report claimed, had 'actually impelled a number of prominent cultural leaders to give up their sophisticated, contemplative detachment in favour of a strong stand against totalitarianism'.[29]

This conclusion was perhaps a little exaggerated, designed to sell the Congress to high-level strategists in government. Certainly, Hugh Trevor-Roper and the British contingent were yet to be convinced. Immediately after his return to England, news reached Trevor-Roper that State Department officials had complained to their Foreign Office counterparts that 'your man spoiled our Congress'. This was enough to confirm Trevor-Roper's suspicions about the role of the American government in the Berlin affair. But it also revealed official irritation with the way Trevor-Roper had conducted himself. Josselson – and his superiors in the CIA – understood that renewed efforts would have to be made to win over British intellectuals to their project.

6

'Operation Congress'

> We must make ourselves heard round the world in a great campaign of truth. This task is not separate and distinct from other elements of our foreign policy.
>
> President Harry Truman, 1950

Despite the recalcitrance of some British delegates, Wisner was satisfied that the Berlin conference had more than repaid his investment. Although its future was still uncertain, it was now added to the CIA's 'Propaganda Assets Inventory', an official list documenting the ever-growing number of conduits and individuals on which the Agency could rely. Known unofficially as 'Wisner's Wurlitzer', the nickname reveals the Agency's perception of how these 'assets' were expected to perform: at the push of a button, Wisner could play any tune he wished to hear.

Wisner returned to the problem of Melvin Lasky, whose peacock presence throughout the Berlin conference had so infuriated him. His earlier command to have Lasky removed from centre-stage having been so blatantly ignored, he wrote an angry internal memo, 'Berlin Congress for Cultural Freedom: Activities of Melvin Lasky', stating that Lasky's visibility was 'a major blunder and was recognized as such by our best friends in the State Department . . . It betrays an unfortunate tendency, apparently more deep-rooted than I expected, to succumb to the temptation of convenience (doing things the easy way) and irrespective of security and other technical considerations of the utmost importance.'[1] Wisner was unequivocal: unless the headstrong Lasky was removed from the Congress for Cultural Freedom, the CIA would not continue to support the organization.

Wisner's memo was cabled to Germany. 'The OPC officer who received it exploded and cabled back a histrionic protest, but there was nothing to be done. Lasky had to go, and OPC contrived to have him removed from the project.'[2] There are two possible explanations for this: either Lasky had some kind of relationship with OPC, and was therefore a real security risk because he refused to lie low; or he was, as he always claimed, an independent operator, in which case his removal represented the first of many such strong-arm tactics on the part of CIA. The OPC officer charged with Lasky's removal was Michael Josselson, whose tendency to explode when provoked would cost him dear in the future. Lasky and Josselson had already developed the strong bond which observers later found to be unbreakable. The psychology of this relationship is hard to fathom: Lasky's influence on Josselson, who was in every way his superior, was unique. 'Josselson was sometimes vexed by Lasky's wilful deafness,' wrote one Congress insider. 'He was sometimes exasperated by Lasky's failure to imagine the consequences of his words and actions, but at the same time he looked on him with indulgent admiration, even wonderment.'[3] To some, Lasky's hold on Josselson had an Oedipal angle. 'Josselson adored Lasky as the son he never had. He always defended him,'[4] Natasha Spender remembered. Lasky objected to this sobriquet, preferring to describe it as a 'brotherly' relationship.[5] Either way, Josselson soon realized that his theatrical defence of Lasky was bad strategy. So he agreed to Wisner's demand that Lasky be officially removed from the project. Unofficially, Lasky would remain Josselson's closest adviser for the entire life of the Congress. And other rewards would follow.

With Lasky apparently out of the way, Wisner now moved to establish the Congress for Cultural Freedom as a permanent entity. Its continuance had been approved by an OPC Project Review Board in early 1950, and it was given the codename QKOPERA.[6] One of Wisner's first decisions was to move the base of operations for the Congress from Berlin to Paris. There were powerful symbolic reasons for leaving the outfit in Berlin, but it was deemed too much of a security risk, too vulnerable to infiltration by the other side.

Wisner offered Josselson the job of running the Congress for the CIA, under Lawrence de Neufville, who was to supervise it from the Agency's French Labor desk. Both men accepted, resigning their cover jobs with the American occupation government in Germany, but taking with them their codenames, 'Jonathan F. Saba' (Josselson), and 'Jonathan Gearing' (de Neufville). Next, Wisner anchored Irving Brown to the Congress by appointing him a key member of the steering committee which had been formed shortly after the Berlin conference. 'More helpful than all the Koestlers and Silones put together,' Brown was once described as a 'one-man OSS' and 'a character out of an E. Phillips Oppenheim novel'. He worked for Jay Lovestone, a former Comintern delegate who now headed up the CIA's secret liaison with the American labour movement. Brown was extremely adroit in pursuing objectives by clandestine routes, and had been shortlisted by George Kennan in 1948 as a candidate to head up OPC, the job that eventually fell to Frank Wisner.[7] 'I don't believe I *ever* saw Irving [Brown] with a nickel that didn't belong to CIA,' remembered Tom Braden, who was soon to take over QKOPERA. 'He would say it was from the labor unions. It was a good cover. Brown was the paymaster, but he enjoyed participation in the planning of operations. He was an intelligent guy with a wide acquaintanceship.'[8]

Also appointed to the steering committee was James Burnham. A constant presence in policy-making and intelligence circles, Burnham was considered indispensable to the success of the Congress, a vital liaison between the intelligentsia and Wisner's office. 'Burnham was a consultant to OPC on virtually every subject of interest to our organization,' wrote Howard Hunt, the CIA dirty trickster who later emerged as one of the Watergate 'plumbers'. 'He had extensive contacts in Europe and, by virtue of his Trotskyite background, was something of an authority on domestic and foreign Communist parties and front organizations.'[9]

Not everybody was happy with Burnham's 'Trotskyite background' though. According to CIA executive Miles

Copeland, there was initially 'some fuss about the Burnham flirtation with the "extreme Left" (wasn't he in a "cell" of some kind that included Sidney Hook, Irving Kristol, and Daniel Bell?), but all was okay when someone remembered [a] remark to the effect that if Jim were a *serious* Communist he would have joined the Party and not been a mere Trotskyist. Besides, as one who had been on the far Left and swung to the far Right, he had good company in the CIA's stable of on-call consultants.' Describing Burnham as 'a hundred per cent capitalist and imperialist, a believer in Mom, apple pie, baseball, the corner drugstore, and . . . American style democracy,' Miles Copeland said that he had learned from him the following principle: 'The first task of any ruling group is to keep itself in power.'[10] One Cold Warrior referred to him as 'a very articulate expounder of the dirty tricks department'.[11] In early 1953, Burnham would play a crucial part in the CIA's Operation AJAX, which unseated Dr Mossadegh in Tehran and replaced him with the Shah. Wisner had decided that the plan was far too crude, and needed 'a touch of Machiavelli', by which he meant a history lesson from Burnham. In his book *The Machiavellians* (which became a manual for CIA strategists), Burnham used, in addition to Machiavelli, the ideas of major modernist European thinkers – Mosca, Pareto, Michels, Sorel – to 'challenge egalitarian political theory and show the persistence and inevitability of elite rule, even in an age of equality'. An old acquaintance of Burnham's once said that the only time she ever saw him manifest any real intellectual enthusiasm was when he talked about Machiavelli.[12]

Alongside Irving Brown, Josselson, de Neufville, and Lasky (undeterred by his earlier dismissal), Burnham worked at giving the Congress for Cultural Freedom a permanent footing. Meeting at the end of November 1950 in Brussels, the steering committee designed a functioning structure for the organization, working from a document drawn up by Lasky in July. Among those present were Ignazio Silone, Carlo Schmid (leader of the Socialists in the German Parliament), the Jewish sociologist Eugene Kogon, Haakon Lie (head of the Norwegian Labour Party), Julian Amery (British MP), Josef Czapski (Polish writer and artist), David Rousset, Irving Brown, and Nicolas Nabokov.

Essentially, the structure sketched out by Lasky was the one adopted: an International Committee of twenty-five was nominated, as were five Honorary Chairmen. Guiding their activities was an Executive Committee of five – Executive Director, Editorial Director, Research Director, Paris Bureau Director, Berlin Bureau Director – who in turn would be kept in check by the General Secretary. In Lasky's diagram, this structure looked like a mirror image of a Cominform apparat. 'They had names just like the Communist Party,' observed one historian. 'The CIA set up these cultural foundations as shadow organizations of the Communist Party, including secrecy being at the core of it. They were really speaking to each other.'[13] Nicolas Nabokov once jokingly referred to the Congress's ruling body as 'our Polit Bureau-Boys'.

Also discussed at the November meeting was a report by Arthur Koestler entitled 'Immediate Tasks for the Transition Period'. Here, Koestler outlined the 'technical tasks' which needed to be accomplished as a follow-up to the Berlin conference. Under the heading 'Political Campaign in the West', Koestler, who had been repeatedly snubbed by the neutralists at the Berlin conference, wrote: 'Our aim is to get those who still hesitate over to our side, to break the influence of the Joliot-Curies on the one hand and of the cultural neutralists like *Les Temps modernes* on the other.'[14]

Challenging the intellectual basis for neutralism was one of the principal objectives of American Cold War policy, and it was now assumed as an official 'line' of the Congress. The CIA's Donald Jameson explained: 'There was a particular concern about those who said, "Well, East is East and West is West and to hell with both of you." [We tried] to move them at least a little bit over on the western side of things. There were a lot of people who felt that neutrality . . . was a position that was compromised. It was an attitude that one hoped would be diminished. But on the other hand I think there was a general recognition that you didn't want to jump on somebody's neutral and say, "You're no good either, you're just like the Commies," because that would push them off to the left, and that was certainly not desirable. But the neutrals were certainly a target.'[15]

Koestler too had become a target. His document was

discussed by the steering committee in his absence. He wasn't even on the committee. Koestler's intolerance of disagreement, his irrational anger and arrogant assertion of his own genius, had now persuaded Washington that he was more of a liability than an asset. Since the June conference, Koestler had been holding regular meetings at his home at Verte Rive with Burnham, Brown, Raymond Aron, Lasky and other members of the 'inner circle'. He had, said Mamaine, become 'quite obsessed with the Congress' and 'barely able to sleep'. These gatherings did not go unnoticed. In August 1950, the French Communist weekly *L'Action* arrived at the imaginative conclusion that Koestler was planning terrorist militia from his home with Burnham and Brown.

Josselson was now persuaded that a moderate tone was essential if the Congress for Cultural Freedom was going to achieve one of its principal tasks: the winning over of the waverers. The response from headquarters was to authorize the removal of Koestler from his central position in the organization. Thus, the man who had drawn up the Manifesto for Cultural Freedom was now eased out. Paragraph 3 of the manifesto stated: 'Peace can be maintained only if each government submits to the control and inspection of its acts by the people whom it governs.'[16] The CIA, by marginalizing Koestler, and by its covert governance of what was to become the largest such agglomeration of intellectuals and 'free thinkers', was effectively acting in breach of the very declaration of rights it had paid for. To promote freedom of expression, the Agency had first to buy it, then to restrict it. The market for ideas was not as free as it appeared. For Koestler it was a devastating betrayal. He suffered some kind of 'nervous crack up', flew to the States, and watched bitterly as the Congress for Cultural Freedom moved away from his ideas.

Arthur Schlesinger was another valuable contact for the Congress. He was part of what Stuart Hampshire, Isaiah Berlin and Stephen Spender nicknamed 'the apparat, the controlling group'. Writing to congratulate Irving Brown after the Berlin meeting, Schlesinger noted enthusiastically, 'I think we may have here an immensely powerful instrument of political and intellectual warfare.'[17] Schlesinger knew something about such matters from his wartime work in the Office of Strategic

Services (OSS), where he had been assigned to the Research and Analysis department, which earned the nickname 'the campus' on account of its tweedy aura.

Schlesinger had maintained close contact with the exclusive 'club' of OSS veterans, many of whom, including himself, went on to become leading statesmen and presidential advisers. He knew Allen Dulles, who in 1950 invited him to sit on the Executive Committee of Radio Free Europe, which was set up that year by the CIA (its participation shielded from public view by its front organization, the National Committee for a Free Europe). Schlesinger had also been exposed to covert operations when he worked as an assistant to Averell Harriman, head of the Marshall Plan in Europe. 'There was a general feeling that the Soviet Union was spending a lot of money on organizing its intellectuals, and we had to do something to respond,'[18] Schlesinger recalled. Under Harriman, he became involved in the secret distribution of counterpart funds to European trades unions, dealing often with Irving Brown.

Schlesinger's relationship with Brown was now soldered by the mutual secret they shared. For Schlesinger was one of the handful of non-Agency people who knew from the outset the true origins of the Congress for Cultural Freedom. 'I knew because of my intelligence links that the original meeting of the Congress in Berlin was paid for by the CIA,' Schlesinger later acknowledged. 'It seemed not unreasonable to help the people on our side. Of all the CIA's expenditures, the Congress for Cultural Freedom seemed its most worthwhile and successful.'[19]

One of Schlesinger's first tasks was to persuade Bertrand Russell, one of the Congress's honorary patrons, not to resign. This the philosopher had threatened to do after reading Hugh Trevor-Roper's 'mischievous reports' in the *Manchester Guardian*, which had described events in Berlin as something uncomfortably close to a Nazi rally. Visiting Russell in London with Koestler on 20 September 1950, Schlesinger listened as Russell told of his alarm at Trevor-Roper's report (which A. J. Ayer had endorsed), and his subsequent decision to withdraw. Russell appeared cold towards Koestler (the philosopher had once made a pass at Mamaine Koestler, and a residual sexual jealousy between the two men continued to hamper their friendship), but finally accepted his and Schlesinger's arguments.

Bertrand Russell, world-renowned mathematician and philosopher, was ubiquitous in 1950, the year which brought him the British Order of Merit and the Nobel Prize. He had met and disliked Lenin: 'His guffaw at the thought of those massacred made my blood run cold . . . My most vivid memories were of bigotry and Mongolian cruelty.' Russell had startled admirers when, in 1948, in a speech in the bomb-damaged main hall of Westminster School, he suggested threatening Stalin with the atomic bomb.[20] At this time, Russell was 'violently anti-Communist [and] insisted that on our side military strength and rearmament took precedence over *all* other matters'.[21] Russell was also prized by IRD, from whom he was happy to receive 'little tit-bits from time to time'. But if Russell was a 'hawk' then, by the mid-1950s he was urging nuclear disarmament ('His aristocratic arse has sat/on London paving stones/along with queens and commies,' wrote one poet).[22] His politics seemed to change with the wind, and he was to cause the Congress and its American backers much heartburn over the years of his patronage, until he finally resigned in 1956. But for now, his name added lustre and satisfied what some detected was Josselson's weakness for the talisman of celebrity.

Like Russell, the other honorary presidents were all philosophers, and all 'representatives for the newborn "Euro-American mind"'.[23] Benedetto Croce was a political conservative and monarchist who had no time for socialism or for organized religion (his works were listed on the Vatican Index of Prohibited Books). Now in his eighties, he was revered in Italy as the eloquent father of anti-Fascism, a man who had openly defied Mussolini's despotism, and who had been adopted as the moral leader of the resistance. He had also been a valuable contact for William Donovan on the eve of the allied landings in Italy. Croce died in 1952, and was replaced by Don Salvador de Madariaga, who was also closely linked to Donovan through the European Movement. John Dewey, who had headed the Committee for the Defense of Leon Trotsky, represented pragmatic American liberalism. Karl Jaspers, the German existentialist, had been an unrelenting critic of the Third Reich. A Christian, he had once publicly challenged Jean-Paul Sartre to state whether or not he accepted the Ten Commandments. Jacques Maritain, a liberal Catholic humanist, was a French resistance hero. He was also a close friend of Nicolas Nabokov. Isaiah Berlin was approached to join this rosary of philosopher-patrons, but refused on the grounds that such public support for an anti-Communist movement would place his relatives in the East in danger. He did, however, promise to support the Congress in any modest way he could. It was Lawrence de Neufville's recollection that Berlin did so in the knowledge that the Congress was being secretly funded by the CIA. 'He knew about our involvement,' said de Neufville. 'I don't know who told him, but I imagine it was one of his friends in Washington.'[24]

As with all professional organizations, the early days were marked by constant shufflings in the ranks as members jostled for jobs. Denis de Rougemont, who had never been a Communist and was from neutral Switzerland, was made President of the Executive Committee. Author of *L'Amour et l'Occident*, de Rougemont hailed from the non-Marxist, anti-Fascist left. After the war, he had been a broadcaster for 'Voice of America', and worked closely with François Bondy in the European Union of Federalists, whose aims he would continue to pursue with covert assistance from the CIA (of which, he later said, he was ignorant) from his Geneva-based Centre Européen de la Culture (which still exists today).

For the job of General Secretary, Josselson lobbied hard for his preferred candidate, Nicolas Nabokov who, even if he didn't know it, had auditioned for a leading role when he had declaimed at the Berlin conference: 'Out of this Congress we must build an organization for war. We must have a standing committee. We must see to it that it calls on all figures, all fighting organizations and all methods of fighting, with a view to action. If we do not, we will sooner or later all be hanged. The hour has long struck Twelve.'[25] Nabokov was duly elected to the post.

Apart from his old friend Josselson, Nicolas Nabokov had powerful sponsors. There was Chip Bohlen, 'that thoroughbred American' who had made America 'a true home' for

Nabokov in the early 1940s, and who was to remain, said Nabokov, 'my model, my source of advice, often my comforter'. And there was George Kennan, who had earlier been so embarrassed when Nabokov's application for government employment had failed. Nabokov's name also appeared on a top-secret list of psychological warfare personnel recommended for employment in sensitive posts, and circulated to the Office of the Secretary of the Army in 1950.[26] This combination of powerful political patrons ensured that Nabokov's security clearance was not held up as it had been a few years earlier.

Irving Brown, the paymaster, offered Nabokov $6,000. Nabokov, with two young sons to put through school, and currently receiving a salary of $8,000 for his teaching jobs at the Peabody Conservatory and Sarah Lawrence College, said he needed more: 'Don't forget that in this job, there will be representational expenses involved. I don't intend to give parties, but I will have to see many people, cajole them, invite them to meals, etc. etc.'[27] Actually, Nabokov loved to give parties, and he would give many and lavish ones at the CIA's expense over the next sixteen years. For the moment, however, the question of Nabokov's salary was unresolved. Irving Brown, who had access to a huge slush fund, had many other pokers in the fire. Whilst he was an energetic supporter of the Congress, his natural inclination was to spend the money available on funding the CIA-backed Force Ouvrière in its attempts to break up the Communist dockers' unions in Marseilles, where Marshall Plan supplies and shipments of American arms were daily being blockaded. The matter was resolved when James Burnham stepped forward in January 1951 with a promise to boost Nabokov's salary. 'Other arrangements to compensate me for my considerable loss of income will be made here, and will not appear on the books of the operation in Europe,'[28] Nabokov told Brown, apparently untroubled by Burnham's flexible approach to accountancy. For the first year or so, Burnham virtually 'ran' Nabokov.

It was decided that Lasky would stay in Berlin editing *Der Monat*, whose office became the headquarters of the German affiliate of the Congress. Josselson and de Neufville would move to Paris and head up the main office there, liaising with Irving Brown, who was instructed to rent and equip a suitable property. As they were preparing to leave Germany, Josselson and de Neufville learned of an exciting new development back at CIA headquarters in Washington: Allen Dulles had just joined the Agency, and he brought with him an assistant called Tom Braden. Things were going to change.

Allen Dulles joined the CIA in December 1950 as Deputy Director of Operations. This was a position of immense scope, giving Dulles responsibility for collecting intelligence, and for supervising Frank Wisner's division, the Office of Policy Coordination. One of his first acts was to recruit Tom Braden, one of his most dashing OSS officers, a man who had cultivated many high-level contacts since his return to civilian life. Wiry, sandy-haired, and with a craggy, handsome visage, Braden looked like a composite of John Wayne, Gary Cooper and Frank Sinatra. Born in 1918 in Dubuque, Iowa, Braden's father was an insurance agent, and his mother wrote romantic novels. She taught him a love for the work of Ring Lardner, Robert Frost and Ernest Hemingway. He graduated in Political Science from Dartmouth in 1940, then got so excited at the outbreak of war that he enlisted in the British Army. He was assigned to the 8th Army, 7th Armoured Division – the famous Desert Rats – where he became best friends with Stewart Alsop. Both were to join OSS, parachuting into occupied France to fight in the woods with the Communist-dominated resistance. After the war, Braden and Alsop co-authored a book, *Sub Rosa: The OSS and American Espionage*, in which they described OSS as providing its men 'with opportunities for the most amazing adventures recorded in any war since that of King Arthur'.

Returning to civilian life, Braden spent the next few years campaigning for a permanent intelligence service. In late 1950, Allen Dulles telephoned and asked him to be his assistant at CIA. Braden accepted. Assigned the codename 'Homer D. Hoskins', Braden was initially without portfolio, nominally assigned to Wisner's OPC, but in reality working directly to Dulles. Within a few months, he had gained an intimate knowledge of the Communist propaganda offensive, and a limited appreciation for the American response. 'How odd, I thought to myself as I watched these developments, that Communists, who are afraid to join anything but the Communist Party, should gain mass allies through organizational war while we Americans, who join everything, were sitting here tongue-tied.'[29]

William Colby, a future CIA director, reached the same conclusion: 'The Communists made no secret of their belief in what they called "the organizational weapon": organize the Party as the key command troop, but then organize all the other fronts – the women's groups, the cultural groups, the trade unions, the farmer groups, the cooperatives – a whole panoply of organizations so that you could include as many of the people in the country as possible within those groups and thereby under basically Communist leadership and even discipline.'[30]

'If the other side can use ideas that are camouflaged as being local rather than Soviet supported or stimulated, then we ought to be able to use ideas camouflaged as local ideas,' Braden reasoned.[31] An overview of Wisner's OPC convinced Braden that it was overburdened with projects which lacked a central focus. One CIA official described it as an 'operational junk heap'. 'There was an International Organizations Branch, but it was a hodgepodge of little jobs the Agency had around, and it was totally unimportant,' Braden recalled. 'I went to Al [Allen Dulles] and said, "Why don't we merge these things into one division?" Maybe Al was hoping I would come up with something like this.'[32]

Whilst Dulles was enthusiastic, Braden's proposal was received with consternation by those CIA staffers who believed that covert operations meant organizing the overthrow of 'unfriendly' foreign leaders like Jacobo Arbenz. If the infant Agency was half faculty (it was already known as 'the campus'), then it was also half cops and robbers. Alongside the pipe-smoking Yalies there were the kind of people, said Braden, who hadn't understood that the war had ended. Dangerously headstrong, their thinking was of a kind with that of men like General MacArthur, who wanted to extend the Korean war by bombing Manchuria, or the Secretary of the Navy, who in 1950 had exhorted the world to prepare itself for another global conflagration. 'I was much more interested in the *ideas* which were under fire from the Communists than I was in blowing up Guatemala,' Braden explained. 'I was more an 'intellectual' than a gung-ho guy.'[33]

Braden's division chief tried to block his proposal by arguing that it 'crossed division lines', a bureaucratic manoeuvre of monumental pettiness. A 'helluva fight' ensued, which Braden lost. He went immediately to Dulles's office and resigned. Dulles, furious, snapped up the telephone and called Frank Wisner. 'What the hell's going on?' he demanded. 'Allen was all over Wisner,' Braden remembered. 'He took my side completely. And that's how I came to set up the International Organizations Division under the DDP [Deputy Director of Plans], who was Wisner. But I didn't pay much attention to Wisner, I just went over his head straight to Allen. I had to handle it carefully, because Frank was ostensibly my superior.'[34]

The formation of this new division (abbreviated to IOD) coincided with – and its activities were sanctioned by – a new National Security directive, NSC-68. Drafted in March 1950 by the new director of the Policy Planning Staff, Paul Nitze (who had replaced Kennan), NSC-68 became 'the supreme documentary symbol of the cold war', and was based on the assumption of a Communist monolith whose guiding spirit resided in the Kremlin.[35] The directive concluded that 'Practical and ideological considerations . . . both impel us to the conclusion that we have no choice but to demonstrate the superiority of the idea of freedom by its constructive application.' 'Truth also needs propaganda,' the philosopher Karl Jaspers had recently declared. Here was the mandate which authorized America's Cold Warriors to take 'constructive' measures to ensure that the truth triumphed over deceit. The budgetary provisions set out by NSC-68 revealed the importance now given to this task: in the next two years, the $34 million spent on psychological warfare in 1950 was to be quadrupled.

'In the contest for men's minds, truth can be peculiarly the American weapon,' Secretary of State Edward Barrett announced. 'It cannot be an isolated weapon, because the propaganda of truth is powerful only when linked with concrete actions and policies . . . a highly skilful and substantial campaign of truth is as indispensable as an air force.'[36] The truth, like the century, was to belong to America. If deceit needed to be used to promote the truth, then so be it. It was what Koestler called 'fighting against a total lie in the name of a half-truth'.

'The purpose of the IOD,' said Braden, 'was to unite intellectuals against what was being offered in the Soviet Union. The idea that the world would succumb to a kind of Fascist or Stalinist concept of art and literature and music [was] a horrifying prospect. We wanted to unite all the people who were artists, who were writers, who were musicians, and all the people who follow those people, to demonstrate that the West and the United States was devoted to freedom of expression and to intellectual achievement, without any rigid barriers as to *what you must write* and *what you must say* and *what you must do* and *what you must paint* [Braden's emphasis], which was what was going on in the Soviet Union. I think we did it damn well.'[37]

The IOD operated according to the same principles that guided Wisner's management of the Non-Communist Left. The purpose of supporting leftist groups was not to destroy or even dominate, but rather to maintain a discreet proximity to and monitor the thinking of such groups; to provide them with a mouthpiece so they could blow off steam; and, *in extremis*, to exercise a final veto on their publicity and possibly their actions, if they ever got too 'radical'. Braden issued clear instructions to his newly established IOD posts in Europe: 'Limit the money to amounts private organizations can credibly spend; disguise the extent of American interest; protect the integrity of the organization by not requiring it to support every aspect of official American policy.'[38]

Braden's new division had been created to provide a better institutional base for entities like the Congress for Cultural Freedom, and it was to him that its managers were now answerable. The real objectives of the Congress were clarified. It was not to be a centre for agitation, but a beachhead in western Europe from which the advance of Communist ideas could be halted. It was to engage in a widespread and cohesive campaign of peer pressure to persuade intellectuals to dissociate themselves from Communist fronts or fellow travelling organizations. It was to encourage the intelligentsia to develop theories and arguments which were directed not at a mass audience, but at that small elite of pressure groups and statesmen who in turn determined government policy. It was not an intelligence-gathering source, and agents in other CIA divisions were warned not to attempt to use it as such. It was to provide 'independent' support for American foreign policy objectives which sought to promote a united Europe (through membership of NATO and the European Movement, the latter being substantially endowed by the CIA), which included a reunified Germany. It was to act as an emissary for the achievements of American culture, and work to undermine the negative stereotypes prevalent in Europe, especially France, about America's perceived cultural barrenness. And it was to respond to negative criticism of other aspects of American democracy, including its civil rights record.

The people who had been chosen by the steering committee to animate the newly consolidated Congress were all subject to security checks, as were those who came to be closely involved with the controlling 'apparat', and all future employees of the Congress. For the CIA, there were Michael Josselson and Lawrence de Neufville. Their needs were serviced by a specially assigned case officer who, in the course of a three-year watch, would liaise with a counterpart of equal rank in Washington who in turn was accountable to an IOD Branch Chief. The Chief of Branch Three looked after the Congress. He answered to the IOD Deputy Division Chief, and the Division Chief (Braden). As the Congress grew, various additional Agency personnel were assigned to look after its finances and activities. Far from being what Koestler had initially envisaged as a 'small, shoestring operation like Willi Munzenberg's', with 'little money, only scant personnel and no Cominform behind us',[39] the Congress had now become an 'asset' of one of the fastest growing divisions in the CIA.[40]

True to form, Braden decided to run operation QKOPERA 'out of lines', and to this end he instructed de Neufville not to tell Wisner's man running the French desk, Robert Thayer, anything about his activities. Above Braden's head, Allen Dulles privately told de Neufville he was 'to keep up with Irving Brown and find out what he was doing', though de Neufville would soon report back to Dulles that this 'was almost impossible because he was running it like it was his own operation, and he never said much about what he was doing'.[41] Not surprisingly, Dulles, Wisner and Braden never acquired reputations as good managers.

Josselson and de Neufville were quick to establish the Paris office and sort out 'the housework', Agency-speak for the domestic arrangements common to all front activities. Whilst they dealt with the fixtures and fittings, Nabokov arrived to take up his new post as General Secretary, moving from New York with Patricia Blake to a little apartment in rue d'Assas, overlooking the Luxembourg Gardens. 'There were no modern precedents, no models in the western world,' he wrote of the organization he now represented. 'No one before had tried to mobilize intellectuals and artists on a worldwide scale in order to fight an ideological war against oppressors of the mind, or to defend what one called by the hackneyed term "our cultural heritage". This kind of ideological war had so far been the appanage of Stalinists and Nazis . . . To lead a rational, ice-cold, determinedly intellectual war against Stalinism without falling into the easy Manichean trap of phony righteousness seemed essential to me, especially at a time when in America that ideological war was getting histrionically hysterical and crusaderishly paranoiac.'[42]

With an energy and enthusiasm which rarely deserted him, Nabokov threw himself into his new career as impresario of the cultural Cold War. In May, the Congress 'presented' a prize intellectual defector at a press conference in Paris. He was the young cultural attaché at the Polish embassy, a poet and translator of *The Waste Land*, Czesław Milosz. Milosz had been a member of the Polish delegation to the Waldorf Astoria conference in 1949, and there, after his 'first exposure to the democratic left he just fell in love with us', according to Mary McCarthy. Brilliantly stage-managed by Nabokov, Milosz's appearance on the side of the angels was an early *coup* for the Congress.

Soon after, Nabokov, accompanied by Denis de Rougemont, went to Brussels to address a dinner sponsored by the magazine *Synthèses*. Then he rushed back to promote the work of the Amis de la Liberté, a kind of rotary club arm of the Congress which organized meetings of French student groups across the country and at the Maison des Jeunesses des Amis de la Liberté in Paris. In mid-June, Nabokov was on the road again, this time bound for Berlin where he was to lecture on 'art under the totalitarian system'. 'This is of course no "Lecture Trip" for me,' he wrote to James Burnham, 'but my first "Prise de Contact" with the German field of operation.'[43] This was the first of many such scouting expeditions undertaken by the Congress's executives, from which mushroomed affiliates not just in Europe (there were offices in West Germany, Great Britain, Sweden, Denmark, Iceland), but across other continents – in Japan, India, Argentina, Chile, Australia, Lebanon, Mexico, Peru, Uruguay, Colombia, Brazil and Pakistan.

Back in Paris, Nabokov played a major part in launching the Congress's first magazine, *Preuves* ('proof' or 'evidence'). The idea of creating a cultural-political magazine in the tradition of the great French reviews was first discussed in February 1951 at the Executive Committee meeting in Versailles. What was needed was a journal which could compete with *Les Temps modernes* and encourage defections from Sartre's stronghold. 'Who was the real antagonist?' one historian later asked. 'It wasn't the Soviet Union or Moscow. What they were really obsessed with was Sartre and de Beauvoir. *That* was "the other side".'[44] 'The Left Bank intellectuals were the target,' a Congress insider confirmed. 'Or, perhaps, the people who listened to them were the target.'[45] But finding an editor who enjoyed enough stature to lure these *compagnons de route* into a more centrist *arrondissement* proved to be difficult. By June 1951, Nabokov was becoming desperate, writing to tell Burnham that 'the question of the French magazine gives me sleepless nights. It is so hard to find someone of the stature of Aron or Camus who would be willing to undertake the editorship . . . the difficulty here is that although people talk a lot about commitment, nobody wants to commit himself. There is a kind of lassitude and apathy or rather tiredness in the air which one has to struggle against daily.'[46]

Having failed to attract a French editor, the Executive Committee decided to give the job to François Bondy, a Swiss writer of German mother tongue who had been a Communist Party activist until the Hitler–Stalin Pact of 1939. A key appointment to the Congress Secretariat in 1950 (as Director of Publications), Bondy had collaborated on *Der Monat* with Melvin Lasky, who called him 'the editorial adviser of our time par excellence'. Under Bondy, the first issue of *Preuves* was finally launched in October 1951. Aimed at establishing an Atlanticist, anti-neutralist, and pro-American consensus, *Preuves* was unmistakably the house organ of the Congress, giving it a voice as well as advertising its activities and programmes. As such, it immediately faced what Manès Sperber called 'une hostilité presque totale', but Bondy stood firm in the face of virulent attacks both from the left and the right.[47]

The Congress in these early days was received with almost universal suspicion. Activists who supported it convinced themselves that these suspicions were simply excrescences of the anti-Americanism so in vogue at the time; those who were unable to do so, simply sublimated their concerns. Detractors, however, took every opportunity to question the Congress's legitimacy as a 'free' and 'independent' organization. That it was able to survive these challenges is a mark of the dogged persistence of those (on the 'inside' and on the 'outside') who believed in its purpose. When Georges Altman, editor of *Franc-Tireur*, and François Bondy were despatched to Rome in late 1950 to engineer support for an Italian affiliate, they were repeatedly asked 'Who's paying for all this?' and 'By "freedom" do you mean American capitalism?' Communist observers seemed to be present, they said, at most of their meetings, and many Italian intellectuals were clearly susceptible to 'the totalitarian temptation'. Others, like Alberto Moravia, were reported to be more concerned about neo-Fascism than Communism. In their report to Josselson, Bondy and Altman stressed the provincialism and anti-Americanism of Italian intellectuals. There were 'great possibilities' for the Congress in Italy, but these would only mature as the result of 'slow, indirect, diversified and extremely discreet action'.[48]

The Italian Association for Cultural Freedom was formed in late 1951 under Ignazio Silone, and became the centre of a federation of about a hundred independent cultural groups to which the association provided speakers, books, pamphlets, films and an internationalist ethos. It produced the bulletin

Libertà della Cultura, and later *Tempo Presente*, edited by Silone and Nicola Chiaromonte. But no sooner was the Italian affiliate assembled, than it started to fall apart. Nabokov was despatched to Rome to try and nudge the Congress's interests along, but like Bondy and Altman before him, he found the intellectuals apathetic and too ready to listen to 'curious rumours' about the Congress. Complaining to Irving Brown about 'the Silonesque lethargy of our Italian outfit', Nabokov said that radical measures were needed to get blood into the Italian 'apparatus'. 'Silone thrones invisible [sic] in heaven and prevents the kids in the office from doing their work. I wrote him two letters, I wire [sic] to ask him to descend from his summer vacation for a day to see me here in Rome . . . no answer to anything. I see dozens of people daily. Most of them are ready to join, work, help (including Moravia) but all say that so long as Silone is the sole master here, no work will be done,' Nabokov whined.[49] Alarmed by its 'quixotic', 'bellicose' and 'arrogant' attitude to the Church, Nabokov also wrote to Jacques Maritain and urged him to write a 'long letter to the Vatican authorities' explaining that the Congress for Cultural Freedom and the Italian Association had 'different policies'.[50]

Nabokov also travelled to London to rally support for the British affiliate, the British Society for Cultural Freedom, which had been founded in January 1951 at The Authors' Society in Whitehall Court. Meeting with T. S. Eliot, Isaiah Berlin, Lord David Cecil, the heads of the British Council, the Third Programme of the BBC, and Richard Crossman, who was now the Secretary General of the Labour Party, Nabokov was able to report back to Paris that the Congress had powerful allies in England. Separately he told Burnham that 'Many [British intellectuals] think of our Congress as some kind of semiclandestine American organization controlled by you . . . I think our constant efforts should be directed towards proving to European intellectuals that the Congress for Cultural Freedom is not an American secret service Agency.'[51] Using language normally favoured by 'witting' collaborators of the intelligence services, Nabokov asked Burnham to communicate to 'our friends in America' the 'fundamental paradox of the situation here: we may have little time left, but we must work as if we had all the time in the world. The process of transforming the "Operation-Congress" into a broad and a solid front opposed to totalitarianism is going to take a lot of time and I am afraid a lot of money.'[52]

7

Candy

> We couldn't spend it all. I remember once meeting with Wisner and the comptroller. My God, I said, how can we spend that? There were no limits, and nobody had to account for it. It was amazing.
>
> Gilbert Greenway, CIA agent

Acquiring a niche in the competitive market-place of Cold War culture required a substantial investment. Initially, it fell to Irving Brown to act as the financial conduit for the CIA's cultural programmes. 'I'd give $15,000, $10,000, $5,000 at a time to Brown, off the budget, but I was never really sure what he did with it,' Tom Braden recalled.[1] But this was small change compared to the total funds at Brown's disposal. 'The key to all this is the counterpart funds,' Lawrence de Neufville later revealed. 'People couldn't say in U.S. Congress, "Oh, look what they're doing with taxpayers' money," because it wasn't our money, it was a biproduct of the Marshall Plan.'[2] In an innovative move under the early years of the Marshall Plan, it was proposed that, in order to make the funds perform double duty, each recipient country should contribute to the foreign aid effort by depositing an amount equal to the US contribution in its central bank. A bilateral agreement between the country and the US allowed these funds to be used jointly. The bulk of the currency funds (95 per cent) remained the legal property of the country's government, while 5 per cent became, upon deposit, the property of the US government. These 'counterpart funds' – a secret fund of roughly $200 million a year – were made available as a war chest for the CIA.

In December 1950, Richard Bissell, who had taught economics at Yale and MIT in the 1930s, was deputy administrator of the Marshall Plan. One day, Frank Wisner called on Bissell in his Washington office. Bissell, who knew Wisner socially through the Georgetown set, described him as 'very much part of our inner circle of people – top-level civil servants who were involved in many of the government enterprises we took on'. Bissell recalled that Wisner said 'he needed money and asked me to help finance OPC's covert operations by releasing a modest amount from the five percent counterpart funds . . . Whether anyone anticipated that these [funds] would include covert activities is difficult to say. This was most definitely a gray area. I was somewhat baffled by the request since I was very uninformed about covert activities. Wisner took the time to assuage at least some of my concerns by assuring me that Harriman had approved the action. When I began to press him about how the money would be used, he explained I could not be told . . . We in the Marshall Plan were dealing directly or indirectly with quite a number of the people who were beneficiaries of the CIA's early covert action programs.'[3]

Counterpart funds had been used under Harriman's administration of the Marshall Plan to subsidize the OPC's counter-move at the International Day of Resistance to Dictatorship and War of April 1949. They had also played a crucial part in the Italian elections of 1948. Now Irving Brown was able to boost his CIA slush fund with Marshall Plan 'candy'. Of the multitude of covert projects financed through Brown, approximately $200,000 (equivalent to $1.5 million in 1999) was earmarked for the basic administrative costs of the Congress for Cultural Freedom in 1951. This paid the salaries of François Bondy, Denis de Rougemont, Pierre Bolomey (a protégé of Altman's who had been appointed Treasurer), an administrator and several secretaries. Bondy and de Rougemont received their salaries in dollars, transferred by Brown through American Express to an account in the Société de Banque Suisse, Lausanne. The others were paid in French francs. The total monthly expenditure for running the

Secretariat at this time was around five million francs. Brown was also bankrolling Les Amis de la Liberté to roughly the same amount. To a private account in Germany, he was depositing 40,000 German marks for the Congress office there, covering salaries and office expenses. The Italian office received several thousand dollars a month through the account of Codignola Trista, editor of the journal *Nuova Italia*. Michael Goodwin, Secretary of the British Society for Cultural Freedom, had access to a monthly subsidy of £700, deposited to his account at Westminster Bank in St James's Park.

Before Brown secured a permanent home for the Congress in Boulevard Haussman, his rooms at the Hôtel Baltimore on Avenue Kleber served as the organization's temporary headquarters. Dropping in unannounced for a drink one evening, a young American woman who was working in the Labor Division of the Marshall Plan noticed a list of names with dollar amounts next to them lying by Brown's telephone. Brown had left the room to make the drinks for his unexpected guest. She thought she detected the presence of somebody other than Brown in the suite. Eventually, unable to hide out any longer, Michael Josselson appeared from the bathroom, whence he had speedily retreated, in order not to be seen. Diana Dodge, who was in two years to become Josselson's wife, thought the scene highly amusing. Josselson was deeply embarrassed.

The scene at the Hôtel Baltimore shows the improvisational nature of the Congress for Cultural Freedom in its early days. 'In the beginning, it was all very well motivated, and we just went along how we thought best,'[4] said de Neufville. Gradually things started to coalesce as the CIA developed a bureaucracy for containing such operations and providing them with 'guidance'. 'There were various meetings [between] some of the top Congress people, including Lasky and others, and the Agency people who were in charge,'[5] recalled Donald Jameson, a CIA expert on Russian affairs who was peripherally involved with QKOPERA. 'Most of the time there would be between ten and fifteen people in a conference room. And we would sit around and talk about what ought to be done, where it ought to be done, and it was very much an open exchange. This was the tone that the people who were in the

Agency chain of command set in, and I think it was very wise to do so. As a matter of fact, if it hadn't been done that way, the people on the other side – on the Congress side – would have quit. I think at least a great many of them. They were not time-servers who were concerned about sticking to the Agency just because they needed a cheque.'[6]

The people on the other side of the table to whom Jameson referred were Josselson, Nabokov, Lasky, Bondy and, occasionally, Malcolm Muggeridge, who provided a line into the British IRD. This was the 'apparat', the group chosen to be party to the CIA's guidance which, despite the genteel nature of its delivery, in effect meant the laying down of the political line that Washington expected the Congress to follow. There was, as Jameson explained, a reciprocity: the CIA would pass on American foreign policy objectives, and by return, they listened attentively to a group whose unique access to the intellectual currents of western Europe could ease or even modify the methods and arguments used to formulate these objectives.

Josselson, although clearly a part of the Agency chain of command, also took his job of representing the Congress's interests very seriously. This was a uniquely hard position to hold, and to hold credibly. Technically, he was subordinate to de Neufville, but de Neufville rarely, if ever, tried to overrule him. 'I saw Josselson every day, or if not, every week, and I would go to Washington with whatever he wanted to accomplish,' said de Neufville. 'If I agreed, which I usually did, I would try and help. I saw my job as trying to facilitate the development of Congress by listening to people like Josselson who knew better than I did. He did a wonderful job.'[7]

'Josselson is one of the world's unsung heroes,' Tom Braden later said. 'He did all this frenetic work with all the intellectuals of Europe, who didn't necessarily agree on much beyond their basic belief in freedom, and he was running around from meeting to meeting, from man to man, from group to group, and keeping them all together and all organized and all getting something done. He deserves a place in history.'[8] Similarly, Arthur Schlesinger remembered Josselson as 'an extraordinary man' who could 'play any instrument in the orchestra'. But there was a darker side to Josselson's heroic temperament. His great talent for listening without talking was occasionally strained by the talent of others for talking without listening. 'Mike sometimes got impatient with all this chatter. Sometimes he felt these people were too precious, too talmudic. Then he would just put his hands over his ears and say, "Enough! I just can't listen to any more of this. Let's just get on with it!"' remembered one colleague. 'He was pretty blunt, and he had a very low boiling point – he'd go up in smoke pretty quickly.'[9] Another Congress insider felt that Josselson was 'almost always on the verge of an emotional explosion'.[10] Josselson, who once revealed that his mother used to 'make scenes', did his best to control his temper. But by avoiding confrontation, he often produced an 'enormously heavy atmosphere', loaded with silent rage and punctuated by piercing looks from his dark eyes. Forty years later, Ben Sonnenberg, a writer who had a brief and infelicitous flirtation with the CIA in the 1950s, shuddered at the memory of Josselson's heart of darkness. 'The name Michael Josselson still gives me the willies,' he said.[11]

Josselson could not stand intellectual shilly-shallying because he regarded the job in hand with such urgency. So when Irving Brown reported that the British Society for Cultural Freedom was stalling in the face of divisiveness and infighting, and was good only for 'receptions and sherry parties' (one member said its 'chief activity was inviting eminent intellectuals to lunch in expensive Soho restaurants'), Josselson resolved to impose his authority on the British affiliate. Formed in January 1951, it had got off to a shaky start. Its chairman, Stephen Spender, soon fell out with the Honorary Secretary, Michael Goodwin, and by the end of 1951 the Executive Committee was disintegrating. Goodwin, as editor of the journal *Twentieth Century*, the famous monthly launched in 1877 as the *Nineteenth Century and After*, was a vital contact for the Paris office, which had saved his journal from liquidation in early 1951 by paying off an angry landlord and financing the move to a new office in Henrietta Street, which also became the headquarters of the British Society. This was followed by two emergency subsidies to *Twentieth Century* of $2,000 and £700, to meet outstanding printing and paper bills in August 1951, plus a further monthly subsidy of £150 to 'cover the magazine's monthly deficit'. Goodwin, who was later to become a

Features and Drama director at the BBC, not only offered Josselson a vehicle in England in the form of *Twentieth Century*, he also provided a useful link to British covert cultural propaganda efforts: he was working as a contract employee for the Information Research Department.

Josselson's subsidy to Goodwin's journal was given on the specific understanding that *Twentieth Century* should address itself to rebutting the *New Statesman and Nation*'s positions. Goodwin confirmed in a letter of January 1952 that this campaign was building up momentum, reporting that *Twentieth Century* is 'keeping up a running fire of comment upon a variety of subjects [in the *New Statesman*] which amounts in total to a systematic critical destruction of their position'. For good measure, he added, it was also preparing to undermine *Soviet Studies*, a Glasgow quarterly 'which is probably the chief source of Stalinist apologetics in this country'.[12]

But Josselson was never entirely happy with the *Twentieth Century* arrangement. 'It wasn't lively enough. It wasn't the right vehicle,' Michael Josselson's wife Diana said.[13] Goodwin's attacks on the *New Statesman* were all well and good, but his journal had not done enough to address the problems indicated by Nabokov in a letter of 19 December 1951, in which Nabokov reported the 'widespread dissatisfaction' of the International Executive Committee. 'Mr Spender will suggest to you and to your Board of Editors urgent and important changes which are fully endorsed by Irving Brown, de Rougemont and myself,' wrote Nabokov sternly.[14] These changes should be effected immediately, he added, or else Congress support would dry up. To which Goodwin replied sharply on 31 December: 'No good can result to anyone unless the review remains, and is known to remain, independent . . . [the review] should be permitted to operate "without strings".'[15]

Things went from bad to worse for Goodwin. In January 1952, Spender was at the centre of what looked like a *coup* to replace Goodwin as Secretary of the British Society, sending him a curt letter of dismissal. Spender himself had resigned in pique a few weeks previously, along with Woodrow Wyatt and Julian Amery, and told Nabokov that he was coming to Paris to explain his reasons for doing so. There, he had convinced the Congress's inner circle that the British affiliate could not function with Goodwin at the helm, and obtained a letter for his dismissal, which he now forwarded to Goodwin. Goodwin in turn blamed Spender for Wyatt's resignation, and urged Nabokov to keep Spender 'within bounds'. But Goodwin was still forced to resign. Spender rejoined the Executive Committee, which from now on was controlled by Malcolm Muggeridge and Fredric Warburg, with Tosco Fyvel 'tailing along as the third person in the trinity'. For somebody who was consistently characterized as a watery, silly soul, Spender displayed a gritty determination to get what he wanted out of this situation.[16] W. H. Auden called him 'a Dostoevskyian Holy Fool' and 'a parody Parsifal'. Isherwood called him an 'essentially comic character' who revealed truth through farce. Others found a 'wincing bewilderment' (Ian Hamilton), or a 'loose-jointed mind, misty, clouded, suffusive', in which 'nothing has outline' (Virginia Woolf). In a life pitted by contradiction and ambiguity, Spender had already developed a talent for retreating behind these dubious aureoles.

Goodwin's resignation was a blow to Josselson, who lost in him a direct contact with the Information Research Department. But IRD soon made good the deficit, inserting their man John Clews into the British Society as its General Secretary. Soon, Clews was using his position as a distribution point for IRD material, writing Nabokov to tell him in June 1952 that he had had 'a long talk with Hannah Arendt and have introduced her to one or two of our Foreign Office experts, as a result of which I am supplying her with a lot of source material that she needs for her new book . . . If you know of any other people that are coming over here and who wish to make similar contacts to those made by Dr. Arendt, just let me know and I will arrange them.'[17] Clews also sent material to Josselson, reminding him (as if he needed to) that the documents could be used freely, 'but their source must not be stated'.

With Clews's appointment, the troubles in the British Society seemed to be temporarily resolved. Tosco Fyvel, editor of *Tribune* and a key member of the Congress steering committee, agreed to 'keep a watching brief on arrangements in London'. But Josselson was still not satisfied. Hugh Trevor-Roper's public criticisms of the Congress after its Berlin inauguration had left a legacy of suspicion, and many British intellectuals were reluctant to identify themselves with an organization whose real origins were deemed to be obscure. The trouble was that the hand of the American government was seen by many British intellectuals to be reaching into their pie. 'We used to joke about it,' said an officer of the British Society for Cultural Freedom. 'We'd take our friends out to lunch, and when they offered to pay, we would say, "Oh no, don't worry, the American taxpayers are paying!"'[18] Many were yet to be persuaded that such blandishments were desirable.

8

Cette Fête Américaine

This Eisenhower splurge . . .
Elizabeth Bishop

In early 1951, Nabokov sent a confidential memo to Irving Brown outlining a plan for a major festival of the arts. With characteristically clumsy syntax (Nabokov never achieved the stylistic ease and grammatical correctness in written English that came so readily to Josselson), he explained that its purpose would be to engineer 'the first close collaboration of top-ranking American artistic organizations in Europe with European ones and also of American artistic production on a *footing of complete equality* with European artistic production. Hence it is bound to have an extremely beneficial all-round effect upon the cultural life of the free world by showing the cultural solidarity and interdependence of European and American civilization. If successful, it will help to destroy the pernicious European myth (successfully cultivated by the Stalinists) of American cultural inferiority. It will be a challenge of the culture of the free world to the un-culture of the totalitarian world and a source of courage and "redressement moral", in particular for the French intellectuals, for it will again give a kind of sense and purposefulness to the dislocated and disintegrated cultural life of France and most of Europe.'[1]

Brown reacted hesitantly to the idea, as did Josselson, de

Neufville and Lasky. Nabokov had to summon up all his powers of persuasion to gain approval – and large amounts of money – for his 'dream festival'. Lasky was always uncomfortable with Nabokov, whom he described sniffily as 'the dandy of the revolution. People like Nicky were absolutely infatuated by the fireworks and the frou-frou and the razzmatazz.' Lasky the City College ideologue had trouble accepting Nabokov's unique brand of aristocratic bohemianism. But even he had to concede that Nabokov's plan to 'introduce a note of flamboyancy, hype, propaganda, fireworks, Mardi-Gras-next-Tuesday, or whatever, to widen the audience and show you're not just grim, bespectacled intellectuals with noses to the ideological grindstone, but aesthetes, fun-loving people' could bring 'positive results'.[2]

Back at the International Organizations Division, Tom Braden was enthusiastic. Nabokov's claim that 'no ideological polemic about the validity and meaning of our culture can equal the products of this culture itself'[3] struck an immediate chord with Braden, who had recently seen a play staged in Warsaw under the auspices of the State Department, and found it 'dreadful, like most of their stuff. It wouldn't impress people in Waterloo, Minnesota, let alone Paris. It was a given that the State Department didn't know its ass from a hole in the road. They weren't with it, they didn't know how to use what they had, everything they did was third or fourth rate.'[4] With a few notable exceptions (like the Frank Lloyd Wright show which toured Europe in 1951–2), this indictment of State Department cultural initiatives was justified. Who would be impressed by window displays given over to celebrating the American way of life which included an exhibit on the 'Manufacture of Nylon in the United States'? And was the 'simplicity and charm of manner' of the Smith College Chamber Singers with 'their fresh and winsome appearance in white gowns' enough to convince French audiences that the centre of culture had shifted to America?[5] 'Who goes to an exhibition of photographs showing the glories of America?' asked Tom Braden. 'I disregarded it as all balderdash. If you're going to do it, get the best. Al [Allen Dulles] and myself, we knew better. It sounds arrogant, but that's what we thought. *We knew*. We knew something about art and music, and State didn't.'[6]

Braden had also clipped an article in the *New York Times* criticizing 'America's foolish disregard of the importance of the "cultural offensive"', and pointing out that the Soviet Union spent more on cultural propaganda in France alone than the US did in the entire world. America needed something big and flashy to make a decisive intervention in the *Kulturkampf*. Nabokov's plan promised just that, and by the end of April 1951, Braden had secured approval for the festival at a CIA project review board.

On 15 May 1951, the Congress for Cultural Freedom's Executive Committee instructed Nabokov, as Secretary General of the International Secretariat, to move the plan forward. Nabokov immediately availed himself of a first-class air ticket to the States, stopping first in Hollywood to see his 'old friend' Igor Stravinsky. Stravinsky (like Schoenberg, Thomas Mann and, for a while, Bertolt Brecht) was one of 'The gods of high culture [who] had disembarked from Europe to dwell, almost incognito, among the lemon trees and beach boys and neo-Bauhaus architecture and fantasy hamburgers' of Southern California.[7] In these incongruous surroundings, Stravinsky greeted his White Russian friend and promised to appear at the festival. Nabokov stayed long enough in Tinseltown to squeeze in a meeting with Jose Ferrer, who was so excited by Nabokov's plans that he later wrote telling him to return to Hollywood, as there was plenty of money there to boost the coffers, and that he, Ferrer, would do everything he could to help.

After a whirlwind tour of America, Nabokov returned to Europe with a clutch of contracts and promises to appear at the festival, whose date had been fixed for April 1952. Igor Stravinsky, Leontyne Price, Aaron Copland, Samuel Barber, the New York City Ballet, the Boston Symphony Orchestra, the Museum of Modern Art in New York, James T. Farrell, W. H. Auden, Gertrude Stein, Virgil Thomson, Allen Tate, Glenway Westcott – works or appearances by all these were pencilled into Nabokov's programme. Returning to Europe, he was soon able to announce that Jean Cocteau, Claude Debussy, William Walton, Laurence Olivier, Benjamin Britten, the Vienna Opera, Covent Garden Opera, the Balanchine troupe, Czesław Milosz, Ignazio Silone, Denis de Rougemont, André

Malraux, Salvador de Madariaga, and Guido Piovene were also on the programme.

Not surprisingly, given Nabokov's own vocation as a composer, the music section began to emerge as the most significant part of the festival. Here, Nabokov intended to counter, composer by composer, Stalinism in the arts. 'The political, cultural and moral meaning of the Festival and of its program should not be overt,' his proposal argued. 'It should be left to the public to make its inevitable logical conclusions. Practically all the works [to be] performed belong to the category branded as "formalist, decadent and corrupt" by the Stalinists and the Soviet aestheticians, including the works of Russian composers (Prokofiev, Schostakovich [sic], Scriabine and Strawinksy [sic]).'[8] The scene at the Waldorf, where Nabokov had challenged Shostakovich to repudiate Stalinism's assault on music, was now set to achieve its crescendo.

Nabokov's grandiose plans represented the first serious challenge for the CIA's newly emergent cultural propaganda machine. The organizational skills and fund-raising powers of Braden's fledgling IOD were truly to be tested. A 'festival account' was opened in New York, with the American Committee for Cultural Freedom acting as the laundry for CIA and State Department funds. The money was channelled through the Farfield Foundation, a dummy front or 'pass-through' set up by the CIA expressly to deal with the cashflow for the festival, but later maintained as the principal conduit for Agency subsidies to the Congress because of its usefulness. Financial support for the British part of the festival was secured through negotiations with IRD and Woodrow Wyatt who, as 'a personal friend of the Secretary of the Exchequer Mr Gaitskell', promised to raise additional cash.

Braden's IOD was also directly involved in negotiating for the Boston Symphony Orchestra. Nabokov had already secured the interest of his old friend Charles Munch, the orchestra's artistic director. But there were problems. The orchestra's travel expenses alone were 'huge', according to Nabokov. The festival also clashed with the highly lucrative Pops season, which meant the orchestra faced the possibility of losing revenue. But Braden was not prepared to lose what was widely considered the best symphony orchestra in America. So he turned to Charles Douglas

Jackson, an ardent Cold Warrior who had taken leave from *Time-Life* to work on Eisenhower's election campaign. 'C. D.', as he was known, was also a trustee of the Boston Symphony Orchestra. Together with Julius Fleischmann, president of the dummy Farfield Foundation and the festival's 'angel', C. D. formally 'invited' the orchestra to play at the festival. Officially, they were acting for the Congress for Cultural Freedom. Unofficially, they were representing the CIA, which had already pledged $130,000 (listed as a donation from 'prominent individuals and associations') towards the costs of the tour. The orchestra was secured.

On 1 April 1952, the Masterpieces of the Twentieth Century, or Oeuvre du Vingtième Siècle, festival opened in Paris with a performance of the *The Rite of Spring* by the Boston Symphony Orchestra, under Pierre Monteux, the same maestro who had conducted it thirty-nine years earlier. It was a glittering event, with Stravinsky, flanked by the French President Vincent Auriol and Madame Auriol, in attendance. Over the next thirty days, the Congress for Cultural Freedom showered Paris with a hundred symphonies, concertos, operas and ballets by over seventy twentieth-century composers. There were performances by nine orchestras, including the Boston Symphony Orchestra, the Vienna Philharmonic, the West Berlin RIAS Orchestra (funded by Marshall Plan counterpart funds), the Suisse Romande of Geneva, the Santa Cecilia orchestra of Rome, the National Radiodiffusion Française. Topping the bill were those composers who had been proscribed by Hitler or Stalin (some, like Alban Berg, had the honour of being banned by both). There were performances of works by the Austrian-born Arnold Schoenberg, driven out of Germany as a Jew and a composer of 'decadent music' in 1933, and characterized as 'anti-aesthetic, anti-harmonic, chaotic and inane' by Russian music 'critics'; Paul Hindemith, another refugee from Nazi Germany, now derided by Stalinists for initiating a whole school of 'graphic, linear pseudo-counterpoint which is slavishly followed by so many pseudo-modernists in Europe and America'; and Claude Debussy, under whose 'Impressionist tree' the 'fleurs du mal of modernism' had been allowed to grow, according to *Sovietskaya Muzyka*.

Also chosen to represent the 'validity of the creative effort of our century' were works by Samuel Barber, William Walton, Gustav Mahler, Erik Satie, Béla Bartók, Heitor Villa-Lobos, Ildebrando Pizzetti, Vittorio Rieti, Gianfranco Malipiero, Georges Auric (listed with Darius Milhaud in *Sovietskaya Muzyka* as 'servile teasers of the snobbish bourgeois tastes of a capitalist city'), Arthur Honegger, Jean Françaix, Henri Sauguet, Francis Poulenc and Aaron Copland (who was grouped with psychiatrists Freud and Borneigg, philosopher Bergson, and 'gangsters' Raymond Mortimer and Bertrand Russell, as false authorities to whom Soviet musicologists and critics should never refer). Stravinsky, who had fled Paris in 1939, conducted his own work, *Oedipus Rex*, for which Jean Cocteau designed the set and directed the choreography. (The American Committee for Cultural Freedom had made a last-minute appeal for Cocteau to be dropped from the festival programme, cabling Nabokov on 9 April 1952 to say they had just learned that Cocteau 'has signed the Communist-inspired document protesting the execution of the Soviet spies in Greece. This is so obviously Communist-inspired that the feeling here is that he should be dropped from the Exposition program.' He wasn't.)

The State Department paid for Virgil Thomson's adaptation of Gertrude Stein's *Four Saints in Three Acts*, which starred Leontyne Price. Nabokov later boasted to Arthur Schlesinger: 'I started her career and because of this she has always been willing to do things for me which she couldn't do for anybody else.' Curiously, Frank Wisner's sister, Elizabeth, also claimed she had discovered and promoted Price, who referred to herself as the Wisners' 'chocolate sister'. One of the great sopranos of her time, Leontyne Price had the added advantage – for her sponsors, at least – of being black. On 15 November 1951, Albert Donnelly Jr, who appeared suddenly in the American Committee as Festival Secretary (and disappeared as soon as the festival was finished), wrote to Julius Fleischmann: 'There has been mention here among interested friends of a certain Negro singer, Leontine [sic] Price, who was, I believe, Mr Nabokov's protégée. She is supposed to be excellent. Could you sound out Mr Nabokov as to whether we should try to get her for *Four Saints*? I have not as yet discussed her with Virgil

Thomson. There is also a strong feeling that for psychological reasons the entire cast of *Four Saints* should be American Negro: to counter the "suppressed race" propaganda and forestall all criticisms to the effect that we had to use foreign negroes because we wouldn't let our own "out".'[9]

The art and sculpture exhibition was curated by James Johnson Sweeney, art critic and former director of New York's Museum of Modern Art, which was contracted to organize the show. Works by Matisse, Derain, Cézanne, Seurat, Chagall, Kandinsky and other masters of early twentieth century modernism were culled from American collections and shipped to Europe on 18 April, aboard the appropriately named SS *Liberté*. Sweeney's press release made no bones about the propaganda value of the show: as the works were created 'in many lands under free world conditions', they would speak for themselves 'of the desirability for contemporary artists of living and working in an atmosphere of freedom. On display will be masterpieces that could not have been created nor whose exhibition would be allowed by such totalitarian regimes as Nazi Germany or present-day Soviet Russia and her satellites, as has been evidenced in those governments' labelling as "degenerate" or "bourgeois" of many of the paintings and sculptures included.'[10] This was to be a kind of reverse *Entartekunst*, in which the 'official' art of the free world was anything the totalitarians loved to hate. And although these were European masterpieces, the fact that all the works in the show were owned by American collectors and museums delivered another clear message: modernism owed its survival – and its future – to America. The art show was a great popular success (despite Herbert Read's criticism that it was too retrospective, and presented the art of the twentieth century as a *fait accompli*, a closed period), attracting the highest attendance of any since the war, according to Alfred Barr, director of the Museum of Modern Art.

Julius Fleischmann, a multi-millionaire famed for his stinginess, was in his element, dishing up CIA money and taking all the credit for it. 'His' contribution of over $7,000 made possible the transfer of the art show to the Tate, and earned the effusive thanks of the Arts Council of Great Britain, who reported that it was 'a resounding success. Already over 25,000 visitors have seen it and it has had an excellent press.'

The literary debates were a mixed affair. Appearing on the podium were Allen Tate, Roger Caillois, Eugenio Montale, Guido Piovene, James T. Farrell, Glenway Westcott, William Faulkner, W. H. Auden, Czesław Milosz, Ignazio Silone, Denis de Rougemont, André Malraux, Salvador de Madariaga and Stephen Spender. The press reaction was tepid. Critics detected a disparity between the calibre of first-rate writers and mediocre writers, and were bored by 'long-winded' speeches. The journalist for *Carrefour* (usually sympathetic, being left-wing and anti-Stalinist) listened to Stephen Spender, but noted only his 'brick-red complexion' and 'shock of hair pointing towards infinity'. Denis de Rougemont was judged to be 'the best by far . . . sober, clear, he skilfully poses the problem of the author in society'. But Guido Piovene gave an address 'as stiff as his collar. It is difficult to understand him; then suddenly you are not listening any more . . . At the door an Italian journalist told me that he had left because he was bored. "Authors were meant to write," he said. I felt this to be another fundamental truth.'[11] Another critic, regretting the absence of Albert Camus and Jean-Paul Sartre, pointed out that the other French intellectuals present – Raymond Aron, André Malraux, René Tavernier, Jules Monneret, Roger Nimier, Claude Mauriac, Jean Amrouche – all had 'the same political ideas', which meant that outsiders listening to them would get a false idea 'of our aesthetic and moral conceptions'.

Sartre had refused to attend the festival, commenting drily that he was 'not as anti-Communist as all that'. Had he been there, he may well have felt, like his hero in *Nausea*, that he was 'alone in the midst of these happy, reasonable voices. All these characters spend their time explaining themselves, and happily recognizing that they hold the same opinions.' In her *roman à clef*, *The Mandarins*, Simone de Beauvoir described the same *ennui*: 'Always the same faces, the same surroundings, the same conversations, the same problems. The more it changes, the more it repeats itself. In the end, you feel as if you're dying alive.'

First there had been *The God That Failed*. Now, apparently, this congregation had found a God who could not: the God of anti-Communism. Certainly, Sartre's brand of selfish, non-collective existentialism could offer nothing to these communicants, who envisaged a progressive culture which was essentially consensual, and presupposed a positive relation between the intellectual and that section of society – political and 'private' – which supported him. Sartre was the enemy not just because of his position on Communism, but because he preached a doctrine (or anti-doctrine) of individualism which rubbed against the federalist 'family of man' society which America, through organizations like the Congress for Cultural Freedom, was promoting. (The Soviet Union, by the way, found Sartre equally uncongenial, branding existentialism 'a nauseating and putrid concoction'.)

The Americans were very happy to be in Paris. Elizabeth Hardwick and Robert Lowell, who were travelling in Europe at the time, 'couldn't resist' dropping in on the festival, and reported that everyone there seemed to be having 'a marvellous time'. Janet Flanner, writing as 'Genet' for *The New Yorker*, devoted the whole of her May 1952 'Letter from Paris' to the festival. 'It has spilled such gallons of captious French newspaper ink, wasted such tempests of argumentative Franco-American breath, and afforded, on the whole, so much pleasure to the eye and ear that it can safely be called, in admiration, an extremely popular fiasco,' she wrote.[12] Like most other reviewers, she found the literary conferences 'dull'. Faulkner 'disappointingly mumbled nothing but a few incoherent words', unable to find anything intelligent to say on the 'absurd topics, set by the Congress committee, such as "Isolation and Communication" or "Revolt and Communion"'. The only Frenchman 'of any literary quality' who agreed to appear was 'General de Gaulle's present political lieutenant, André Malraux who [merely] said, "America is now part of Europe."'[13]

'Cette fête américaine' became a piping hot French dinner-table conversation piece. *Combat*, a Non-Communist Left daily, ran a series by Guy Dumur, who concluded: 'Confusedly, these cultural entertainments were tied to the signing of the treaty for a European Army and to the Admiral Fechteler report [a reference to a report, possibly spurious, in which the Admiral was supposed to have advised the National Security Council of the inevitability of war by 1960] which, true or false, has fed the anti-American mythology and rekindled Europe's great fear. And this irritating mixture of chauvinism and inferiority complex as regards America (so little known by the French) . . . has bizarrely, but not inexplicably, found an outlet in decrying this exposition of the arts of Europe, to which the Americans, somewhat clumsily, wished to render homage.'[14]

But another piece in *Combat* derided 'NATO's Festival' and complained about the 'noisy presentation of these events' from which 'French musicians among the best have been forgotten, probably because they have never been heard of in Alabama or Idaho . . . But we would overcome our national pride if a very special target was not hidden behind the whole venture. Freedom and culture do not have to be defined by a Congress; their main characteristic being to bear neither limitation nor prejudice, nor sponsorship . . . For our part, in this newspaper where the words "freedom" and "culture" are always understood without any idea of compromising, we can but deplore the use which is made of these words in connection with the Festival's manifestations. The value and interest of these events do not need the help of an "inspired" Barnum, nor an "Atlantic" flag.'[15]

Nabokov's original intention of concealing the propaganda value of the festival had failed. This had been, said Janet Flanner, 'the biggest cultural propaganda effort, either private or governmental, since the war . . . the propaganda focus [being] naturally anti-Communist'. In a France weary of the subvention of art to *parti pris*, the Congress's attempt to lasso the masterpieces of the twentieth century to a political agenda was widely resented. In an open letter to the festival organizers, the famously intemperate head of the ballet troupe at the Paris Opera, Serge Lifar, angrily accused the Congress of undertaking an 'absolutely meaningless' crusade in France 'against a possible and unforeseeable cultural subjection [by Communism]'. Apparently forgetting the Vichy years, Lifar asserted that 'France is the only country where "spiritual domestication" is unthinkable. If one considers France's long past struggle for freedom of thought and individual independence, one can hardly understand how you dare come here and talk about freedom and criticize our intellectual activities. Dear sirs, you have made a big mistake: from the point of view of spirit, civilization and culture, France does not have to ask for anybody's opinion; she is the one that gives advice to others.'[16]

Franc-Tireur, the leftist daily, challenged Lifar's right to speak as a champion of France, 'the cause of which he is not well qualified to support, inasmuch as the service of art is not incompatible with the devotion to the cause of freedom and human dignity, especially at a time when these causes were oppressed as they were during the German occupation which did not prevent Mr. Lifar from dancing.' *Touché*. The article went on: 'Please let us forget about politics or propaganda. That gloomy mystification which puts creative minds in the artistic or scientific fields at the service of the state or the chief, has not been established by the free world [which] allows the spirit to blow anywhere . . . Freedom's wings have not been cut yet.'[17]

Franc-Tireur seemed to have recovered from that 'barely concealed anti-Americanism' of a few years earlier, and supported the festival wholeheartedly. It was now edited by Georges Altman – a member of the Congress steering committee. Also favourable was *Figaro Littéraire*, which praised the festival as 'great proof of unbiased artistic activity'. Again, not surprising, given that the paper's editor-in-chief was Maurice Noel, a friend of Raymond Aron, who in turn introduced him to the Congress. The main paper, *Le Figaro*, was also closely aligned to the Congress through the good offices of Mr Brisson, the editor-in-chief, whom Nabokov fastidiously cultivated over long lunches.

At the hands of the Communist press, the Congress received a thorough mauling. *L'Humanité* attacked the festival as part of a sinister design 'to facilitate the ideological occupation of our country by the United States, to have French minds imbued with bellicist and fascist ideas, the acceptance of which would permit the enrolment of French intellectuals in a "cultural army", a reinforcement of the European army . . . Cultural exchanges become for the Americans a means . . . to reinforce the infiltration, spying and propaganda programs set up by Burnham and approved by the American Congress, through the so-called "security credits" . . . The famous statement made by Mr Henry Luce, that "The Twentieth Century must, to a great extent, become an American century" gives us the true meaning of the venture called "Twentieth Century Festival"'.[18] 'The United States nowadays are playing the part that Rome once played towards Greece. New Hadrians are not emperors any more (not even "presidents"): they are bankers or car manufacturers,' read one article in *Combat*.

Diana Josselson remembered the Paris of this period as brimful with anti-Americanism, a 'Yanqui Go Home' mentality everywhere: 'the people one met weren't really like that, but they did have an idea that the typical American was gross'. Many Americans were irked by this ungenerous response to their largesse. 'I could get quite distressed at Europeans if I allowed myself to,' confessed C. D. Jackson. 'How Europeans can indulge in "Americans, go home" out of one corner of their mouth, while out of the other corner it is, "If a single American division leaves European soil it is the end of the world," seems a little silly to me, and not in keeping with Europe's famed logical mind.'[19]

Overall, Nabokov's festival ultimately contributed 'a further painful twist to knotted Franco-American propaganda relations'.[20] De Neufville, who was never persuaded that the festival was a good idea, later said that it 'seemed a very expensive cover story. But then it was picked up by Washington, and they pushed money at us because they thought it was a great idea. It just had a kind of snowball effect. Was it a success? Well, what was it trying to do? Did it spread the message of cultural freedom? I don't know. It served its purpose as a cover story, I suppose. I mean, it introduced Fleischmann as the patron of all this stuff. It was a mixed effort. I guess it was a big show-window for things from the U.S. to be shown competitively with European culture, and [Washington] got enthusiastic about that.'[21]

Melvin Lasky was unmoved. 'The Boston Symphony Orchestra cost a packet,' he complained. (In fact, the total cost of bringing the orchestra to Europe was $166,359.84.) Lasky continued, 'I thought [the festival] was trivial. It's unimportant whether foreigners think Americans can play music or not. This whole thing wasn't a gravy train, there weren't oodles of money, as people have said – it was skimpy. So to spend such large sums on this kind of spectacular hype – it didn't make sense.'[22] 'Anti-Americanism in France then was very strong, and Nicolas's festival was designed to counter that. It was thrilling. But it gave more weight to the idea that America was behind the Congress,' Diana Josselson concluded.[23]

Nevertheless, the festival had two tangible results. First, it launched the Boston Symphony Orchestra as a billboard for America's symphonic virtuosity. After its triumphant appearance at the Paris festival, the orchestra travelled through most major cities in Europe, taking in The Hague, Amsterdam, Brussels, Frankfurt, Berlin, Strasbourg, Lyons, Bordeaux, and London. The juggernaut of American culture, it became the CIA's answer to the agitprop trains of old.

C. D. Jackson wrote excitedly of the 'overwhelming success and acceptance of the Boston Symphony on its European tour . . . It was not an easy job to put across, but from the standpoint of the Great Cause, it was essential, and it more than justified the preliminary blood, sweat, and tears. One of the greatest, if not the greatest, hazards that we face in Europe is European non-acceptance of America on matters other than Coca-Cola, bathtubs, and tanks . . . The contribution of the BSO in this intellectual and cultural area is immeasurable but immense.'[24] Braden was similarly enthused, and later remembered 'the enormous joy I got when the Boston Symphony Orchestra won more acclaim for the U.S. in Paris than John Foster Dulles or Dwight D. Eisenhower could have brought with a hundred speeches.'[25]

The second positive achievement of the festival was that it established the Farfield Foundation as an apparently credible backer for the Congress. This meant that Irving Brown no longer needed to fork out cash from his slush fund, and he now began to recede into the background. The Farfield was incorporated on 30 January 1952 as a 'non-profit organization'. According to its brochure, 'It was formed by a group of private American individuals who are interested in preserving the cultural heritage of the free world and encouraging the constant expansion and interchange of knowledge in the fields of the arts, letters, and sciences. To this end, the Foundation extends financial aid to groups and organizations engaged in the interpreting and publicizing of recent cultural advances and to groups whose enterprises in literary, artistic or scientific fields may serve as worthy contributions to the progress of culture. The Foundation offers assistance to organizations whose programs tend to strengthen the cultural ties which bind the nations of the world and to reveal to all peoples who share the traditions of a free culture the inherent dangers which totalitarianism poses to intellectual and cultural development.'[26]

First president of the Farfield, and the CIA's most significant single front-man, was Julius 'Junkie' Fleischmann, the millionaire heir to a huge yeast and gin fortune, who lived at Indian Hill, outside Cincinnati. He had helped finance *The New Yorker*, and boasted a bulging portfolio of artistic patronage: he was a director of New York's Metropolitan Opera, a fellow of the Royal Society of the Arts, London, a member of the advisory committee of the Yale Drama School, a director of Diaghilev's Ballet Russe de Monte Carlo, and of the Ballet Foundation of New York, and a financial backer of many Broadway productions. Michael Josselson referred to him as 'The American Maecenas for the world of culture'. His personal wealth and varied artistic patronage made him an ideally plausible angel for the CIA's sponsorship of the Congress for Cultural Freedom.

Braden later described Junkie as one of the many 'rich people who wanted to be of service to government. They got a certain amount of self-esteem out of it. They were made to feel they were big shots because they were let in on this secret expedition to battle the Communists.'[27] A fully roped-up member of Wisner's OPC from its early days, Junkie was an habitué of the dusty corridors of the sheds on the Washington Mall, proud of his role as a front (initially through the Fleischmann Foundation) for covert activities. But in the shake-up that followed the formation of the International Organizations Division, Junkie got pushed around. 'The trouble was he took it too seriously,' said Braden. 'He began to think he was the boss of these fronts. They were just using his name, but he started to believe it was for real. I remember he started telling me what he wanted. He'd tell me he wanted his foundation to do this, and not that. And that was the last thing I needed . . . In the end, we offered him the Farfield as a kind of substitute. But it was only ever a front. Whoever was president was just a name, and those old guys from New York all sat on the board just to do us a favour.'[28]

'The Farfield Foundation was a CIA foundation and there were many such foundations,' Tom Braden went on to explain. 'We used the names of foundations for many purposes but the foundation *didn't exist* except on paper. We would go to somebody in New York who was a well known rich person and we would say, "We want to set up a foundation," and we would tell him what we were trying to do, and pledge him to secrecy and he would say, "Of course I'll do it." And then you would publish a letterhead and his name would be on it, and there would be a foundation. It was really a pretty simple device.'[29] As president of the Farfield Foundation, Junkie could be presented to unwitting outsiders as the private angel of the Congress for Cultural Freedom. 'It was good to have a patron to display,' Diana Josselson commented, 'and he loved his role. But the relationship became a chore and a bore, because it diverted Michael from more substantive things while he made a big show of being deferential to the big patron.'[30]

The directors of the Farfield met every other month in New York where there would usually be a 'guest' from the Congress – Nabokov, Josselson or Muggeridge. They approved the payments, asking no questions, acting out what Muggeridge called 'the comedy' as a patriotic duty. There was also an annual board meeting, which Diana Josselson described as 'a very big farce, of course. Michael would go, and Junkie. The whole relationship was farcical, in a way, because we just played it straight. They would just pass on a set of pre-prepared actions.'[31]

As the Congress's Secretary General, Nabokov surely knew to which government agency he owed the extraordinary largesse enjoyed by the Paris office during his mammoth festival. Years later, he would confess to Josselson that 'Queen Juliana Fleischmann' had never been plausible. He had always thought of 'the plutocratic Junkie' as 'a poor conduit'. But officially, Nabokov knew nothing, and maintained (just as implausibly) that 'Curiously enough, not for a moment did the question of money cross my mind. It probably should have, because it was hard to imagine the American labor unions subsidizing a grandiosely expensive modern-arts festival and not in America, but in Paris, of all places . . . Not in my wildest dreams could I have expected that my "dream festival" would be supported by America's spying establishment, nor did I know that the fare for my delightful first class flight to Paris was being paid by the CIA via the labor union's European representative, the cheerful Mr. Brown. And soon, very soon, that same spy mill would be using "passing" foundations to pump money to such groups as our Cultural Committee, to American colleges, to refugee orchestras, and whatnot.'[32]

Could Nabokov really have been in ignorance, unaware that he was entangled in a deliberate deception? Or had he, like so many of his contemporaries, become, like Graham Greene's Alden Pyle, just another Quiet American. 'He didn't even hear what I said; he was absorbed already in the dilemmas of Democracy and the responsibilities of the West; he was determined – I learnt that very soon – to do good, not to any individual person but to a country, a continent, a world. Well, he was in his element now with the whole universe to improve.'[33]

9

The Consortium

'Sire – over what do you rule?'
'Over everything,' said the king, with magnificent simplicity.'

Le Petit Prince, Antoine de Saint-Exupéry

Cultural freedom did not come cheap. Over the next seventeen years, the CIA was to pump tens of millions of dollars into the Congress for Cultural Freedom and related projects. With this kind of commitment, the CIA was in effect acting as America's Ministry of Culture.

A central feature of the Agency's efforts to mobilize culture as a Cold War weapon was the systematic organization of a network of 'private' groups or 'friends' into an unofficial consortium. This was an entrepreneurial coalition of philanthropic foundations, business corporations and other institutions and individuals, who worked hand in hand with the CIA to provide the cover and the funding pipeline for its secret programmes in western Europe. Additionally, these 'friends' could be depended on to articulate the government's interests at home and abroad, whilst appearing to do so solely on their own initiative. Maintaining their 'private' status, these individuals and bodies were in fact acting as the CIA's designated Cold War venture capitalists.

The inspiration behind this consortium was Allen Dulles, who had started to build its foundations after the war, when he and his brother John Foster Dulles were partners at the law firm of Sullivan and Cromwell. In May 1949, Allen Dulles presided over the formation of the National Committee for a Free Europe, ostensibly the initiative of a 'group of private American citizens', but in reality one of the CIA's most ambitious fronts. Incorporated on 11 May 1949 in New York, the declared purpose of the National Committee for a Free Europe, Inc. was 'to use the many and varied skills of exiled East Europeans in the development of programs which will actively combat Soviet domination'.[1] Committed to 'the belief that this struggle can be resolved as much by force of ideas as by physical means', the Committee was soon to extend its reach into all areas of the cultural Cold War. 'The State Department is very happy to see the formation of this group,' announced Secretary of State Dean Acheson. 'It thinks that the purpose of this organization is excellent, and is glad to welcome its entrance into this field and give it its hearty endorsement.'[2] This public blessing was intended to mask the official origins of the Committee and the fact that it operated solely at the discretion of the CIA, which provided 90 per cent financial support through unvouchered funds. Behind Acheson's endorsement was another concealed truth. Although the Committee's founding statute included the clause, 'No part of the activities of the corporation shall be the carrying on of propaganda,' this was precisely and specifically what it was designed to do.[3]

Moving to the CIA in December 1950, Allen Dulles became 'the Great White Case Officer' of the National Committee for a Free Europe, working with Carmel Offie, who had overseen it for Wisner's OPC since its creation a year earlier. Dulles now took charge of organizing its committees, securing its budget allocation, and designing its strategies. One of the earliest pioneers of the quango, Dulles understood that the success of America's Cold War programme depended on 'its ability to appear independent from government, to seem to represent the spontaneous convictions of freedom loving individuals'.[4] For this aspect alone, the National Committee for a Free Europe, Inc. serves as the paradigm for the CIA-led 'corporatization' of the foreign policy machinery in the Cold War period.

Proliferating committees and sub-committees, boards of directors and trustees, the National Committee for a Free Europe boasted a membership which read like *Who's Who in America*. Interconnectedness was vital, and gave new meaning to Paul Valéry's jokey comment that it was the ambition of Europeans to be governed by a committee of Americans. There was Lucius Clay, who as High Commissioner in Germany had given the green light to *Der Monat*; Gardner Cowles, president of the Cowles publishing group, and a trustee of the Farfield Foundation; Henry Ford II, president of General Motors; Oveta Culp Hobby, a Museum of Modern Art trustee who allowed several family foundations to be used as CIA conduits; the Cold War cardinal, Francis Spellman; C. D. Jackson, psychological warfare veteran and *Time-Life* executive; John C. Hughes, US Ambassador to NATO; Junkie Fleischmann; Arthur Schlesinger; Cecil B. DeMille; Spyros Skouras; Darryl Zanuck; and Dwight D. Eisenhower. There were businessmen and lawyers, diplomats and Marshall Plan administrators, advertising executives and media moguls, film directors and journalists, trades unionists and, of course, CIA agents – plenty of them.

These men were all witting. To the Agency, a 'witting' individual was 'a man of their world, he knew the language, the code words, the customs, the recognition symbols. To be "witting" was to belong to the club. To talk the language. To understand the high signs. To know the fraternity grip. The "unwitting" was out in the cold, unaware of what went on around him, ignorant of the elite conceptions that guided the closed circle of intelligence.'[5] Recalling the ease with which he could engage his fellow Americans in covert projects, CIA agent Donald Jameson said, 'There was almost nobody in this country that I couldn't go to in those days and say, "I'm from the CIA and I'd like to ask you about so and so," and at the very least get a respectful reception and a discussion.'[6] CIA agents rarely had to knock – the door was open.

Just twelve months after its creation, this nucleus of 'private' operators had advanced Dulles's Free Europe Committee (as it became known) from its 'tentative beginnings into a broad and well-defined program, with operations on a very substantial scale'. It was 'an instrument in hand – timely, already well-fashioned' for pursuing 'the victory of ideas'. Its personnel numbered 413, of which 201 were Americans, many of European origin, and 212 'specialist' exiles from Eastern Europe.[7] The budget for its first year alone was $1,703,266. A separate budget of $10 million was set aside for Radio Free Europe (RFE), founded in Berlin in 1950 under the auspices of the committee. Within a few years, RFE had twenty-nine stations broadcasting in sixteen different languages and was using 'every trick of oratory known to Demosthenes or Cicero in [its] "Phillippics" against every individual who supports the Stalinist regime'.[8] It was also soliciting the services of informers behind the Iron Curtain, monitoring Communist broadcasts, underwriting anti-Communist lectures and writings by western intellectuals, and distributing its 'research' internationally to scholars and journalists (including those affiliated with the Congress for Cultural Freedom).

The fund-raising arm of the Free Europe Committee was the Crusade for Freedom, for which a young actor named Ronald Reagan was a leading spokesman and publicist. The Crusade for Freedom was used to launder money to support a programme run by Bill Casey, the future CIA director, called the International Refugee Committee in New York, which allegedly coordinated the exfiltration of Nazis from Germany to the States where they were expected to assist the government in its struggle against Communism.

Dulles kept a firm grip on the committee by placing CIA officers in key positions. If a problem arose which needed to be resolved 'out of channels', Dulles would simply call a meeting with the committee's principals in a New York club or hotel. Top-secret documents record a series of such meetings convened by Dulles at the Knickerbocker Club and the Drake Hotel (in this case, in a bedroom booked for the occasion. How many Cold War campaigns were waged from hotel bedrooms?) Other meetings were held in Allen Dulles's or Frank Wisner's offices at CIA headquarters.

'The USA was a big operation, very big,' says the narrator of *Humboldt's Gift*. Commenting on the dedication of America's elite as they manned this privateer, Henry Kissinger wrote: 'It is to the lasting credit of that generation of Americans that they assumed these responsibilities with energy, imagination and skill. By helping Europe rebuild, encouraging European unity, shaping the institutions of economic cooperation, and extending the protection of our alliances, they saved the possibility of freedom. This burst of creativity is one of the glorious moments of American history.'[9] Henry Breck, a CIA case officer and alumnus of Groton School, expressed it another way: 'Of course, if you're in a real war you must fight hard – and the upper classes fight the hardest. They have the most to lose.'

When they were not huddled together in clubs or hotel rooms, Breck's upper classes applied themselves with equal commitment to the business of entertaining. Lively, self-confident, voluble, Wisner and his colleagues were driven to enjoy a good party, just as they were driven to save the world from Communism. Wisner loved to do a dance called the Crab Walk. Angleton, a legendary consumer of martinis (and, sometimes, anything he could get hold of), used to dance free form to Elvis Presley tunes at parties, weaving enthusiastically, and often by himself. Maurice Oldfield, chief of MI6, known as 'C', also loved to dance. 'Maurice . . . would come visit us in Rhode Island and dance under the trees at night,' recalled Janet Barnes.[10] As the world became stranger, 'the pattern more complicated', theirs was indeed 'a lifetime burning in every moment'.

It seems amazing that men who partied so hard and drank so prodigiously continued to function in their day jobs. The brokers of a new world order, they delayed burn-out only because the potential gains were so immense. Back at their desks the next day, they busied themselves with finding new ways of securing their investments and enlarging their assets. 'We generally reached out to find Americans who would consent to take the money into their accounts and then use it to contribute in various ways,' said covert action agent William Colby. 'If you went to any American institution, company, anything else, and said, "Will you help your country by passing this money?" they'd salute and say, "Absolutely, I'd be delighted." It's easy to pass money around the world to the desired end objective. It might not be one bulk payment but various small payments going in the right direction. This goes all the way to the rather more naked thing that I was sometimes engaged in, putting bundles of local currency in the back of my car and driving out and transferring them to another fellow's car.'[11]

The American companies and individuals who agreed to collaborate with the Agency in this way were known as 'quiet channels'. These channels could also be established after contact was made the other way round. 'Often times, private American groups came to us,' remembered case officer Lee Williams. 'We didn't just always go to them. There was a commonality of purpose that seemed to us to dissolve any major concern about the morality of what we were doing.'[12]

In 1956, in the wake of the Hungarian uprising, J. M. Kaplan, president of the Welch Grape Juice Company, and president and treasurer of the Kaplan Foundation (assets: $14 million), wrote to Allen Dulles offering his services in the fight against Communism. Kaplan offered to devote his 'unending energy to utilize every idea and ingenuity to the over-riding aim of breaking up the Communist conspiracy, searching out and working out every practical opportunity'.[13] Dulles subsequently arranged for a CIA 'representative' to make an appointment with Kaplan. The Kaplan Foundation could soon be counted as an asset, a reliable 'pass-through' for secret funds earmarked for CIA projects, amongst them the Congress for Cultural Freedom, and an institute headed by veteran socialist and chairman of the American Committee for Cultural Freedom, Norman Thomas.

The use of philanthropic foundations was the most convenient way to pass large sums of money to Agency projects without alerting the recipients to their source. By the mid 1950s, the CIA's intrusion into the foundation field was massive. Although figures are not available for this period, the general counsel of a 1952 Congress committee appointed to investigate US foundations concluded that 'An unparalleled amount of power is concentrated increasingly in the hands of an interlocking and self-perpetuating group. Unlike the power of corporate management, it is unchecked by stockholders; unlike the power of government, it is unchecked by the people; unlike the power of the churches, it is unchecked by any firmly established canons of value.'[14] In 1976, a Select Committee appointed to investigate US intelligence activities reported on the CIA's penetration of the foundation field by the mid-1960s: during 1963–6, of the 700 grants over $10,000 given by 164 foundations, at least 108 involved partial or complete CIA funding. More importantly, CIA funding was involved in nearly half the grants made by these 164 foundations in the field of international activities during the same period.

'Bona fide' foundations such as Ford, Rockefeller and Carnegie were considered 'the best and most plausible kind of funding cover'.[15] A CIA study of 1966 argued that this technique was 'particularly effective for democratically run membership organizations, which need to assure their own unwitting members and collaborators, as well as their hostile critics, that they have genuine, respectable, private sources of income'. Certainly, it allowed the CIA to fund 'a seemingly limitless range of covert action programs affecting youth groups, labor unions, universities, publishing houses, and other private institutions' from the early 1950s.[16]

'There was a cover branch at CIA whose job it was to help provide cover, like the foundations we used for our operations,' Braden explained. 'I paid no attention to the details. The Finance Department would handle it, and talk to the cover officer. It was just a mechanism which you used. The Farfield Foundation was one of them. I don't know the names of all of them, I can't remember. But it was a criss-cross of money. There was never any danger of the CIA running out of money.'[17]

The criss-cross of money filtered its way through a raft of host foundations, some acting as fronts, some as conduits. Known to have wittingly facilitated CIA funding 'passes' were over 170 foundations, including the Hoblitzelle Foundation (a pass-through for the Farfield), the Littauer Foundation (a donor to the Farfield), the Miami District Fund (another 'donor' to the Farfield), the Price Fund (a CIA dummy), the Rabb Charitable Foundation (which received CIA money from the phoney Price Fund, then passed it to the Farfield), the Vernon Fund (like the Farfield, a CIA dummy front with a rubber-stamp board of directors), and the Whitney Trust. On their boards sat the cream of America's social, financial and political establishment. Not for nothing did these foundations announce themselves as 'private'. Later, the joke was that if any American philanthropic or cultural organization carried the words 'free' or 'private' in its literature, it must be a CIA front. This was the consortium at work, calling in favours across the old school tie network, the OSS network, the boardrooms of America.

The board of the Farfield Foundation alone provides a fascinating map of these intricate linkages. Junkie Fleischmann, its president, was a contract consultant for Wisner's OPC, and thereafter a witting CIA cover for the Congress for Cultural Freedom. His cousin, Jay Holmes, was President of the Holmes Foundation, incorporated in 1953 in New York. Holmes began making small contributions to the Congress for Cultural Freedom in 1957. From 1962, the Holmes Foundation acted formally as a pass-through for CIA money to the Congress. The Fleischmann Foundation, of which Junkie was president, was also listed as a donor to the Farfield Foundation. Also on the board of the Fleischmann Foundation was Charles Fleischmann, Junkie's nephew, who was brought into the Farfield as a director in the early 1960s.

Another Farfield trustee was Cass Canfield, one of the most distinguished of American publishers. He was a director of Grosset and Dunlap, Bantam Books, and director and chairman of the editorial board of Harper Brothers. Canfield was the American publisher of *The God That Failed*. He enjoyed prolific links to the world of intelligence, both as a former psychological warfare officer, and as a close personal friend of Allen Dulles, whose memoirs *The Craft of Intelligence* he published in 1963. Canfield had also been an activist and fund-raiser for the United World Federalists in the late 1940s. Its then president was Cord Meyer, later Tom Braden's deputy, who revealed that 'One technique that we used was to encourage those of our members who had influential positions in professional organizations, trade associations, or labor unions to lobby for passage at their annual conventions of resolutions favourable to our cause.'[18] In 1954 Canfield headed up a Democratic Committee on the Arts. He was later one of the founding members of ANTA (American National Theatre and Academy), reactivated in 1945 as the equivalent of the foreign affairs branch of American theatre, alongside Jock Whitney, another of the CIA's 'quiet channels'. Canfield was a friend of Frank Platt, also a Farfield director, and a CIA agent. In the late 1960s, Platt helped Michael Josselson get a job with

Canfield at Harper's. Canfield was also a trustee of the France–America Society, alongside C. D. Jackson, Grayson Kirk (president of Columbia University), David Rockefeller, and William Burden (who was its president).

William Armistead Moale Burden, as well as being president of the France–America Society, was a director of the Farfield. A great-great-grandson of Commodore Vanderbilt, Burden was a key presence in the American establishment. He was a member and director of the Council on Foreign Relations, a private think-tank made up of America's corporate and social elite, which acted as a kind of shadow foreign policy-making unit (other members included Allen Dulles, John McCloy and David Rockefeller). During the war, he worked for Nelson Rockefeller's intelligence outfit, and sat as chairman of an advisory committee of the Museum of Modern Art in New York. In 1956, he became president of the museum. In that year, he also sat on the State Department's 'Books Abroad' Advisory Committee. Formerly Assistant Secretary of State for Air, he was a financier who had special interests in aviation financing, having been associated with Brown Brothers, Harriman and Company, and Scudder, Stevens and Clark, in New York, and a director of numerous companies, including American Metal Company Ltd, Union Sulphur and Oil Corporation, Cerro de Pasco Corporation, and the Hanover Bank. He was a visiting member of faculty committees at Harvard and MIT, co-chairman of the government-sponsored 'Salute to France' (Paris, spring 1955), and US Ambassador to Brussels in 1960.

Another Farfield executive was Gardner Cowles, a donor of the Iowa-based Gardner Cowles Foundation, whose substantial tax-exempt assets came from the huge profits of the Cowles Magazines and Broadcasting company, of which he was president. He was also a corporate member of the Crusade for Freedom, and a sponsor of the periodical *History*, published by the Society of American Historians, and funded by 'private donations'. The journal was as much a product of the Cold War as the Crusade for Freedom, and included in its list of 'sponsors' William Donovan, Dwight D. Eisenhower, Allen Dulles and Henry Luce.

The longest serving Executive Director of the Farfield Foundation was John 'Jack' Thompson, who held the post from 1956 to 1965. Thompson was recruited to the CIA by Cord Meyer, whom he had known since 1945, when both were assistants to the US delegation at the San Francisco conference convened to establish the structure of the new United Nations organization. Formerly a student at Columbia under Lionel Trilling, Thompson was well known in New York literary circles. Jennifer Josselson, Michael's daughter, referred to him as 'Uncle Jack'.

Other Farfield directors included William Vanden Heuvel, a New York lawyer who was close to both John and Bobby Kennedy, and to Arthur Schlesinger (he was also a board member of the Emergency Rescue Committee, alongside William Donovan and Cass Canfield); Joseph Verner Reed, president of Triton Press, vice-president of the Hobe Sound Company, Florida, and a member of the Drama Advisory Panel for the International Exchange Program of ANTA; Fred Lazarus Jr., chief donor of the Fred Lazarus Foundation (which in 1956 made a substantial contribution to the Farfield) and later an advisory member of the National Endowment for the Arts; Donald Stralem, president of United Community Defense Services Inc., and donor, along with his wife Jean, to the Shelter Rock Foundation (which 'piggy-backed' CIA money destined for the Congress for Cultural Freedom into the Farfield coffers in 1962, the year in which Stralem replaced Fleischmann as president of the Farfield); Whitelaw Reid, former editor of the *New York Herald Tribune*; Ralph P. Hanes, director of the Hanes Foundation, North Carolina. A good friend of Junkie's, Hanes and his wife Barbara cruised with the Fleischmanns and the Wisners in the Bahamas. Finally, of course, there was Michael Josselson, whose name appeared on the foundation's letterhead as its International Director, and who received his CIA salary through the foundation.

Farfield was by no means exceptional in its incestuous character. This was the nature of power in America at this time. The system of private patronage was the pre-eminent model of how small, homogenous groups came to defend America's – and, by definition, their own – interests. Serving at the top of the pile was every self-respecting WASP's ambition. The prize was a trusteeship on either the Ford Foundation or the Rockefeller Foundation, both of which were conscious instruments of covert US foreign policy, with directors and officers who were closely connected to, or even members of American intelligence.

Incorporated in 1936, the Ford Foundation was the tax-exempt cream of the vast Ford fortune, with assets totalling over $3 billion by the late 1950s. Dwight Macdonald described it memorably as 'a large body of money completely surrounded by people who want some'. The architects of the foundation's cultural policy in the aftermath of the Second World War were perfectly attuned to the political imperatives which supported America's looming presence on the world stage. At times, it seemed as if the Ford Foundation was simply an extension of government in the area of international cultural propaganda. The foundation had a record of close involvement in covert actions in Europe, working closely with Marshall Plan and CIA officials on specific projects. This reciprocity was further extended when Marshall planner Richard Bissell, under whose signature counterpart funds were signed over to Frank Wisner, came to the Ford Foundation in 1952, accurately predicting there was 'nothing to prevent an individual from exerting as much influence through his work in a private foundation as he could through work in the government'.[19] During his tenure at Ford, Bissell met often with Allen Dulles and other CIA officials, including former Groton classmate Tracy Barnes, in a 'mutual search' for new ideas. He left suddenly to join the CIA as a special assistant to Allen Dulles in January 1954, but not before he had helped steer the foundation to the vanguard of Cold War thinking.

Bissell had worked directly under Paul Hoffman, who became president of the Ford Foundation in 1950. Arriving straight from his job as administrator of the Marshall Plan, Hoffman had received a full immersion course in the problems of Europe, and in the power of ideas to address those problems. He was fluent in the language of psychological warfare and, echoing Arthur Koestler's cry of 1950 ('Friends, freedom has seized the offensive!'), he talked of 'waging peace'. He also shared the view of Ford Foundation spokesman Robert Maynard Hutchins that the State Department was 'subjected to so much domestic political interference that it can no longer present a rounded picture of American culture'.

One of the Ford Foundation's first post-war ventures into international cultural diplomacy was the launch in 1952 of the Intercultural Publications programme under James Laughlin, the publisher of the New Directions series (which published George Orwell and Henry Miller), and a revered custodian of the interests of the avant-garde. With an initial grant of $500,000, Laughlin launched the magazine *Perspectives*, which was targeted at the Non-Communist Left in France, England, Italy and Germany (and published in all those languages). Its aim, he emphasized, was not 'so much to *defeat* the leftist intellectuals in dialectical combat as to *lure* them away from their positions by aesthetic and rational persuasion'. Further, it would 'promote peace by increasing respect for America's non-materialistic achievements among intellectuals abroad'.[20]

Its board packed with cultural Cold Warriors, the Intercultural Publications programme also targeted those American intellectuals who felt their work was 'undermined by the prevailing stereotype of America as a mass-cult hell'. Malcolm Cowley was an early supporter of *Perspectives*, which offered a version of America far removed from 'movies, hard-boiled detective stories, comic books and magazines in which there is more advertising than text'. One academic, Perry Miller, argued that 'no propaganda for the American way should be included; that omission will, in itself, become the most important element of propaganda, in the best sense'.[21] *Perspectives* never lived up to these expectations. Irving Kristol referred to it as 'that miserable Ford Foundation journal'.[22] In the wake of its failure, the Ford Foundation was easily persuaded to take over sponsorship of Lasky's *Der Monat*. Set up under Lucius Clay's backing in October 1948, and financed through the 'Confidential Fund' of the American High Commission, *Der Monat*'s official auspices strained its claims to be independent. Lasky longed to replace this subsidy, and with the help of Shepard Stone, a foundation executive who had worked under Clay in Germany, he finally secured a grant from the Ford Foundation, declaring in the October 1954 issue, 'From now on we are absolutely and completely free and independent.'

On 21 January 1953, Allen Dulles, insecure about his future

in the CIA under the newly elected Eisenhower, had met his friend David Rockefeller for lunch. Rockefeller hinted heavily that if Dulles decided to leave the Agency, he could reasonably expect to be invited to become president of the Ford Foundation. Dulles need not have feared for his future. Two days after this lunch, the *New York Times* broke the story that Allen Dulles was to become Director of Central Intelligence.

The new president of the Ford Foundation was announced shortly after. He was John McCloy, the archetype of twentieth-century American power and influence. By the time he came to the Ford Foundation, he had been Assistant Secretary of War, president of the World Bank, and High Commissioner of Germany. In 1953 he also became chairman of the Rockefellers' Chase Manhattan Bank, and chairman of the Council on Foreign Relations. After John F. Kennedy's assassination, he was a Warren Commission appointee. Throughout, he maintained his career as a Wall Street attorney for the seven big oil companies, and as director of numerous corporations.

As High Commissioner in Germany, McCloy had agreed to provide cover for scores of CIA agents, including Lawrence de Neufville. Although officially employees in his administration, unofficially they were accountable to their chiefs in Washington, who were under few obligations to tell McCloy what they were really up to. A political sophisticate, McCloy took a pragmatic view of the CIA's inevitable interest in the Ford Foundation when he assumed its presidency. Addressing the concerns of some of the foundation's executives, who felt that its reputation for integrity and independence was being undermined by involvement with the CIA, McCloy argued that if they failed to cooperate, the CIA would simply penetrate the foundation quietly by recruiting or inserting staff at the lower levels. McCloy's answer to this problem was to create an administrative unit within the Ford Foundation specifically to deal with the CIA. Headed by McCloy and two foundation officers, this three-man committee had to be consulted every time the Agency wanted to use the foundation, either as a pass-through, or as cover. 'They would check in with this particular committee, and if it was felt that this was a reasonable thing and would not be against the foundation's long-term interests, then the project would be passed along to the internal staff and other foundation officers [without them] knowing the origins of the proposal,'[23] explained McCloy's biographer, Kai Bird.

With this arrangement in place, the Ford Foundation became officially engaged as one of those organizations the CIA was able to mobilize for political warfare against Communism. The foundation's archives reveal a raft of joint projects. The East European Fund, a CIA front in which George Kennan played a prominent role, got most of its money from the Ford Foundation. The fund forged close links with the Chekhov Publishing House, which received $523,000 from the Ford Foundation for the purchase of proscribed Russian works, and translations into Russian of western classics. The foundation gave $500,000 to Bill Casey's International Rescue Committee, and substantial grants to another CIA front, the World Assembly of Youth. It was also one of the single largest donors to the Council on Foreign Relations, an independent think-tank which exerted enormous influence on American foreign policy, and which operated (and continues to operate) according to strict confidentiality rules which include a twenty-five-year embargo on the release of its records.

Under a major grant from the Ford Foundation, the Institute of Contemporary Arts, founded in Washington in 1947, expanded its international programme in 1958. On the ICA's board of trustees sat William Bundy, a member of the CIA's Board of National Estimates, and son-in-law of former Secretary of State Dean Acheson. His brother, McGeorge Bundy, became president of the Ford Foundation in 1966 (coming straight from his job as Special Assistant to the President in Charge of National Security, which meant, among other things, monitoring the CIA). Benefiting from the foundation's largesse were Herbert Read, Salvador de Madariaga, Stephen Spender, Aaron Copland, Isak Dinesen, Naum Gabo, Martha Graham, Robert Lowell, Robert Penn Warren and Robert Richman, who were all Fellows of the ICA's Congress of Cultural Leaders. This was in effect an extension of the work of the Congress for Cultural Freedom, which itself was one of Ford Foundation's largest grantees, receiving $7 million by the early 1960s.

One of the earliest CIA supporters of the Congress for

Cultural Freedom was Frank Lindsay, to whom de Neufville was reporting in the build-up to the 1950 Berlin conclave. Lindsay was an OSS veteran who in 1947 had written one of the first memos recommending that the US create a covert action force to fight the Cold War. The paper attracted the attention of Frank Wisner, who asked him to come on board and run his European operations at OPC. As Deputy Chief of OPC (1949–51), Lindsay was responsible for setting up the 'stay-behind' groups in western Europe. In 1953, he joined the Ford Foundation, and from there he maintained close contact with his confrères in the intelligence community.

Lindsay was later joined at the foundation by Waldemar Nielsen, who became its staff director. Throughout his tenure there, Nielsen was a CIA agent. In 1960, he became Executive Director of the President's Committee on Information Activities Abroad. In his various guises, Nielsen worked closely with C. D. Jackson, with whom he shared a contempt for the 'fundamental disregard for psychological factors among a good many of the hautes fonctionnaires in this town'. Nielsen was also a close friend of the Congress for Cultural Freedom, whose efforts he wholeheartedly supported.

The key link between the Congress and the Ford Foundation was Shepard Stone, who had established a reputation as an expert in the structure and procedures by which the American government and private groups participated in world affairs. The Sunday editor of the *New York Times* before the war, he went on to serve with G-2 (army intelligence), before becoming Director of Public Affairs under John McCloy in Germany, in which guise he had secured government sponsorship for *Der Monat*. An old hand at psychological warfare, John McCloy thought highly enough of Stone to recommend him as a worthy successor to the outgoing director of the Psychological Strategy Board in 1951. Stone did not get the job, and instead joined the Ford Foundation. Throughout his career, he was so closely connected to the CIA that many believed he was an Agency man. 'Shep was not a CIA man, though he may have fished in those waters,'[24] one agent commented vaguely. In 1953, he spent a month in Europe, at Josselson's invitation, visiting key Congress people. As director of the Ford Foundation's

International Affairs division from 1954, Stone's value to the Congress was further enhanced.

The Rockefeller Foundation, no less than the Ford, was an integral component of America's Cold War machinery. Incorporated in 1913, its principal donor was the legendary John D. Rockefeller III. It had assets exceeding $500 million, not including an additional $150 million in the Rockefeller Brothers Fund Inc., a major think-tank which was incorporated in New York in 1940. In 1957 the fund brought together the most influential minds of the period under a Special Studies Project whose task was to attempt a definition of American foreign policy. Subpanel II was designated to the study of International Security Objectives and Strategy, and its members included Henry and Clare Booth Luce, Laurence Rockefeller, Townsend Hoopes (representing Jock Whitney's company), Nelson Rockefeller, Henry Kissinger, Frank Lindsay and William Bundy of the CIA.

The convergence between the Rockefeller billions and the US government exceeded even that of the Ford Foundation. John Foster Dulles and later Dean Rusk both went from the presidency of the Rockefeller Foundation to become secretaries of state. Other Cold War heavies such as John J. McCloy and Robert A. Lovett featured prominently as Rockefeller trustees. Nelson Rockefeller's central position on this foundation guaranteed a close relationship with US intelligence circles: he had been in charge of all intelligence in Latin America during the Second World War. Later, his associate in Brazil, Colonel J. C. King, became CIA chief of clandestine activities in the western hemisphere. When Nelson Rockefeller was appointed by Eisenhower to the National Security Council in 1954, his job was to approve various covert operations. If he needed any extra information on CIA activities, he could simply ask his old friend Allen Dulles for a direct briefing. One of the most controversial of these activities was the CIA's MK-ULTRA (or 'Manchurian Candidate') programme of mind-control research during the 1950s. This research was assisted by grants from the Rockefeller Foundation.

Running his own intelligence department during the war, Nelson Rockefeller had been absent from the ranks of OSS, and indeed had formed a lifelong enmity with William

Donovan. But there was no prejudice against OSS veterans, who were recruited to the Rockefeller Foundation in droves. In 1950, OSS-er Charles B. Fahs became head of the foundation's division of humanities. His assistant was another OSS veteran named Chadbourne Gilpatric, who arrived there directly from the CIA. These two were the principal liaisons for the Congress for Cultural Freedom, and responsible for dispensing large Rockefeller subsidies to Josselson's outfit.

As important as Nelson Rockefeller was his brother, David. He controlled the donations committee of the Chase Manhattan Bank Foundation, was vice-president then president of the bank itself, a trustee of the Council on Foreign Relations, chairman of the Executive Committee for International House, and a close personal friend of Allen Dulles and Tom Braden. 'I often briefed David, semi-officially and with Allen's permission, on what we were doing,' recalled Braden. 'He was of the same mind as us, and very approving of everything we were doing. He had the same sense as I did that the way to win the Cold War was *our* way. Sometimes David would give me money to do things which weren't in our budget. He gave me a lot of money for causes in France. I remember he gave me $50,000 for someone who was active in promoting a united Europe amongst European youth groups. This guy came to me with his project, and I told David, and David just gave me the cheque for $50,000. The CIA never came into the equation.'[25]

These freelance transactions gave new meaning to the practice of governmental buccaneering, and were an inevitable bi-product of the semi-privatization of American foreign policy during these Cold War years. Out of the same culture, however, came later Oliver North-type disasters. The comparison is apt: for, just like the architect of Irangate, 'with his steadfast gaze, his inexorable sense of mission and his palpable conviction that the end justifies the means',[26] these earlier friends of the CIA were never once afflicted by doubt in themselves or their purpose.

10

The Truth Campaign

It is not enough to write in Yiddish; one must have something to say.

Y. L. Peretz

Nicolas Nabokov's massive festival of the arts of 1952 had provided an opportunity to test the range of America's covert propaganda capability. But, in an era which had yet to discover Marshall McLuhan's maxim that 'the medium is the message', government strategists now wondered exactly what the message was. Or, as Walt Rostow, former OSS-er and special adviser to Eisenhower, would later put it: 'The problem with dirty tricks was that we did not know what to say.'[1] Who better than an advertising executive to define the message?

In the early 1950s, one man alone did more than any other to set the agenda for American cultural warfare. As president of the National Committee for a Free Europe, and later, special adviser to Eisenhower on psychological warfare, C. D. Jackson was one of the most influential covert strategists in America. Born in New York in 1902, his father was a wealthy industrialist importing marble and stone from Europe. Graduating from Princeton in 1924, 'C. D.' joined the family firm and travelled extensively in Europe, cultivating contacts which would provide a valuable resource during later years. In 1931 he joined Henry Luce's *Time-Life* empire as an advertising executive. During the war, he was one of America's leading psychological warfare specialists, serving as deputy chief for the Office of War Information Overseas, North Africa and Middle East, and then deputy chief of the Psychological Warfare Division (PWD) of SHAEF (Supreme Headquarters Allied Expeditionary Force, which was under Eisenhower's command).

After the war, C. D. returned to Time-Life Inc., where he became vice-president of *Time*. He was an early activist in Allen Dulles's New York crowd, one of the Park Avenue Cowboys. Then, in 1951, he was invited to take part in a CIA-sponsored study recommending the reorganization of the American intelligence services. This led to a job as an 'outside' director of CIA covert operations via The Truth Campaign and the National Committee for a Free Europe, of which he became president. There, he rounded up a roster of prominent Americans – including General Eisenhower – ready to lend their names to the Committee. He sat on the Radio Free Europe Executive Committee, alongside Jay Lovestone, and, occasionally, Arthur Schlesinger. He was also a director of the United Negro College Fund, a trustee of the Boston Symphony Orchestra (alongside Cold Warriors Henry Cabot Lodge, Jacob Kaplan and Edward Taft), and sat on the boards of the Lincoln Center for the Planning of Arts, the Metropolitan Opera Association (alongside Cornelius Vanderbilt Whitney), and the Carnegie Corporation of New York.

Eisenhower knew C. D. Jackson well from his wartime campaigns in Europe and Africa, and had been tutored by him in the art of manipulating audiences. It was under C.D.'s influence that Eisenhower had been persuaded to hire a public relations company during his election campaign, making him the first presidential candidate to do so (and leading one writer to invent the jokey mantra, 'Philip Morris, Lucky Strike, Alka-Seltzer, I Like Ike'). No sooner had Eisenhower entered the White House in January 1953 as thirty-fourth president of the United States, he made a key appointment to his staff: C. D. Jackson was to be Special Adviser to the President for Psychological Warfare, a position which made C. D. an unofficial minister for propaganda with almost unlimited powers.

C. D.'s first task was to consolidate America's covert warfare capability. Psychological warfare and propaganda operations at this time were split amongst the State Department, the Economic Cooperation Administration (which ran the Marshall Plan), military intelligence, the CIA and, within the CIA but often quite independently, Wisner's OPC. Seeing these government departments riddled with organizational disputes and interdepartmental rivalry, C. D. took the view that they were behaving like 'professional amateurs', and complained of an 'absolute paucity of policy in Washington, a complete vacuum'. There was, he argued, 'an opportunity and a problem. The opportunity is to recapture our world dynamic, which is not dollars but ideas. Our dynamic up to now – self-protection and dollars – must be replaced by the earlier American dynamic of dedication to an ideal. Here we are faced with the possibility of a resurgence of the American proposition throughout the world . . . the problem is how to preserve the dynamic of this thing without having to pull in our horns.' In short, what was needed was a comprehensive 'policy blueprint and plan for US psychological warfare', whose target was 'winning World War III without having to fight it'.[2]

'Our aim in the Cold War is not conquering of territory or subjugation by force,' President Eisenhower explained at a press conference. 'Our aim is more subtle, more pervasive, more complete. We are trying to get the world, by peaceful means, to believe the truth. That truth is that Americans want a world at peace, a world in which all people shall have opportunity for maximum individual development. The means we shall employ to spread this truth are often called "psychological". Don't be afraid of that term just because it's a five-dollar, five-syllable word. "Psychological warfare" is the struggle for the minds and wills of men.'[3]

To overcome the fragmented and self-competing proliferation of covert operations across the government, the Department of Defence and the CIA had proposed an independent board to coordinate psychological operations. Despite State Department resistance, George Kennan championed the idea and was instrumental in persuading President Truman to sign a secret directive establishing the Psychological Strategy Board on 4 April 1951. It was this board (its Orwellian title was soon reduced to its initials, PSB) which was now instructed to draw up the 'policy blueprint' that C. D. Jackson had called for.

The PSB's 'doctrinal' or 'ideological' plan was first proposed in a strategy paper called PSB D-33/2. The paper itself is still classified, but in a lengthy internal memo a worried PSB officer, Charles Burton Marshall, quoted freely from the passages which most exercised him. 'How [can] a government interpose with a wide doctrinal system of its own without taking on the color of totalitarianism?' he asked. 'The paper does not indicate any. Indeed, it accepts uniformity as a substitute for diversity. It postulates a system justifying "a particular type of social belief and structure", providing "a body of principles for human aspirations", and embracing "all fields of human thought" – "all fields of intellectual interests, from anthropology and artistic creations to sociology and scientific methodology."' Marshall (who was to become a staunch opponent of the PSB) went on to criticize the paper's call for '"a machinery" to produce ideas portraying "the American way of life" on "a systematic and scientific basis."' 'It anticipates "doctrinal production" under a "coordination mechanism,"' Marshall observed. 'It asserts "a premium on swift and positive action to galvanize the creation and distribution of ideas" . . . It foretells a "long-term intellectual movement" as growing out of this effort and having the aim not only to counter communism but indeed to "break down worldwide doctrinaire thought patterns" providing an intellectual base for "doctrines hostile to American objectives."' His conclusion was adamant: 'That is just about as totalitarian as one can get.'[4]

Marshall also took issue with the PSB's reliance on '"non-rational social theories"' which emphasized the role of an elite '"in a manner reminiscent of Pareto, Sorel, Mussolini and so on"'. Weren't these the models used by James Burnham in his book *The Machiavellians*? Perhaps there was a copy usefully to hand when PSB D-33/2 was being drafted. More likely, James Burnham himself was usefully to hand. Certainly, it was Burnham's theory of elite rule that Marshall was now challenging. 'Individuals are relegated to tertiary importance,' Marshall continued. 'The supposed elite emerges as the only group that counts. The elite is defined as that numerically "limited group capable and interested in manipulating doctrinal matters", the men of ideas who pull the intellectual strings "in forming, or at least predisposing, the attitudes and opinions" of those who in turn lead public opinion.'[5] According to Marshall's exegesis, the PSB planned to work on the elite in each area so as to predispose its members to 'the philosophy held by the planners'. Use of local elites would help conceal the American origin of the effort 'so that it appears to be a native development'. But it wasn't just aimed at foreigners. Though the paper disavowed any intention of propagandizing Americans, it did commit itself to a programme of indoctrination in the military services by injecting the right ideas into servicemen's comic books, and having their chaplains propagate them.[6]

Mr Marshall's trenchant criticisms struck right at the very fundamentals of America's secret cultural warfare programme. The theory of the elite which underpinned the PSB's doctrinal paper was exactly the same model as that used by the CIA to justify its embrace of the Non-Communist Left and its support of the Congress for Cultural Freedom. Commenting on the use of the intellectual elite to develop 'the philosophy held by the planners', CIA agent Donald Jameson intended no irony when he said, 'As far as the attitudes that the Agency wanted to inspire through these activities are concerned, clearly what they would like to have been able to produce were people, who *of their own reasoning and conviction*, were persuaded that everything the United States government did was right.'[7]

But Marshall's criticisms fell on deaf ears. PSB director Raymond Allen was moved to the lofty announcement that 'The principles and ideals embodied in the Declaration of Independence and the Constitution are for export and . . . are the heritage of men everywhere. We should appeal to the fundamental urges of all men which I believe are the same for the farmer in Kansas as for the farmer in the Punjab.'[8] And in May 1952, the newly strengthened PSB formally took over supervision of the pace and timing of CIA's psychological warfare programme, codenamed 'Packet'. This gave it oversight of the CIA's campaign to exert pressure on overseas 'opinion leaders', including journalists and commentators, artists, professors and scientists, to whom Communism had appealed so successfully. Winning back these influential figures to the cause of 'liberty and freedom' required a programme of 'learned operations like seminars, symposia, special tomes, learned journals, libraries, exchange of persons, endowed professorships etc'. Under this rubric, the PSB now assumed supervision of the Moral Rearmament Movement, the Crusade for Freedom, Radio Free Europe, Paix et Liberté, the American Committee for Cultural Freedom, and even operations involving broadcasting from ships, 'three-dimensional moving pictures', and 'the use of folk songs, folklore, folk tales, and itinerant storytellers'. By June 1953, 'Packet' was just one part of the PSB's 'Doctrinal Program', whose 'psychological objectives' were defined in a new paper as 'appealing to intellectuals, scholars and opinion-forming groups' in order to 'break down worldwide doctrinaire thought patterns which have provided an intellectual basis for Communism and other doctrines hostile to American and Free World objectives'. This campaign of persuasion, it was reasoned, would 'create confusion, doubts and loss of confidence in the accepted thought patterns of convinced Communists [and] captive careerists'. The CIA was ordered to 'give high and continuing priority to all activities supporting the objectives of this program'.[9] Less than two years after its creation, the PSB 'had finally succeeded in establishing itself as an integral part of the development and implementation of foreign policy.'[10]

Enjoying unrivalled access to the secret machinations of the PSB and the government departments it embraced, C. D. Jackson became the most sought-after figure in that tight circle of power which came to be known as 'the invisible government'. Sitting like some eastern potentate or Delphic oracle, he received a steady flow of visitors seeking his wisdom on a wide range of matters. His detailed log files of these visits provide a unique insight into the world of clandestinity. From the PSB came officers armed with plans for doctrinal warfare, which included floating all manner of printed propaganda over the Iron Curtain in helium balloons. From the Information Research Department came Adam Watson, to present C. D. with a memorandum on British psychological warfare policy, 'which Watson assured me was absolutely unique and unprecedented action on HMG's part. In this connection he brought up problem of British sharing virtually all intelligence with us and we sharing nothing with them. I told him operators here very much aware of that situation, and that I had hopes it would be accelerated very soon.' Watson became a valued contact for C. D., whom he had first met in 1951 at the British Embassy in Washington, where Watson was liaising with the CIA. Thereafter, C. D. 'worked very closely with him', and recommended Watson to Nelson Rockefeller (who succeeded C. D. in his White House post in 1954) as someone who 'would really like [a] much more useful unofficial, relaxed, give-and-take relationship'.[11] Watson was also to prove a powerful, if discreet, ally of the Congress for Cultural Freedom for many years. From the Congress for Cultural Freedom came Julius Fleischmann, 'to discuss possibilities of Congress for Cultural Freedom sponsoring European junket for Metropolitan Opera', and later Daniel Bell, 'to talk about Miloscz [sic] and upcoming scientific meeting under sponsorship of Congress for Cultural Freedom'.[12]

With C. D. Jackson in the White House, the Congress for Cultural Freedom gained a powerful ally in Washington. Tom Braden moved quickly to establish a relationship with C. D., and the two met regularly to discuss 'accumulated matters'. Their collaboration on the Boston Symphony Orchestra tour of 1952 had convinced C. D. of the usefulness of the Congress, which he praised as 'the only outfit I know of that is really making an anti-Communist anti-neutralist dent with intellectuals in Europe and Asia'.[13] And he held many of its activists in high regard, recommending several of them as candidates for government work, including Sidney Hook, James Burnham ('a very articulate expounder of the "dirty tricks department"'), *New Leader* editor Sol Levitas ('definitely on the side of the angels'), and Daniel Bell, who had worked for the Luce-owned *Fortune* and was, said C. D., 'thoroughly knowledgeable on Communist cold war techniques'.[14] He was also a long-time admirer of Nicolas Nabokov. It was C. D. who had recommended Nabokov in the list of psychological warfare personnel suitable for employment in sensitive posts which was submitted to the Office of the Secretary of the Army in 1950.

C. D.'s alliance with the Congress extended over many years (in 1954 he became a board member of the American Committee), and brought it numerous benefits, besides the prestige of his discreet support. If the Congress needed coverage in Luce's magazines, C. D. was there to secure it. If it sought convergence with the Free Europe Committee and Radio Free Europe, C. D. would act as liaison. If it needed 'private' donations, C. D. could call upon his vast range of business contacts to provide the necessary cover. But most important was the political cachet C. D. brought to an organization which had surprisingly few defenders in the capital. 'Nobody had a reputation in Washington for supporting it, and nobody was sure they wanted a reputation for supporting it,' Lawrence de Neufville said. 'Most people were mystified by it. We created it, but we didn't have any real machinery for it in Washington.'[15] That the Congress for Cultural Freedom survived, and even thrived, in the context of such scepticism must be credited to the heroic efforts of Michael Josselson.

After the hectic workload of the past few years, Michael Josselson took a short break from the struggle for the minds and wills of men. On 14 February 1953 he married Diana Dodge in a civil ceremony with Lawrence de Neufville as witness. Both had been married before. Josselson had married Colette Joubert in Havana in 1940, but they had divorced and were estranged. Always fiercely private, he never spoke of her to anyone. But he did preserve a faded clipping from a New York newspaper of February 1963 reporting Colette's gruesome murder – she was found bound and choked to death with a gag after being sexually assaulted in her Upper East Side apartment.

Michael and Diana honeymooned in Majorca. Shortly after their return to Paris, Michael 'came clean', telling his new wife he was employed by the CIA, and that the Congress for Cultural Freedom was an Agency 'proprietary'. Diana, who had already observed from Michael's involvement with the Congress that there was more to him than his import-export business card announced, had once entertained the idea he might be working for the Russians. To her relief, she now discovered he was on the 'right' side. Diana was assigned a codename – 'Jean Ensinger' – and from then on they formed a kind of partnership.

Diana Josselson was well suited to the task. A former Fulbrighter, she had an intricate knowledge of labour affairs, first from working as an editor of a digest of the US labour press, then from her work in the Labor Division of the Marshall Plan, which operated under the influence of Jay Lovestone and Irving Brown. 'I was young and fresh-faced, and a great success with all the labor leaders,' Diana recalled brightly. Her job in the Labor Division entailed writing reports on Communist trade unions in Europe, for which she had access to top-secret intercepts. This sensitive work required clearance from the CIA. Diana later learned that counterpart funds at the disposal of the CIA were being used to cover her salary.

Together, 'Jean Ensinger' and 'Jonathan F. Saba' would write cables and memos encoded for despatch to Washington. These would be handed over to a CIA case officer over martinis in the Josselson apartment. 'All case officers had the same attaché case with a false bottom, and they put the cables in there. It really was very funny, because you could recognize them a mile away – they all had the same standard model case. It was a riot. We'd read the incoming cables, then I'd flush them down the toilet,'[16] Diana remembered. She was well cut out for the job, and knew how to keep a secret, even from her own mother. Once, case officer Lee Williams went out to buy jars of baby food for Jennifer, the Josselsons' first and only child. When he returned, Diana was obliged to introduce him to her mother, who had come over from the States to help with the baby. Noticing a copy of *Jane Eyre* lying on the table, Diana stammered, 'This is, er – Mr Rochester.' 'How strange! Mr Rochester. Just like in *Jane Eyre*!' exclaimed her unsuspecting mother. That Diana didn't simply use Lee Williams' real name, which of itself would have revealed nothing, indicates how intricately her imagination was caught up in the Great Game. When Diana's mother was eventually told the truth, she too was 'very excited by the whole thing'.[17]

Now completely *au fait* with Michael's job, Diana was daily more admiring of his extraordinary expertise. His ability to coordinate the exigencies of Washington and the often volatile temperaments of the Congress intellectuals left her amazed. 'There's no way the Congress could have happened without him,' she later said. 'The atmosphere of the Congress in its heyday was as I imagine the first hundred days of the Kennedy administration were. It was electric. You felt you were in touch with everything going on everywhere. Things were blossoming, it was vital. Michael would know everything. It was dazzling how in the morning he could be talking about playwrights in Bolivia, and then about writers in Asia in the afternoon, and then he and Nicolas would be on the phone in the evening talking in four different languages. I remember sitting with Stravinsky at a café in Paris, and his wife telling me how to make blinis. It was an extraordinary time for us. The Cold War, the Congress for Cultural Freedom – it was like the French Revolution or the Oxford Movement. That's what it felt like.'[18]

The Josselsons met often with Tom Braden, who regularly toured his operations in Europe. They would go to a restaurant, or the Roland-Garros tennis tournament, or they would take Braden to the bicycle races at the Vélodrome d'Hiver, 'that stadium of dreadful memory' where the Jews had been taken during the massive round-up under Vichy. The Josselsons also maintained regular contact with Irving Brown, sometimes meeting him at his table at a gay nightclub called L'Indifférent. On one occasion, they arrived there to find Brown handing over large amounts of cash to 'a thug from Marseilles'.[19] Brown at this time was building up 'the Mediterranean Committee', a group of vigilantes paid to stand guard at French ports while dockworkers unloaded Marshall Plan supplies and US arms for NATO. On Brown's ability to syncopate these activities, Braden commented wryly that 'It was unusual for somebody who was taking a highly visible part in beating up commie goons in the docks of Marseilles to also be interested in the Congress for Cultural Freedom.'[20]

'The American Federation of Labor had real experience of Communism, and that was the obvious place to stage the fight from,' Diana Josselson explained. 'Brown loved all the strong-arm business, strike-breaking in Marseilles and so forth. Michael and I were amused by the whole thing of going to a nightclub and meeting a union tough whom Irving would be giving money to, and I'm sure Irving was equally amused by the intellectuals. I suppose the attraction of the Congress crowd for Irving – who didn't know his Picassos or his Baudelaires – was that it was glamorous, and the contacts were good.'[21]

At weekends, Michael and Diana relaxed by trawling the antique shops and galleries of the Left Bank. They lunched on open sandwiches and aquavit, followed by tea at the Café de Flore (Sartre's favourite) or the Deux Magots. On Sundays, they would picnic at Fontainebleau, or take a boat out on the Seine. Sometimes they would meet up with de Neufville, forming a congenial trio, bound both by genuine friendship and by the secret they shared. De Neufville returned from one shopping excursion with Josselson the proud owner of two paintings by Braque. Years later, when Josselson's daughter Jennifer had become an expert in modern art, she reluctantly declared them to be fakes.

With Josselson's imprimatur stamped on the Paris office, the Congress was acquiring a reputation as a well-organized centre of intellectual resistance to Communism. Through *Preuves*, it projected a sophisticated political voice which also spoke to the major artistic and cultural issues of the period. Although the German affiliate of the Congress wobbled from one crisis to the next, Josselson could rely on Melvin Lasky (and soon, *Der Monat*, which the Congress took over from the Ford Foundation in 1954) to carry the Congress's interests there. Affiliates in other countries experienced a variety of teething problems, all of which testified to the near impossibility of getting intellectuals to work together without falling prey to faction fights and wounded sensibilities. But their problems seemed like so many storms in a teapot compared to the hurricanes which raged in the American Committee.

11
The New Consensus

> An artist must be a reactionary. He has to stand out against the tenor of his age, and not go flopping along; he must offer some little opposition.
>
> Evelyn Waugh

> I choose the West.
>
> Dwight Macdonald, 1952

Founded in New York in January 1951, the principal force behind the American Committee for Cultural Freedom was Sidney Hook, who became its first chairman and who was, according to Lawrence de Neufville, a 'contract consultant' for the CIA. Irving Kristol, another graduate of New York City College, served as Executive Director, for which he was paid an annual salary of $6,500. This rose to $8,500 in 1954, when Kristol was replaced by Sol Stein, who arrived straight from the United States Information Service, where he had worked in a unit dedicated to ideological analysis. The Committee, as the official American affiliate of the Congress, was intended to reflect the broad coalition of liberal and left-of-centre constituencies which made up the host organization. But where the Congress had been able to marginalize its hard-line activists like Koestler, it had no such power over the American Committee, which soon divided down the middle between the moderates and the militants. 'In those days you were either "hard" or "soft" on Communism,' explained Jason

Epstein, who remembered Diana Trilling, in carnal mood, 'standing behind Lionel's [Trilling] chair at a dinner party once and saying, "None of you men are HARD enough for me!" They were ridiculous people, really, who lived in a teacup.'[1]

Living in the teacup with the Trillings was a powerful combination of conservative intellectuals from what was jokingly referred to as 'the Upper West Side kibbutz'. They included James Burnham, Arnold Beichmann, Peter Viereck (whose father had been a notorious Fascist sympathizer), the art critic Clement Greenberg, and Elliot Cohen, editor of *Commentary* and an unofficial adviser on Communism to executives at the Luce publications. In style as well as content, theirs was *haute* anti-Communism. 'Some people like Beichmann and the Trillings (mostly Diana) were violently pro-American, and they thought we were falling down on the job. Diana in particular was quite vitriolic,' recalled Irving Kristol.[2] Another insider remembered 'a kind of feverish sense of superiority amongst many Americans: we've won the war, now we're going to reorganize Europe our way. These people were mostly gun-slingers from New York, and they favoured a moral high road of intransigence, and considered ours to be a lower road of appeasement. Some even thought that the Congress had been penetrated by Communists.'[3]

Representing the moderate element of the American Committee were Arthur Schlesinger, the Cold War theologian Reinhold Niebuhr, James T. Farrell, Richard Rovere of *The New Yorker*, former Socialist Party chairman and six times candidate for American president Norman Thomas, and *Partisan Review* editor Philip Rahv. Swinging between the two factions were Irving Kristol (who later became an ardent Reaganite), the other *Partisan Review* editor William Phillips, and Sidney Hook. Hook, in particular, had an interest in maintaining peace between the two groups: he was at this time promoting the Committee's interests with CIA director Walter Bedell Smith (whom Allen Dulles replaced in 1953), and Gordon Gray, first director of the Psychological Strategy Board (meetings which failed to merit a mention in Hook's autobiography).[4] These contacts with high-level intelligence operatives testify to a much more knowing engagement with clandestine cultural warfare than Hook was ever ready to admit to. His article in the *New York Times Magazine* of March 1951 – 'To Counter the Big Lie – A Basic Strategy' – was clipped and filed by the PSB, C. D. Jackson, and the CIA. In it, Hook described the threat to democracy posed by international Communism, and called for 'the [exhaustion] of every possibility of effective political warfare in defense of democratic survival . . . The democracies must take the offensive in political warfare against the totalitarian regime of the Soviet Union and keep the offensive . . . How successful this political warfare would be cannot be foretold in advance. But it is surely worth the cost of a half dozen bombers to launch it.'[5] For Hook, the American Committee was a bazooka in America's political arsenal, and he worked with his customary zeal to consolidate its position.

It was to the moderates that Josselson turned in an effort to keep the American Committee politically attuned to the Congress. But Schlesinger and his allies were unable to contain the unruly clique of hardliners, and disagreements between the Committee and the Paris office surfaced almost immediately. The Americans scorned Nabokov's massive festival in Paris, accusing the Congress of frivolity. Elliot Cohen, who in his politics was only slightly less extreme than James Burnham, asked whether, 'With this kind of hoopla, we are losing sight of our function and goals, and if we lose sight, who else is there around?'[6] Another critic mocked it as 'appealing to snobs and esthetes' and destroying the Congress's reputation as 'a serious intellectual power'.[7]

The fascination with power was much evident in the American Committee, and culminated in 1952 with a *Partisan Review* symposium which confirmed a new and positive relationship between intellectuals and the nation state. Running in issue after issue, the symposium was called 'Our Country and Our Culture'. Its purpose, wrote the editors, was 'to examine the apparent fact that American intellectuals now regard America and its institutions in a new way. Until little more than a decade ago, America was commonly thought to be hostile to art and culture. Since then, the tide has begun to turn, and many writers and intellectuals now feel closer to their country and its culture . . . Politically, there is recognition that the kind of democracy which exists in America has an intrinsic and positive value: it is not merely a capitalist myth but a reality which must be defended against Russian totalitarianism . . . Europe is no longer regarded as a sanctuary; it no longer assures that rich experience of culture which inspired and justified a criticism of American life. The wheel has come full circle, and now America has become the protector of western civilization'.[8]

Intellectual life in New York during the 1930s had been gauged almost exclusively in relation to Moscow, and there to articulate its concerns was *Partisan Review*, created by a group of Trotskyites from City College. Starting its life as a house organ of the Communist-dominated John Reed Club, *Partisan Review* created a sophisticated language to articulate Marxist ideas. But the events of 1939–40 destroyed its moorings. With the signing of the German–Soviet Non-Aggression Pact, many intellectuals began to veer away from the orthodoxies of Leninist Communism towards the dissident radicalism of Trotsky. Some simply abandoned the left altogether, moving towards the political centre and even the right. *Partisan Review* now found itself creating a counter-language to articulate anti-Stalinism and redefine radicalism in a non-Communist context.

Returning to the *idea* of America like so many repentant prodigals, intellectuals and artists emerged from the 'dark period' of the 1930s to discover 'an exhilaration at the sudden and overwhelming appearance of new possibilities, in life as in consciousness. There was a world out there which no-one, it seemed, had bothered to look at before, and everyone, happily shedding his Marxist blinkers, went rushing off to look.'[9] These born-again intellectuals, in their search for something to replace the historical absolutes which had failed them so absolutely, found the answer in 'America', or more glibly, 'Americanism'. The literary equivalent of Aaron Copland's 'Fanfare for the Common Man', *Partisan Review*'s symposium signalled this act of discovery of America as if for the first time. 'American artists and intellectuals have acquired a new sense of belonging to their native land,' wrote William Phillips, 'and have generally come to feel that their own fate is tied to the fate of their country.'[10] As intellectuals developed a congenial connection to America, so America came to see them in a new light. 'Intellect has associated itself with power, perhaps as never before in history, and is now conceived to be in itself a kind of power,' Lionel Trilling observed.[11]

'It was perhaps the first time since the French Revolution when the significant components of an intellectual community decided that it was no longer *de rigueur* to be adversarial; that you could support your country without cheapening intellectual and artistic integrity,' noted the historian Carol Brightman.[12] This new perception of intellectuals was confirmed when *Time* magazine ran a cover story called 'Parnassus: Coast to Coast', which concluded that 'The Man of Protest has . . . given way to the Man of Affirmation – and that happens to be the very role that the intellectuals played when the nation was new.'[13] This was the moment at which deviationist Marxists began to transform themselves from refusniks into 'all-rightniks'; when City College ideologues, together with their more waspish *compagnons de guerre*, like Dwight Macdonald, lost their taste for the class struggle and were being improbably asked for letters of recommendation by aspiring students. 'The speed with which I evolved from a liberal into a radical and from a tepid Communist sympathizer into an ardent anti-Stalinist still amazes me,' Dwight Macdonald later wrote.[14] Describing this political transformation, his biographer concluded: 'Dwight's independence, his self-proclaimed negativism, his refusal to accept any kind of nationalist loyalty had marked his political vision and sustained his political life. It was not a matter of betrayal of commitment: he had simply arrived through his own painful analysis to a point where he had no viable political position other than the "lesser evil". For him it was a discouraging dilemma. Even as he continued to identify with a radical, or at least dissenting, tradition, and still felt himself to be a member of an alienated elite in opposition to American nationalism, imperialism and mass culture, he was, even if inadvertently, coming to support the maintenance of American power abroad and established institutions at home.'[15] Philip Rahv observed such developments with growing alarm, and warned: 'Anti-Stalinism has become almost a professional stance. It has come to mean so much that it excludes nearly all other concerns and ideas, with the result that they are trying to turn anti-Stalinism into something which it can never be: a total outlook on life, no less, or even a philosophy of history.'[16]

The headquarters of 'professional' anti-Stalinism was the American Committee for Cultural Freedom, and the magazines whose editors sat on its board, namely *Commentary*, the *New Leader* and *Partisan Review*. But now, just as the centre was beginning to hold, *Partisan Review* was on the brink of folding, in part because the US Treasury was threatening to strip it of its tax-exempt status. Sidney Hook wrote a dramatic plea to Howland Sargeant, Assistant Secretary of State on 10 October 1952, defending *Partisan Review*'s record as an effective vehicle for 'combatting communist ideology abroad, particularly among intellectuals', and begging for its tax-exemption to be preserved. Daniel Bell also took the initiative, acting as an 'intermediary' in discussions with Henry Luce, who saved the magazine with a grant of $10,000 (at the same time, Luce donated seventy-one shares of Time Inc. stock to the American Committee). 'To the best of my knowledge, that grant was never publicly disclosed, not even to the contributors and some of *Partisan Review*'s associate editors,' Daniel Bell later wrote.[17] Quite what Luce expected in return for his investment is not clear. Jason Epstein later claimed that 'what was printed in *Partisan Review* soon became amplified in *Time* and *Life*'.[18] Certainly, Luce's generous financial support of what had once been an authorized voice of the American Communist Party lends new meaning to the much discussed 'de-radicalization' of American intellectuals during the Cold War.

The CIA had first been alerted to the financial difficulties of *Partisan Review* through Irving Brown. A year before the Luce grant was made, Sidney Hook had written to Brown asking for help in the fight to keep *Partisan Review* and the *New Leader* alive. 'Our advices are from many of our European friends that anti-American and especially *neutralist* sentiment is rising in Western Europe. This at the same time as that splendidly anti-neutralist democratic organ the *New Leader* really faces extinction because of rising costs. Its disappearance,' wrote Hook, 'would be a cultural calamity.'[19] He made the same case for *Partisan Review*, and asked Brown to help secure a guaranteed foreign circulation of four to five thousand for both magazines. Brown passed the problem on to Braden at the International Organizations Division. Shortly afterwards, the *New Leader*'s editor, Sol Levitas, found himself in Tom Braden's office. 'God, I can remember that guy sitting across the table, pleading with me for money,' Braden recalled.[20]

Levitas, a Russian émigré who had worked with Trotsky and Bukharin, had powerful supporters in America's intelligence community. C. D. Jackson praised him for doing 'an excellent job in providing virtually the only objective, unslanted, pro-American, high-quality, left-wing literature that exists on either side of the Atlantic,' and said he was 'definitely on the side of the angels.'[21] Certainly, Allen Dulles thought so. In 1949, Levitas had run a piece by Dulles advocating a 'commission of internal security' to examine subversive influences in the US and to 'use the institutions of democracy to destroy them'. With Allen Dulles helping the White House reorganize America's intelligence service, this 'was rather like the head of MI5 writing for the *New Statesman*'.[22] At this time too, although the *New Leader* was issuing frantic appeals for funds to pay off its $40,000 debts, it started appearing in April 1950 as a new *New Leader* with an expensive *Time*-like magazine format. Sitting opposite Braden a couple of years later, Levitas had found another angel who could save his magazine. Braden agreed to subsidize the *New Leader*, arranging to hand over cash sums to Levitas at his, Braden's, office, on at least three occasions. 'It wasn't a huge sum,' Braden said, 'probably in the region of $10,000 a time. But that was enough to keep the magazine from going under.'[23]

Meanwhile, Braden's deputy, Cord Meyer, had taken up *Partisan Review*'s cause. Further to the Luce grant of $10,000, the magazine received a subsidy of $2,500 in early 1953 from the American Committee's 'festival account', which still contained some residual funds left over from Nabokov's extravaganza of the previous year. The festival account, it will be remembered, was the pipeline for CIA dollars, which were 'piggy-backed' through the phoney Farfield Foundation. When this grant was made to *Partisan Review*, its co-editor William Phillips was Cultural Secretary of the American Committee. Phillips later said he did not recall this grant, and was always adamant that his magazine had never been the recipient of CIA support.

By subsidizing American journals, the CIA was acting in breach of its own legislative charter, which prohibited support of domestic organizations. In the case of *Partisan Review* and the *New Leader*, there were two very persuasive reasons for ignoring this legal nicety: first, the journals provided an ideological bridgehead for American and European intellectuals whose common ground was anti-Communism, but who were separated by geopolitical and cultural differences; secondly, financial support provided what Josselson described as a 'shield' against the anticipated 'anger' of *Partisan Review* and the *New Leader* when they discovered – as they soon would – that their position in the market-place of ideas was about to be seriously challenged.

12

Magazine 'X'

> What, then, shall we do? Stick, so far as possible, to the empirical facts – always remembering that these are modifiable by anyone who chooses to modify the perceiving mechanism.
>
> Aldous Huxley, *Eyeless in Gaza*

Encounter magazine, which ran from 1953 to 1990, held a central position in post-war intellectual history. It could be as lively and bitchy as a literary cocktail party. It was here Nancy Mitford published her famous article 'The English Aristocracy', a bitingly witty analysis of British social mores which introduced the distinction between 'U and Non-U'. It printed Isaiah Berlin's 'A Marvellous Decade', four memorable essays on Russian literature, Vladimir Nabokov on Pushkin, Irving Howe on Edith Wharton, David Marquand on 'The Liberal Revival', stories by Jorge Luis Borges, critical essays by Richard Ellmann, Jayaprakash Narayan, W. H. Auden, Arnold Toynbee, Bertrand Russell, Herbert Read, Hugh Trevor-Roper – some of the best minds of those decades. It was read in England and America, Asia and Africa. Promiscuous in its attention to cultural subjects, it was strangely silent, or simply obscure, on many political issues. In all cases, it was resolutely ideological, an integer of anti-Communist Cold War thinking. It never broke even, but ran at a substantial deficit, needing to double its circulation in order to get out of the red. It was intelligent. And it was profligately linked to the intelligence world. Michael Josselson referred to it as 'our greatest asset'.

Post-war austerity had claimed Cyril Connolly's *Horizon* in 1950, followed shortly thereafter by John Lehmann's *Penguin New Writing*. The *London Magazine* was teetering financially, and F. R. Leavis, despite a generous grant from the Rockefeller Foundation, was almost through with *Scrutiny*. Only the *New Statesman and Nation* flourished, its weekly circulation of 85,000 showing an impressive resilience to attempts to undermine it. Josselson's secret subsidies to *Twentieth Century* were part of this campaign. As well as cash, the journal, together with the British Society for Cultural Freedom, had received explicit instructions to 'engage in a permanent polemic with The New Statesman and Nation'.[1] The CIA, mindful of the lacklustre British performance at the Berlin conference of 1950, was eager to penetrate the fog of neutralism which dimmed the judgement of so many British intellectuals, not least those close to the *New Statesman*. That Kingsley Martin's magazine had not embraced the idea of a socialist vision fully divorced from Moscow rankled deeply with American Cold Warriors.

British intelligence, too, was interested in projecting a voice which could oppose the *New Statesman*'s policy of ambivalence, its 'soft-headedness' and 'terrible simplifications'. The Information Research Department's support of *Tribune*, whose material was excerpted and distributed internationally by foreign service officers, was a gesture in this direction. Malcolm Muggeridge and Woodrow Wyatt, both closely linked to IRD, met with *Tribune* editor Tosco Fyvel in April 1950 to discuss the future of the magazine, but Muggeridge concluded, 'They are obviously badly on the rocks, and I said that in the interests of the cold war they should be kept going as a counterblast to the *New Statesman*. Developed one of my favourite propositions – that the *New Statesman*'s great success as propagandists had been to establish the proposition that to be intelligent is to be Left whereas almost the exact opposite is true.'[2]

IRD's support of *Tribune* was not enough to persuade Fyvel of its long-term future, and by late 1951 he was talking of a new 'Anglo-American Left-of-Centre publication'. Writing to

Irving Brown, Fyvel said that plans for such a publication 'have advanced, and several people are anxious that I should make a start. I have discussed the idea directly or by letter with Denis Healey, Maurice Edelman, Dick Crossman, Arthur Schlesinger, David Williams and others – for obvious reasons this is something quite outside Congress for Cult. Freedom activities.'[3] The obvious reason for keeping the magazine separate from the Congress was, as Fyvel well knew, because the American government had agreed not to conduct propaganda activities in Britain. The CIA had 'virtually declared a moratorium on [Agency] money . . . being used in that particular country. There is a sort of gentlemen's agreement on that matter.'[4] But this was about to change.

Independently of each other, British intelligence and the CIA had been batting around the idea of creating a new magazine which could address the perceived deficit in the bank of intellectual anti-Communism in Britain. This duplication of effort came to light during a series of meetings held at Frank Wisner's initiative in London in early 1951. Accompanied by Washington-based MI6–CIA liaison Kim Philby (whose friends Burgess and Maclean were just months away from their defection to the Soviet Union), Wisner had travelled to London to discuss with British intelligence 'matters of common interest'. During a series of meetings attended by MI6 and members of the Foreign Office, according to Philby, Wisner 'expatiated on one of his favourite themes: the need for camouflaging the source of secret funds supplied to apparently respectable bodies in which we were interested. "It is essential," said Wisner in his usual informal style, "to secure the overt cooperation of people with conspicuous access to wealth in their own right."' At this, Philby was amused to see a Foreign Office official scribbling a note which read: 'people with conspicuous access to wealth in their own right = rich people'.[5]

It was during the Wisner 'mission' to London that the question of a high-level publication aimed at encouraging a leftist lexicon free of Kremlin grammar was first aired. The two services realized they had been pursuing the same idea. Wisner and his Secret Intelligence Service (SIS) counterparts agreed this would be folly, and they settled on a joint operation. By late 1951, the joint proposal had been cleared at the highest levels, and it was now passed down the lines. Philby delegated to his assistant in Washington, John Bruce Lockhart, nephew of the great Robert Bruce Lockhart, an intelligence supremo of both wars who in 1917 had been arrested by the Soviets as a spy and imprisoned in the Kremlin. As his uncle's star faded, Lockhart the younger had himself forged ahead as a model intelligence officer. He had headed up the military branch of 'C' (SIS) in Italy during the war, and was an expert on penetrating Communist organizations in Europe. Lockhart was well respected in Washington, where he had forged a close relationship with Frank Wisner. When Wisner wanted to get his son, Frank Wisner Jr., into Rugby College, Lockhart, who had been schooled there, was happy to arrange it. Wisner trusted Lockhart, but not Philby. Philby in turn was unable to repress his dislike of Wisner, whom he described witheringly as 'a youngish man for so responsible a job, balding and running self-importantly to fat'.[6]

John Bruce Lockhart also enjoyed a good relationship with Lawrence de Neufville, with whom he had liaised in Germany after the war. It was Lockhart who now set up a meeting for de Neufville and Josselson with IRD's Christopher Monty Woodhouse in London. Woodhouse was a man of profligate talent. He had been introduced to the writings of Euripides and Lucretius at the age of eleven, and before the war had been tutored at New College, Oxford, by Richard Crossman and Isaiah Berlin (who deployed 'an intense, low-pitched buzz of monologue' in tutorials, and 'was known as the only man in Oxford who could pronounce "epistemological" as one syllable').[7] Taking a double first in 1939, Woodhouse was dreaming of an academic career lecturing on Plato and Aristotle when war broke out. His education thereafter was quite different – 'barrack-square, gun-drill, parachuting, guerrilla warfare, sabotage, intelligence' – and eventually led him to fight an heroic guerrilla war in occupied Greece.[8]

A dashing, daring spy of the old school, Woodhouse was a key player in preparations to overthrow Iran's premier, Mohammed Mossadegh, working alongside Kim Roosevelt in a *coup* engineered jointly by the CIA and SIS which installed the ultra-right monarchy of the Shah.[9] On his return from Tehran, Woodhouse was assigned to deep cover work for the

Information Research Department. He ran a separate office, provided by SIS, opposite St James's Park tube station. This office was staffed by a handful of junior Foreign Office people who were nominally registered to IRD, but were in effect run as a semi-autonomous team by Woodhouse.

Reluctant to 'do business' in his own club, The Reform, Woodhouse agreed to meet at the Royal Automobile Club on Pall Mall, where de Neufville held an overseas membership. De Neufville and Josselson travelled to London from Paris for the meeting. It was here, in the late spring of 1952, that British and American intelligence made one of the most significant interventions in the course of post-war intellectual history. Over lunch in the RAC's dining room, they outlined their plan for the launch and covert sponsorship of a new highbrow magazine. Woodhouse, who was authorized to clear the project, did so without hesitation. Working for various different geographical divisions of the Foreign Office, this project stood at the more 'mundane end of the spectrum' for Woodhouse. But he was a keen advocate of psychological warfare, into which the proposal so neatly fell. The tone of the conversation at the RAC left him in no doubt that this was to be a subtle contribution to the covert propaganda struggle.

His only caveat was that the British should be allowed to keep a finger on the pulse. It was agreed that the Congress for Cultural Freedom, through a designated CIA case officer, would consult with Woodhouse on 'operational' procedures relating to the magazine. In addition, SIS wished to maintain a financial interest in the project, a small contribution which would come from IRD's secret vote. Woodhouse suggested that this contribution be earmarked for the salaries of the British editor and his secretary. This would avoid the impropriety of the CIA remunerating British subjects.

Further, he said that the Foreign Office's principal interest in such a project was to acquire a vehicle for communicating anti-Communist ideas to intellectuals in Asia, India and the Far East. To guarantee distribution of the magazine in these spheres of influence, the Foreign Office would buy up a specified number of copies to be shipped and distributed through the British Council. Beyond this, the financial liability for the magazine rested with the Congress for Cultural

Freedom. Josselson confirmed that funds were to be made available through the Farfield Foundation, although the magazine would be encouraged to function as a business, to allay suspicion. Finally, Josselson told Woodhouse that two candidates had been short-listed for the job of co-editing the magazine. Subject to security clearance by both services, it was agreed that these two candidates be approached by the Congress for Cultural Freedom. With the working structure in place, the meeting closed with an agreement that Josselson and de Neufville would advance the project, and then meet again with Woodhouse. Woodhouse, meanwhile, started looking for suitable 'fronts' – Wisner's 'rich people' – through which to channel IRD money to the new magazine.

The American candidate for the post of co-editor was Irving Kristol, the Executive Director of the American Committee for Cultural Freedom. Born in 1920, the son of a New York clothing subcontractor, in 1936 he went to City College, where he befriended Irving Howe, Daniel Bell and Melvin Lasky. There, he became involved with the Young People's Socialist League, an anti-Communist leftist organization at the college, and the Trotskyites. Small in stature, Kristol compensated by developing the muscular political stance so typical of City College undergraduates, accompanied by a readiness to jump his opponents, which would acquire him a reputation as an intellectual bruiser. Graduating *cum laude* in 1940, he went to work as a freight handler in Chicago and helped edit the ex-Trotskyist magazine *Enquiry* until he was called up. Drafted as an infantryman in 1944, he saw combat in France and Germany, and was discharged in 1946. He went to England and began working for *Commentary*, returning to New York in 1947 to become its managing editor.

The British candidate was Stephen Spender. Born in 1909 to a famous liberal family, he had a protected childhood ('My parents kept me from children who were rough'),[10] and developed a languid, easy-going nature and an attraction to utopian ideas. At Oxford in the 1920s he came under the lifelong influence of W. H. Auden, and achieved fame soon after with his first book, *Poems*, which oozed the sexual and political mood of the inter-war period. He was immediately identified with Auden, Cecil Day Lewis and Louis MacNeice as a Poet of the

Thirties, the decade which brought politics into the deepest chambers of literature and saw Spender joining the Communist Party, though only for a few weeks. His was more that kind of 'English parlour Bolshevism' than anything else, typical of Spender's butterfly politics. Later, he was to describe his changes of belief and commitment as a matter of 'my utter vulnerability and openness'.[11] Anita Kermode inverted Henry James Sr.'s famous remark (of Emerson) that he was like 'a clue without a labyrinth', to describe Spender as 'a labyrinth without a clue'.[12] Another Jamesian phrase suited Spender well: he was 'a man without a handle'.

Spender later surmised that the reason he had been chosen to co-edit the Congress's new magazine 'was a consequence of my essay in *The God That Failed*'. More perhaps than his disavowal of Communism, it was Spender's positive relationship with the US which made him an ideal candidate. In 1948, Spender had written a paean to America – 'We Can Win the Battle for the Mind of Europe' – in which he claimed that 'where American policy finds dubious allies and half-hearted friends, American freedom of expression in its greatest achievements has an authenticity which can win the most vital European thought today . . . If America chose to do so she could play an educational role in Europe today which would bring thousands of students to understand the best in American civilization and the American conception of freedom . . . For what is realistic today is to expect nothing of propaganda and political bludgeoning, but to take part in showing Europeans the greatest contemporary achievements of American civilization, education and culture.'[13] Spender could barely contain his excitement, going on to state that 'a word from the mouth of an American or English man of letters' is regarded as 'almost something miraculous' by European students. The Marshall Plan, he wrote, was well and good, but 'It is necessary also to strengthen the old civilization of the West in Europe with the faith and the experience and the knowledge of the new Europe which is America.'[14] Such sentiments were echoed by many other western intellectuals. Raymond Aron announced that he was 'entirely convinced that for an anti-Stalinist there is no escape from the acceptance of American leadership'.[15] It could hardly be said (as it later was) that

America's intervention in the *Kulturkampf* had no native support when people like Spender and Aron identified the survival of Europe with the American saviour.

Spender had other attractive qualities for his prospective employers. As part of the 'MacSpaunDay' (MacNeice, Spender, Auden, Day Lewis) group, he provided an important link to London's literary aristocracy, which still clung to many of the snobbish excrescences of the Bloomsbury period, but whose members surrendered promptly to Spender's charm. Josselson had experienced at first hand the intransigence of the British element at the Congress's Berlin début, and many American strategists were irked by the superior air affected by the British intelligentsia. 'There's some important background to all this,' Stuart Hampshire explained. 'In 1949, I believe, the Ford Foundation came to London, and they held a big meeting in a hotel, to which they summoned the leading intellectuals. At that time, they had capital reserves which were worth more than the whole of the sterling area. So, the intellectuals come, and the Ford Foundation offers them the earth, but they say, "We're fine, thank you. We've got All Souls, and that's enough for us." The British were underwhelmed. They did ask for a few things, but they were so small the Americans thought they were mad. And the context for this is that there was a very deep, Freud-like anti-Americanism; a kind of Wykehamish snobbery meets Chinese left-wingery, epitomized by people like Empson and Forster. I remember Forster staying with Lionel Trilling in New York once. Trilling (who'd written a book about Forster, and was a rather pathetic Anglophile who'd never been to England at that point) was very nervous. Forster told him he needed to buy a shirt for some occasion, and Trilling took him to Brooks Brothers. But when Forster got there, he took one look and said, "My God, I can't possibly buy anything here." That summed it up.'[16]

Spender, who had worked for the British Control Commission in occupied Germany after the war, was well attuned to the needs of government in the area of cultural politics. Since then, he had spent a good deal of time in America, where he found himself under the wing of John Crowe Ransom, Allen Tate, and the conservative duo Ben Tate and Senator Edward Taft. Cultivating his British colleagues with equal charm, Spender was just the bridge the Americans needed to make an advance on their recalcitrant allies. But his most irresistible talent, claimed his wife Natasha, was for being easily conned. 'Of course,' she said, 'Stephen had all the right credentials to be chosen as a front: he was one of the great recanters [of Communism], and he was eminently bamboozable, because he was so innocent. His father was bamboozled by Lloyd George. They're a very trusting family; it never occurs to them to think that people are telling them lies.'[17] The cost of this congenital *naïveté* would later prove to be high.

In February 1953, Spender, who was teaching in Cincinnati, received a letter from Josselson inviting him to come to Paris to discuss 'an English edition of *Preuves*'. From Kristol, Spender learned that 'During a quick trip to Paris which I made a couple of weeks back I spent a great deal of time discussing [this matter] with Mike Josselson, François Bondy and Mel Lasky; moreover, Josselson and myself went to London for a day to talk the matter over with Warburg, Muggeridge and Fyvel.'[18]

Shortly before this London meeting, de Neufville and Josselson had met again with Woodhouse. They agreed on an arrangement for a publishing 'deal' whereby Fredric Warburg, the publisher of Orwell, would lend his company's name to the magazine. In a letter from Josselson to Warburg he confirmed that the Congress 'assumed full responsibility for the prompt payment of all bills presented in connection with the production and distribution of *Encounter*', and full liability for libel. Josselson made it clear to Warburg that 'neither he nor his firm is to have any influence whatsoever over the editorial side of the magazine'.[19]

By the time of their second meeting, Woodhouse and de Neufville had struck up a firm rapport. De Neufville's credentials were no less impressive than Woodhouse's. Born in London, he had taken degrees at New College and Harvard, before becoming a Reuters correspondent. 'We got on extremely well, saw very much eye to eye,' Woodhouse remembered. 'I always got on extremely well with my American colleagues, provided they weren't lunatics,' he added, in a tone which suggested many were. 'Whenever Larry came over to London, I met him. Or if I went to Washington,

I'd meet him there, with my man in Washington, Adam Watson.'[20] The two were to meet regularly over the next couple of years, until de Neufville returned to America, and Woodhouse went on to become Director of the Royal Institute of International Affairs. As this was the only area where their responsibilities overlapped, they discussed 'operations and methods' for *Encounter* and 'the British operation' in general over drinks at the RAC.

'Operations and methods' initially meant putting in place what Woodhouse described as 'a cash flow and a line of contact'. 'Be careful of thinking there was a system for anything in those days. It was all improvised,' de Neufville later explained.[21] Brought in to help with the improvisation, and to act as a go-between for MI6 and the Congress for Cultural Freedom was Malcolm Muggeridge. Muggeridge had made a long journey from those days as a boy when he had sung 'The Red Flag' with his father from a Labour Party platform in Croydon. His book *Winter in Moscow* (1933), which presented the shattering of his Russian utopia, was one of the first exposures of the Soviet myth written from the left, and had marked the beginning of his political transformation into an agent for MI6. A member of the Congress for Cultural Freedom's steering committee, he was firmly aligned with its anti-neutralist, pro-American stance, reasoning that 'If I accept, as millions of other Western Europeans do, that America is destined to be the mainstay of freedom in this mid-twentieth century world, it does not follow that American institutions are perfect, that Americans are invariably well behaved, or that the American way of life is flawless. It only means that in one of the most terrible conflicts in human history, I have chosen my side, as all will have to choose sooner or later, and propose to stick by the side I have chosen through thick and thin, hoping to have sufficient courage not to lose heart, sufficient sense not to allow myself to be confused or deflected from this purpose, and sufficient faith in the civilization to which I belong, and in the religion on which that civilization is based, to follow Bunyan's advice and endure the hazards and humiliations of the way because of the worth of the destination.'[22]

'Secrecy,' wrote Muggeridge in *The Infernal Grove*, 'is as essential to Intelligence as vestments and incense to a mass, or darkness to a spiritual seance, and must at all costs be maintained, quite irrespective of whether or not it serves any purpose.'[23] Ever excited by a bit of cloak and dagger intrigue, even if he doubted its necessity, Muggeridge was delighted to be involved with the Congress's new publishing venture. His first job was to secure the 'rich people' who could pose as credible private backers of the magazine. At a meeting in a Fleet Street pub, Muggeridge was able to report to Woodhouse that his search for financial conduits had turned up two willing candidates.

The first was émigré film director Alexander Korda. As a friend of Ian Fleming and a former employer of Robert Bruce Lockhart (who worked for him as an adviser on the international distribution of films), Korda enjoyed close links to British intelligence. Following the approach from Muggeridge, Korda agreed to allow IRD to use his bank account as a 'piggy back' for subsidies to the new magazine. The other conduit brought in by Muggeridge was his old friend Lord Victor Rothschild. Rothschild was closely connected to the magazine until the mid-1960s, but always as a shadow, never in the open.

There were still practical issues to be resolved, and Muggeridge and Warburg – now referred to by CIA case officers as 'The Cousins' – went to Paris at the end of February 1953 to thrash matters out. Jasper Ridley, then Secretary of the British Society for Cultural Freedom, was instructed to buy their tickets and pay for their hotels. On his return, Warburg asked Ridley to write him a cheque on the British Society's account for £100 for his 'expenses' in Paris. Ridley, whose weekly salary was about £10, was amazed. 'I think that Warburg either pocketed the £100 or spent it in buying jewellery for his attractive wife Pamela de Bayou,'[24] he later surmised.

On 5 March 1953, Michael Josselson wrote to Stephen Spender with an account of the meeting between Muggeridge, Warburg, Fyvel, Nabokov, Bondy and Josselson. 'We need a magazine with wider appeal than *Horizon*; more like *Der Monat*. You and Kristol would be an ideal team of editors. There should be an editorial board with, perhaps, Muggeridge and Hook, who will be spending a whole year in Europe from

July 1953. Muggeridge and Warburg are willing to put all the funds which Mr Muggeridge has meanwhile been successful in raising for the British Society into the magazine.'[25] Referring to this arrangement, Spender wrote to Kristol, 'it looks as if we are both to be employed by the British Committee'.[26] He was half right. Kristol, the American, would be paid with funds from the CIA's Farfield Foundation; Spender, with money from the British treasury's secret vote.

By March 1953, Kristol had moved to Paris and was busy collecting copy for the magazine. The Paris office, which envisioned a journal that would serve 'as the mouthpiece of the Congress', produced four drafts for a cover, under Josselson's direction. Neither Kristol nor Spender (who was still in the States) could agree on a title. The working title, 'Outlook', was judged to be banal, so they racked their brains and thumbed the thesaurus, and bandied about 'Symposium', 'Culture and Politics', 'Congress', 'Witness', 'Vista', 'Testimony', 'Writing and Freedom' (Kristol wanted to avoid the words 'freedom' and 'liberty' because of an 'aroma of boredom'), 'Messenger', 'Across Seas', 'East-West Review', 'Compass', 'Connect', 'Exchange', 'Interchange', 'Present', 'Turning Point', 'Circumference'. At one point, Kristol simply referred to it as 'Magazine X'.[27] Perhaps this would have been the most appropriate title, in the light of the clandestine spirit behind it. The title 'Encounter' first surfaced in a letter dated 27 April 1953 from Kristol to Warburg, but Kristol said he was not enthusiastic about it.

On 30 April 1953, Alexander Korda wrote his first cheque for £250. So, presumably, did Victor Rothschild, though no record exists to confirm when his 'donations' started. Thus camouflaged, British intelligence passed funds to *Encounter* from its inception. The cash-flow was boosted by the regular arrival of a brown envelope at *Encounter*'s office. The courier was a member of Woodhouse's staff. So, too, was the magazine's office manager (and later managing editor), Margot Walmsley, who came straight from her job as a clerical officer with IRD, and remained the Foreign Office's 'line of contact' into *Encounter* for over two decades. Walmsley later remarked to a bemused Frank Kermode that if he wanted to know anything about *Encounter*, she could tell him 'everything'. Dying in 1997, Walmsley never disclosed that she was a Foreign Office employee.

Later, the IRD paid the money into a private account at publishers Secker and Warburg, and Warburg would then arrange for a cheque for the same amount to be made out to the British Society for Cultural Freedom, of which he was treasurer. The British Society, by now no more than a front for IRD's cash-flow to *Encounter*, then made over the same amount to the magazine. In intelligence phraseology, this kind of funding mechanism was known as a 'triple pass'. Thus, circuitously, Her Majesty's Government paid Stephen Spender's salary. Woodhouse himself never spoke to Spender of this arrangement, though he had ample opportunity to do so. 'His children and my children were at the same kindergarten, and we used to meet each other there,' Woodhouse recalled. 'I would've tended to assume that he did know, and therefore didn't particularly feel the need to talk to him about it. This was our sort of drill in that kind of world.'[28] Spender was later adamant that he had never been told of these arrangements.

By June 1953, *Encounter* magazine was up and running, operating out of the British Society for Cultural Freedom's office on 119b Oxford Street, before moving in September to offices in the Haymarket. Printing bills and other expenses for its first twelve months were met by a grant of $40,000 from the Farfield Foundation, a figure Kristol and Spender were advised by Josselson to 'keep to yourselves'. Kristol, who had been in London since May, was joined by his wife, the historian Gertrude Himmelfarb, and their young child William. Shortly afterwards, Spender arrived from Cincinnati. Both were listed as shareholders in Encounter Ltd., which was registered in December 1953, with the majority shares held by Junkie Fleischmann, as president of the Farfield Foundation, and Pierre Bolomey, as treasurer of the Congress for Cultural Freedom.

In a notable rewriting of history, both Spender and Kristol would later record their collaboration as some kind of honeymoon. 'In view of the fact that Stephen and I were two such very different people I think we got along surprisingly well,'[29] said Kristol. 'I worked very happily with Irving Kristol,'[30] said Spender. They did consider each other friends, then as later. But their professional relationship was problematic from the start. Spender was willowy, emotional, wincingly non-confrontational, and as an editor sometimes didn't 'know his arse from his elbow'.[31] Kristol, by contrast, was mulish and uncompromising, inured by years of Brooklyn arguments to sentimental or intellectually precious behaviour. Small in stature, he shared with Lasky and Hook both this and a shortness of temper. 'It's crazy to think that Irving Kristol – a former Trotskyite from Brooklyn – could go over there and deal with all those British intellectuals and correct their prose!' said one CIA agent.[32] But it wasn't just Spender and his British friends who needed to watch out for Kristol. Josselson discovered very early on the calibre of the man he had chosen. 'Irving had stand-up rows with the Paris office,' said Natasha Spender, who recalled hearing from Stephen that Kristol was given to shouting down the telephone at Josselson that if he wanted a 'house magazine' he could go find himself another editor.[33]

In July, Kristol sent Josselson the prospective table of contents for the first issue: Denis de Rougemont on India, a short meditation on death by Albert Camus, pages from the notebooks of Virginia Woolf, two Japanese short stories, a memoir of Ernst Toller by Christopher Isherwood, Leslie Fiedler on the Rosenbergs, Nicolas Nabokov on Soviet music, Josef Czapski on André Malraux's *Voices of Silence*, Irving Kristol on the Congress's 'Science and Freedom' conference, Herbert Lüthy on the recent revolts in East Germany and Czechoslovakia, and Edith Sitwell on Hollywood. Book reviews had been promised by Muggeridge, Spender, Hugh Seton-Watson, J. K. Galbraith, and Nathan Glazer. Pieces by Koestler and Aron were dropped from the first issue after Nabokov warned Kristol that they were too militantly anti-Communist.

Concerned that the line-up for the first issue was not political enough, Josselson wrote as much to Kristol. Kristol replied tartly: 'I'm not sure about your cryptic remark about the "political contents" living up to expectations. The magazine, obviously, should be a "cultural" periodical – with politics taken, along with literature, art, philosophy, etc. as an intrinsic part of "culture," as indeed it is. The ratio of specifically political to literary etc. articles will naturally vary from number to number. In the first number, politics is relatively subordinate, since we are aiming to capture the largest possible audience. I have a very clear idea of what the Congress wants, and of how one should go about getting it. But I can't operate efficiently with the Paris office breathing down my neck, sending editorial directives, etc.'[34]

In another fiery letter, Kristol again remonstrated with Josselson, telling him: 'We here in London are not inept morons, and I sincerely believe that we can better judge the situation than you can in Paris. You and your colleagues in Paris think the cover is lousy? Well, maybe you're right. Then again, maybe you're wrong – magazine covers are not, after all, your specialty. I think the cover is good, though doubtless capable of improvement; Muggeridge thinks it's very good . . . You think the first issue is insufficiently political? But then you obviously haven't studied the table of contents carefully . . . You think the first issue is too literary? Well, you're wrong . . . Perhaps I'm deluding myself, but I really think that, in *Encounter*, the Congress has hold of something far more important than even you realize. You, apparently, would be satisfied if we could achieve the standing of *Preuves*. My god, man, we're way past that (again, unless I'm deluding myself). Potentially, we have it in us to become, in a few months, *the* English language cultural periodical, and not only in England but for Asia too. Give us a few months, and we'll be the idol of the intelligentsia, East and West – a magazine in which an Asian – or European and American! – writer would give his eye-teeth to appear. I mean this seriously; and if I'm wrong, then you ought to get yourself another editor. But you've got to give us time, and editorial freedom, to achieve this . . . Your attitude to sales puzzles me: you say you're less interested in them than in the magazine's "impact". But isn't one a measure of the other?'[35] Had Kristol known of the financial scaffolding by which *Encounter* was to be held up, he would have realized this last question was redundant.

Clearly, Kristol was not going to play the role of megaphone soap-boxer for Josselson. Spender invented the concept of 'Kristol Power' to describe his colleague's adamantine pose. After one threat too many, Josselson would indeed find himself another editor. But for the time being, *Encounter* needed stability, and Josselson had no choice but to stick with Kristol.

The Paris office had won the fight with Kristol to drop Koestler and Aron, but in return they had to concede an article by Leslie Fiedler which made them deeply uneasy. Kristol had originally invited his friend Fiedler to submit an article on Karl Marx, but Fiedler showed no enthusiasm, and offered him instead a piece on the Rosenbergs. If Kristol wanted something 'provocative' for the first issue, he had got it.

On the morning of their execution, Julius and Ethel Rosenberg sat down in their cell at Sing Sing prison to write a letter to their two young children, Robert and Michael. 'Always remember that we were innocent and could not wrong our conscience,' the letter ended. Just after eight o'clock on the evening of 19 June 1953, minutes before sundown announced the start of the Jewish Sabbath, and on the eve of their fourteenth wedding anniversary, the Rosenbergs were put to death in the electric chair. First Julius, then Ethel. Before being strapped into the chair, Ethel turned to the prison matron, reached out her hand, and drew her close to kiss her on the cheek.

The Rosenbergs had been convicted in March 1951 of transmitting American atomic secrets to the Soviets. After retreating to a synagogue to contemplate his sentence, Judge Kaufman returned to the court to condemn the Rosenbergs to death for their part in what he described as a 'diabolical conspiracy to destroy a God-fearing nation'.[36] Never before in America had capital punishment been imposed on anyone convicted in peacetime of espionage. The international outcry which followed presented America's propagandists with their most urgent challenge since the opening sallies of the Cold War. The question of the Rosenbergs' guilt (and there could be little real doubt that they *were* guilty), was not the central issue: to most observers, the case against them was incontrovertible. But it fell to American strategists to convince the world not simply that the verdict was incontestable, but that the punishment fitted the crime.

'When two innocents are sentenced to death, it is the whole world's business,' Jean-Paul Sartre exclaimed, defining Fascism not 'by the number of its victims but by the way it kills them'.

He added that the execution was 'a legal lynching that has covered a whole nation in blood'.[37] To make sure the whole world knew it was its business, the Communists orchestrated a massive campaign for clemency, organizing coverage in the Communist-controlled press, and arranging for Communist-front organizations to petition American embassies. London received thousands of petitions and protests bearing several thousand signatures. Paris reported that it was receiving telegrams, letters and petitions at the rate of approximately fifty per day.

In France, especially, the Rosenberg case became the symbolic rallying point for anyone who had a bone to pick with the American government. Protests were staged all over France, and many of them turned into anti-American riots. One man was killed in a 'Libérez les Rosenbergs' rally in the Place de la Concorde.[38] Melvin Lasky, although 'queasy' about the use of capital punishment during peacetime, ridiculed these protests as the product of 'fashionable anti-American resentments'.[39] Certainly, none of the Communist-backed lobbies formed to defend the Rosenbergs publicized the fact that on the same day that the Rosenberg Defence Committee was founded in France, eleven former leaders of the Czech Communist party were executed in Prague. Nor did they discuss the fact that more Communists had been shot by Stalin than in any Fascist country; or that in the Soviet Union workers were sent to hard labour camps if they were more than five minutes late for work on two occasions; nor that when artists were told to enter a competition for a statue to celebrate Pushkin's centenary, the first prize went to a sculptor whose statue showed Stalin reading Pushkin's work.

Yet Melvin Lasky's analysis remains fantastically simplistic. The US Ambassador in Paris, Douglas Dillon, had pointedly cautioned the Secretary of State in a cable dated 15 May 1953 that the majority of people in France were 'overwhelmingly of [the] opinion that [the] death sentence [is] unjustifiable' and warned that 'people who urge clemency should not all be taken as unconscious dupes of [the] Communists'.[40]

Clearly, the clemency drive could not be passed off solely as a Communist conspiracy. One American intelligence report stated that in western Europe, 'pleas for clemency have very recently emerged in the Socialist and independent press and from official Socialist groups, and in England some Labor opinion supports clemency. Such non-Communist pleas for clemency are based on certain doubts about the guilt of the Rosenbergs, and on the ground that clemency will play less into the hands of Communist propagandists than will execution and consequent martyrdom.'[41]

The whole American psychological warfare apparatus now faced a massive challenge. For the next six months, right up to the Rosenbergs' execution in June, it pulled together all its resources to convince the non-Communist world that American justice was just. The Psychological Strategy Board (PSB) was ordered to coordinate the campaign, whose central objective was to place the Rosenbergs in the context of a negative Communist archetype – the Communist as monster, which needed 'bloody sacrifices'. It compiled reports for briefing the President and all his men, based on embassy despatches and CIA reports, and issued a volley of instructions to all American posts abroad. But whilst PSB-generated reports which showed the Rosenbergs were 'fairly convicted and guilty as charged' were well amplified in the European press, many US diplomatic representatives continued to press for clemency. In France, Ambassador Dillon remained deeply concerned 'with the adverse effect in Western Europe of the execution', and pressed for the sentence to be reappraised 'in terms of the higher national interest'.[42]

As PSB examined 'the entire scope of the Rosenbergs' execution, particularly the impact of such a decision on foreign psychology, and its effect on U.S. prestige and U.S. leadership,'[43] C. D. Jackson was taking a slightly different tack. Though he was confident that the Rosenbergs 'deserve to fry a hundred times for what they have done to this country', he was bent on extracting a confession of guilt from them. This of course would have changed the whole complexion of the case. In a hand-delivered letter to the Attorney General, Herbert Brownell, dated 23 February 1953, C. D. wrote: 'it is worth one more try to crack at least one of the Rosenbergs . . . Cracking the Rosenbergs', he went on, 'is not a "third degree" problem, but a psychiatric problem. Therefore, would it not be possible to get some really skillful Jewish psychiatrist, say

Dr Karl Binger, to attempt to insinuate himself into their confidence during these next 30 days, and if they did show signs of coming along, a stay of execution for another 30 or 60 days could be arranged while the work progressed.'[44]

In May, C. D. came up with another idea. In a 'memo for the file' on White House notepaper, C. D. wrote: 'Spoke to Brownell and urged him to play war of nerves with Rosenbergs, including if necessary temporary stay of execution by the President. Brownell advised that the matron had managed to ingratiate herself, and that they had hopes in that direction. Urged upon Brownell that the warden, matron, prison doctor, and anybody else involved should have impressed upon them the subtleties of the situation and the game that was being played, rather than let them play it by ear. This was no longer a police matter. Brownell agreed to do something along these lines.'[45] Just how far the matron was able to ingratiate herself remains a matter of speculation. From Ethel's last gesture, however, one can deduce that she came pretty close.

Meeting in cabinet on 19 June 1953, the date set for the execution, a nervous Eisenhower admitted he was 'struck by the element in his mail reflecting honest doubt' about the Rosenberg judgement, and said it seemed 'strange our judicial system should be attacked in so clear-cut a case'.[46] Herbert Brownell assured Eisenhower there was 'no question of doubt here . . . merely a technicality'. 'The public doesn't know of technicalities,' snapped Eisenhower. To which Brownell answered, 'Who's going to decide, pressure groups or the judicial system? The Communist objective is to show that Dwight Eisenhower can be pressured.'[47] Again, Eisenhower showed his impatience, telling Brownell he was 'concerned only with honest citizens'. C. D. Jackson now cut in, and acknowledged that some people were finding the death sentence hard to understand in light of the fact it had not been passed down on other convicted spies like Klaus Fuchs. To which C. D.'s friend Henry Cabot Lodge (recently appointed Eisenhower's tactical expert on Communism) replied confidently, 'All can be easily explained.' 'Not easily to me,' snorted Eisenhower.[48]

As all hope of clemency began to recede, even Michael Josselson had been moved to call for mercy. 'Michael thought they were guilty, but that they shouldn't be executed, because it was such bad PR. He sent a personal telegram to Eisenhower asking for clemency,'[49] Diana recalled. Additionally, Josselson organized for Denis de Rougemont to cable an appeal to the White House on 13 June 1953. 'The Writers, Scientists and Artists Association with the International Congress for Cultural Freedom appeal to you for clemency for the Rosenbergs,' read the Western Union telegram. 'We believe that such an action on your part would be in the humane tradition of western democracy and would serve the cause of freedom throughout the world.'[50] Even Pope Pius XII intervened, asking Eisenhower to temper justice with charity, but to no avail. 'We were devastated at the execution. It was *so* stupid,' said Diana Josselson.[51]

In late July, Irving Kristol received Leslie Fiedler's piece, titled 'A Postscript to the Rosenberg Case'. Fiedler, a former member of the Young Communist League and the Socialist Workers Party, had drifted away from the left by the early 1940s and was now writing 'virulent anti-Communist essays so full of dubious psychologizing and calls for atonement by the entire left that Harold Rosenberg felt compelled to publish a lengthy rebuttal called "Couch Liberalism and the Guilty Past"'.[52] It was in this mood that Fiedler had penned his thoughts on the Rosenberg case.

Fiedler noted that, at first, not even the Communists were interested in identifying themselves with the couple, as they were 'so central to their whole espionage effort and so flagrantly guilty'. He made a distinction between the 'factual' Rosenberg case, and a second, 'legendary' Rosenberg case in which, thanks to a carefully orchestrated fellow-travelling mythology, they had been built up as martyrs in the tradition of Dreyfus. And thus, as 'the flags of the gallant old causes were unfurled', liberal-minded people everywhere had been the victims of 'a kind of moral blackmail'.[53] He went on to blame the Communists for the Rosenbergs' suffering and death, alleging that it was 'willed by the makers of Communist opinion and relished by them, as every instance of discrimination against a Negro in America is willed and relished, as further evidence that they are right'. He had been there, said

Fiedler, right in the thick of a Europe revelling in its anti-Americanism. He had seen 'the faces of the Communist crowds surging and screaming before the American Embassy' in Rome, and he had seen 'nothing but joy'. 'Death to the Killers of the Rosenbergs!' the crowd had chanted, before going off 'to sit afterwards over a bottle of wine, content with a good day's work'. As for the Rosenbergs, well, they were 'unattractive and vindictive' but 'human', taking an interest in their children, 'concerned with operations for tonsillitis and family wrangles'. But Fiedler was so repulsed by the couple that he had difficulty fitting the Rosenbergs to a 'human' story, so he went on to claim that they had in fact 'dehumanized' themselves by becoming 'official clichés', even up to the moment of their death. 'It is a parody of martyrdom they give us, too absurd to be truly tragic,' he wrote. Commenting on the letters the couple wrote to each other from their separate cells in Sing Sing prison, Fiedler seemed affronted as much by Ethel Rosenberg's literary style (or lack of) as by Julius's failure to be sufficiently intimate with his wife and accomplice. 'We have grown used to Communist spies lying in court with all the conviction and fervour of true victims; there was the recent example of Alger Hiss, to name only one;[54] but we had always hoped that to their wives at least, in darkness and whispers, they spoke the truth.' But they couldn't speak in anything other than code, even to each other, and so, Fiedler asked, as they were not 'martyrs or heroes – or even human beings . . . What was there left to die?'[55]

Sidney Hook, when he saw proofs of the article, was alarmed. James T. Farrell had once said of Hook that 'he submits the living complex reality of history to a logic machine, and chops it up. The way in which he practises "selective emphasis" amounts to ledgerdemaine [sic] . . . All kinds of problems and contradictions . . . are going to get in his hair, and he'll have to wash them out.'[56] Hook could quickly identify these defects in others, if not in himself, and he was sure that Fiedler's analysis was going to stick in the Congress's hair. Writing to Kristol (who had sent him the proofs), he counselled that the piece be run with the following *apologia*: 'These remarks should not be construed as an attack against human beings who are dead – for we must respect the dead as human beings – but the point is that in their political life the Rosenbergs abandoned their role as human beings and put themselves forward as political symbols. We are therefore making an analysis not of human personalities but of a political myth.'[57] A less succinct version of Hook's suggested addition did find its way into Fiedler's text, but its impact was lost in an article which remained striking for its human meanness.

News of the Fiedler piece spread fast, and within a week, the entire print run of 10,000 copies of *Encounter*'s first issue sold out (how many of these were advance 'purchases' by the Foreign Office is not known. According to Tom Braden, the CIA also 'paid circulation funds to get it accepted'). Given the dearth of high-level journals in England, there was never any chance that *Encounter*'s début would be met with indifference. Now its name was on everybody's lips, and no dinner party passed without a heated discussion of its contents. Within days, the fall-out began to reach the *Encounter* office in the form of a bulging mail bag. From Christopher Isherwood came praise for an 'exciting and unstuffy' début. Leonard Woolf wrote that he found every article 'above the average', and described the Fiedler piece as 'exceptionally good'.

From a distance, Melvin Lasky deduced that the Fiedler piece would guarantee a bitter struggle for *Encounter*. Signs that this was the case appeared in a trio of letters received by Spender on the morning of 22 October 1953. Writing to Josselson, Spender quoted from E. M. Forster's letter, which expressed particular resentment at the Rosenberg article, 'not for its factual findings which may be correct, but for the contempt and severity with which it treats Ethel Rosenberg's last days. Most offensive was the "compassionate" ending with its mysterious assertion that here was a human being who had acted in a non-human fashion and who would be pardoned by the human being who had written the article. I wonder how *he* will act if he is ever condemned to death?'[58]

Czesław Milosz didn't like the Rosenberg piece either, Spender told Josselson. Worse still, T. S. Eliot, writing in answer to Spender's request for an article, said he had doubts about the effectiveness of *Encounter*, as it was so 'obviously published under American auspices'. If he wanted to say something to influence American opinion, wouldn't he be better off saying it in a paper published in America for American consumption? 'The point is that Eliot here states the kind of reputation we have to try and live down of being a magazine disguising American propaganda under a veneer of British culture,'[59] Spender explained. Agreeing with Hugh Gaitskell's comment that 'any politics we published would be suspect through people knowing that we had American support,' Spender concluded that 'any direct anti-Communist sentiments simply defeat their own ends'. He went on to tell Josselson that he found the letters 'deeply disturbing', adding that, 'As far as my own personal position is concerned, the implied criticism that I am putting in articles which serve American purposes is naturally very painful to me.'[60] 'There was a puerile anti-Americanism in England at that time,' said Natasha Spender. 'Eminent, respectable people were full of reactionary clichés about America being an adolescent country, and all that. And Stephen was constantly being criticized by these people, who said they wouldn't even have a copy of *Encounter* in their house, because it was so obviously "American". And this made him very angry, because he wanted to defend those colleagues whom he admired from his time in America.'[61]

Fiedler, apparently, was one defence too far for Spender. Monty Woodhouse remembered being 'staggered' when Spender 'more or less exploded and said he wasn't going to take part in a "propaganda exercise" any more. I assumed he shared my views and the views of all of us on the desirability of intellectual reaction to the Communists. I thought it was intellectually too simple for him to say he was being frustrated in some way.'[62] Spender did acknowledge that the Rosenberg article had not offended everyone, and he defended it as 'not at all propaganda'. But he was deeply worried that it was broadly regarded 'as being the kind of Trojan Horse contained within *Encounter*'.[63]

This, and more, was implied in Anthony Hartley's review in the *Spectator*, which claimed to have detected 'something of the pomposity of official culture' in the magazine's first issue, and remarked, 'It would be a pity if *Encounter*, in its turn, were to become a mere weapon in the cold war.'[64] The

Cambridge don and critic Graham Hough referred to *Encounter* as 'that strange Anglo-American nursling' and claimed it was not as free as it declared: 'It's not free from "obsession" or "idées fixes,"' he said, adding that it had 'a very odd concept of culture indeed.' In a sideswipe at *Encounter*'s sponsors, he remarked that he did 'not like to contemplate the concept of cultural freedom that could make it possible to write or to print [the Fiedler] piece'.[65]

More mischievous was an item in the *Sunday Times* 'Atticus' column which referred to the magazine as 'the police-review of American-occupied countries'. A. J. P. Taylor, writing in the *Listener*, simply ignored the fuss about the Rosenberg piece to complain, 'There is no article in the present number which will provoke any reader to burn it or even to throw it indignantly into the waste-paper basket. None of the articles is politically subversive . . . All are safe reading for children. Most of them are written by the elderly and the established.'[66] 'Have you seen *Encounter*?' Mary McCarthy asked Hannah Arendt. 'It is surely the most vapid thing yet, like a college magazine got out by long-dead and putrefying undergraduates.'[67]

Privately, Spender told friends that he had always been against running the Fiedler piece, but had felt 'he could not oppose Kristol on everything in the first issue', and appreciated Kristol's need to make his mark in his new milieu. But he also confided that the Fiedler piece was as good a way as any of 'letting British readers know just how awful a certain type of American intellectual could be'.[68] This echoed the view of Harold Rosenberg who, despairing at Fiedler's lack of depth, wrote that the article had achieved nothing beyond confirming the widely held belief that 'everyone in America lives on a billboard'.

Just as Fiedler's piece divided *Encounter*'s readers, so it drove a wedge between its co-editors, and broadened the gap between them. By March 1954, Spender was writing to Josselson to complain that Kristol never agreed to any of his suggestions, and that unless Kristol would 'admit his own ignorance' in certain matters, *Encounter* risked losing the position it had attained. He further accused Kristol of running the magazine as if he, Spender, were not there (indeed, for much of that year he wasn't, as he had been, according to Natasha Spender, 'coerced by Josselson and Nabokov' into undertaking a foreign tour on behalf of the Congress): 'I am writing to you now because I have complained dozens of times verbally to you without it having the slightest effect,' Spender admonished Kristol. 'I must be certain that plans for improving the magazine are not simply blocked by your unwillingness to consult me, or anyone else.'[69] Josselson took up Spender's corner, writing frequently to chastise Kristol for ignoring advice, and warning him to improve the look of the magazine and 'to offer the readers something worthwhile instead of the "crap" we have been offering them so far and which can only have hurt the magazine'.[70]

Within two years of *Encounter*'s launch, the Spender–Kristol relationship had frayed beyond repair. 'I find it impossible to work with Irving because there is no basis and no machinery for cooperating,' Spender told Josselson. 'I therefore think it would be quite dishonest to go on working with [him].'[71] Whilst Josselson battled to resolve the situation, another, more serious problem arose.

13
The Holy Willies

> Then let no cantankerous schism
> Corrupt this our catechism.
>
> John Crowe Ransom, 'Our Two Worthies'

The Rosenberg case had thrown up a painful dilemma for America. When McCarthy's minion Roy Cohn had publicly boasted to the Europeans of his role in the prosecution of the Rosenbergs, he had reinforced a suspicion that the trial was linked to the McCarthy witch-hunt. Although technically quite separate issues, the feeling spread in Europe that the two phenomena were conflated.

McCarthy emerged at a time when many Europeans were alert to evidence of a 'parallel nastiness' in America and the Soviet Union. 'The poison blows across the Atlantic like some horrible prevailing wind,'[1] wrote a young American diplomat's wife in France at the height of McCarthy's campaign. The senator from Wisconsin compensated for his meagre intellect with a loud mouth and an inveterate dishonesty (his limp, he claimed, was the result of a war wound, though actually it was acquired by slipping on a staircase). Mamaine Koestler found him repellent, describing him as 'a hairy-pawed thug' (though she believed he was doing a rather fine job of exposing 'infiltrators'). Richard Rovere wrote that no other politician of the age had 'surer, swifter access to the dark places of the

American mind'.[2] By the early 1950s, McCarthy was ranting about 'a great conspiracy, on a scale so immense and an infamy so black as to dwarf any previous venture in the history of men'. Encouraged by the trials of Alger Hiss, the Rosenbergs, and other pro-Soviet agents in the US, which contributed some plausibility to his Orwellian fixations, Joe McCarthy even accused General George Catlett Marshall of serving Kremlin policy. Under his hectoring chairmanship of the House Un-American Activities Committee hearings, accusations and blacklists became the order of the day. Arthur Miller was given a prison sentence (later quashed on appeal). Lillian Hellman was blacklisted and dubbed the era the 'Scoundrel Time'.

'Apart from I. F. Stone, whose four-page self-published weekly newsletter persistently examined the issues without obeying the rule that every question had to be couched in anti-Communist declarations, there was no other journalist I can now recall who stood up to the high wind without trembling,' wrote Arthur Miller. 'With the tiniest Communist Party in the world the U.S. was behaving as though on the verge of bloody revolution.'[3] Membership of the Communist Party was some 31,000 in 1950, skidding to just a few thousand by 1956, the majority of whom were said to be FBI undercover agents. 'I always believed the old adage that the FBI kept the Communist Party alive through their dues payments of their agents,'[4] said William Colby. For writer Howard Fast, 'The Communist Party of the United States, in fact, at that moment, was practically a branch of the Justice Department.'[5]

Chrome fin tails on new Cadillacs, bobby socks and Jell-O, Hula Hoops and Frigidaires, Chesterfields and food blenders, golf, Uncle Ike's grin, Mamie's hats: welcome to the Nifty Fifties. This was the America of *Life* magazine, a place with a booming consumer economy, a society at ease with itself. But behind this there was another America – brooding, dark, ill at ease; an America where owning a Paul Robeson record could be considered an act of subversiveness; where a school textbook called *Exploring American History*, co-authored by a Yale historian, offered children the following advice: 'The FBI urges Americans to report directly to its offices any suspicions they may have about Communist activity on the part of their fellow Americans. The FBI is expertly trained to sift out the truth of such reports under the laws of our free nation. When Americans handle their suspicions in this way, rather than by gossip and publicity, they are acting in line with American traditions.'[6] 'Exalting young tattlers was a mark of totalitarian societies, but it took the Cold War to include informing among the inventory of "American traditions",' wrote one historian.[7] The tenor of this sullen mood was registered in James Dean's *Weltschmerz*, Marlon Brando's nose-picking insouciance, Lenny Bruce's verbal violence, early manifestations of what would later become mass protest movements. But these were isolated moments, dark hints which were lost in the clamour of 'official' culture, in the din of Mickey Spillane's hate-filled and corrosive logorrhoea, or in the noisy exploits of Captain America, the *Marvel* comic hero who had switched so easily from battling Nazis to exposing Communists and who now warned: 'Beware, commies, spies, traitors, and foreign agents! Captain America, with all loyal, free men behind him, is looking for you, ready to fight until the last one of you is exposed for the yellow scum you are!'[8]

This was the America of Roy Cohn and David Schine, McCarthy's 'dreadful duo'. One commentator described Cohn as 'unspeakable', Schine as 'a gilded jackanapes'. Cohn was a brilliant lawyer who got his law degree from Columbia when he was still nineteen, and at twenty-five became McCarthy's counsel on the House Un-American Activities Committee. Highly ambitious and arrogant, Cohn wept every time he heard 'The Star-Spangled Banner'. David Schine, the son of a wealthy hotel magnate, educated at Andover and Harvard, was Cohn's closest friend. Schine loved nightclubs, fast cars and attention. In early 1953, Cohn got him a job on McCarthy's subcommittee. Schine had few qualifications, except the authorship of a nutty book called *Definition of Communism*, copies of which were placed next to Gideon's Bible in hotels owned by his father.

In the spring of 1953, when the impact of the Rosenberg trial was exposing a widespread resentment at America's presence in Europe, Cohn and Schine undertook a tour of inspection of America's official information outposts. They arrived in the wake of Stalin's death, which was announced by the Kremlin on

5 March. But their next move was as powerful a reminder as any that the mental halitosis of Stalinism was still abroad. After visiting United States Information Agency (USIA) libraries in seven countries, they announced that 30,000 books of the two million on the shelves were by 'pro-Communist' writers, and demanded their removal. The State Department, far from defending its libraries (which were visited by 36 million people annually) issued a craven directive prohibiting any material, including paintings, by 'any controversial persons, Communists, fellow-travellers, et cetera'. Thus, with Kafkaesque vagueness, were the works of hundreds of American writers and artists consigned to the dustbin of politics.

There followed a volley of telegrams between the State Department and all USIA missions (Berlin, Bremen, Düsseldorf, Frankfurt, Hamburg, Munich, Hanover, Stuttgart, Freiburg, Nuremberg, Paris) as the book-banning gathered pace: 'Remove all Sartre volumes from all Amerika Hauser collections.' 'All books by following listed authors to be removed: Hammett, Dashiell; Kay, Helen; Weltfish, Gene; Hughes, Langston; Seaver, Edwin; Stern, Bernhard; Fast, Howard.' 'Remove all (repeat all) works of following listed individuals: Abt, John; Julius, J.; Singer, Marcus; Witt, Nathan.' 'All works by the following authors are hereby ordered removed: Dubois, W. E. B.; Foster, William; Gorki, Maksim [sic]; Lysenko, Trofim; Reed, John; Smedley, Agnes.'[9] Herman Melville was harpooned, and all books illustrated by Rockwell Kent were withdrawn. On 20 April 1953, the US Embassy in Paris cabled the Department of State: 'The following books have been withdrawn from the USIA library in Paris and in the provinces: Howard Fast, *The Proud and the Free*, *The Unvanquished*, *Conceived in Liberty*; Dashiell Hammett, *The Thin Man*; Theodore Haff, *Charlie Chaplin*; Langston Hughes, *Weary Blues*, *Ways of White Folks*, *Big Sea*, *Fields of Wonder*, *Montage of a Dream Deferred*, *Not Without Laughter*, *Histoires des Blancs*.'[10]

American cultural prestige was being ground underfoot as government agencies and missions truckled to McCarthy. The average number of titles shipped abroad by USIA in 1953 plunged from 119,913 to 314. Many books removed from libraries had been burned under the Nazis. Committed to the pyre for a second time were Thomas Mann's *The Magic Mountain*, Tom Paine's *Selected Works*, Albert Einstein's *Theory of Relativity*, Sigmund Freud's writings, Helen Keller's *Why I Became a Socialist*, and John Reed's *Ten Days That Shook the World*. Thoreau's essay on 'Civil Disobedience' was banned by the US at the same time as it was outlawed by Maoist China. Seemingly unstoppable, the McCarthy-inspired cultural cleansing bankrupted America's claims to be the harbinger of freedom of expression.

Nobel Prize-winner and famed anti-Nazi Thomas Mann now found that his American citizenship offered less than the hoped-for protection from the totalitarian impulses he had escaped. Denounced by the McCarthyites for being soft on Communism, and labelled 'America's Fellow-Traveler Number One' by *Plain Talk* magazine, he longed to leave America, which he called 'an air-conditioned nightmare'.[11] Another prize for Cohn and Schine was Dashiell Hammett, who in 1951 served twenty-two weeks of a six-month jail sentence for refusing to identify the contributors to the Civil Rights Bail Fund, which had been set up to provide bail for arrested Communists. In 1953, he was called to testify at McCarthy's Senate Permanent Investigations Subcommittee, where he again refused to name names, this time invoking the Fifth Amendment. Cohn and Schine now demanded the removal of all his books from State Department libraries. With *The Adventures of Sam Spade* taken off the radio by NBC, Hammett was deprived of his main source of income. Having fought for America in two world wars, he died in poverty in 1961. In spite of FBI efforts to prevent it, he was buried at his own request in Arlington National Cemetery.[12]

Most of the living authors banned under State Department directives were also the subjects of voluminous – and often ridiculous – files at J. Edgar Hoover's FBI. The activities and movements of Robert Sherwood, Archibald MacLeish, Malcolm Cowley (in whose file Sidney Hook was named as the FBI's informant), John Crowe Ransom, Allen Tate, Howard Fast, F. O. Matthiessen, Langston Hughes and, of course, all the old *bêtes noires* from the Waldorf Astoria conference were monitored. When Ernest Hemingway complained to his friends that he was under surveillance by the FBI, they thought he was losing touch with reality. His file, released in the mid-1980s, and running to 113 pages, confirmed Hemingway's suspicions: he was followed, tapped and harassed by Hoover's men for over twenty-five years. Shortly before he took his life, and suffering from deep depression, Hemingway checked into a clinic in Minnesota under an assumed name. A psychiatrist at the clinic contacted the FBI to check that there were no objections to Hemingway registering himself in this way.[13]

The file on poet William Carlos Williams describes him as 'a sort of absent minded professor type' who uses 'an "expressionistic" style which might be interpreted as being "code"'. This was enough to ensure that when Williams was appointed Consultant in Poetry to the Library of Congress in 1952, he did not serve because he failed to pass the security test (the post remained vacant until 1956). The poet Louis Untermeyer was placed on the FBI's Security Index (which classified him as a national security risk) in 1951.[14] Shortly afterwards, Untermeyer locked himself in his apartment, refusing to come out for almost a year and a half, hostage to an 'overwhelming and paralysing fear'.[15] The essayist Murray Kempton believed that Hoover was 'stark, raving mad', and imagined that his 'nights were haunted by the suspicion that somewhere there might be someone who didn't revere him'.[16]

Discussing the problem of cultural censorship on 10 July 1953, Eisenhower's cabinet concluded weakly that 'we cannot screen without looking like a fool or a Nazi. Can be done quietly if enough time and intemperate souls were taken out. Definite intention now to select new books to conform with law.'[17] This was hardly the robust response needed. Letters were flooding in to American posts all over Europe, criticizing the book-banning. The British – who had taken the decision to leave copies of *Mein Kampf* on the shelves of German libraries after the war 'until it becomes a joke' – took a very dim view. Part of the problem was that Eisenhower, instead of getting down in the mud with McCarthy, thought he could eclipse him with his own anti-Communist crusade, a strategy endorsed by his Secretary of State, John Foster Dulles. McCarthy, meanwhile, had his doubts even about Eisenhower. Rumours were circulating that, under Ike's supreme command in post-war Europe, there had been massive penetration of American government offices – especially in Germany – by Communists. Surprisingly, it was Nicolas Nabokov who fanned the flames of this allegation, feeding information to the Alsop brothers about the seriousness of the infiltration, claiming that the Communist Fifth Column had virtually controlled the Eisenhower command.

Also under attack was the State Department's Voice of America. As McCarthy staged televised hearings featuring wild tales of Communist penetration of America's foreign broadcast service, employees who had helped build the service up were summarily sacked. In March 1953, a Voice of America producer called down to the music library for a recording of the 'Song of India', but was told by the librarian he couldn't have it, as 'it's by Rimsky-Korsakov, and we're supposed not to use anything by Russians'.

McCarthy's attacks on the State Department were relentless, and culminated in the accusation that Dean Acheson – 'this pompous diplomat in striped pants with a phony British accent' – was 'coddling communists'. The charge that Acheson, the architect of the Truman Doctrine, was soft on Communism rang a little hollow. McCarthy himself most likely didn't believe it. But the fact that Acheson waxed his moustache and bought his suits in Savile Row was a real indictment. Like Mussolini before him, McCarthy was an autarchist – he wanted 'Made in America'. His was the voice of the yahoos who rejected the anglicized values of people like Acheson. McCarthyism was a movement – or a moment – fired with populist resentment against the establishment. In turn, McCarthy's vulgar demagoguery was received as an insult by the ruling elite. He represented what A. L. Rowse in England scorned as 'the Idiot People'; he offended brahmin taste, which recoiled at mediocrity, hick mentality, the dreaded mid-cult. Political mandarins like the Alsop brothers, Joseph and Stewart, viewed McCarthy as 'a heartland populist stirring up passions against the country's foreign policy elite . . . They also viewed [his] attack on the State Department as an attack on the internationalist philosophy that had guided American foreign policy since the end of the war. Nobody was saying it explicitly, but it seemed clear to the brothers that if McCarthy succeeded in bringing down the

Department's internationalists, the result would be a new wave of isolationism.'[18]

'Nearly every liberal in the federal government was viewed with suspicion,' said Lyman Kirkpatrick, who served as CIA Inspector General during the McCarthy period. 'It had something of the atmosphere that must have been present during the French Revolution when denunciations and trials led to the guillotine. While there was no guillotine in Washington, there was perhaps an even worse fate in the destruction of an individual's career, and the wrecking of his life.'[19] Having permanently damaged the morale of the State Department, McCarthy turned an eye towards the CIA, a 'major and much more important target, particularly from the point of view of getting him greater personal publicity'.[20]

It was those 'internationalists' grouped around the CIA's International Organizations Division who had most to lose. By late 1952, McCarthy's suspicions had transferred to Braden's outfit, after the Senator learned that it had 'granted large subsidies to pro-Communist organizations'.[21] This was a critical moment: McCarthy's unofficial anti-Communism was on the verge of disrupting, perhaps sinking, the CIA's most elaborate and effective network of Non-Communist Left fronts. 'One of the oddities of the CIA's venture in cultural politics was that what it did should have been done openly and publicly through the United States Information Agency, or some other such body,' explained Arthur Schlesinger. 'The reason it couldn't be was because of Joe McCarthy, because if Joe McCarthy knew that the U.S. government was funding Non-Communist Left magazines, and socialist and Catholic trade unions, that would have caused great trouble. So it was in order to avoid McCarthy that the CIA did these things in a covert way.'[22] 'It all had to be off the budget,' said one CIA officer attached to the Congress for Cultural Freedom, 'as none of this would ever have got through Congress. Imagine the ridiculous howlings that would've gone up: "They're all Communists! They're homosexuals!" or whatever.'[23]

'A lot of these covert operations ironically were placed at risk because of McCarthy, who threatened at one point to blow their cover because, from his perspective, this was an American agency, the CIA, going into cahoots with lefties,' explained historian Kai Bird. 'It was an embarrassment, it was discrediting the idea that America was a sophisticated, democratic society capable of having a rational political debate. But it was also threatening to blow major intelligence operations that had long term implications for building a political consensus and keeping western Europe within NATO, and within a western alliance.'[24]

With McCarthy's bloodhounds sniffing around the Agency's Non-Communist Left programme, the CIA needed to recede as far as possible into the background. But at this critical moment, the American Committee for Cultural Freedom opened its mouth. In early March 1952, the Committee held a closed meeting to discuss what its response to McCarthy should be. It was immediately apparent that the Committee was hopelessly divided. James T. Farrell and Dwight Macdonald were in no doubt about the dangers of McCarthyism. 'The Stalinist menace is largely licked in America, although not on the world plane,' argued Farrell. 'But we are seeing the development of a group of McCarthyite intellectuals.'[25] He went on to define McCarthyism as 'know-nothingism', as an undue pressure to conformity and orthodoxy. Macdonald offered two positions: 'the "pure" one . . . which means making no distinction between Communists and non-Communists in matters of civil rights and cultural freedom; and the "impure" one, which means defending only people . . . who are penalized on false or unproven charges of Communism.'[26] He hoped the Committee would take the former position, but thought it should at least take the latter. Bertram Wolfe countered that 'the dangers in America today are a direct result of "our" failure to do the job of exposing Stalinists. If we don't do it, the "men with clubs" will.'[27]

Another member warned the Committee against its 'tendency to attach itself to ready-made controversies and then take the "official" position . . . it has fallen into the role of defending the present line of the government. What it should be concerned with is discovering new problems and issues. The others will be taken care of by a vast propaganda machine.'[28] Supporting this view was Richard Rovere, associate editor of *The New Yorker*, who said, 'It is clearly our job to let the country know and let Europe know that it is possible to be against McCarthyism as well as against Communist totalitarianism. The main problem here is that politics are beginning to determine culture.'[29] But Sidney Hook, Daniel Bell, Clement Greenberg, and William Phillips, speaking for the majority view, refused to support a general condemnation of McCarthy.

Writing to Hannah Arendt with news of these divergent positions, Mary McCarthy revealed that she had 'got an intimation of the Hook group's line, which seems to be that the goings-on of McCarthy . . . are not within the province of a committee for *cultural* freedom'.[30] She had also been told, in confidence, 'that the Committee, acknowledging that there is really no Communist menace here, is principally interested in raising funds to fight Communism in Western Europe, or, rather, to fight neutralism, which is taking first place as a Menace. This was proffered [to] me as "between ourselves."'[31] On the other hand, continued Mary McCarthy, there was a feeling that 'the great thing to be combated was a relapse into neutralism over here. That if Hook and Co. relaxed their efforts for a moment, stalinism [sic] would reassert itself in government and education, culminating in appeasement abroad. I couldn't tell whether this was a genuine fear (it seems so fantastic) or a rationalization. I can't believe that these people seriously think that stalinism on a large scale is latent here, ready to revive at the slightest summons . . . They live in terror of a revival of the situation that prevailed in the thirties, when the fellow-travelers were powerful in teaching, publishing, the theatre, etc., when stalinism was the gravy-train and these people were off it and became the object of social slights, small economic deprivations, gossip and backbiting. These people, who are success-minded, think in terms of group-advancement and cultural monopoly and were really traumatized by the brief stalinist apogee of the thirties . . . In their dreams, this period is always recurring; it is "realer" than today. Hence they scarcely notice the deteriorating actuality and minimize Senator McCarthy as not relevant.'[32]

To date, the split in the American Committee over McCarthyism had been kept relatively private. But on 29 March, it aired its divisions publicly in an open debate sponsored by the Committee entitled 'In Defense of Free Culture', which was staged, appropriately enough, in the Starlight Room of the Waldorf Astoria. In the morning session, Dwight Macdonald, Mary McCarthy and Richard Rovere spoke out against Senator McCarthy. But in the afternoon, Max Eastman, the darling of the American left in the early 1930s, delivered a speech which showed how complete the process of deradicalization could be. Denying there was a witch-hunt going on, he accused the Communists and their fellow travellers of inventing the term as 'a smear tactic'. 'As a half-burned witch from those hysterical days,' said Eastman, 'I beg to assure you that what you call a witch-hunt is child's play at a Sunday School picnic compared to what American people can do when they really get going.'[33] He went on to accuse the national executive of 'failing us in [the] struggle against infiltration by the enemies of freedom', and for good measure, he levelled the same charge at Freedom House, Americans for Democratic Action, and the American Civil Liberties Union (of which he himself was a member), denouncing them all as so many 'fuzzy-minded liberals who, in the name of cultural freedom, are giving their best help to an armed enemy bent on destroying every freedom throughout the world'.[34]

Some reports say the audience was stunned, some say it was jubilant. In his speech that morning, Richard Rovere had taken Irving Kristol to task for seldom coming out 'with the kind of blunt truth about McCarthy that he wishes other people to speak about the Communists'. He had accused McCarthy of having 'as low a regard for the truth as any Soviet historian', and concluded gloomily that 'the certain, and perhaps inevitable, truth is that the Holy Willies are on the march everywhere today'.[35] Now, according to Max Eastman, such sentiments simply indicated that Rovere was himself a sucker for Soviet propaganda.

After the meeting, Rovere wrote to Schlesinger expressing his desolation at Eastman's outburst, and begged him to do something about it. Who did Schlesinger turn to? Frank Wisner. Schlesinger later recalled, rather improbably, that although he had known of the CIA's initial investment in the Berlin launch of the Congress for Cultural Freedom, he had thereafter 'assumed that the foundations were paying. Like everybody else, I thought they were bona fide . . . I didn't know it was CIA paying for it all.' Half a century later, Schlesinger was still reticent about any formal relationship with the CIA in this matter: 'Sometimes I'd meet Frank Wisner at Joe Alsop's house, and he would ask me in a kind of social way what was happening at the American Committee, and I would tell him.'[36] So presumably it was in the form of a 'social' gesture that Schlesinger wrote to Wisner on 4 April 1952, together with certain enclosures 'all of which', noted Wisner, 'present a rather alarming picture'.[37] In response to Schlesinger's communication, Wisner penned an internal memo, 'Reported Crisis in the American Committee for Cultural Freedom', which is extraordinarily revealing and worth quoting in full:

> CIA memo from Deputy Director, Plans (Wisner) to Deputy Assistant Director for Policy Coordination re: Reported Crisis in the ACCF
>
> 1. Attached hereto is a letter dated 4 April from Arthur Schlesinger Jr. to myself, together with certain enclosures, all of which present a rather alarming picture. I had not heard about these developments prior to my receipt of Schlesinger's letter, and I am most anxious to have an OPC evaluation of this matter, which very well may *not* be a tempest in a teapot.
>
> 2. My offhand reaction to this mess is that the position of neither the pro-McCarthyites or anti-McCarthyites is the correct one from our standpoint, and that it is most unfortunate that the matter ever came up in such a way as to bring it to this kind of head. I can understand how an American committee for cultural freedom, standing alone, and being in fact a group of American private citizens interested in cultural freedom, would feel that it would *have* to take a position on McCarthyism. However, that is not the nature of the American Committee for Cultural Freedom which, according to my recollection, was inspired if not put together by this Agency for the purpose of providing cover and backstopping for the European effort. If such is the case, we are stuck with the Committee in that we have an inescapable responsibility for its conduct, its actions and its public statements. Under the

circumstances the raising of the issue of McCarthyism, whether to condemn it or to support it, was a serious mistake in my opinion. The reason is simply that this injects us into an extremely hot American domestic political issue, and is sure to get us into trouble and to bring down on our heads criticism for interference in a matter that is none of our concern whatsoever.

3. If you agree with the foregoing analysis and reaction, we should consider *promptly* what should be done now that the fat is in the fire. If it were possible to do so, it would be my thought that the entire debate on this subject, from the beginning, be expunged from the record and the matter thus laid to rest. I know that this will not satisfy either faction, but it might be possible for us to put across to the members of both factions that we are talking about Europe and the world outside the U.S., and that we should stick to our last — and that if we do not do so the entire effort will be exposed and shot down because of our involvement in domestic political issues. An appeal to unity and concord and the preservation of this valuable effort might be successful. In any case it is the only approach that I can think of.[38]

The significance of the memo is manifold. It shows Arthur Schlesinger alerting Frank Wisner to developments in the American Committee which he, Schlesinger, finds disturbing (Schlesinger had earlier complained to Nabokov that the organization was riddled with 'neurotic' anti-Communists, and was becoming 'an instrument for these bastards'.)[39] It reveals the origins of that Committee, which advertised itself as a 'free' and 'independent' body, as a 'backstop'[40] for a larger CIA effort in western Europe. It shows that Wisner was in no doubt as to the Agency's responsibility for the American Committee's conduct, actions and public statements. Created by the Agency, the question of its freedom to do and say as it wanted was, to Wisner's mind, academic. If it were indeed what it said it was – an independent group of private citizens – then it could do what it wanted. But it wasn't what it said it was: it was part of Wisner's Wurlitzer, and as such it could be expected to play the right tune or, if necessary, remain silent. Legally, of course, the

CIA had no right to interfere in the business of a domestic organization. Wisner admits as much in the memo.

Further, that Wisner could write so freely of 'expunging the record' offers a disturbing picture of the CIA's attitude to such groups. The Agency had a power of veto over its front activities, and Wisner was now advocating the use of that veto. Also clear from the memo is the fact that Wisner felt he had a direct line into the American Committee, which he now wanted to activate to persuade both factions within the group to forget their differences, and to drop the subject of McCarthyism altogether.

'The American Committee for Cultural Freedom was just a front in order to create the impression of some American participation in the European operation,' said Tom Braden. 'When they started raising the McCarthy issue, Oh God, was that embarrassing, especially for Allen [Dulles]. That was a good enough reason why there shouldn't be an American Committee, certainly in Allen's mind. He would've been aghast at such public acknowledgement of someone in the Congress for Cultural Freedom opposing McCarthy. He of course hated McCarthy, but he knew you gotta handle him with very, very delicate kid gloves: don't cross him, or get him involved in anything. The idea that people like Burnham or Schlesinger – people of that stature – would be getting up and making a big stink about McCarthy was really out of the question, at least in Allen's mind.'[41]

Plainly, it was a matter of policy that the Congress for Cultural Freedom and its affiliates leave McCarthyism well alone, as one English activist later recalled: 'It was clearly understood that we must not criticize the American government, or the McCarthyism which was then at its height in the U.S.'[42] This was one of the matters discussed by de Neufville and Monty Woodhouse in their 'operations and methods' meetings, and complemented a Foreign Office directive to the Information Research Department that none of its activities 'should appear to be attacking the United States in any way'. *Encounter*'s contribution to the subject of McCarthyism should be viewed in this context. Generally managing to avoid the issue altogether, when it did examine it, the tone was far from condemnatory. In an essay of extraordinary obfuscation,

Tosco Fyvel ventured that the mood in America which attended the rise of McCarthy was akin to the mood of England in 1914, when 'a century of English security crumbled'. 'The cold hate for the enemy (the Hun), passionate faith in the justice of Britain's cause, angry intolerance towards socialists, pacificists, other dissenters' – these, argued Fyvel, were emotions comparable to America's 'abrupt loss of [its] sense of security' on the day peace broke out in 1945, with the 'inaugural of the new atomic-bomb age, and with the Soviet Union looming up as a powerful opponent'. All that had followed had been an attempt, albeit 'painful', to adjust. Although McCarthy was to be regretted, he had to be viewed in the context of America's 'insistent search for new national security, for a world, indeed, made safe for democracy'. This, concluded Fyvel, was infinitely preferable to 'European weariness, and scepticism of any such achievement'.[43]

The idea that Europeans had fundamentally misunderstood the circumstances surrounding McCarthyism was taken up by Leslie Fiedler, who argued that it was wrong to assume, as did so many 'vague anti-capitalists all over the world', that 'because McCarthy bellows against Communist infiltration, this is sufficient proof that the whole idea is absurd'. Assuming 'innocence by association', these people rushed to defend *anyone* who was accused by McCarthy. Dismissing as 'comedy' claims that Americans were constantly 'twittering back and forth' in fear of McCarthy, Fiedler concluded that the Wisconsin senator was a windmill against whom it was futile to 'waste one's blows' when there were 'real monsters' to be fought.[44]

The 'lesser evil' card was also played by the young British conservative Peregrine Worsthorne, who announced in the November 1954 issue of *Encounter* that 'America has a chequered past, and will no doubt have a chequered future, and the sooner we accept this inevitable fact the sooner we will be able to take full advantage of her manifold blessings without harping on the blemishes. Legend created an American God. The God has failed. But unlike the Communist God which, on closer examination, turned out to be a devil, the American God has just become human.'[45] *Encounter* is rightly remembered for its unflinching scrutiny of cultural curtailment in the

Communist bloc. But its mitigation of McCarthyism was less clear-sighted: where the journal could see the beam in its opponent's eye, it failed to detect the mote in its own.

Surely it was to be expected that those who claimed to honour the cause of freedom should find a way to deplore that which assaulted or dishonoured it? The American Committee had been right to raise the issue of McCarthyism, and the CIA was at fault for trying to suppress the debate. But Wisner was not a man to be delayed by such niceties. In his memo, he had suggested that an 'appeal to unity and concord and the preservation of this valuable effort might be successful'. This appeal was swiftly organized. Nabokov's letter to Arthur Schlesinger, written in the fullness of preparations for the Paris 'Masterpieces' festival in April 1952, echoes Wisner's memo with uncanny precision: 'Frankly, I would deplore a split in the American Committee. It would endanger the work of the Congress, and our French Organization, to an incalculable degree,' he warned. 'It should be made clear to Europeans that McCarthy is a man, not a movement[46] . . . I am convinced that we must attack the individual actions and methods of *McCarthy*, but I question the utility and the logic of resolutions against '*McCarthyism*', which would tend to imply, at least for Europeans, that McCarthy represents an authentic popular movement in the United States.' Nabokov went on to urge Schlesinger 'to do everything you can to prevent a split in the American Committee. I cannot put my conviction strongly enough that such a rupture would virtually represent a death blow to our work here.'[47]

Case officer Lee Williams revealed that if there were problems with Congress committees or affiliates or editors stepping too far out of line, then one way of getting the Agency's veto in place without it being seen as such was to leap-frog all the bureaucracy and get a message directly to the offenders from someone 'on high' within the Congress structure.[48] This job usually fell to Julius Fleischmann, who on one famous occasion warned the editors of *Encounter* that their funding might be jeopardized if they insisted on running a controversial article. Nabokov appears to have assumed a similar function, both here over the question of the American Committee's intrusion into the McCarthy minefield, and on future occasions. Either

Nabokov was 'positioned' to intercede in such instances without his knowing at whose behest; or, more likely, he did so wittingly.

'If we had fought back from the beginning instead of running away, these things would not be happening now,'[49] wrote John Steinbeck, at the height of the McCarthy crusade. 'The terrible thing is that many of those victimized, and the American people as a whole, accepted this sentence of Guilty,' wrote John Henry Faulk. 'They accepted the right of vigilantes to bring charges, to make the decision and to pronounce the sentence. And we all kept quiet. We felt that silence would make us safe.'[50]

Whilst Soviet writers and artists were persecuted on a scale which does not, and cannot, bear comparison with the McCarthy campaign in America, both scenarios shared similar elements. A visit by the Alsop brothers to 'the McCarthy lair on Capitol Hill' contained all the motifs of the Soviet nightmare, with McCarthy himself bearing more than a passing resemblance to a Stalinist apparatchik or secret policeman. 'The anteroom is generally full of furtive-looking characters who look as though they might be suborned State Department men,'[51] the Alsops wrote. 'McCarthy himself, despite a creeping baldness and a continual tremor which makes his head shake in a disconcerting fashion, is reasonably well cast as the Hollywood version of a strong-jawed private eye. A visitor is likely to find him with his heavy shoulders hunched forward, a telephone in his huge hands, shouting cryptic instructions to some mysterious ally. "Yeah, yeah. I can listen, but I can't talk. Get me? Yeah? You really got the goods on this guy?" The senator glances up to note the effect of this drama on his visitor. "Yeah? Well, I tell you. Just mention this sort of casual to Number One, and get his reaction. Okay?" The drama is heightened by a significant bit of stage business. For as Senator McCarthy talks he sometimes strikes the mouthpiece of his telephone with a pencil. As Washington folklore has it, this is supposed to jar the needle off any concealed listening device. In short, while the State Department fears that Senator McCarthy's friends are spying on it, Senator McCarthy apparently fears that the State Department's friends are spying on him.'[52]

Here was the rationale for Wisner's memo: the reason for stopping the debate was because McCarthy was breeding a 'miasma of neurotic fear and internal suspicion', and outside the US this threatened the very fundamentals of the CIA's efforts to achieve convergence with the Non-Communist Left.

But within the conservative element of the American Committee, the Alsop account was dismissed as the product of a fevered imagination. 'There are some, who should know better, who have asserted that we were going through the worst period of political terror and hysteria in our history,' wrote Sidney Hook. 'This description of the present state of America [is] a fantastic exaggeration of the facts.'[53] Kristol, too, mocked claims that McCarthyism was creating 'an atmosphere of dread'. Answering Arthur Miller's claim that Broadway was suffering from the 'knuckle-headedness of McCarthyism' with its 'Congressional investigations of political unorthodoxy', Kristol wrote in the *New York Times* that Miller was guilty of 'expressing absurdities'.[54] In 1953, Kristol stated famously that 'there is one thing the American people know about Senator McCarthy; he, like them, is unequivocally anti-Communist. About the spokesmen for American liberalism, they feel they know no such thing.' At the same time, Stephen Spender concluded gloomily that 'Every now and then an American writer crosses himself with a pious anti-communist sentiment, and one suspects that instead of saying Ave Maria, he is really saying Ave McCarthy.'[55]

Josselson had been against setting up the American Committee from the very beginning, and in the wake of the McCarthy 'flap', he felt vindicated. Braden, too, had considered it unwise, saying later: 'I think it was Sidney Hook's idea, but I thought it was a mistake. It seemed to me it was setting up a rival organization to the Congress in Paris, and also it would be full of hardliners. Some of the American Committee people were pretty close in character to McCarthy. Worse, these were people who had access to the ears of influential people in the State Department, and this could create problems for the Agency.'[56] Despite these reservations, Frank Wisner had managed to convince Allen Dulles, then still Deputy Director for Operations, that an American branch of the Congress for Cultural Freedom was an unavoidable necessity.

It was, said Melvin Lasky later (and perhaps at the time?) 'part of the endemic, integral nature of the covert thing. The Agency couldn't participate in domestic affairs, and yet you had to have an American committee. How could you not? It would've been an inexplicable anomaly. You say you're international, so where are the Americans? It would've been like going into a prize fight with only one glove. It was the weakest side of this covert thing, but you had to have it. How not?'[57]

However, faced with the Committee's disintegration in a public display of acrimony and recrimination over whether or not to oppose McCarthy, Josselson and his CIA superiors had real reason to be concerned. The danger was that if the American Committee folded, it would regroup under the same name, but without the moderate wing represented by Schlesinger and Rovere and their 'sensible' friends. The last thing Josselson needed was a hardline pressure group quite at odds with the European effort.

Those who expected the American Committee to defend cultural freedom from the depredations of McCarthyism were disappointed. 'Its wishy-washy stand on this question caused the Congress much embarrassment throughout the world,'[58] Josselson later said. It did publish a book, *McCarthy and the Communists* (by Midge Decter and James Rorty), but its main attack was aimed at McCarthy's lazy methods rather than his pursuit of alleged Communists. Appearing in 1954, it was a belated and rather ambiguous contribution (that it was published at all provoked James Burnham to lead a walkout of the conservative wing of the American Committee. At about the same time, Burnham also ended his lifelong association with *Partisan Review*). That the American Committee for Cultural Freedom, like *Encounter*, sought to deny or minimize the risks to culture of McCarthy is a troubling legacy. Depressed by the lack of any sustained analysis of the problem, Mary McCarthy wrote to Hannah Arendt of her vision of a 'curious amalgam of left elements, anarchist elements, nihilist elements, opportunist elements, all styling themselves conservative, in a regular *Narrenschiffe* [ship of fools] . . . The great effort of this new Right is to get itself accepted as *normal* . . . and this, it seems to me, must be scotched, if it's not already too late.'[59]

*

While Senator McCarthy planned his assault on the CIA, Allen Dulles took over as its director. Unlike his brother, John Foster Dulles, whose 'Black Protestantism' and aggressive anti-Communism restrained him from challenging McCarthy, Allen Dulles was determined to prevent a 'jumped-up hack from Wisconsin' from destroying the Agency. He warned his employees that he would fire anyone who went to McCarthy without his personal authorization. Some CIA personnel had already received mysterious phone calls from McCarthy's associates, who included a shady Baltimore figure called Ulius Amoss, a Greek-American who had been booted out of the OSS (itself quite an achievement), and now ran a private intelligence agency called the International Services of Information Foundation, which McCarthy quietly subcontracted to dig up the dirt on CIA staffers. Suddenly, Agency personnel were being told by anonymous callers that 'it was known that they drank too much, or were having an "affair", and the caller would make no issue of this if they would come around and tell everything they knew about the Agency' to a McCarthy devotee.[60]

But Amoss proved he could not handle the opening of an envelope, much less a serious investigation into members of the espionage establishment. McCarthy's first shot – an attack on William Bundy in July 1953 – blew up in his face. Bundy, a member of the CIA's Board of National Estimates (and Dean Acheson's son-in-law) had contributed $400 to the Alger Hiss defence fund. This, deduced McCarthy, meant that Bundy must be a Communist. 'I just happened to be in Allen's office when this came up,' recalled Tom Braden, 'and Bundy was there. Allen told him, "Get out of here, and I'll deal with it." Bundy took a few days leave, and Allen went directly to Eisenhower, and said he wasn't going to fuck about with this mess from Wisconsin.'[61] Dulles actually told the president he would resign unless McCarthy's attacks were stopped.

This, finally, is what seems to have prompted Eisenhower to action. After vice-president Richard Nixon was despatched to pressurize McCarthy into dropping his plans for a public investigation, the senator suddenly became 'convinced' that 'it would not be in the public interest to hold public hearings on the CIA, that that perhaps could be taken care of administratively'.[62] This took the form of a compromise, whereby McCarthy agreed to make his complaints against the Agency in the privacy of Allen Dulles's office. Bringing with him lists of alleged 'homosexuals' and 'rich men' in CIA employ, he demanded a vast internal purge of the CIA. If Dulles failed to comply, McCarthy threatened to pursue a public investigation. 'The pressure took its toll. Security standards were tightened. In one case, the CIA's loss was Hollywood's gain. A young political science graduate with a classic New York accent called Peter Falk [of *Columbo* fame] applied for entrance to the CIA's training program in 1953, but his application was rejected because he had once belonged to a left-wing union.'[63]

The employees of Braden's IOD were subject to special scrutiny because of their alleged political liberalism. Braden's director of trade union operations was fired because he had briefly belonged to the Young Communist League in the 1930s. But worse was to come. In late August 1953, Braden was sailing in Maine with Richard Bissell, who had taken a short break from his job at the Ford Foundation to enjoy his yacht, the *Sea Witch*. Anchored in Penobscot Bay, Braden received an urgent message informing him that the McCarthyites had discovered 'a red' at the Agency. The man in question was Braden's deputy, Cord Meyer Jr., who had been recruited by Allen Dulles in 1951. With Dulles and Braden both away on vacation, there was nothing to stand between Meyer's pants and the force of McCarthy's boot. He was suspended without pay pending a security investigation, and found himself rereading Kafka's *The Trial*, understanding as never before 'the plight of his bewildered hero, who could never discover why or by whom he had been accused'.[64]

Cord Meyer wasn't red. He wasn't even pink. Among the charges listed in a three-page document was the fact that he had once shared a lecture platform with Harlow Sharpley, a Harvard astronomer known for his leftist political views. Also noted was Meyer's association with the National Council of the Arts, Sciences and Professions, which had been cited as a Communist front by the House Un-American Activities Committee. Both alleged crimes dated to the immediate post-war years when Meyer had been a leader of the American

Veterans' Committee, a liberal organization designed to offer an alternative to the ultra-conservative American Legion, and a founder of the United World Federalists, which called for world government, and was more utopian than liberal.

'My immediate boss, Tom Braden, was consistently supportive and encouraged me to believe that there was never any doubt that I would be able to clear myself,'[65] Meyer later wrote. And indeed, there was never any real chance that McCarthy's charges would stick. On Thanksgiving Day 1953, two months after his suspension, Meyer received a telephone call from Allen Dulles: he had been entirely cleared of the disloyalty charges, and was free to come back to the Agency. The episode was to mark Meyer for the rest of his life, and it serves to illustrate one of the great paradoxes of Cold War America: whilst CIA men worked around the clock to defeat Communism, they were being tailed by fellow Americans who claimed to be bent on the same objective. If Juvenal had wondered who was guarding the guards, the question here was more who was slaying the dragon-slayers?

McCarthy was finally eclipsed in late 1954, and died an alcoholic in 1957. But Dwight Macdonald's characterization of McCarthyism as a 'mock-heroic epic . . . an interlude in our political history so weird and wonderful that future archeologists may well assign it to mythology rather than history'[66] was wishful thinking. America would struggle to exorcize the demons McCarthy had raised for years to come; at the time, 'the values he espoused and the assumptions on which he had based his crusade remained mostly unchallenged'. As one observer put it, 'McCarthy was censured and quashed, but not McCarthyism.'[67] The search for the truth, the desire to get to the bottom of things, the very process of intellectual enquiry, became tainted by its association with witch-hunts.

Or was it the other way around? Perhaps the question is, could McCarthyism have happened without the Truman Doctrine? Was the departure from the elementary rules for the ascertainment of truth, where judgement was clouded by fear and hostility, where what Murray Kempton described as 'over attendance upon the excessive' distracted men 'from noticing how bad the normal is', the essence of Cold War thinking? 'Our leaders became liberated from the normal rules of evidence and inference when it came to dealing with Communism,' Senator William Fulbright later argued. 'After all, who ever heard of giving the Devil a fair shake? Since we know what he has in mind, it is pedantry to split hairs over what he is actually doing . . . The effect of the anti-Communist ideology was to spare us the task of taking cognizance of the specific facts of specific situations. Our "faith" liberated us, like the believers of old, from the requirements of empirical thinking . . . Like medieval theologians, we had a philosophy that explained everything to us in advance, and everything that did not fit could be readily identified as a fraud or a lie or an illusion . . . The perniciousness of [anti-Communist orthodoxy] arises not from any patent falsehood but from its distortion and simplification of reality, from its universalization and its elevation to the status of a revealed truth.'[68]

Far from denting the CIA, McCarthy eventually contributed to its enhanced prestige. Thanks to him, the CIA's reputation as something of a haven for foreign policy 'freethinkers' was confirmed. Richard Bissell, who joined the Agency in January 1954, remembered it as 'a place where there was still intellectual ferment and challenge and things going on [while] much of the challenge and sense of forward motion had gone out of other parts of the government'.[69] Its director, Allen Dulles, emerged even stronger than before. According to Tom Braden, 'Power flowed to him and, through him, to the CIA, partly because his brother was Secretary of State, partly because his reputation as the master spy of the Second World War hung over him like a mysterious halo, partly because his senior partnership in the prestigious New York law firm of Sullivan and Cromwell impressed the small-town lawyers of Congress.' And now, in the face of McCarthy's attack on the Agency, Dulles had won, and 'his victory vastly increased the respectability of what people then called "the cause" of anti-Communism. "Don't join the book burners," Eisenhower had said. That was the bad way to fight Communism. The good way was the CIA.'[70]

14

Music and Truth, *ma non troppo*

It occurs to me that the apparatus for the creation and maintenance of celebrities is vastly in excess of material fit to be celebrated.

Philip Larkin

In contrast to the American Committee, whose failure to take a coherent stand on a single major issue accelerated its imminent demise, the Congress in Europe had, by the mid-1950s, clearly staked out its territory. Under Josselson's firm hand, it had established a reputation as a serious alliance of intellectuals committed to demonstrating the fallibility of the Soviet mythos, and the superiority of western democracy as a framework for cultural and philosophical enquiry. Whilst the composition of its inner circle – or 'apparat' – remained unchanged, the Congress could now boast a membership studded with the names of eminent intellectuals and artists.

Julian Huxley, Mircea Eliade, André Malraux, Guido Piovene, Herbert Read, Allen Tate, Lionel Trilling, Robert Penn Warren, W. H. Auden, Thornton Wilder, Jayaprakash Narayan – these and many other luminaries graced the pages of *Encounter*, *Preuves*, and the raft of other magazines created by or affiliated to the Congress. Directed at Latin American intellectuals was *Cuadernos*, launched in 1953 from Paris under the editorship of novelist and playwright Julian Gorkin. In Vienna, the Congress launched *Forum* magazine in early

1954 as a monthly edited by novelist and critic Friedrich Torberg. 'Freddy the Torte', as he was nicknamed, was an extraordinary character who repelled and attracted people in equal measure. Koestler wrote admiringly that he was 'the last Mohican of the Danube, of an Old Vienna which perhaps existed only in our fantasy'. Others found him arrogant and intolerant. The Communists attacked him as 'an American agent . . . slanderer . . . and informer', and dismissed the anti-neutralist tone of his magazine as an American conspiracy. *Forum* developed the usual Congress themes, and Torberg enjoyed a good working relationship with the Paris secretariat. But Josselson sometimes had to discipline him, as on one occasion in 1957 when *Forum* reprinted an article from the right-wing *National Review*. This, said Josselson, was 'beneath the dignity of a Congress journal'. 'It will not happen again,' a chastened Torberg replied.

Science and Freedom was launched in autumn 1953 after a Congress conference of the same name. Held in Hamburg in July 1953, the conference had attracted grants of $10,000 from the Rockefeller Foundation and $35,000 from the Farfield Foundation. The eponymous journal was edited by Michael Polanyi, who was appointed to the Executive Committee in the same year. In drawing attention to racial segregation in America, as well as apartheid in South Africa, Polanyi's journal spoke about issues on which the Congress was, on the whole, muted. It also recognized *détente* long before most people knew the meaning of the word, encouraging intellectual exchanges with the Soviet bloc and a softening of the West's Cold War stance. But as a bi-annual bulletin with a tiny readership, its voice was never more than a reed in the strong gusts of Cold War polemics.[1]

Soviet Survey started in 1955 as a monthly newsletter edited by the historian Walter Laqueur, who was also the Congress's official representative in Israel. Described by Josselson as 'one of the best international experts on the Soviet Union', Laqueur wrote extensively on the Russian affairs under the pen name Mark Alexander. Under him, *Soviet Survey* produced investigations of intellectual, artistic and political life in the eastern bloc which offered an insight 'unique amongst Western publications'.[2] Whilst claims that it 'crackled with excitement'[3] may be overstated, it certainly earned a wide and dedicated readership. Bizarrely, even some Communist journals felt they could usefully borrow material from *Soviet Survey*, causing Josselson to write anxiously to Laqueur that 'we don't want pro-Soviet publication[s] to sugarcoat their propaganda with some of our material'.[4]

In April 1956, the first issue of *Tempo Presente* appeared in Italy. Edited by Ignazio Silone and Nicola Chiaromonte, it was the first serious challenge to *Nuovi Argomenti*, a journal founded in 1954 by Alberto Moravia which closely resembled Sartre's *Les Temps modernes*. *Tempo Presente* took the resemblance one step further, its title a deliberate echo of Sartre's. Cynics would later argue that this amounted to intellectual theft, and illustrated claims that one major CIA strategy was to create or support 'parallel' organizations which provided an alternative to radicalism over which they had no control. Certainly, *Tempo Presente* 'opened its pages to many defectors from the Italian Communist Party in the late 1950s',[5] including the writers Italo Calvino, Vasco Pratolini and Libero de Libero. Its pages were also open to dissident writers from the eastern bloc who, together with the regular stable of Congress contributors, kept up a sustained attack on the vagaries of Communist totalitarianism.

The Congress also established a presence further afield, projecting its voice into areas which were considered susceptible to Communism or neutralism. It had a magazine in Australia, *Quadrant*, which aimed to reduce the influence of that large corps of Australian intellectuals who were drawn 'to an alarming extent to the magnetic field of Communism'. Its editor, Catholic poet James McAuley, believed that 'men's minds will be won only when anti-Communist positions can radiate a counter-attraction', and under him *Quadrant* (which still exists) became a lively focus for the Australian Non-Communist Left.[6]

In India, the Congress published *Quest*, which first appeared in August 1955. Culturally limited by being in English, the language of administration and not literature, it was attacked by Indian Communists for 'insidious' American propaganda, but like *Cuardernos* in Latin America, at least it gave the Congress a foothold in difficult terrain. It probably didn't deserve J. K. Galbraith's sneer that 'it broke new ground in ponderous, unfocused illiteracy'. Certainly, Prime Minister Nehru didn't like it, as he always distrusted the Congress as an 'American front'. In Japan, there was *Jiyu*, one of the most heavily subsidized of all the Congress magazines. Its attempts to moderate anti-American opinion among Japanese intellectuals were initially too watery, and in 1960 the Congress decided to break entirely with the publisher and relaunch with a team under direct control of the Paris office. Japan, it was deemed, was 'far too tricky ideologically' to leave the magazine in even semi-independent hands.[7] By the mid to late 1960s, the Congress had extended its publications programme to include other areas of strategic interest: Africa, the Arab world and China.

'The real mystery is how those magazines worked,' said one CIA agent. 'All those intellectuals wouldn't go to a cocktail party together, but they were all in *Preuves*, *Tempo Presente*, *Encounter*. You just couldn't have done it in America. *Harpers* couldn't do it, *The New Yorker* couldn't do it. They couldn't get Isaiah Berlin and Nancy Mitford and all the others. Even Irving Kristol couldn't do it when he came back from London. I suppose the answer is: Michael Josselson.'[8] Well, that was half the answer. There was Michael Josselson, and there was Melvin Lasky. Diana Josselson explained the relationship: 'Michael was publisher and editor-in-chief. Lasky was vice-president, and, to a certain extent, Michael's mouthpiece. Michael tried to arrange periodic meetings between the various editors, and Lasky was understood to be the main guy if Michael wasn't there. They were in close contact, and saw things similarly.'[9]

Melvin Lasky later claimed that Josselson had initially wanted him to be Spender's co-editor at *Encounter*, but that he, Lasky, did not want to leave Berlin, so he recommended Irving Kristol instead. It seems more probable that the reason Lasky did not find himself at the helm of the Congress's flagship magazine was the same as that given by Wisner in 1950 when he ordered Lasky to be removed from the organizing body of the Congress in Berlin: he was too closely connected to the American government. By 1953, Lasky could argue that this was no longer the case. His magazine, *Der Monat*, was now sponsored by the Ford Foundation, which had recently given him a further grant of $275,000 to publish books under *Der Monat*'s auspices. But there remained a haze of suspicion around Lasky which was hard to dispel. Josselson did his best, receiving *Der Monat* into the fold of Congress magazines at the end of 1953, when the initial Ford Foundation grant expired. In this way, Josselson was able to legitimize Lasky's relationship with the Congress. As the editor of one of its magazines, Lasky now found himself officially at the centre of its policy-making apparat.

As a member of the 'Tri-Magazine Editorial Committee' which was set up to coordinate editorial policy for *Encounter*, *Der Monat* and *Preuves*, Lasky was now part of a small team which decided how the Congress's themes were articulated. Meeting regularly in Paris, and joined by Josselson, Nabokov and de Rougemont, this committee analysed the performance of the magazines and agreed on subjects for discussion in forthcoming issues. Lasky argued consistently for a deeper commitment to States-side themes (Eudora Welty should be approached to do a 'De-Segregation' piece; someone should write about 'the Great American Boom'; Gian Carlo Menotti could do something on the theme of 'highbrow and lowbrow'), and increased emphasis on Soviet affairs. Another favourite *bête noire* – and consistently the target of a kind of insensate hatred in Congress magazines – was Jean-Paul Sartre, whose break with Merleau-Ponty in 1955 (after Merleau-Ponty announced his divorce from Communism) should, said Lasky, be signalled in Congress magazines under the heading 'Sartre est mort'.[10] Sartre was repeatedly dismissed in the pages of *Encounter* and *Preuves* as a lackey of Communism, a miserable time-server whose political and creative writings perpetuated the Communist delusion and 'rejoiced in violence'.

The extent of Lasky's influence on the three magazines is revealed in a report dated April 1956 – 'Some Notes on Preuves, Encounter and Der Monat' – in which he summarised their achievements and set forth his agenda for their future. The magazines had established themselves, he wrote, as 'part of the community, a piece of the environment, with their own institutional weight. They have become symbols in the cultural life of two ancient nations of free, humane, and democratic international (and transatlantic) exchange.'[11] But he cautioned his fellow editors against 'insisting, in the matter of American material, that the USA be constantly projected "positively", that all the European anti-American stereotypes be made short shrift of'. Although he conceded that some 'anti-American slips' which had appeared in the magazines were 'regrettable and to be avoided in the future', Lasky argued against straining the quality of transatlantic understanding. 'Let's not always be forcing the matter. (And-what-have-we-done-today-to-stop-people-thinking-of-us-as-Barbarians?) We – not unlike everybody else – have too many problems (including materialism, cynicism, corruption, violence) consistently to come out with a positive word of cheer for the Stars-and-Stripes forever. Let European writers grumble. Let's grumble a bit ourselves (paradoxically, one of our most sympathetic sounds).'[12]

In effect, Lasky was conceding that critics of the Congress magazines who complained of a pro-American bias were basically right. *Encounter*, in particular, must now address the charge that it was a 'Trojan horse' for American interests, that it 'had a peculiar blind spot – it hardly ever contained any critical articles about the U.S., as if this was forbidden territory'.[13] In the early years, certainly, *Encounter* went to great lengths to erode any antipathy towards America and its institutions. Anti-Americanism was variously characterized as 'a psychological necessity to many Europeans', a device which enabled them 'to indulge simultaneously in self-hatred' (America as 'mythicized image of all [they] hate') and 'self-righteousness' (Fiedler); or as a way of heightening 'the gratification which British intellectuals derive from their national self-contemplation' (Edward Shils); or as a mechanical reflex of 'modern liberalism', epitomized by the *New Statesman and Nation*, with its 'pernicious anaemia', 'stereotyped reactions', and 'moral smugness' (Dwight Macdonald in 1956, at the height of his Cold Warriorism). Lasky's recommendations only partially succeeded. Although A. A. Alvarez, writing in 1961, noticed a change – 'the paranoiac throb of genuine propaganda is rarely heard in *Encounter* these days'[14] – others remained unconvinced, sharing Conor Cruise O'Brien's view that '*Encounter*'s first loyalty is to America.'[15]

Back at CIA headquarters in Washington, *Encounter* was

regarded proudly as a 'flagship', a congenial vehicle for advancing the notion of a cultural community linked, and not separated, by the Atlantic. It even became a kind of calling card for CIA agents. Arranging a meeting with Ben Sonnenberg, a rich young wanderer who worked briefly for the CIA in the mid-1950s, an agent told him, 'I'll be carrying a copy of *Encounter*, so you'll know who I am.'

The CIA's faith in the Congress's journals was matched by its financial commitment. Although the details are, *de facto*, hard to come by, some financial accounts have survived, scattered around the dusty recesses of a number of archives. According to the Statement of Disbursements for the period ending 31 December 1958, the Farfield Foundation paid the salaries of the 'editorial secretariat' of the Congress to the tune of $18,660 per annum. This covered Bondy, Lasky (presumably), and the American editor of *Encounter* (the British editor's salary, it will be remembered, was the responsibility of British intelligence). In 1959, *Encounter* received $76,230.30 from the Farfield (almost double the initial annual grant of $40,000). In the same year, *Cuadernos* received $48,712.99, and *Preuves* $75,765.07. Additionally, $21,251.43 was allocated for the 'administration' of Congress periodicals. Grants to *Der Monat* (approximately $60,000 per annum) were channelled through a variety of fronts. In 1958, earmarked funds were piggy-backed through the Miami District Fund. By 1960, the grant was diversified, this time coming via the Florence Foundation ($27,000), and the Hoblitzelle Foundation ($29,176), an improbable donor, given that its 'Purpose and Activities' were listed in the Directory of American Foundations as providing 'support to organizations within Texas, primarily in Dallas, with emphasis on aid for the handicapped'. This route was also used for supplying funds to *Tempo Presente*, which received $18,000 and $20,000 respectively from the same foundations in 1960. The total disbursements for Congress periodicals in 1961 was $560,000, rising to $880,000 in 1962. At the same time, Farfield's commitment to the Congress (in other words, the direct cost to the CIA in salaries, administration, rent, etc.) was running at approximately $1 million (or $6 million in 1999) per annum.

Despite Lasky's claim that this was no gravy train, it

certainly began to look like one. 'Suddenly there were limousines, parties with lashings of smoked salmon and so on, and people who couldn't normally afford the bus ticket to Newark were now flying first class to India for the summer,'[16] recalled Jason Epstein. 'In the heyday of all this activity the airlines were crowded with dons and writers carrying branded culture to every corner of the habitable globe,'[17] Malcolm Muggeridge later wrote. Even British intelligence was aghast at the scale on which its American counterpart was endowing the cultural Cold War. Remembering those 'Elysian days' in London 'when the first arrivals came among us, straight from their innocent nests in Princeton or Yale or Harvard, in Wall Street or Madison Avenue or Washington, D.C.', Muggeridge was amazed at 'How short a time the honeymoon period lasted! How soon our British setup was overtaken in personnel, zest and scale of operation, above all, in expendable cash! . . . The OSS–CIA network, with ramifications all over the world, came to outclass our once legendary Secret Service as a sleek Cadillac does an ancient hansom cab.'[18]

Travelling happily in that Cadillac was Nicolas Nabokov, busy doing what he did best: arranging the glamour. Nabokov's bewildering range of contacts and friendships were invaluable in gaining credibility and status for the Congress. His terms of endearment were testimony to his capacity for guaranteeing the affection and loyalty of these friends. Schlesinger was addressed as 'Arthuro', Isaiah Berlin as 'Carissimo', 'Dear Doctor' and 'Uncle', Natasha Spender as 'Sweetie Pie' and Stephen as 'Milyii Stiva', George Weidenfeld as 'Dear Little Königskind', Edward Weeks, editor of *Atlantic Monthly*, as 'Caro Ted', Edward d'Arms of the Rockefeller Foundation as 'Chat'.

Nabokov, though a mediocre composer himself, and certainly no intellectual, was one of the great impresarios of the post-war years, recognizing talent and encouraging creative genius. During the winter of 1953–4, he settled into a temporary residency as musical director of the American Academy in Rome. This meant he was well placed to organize the Congress's first major foray into the music scene since the Masterpieces festival of 1952. Indeed, in many ways, the festival which Nabokov now set about arranging was the official answer to Herbert Read's criticism of the retrospective nature of the Paris venture. 'Let our next exhibition be, then, not a complacent look at the past, but a confident look into the future,'[19] Read had urged. Now, after flying to New York to hold a press conference in February 1953, Nabokov took up the challenge. 'With that festival we shut the door of the past,' he said. 'We said, in effect, here are great works. They are no longer "modern" even though they originated in the twentieth century. They are now a part of history. Now, I have a new plan . . . we are going to have a composers' contest that is unlike any other competition ever held. Twelve young and promising but internationally unknown composers are to be invited to Rome, all expenses paid. Each will bring a score and these will be performed . . . Finally, a special jury, democratically elected by all those attending the conference, will pick out of these twelve a winning work. And the award itself is staggering: first, there will be a cash prize; second, there will be a promise of performance by three major orchestras in Europe and three in America; third, the work will be published, and fourth, it will be recorded by a leading company. Not only that – even the eleven losers can't really lose,' Nabokov went on, sounding more and more like a Chicago booster. 'They will get, in addition to a free trip to Rome, a guarantee by the conference that their works will also be published and the copying of the parts paid for. Now,' he asked, 'is that a prize or isn't it?'[20]

The International Conference of Twentieth Century Music, scheduled to take place in Rome for two weeks in mid-April 1954, announced the Congress's commitment to the promotion of avant-garde composition. It was to place the Congress firmly on the map as part of the vanguard in musical experiment. And it offered the world a rich sample of the kind of music expressly forbidden by Stalin.

The Italian government was meant to deposit 2.5 million lire into Nabokov's American Express account in Rome by way of a subsidy for this event, but the money never arrived (confirming Nabokov's fear that it would end up 'getting lost somewhere in the ruins of the Forum'). No matter, there was money enough pouring in from the Farfield Foundation, a portion of which was used to endow the competition with prizes totalling 25,000 Swiss francs ($6,000) for the best concerto for violin and orchestra, short symphony, and chamber music for solo voice and instruments. The press release announced that the festival, 'designed to prove that art thrives on freedom', was the beneficiary of a generous donation from 'U.S. gin and yeast heir Julius Fleischmann'. Junkie was also brought in once again to negotiate with the Boston Symphony Orchestra, which agreed to give the winning composition its first American performance at its subsidiary, Tanglewood (by 1953, eight of the eleven members of the international music advisory board of the Congress were associated with the Tanglewood music school).

As was his custom, Nabokov sent the first invitation to his old friend, Igor Stravinsky, offering to pay expenses up to $5,000 for the maestro and his wife, plus their secretary, to attend the festival in Rome. In addition, Stravinsky agreed to head up the music advisory board for the festival, alongside Samuel Barber, Boris Blacher, Benjamin Britten, Carlos Chavez, Luigi Dallapiccola, Arthur Honegger, Francesco Malipiero, Frank Martin, Darius Milhaud and Virgil Thomson (who, according to Nabokov, 'knew all the boys and girls at the Rockefeller Foundation'). Charles Munch had proposed that Arturo Toscanini be invited to join the board, but Nabokov objected on the grounds that 'The name of Toscanini connected with a project concerning contemporary music sounds, to say the least, anachronistic. The good Maestro . . . has been a consistent and determined enemy of contemporary music, and has at many occasions attacked its main protagonists.'[21]

In early 1954, the Congress set up a festival office in the noble surroundings of the Palazzo Pecci, courtesy of Count Pecci-Blunt, a close friend of Nabokov's, and, despite his sumptuous title, an American citizen. Treasurer Pierre Bolomey organized a credit line with the Congress's Chase National Bank account at Basle, through which CIA money was funnelled. Pecci-Blunt made a personal contribution of $1,300 to the festival's slush fund. A further $10,000 was channelled through Denis de Rougemont's Centre Européen de la Culture, which in turn was receiving money from the Farfield Foundation. De Rougemont's outfit was given top billing on the programme. Arrangements were also secured for the travel of Leontyne Price, and round trip tickets were despatched to Aaron Copland, Michael Tippett, Joseph Fuchs and Ben Weber.

By March 1954, Nabokov was ready to announce the line-up for the festival. With a heavy concentration on atonal, dodecaphonic composition, the aesthetic direction of the event pointed very much to the progressive avant-garde of Alban Berg, Elliott Carter, Luigi Dallapiccola and Luigi Nono. Amongst the 'new' composers were Peter Racine Fricker, Lou Harrison and Mario Peragallo, whose work was influenced in varying degrees by twelve-tone composition. They were, on on the whole, well received. *Musical America* noted that 'most of the composers and critics making up the advisory and executive committees responsible for the concerts . . . have not been known in the past for the friendliness to dodecaphonic principles or proponents. For this reason, the programs they offered were not only surprising, but encouraging as well.'[22] A recent convert to twelve-tone music was Stravinsky, whose presence in Rome signalled a major moment in the convergence of modernist tributaries in the 'serialist orthodoxy'. For Nabokov, there was a clear political message to be imparted by promoting music which announced itself as doing away with natural hierarchies, as a liberation from previous laws about music's inner logic. Later, critics would wonder whether serialism had broken its emancipatory promise, driving music into a modernist cul-de-sac where it sat, restricted and difficult, tyrannized by despotic formulae, and commanding an increasingly specialized audience. Towards its 'squawks and thumps', wrote Susan Sontag, 'we were deferential – we knew we were supposed to appreciate ugly music; we listened devoutly to the Toch, the Krenek, the Hindemith, the Webern, the Schoenberg, whatever (we had enormous appetites and strong stomachs).'[23] Even the most deferential amongst those attending the Congress festival in Rome broke into whistles and shouts when one performance turned into a 'private soliloquy'. And when Hans Werner Henze's twelve-tone opera *Boulevard Solitude* was premiered, the audience could be forgiven for feeling as if it were travelling along a via Dolorosa.

Perhaps sensing a challenge to his own brand of difficulty, Pierre Boulez wrote Nabokov a furious letter larded with insults. Nabokov, he said, was encouraging a 'folklore of mediocrity', nurtured by petty bureaucrats who were obsessed with the number twelve – 'A Council of Twelve, a Committee of Twelve, a Jury of Twelve' – but who understood nothing of the creative process. Boulez went on to accuse the Congress of manipulating young composers by offering large prizes (the winners were Lou Harrison, Giselher Klebe, Jean-Louis Martinet, Mario Peragallo, and Vladimir Vogel). It would be more honest, he said, to give them hand-outs, rather than go through with the charade of the 'spectacular public gestures of a Cincinnati banker'. He ended with the suggestion that the Congress's next venture be a conference on 'the role of the condom in the Twentieth Century', a subject he deemed to be 'in better taste' than its previous initiatives.[24] A stunned Nabokov wrote in response that he hoped Boulez's letter would not be found in a bottom drawer by somebody in the future, as it 'dishonoured both his intelligence and his judgement'. Having neither the time nor the energy to pursue the matter, Nabokov asked Boulez to refrain from ever writing to him again.

As well as subsidizing those composers and performers who attended the Rome festival, the Farfield Foundation was endowing other groups and artists through a series of grants made mostly at Josselson's discretion. In January, it gave $2,000 to the Mozarteum Akademie Orchester of Salzburg, for an International Youth Orchestra Course. From his 'special discretionary fund' at the Farfield, Josselson rewarded the exiled Polish composer Andrzej Panufnik, who had made a hair-raising escape from Warsaw via Zurich to London, with an obligation-free 'yearly fellowship of $2,000 to be paid in 12 monthly instalments', starting in September 1954. According to Nabokov, the grateful Panufnik declared himself 'entirely ready to cooperate and collaborate with us for he is entirely sold on the ideals of the Congress for Cultural Freedom'.[25]

Also in September 1954, Josselson initiated a monthly grant of $300 to Yehudi Menuhin's *maître*, the exiled Romanian musician Georges Enesco. A year after Enesco's death in 1955, the Farfield paid for a memorial concert given by the Boston Symphony Orchestra, which was again touring Europe largely at the CIA's expense (via the Free Europe Committee).[26]

Referring to the orchestra's triumphant 1956 tour, C. D. Jackson was moved to declare: '"Culture" is no longer a sissy word. A nation like ours can be virile. A nation like ours can be fantastically successful economically. But in a strange way the glue that holds things together is the nation's coefficient of idealism . . . The tangible, visible and audible expression of national idealism is culture. Of all the expressions of culture, music is the most universal. Of all the expressions of present-day musical culture, the Boston Symphony Orchestra is the best.'[27]

The year 1956 also saw the launch of the Metropolitan Opera in Europe. Once again, C. D. was there to lend his every support, arguing that 'The United States engages in many activities designed to project the correct image of the U.S. abroad. Sometimes we are successful, sometimes not. It is admittedly a nebulous and imprecise business. But the one area which is as close to sure-fire as any that have been tried, is the cultural projection of America – provided, of course, that the selection of what constitutes American culture is intelligently made and that nothing is sent over except highest quality. I believe that the Met would wow them.'[28] The Psychological Strategy Board, which in 1953 had invited Junkie Fleischmann to negotiate the tour, agreed with Jackson, and pulled together a massive $750,000 to finance it. Most of this appears to have come from the CIA. Although C. D. acknowledged that this was 'an awful lot of money for a cultural propaganda impact', he urged Allen Dulles not to underestimate the potential gains, adding that 'this impact would be absolutely terrific in the capitals of Western Europe, including Berlin'.[29] Junkie agreed, and produced his own exquisitely opportunistic rationale for the tour: 'We, in the United States, are a melting pot,' he said, 'and, by being so, have demonstrated that peoples can get along together irrespective of race, color or creed. Using the "melting pot" or some such catch phrase for a theme we might be able to use the Met as an example of how Europeans can get along together in the United States and that, therefore, some sort of European Federation is entirely practicable.'[30] Thus did America's Cold Warriors weave their tangled web, wherein the Metropolitan Opera could be used to rally audiences to the concept of free world federalism.

At the same time as C. D. was working on the Psychological Strategy Board's idea of a Metropolitan Opera tour, he was dealing with another, more controversial aspect of the company's plans. In March 1953, he had learned that Rudolf Bing, the Met's general manager, wanted to engage Wilhelm Furtwängler as guest conductor for the 1953–4 season. Asked whether he thought the State Department might object to this appointment, C. D. was able to report that there would be no 'Departmental eyebrow-raising on the subject of Mr Furtwaengler'. He did warn that there may be 'a public relations problem' from the Met's standpoint, but concluded with the following words of encouragement: 'My five cents' worth is that by the time he will be getting over here, no one would care if he had been the Beast of Belsen.'[31]

Though they were to express it more delicately, the American Committee for Cultural Freedom apparently felt much the same way. When, in February 1955, the Jewish group Betar protested against the appearance of Herbert von Karajan at a New York performance given by the Berlin Philharmonic – 'Music Lovers, do not attend tonight's bloody concert!' – the Committee lobbied the American Federation of Musicians to oppose such protests. In a cable signed by James T. Farrell, on behalf of 'three hundred leaders of the American cultural community', the Committee denounced Betar's protest as 'an encroachment on cultural freedom'. Interestingly, at no point did the Committee take issue with Betar's allegation that von Karajan had been a member of the Nazi party. On the contrary, it conceded this was a 'deplorable' fact. But the charge was not 'relevant to the non-political nature of the orchestra's appearance here', and ignored the fact that the Berlin Philharmonic 'has rendered signal service to the cause of free culture in Europe and symbolizes the courageous resistance of the people of Berlin to Communist totalitarianism, which surrounds their isolated outpost'.[32] The cable concluded with the suggestion that a portion of the profits from the orchestra's tour be donated to victims of the Nazis.

The American Committee was apparently unaware of how far it was straying from its 1953 'Statement of Principles', in which it declared itself to be 'vitally concerned with political issues as these affect the conditions of cultural freedom and cultural creativity. It is consequently intractably opposed to totalitarianism of whatever kind, for totalitarianism is the very negation of these conditions.'[33] This same statement had deplored 'the plain and shameful fact that, even today, Communists and Communist sympathizers are conceded a measure of respectability in intellectual and cultural circles which would never have been accorded to a Nazi or neo-fascist'.

That the American Committee could be so blind to the contradictory – and morally inconsistent – nature of its attitude to individuals like von Karajan or Furtwängler seems astonishing. Three months later, George Kennan, one of the architects of the strategy of harnessing culture to the political imperatives of the Cold War, was to demonstrate that he too was vulnerable to the same confusion. Addressing the International Council of the Museum of Modern Art on 12 May 1955, Kennan deplored the fact that, 'In recent years, there has grown up among us a most reprehensible habit, a totalitarian habit in fact, of judging the suitability of cultural contributions by whatever political coloration we conceive their creators to have acquired. I know of nothing sillier than this. A painting is not more or less valuable because the artist once belonged to this or that party or contributed to this or that group. The value of a symphony concert seems to me to be quite unaffected by the nature of the political regime under which the conductor may once have plied his trade . . . After all, cultural events are not political livestock exhibits in which we put forward human figures to be admired for the purity of their ideological features.'[34]

America's cultural Cold Warriors found themselves caught in a dangerous paradox: where the bogeyman of Nazism was raised, they campaigned vigorously for the separation of art and politics; but where dealing with Communism, they were unwilling to make such a distinction. This egregious illogicality had first surfaced back in the late 1940s, during the 'denazification' of Germany. Then, whilst Furtwängler had been rewarded with high-profile concerts alongside Yehudi Menuhin, Bertolt Brecht was ridiculed by Melvin Lasky in *Der Monat*.[35] The whole premise of the cultural Cold War, of the Congress for Cultural Freedom, was that writers and artists had to *engage* themselves in the ideological struggle. 'You're talking about the leading writers, the leading musicians, and painters – whoever was willing to associate with the idea of fighting for what Camus called literature "engagé", someone who was committed not just to writing but to writing as an expression of a system of values. And we were for that, we were for that, and we supported it,'[36] explained the CIA's Lee Williams. That America's cultural Cold Warriors could so easily 'disengage' when it suited them to do so is disturbing.

No such tolerance was accorded to the fellow travellers and neutralists whom the American Committee was bent on exposing. Nobody could seriously argue, at least by the mid-1950s, that Communism could plausibly be considered the central and overriding enemy of cultural freedom within the United States. But professional anti-Communists, like all professionals, wanted to protect and even expand their market. A rough count of organized anti-Communist lobbies and pressure groups in America during the 1950s – a time generally acknowledged to mark the Fifth Column's lowest point – suggests unparalleled proliferation. There being no real Communist threat in America to fight, anti-Communists were in reality, to recycle Churchill's phrase, 'chained to a dead body'.

'Slowly and gradually one's colleagues will get around to one,' James T. Farrell had accurately predicted in 1942. 'I trust my colleagues to do this. I have great confidence in their developing capacities to become my policemen, and the guardian of my soul. My faith in their potentialities to be shameful is invincible: you cannot shake that dogma of my faith. All these little guardian angels of the soul of America.'[37] By now, the hardline element of the Committee had earned it a dubious reputation as a 'truth squad'. It appeared to have lost all sense of proportion, and wandered far from its declared purpose, which was to strengthen the social and political conditions for cultural creativity and free intellectual enquiry. Schlesinger wrote of a feeling of disgust at the 'elements of vindictiveness in the harrying of fellow travelers, as if we were refighting in the fifties the old, dead battles of the thirties and the forties . . . we now have better things to do than to pay off old scores. A committee dedicated to cultural freedom can hardly err in being

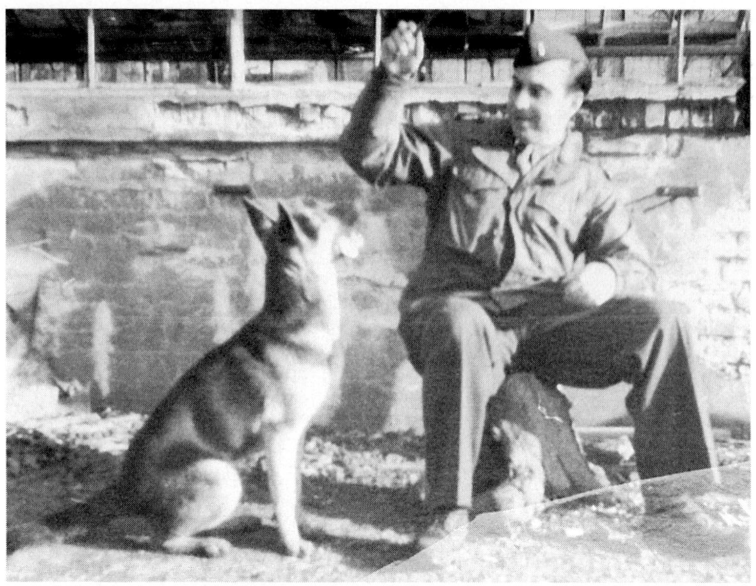

First Lieutenant Michael Josselson, Berlin, 1948. A Cultural Affairs Officer for the American Military Government, he would shortly be recruited to the CIA.

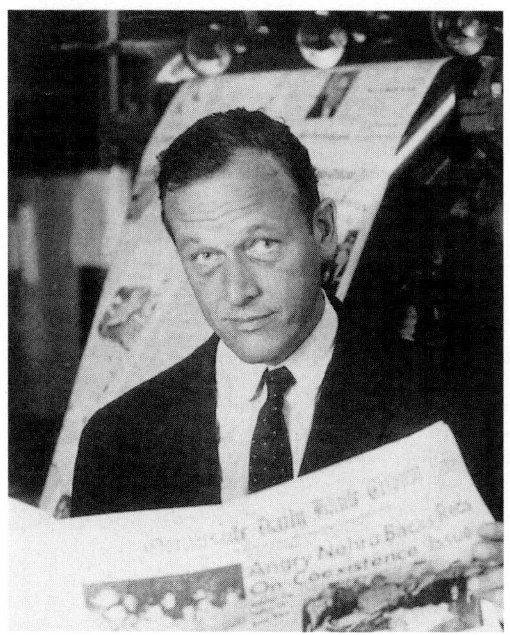

Tom Braden, the CIA agent who put together the International Organizations Division, the nerve centre of America's secret cultural Cold War. Braden's division ran dozens of 'fronts', including the Congress for Cultural Freedom.

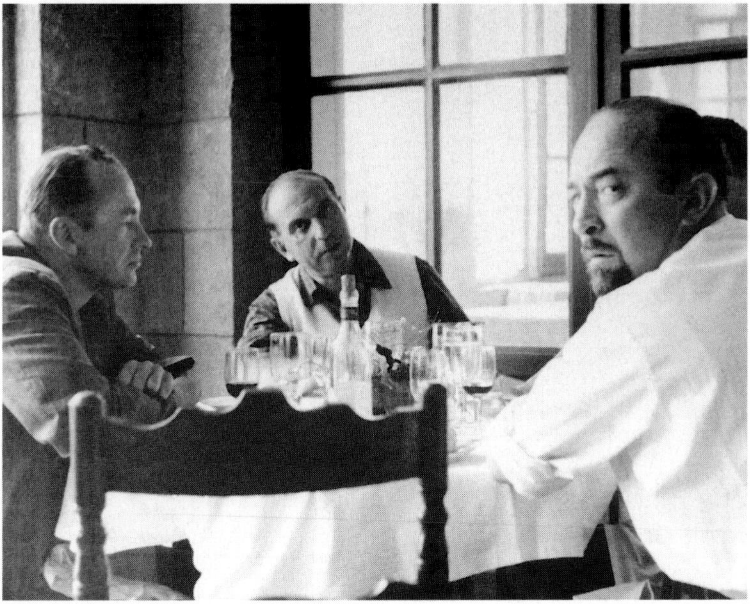

The 'apparat' at a working lunch. John Hunt, Michael Josselson and Melvin Lasky.

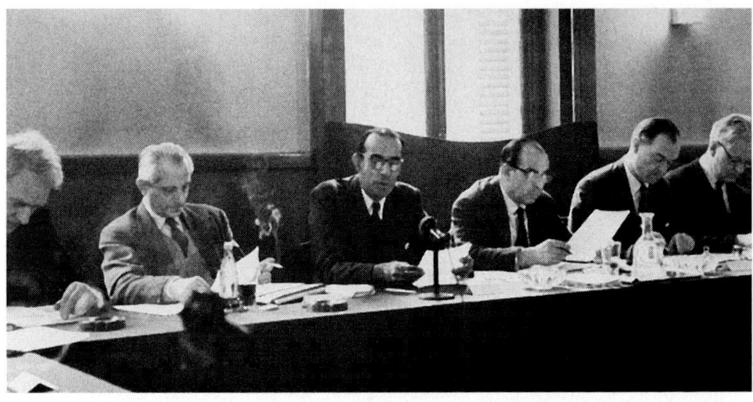

Stephen Spender, Manès Sperber, Minoo Masani, Michael Josselson, Denis de Rougemont, Nicolas Nabokov at the meeting of the Executive Committee of the Congress for Cultural Freedom, January 1957.

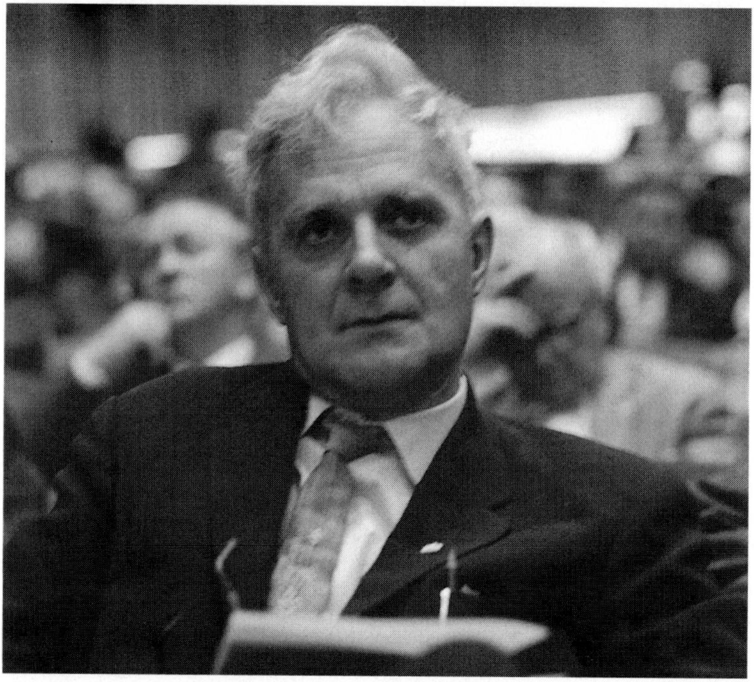

Stephen Spender, chosen by the CIA and MI6 to co-edit *Encounter* magazine. 'Stephen had all the right credentials to be chosen as a front,' said Natasha Spender. 'He was eminently bamboozable, because he was so innocent.'

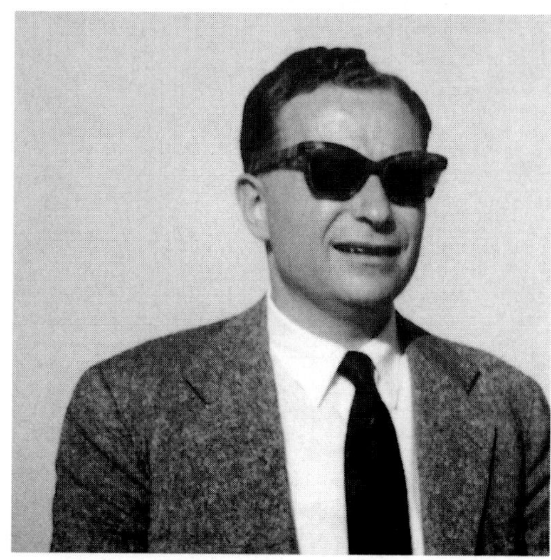

Irving Kristol, co-editor of *Encounter* from 1953 to 1958.

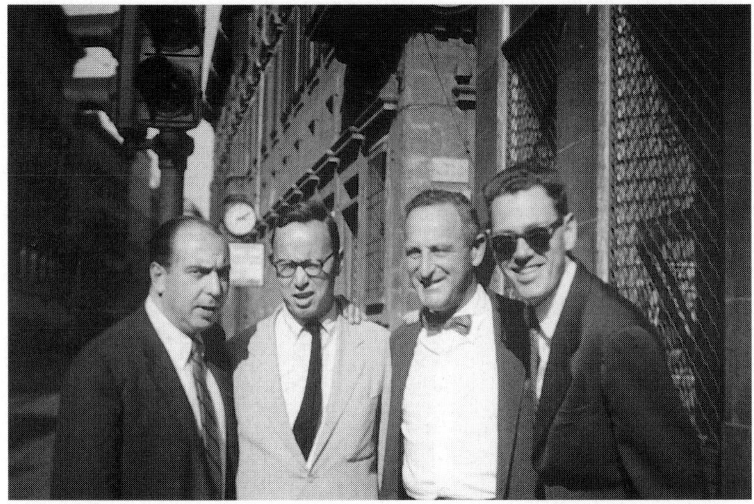

Michael Josselson, Arthur Schlesinger Jr, Julius Fleischmann, and the sociologist Peter Dodge in Milan, September 1955, to discuss 'The Future of Freedom'.

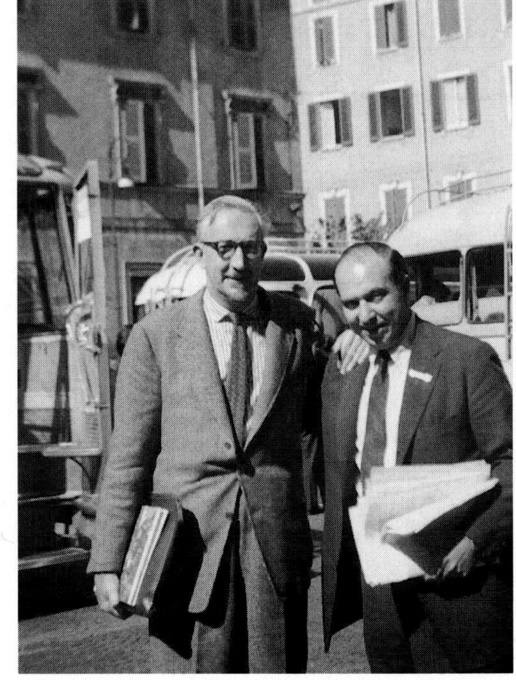

Dwight Macdonald with Michael Josselson, Milan, September 1955, during 'The Future of Freedom' conference. The debates, said one observer, were 'deadly boring', but there were heated exchanges behind the scenes over the proposal to put Dwight Macdonald in the editorial chair at *Encounter*.

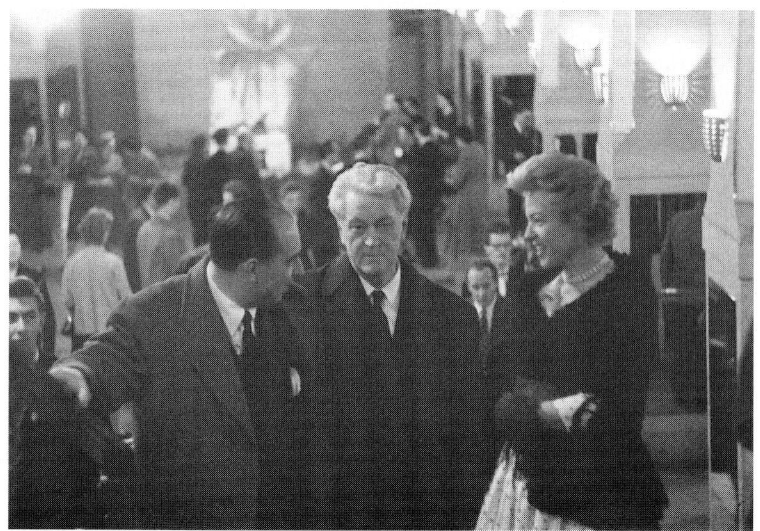

Nicolas Nabokov, composer and impresario, the 'front man' for the Congress for Cultural Freedom. Nabokov is flanked by his wife, Marie-Claire, and Michael Josselson. Vienna Opera House, 1957.

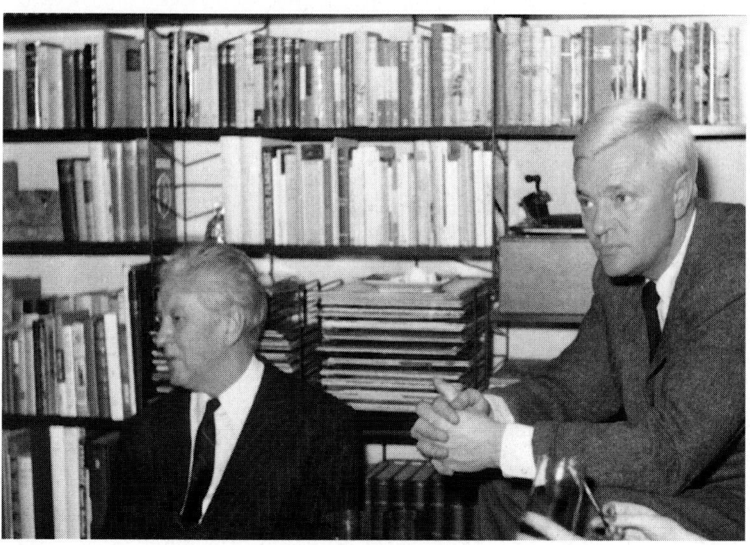

Nicolas Nabokov and the actor Peter van Eyck in the Josselsons' apartment, Paris, March 1958, to celebrate Michael Josselson's birthday. Van Eyck and Josselson had shared a billet in post-war Berlin.

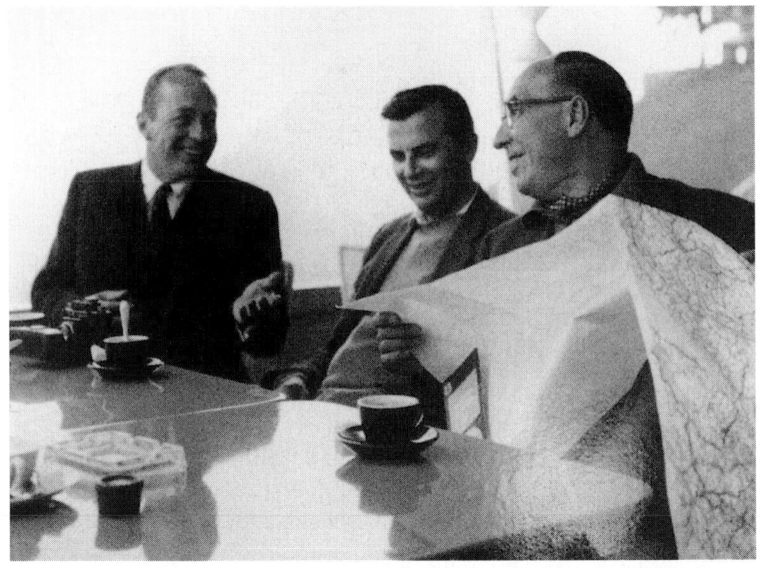

John Hunt, Robie Macauley and Michael Josselson mapping things out in the hills above Geneva.

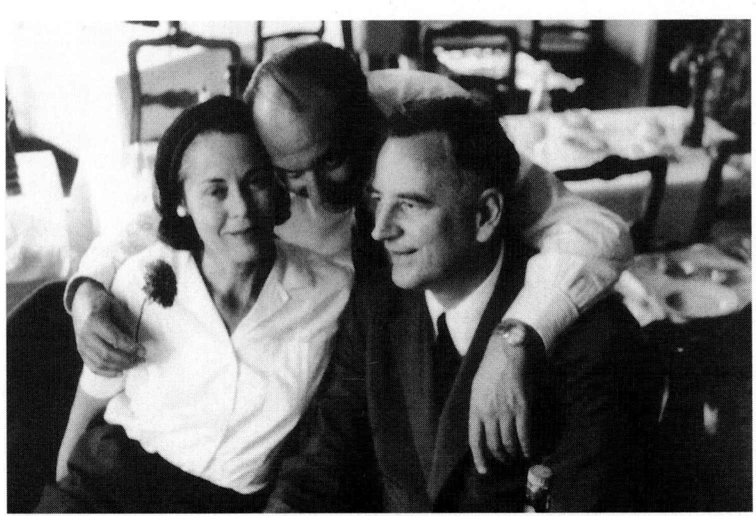

Michael Josselson embraces his friend and colleague, Lawrence de Neufville, and de Neufville's wife, Adeline. De Neufville had recruited Josselson to the CIA in 1948, and together they set up the Paris-based Congress for Cultural Freedom as a permanent body in 1950. De Neufville returned to the US in 1954, leaving Josselson to cope with a series of disappointing successors.

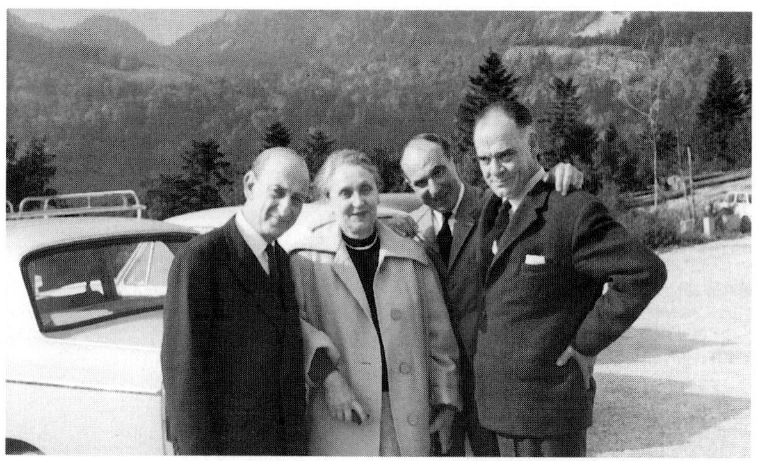

Raymond Aron and his wife Susanne, Michael Josselson, and Denis de Rougemont, enjoying a day out in the Swiss mountains. Aron felt deeply compromised by the exposure of the Congress as a CIA front, though it is alleged he had been in on the secret for years.

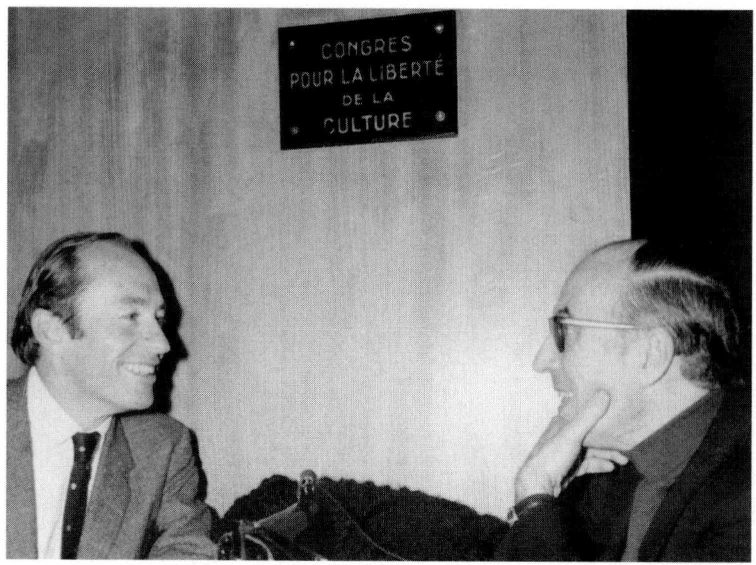

John Hunt and Michael Josselson, sitting beneath the brass wall plate of the Congress. The plate had been stolen from outside the Paris office some years previously, and, to their amazement, had been spotted on the wall of a Geneva restaurant, where Diana Josselson took this photograph in 1969.

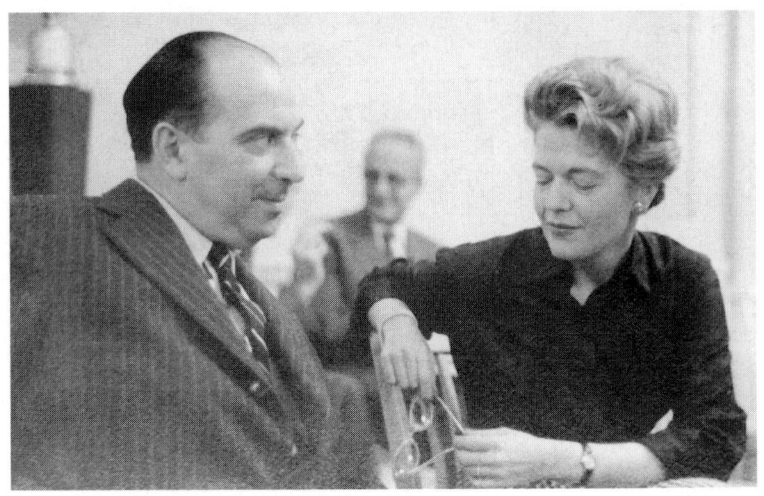

A most effective partnership: Michael Josselson, code-name 'Jonathan F. Saba', and his wife Diana, code-name 'Jean Ensinger'.

magnanimous.'[38] From Cornell University, a colleague of Sol Stein wrote in similar vein: 'Sol, my boy, what you need is a whiff of the fresh air of upstate New York or Kansas or Seattle or just about any other place but the middle of Manhattan. Are you really so sure that all those bitter literary battles of the late 1930s, and the battles of today as well, are really that important in the history of the United States?'[39]

And this was the point. American intellectual history had see-sawed over the past two decades from the left dissecting the right to the right dissecting the left, and the sight of men tearing at each other's viscera in this way was unedifying. Balkanized into squabbling academic fiefdoms, both factions missed the one important truth: absolutism in politics, whether in the form of McCarthyism, or liberal anti-Communism, or Stalinism, was not about left or right, it was about refusing to let history tell the truth. 'It's so corrupt, it doesn't even know it,' said Jason Epstein, in uncompromising mood. 'When these people talk about a "counter-intelligentsia", what they do is to set up a false and corrupt value system to support whatever ideology they're committed to at the time. The only thing they're really committed to is power, and the introduction of Tzarist-Stalinist strategies in American politics. They're so corrupt they probably don't even know it. They're little, lying apparatchiks. People who don't believe in anything, who are only *against* something, shouldn't go on crusades or start revolutions.'[40]

Commenting on the 'contrapuntal relationship with Communism' of many intellectual Cold Warriors, George Urban, a director of Radio Free Europe, concluded that this responded to a 'compulsion to argue, fence, and fight, almost regardless of the objectives[41] . . . Their protestations were too intense, their cynicism too stark, and their analyses too reflective of the world they thought they had left behind. They marched in negative step, but in step all the same.'[42]

Josselson, who at this time was recovering from an operation which left him stranded – though clearly not inactive – in a deckchair, wrote to Sidney Hook that he was 'more convinced than ever that a natural death of the present [American Committee] would be the best thing to happen for everyone concerned . . . this group is incompatible [sic] to do anything in any field except in the field of petty quarrels.'[43] One way of ensuring the Committee's demise was to withdraw its subsidies, and in October 1954 Josselson did just that. The monthly deposits from the Farfield Foundation to the American Committee had already been stopped in early 1953, and now, with the withdrawal of an annual payment of $4,800 from the Paris office, the group faced imminent financial ruin.

Sidney Hook, who had set the Committee up in consultation with the CIA, was appalled at the Congress's decision to cut its financial ties. Ignoring Josselson's determination to see the Committee extinguish itself, he went directly to Allen Dulles to plead for more money. Sol Stein (who warned that 'if American intellectuals lose their voice in West Europe for want of $20,000 a year, then some new Gibbon better start sharpening his pencil now') was fully briefed on this development, as was Norman Thomas, the former socialist candidate for US president, who now occupied an executive position in the American Committee. Furthermore, both men were separately lobbying the intelligence community through 'our friend Dr. Lilly', a Psychological Strategy Board officer and CIA consultant. Knowing that Norman Thomas was a close friend and neighbour of Allen Dulles, Stein further suggested that Thomas telephone Dulles, to 'remind [him] of his interest in our work and suggest that speed is essential in coming to our assistance'.[44] Thomas replied that he thought it 'would do harm rather than good to call Allen Dulles without some more immediate excuse', but said that 'on the fair chance that Dulles may be up in the country this weekend, I will try to get in touch with him on Sunday'.[45] This was April 1955. By May, the Committee's coffers were swollen with a grant of $4,000 from the CIA's Asia Foundation and $10,000 from the Farfield Foundation. Josselson had been overruled.

Arthur Schlesinger now wrote plaintively to Cord Meyer to extend his complaints about 'certain members' of the Executive Committee, who, bolstered by the CIA's renewed largesse, were once again experiencing an inflation of their own importance. Meyer explained by return that 'We certainly don't plan on any continuing large scale assistance, and the single grant recently made was provided as the result of an urgent request directly from Sidney Hook and indirectly from Norman Thomas. Our hope is that the breathing space provided by this assistance can be used by those gentlemen, yourself, and the other sensible ones to reconstitute the Executive Committee and draft an intelligent program . . . If this reconstitution of the leadership proves impossible we then, I think, will have to face the necessity of allowing the Committee to die a natural death, although I think this course would result in unhappy repercussions abroad.' Meyer ended the letter thanking Schlesinger for 'sitting on top of the loose talk', suggesting that they meet together soon to 'discuss the whole problem in some detail'.[46]

The Dulles–Meyer strategy proved completely fallible, as Josselson had always feared. The injection of extra dollars simply served to defer the moment of final conflict between the gun-slingers in New York and the sophisticates of the Paris operation. Within less than a year, the mutual distrust and acrimony, which had first surfaced after Nabokov's 1952 Paris festival, broke into the open. On 26 March 1956, the *Manchester Guardian* published a letter from Bertrand Russell which referred to 'atrocities committed by the FBI' during the Rosenberg trial, and compared America with 'other police states such as Nazi Germany and Stalin's Russia'. Josselson reacted immediately, suggesting to Irving Kristol that he find an 'intelligent American correspondent in London' to interview Russell in such a way as to 'show that Russell has not seen any new evidence in the Rosenberg case and that his statement was based on some Communist propaganda which in his senility he can no longer distinguish from truth'.[47]

But whilst Josselson was preparing to undermine Russell's claims through a carefully angled interview, the American Committee decided to wade in feet first. A letter of protest was sent directly to Russell, accusing him of an 'extraordinary lapse from standards of objectivity and justice' and doing 'a major service to the enemies we had supposed you engaged to combat'. Had it occurred to Russell to consider 'the propriety of any friend of cultural freedom, and in particular an officer of the Congress for Cultural Freedom . . . in making false and irresponsible statements about the process of justice in the United States'?[48] Not surprisingly, Russell's response to the letter was to resign as Honorary Chairman of the Congress.

Josselson was furious, not least because the letter to Russell was 'transmitted to us in the most peremptory fashion'. It was unthinkable that such a communication could have been sent by any other affiliate of the Congress without Josselson's prior approval. After calling an emergency quorum of the Executive Committee in Paris, Josselson forwarded its official censure of the American outfit for its failure to 'consult with us when taking actions, within the body of the Congress, which can have serious international consequences'.[49] It was too late to retrieve Russell, whose fourth resignation from the Congress really was his last. In June 1956, his name was removed from the letterhead of all Congress stationery.

The trouble did not end there. Two months later, the resignation of James T. Farrell as National Chairman of the American Committee was splattered across the headlines. Farrell was a complex man. Whilst an avowed anti-Communist, he could not abide the posturing of so many New York intellectuals whose 'Park Avenue avant-gardism' was simply an excuse not to get down to better work. He himself had renounced politics once before, writing to Meyer Schapiro in 1941, 'I've decided that there is not much I can do in the world today, and there are enough people posing as statesmen. So, I am going to work hard at my own work.'[50] But then the temptations of a crusade against Communism had proved hard to resist, and he too had taken up the charge. In the end, he was defeated not by Communism, but by the petty vigilantism of his fellow crusaders. 'Monomania,' George Orwell had once warned, 'and the fear of uttering heresies are not friendly to the creative faculties.' Farrell's letter of resignation reeked of Cold War fatigue. 'We have never been able to sink our roots deeply into American life,' he complained. 'We have not been able to contribute sufficiently to the fight against censorship in this country . . . the time has come for all who believe in the liberal spirit to make a new effort towards achieving its resurgence . . . We are constantly standing on the edge of becoming a political Committee with views on foreign policy and many other issues. In doing that, we are in danger of mixing politics and culture.' He also stressed his personal reason for resigning, which was a thinly veiled warning to other writers on the American Committee: 'If I want to write better, I must give more time to it and to study.'[51]

This might have been the end of it, but for the fact Farrell chose to announce his resignation first to the *New York Times*. He called the paper late on Monday night, 27 August 1956, apparently much disinhibited by drink. He cavilled at the American Committee's failure to cohere as a mass organization, its failure to do anything about censorship in the United States, its lack of concern with American civil liberties, and its weaselling on the McCarthy issue. Diana Trilling was elected by the board of directors to accept Farrell's resignation, which she did in a letter ringing with icy contempt.

In Paris, the news of Farrell's resignation was met with incredulous rage by Michael Josselson, who wrote angrily: 'We fail to understand why the Committee did not use the 24 hour period of grace between the time when Mrs Trilling received the call and the time that the story actually went to press to have Jim Farrell withdraw his original statement and have it replaced by a statement of his resignation which would have been agreeable to everyone concerned.'[52]

Enough was enough. When Irving Brown received a letter asking him to backpay three years of membership dues to the American Committee, he simply ignored it. Junkie Fleischmann withdrew from its board in October 1956, saying he was far too busy with the Paris operation. On 31 January 1957, Sidney Hook wrote to Nabokov that the American Committee had 'reluctantly decided to suspend its active organizational life' because of financial straits.

15

Ransom's Boys

> It's my contention that the CIA not only engaged in a cultural cold war in the abstract and purely pragmatic way, but that they had very definite aims in view, and they had a very definite aesthetic: they stood for High Culture.
>
> Richard Elman

In September 1954, Cord Meyer took over the International Organizations Division from Tom Braden, who 'retired'[1] from the CIA and moved to California to edit a newspaper purchased for him by Nelson Rockefeller. Meyer inherited a division which constituted the greatest single concentration of covert political and propaganda activities of the by now octopus-like CIA.[2] Furthermore, he did so in an atmosphere increasingly favourable to covert activity, as a top-secret report submitted to President Eisenhower in the same month shows: 'As long as it remains national policy, another important requirement is an aggressive covert psychological, political and paramilitary organization more effective, more unique, and if necessary, more ruthless than that employed by the enemy. No one should be permitted to stand in the way of the prompt, efficient, and secure accomplishment of this mission. It is now clear that we are facing an implacable enemy whose avowed objective is world domination by whatever means and at whatever cost. There are no rules in such a game. Hitherto acceptable norms of human conduct do not apply. If the U.S. is to survive, longstanding American concepts of "fair play" must be reconsidered . . . It may become necessary that the American people be made acquainted with, understand and support this fundamentally repugnant philosophy.'[3]

Yet the importance of the International Organizations Division was not always reflected in the calibre of the staffers assigned to it. Tom Braden had struggled to inspire his own assistant, only to be met with total indifference. 'His name was Lieutenant Colonel Buffington. He left memos everywhere, but he didn't do jack-shit,' said Braden. 'He was a total waste of time, he did nothing all day. He would come in at nine, hang up his hat, read the *New York Times*, then go home again.'[4] In a jokey attempt to trace the genealogy of case officers arriving in Paris, Josselson and his intimates referred to them as George I, George II, George III, and so on. George IV was Lee Williams, also jokingly known as 'Nickel and Dime' (a play on his codename) and, fleetingly, as 'Mr Rochester'. Williams made a better impression than most of his predecessors, valiantly straddling the two cultures of an increasingly bureaucratized CIA and the Congress, which was almost bohemian in contrast. 'I remember driving along in Paris with Cord [Meyer] once after a meeting with Mike, and Cord turned to me and said, "You know, Lee, Mike really *likes* you",' Williams remembered. 'Son of a bitch! It's like he was surprised. But Mike liked me because I never tried to teach him his job – I sat at his feet, I was deferential to him.'[5] But Josselson's real ally was Lawrence de Neufville, and he, after ten years in Europe, wanted to go home. Assigned new cover in the New York office of Radio Free Europe, he left Paris in late 1953.

De Neufville was never going to be an easy act to follow, and after him, Josselson came increasingly to think of the Congress case officers as 'messenger boys'. 'At the beginning the CIA were good, interesting people like Lawrence de Neufville, whose hearts were in the right places,' said Diana Josselson. 'But then they became less and less impressive, and Michael came to like them less. Every now and then a case officer would appear and I could see Michael trying to disengage, but they would cling on. Michael would never have asked anything substantive of them. He was friends with them, talked about their families and careers, and I had the idea that they admired him, but Michael was determined to protect the Congress from the Agency, and from the possibility the relationship might be revealed.'[6] According to Diana, the relationship between Michael and his Agency colleagues became increasingly a charade: 'Since they wanted to pretend they were in control, Michael probably welcomed the opportunity to inform them of developments, to help the illusion along.' Diana, who dutifully served case officers with the obligatory martini cocktails when they came to the Josselsons' apartment, later dismissed them as 'a necessary evil. They weren't half as important to me as my maid.'[7]

One of the problems for Cord Meyer was that it was difficult to attract Agency staffers to his division. Not that there was any shortage of suitable candidates. By the mid-1960s, it was the Agency's boast that it could staff any college from its analysts, 50 per cent of whom held advanced degrees, 30 per cent doctorates, prompting one State Department official to say 'there are more liberal intellectuals per square inch at CIA than anywhere else in government'. But these collegiate types had not joined the Agency to do what they could do on campus. They were seeking adventure, not a job looking after the kind of people they could meet at high table. 'The people in the International Organizations Division were looked upon by a great many [Agency] people as some kind of fluff on the side, particularly by those who felt what we ought to be doing is hard intelligence and let's recruit the spies and get the documents and the rest of this is just a bunch of nonsense,'[8] said CIA officer Donald Jameson. 'Some people in CIA didn't think it was proper to be spending all this money on all these leftists,'[9] Lawrence de Neufville confirmed. So Cord Meyer began to look elsewhere.

'Cord brought unique intellectual cachet,' said Lee Williams. 'He had unique access to the intellectual community in America, and he had huge respect for literary men.'[10] Entering Yale in 1939, Meyer had studied English verse 'from the metaphysical poets of the Seventeenth Century to the modern poetry of Yeats and T. S. Eliot under Professor Maynard Mack, who left us a permanent respect for the graceful majesty of that achievement and an ambition in some of us to try to write as well'.[11] Meyer tried his hand at poetry, publishing some 'passable' verses in the *Yale Lit*, of which he subsequently became editor.

In 1942, Meyer graduated in English literature with a brilliant *summa cum laude*. His literary ambitions were thwarted by the war, in which his twin brother was killed, and Meyer himself lost an eye in Guam when a Japanese grenade exploded at his feet (subsequently earning him the CIA nickname 'Cyclops'). Thereafter, he penned a few articles and, in 1980, his memoirs, *Facing Reality*.

As editor of the *Yale Lit*, Meyer was following in the footsteps of James Jesus Angleton, who became the CIA's legendary chief of counter-intelligence. A literary radical, Angleton had introduced Ezra Pound to Yale, and founded the magazine of verse, *Furioso*, in 1939 (his name as editor appeared on the masthead even when he was chief of counter-espionage in Rome). Angleton was the vital link in what became known as 'the P source' ('P' standing for 'Professor'), which described the Agency's connection with the Ivy League. Prominent members of 'the P source' included William Sloane Coffin, a graduate of Yale who was recruited by Allen Dulles. Recalling his decision to join the Agency, Coffin later said: 'Stalin made Hitler look like a Boy Scout. I was very strongly anti-Soviet. In that frame of mind I watched the Korean War shape up. But I didn't follow it too closely, or question the causes. When I graduated from Yale in 1949, I was thinking of going into the CIA, but I went into the seminary instead. After a year at the Union Theological Seminary, when war with the Soviet Union seemed to be threatening, I quit to go into the CIA, hoping to be useful in the war effort. The CIA financed the non-Communist left; they gave with minimal strings attached. In those days, I had no quarrel with American policy – but, in retrospect, I wouldn't be so innocent and smirchless.'[12] Coffin's Ivy League recruits included Archie Roosevelt, who had read English at Harvard under the famous head of Wadham College, Maurice Bowra (who was on exchange from Oxford for a year), and Archie's cousin, Kermit 'Kim' Roosevelt, who was a few years ahead of him at Groton School and Harvard.

Another major Ivy League connection – and the epitome of 'the P source' – was Professor Norman Holmes Pearson, a revered humanist famous for editing the Viking five-volume

Poets of the English Language with W. H. Auden, and an officer of both the American Studies Association and the Modern Language Association, a trustee of the Bryher Foundation, and an executor of the poet H. D.'s estate. Pearson was also an OSS–CIA *incunabula*. He trained many of the most promising minds at Yale, including Angleton and Richard Ellmann, whom he recruited to OSS.[13] He himself worked with X-2, the counter-intelligence branch of OSS, working in London during the war under Kim Philby, who later described him as 'naïve'. Pearson supervised the wartime accumulation of files on a million enemy agents and organizations, a practice he 'strongly felt should be continued after the war, despite its offensiveness to traditional Jeffersonian notions of government. Such quaint objections . . . were quickly overcome, as the term "enemy" acquired a very liberal definition.'[14] Returning to Yale, he presided over 'the promotion of American studies at home and abroad. Like foreign-area studies, this new discipline was of clear imperial import, in that it allowed us to understand our unique fitness for our postwar role as the world's governor, and encouraged a finer appreciation of our cultural sophistication among the ruled.'[15] Consistent with this view was Pearson's preface to the Rinehart edition of Thoreau's *Walden*, where he minimized the radicalism of the great American individualist and sought to release him from any association with anarchy, stressing that his writings were in support of better government, 'a symbol of the individual freedom on which we like to think the American way of life is based'.

Pearson's most famous protégé was James Jesus Angleton. Born in Idaho in 1917, as a teenager Angleton was sent to Malvern College in Worcestershire, where he worked at becoming 'more English than the English. He absorbed Old World courtesy and the quiet good manners that never deserted him. Indeed, the years gave him a European persona (he also spent long holidays in Italy) that obscured his Yank background, and gave him a slight English accent.'[16] He was at Yale from 1937 to 1941, where he worked on the *Yale Lit* alongside McGeorge Bundy, the future National Security Adviser, Walter Sullivan, who later became science editor of the *New York Times*, and the poet E. Reed Whittemore Jr. In 1938, Angleton met Ezra Pound in Rapallo, and they became firm friends, Pound later describing him as 'one of the most important hopes of literary magazines in the U.S.' When Angleton wrote his will in 1949, he left 'a bottle of good spirits' to Ezra Pound, ee cummings and other poet friends from *Furioso*, and concluded with the following credo: 'I can say this now, that I do believe in the spirit of Christ and the life everlasting, and in this turbulent social system which struggles sometimes blindly to preserve the right to freedom and expression of the spirit. In the name of Jesus Christ I leave you.' Despite these sentiments, Reed Whittemore remembered that Angleton (whose mother was Mexican) was embarrassed by his middle name because 'it suggested he was not an upper-class Englishman, which was then the image he was trying to project'.[17]

An old hand at conspiracy from OSS, Angleton carried his talents to the CIA, where he developed a seemingly limitless capacity for Byzantine intrigue. He first major success was the orchestration of America's covert campaign to secure victory for the Christian Democrats in the 1948 Italian elections. This campaign, closely watched and supported by George Kennan and Allen Dulles, was America's first successful act of political Cold Warfare. According to Kim Philby, Angleton was promoted to chief of the CIA's Office of Special Operations in 1949. For twenty years he was in charge of the Agency's Counterintelligence Staff (CI), and responsible for all liaison with allied intelligence from 1954. He also ran a completely independent group of journalist-operatives who performed sensitive and frequently dangerous assignments. CIA contemporaries knew virtually nothing of this group, which worked under 'deep snow' cover, and whose secrets Angleton kept locked away in a safe in his office to which only he had access.

An accomplished grower of wild orchids (and the model for 'Mother' in Aaron Latham's *roman à clef*, *Orchids for Mother*), a world-class fly fisherman, a published photographer, a skilful worker in gemstones and leather, a fan of Italian opera, Paul Newman, Robert Redford, Marlon Brando, Peter Sellers, Shirley MacLaine, cricket matches and European soccer, Angleton was an extraordinary, eclectic figure. Clare Booth Luce once told him, 'There's no doubt you are easily the most interesting and fascinating figure the intelligence world has produced, and a living legend.'[18] Standing six feet tall, always dressed in dark clothes, Angleton, said one admirer, had 'the look of a Byron – very lean and starved about the jaws'. He was the very image of the poet-spy, the inspiration for many romantic myths about the CIA as an extension of the American liberal literary tradition.

Cord Meyer's own extensive network of 'P source' contacts now drew him to Kenyon College, where his favourite poets Allen Tate and John Crowe Ransom taught. It was here, in 1938, that Ransom had founded the *Kenyon Review*, a magazine which shaped the literary sensibility of a generation, its prestige securing a high place on the cultural Dow-Jones for the lazy backwater town of Kenyon. Here, also in 1938, a pool of talent had been residing at Douglass House, a 'carpenter-Gothic' building in the centre of campus, earmarked as the ideal 'isolation block' for John Crowe Ransom's studious, eccentric poet protégés. Known as 'Ransom's Boys', this group included Robie Macauley, Randall Jarrell, John Thompson, David Macdowell, Peter Taylor, and the more senior Robert Lowell, a faculty member.[19]

As a student at Olivet College, Michigan, in 1937 Robie Macauley had listened to lectures by Katherine Anne Porter and Allen Tate, and observed Ford Madox Ford wandering around the campus 'like a pensioned veteran of forgotten wars' (Macauley later wrote the preface to the 1961 edition of Ford's *Parade's End*). During the war, Macauley served for four years with G-2, the US Army Counter-intelligence Corps, working as a special agent hunting down Nazis. He later fictionalized the experience in a collection of short stories, *The End of Pity*, which won him the *Furioso* Fiction Prize. After taking a post-graduate degree at the University of Iowa, he returned to Kenyon College to join John Crowe Ransom as an assistant on the *Kenyon Review*. In August 1953, Ransom told a colleague that he had 'high hopes of making a Fellow out of Robie if he doesn't take a job with Central Intelligence, as I've heard he's going to'.[20] Cord Meyer had personally offered Macauley a job in the International Organizations Division. After considering the offer over the summer, Macauley accepted. 'Cord recruited him to be a case officer to work with Josselson because I guess he thought he could speak the right language,' said Lee Williams.[21]

Meyer scooped his second Ransom's boy when he recruited John 'Jack' Thompson, who in 1956 became Executive Director of the Farfield Foundation, a job he held, under contract to the CIA, for over a decade. After Kenyon, Thompson had authored a number of scholarly articles, and commanded quite a degree of influence amongst the New York literati. 'He got picked up by John Crowe Ransom and the Fugitive Group, then later by Lionel and Diana Trilling in New York, where Thompson was teaching English at Columbia University,' remembered his close friend Jason Epstein. 'The Trillings, who were fantastic snobs, were obsessed with Thompson and his wife. So Trilling suggested Jack as director of the Farfield Foundation, probably because he [Trilling] hoped to get money from it for the American Committee for Cultural Freedom.'[22] At the time, it all seemed like a good idea to Thompson. 'The KGB was spending millions,' he said, 'but we had our friends, too. We knew who was deserving, and who was not; we knew what the best stuff was, and we were trying to avoid the standard democratic crap of seeing that funds went to one Jew, one black, one woman, one Southerner. We wanted to reach our friends, and help them, the people who agreed with us, and were trying to do good things.'[23] Despite his long collaboration with the CIA, Thompson's entry in one edition of the Directory of American Professors, under 'Politics', reads 'radical'.

As well as Thompson and Macauley, one other member of the Douglass House group would also be played as an 'asset' by Cord Meyer, but to disastrous, if darkly comic, effect. To Ransom he was 'more than a student, he's more like a son to me'. His name was Robert Lowell.

From the less prestigious classrooms of a small experimental boys' school in St Louis, Missouri, Cord Meyer now added the young novelist John Hunt to his list of new recruits. Born in Muskogee, Oklahoma, in 1925, Hunt had attended Lawrenceville School in New Jersey, before leaving to enlist in the Marine Corps in 1943. Discharged in 1946 with the rank of Second Lieutenant, he entered Harvard on a scholarship in the same year. There, he was editor of *Student Progressive*, the publication of the Harvard Liberal Union. Graduating in

1948 with a major in English Literature and a minor in Greek, Hunt married that autumn and moved to Paris, where he started writing fiction, took classes at the Sorbonne, and found himself enchanted and fascinated by the Hemingway notion of an American in Paris. Following the birth of a daughter in July 1949, he returned to the US to enter the Writer's Workshop of the University of Iowa, where he also taught in the classics department. There, he met Robie Macauley. In 1951 Hunt joined the faculty of the Thomas Jefferson School in St Louis, where he stayed until June 1955, when the novel he had begun in Paris – *Generations of Men* – was accepted for publication by Atlantic, Little Brown. It was around this time that Meyer recruited Hunt as a case officer for the Congress for Cultural Freedom.

A combination of the enormous pressure of work and his own highly strung temperament had begun to affect Michael Josselson's health, and in October 1955, aged forty-seven, he suffered his first heart attack. So Meyer decided to send in Second Lieutenant John Hunt to lighten the load. There followed the peculiar charade of John Hunt being formally interviewed by Josselson, who had already been supplied with a curriculum vitae and a list of glowing references. John Farrar, of Farrar Straus, recommended Hunt for his 'executive ability, a careful head and a sense of mission for the things we all believe in'. Timothy Foote, assistant editor of *Time-Life* in Paris, was confident that he would be 'awfully useful to have around in almost any reasonable enterprize [sic],' adding that 'he is a strong believer in American responsibilities overseas, but he does not feel that the United States should apologize for her efforts or influence in foreign countries'.[24] Interviewed by Josselson in February 1956, Hunt was formally appointed to the Congress Secretariat shortly afterwards. It can only be assumed that the resumé and the letters of recommendation were part of Hunt's cover, useful to have in the files in order to give the appearance that his appointment was entirely above board.

For Hunt, the Congress was, like Melville's sea, 'my Yale College and my Harvard'. Although he could not expect to achieve the authority that Josselson had won after years of diligent and scrupulous management of both dollars and temperaments, the Congress benefited from the injection of new blood. The advent of Meyer's recruits signalled a new era in the Congress's relationship with the CIA. It ended the drought of case officers properly suited to the job, providing Josselson with adjutants who were intellectually compatible with the demands of the Congress. Josselson and Macauley in particular got on extremely well. They took motoring trips together with their wives, sometimes joined by Hunt and his wife. Photographs show them tanned and relaxed, with Macauley and Hunt looking the archetypal 1950 Americans, handsomely sporting crew cuts, chino pants, and black-framed sunglasses. Back on the job, they often shared a joke at Agency expense. When newly arrived CIA agent Scott Charles revealed that he was taking a different route to the office each day in case he was being followed, Josselson, Macauley and Hunt thought this was hysterically funny.

'Robie Macauley didn't think like them [the CIA] or act like them. He wasn't cynical or smart Alecky,' said Diana Josselson, who had been a friend of Macauley's since 1941. 'He only ever got one thing wrong with Michael, which was that he wouldn't respond when Michael asked angrily or explained angrily about some situation. Michael would get more and more angry, and his blood pressure would rise, and he'd repeat himself again, and Robie would just sit there and say nothing. I told him once that he wasn't handling Michael properly, that he should say something and not let Michael get all steamed up like this.'[25]

Meyer's recruitment drive demonstrated a strengthened commitment to the Congress, but this was proving to be a mixed blessing. The arrival of Warren Manshel in 1954, for example, was resented by Josselson, who felt that the Agency's presence within the Congress 'apparat' was becoming disproportionate. Manshel, said Diana Josselson, 'was sent over by the CIA to report on the Congress. He was planted on Michael, who had to find some kind of cover for him. He was part of a series of shifting relationships outside of the immediate staff, and Michael just had to put up with him.'[26] He also had to put up with Scott Charles, who was placed in the Paris office as an auditor. 'I rather liked him,' said Diana. 'Later, after Michael had died, I edited his guidebook on Geneva.'[27]

By the mid-1950s, Josselson's allegiance was primarily to the Congress, whose needs he instinctively ranked higher than those of the CIA. He felt that the Congress needed the Agency only for the money (and Cord Meyer was keeping a close eye on his dollars, inserting CIA accountant Ken Donaldson into the Congress as its London-based 'Comptroller General'). Josselson had even tried to free the Congress from its financial dependency on the Agency, making his own overtures to the Ford Foundation. As Ford had already supported the Congress to the tune of several million dollars by the mid-1950s, it might reasonably be expected that it would consider assuming the full financial burden. But the Agency refused to relinquish its grip on the Congress, and Josselson's discussions with the Ford Foundation were doomed from the outset.

Far from diminishing, the CIA's presence in the cultural life of the period now increased. From New York, Lawrence de Neufville wrote to Josselson with ideas for discussion in *Encounter*, including a piece on the subject of 'the conscience of the individual versus the requirements of hierarchy', which Josselson hastily recommended to Spender and Kristol. They, presumably, were ignorant of the special interest Josselson had in the intricacies of such a subject. Other Agency men were unable to resist the pull of the pen. Jack Thompson continued to write for scholarly journals like the *Hudson Review*, and in 1961 he published *The Founding of English Metre*, a brilliant study of English poetry. Robie Macauley wrote for the *Kenyon Review*, *The New Republic*, *The Irish University Review*, *Partisan Review*, and the *New York Times Book Review*. During his tenure at the CIA, he continued to write fiction, notably *The Disguises of Love* (1954) and *The End of Pity and Other Stories* (1958).

The London firm of Hodder and Stoughton published a book on Afghanistan by Edward S. Hunter, another CIA operative who used the cover of a freelance writer, and roamed Central Asia for years. Frederick Praeger, a propagandist for the American military government in post-war Germany, published between twenty and twenty-five volumes in which the CIA had an interest, either in the writing, the publication itself, or the distribution. Praeger said they either reimbursed him directly for the expenses of publication, or guaranteed, usually through a foundation, the purchase of enough copies to make it worthwhile.

'Books differ from all other propaganda media,' wrote a chief of the CIA's Covert Action Staff, 'primarily because one single book can significantly change the reader's attitude and action to an extent unmatched by the impact of any other single medium [such as to] make books the most important weapon of strategic (long-range) propaganda.'[28] The CIA's clandestine books programme was run, according to the same source, with the following aims in mind: 'Get books published or distributed abroad without revealing any U.S. influence, by covertly subsidizing foreign publications or booksellers. Get books published which should not be "contaminated" by any overt tie-in with the U.S. government, especially if the position of the author is "delicate". Get books published for operational reasons, regardless of commercial viability. Initiate and subsidize indigenous national or international organizations for book publishing or distributing purposes. Stimulate the writing of politically significant books by unknown foreign authors – either by directly subsidizing the author, if covert contact is feasible, or indirectly, through literary agents or publishers.'[29]

The *New York Times* alleged in 1977 that the CIA had been involved in the publication of at least a thousand books.[30] The Agency has never made public its publications backlist, but it is known that books in which it had an involvement include Lasky's *La Révolution Hongroise*, translations of T. S. Eliot's *The Waste Land* and *Four Quartets*, and, naturally, those books published by the Congress for Cultural Freedom or its affiliates, including anthologies of verse, Herbert Lüthy's *Le Passé Présent: Combats d'Idées de Calvin à Rousseau*, Patricia Blake's *Half-Way to the Moon: New Writing from Russia* (1964, an Encounter book), *Literature and Revolution in Soviet Russia*, edited by Max Hayward and Leopold Labedz (Oxford University Press, 1963), *History and Hope: Progress in Freedom* by Kot Jelenski, Bertrand de Jouvenel's *The Art of Conjecture*, *The Hundred Flowers*, edited by Roderick MacFarquhar, Nicolo Tucci's autobiographical novel *Before My Time*, Barzini's *The Italians*, Pasternak's *Doctor Zhivago*, and new editions of Machiavelli's *The Prince*. Under the imprint of the Chekhov Publishing Company, Chekhov's works were widely translated and distributed. The Chekhov Publishing Company was secretly subsidized by the CIA.

In addition to John Hunt, whose first calling was as a writer, the Agency boasted several other active novelists. In Paris, Yale graduate Peter Matthiessen, later the celebrated author of *The Snow Leopard*, co-founded and wrote for the *Paris Review*, and penned the novel *Partisans* whilst he was working for the CIA. Another of Cord Meyer's recruits was Charles McCarry, who was later seen as America's answer to John Le Carré. There was also James Michener, whose long career writing blockbusters with such modest titles as *Poland*, *Alaska*, *Texas*, *Space*, was punctuated by a spell with the Agency. In the mid-1950s, Michener used his career as a writer as cover for his work in eliminating radicals who had infiltrated one of the CIA's Asian operations. To this end, he was placed in the CIA's Asia Foundation. He later said that 'a writer must never serve as a secret agent for anything or anybody'.

Then there was Howard Hunt, author of such novels as *East of Farewell*, *Limit of Darkness*, and *Stranger in Town* (which won him a Guggenheim Fellowship). Whilst working for Wisner's OPC, Howard Hunt was signed to do several paperback originals with the Fawcett Publishing Corporation under the Gold Medal imprint. In Mexico, he was responsible for the Marxist writer-intellectual El Campesino's book *Life and Death in the USSR*, one of the first personal revelations of Stalinist terror to come out of Latin America. The book was widely translated and distributed with CIA assistance. He also assigned case officer William Buckley to help another intellectual, Chilean Marxist Eudocio Ravines, finish his equally influential book, *The Yenan Way*.

In late 1961, Howard Hunt joined Tracy Barnes's newly established Domestic Operations Division. Barnes, who served as deputy director of the Psychological Strategy Board, was a strong advocate of the use of literature as an anti-Communist weapon, and worked hard to strengthen the CIA's publishing programme. 'The new division accepted both personnel and projects unwanted elsewhere within CIA,' Howard Hunt later wrote, 'and those covert-action projects that came to me were almost entirely concerned with publishing and publications. We subsidized "significant" books, for example, *The New Class* by Milovan Djilas (the definitive study of Communist oligarchies), one of a number of Frederick A. Praeger Inc. titles so supported.'[31]

'Under one ghost's name or another, I was helping on a few pro-CIA novels . . . as well as overseeing one or two scholarly works, not to mention dashing off an occasional magazine piece on the new invidiousness of the old Commie threat,' says Harry Hubbard in Mailer's *Harlot's Ghost*. Even travel guides could contain the insights of CIA agents, several of whom floated about Europe using the celebrated Fodor guides as cover. Eugene Fodor, a former OSS Lieutenant, later defended this practice, saying the CIA contributors 'were all highly professional, high quality. We never let politics be smuggled into the books.'[32] Lyman Kirkpatrick, executive assistant to the director of CIA, contributed the 'Armies of the World' article each year to the *Encyclopaedia Britannica*, which was owned by former Assistant Secretary of State for Public Affairs, William Benton. Sometimes, reviews of books in the *New York Times* or other respected broadsheets were penned by CIA writers under contract. CIA agent George Carver signed articles under his own name in *Foreign Affairs* (though he omitted mention of who his employers were). In England, Monty Woodhouse wrote articles for *Encounter* and the *Times Literary Supplement*.

The phenomenon of writer as spy, spy as writer, was by no means new. Somerset Maugham used his literary status as cover for assignments for the British Secret Service during the First World War. His later collection of autobiographical stories, *Ashenden*, was a bible for intelligence officers. Compton Mackenzie worked for MI5 in the 1930s, and was later prosecuted by Her Majesty's government for revealing the names of SIS personnel in his book *Aegean Memories*. Graham Greene derived much fictional material from his experience as an undercover agent for MI5 during – and, it is said, after – the Second World War. He once famously referred to MI5 as 'the best travel agency in the world'.

'Intellectuals, or a certain sort of intellectuals, have always had a romance about intelligence services,' observed Carol Brightman. 'It's a kind of coming of age experience, going into the intelligence services, especially on certain campuses such as Yale.'[33] For novelist Richard Elman (not to be confused with Joyce biographer, Richard Ellmann), there was also a shared aesthetic concern: 'It's worth considering what these people had in common. They were all Christians, in a non-sectarian, T. S. Eliot kind of way. They believed in a higher authority, a higher truth which sanctioned their anti-Communist, anti-atheist crusade. T. S. Eliot, Pound, and other modernists appealed to their elitist sensibilities. The CIA even commissioned a translation of Eliot's *Four Quartets* and then had copies air-dropped into Russia. These were men, as much as Shaw and Wells, for whom the socialist "century of the common man" was unwelcome – they wanted the Uncommon Man and High Culture. So, they weren't just putting money into culture willy-nilly.'[34]

Allen Ginsberg even fantasized that T. S. Eliot was part of a literary conspiracy mounted by his, Eliot's, friend James Jesus Angleton. In a 1978 sketch called 'T. S. Eliot Entered My Dreams', Ginsberg imagined that 'On the fantail of a boat to Europe, Eliot was reclining with several passengers in deck seats, blue cloudy sky behind, iron floor below us. "And yourself," I said, "What did you think of the domination of poetics by the CIA. After all, wasn't Angleton your friend? Didn't he tell you his plan to revitalize the intellectual structure of the West against the so-to-speak Stalinists?" Eliot listened attentively – I was surprised he wasn't distracted. "Well, there are all sorts of chaps competing for dominance, political and literary . . . your Gurus for instance, and the Theosophists, and the table rappers and dialecticians and tea-leaf-readers and Ideologues. I suppose I was one such, in my middle years. But I did, yes, know Angleton's literary conspiracies, I thought they were petty – well meant but of no importance to Literature." "I thought they were of some importance," I said, "since it secretly nourished the careers of too many square intellectuals, provided sustenance to thinkers in the Academy who influenced the intellectual tone of the West . . . After all, Intellectual tone should be revolutionary, or at least Radical, seeking roots of dis-ease and Mechanization and dominance by unnatural monopoly . . . And the Government through foundations was supporting a whole field of 'Scholars of War' . . . The subsidization of magazines like *Encounter* which held Eliotic style as a touchstone of sophistication and competence . . . failed to create an alternative free vital decentralized individualistic culture. Instead, we had the worst of Capitalist Imperialism."'[35]

The defence of 'high' culture mounted by people like Angleton was automatic. 'It would never have occurred to us to denounce anyone or anything as "elitist",' Irving Kristol once said. 'The elite was us – the "happy few" who had been chosen by History to guide our fellow creatures toward a secular redemption.'[36] Raised on modernist culture, these elitists worshipped Eliot, Yeats, Joyce, and Proust. They saw it as their job 'not to give the public what it wants, or what it thinks it wants but what – through the medium of its most intelligent members – it ought to have'.[37] In other words, high culture was not only important as an anti-Communist line of defence, but also the bastion against a homogenized mass society, against what Dwight Macdonald viewed with horror as 'the spreading ooze of Mass Culture'.[38]

The paradox of a defence of democracy mounted by patricians who were essentially deeply suspicious of it is hard to ignore. Positioning themselves like an elite of princes holding the pass against barbarism, they were modernists terrified of modernity and its blood-dimmed tide. In a valedictory address to Kenyon College in 1940, Robert Lowell had given voice to the darkest fears of this aristocracy: 'For all of you know that as the Philistines and Goths proceed in their spiritless way to dismember civilization, they will come to all the golden palaces of learning, they will come at last to Milton, Groton, St Paul's and St Mark's and there, the students who are neither efficient nor humane nor cultured will be doing what they are doing. And the indignant Goths and Philistines will turn these poor drones out of the hive and there will be no old limbs, for the new blood, and the world will revert to its unwearied cycles of retrogression, advance and repetition.'[39]

Convinced that they had to shore up their defences against the coming ruin, these were the Aurelians who in 1949 had decided to award Ezra Pound the Bollingen Prize for Poetry for his *Pisan Cantos*. One anecdote tells how one day Paul Mellon, a generous philanthropist, complained to Allen Tate and John Crowe Ransom about how many writers were leftists. Mellon himself was advanced in his taste in art, but conservative in politics, almost a *sine qua non* of Cold War angels. Tate replied to the effect that writers were always needy, so why didn't Mellon put up some money for fellowships, awards or whatever, which would make the recipients much happier and less inclined to be revolutionary? So Mellon put up the Bollingen-Mellon awards as private endowments worth about $20,000 each.

'Why did they propose Pound?' asked Richard Elman. 'Because he represented the ultimate in the mandarin culture they were trying to preserve and promote.'[40] The award sparked a huge controversy, not least because Pound was in a hospital for the criminally insane at the time, the only American charged with treason in the Second World War. His wartime broadcasts for Mussolini's Minculpop had included tirades against 'Mr Jewsevelt', 'Franklin Finkelstein Roosevelt', 'Stinkie Roosenstein' and 'kikes, sheenies, and the oily people'. He argued that *Mein Kampf* was 'keenly analysed history', and called its author 'a saint and a martyr' in the tradition of Joan of Arc. America, he said, 'had been invaded by vermin'. Karl Shapiro, editor of *Poetry* magazine, wrote that he was 'the only dissenter from the Bollingen Prize to Pound, except Paul Green, who abstained. Eliot, Auden, Tate, Lowell – all voted the prize to Pound. A passel of fascists.' When William Barrett attacked the jury's decision, Allen Tate challenged him to a duel.

The decision to award Pound the prize re-inflamed all the art-versus-politics disputes that had been raging since the 1930s, and seemed to confirm what many on the left feared: that there was a disposition amongst those who called themselves liberals to forgive, or at least ignore, the historic compromises which had led many artists – many of whom were now comfortably relocated in America – to use their creative talent in flattery of Fascism. At a time when art and artists were so highly politicized, it seemed insufficient to state, as the Bollingen jury did, that 'To permit other considerations than that of poetic achievement to sway the decision would destroy the significance of the award and would in principle deny the validity of that objective perception of value on which civilized society must rest.'[41] How could art be autonomous on the one hand and, where convenient, pressed into political service on the other?

16

Yanqui Doodles

> I can paint better than anybody!
>
> Jackson Pollock, in de Kooning's dream

During his presidency, Harry Truman liked to get up early and make for the National Gallery. Arriving before the city had risen, he would nod silently to the guard whose special duty it was to unlock the door for the President's pre-breakfast stroll through the gallery. Truman relished these visits, and recorded them in his diary. In 1948, after gazing at assorted Holbeins and Rembrandts, he entered the following observation: 'It's a pleasure to look at perfection and then think of the lazy, nutty moderns. It is like comparing Christ with Lenin.' Publicly, he arrived at similar judgements, claiming that the Dutch masters 'make our modern day daubers and frustrated ham and egg men look just what they are'.

In his scorn for the moderns, Truman articulated a view held by many Americans that linked experimental, and especially abstract art to degenerate or subversive impulses. Those European vanguardists who had fled the Fascist jackboot were now startled to find themselves in an America where modernism was once again being kicked about. This was, of course, consistent with the cultural fundamentalism of figures like McCarthy, and part of the confusing process by which

America, whilst advocating freedom of expression abroad, seemed to begrudge such freedoms at home. On the floor of Congress, a high-octane assault was led by a Republican from Missouri, George Dondero, who declared modernism to be quite simply part of a worldwide conspiracy to weaken American resolve. 'All modern art is Communistic,' he announced, before moving on to a deranged but poetic exegesis of its various manifestations: 'Cubism aims to destroy by designed disorder. Futurism aims to destroy by the machine myth . . . Dadaism aims to destroy by ridicule. Expressionism aims to destroy by aping the primitive and insane. Abstractionism aims to destroy by the creation of brainstorms . . . Surrealism aims to destroy by the denial of reason.'[1]

Dondero's neurotic assessment was echoed by a coterie of public figures, whose shrill denunciations rang across the floor of Congress and in the conservative press. Their attacks culminated in such claims as 'ultramodern artists are unconsciously used as tools of the Kremlin', and the assertion that, in some cases, abstract paintings were actually secret maps pinpointing strategic United States fortifications.[2] 'Modern art is actually a means of espionage,' one opponent charged. 'If you know how to read them, modern paintings will disclose the weak spots in US fortifications, and such crucial constructions as Boulder Dam.'

This was not a propitious time for modernists. Most vulnerable to the attacks of the Dondero caucus was a group of artists that emerged in the late 1940s as the Abstract Expressionists. In reality, they were not a group at all – 'it is disastrous to name ourselves,' de Kooning once warned – but a disparate band of painters bound more by a taste for artistic adventure than by any formal aesthetic common denominator. But they were linked by a similar past: most of them had worked for the Federal Arts Project under Roosevelt's New Deal, producing subsidized art for the government and getting involved in left-wing politics. Foremost amongst them was Jackson Pollock, who in the 1930s had been involved in the Communist workshop of the Mexican muralist David Alfalo Siquieros. Adolph Gottlieb, William Baziotes and several other Abstract Expressionists had all been Communist activists. The fact that theirs had been more an 'untheorized affiliation with the "left"' than anything deeper was immaterial to Dondero and his allies, who, unable or unwilling to distinguish between the biography and the work, conflated the political record of the artist with his aesthetic expression, and damned both.[3]

Where Dondero saw in Abstract Expressionism evidence of a Communist conspiracy, America's cultural mandarins detected a contrary virtue: for them, it spoke to a specifically anti-Communist ideology, the ideology of freedom, of free enterprise. Non-figurative and politically silent, it was the very antithesis to socialist realism. It was precisely the kind of art the Soviets loved to hate. But it was more than this. It was, claimed its apologists, an explicitly *American* intervention in the modernist canon. As early as 1946, critics were applauding the new art as 'independent, self-reliant, a true expression of the national will, spirit and character. It seems that, in aesthetic character, US art is no longer a repository of European influences, that it is not a mere amalgamate of foreign "isms", assembled, compiled and assimilated with lesser or greater intelligence.'[4]

Elevated as chief representative of this new national discovery was Jackson Pollock. 'He was *the* great American painter,' said fellow-artist Budd Hopkins. 'If you conceive of such a person, first of all, he had to be a real American, not a transplanted European. And he should have the big macho American virtues – he should be rough-and-tumble American – taciturn, ideally – and if he is a cowboy, so much the better. Certainly not an easterner, not someone who went to Harvard. He shouldn't be influenced by the Europeans so much as he should be influenced by our own – the Mexicans and American Indians, and so on. He should come out of the native soil, not out of Picasso and Matisse. And he should be allowed the great American vice, the Hemingway vice, of being a drunk.'[5]

Everything about Pollock was right. Born on a sheep ranch in Cody, Wyoming, he entered the New York scene like a cowboy – hard-talking, heavy-drinking, shooting his way from the Wild West. This was, of course, a mythical past. Pollock had never ridden a horse, and had left Wyoming as a young child. But the image was so apt, so *American*, and no one disbelieved it. Willem de Kooning once told of a dream he'd had of Pollock flinging open the doors of a bar like a screen cowboy and shouting, 'I can paint better than anybody!' He had the grittiness of Marlon Brando, the brooding rebelliousness of James Dean. Next to Matisse – by now barely able to lift a paintbrush, the compromised and impotent figurehead of an ageing European modernism – Pollock was virility incarnate. He came up with a technique known as action painting, which involved laying a huge canvas flat on the ground – preferably outdoors – and dripping paint all over it. In the splurgy, random knot of lines which threaded their way across the canvas and over the edges, he seemed to be engaged in the act of rediscovering America. Ecstatic, loose, fuelled by drink, modernism in Pollock's hands was a kind of tremendous delirium. Although one critic described it as 'melted Picasso', others rushed to celebrate it as 'the triumph of American painting', which spoke for what America was: vigorous, energetic, free-wheeling, big. It was seen to uphold the great American myth of the lone voice, the intrepid individual, a tradition which Hollywood enshrined in films such as *Mr Smith Goes to Washington* and, later, *Twelve Angry Men* (the Abstract Expressionists once styled themselves 'The Irascibles').

By 1948, the art critic Clement Greenberg, himself a brawling, boozing, one-man slugfest, was making prodigal claims for the new aesthetic: 'When one sees . . . how much the level of American art has risen in the last five years, with the emergence of new talents so full of energy and content as Arshile Gorky, Jackson Pollock, David Smith . . . then the conclusion forces itself, much to our own surprise, that the main premises of Western Art have at last migrated to the United States, along with the center of gravity of industrial production and political power.'[6] America, in other words, was the place an artist no longer felt he had to 'escape *from*, in order to mature in Europe'.[7] Commenting on this claim, rather than agreeing with it, Jason Epstein later said: 'America – and especially New York – had now become the centre of the world politically and financially and, of course, it had become the centre culturally too. Well, what would a great power be without an appropriate art? You couldn't be a great power if you didn't have art to go with it, like Venice without Tintoretto or Florence without Giotto.'[8] The idea that Abstract Expressionism could become a vehicle for the imperial burden began to take hold. But its emergence at a time of such political and moral odium presented its would-be promoters with a substantial dilemma.

Despite the patent idiocy of Dondero's protests, by the late 1940s he had achieved the collapse of successive attempts on the part of the State Department to deploy American art as a propaganda weapon. The philistines scored an early victory in 1947 when they forced the withdrawal of a State Department exhibition called 'Advancing American Art', a selection of seventy-nine 'progressive' works, including those of Georgia O'Keeffe, Adolph Gottlieb and Arshile Gorky, which was scheduled to travel to Europe and Latin America. The show reached Paris, then moved on to Prague, where it was such a success that the Russians immediately sent in a rival exhibition. The official rationale for this venture was to 'dispel for the foreign audience any notion of the academic or imitative character of contemporary American art'.[9] 'This time we are exporting neither domestic brandy in imitation cognac bottles nor vintage non-intoxicating grape juice, but real bourbon, aged in the wood – what may justly be described as the wine of the country,'[10] eulogized one critic.

Far from advancing the cause of American art, the show signalled its ignominious retreat. Vigorously contested in Congress, it was denounced as subversive and 'un-American'. One speaker detected a malicious intent to 'tell the foreigners that the American people are despondent, broken down or of hideous shape – thoroughly dissatisfied with their lot and eager for a change of government. The Communists and their New Deal fellow travelers have selected art as one of their avenues of propaganda.'[11] 'I am just a dumb American who pays taxes for this kind of trash,' cried another, a worthy progenitor of Jesse Helms. 'If there is a single individual in this Congress who believes this kind of tripe is . . . bringing a better understanding of American life, then he should be sent to the same nut house from which the people who drew this stuff originally came.'[12] The show was cancelled, and the paintings were sold off at a 95 per cent discount as surplus government property. Responding to the charge that many of the artists represented in the exhibition had dabbled in left-wing politics (then a *sine qua non* of any self-respecting vanguardist), the State Department issued a craven directive ordering that in future no

American artist with Communist or fellow-travelling associations be exhibited at government expense. And with this, 'the perception of avant-garde art as un-American had now been incorporated into official policy'.[13]

A terrible vision of the barbarians at the gates of the palace of high art now insinuated its way into the imagination of the cultural elitists. Dwight Macdonald denounced these attacks as *Kulturbolschewismus*, and argued that while they were proposed in the name of American democracy, they actually mirrored totalitarian attacks on the arts. The Soviets – and indeed much of Europe – were saying that America was a cultural desert, and the behaviour of US Congressmen seemed to confirm that. Eager to show the world that here was an art commensurate with America's greatness and freedom, high-level strategists found they couldn't publicly support it because of domestic opposition. So what did they do? They turned to the CIA. And a struggle began to assert the merits of Abstract Expressionism against attempts to smear it.

'We had a lot of trouble with Congressman Dondero,' Braden later recalled. 'He couldn't stand modern art. He thought it was a travesty, he thought it was sinful, he thought it was ugly. He put up a heck of a fight about painting, and he made it very difficult to get Congress to go along with some of the things that we wanted to do – send art abroad, send symphonies abroad, publish magazines abroad, whatever. That's one of the reasons why it had to be done covertly; it had to be covert because it would have been turned down if it had been put to a vote in a democracy. In order to encourage openness we had to be secret.'[14] Here again was that sublime paradox of American strategy in the cultural Cold War: in order to promote an acceptance of art produced in (and vaunted as the expression of) democracy, the democratic process itself had to be circumvented.

Once again, the CIA turned to the private sector to advance its objectives. In America, most museums and collections of art were – as they are now – privately owned and privately funded. Pre-eminent amongst contemporary and avant-garde art museums was the Museum of Modern Art (MoMA) in New York. Its president through most of the 1940s and 1950s was Nelson Rockefeller, whose mother, Abby Aldrich

Rockefeller, had co-founded the museum in 1929 (Nelson called it 'Mommy's Museum'). Nelson was a keen supporter of Abstract Expressionism, which he referred to as 'free enterprise painting'. Over the years, his private collection alone swelled to over 2,500 works. Thousands more covered the lobbies and walls of buildings belonging to the Rockefeller-owned Chase Manhattan Bank.

Supporting left-wing artists was familiar territory for the Rockefellers. When challenged over her decision to promote the Mexican revolutionary Diego Rivera (who had once chanted 'Death to the Gringos!' outside an American embassy), Abby Aldrich Rockefeller had argued that Reds would stop being Reds 'if we could get them artistic recognition'. A one-man show for Rivera, the second in MoMA's history, duly followed. In 1933, Nelson Rockefeller had supervised Rivera's commission to paint a mural at the newly erected Rockefeller Center. Inspecting Rivera's work one day, Nelson noticed that one figure had taken on the unmistakable features of Vladimir Ilich Lenin. He politely asked Rivera to remove it. Rivera politely refused. At Nelson's instruction, the mural was surrounded by guards whilst Rivera was handed a cheque for his full fee ($21,000), and served notice that his commission was cancelled. In February 1934, the mural, which had been nearly completed, was destroyed with jack-hammers.

Although this particular piece of patronage was unsuccessful, the principle which guided it was not abandoned. Establishment figures continued to believe that leftist artists were worth supporting. In the process, it could be hoped that the political clamour of the artist might be drowned out by the clink of the patron's coin. In a famous article entitled 'Avant-Garde and Kitsch', Clement Greenberg, the art critic who did most to put Abstract Expressionism on the map, set out the ideological rationale for accepting sponsorship from an enlightened patron. Published in *Partisan Review* in 1939, the article still stands as the definitive article of faith for the elitist, and anti-Marxist view of modernism. The avant-garde, wrote Greenberg, had been 'abandoned by those to whom it actually belongs – our ruling class'. In Europe, traditionally, support was provided 'by an elite among the ruling classes . . . from which [the avant-garde] assumed itself to be cut off, but to which it had always remained attached by an umbilical cord of gold'.[15] In the United States, he argued, the same mechanism must prevail. The really deep connection between Abstract Expressionism and the cultural Cold War can be found here. It was according to this principle that the CIA, together with its private venture capitalists, operated.

Tom Braden, in particular, was attracted to the Greenbergian proposition that progressive artists need an elite to subsidize them – just like their Renaissance forbears. 'I've forgotten which pope it was who commissioned the Sistine Chapel,' he said, 'but I suppose that if it had been submitted to a vote of the Italian people there would have been many, many negative responses: "It's naked," or, "It isn't the way I imagined God," or whatever. I don't think it would have gotten through the Italian parliament, if there had been a parliament at the time. It takes a pope or somebody with a lot of money to recognize art and to support it. And after many centuries people say, "Look! the Sistine Chapel, the most beautiful creation on earth." It's a problem that civilization has faced ever since the first artist and the first multi-millionaire – or pope – who supported him; and yet if it hadn't been for the multi-millionaires or the popes, we wouldn't have had the art.'[16] Patronage, in Braden's terms, carried with it a duty to instruct, to educate people to accept not what they want, or think they want, but what they ought to have. 'You have always to battle your own ignoramuses, or, to put it more politely, people who just don't understand.'[17]

'There is a perverse way of looking at this question, which is to say the CIA took art very seriously,' commented art critic Philip Dodd. 'The great thing about politicians when they get involved in art is it *means* something to them, whether it's the Fascists or the Soviets or the American CIA. So there may be a really perverse argument that says the CIA were the best art critics in America in the fifties because they saw work that actually should have been antipathetic to them – made by old lefties, coming out of European surrealism – and they saw the potential power in that kind of art and ran with it. You couldn't say that of many of the art critics of the time.'[18]

'Regarding Abstract Expressionism, I'd love to be able to say that the CIA invented it all, just to see what happened in New

York and downtown SoHo tomorrow!'[19] joked Agency man Donald Jameson, before moving to a more sober explanation of the CIA's involvement. 'We recognized that this was the kind of art that did not have anything to do with socialist realism, and made socialist realism look even more stylised and more rigid and confined than it was. And that relationship was exploited in some of the exhibits. Moscow in those days was very vicious in its denunciation of any kind of non-conformity to its own very rigid patterns. So one could quite adequately and accurately reason that anything they criticized that much and that heavyhandedly was worth support one way or another. Of course, for matters of this sort [it] could only have been done through the organizations or the operations of the CIA at two or three removed, so that there wouldn't be any question of having to clear Jackson Pollock, for example, or do anything that would involve these people in the organization – they'd just be added at the end of the line. I don't think that there was any significant relationship between us and Robert Motherwell, for example. And it couldn't have been any closer and certainly shouldn't have been any closer either, because most of them were people who had very little respect for the government in particular and certainly none for the CIA. If you had to use people who considered themselves one way or another closer to Moscow than to Washington, well, so much the better perhaps.'[20]

Operating at a remove from the CIA, and therefore offering a plausible disguise for its interests, was the Museum of Modern Art. An inspection of MoMA's committees and councils reveals a proliferation of links to the Agency. First and foremost was Nelson Rockefeller himself, who had headed up the government's wartime intelligence agency for Latin America, named the Coordinator of Inter-American Affairs (CIAA). This agency, among other activities, sponsored touring exhibitions of 'contemporary American painting'. Nineteen of these shows were contracted to MoMA. As a trustee of the Rockefeller Brothers Fund, a New York think-tank subcontracted by the government to study foreign affairs, Rockefeller presided over some of the most influential minds of the period as they thrashed out definitions of American foreign policy. In the early 1950s, he received briefings on covert activities from

Allen Dulles and Tom Braden, who later said 'I assumed Nelson knew pretty much everything about what we were doing.' A reasonable assumption, given Nelson's appointment as Eisenhower's special adviser on Cold War strategy in 1954 (replacing C. D. Jackson), and his chairmanship of the Planning Coordination Group which oversaw all National Security Council decisions, including CIA covert operations.

Rockefeller's close friend was John 'Jock' Hay Whitney, a long-time trustee of MoMA, who also served as its president and chairman of the board. Educated at Groton, Yale and Oxford, Jock had converted a substantial inheritance into a vast fortune by bankrolling fledgling companies, Broadway plays and Hollywood movies. As director of Rockefeller's motion picture division at CIAA in 1940–2, Jock oversaw production of such films as Disney's *Saludas Amigos*, which brimmed with inter-American goodwill. He joined the Office of Strategic Services (OSS) in 1943, was captured in southern France by German soldiers in August 1944, and loaded on to a train heading east before making a daring escape. After the war, he set up J. H. Whitney & Co., as 'a partnership dedicated to the propagation of the free-enterprise system by the furnishing of financial backing for new, undeveloped, and risky businesses that might have trouble attracting investment capital through more conservative channels'.[21] A prominent partner was William H. Jackson, a polo-playing friend of Jock's who also happened to be deputy director of the CIA. Jock had a position on the Psychological Strategy Board, and found 'many ways of being useful to the CIA'.[22]

Another link was William Burden, who first joined the museum as chairman of its Advisory Committee in 1940. Descended from 'commodore' Vanderbilt, Burden epitomized the Cold War establishment. Formerly Secretary of State for Air, he too had worked for Rockefeller's CIAA during the war. He had also earned a personal fortune and a reputation as 'a venture capitalist of the first rank'. Chairing numerous quasi-governmental bodies, and even the CIA's Farfield Foundation (of which he was president), he seemed happy to perform as a front-man. In 1947, he was appointed chairman of the Committee on Museum Collections, and in 1956 he became MoMA's president.

Under Burden's presidency, 'policy was made by [René] d'Harnoncourt so far as the operations of the museum were concerned', with consultations conducted 'pretty much on a rubber-stamp basis'.[23] This gave d'Harnoncourt scope to exercise his considerable talents as the Cardinal Wolsey of the court circles surrounding MoMA. Standing at six feet five inches, and weighing 230 pounds, the Viennese-born d'Harnoncourt was an extraordinary figure, 'a descendant, direct and collateral, of a cloud of Middle European noblemen who flourished as chamberlains and provosts to a cloud of Dukes of Lorraine, Counts of Luxembourg, and Hapsburg emperors'.[24] He emigrated to the States in 1932, and during the war worked in the arts section of the CIAA. Nelson then recruited him to the museum, of which he became director in 1949. D'Harnoncourt believed that 'modern art in its infinite variety and ceaseless exploration' was the 'foremost symbol' of democracy, and openly lobbied Congress during the 1950s to finance a cultural campaign against Communism. Although Braden maintained that 'the guys at MoMA liked to handle things in-house,' he concluded that René d'Harnoncourt was 'most likely the Agency's contact at the museum'. Certainly d'Harnoncourt was consulting with the National Security Council's Operations Coordinating Board (which had replaced the Psychological Strategy Board). He also reported regularly to the State Department. These liaisons give a certain piquancy to the comment that, like his ancestors, d'Harnoncourt 'exhibited a gift for making himself indispensable to a succession – and quite often an overlapping – of patrons'.[25]

William Paley, heir to the Congress Cigar Company, was yet another MoMA trustee with close links to the intelligence world. A personal friend of Allen Dulles, Paley allowed CBS, the network he owned, to provide cover for CIA employees, in an arrangement similar to that authorized by Henry Luce at his Time-Life empire (Luce was also a MoMA trustee). At the height of this relationship, CBS correspondents joined the CIA hierarchy once a year for private dinners and briefings. These dinners, 'grown-up affairs with good table talk and good cigars', were held at Dulles's home or at his private club, the Alibi, in Washington. Of Paley's involvement with the CIA, one CBS executive said, 'It's the single subject about which his memory has failed.'[26]

On and on go the names, on and on go the links. Joseph Verner Reed, for example, was a MoMA trustee at the same time as he was a trustee of the Farfield Foundation. So was Gardner Cowles. So was Junkie Fleischmann. So was Cass Canfield. Oveta Culp Hobby, a founding member of MoMA, sat on the board of the Free Europe Committee, and allowed her family foundation to be used as a CIA conduit. While she was Secretary of State for Health, Education and Welfare under Eisenhower, her assistant was one Joan Braden, who had previously worked for Nelson Rockefeller. Joan was married to Tom. Tom, before he joined the CIA, had also worked for Nelson Rockefeller, as the Museum of Modern Art's executive secretary from 1947 to late 1949.

As Gore Vidal once said, 'Everything has so many chains of association in our unexpectedly Jacobean republic that nothing any longer surprises.' Of course it could be argued that this congruity revealed nothing more than the nature of American power at the time. Just because these people knew each other, and just because they were socially (and even formally) enjoined to the CIA, doesn't mean that they were co-conspirators in the promotion of the new American art. But the cosiness of the relationship ensured the durability of claims that MoMA was in some official way connected to the government's secret cultural warfare programme. This rumour was first examined in 1974 by Eva Cockroft, in a seminal article for *Artforum* called 'Abstract Expressionism: Weapon of the Cold War', which concluded: 'Links between cultural cold war politics and the success of Abstract Expressionism are by no means coincidental . . . They were consciously forged at the time by some of the most influential figures controlling museum policies and advocating enlightened cold war tactics designed to woo European intellectuals.'[27] Moreover, Cockroft asserted, 'In terms of cultural propaganda, the functions of both the CIA's cultural apparatus and MoMA's international programs were similar and, in fact, mutually supportive.'[28]

'I didn't have anything to do with promoting Pollock or whomever,' said Lawrence de Neufville. 'I don't even remember when I first heard of him. But I do remember hearing that Jock Whitney and Allen Dulles agreed they had to do something about modern art after the State Department caved in.

Perhaps that's how you might define "mutually supportive."'[29] There is no *prima facie* evidence for any formal agreement between the CIA and the Museum of Modern Art. The fact is, it simply wasn't necessary.

MoMA's defenders have consistently attacked the claim that the museum's support of Abstract Expressionism was in any way linked to the covert advancement of America's international image. Curiously, one argument they use is that MoMA actually neglected the movement when it first emerged. 'The Modern's exhibitions of Abstract Expressionism, more so at home, but also abroad, came on the whole only during the later fifties, by which time the movement's first generation had already been followed by a second,'[30] wrote Michael Kimmelman, in a rebuttal commissioned by MoMA. To argue that MoMA simply missed what was right under its nose is disingenuous, and ignores the fact that the museum had steadily and consistently collected works by the Abstract Expressionists from the time of their earliest appearance. From 1941, MoMA acquired works by Arshile Gorky, Alexander Calder, Frank Stella, Robert Motherwell, Jackson Pollock, Stuart Davis and Adolph Gottlieb. In May 1944, the museum sold at auction 'certain of its nineteenth century works of art to provide funds for the purchase of twentieth century works'. Although receipts from the sale were disappointing, enough cash was made available to purchase 'important paintings by Pollock, Motherwell, and Matta'. Thus, as might be expected of a museum of *modern* art, and particularly one which acknowledged that it held 'a tremendous moral responsibility toward living artists whose careers and fortunes can be drastically affected by the Museum's support or lack of it',[31] was the new generation of American painters brought into its fold.

That these acquisitions were made in the face of internal opposition further demonstrates a resolve to consolidate Abstract Expressionism's right to canonical recognition. When some members of the Committee of Museum Collections, encouraged by adverse newspaper criticism, 'vigorously questioned the validity of certain acquisitions, including paintings called "abstract expressionist"',[32] their protests were ineffectual; and nobody stood in the way when one committee member resigned in protest against the purchase of a Rothko. As for foreign tours, Motherwell, Mark Tobey, Georgia O'Keeffe and Gottlieb were all selected for the exhibition 'American Painting from the 18th Century to the Present Day', which opened in London in 1946, before proceeding to other European capitals. This was one of the earliest appearances of Abstract Expressionism in a group show under official auspices (sponsorship was provided by the State Department and the Office of War Information). The same year, the MoMA show 'Fourteen Americans' included Gorky, Motherwell, Tobey and Theodore Roszak. By 1948, Lincoln Kirstein, a former MoMA activist, was moaning in *Harper's* that the museum 'has done its job almost too well' by making itself into 'a modern Abstract Academy' whose tenets he defined as 'improvisation as method, deformation as formula, and painting . . . as an amusement manipulated by interior decorators and high-pressure salesmen'.[33] In 1952, some fifty American artists, including Edward Hopper, Charles Burchfield, Yasuo Kuniyoshi and Jack Levine, attacked MoMA, in what came to be known as the 'Reality Manifesto', for 'coming to be more and more identified in the public eye with abstract and non-objective art', a 'dogma' which they felt stemmed 'very largely from the Modern Museum and its unquestioned influence throughout the country'. In the same year, the Communist monthly *Masses and Mainstream* lampooned abstract art and its 'shrine', the Museum of Modern Art, in a tirade whose title – 'Dollars, Doodles, and Death' – was eerily prophetic.

Is it really possible to argue that MoMA came on board late? When Sidney Janis took the group show 'American Vanguard Art for Paris' to the Galerie de France in late 1951, it was a resounding failure. Reviews were lukewarm at best, and mostly downright hostile. Not one picture was sold. 'It was too early,' Janis concluded. Other private gallery owners who championed the New York School were in no doubt that it was indebted to MoMA's early recognition. 'I must say that the Modern Museum was one of the first to accept people like Motherwell, Gottlieb, Baziotes,' said Samuel Kootz of the Kootz Gallery. '[Alfred] Barr was an enthusiast for those particular three men and conveyed this enthusiasm to people like Burden, or Nelson Rockefeller, and others of the Modern group of Trustees.'[34]

As the authoritative tastemaker of his day, Alfred Barr's advocacy of Abstract Expressionism was integral to its success. Born in 1902 in Detroit, Barr entered Princeton in 1918, and emerged with a burning interest in art, military history and chess (reflecting his concern with strategy and tactics). In 1929, at Abby Aldrich Rockefeller's invitation, he became MoMA's first director, a post he held until 1943, when he was replaced by René d'Harnoncourt. Barr continued to keep an office in the museum, and in February 1947 was appointed director of Museum Collections. In a *New Yorker* profile, Dwight Macdonald described him as 'shy, frail, low of voice, and scholarly of mien, the austerity of his beak-nosed, bespectacled face relieved only by the kind of secret smile one sees on archaic Greek statues or on the carefully locked features of a psychoanalyst'. But Macdonald noticed that there was more to Barr than 'simply another nice old absent-minded professor. In his quiet, rectitudinous way, he is more than something of a politician . . . "the fine Italian hand of Alfred Barr" has had its part in creating an atmosphere of intrigue in the museum, where things are not necessarily what they seem to such an extent that one bewildered artist has called the place "The House of Mystery if not Mirth".' Macdonald went on to quote Peggy Guggenheim – who once said of Barr that she 'hated his cagey quality' – and another contemporary who detected 'something of the Jesuit about Alfred. But as the Jesuits practiced their wiles *ad majorem Dei gloriam*, so Barr manoeuvres away for the greater glory of modern art and the museum.'[35]

Behind MoMA's strategies in this highly politicized period, there is evidence of Barr's 'Italian hand'. As part of a deliberate manoeuvre to quieten opposition to the museum's cultivation of Abstract Expressionism, he followed 'a two-pronged policy that, for reasons of tact or diplomacy, was never acknowledged, but was manifested, especially in the museum's exhibition program'.[36] Thus, there was no shortage of exhibitions catering to the prevailing taste for romantic or representational painting, leading one critic to charge that the museum was dedicated less to the 'art of our time' than to the 'art of our grandfathers' time'.[37] But simultaneously, Barr was acquiring works by the New York School, and canvassing discreetly for broader institutional support. It was he who persuaded Henry Luce of *Time-Life* to change his editorial policy toward the new art, telling him in a letter that it should be especially protected, not criticized as in the Soviet Union, because this, after all, was 'artistic free enterprise'.[38] Thus was Luce – who held the phrase 'America's intellectual health' permanently on the end of his tongue – won over to Barr's and MoMA's interests. In August 1949, *Life* magazine gave its centre-page spread to Jackson Pollock, landing the artist and his work on every coffee table in America. Such coverage (and Barr's effort to secure it) destroys the case for neglect.

But it was loans to Europe from MoMA's collection which best illustrate the fortunes of the New York School. Under the auspices of the International Program, which was established in 1952 through a five-year annual grant of $125,000 from the Rockefeller Brothers Fund, the museum launched a massive export programme of Abstract Expressionism, which Barr himself referred to as a form of 'benevolent propaganda for foreign intelligentsia'[39] (another MoMA activist called it 'an immense asset toward foreign understanding'). Director of the programme was Porter McCray, Yale graduate and yet another veteran of Nelson Rockefeller's South American intelligence outfit. In December 1950, McCray took a year's leave of absence from his job as director of MoMA's Department of Circulating Exhibitions to become an attaché in the US Foreign Service, assigned to the cultural section of the Marshall Plan in Paris. Of this move, Russell Lynes wrote in his history of MoMA that 'The Museum now had, and was delighted to have, the whole world (or at least the world outside the Iron Curtain) in which to proselytize – though this time the exportable religion was home-grown rather than what had been in the past its primary message, the importable faith from Europe.'[40] In France, McCray saw at first hand the negative impact of the State Department's official proscription of (so-called) left-wing artists, leaving what one American Embassy official called 'a gap in American interests and activities which not only is impossible for Europeans to understand but which plays into the hands of the Communists by appearing to justify their charge that America fails to share the basic values of western civilization'.[41] McCray returned to MoMA with a mission to correct this impression. Under him, the museum's loans for touring exhibitions increased dramatically, even 'to a somewhat disquieting degree', according to one internal report, leaving the museum 'deprived of most of its best American paintings for 18 months' in 1955. By 1956 the International Program had organized thirty-three international exhibitions, including the US participation in the Venice Biennale (the only country to be privately represented). At the same time, loans to US embassies and consulates increased dramatically.

'There was a series of articles relating the Museum of Modern Art's International Program to cultural propaganda; and even suggestions that it was associated with the CIA, and since I worked there through those years I can say, categorically, untrue!'[42] said Waldo Rasmussen, assistant to McCray. 'The main emphasis of the International Program was about art – it wasn't about politics, and it wasn't about propaganda. And in fact it was important for an American museum to avoid the suggestion of cultural propaganda, and for that reason it wasn't always advantageous to have connections with American embassies, or American government figures, because that would suggest that the exhibitions were intended as propaganda, and they were not.'[43]

The Museum of Modern Art was neither free from propaganda, nor from government figures. When, for example, it accepted the contract to supply the art exhibit for the Congress for Cultural Freedom's 1952 Masterpieces festival in Paris, it did so under the auspices of trustees who were fully cognizant of the CIA's role in that organization. Moreover, the exhibit's curator, James Johnson Sweeney (a member of MoMA's advisory committee, and of the American Committee for Cultural Freedom), publicly endorsed the propaganda value of the show when he announced: 'On display will be masterpieces that could not have been created nor whose exhibition would be allowed by such totalitarian regimes as Nazi Germany or present-day Soviet Russia and her satellites.'[44] The view that abstract art was synonymous with democracy, that it was 'on our side', was also stressed by Alfred Barr, who borrowed from Cold War rhetoric when he maintained that 'The modern artist's nonconformity and love of freedom cannot be tolerated within a monolithic tyranny and modern art is useless for the dictator's propaganda.'[45]

Of far greater significance than Nabokov's Masterpieces exhibition was the 1953–4 tour of the show 'Twelve Contemporary American Painters and Sculptors',[46] the first by MoMA dedicated exclusively to the New York School. Opening at the Musée National d'Art Moderne in Paris, it was the first significant exhibition of American art to be held in a French museum for over fifteen years. To pre-empt the accusation that it was spearheading a 'cultural invasion' of France (whose own cultural chauvinism could not be underestimated), MoMA claimed that the show was the result of requests initiated by the host museum. In fact, the opposite was the case. According to a despatch from the American Embassy in Paris, 'In early February 1953, the Museum [of Modern Art] requested the Cultural Relations Section of the Embassy to discuss with Jean Cassou, Director of the Musée National d'Art Moderne at Paris, the possibility of putting on the present show. M. Cassou had already scheduled all of his exhibition space until the spring of 1954. On learning, however, that this exhibition would be available, he reorganized his plans and put off an exhibition of the Belgian painter, Ensor, which had been planned.'[47] The despatch complained of the embassy's inability 'to take any action on this request because of the absence of any art program under the auspices of the United States Government', but went on to state that 'In the case of the exhibition of American art under consideration, however, this deadlock was broken by action of the Nelson Rockefeller Fund, which allotted funds to the Museum of Modern Art in New York to be used for international exhibitions.'[48]

Unable to assume any official role in the exhibition, the American Embassy confined itself to acting as a quiet liaison between MoMA and its French hosts. These included the Association Française d'Action Artistique, which was attached to both the Ministry of Foreign Affairs and the Ministry of National Education. The Association came forward with a significant 'donation' for a de luxe catalogue, posters and 'all publicity for the show'. The link is interesting: the Association was also a 'donor' to the Congress for Cultural Freedom, and its director, Philippe Erlanger, was, according to Junkie Fleischmann, 'one of those people in France who has been most helpful and cooperative every time that we have approached him with any problems having to do with the Congress'.[49] Erlanger was, in fact, a designated CIA contact at the French Foreign Office. Through him, the Congress for Cultural Freedom (and, on this occasion, MoMA), acquired a credible conduit for official French funds to cultural propaganda initiatives. René d'Harnoncourt, who attached sufficient importance to the show to install it in person, could not have been ignorant of this connection. Elements of the French press picked up on the political manoeuvring behind the show, and snide reference was made to the Musée d'Art Moderne as a new outpost of 'United States territory', and to the painters on show there as 'Mr Foster Dulles' twelve apostles'.

As 'Twelve Contemporary American Painters and Sculptors' was being packed up for its next destination (it travelled on to Zurich, Dusseldorf, Stockholm, Oslo and Helsinki), MoMA was already preparing for its participation in an exhibition which would bring it once again into a direct relationship with the Congress for Cultural Freedom. Writing to Nabokov on 9 April 1954, Monroe Wheeler, MoMA's director of Exhibitions and Publications, confirmed that 'Our Coordination Committee has agreed that we should cooperate as much as we can with your project for an exhibition of paintings by artists between the ages of 18 and 35. We would like to suggest for membership on your International Advisory Committee the Museum's Director of Painting and Sculpture, Mr Andrew Carnduff Ritchie.'[50]

The result of this collaboration was the 'Young Painters' show, which opened at the Galleria Nazionale d'Arte Moderna in Rome, then moved to the Palais des Beaux-Arts in Brussels, the Musée National d'Art Moderne in Paris, and the Institute of Contemporary Arts (ICA) in London. Of the 170 paintings in the exhibit, nearly all were abstract works. Ritchie, who believed that artists working in the abstract mode were in some way responding to 'the weakness, even sterility, of most non-Communist figurative painting', selected works by Richard Diebenkorn, Seymour Drumlevitch, Joseph Glasco, John Hultberg, Irving Kriesberg and Theodoros Stamos. Thus, whilst European audiences were still being introduced to the first wave of Abstract Expressionists, Ritchie was already delivering the second.

As usual, the Congress for Cultural Freedom rustled up large cash prizes, to be awarded to the three best paintings (Hultberg shared the first prize for best painting with Giovanni Dova and Alan Reynolds, each receiving 1,000 Swiss francs, or $2,000, 'donated' by Fleischmann). Funds to organize the show, and for its transportation and publicity during the year that it toured, were provided directly by the Farfield Foundation. MoMA's International Program picked up the tab for transporting the works to and from Europe, using money supplied by the Rockefeller Brothers Fund. The Congress's media network did its part in amplifying the show's influence. *Preuves* devoted half of its October 1956 issue to the exhibition, and published an international survey of young painters on the subject of abstraction versus figurative art.[51] Josselson, who averred that 'the problems of modern painting happen to be a hobby of mine', forwarded the survey to Nelson Rockefeller, and said that it ranked 'high among the topics of discussion in Paris today'.[52]

The collaboration with the Congress brought MoMA access to the most prestigious art institutions in Europe. Sitting on the Congress Arts Committee were the directors of the Palais des Beaux-Arts in Brussels, Switzerland's Museum of Modern Art, London's ICA, the Kaiser Friedrich Museum in Berlin, the Musée National d'Arte Moderne in Paris, the Guggenheim Museum (New York and Venice), and the Galleria Nazionale d'Arte Moderna in Rome. Combined with the economic strength of MoMA (and, behind the scenes, the Farfield Foundation), this committee had the breadth and scope to influence aesthetic tastes across Europe. As one reviewer of 'Young Painters' wrote, 'The fact that the exhibition conforms to the prevailing taste for various currents of abstract art and offers no surprises is probably attributable to the composition of the selection jury. Almost all members of the jury are museum directors and as such cannot be expected to outpace the established best.'[53]

There can be little doubt that this prevailing orthodoxy was carved out according to a political, and not a solely aesthetic, agenda. It was an agenda personally sanctioned by President Eisenhower who, unlike Truman before him, recognized the value of modern art as a 'pillar of liberty'. In an address which explicitly endorsed the work of MoMA, Eisenhower declared: 'As long as artists are at liberty to feel with high personal intensity, as long as our artists are free to create with sincerity and conviction, there will be healthy controversy and progress in art . . . How different it is in tyranny. When artists are made the slaves and the tools of the state; when artists become chief propagandists of a cause, progress is arrested and creation and genius are destroyed.'[54] These sentiments were echoed by a former chairman of MoMA's International Program, August Heckscher, who claimed the museum's work was 'related to the central struggle of the age – the struggle of freedom against tyranny. We know that where tyranny takes over, whether under Fascism or Communism, modern art is destroyed and exiled.'[55]

George Kennan rallied to this 'free art' ideology, telling an audience of MoMA activists in 1955 that they had a duty 'to correct a number of impressions that the outside world entertains of us, impressions that are beginning to affect our international position in very important ways'.[56] These 'negative feelings', said Kennan, were 'related to cultural rather than political conditions'. His next point startled everyone: 'The totalitarians recognized that only if they appeared outwardly to enjoy the confidence and enthusiasm of the artists could they plausibly claim to have created a hopeful and creditable civilization . . . And I find it sad that they should have come to this appreciation so much sooner than many of our own people.'[57] What, asked Kennan, was the nature of the task ahead? 'We have . . . to show the outside world both that we have a cultural life and that we care something about it. That we care enough about it, in fact, to give it encouragement and support here at home, and to see that it is enriched by acquaintance with similar activity elsewhere. If these impressions could only be conveyed with enough force and success to countries beyond our borders, *I for one would willingly trade the entire remaining inventory of political propaganda for the results that could be achieved by such results alone* .'[58]

The Congress for Cultural Freedom's support for experimental, predominantly abstract painting over representational, or realist aesthetics, must be viewed in this context. From the statements of Tom Braden and Donald Jameson, it is evident that the CIA felt it had a part to play in encouraging consent for the new art. From the records of the Farfield Foundation, it can also be shown that the Agency expressed its commitment with dollars. In addition to supporting the 'Young Painters' show, several donations were passed from the Farfield to MoMA, including $2,000 to its International Council in 1959, for the provision of books on modern art to Polish readers.

There is further, incontrovertible evidence that the CIA was an active component in the machinery which promoted Abstract Expressionism. Immediately after the 1955–6 'Young Painters' show closed, Nicolas Nabokov had started to plan a follow-up. Despite a faltering start, the proposal was finally approved in early 1959. Junkie Fleischmann, by now chairman of the Congress Music and Arts Committee, as well as a member of MoMA's International Arts Council (an expanded version of the International Program), provided the link between the two organizations. Once again, MoMA selected the American participation for the show, mostly from works which had already been shipped to Europe for the Biennale de Paris. By the end of the year, Nabokov's secretary was able to tell Junkie that news of the planned exhibition had 'swept through the artistic circles like a tornado. Every young painter in Paris, every gallery director, every art critic are [sic] telephoning [the Congress] to find out what it's all about. It's going to be a terrific hit.'[59]

Originally entitled 'Sources poétiques de la peinture actuelle', the show which finally opened in January 1960 at the Louvre's Musée des Arts Décoratifs was called, more provocatively, 'Antagonismes'. Dominating the exhibition were works by Mark Rothko (who was in France at the time), Sam Francis, Yves Klein (in his first showing in Paris), Franz Kline, Louise Nevelson, Jackson Pollock, Mark Tobey and Joan Mitchell. Many of the paintings had been brought to Paris from Vienna, where the Congress had exhibited them as part of a wider, CIA-orchestrated campaign to undermine the 1959 Communist youth festival. This show had cost the CIA $15,365, but for its expanded version in Paris they had to dig deeper. A further $10,000 was laundered through the Hoblitzelle Foundation, to which was added $10,000 from the Association Française d'Action Artistique.

Although the press paid 'lavish attention' to the 'Antagonismes' show, the Congress was obliged to acknowledge that reviews were 'on the whole very spiteful'. Although some European critics had been won over to the 'magnificent resonances' and the 'breathless, dizzy world' of Abstract Expressionism, many others were baffled or outraged by it. In Barcelona, a critic reviewing 'The New American Painting', which MoMA toured that year, was appalled to learn that two canvases – one by Jackson Pollock, the other by Grace Hartigan – were so big that the upper part of the metal entrance door of the museum had to be sawn off to get them in. 'The Biggest in the World', announced *La Libre Belgique*, which worried that 'this strength, displayed in the frenzy of a total freedom, seems a really dangerous tide. Our own abstract painters, all the "informal" European artists, seem pygmies before the disturbing power of these unchained giants.'[60] References to the size, the violence, the Wild West abounded, 'as if the critics had got hold of the wrong catalogue, and thought the pictures were painted by Wyatt Earp or Billy the Kid'.[61]

It was not only European artists who felt dwarfed by the gigantism of Abstract Expressionism. Adam Gopnik later concluded that 'oversized abstract watercolors [had become] the single style of the American museum, forcing two generations of realists to live in basements and pass still-lifes around like samizdat'.[62] John Canaday reflected that, by 1959, 'Abstract Expressionism was at the zenith of its popularity, to such an extent that an unknown artist trying to exhibit in New York couldn't find a gallery unless he was painting in a mode derived from one or another member of the New York School.'[63] Critics who 'suggested that Abstract Expressionism was abusing its own success and that the monopolistic orgy had gone on long enough' could find themselves, said Canaday, in a 'painful situation' (he claimed his own lack of appreciation for the New York School had earned him a death threat).[64] Peggy Guggenheim, returning to the States in 1959 after a twelve-year absence, was 'thunderstruck, the entire art movement had become an enormous business venture'.

The Museum of Modern Art, described by one critic as the 'overgeared cartel of Modernism,' held tenaciously to its executive role in manufacturing a history for Abstract

Expressionism. Ordered and systematic, this history reduced what had once been provocative and strange to an academic formula, a received mannerism, an *art officiel*. Thus installed within the canon, the freest form of art now lacked freedom. More and more painters produced more and more paintings which got bigger and bigger and emptier and emptier. It was this very stylistic conformity, prescribed by MoMA and the broader social contract of which it was a part, that brought Abstract Expressionism to the verge of kitsch. 'It was like the emperor's clothes,' said Jason Epstein. 'You parade it down the street and you say, "This is great art," and the people along the parade route will agree with you. Who's going to stand up to Clem Greenberg and later to the Rockefellers who were buying it for their bank lobbies and say, "This stuff is terrible"?'[65] Perhaps Dwight Macdonald was right when he said 'few Americans care to argue with a hundred million dollars'.[66]

What of the artists themselves? Did they not object to the Cold War rhetoric – what Peter Fuller called 'the ideological laundering' – that often accompanied exhibitions of their work? One of the extraordinary features of the role that American painting played in the cultural Cold War is not the fact alone that it became part of this enterprise, but that a movement which so deliberately declared itself to be apolitical could become so intensely politicized. 'Modern painting is the bulwark of the individual creative expression, aloof from the political left and its blood brother, the right,'[67] the artist Paul Burlin had declared. For critic Harold Rosenberg, post-war art entailed 'the political choice of giving up politics'. 'Yet in its politically shrewd reaction against politics, in its ostensible demonstration that competing ideologies had depleted themselves and dissipated adherents . . . the new painters and their supporters had of course become fully engaged in the issues of the day.'[68]

Was their work entirely at odds with the social and political function to which it was put? Barnett Newman, in his introduction to the catalogue of the 1943 show 'First Exhibition of Modern American Artists', wrote: 'We have come together as American modern artists because we feel the need to present to the public a body of art that will adequately reflect the new America that is taking place today and the kind of America that will, it is hoped, become the cultural center of the world.'[69] Did Newman come to regret this national context? Willem de Kooning found 'this American-ness' to be 'a certain burden' and said, 'If you come from a small nation, you don't have that. When I went to the Academy and I was drawing from the nude, I was making the drawing, not Holland. I feel sometimes an American artist must feel like a baseball player or something – a member of a team writing American history.'[70] Yet in 1963, de Kooning was proud to receive the President's Medal. 'The idea of an isolated American painting . . . seems absurd to me, just as the idea of creating a purely American mathematics or physics would seem absurd,'[71] said Jackson Pollock, who died at the wheel of his Oldsmobile before he faced the choice of whether or not to accept such honours.

Robert Motherwell, who was initially happy to be part of the 'mission to make painting in America equal to painting elsewhere' later thought it 'strange when a commodity is more powerful than the men who make it'.[72] Repudiating nationalist claims for Abstract Expressionism, in the 1970s he supported the English abstract artist Patrick Heron when he challenged America's right to exert a monopoly in cultural leadership, and wrote of Heron's 'gallant efforts re. N[ew] Y[ork] Imperialism . . . your generation in England made a heroic effort to reach beyond gentlemanly art [which] was not then or now given its just due' because of New York's 'want of generosity toward your generation in Britain'. Motherwell added that he looked forward to 'an unchauvinistic story of modern art', and ended by reassuring Heron that 'not all Americans are mongols'.[73]

Motherwell was a member of the American Committee for Cultural Freedom. So were Baziotes, Calder and Pollock (though he was sodden with drink when he joined). The realist painter Ben Shahn refused to join, referring to it as the 'ACCFuck'. Former fellow travellers Mark Rothko and Adolph Gottlieb both became committed anti-Communists during the Cold War. In 1940 they helped found the Federation of Modern Painters and Sculptors, which started by condemning all threats to culture from nationalistic and reactionary political movements. In the following months, the Federation became an active agent for anti-Communism in the art world. It sought to expose Party influence in various art organizations. Rothko and Gottlieb led these efforts to destroy Communist presence in the art world. Their dedication to that cause was so strong that when the Federation voted to cease its political activities in 1953, they resigned.

Ad Reinhardt was the only Abstract Expressionist who continued to cleave to the left, and as such he was all but ignored by the official art world until the 1960s. This left him in a perfect position to point out the inconsistencies in the lives and art of his former friends, whose drunken evenings at the Cedar Tavern had given way to homes in the Hamptons, Providence and Cape Cod; and whose group photos like 'The Irascibles' of 1950 had been replaced by features in *Vogue* magazine showing these angry young men looking more like the stockbrokers who listed them as 'speculative' or 'growth' painters, and reported a market for Abstract Expressionism 'boiling' with activity. Reinhardt roundly condemned his fellow artists for succumbing to the temptations of greed and ambition. He called Rothko a '*Vogue* magazine cold-water-flat-fauve', and Pollock a 'Harpers Bazaar bum'. Barnett Newman was 'the avant-garde huckster-handicraftsman and educational shopkeeper' and 'the holy-roller explainer-entertainer-in-residence' (a comment which provoked Newman to sue). Reinhardt didn't stop there. He said that a museum should be 'a treasure house and tomb, not a counting house or amusement centre'.[74] He compared art criticism to 'pigeon droolings', and ridiculed Greenberg as a dictator-pope. Reinhardt was the only Abstract Expressionist to participate in the March on Washington for black rights in August 1963.

It is hard to sustain the argument that the Abstract Expressionists merely 'happened to be painting *in* the Cold War and not *for* the Cold War'.[75] Their own statements and, in some cases, political allegiances, undermine claims of ideological disengagement. But it is also the case that the work of the Abstract Expressionists cannot be reduced to the political history in which it is situated. Abstract Expressionism, like jazz, was – is – a creative phenomenon existing independently and even, yes, triumphantly, apart from the political use which was made of it. 'There's no doubt that we need to understand all art in relationship to its time,' argued Philip Dodd. 'In order to make sense of Abstract Expressionism, we need to understand how it was made during an extraordinary moment in European and American relationships. At a political level these were a generation of radicals beached by history, and at a national level they emerged just at the moment when America became *the* great cultural imperium of the post-war period. All these things need to be understood in order to be able to assess their achievements. But their art cannot be reduced to those conditions. It is true that the CIA were involved – I lament that as much as anybody else laments it – but that doesn't explain why it became important. There was something in the art itself that allowed it to triumph.'[76]

Jackson Pollock was killed in a car crash in 1956, by which time Arshile Gorky had already hanged himself. Franz Kline was to drink himself to death within six years. In 1965, the sculptor David Smith died following a car crash. In 1970, Mark Rothko slashed his veins and bled to death on his studio floor. Some of his friends felt that he killed himself partly because he could not cope with the contradiction of being showered with material rewards for works which 'howled their opposition to bourgeois materialism'.

'The country is proud of its dead poets,' says the narrator of *Humboldt's Gift*. 'It takes terrific satisfaction in the poets' testimony that the USA is too tough, too big, too much, too rugged, that American reality is overpowering . . . The weakness of the spiritual powers is proved in the childishness, madness, drunkenness, and despair of these martyrs . . . So poets are loved, but loved because they just can't make it here. They exist to light up the enormity of the awful tangle.'[77]

7

The Guardian Furies

> In 1787, at an inn near Moulins, an old man was dying – a friend of Diderot's, whose ideas had been moulded by the philosophes. The local priests were baffled: they had tried everything in vain; the good man refused the last sacraments, saying he was a pantheist. Monsieur de Rollebon, who was passing by and who believed in nothing, bet the Curé of Moulins that he would take less than two hours to bring the sick man back to Christian sentiments. The Curé took the bet and lost: taken in hand at three in the morning, the sick man confessed at five and died at seven. 'You must be very good at arguing,' said the Curé, 'to beat our own people!' 'I didn't argue,' replied Monsieur de Rollebon, 'I made him frightened of hell.'
>
> Jean-Paul Sartre, *Nausea*

Whilst Abstract Expressionism was being deployed as a Cold War weapon, America had turned up an even more potent discovery – God. Religious faith in the moral law had been enshrined in the Constitution of the United States in 1789, but it was during the height of the Cold War that America discovered how useful the invocation of the highest hosanna could be. God was everywhere: He was in 10,000 balloons containing bibles which were floated across the Iron Curtain by the Bible Balloon Project in 1954; His imprimatur was stamped on an act of Congress of 14 June 1954 which expanded the Pledge of Allegiance to include the words 'One Nation Under God', a phrase which, according to Eisenhower, reaffirmed 'the transcendence of religious faith in America's heritage and future; in this way we shall constantly strengthen those spiritual weapons which forever will be our country's most powerful resource in peace and war';[1] He even began to appear on dollar bills after Congress ordained that the words 'In God We Trust' become the nation's official motto in 1956.

'Why should *we* make a five-year plan for ourselves when God seems to have had a thousand-year plan ready-made for us?'[2] asked one American historian. Under the terms of this logic, political virtue was to be submitted to a long-standing Christian tradition of obedience to the law of God. By invoking the ultimate moral authority, America acquired an unanswerable sanction for her 'manifest destiny'.

Destiny's elect had been taught, like the boys at Groton School, that 'In history, every religion has greatly honored those members who destroyed the enemy. The Koran, Greek mythology, the Old Testament . . . Doing in the enemy is the right thing to do. Of course, there are some restraints on ends and means. If you go back to Greek culture and read Thucydides, there are limits to what you can do to other Greeks, who are part of your culture. But there are no limits on what you can to do a Persian. He's a barbarian. The Communists were barbarians.'[3]

The religious imperative motivated Cold Warriors such as Allen Dulles who, brought up in the Presbyterian tradition, was fond of quoting from the Bible for its use of spies (by Joshua into Jericho). When the CIA moved into its vast new complex in the Virginian woods in 1961, Dulles arranged for one of his favourite quotes from scripture to be engraved on the wall of the Langley lobby: 'And ye shall know the truth, and the truth shall make you free' (John: 8,32). Henry Luce, the child of American missionaries, was fond of drawing on the same divine reference: 'The great Christian promise is this: Seek and ye shall find . . . That is the promise and the premise on which American is founded.' Luce seldom missed Sunday church or went to bed without first praying on his knees. His wife, Clare Booth Luce, converted to Roman Catholicism after her daughter Anne had been killed in a car accident in 1943. The country's most publicized conversion, it prompted some detractors to derision. According to one widely repeated jape, the Pope interrupted a doctrinal argument with Mrs Luce, when she was American ambassador to Italy, to remind her, 'But, Madam, I too am a Catholic.' She claimed credit for persuading Eisenhower to become a Presbyterian in the run-up to the 1952 election campaign.[4]

'Neither profit nor personal glory motivated Luce as deeply as his missionary urge to improve his countrymen, and he exercised his power in the sincere, if not unanimously shared belief that he knew what was good for them,' wrote one early biographer.[5] He insisted that 'the American capacity for successful cooperation is directly related to our country's constitutional dependence on God', and believed that 'no nation in history, except ancient Israel, was so obviously designed for some special phase of God's eternal purpose'.[6] To Luce, the Cold War was a holy war, in which Time Inc. was committed to the 'dominant aim and purpose' of defeating Communism throughout the world. 'Is that a declaration of private war?' he once asked Time Inc. executives. 'And if so, may it not be unlawful and probably mad? Perhaps so, but there are some mighty fine precedents for the declaration of private war.'[7] Nowhere was the parallel with the mercenaries of the crusades, or the private armada of Francis Drake, so powerfully drawn.

The theologian most favoured by Luce was Reinhold Niebuhr, an honorary patron of the Congress for Cultural Freedom, and a Cold War 'realist' who believed that the establishment of a calculated balance of power was paramount, with foreign policy the exclusive responsibility of an elite authority. For members of that elite, Niebuhr was, of course, a congenial authority figure. Martin Luther King, on the other hand, claimed to have learned from him the 'potential for evil'. Niebuhr served up liberal helpings of theology to *Time-Life* readers, winning Sidney Hook's approval for successfully reviving the doctrine of original sin as a political tool, and making 'God an instrument of national policy'.[8] Indeed, with the religious imperative insinuating its way into every major Cold War policy plank, the whole edifice of American power in the 1950s seemed to rest on one fundamental, monist proposition: that the future would be decided 'between the two great camps of men – those who reject and those who worship God'.[9] 'We must not be confused about the issue which confronts the world today,' President Truman had warned. 'It is tyranny or freedom . . . And even worse, communism denies the very existence of God.'[10] The manufacturing of such a concept – which reduced the complexity of world relations to a struggle between the powers of light and darkness – meant that the rhetoric of American foreign policy had come to rest on distinctions which resisted the processes of logic or rationality. George Santayana, writing in 1916, had described the philosophical process by which such distortions come to dominate the historical process: 'Imagination that is sustained is called knowledge, illusion that is coherent is called truth, and will that is systematic is called virtue'.[11]

Such distinctions were lost on the young preacher Billy Graham, who amplified Truman's warnings with the theory that 'Communism is . . . master-minded by Satan . . . I think there is no other explanation for the tremendous gains of Communism in which they seem to outwit us at every turn, unless they have supernatural power and wisdom and intelligence given to them.'[12] Norman Mailer inferred a different diagnosis: 'America's deepest political sickness is that it is a self-righteous nation.'[13]

It was in this climate of doctrinal dogmatism that Senator Joe McCarthy flourished. In *The Crucible*, Arthur Miller compared the Salem witch-hunts with the McCarthy period to demonstrate a parallel guilt, two centuries apart, 'of holding illicit, suppressed feelings of alienation and hostility toward standard, daylight society as defined by its most orthodox opponents. Without guilt the 1950s Red-hunt could never have generated such power.'[14] The main point of both inquisitions was to establish guilt by public confession, with the accused expected to 'damn his confederates as well as his Devil master, and guarantee his sterling new allegiance by breathing disgusting old vows – whereupon he was let loose to rejoin the society of extremely decent people'.[15] A curious feature of McCarthy's Un-American Activities hearings was that they showed 'less interest in the names supplied than in testing the sincerity of the witness's confession'. Leslie Fiedler, who, like his friend Irving Kristol, discovered religion in the early 1950s, described the process as a kind of symbolic ritual when he said that 'The confession in itself is nothing, but without the confession . . . we will not be able to move forward from a liberalism of innocence to a liberalism of responsibility.'[16]

Much drawn to the symbolism of public confession was the American Committee for Cultural Freedom. Elia Kazan, who had named names at a McCarthy hearing in April 1952, had been rewarded with membership of the American Committee, which was now happy to fight his battles for him. Defending Kazan's Actor's Studio from the attacks of a hardline anti-Communist group, Sol Stein, in Jesuitical mood, argued that Kazan was fulfilling the 'proper role for anti-Communists in the theatre [which] is that of missionary to their politically backward brethren who have taken much too long a time in appreciating the fact that service to front groups in this country contributes to the power of the Soviet mammoth'.[17] 'Those who sided with the Communists in the past ought to be given an opportunity to direct their energies into genuinely anti-Communist enterprises and efforts, if that is in line with their present convictions,' reasoned Stein.[18] Kazan, he said, should be given space to offer the 'political Johnny-come-latelies an opportunity for redemption in order that their talents might be enlisted against our common enemy'.[19] This was not enough to reassure the extreme anti-Communist pressure group, Aware, Inc., who complained that Kazan was continuing to work with 'unregenerates' like Marlon Brando, Frank Silvera and Lou Gilbert, and had failed to employ 'any active anti-Communists'.[20]

The American Committee also saw fit to appoint to its executive body America's most famous informer, Whittaker Chambers, whose testimony had sunk the career of Alger Hiss. Whittaker had elevated the art of snitching to new heights, provoking one senior colleague at *Time-Life* (where Chambers was an editor) to tell him, in Luce's presence, 'I think your favourite movie would be *The Informer*.' Sol Stein wrote excitedly to Chambers that his nomination had precipitated 'a number of post-midnight anonymous calls threatening to wipe the [board members] "off the face of the earth". Dear God, I suppose this foolishness will always be with us,' he concluded.[21]

'At issue,' wrote Chambers in *Witness*, his 1952 autobiography, 'was the question whether this sick society, which we call Western civilization, could in its extremity still cast up a man whose faith in it was so great that he would voluntarily abandon those things which men hold dear, including life, to defend it.'[22] Presenting himself as just such a David, Chambers got $75,000 for taking up his sling against Communism from the *Saturday Evening Post*, which serialized the book over eight weeks. 'You are one of those who did not return from Hell with empty hands,'[23] André Malraux told him after reading *Witness*.

With God and Mammon on their side, American anti-Communists were able to reap the benefits of what had become a flourishing sub-profession. In Hollywood, the crusade to cleanse American culture of all godless impurities was seized upon by Hedda Hopper and Louella Parsons, two syndicated gossip columnists who were to moral hygiene what Mrs Beeton was to a clean kitchen. Richly salaried, they were 'the guardian Furies, the police matrons planted at the portals to keep out the sinful, the unpatriotic, and the rebels against propriety unworthy to breathe the same pure air as such apostolic exemplars as Louis B. Mayer, Harry Cohn, Jack Warner, Darryl Zanuck, Sam Goldwyn, and a handful of others. The ladies' ferocity towards Communism was matched only by their duplication of some of its practices.'[24]

Hopper and Parsons, though they may not have thought of themselves as such, were 'militant libertists', the phrase which designated a top-secret campaign on the part of the Pentagon, the Navy, the National Security Council and the Operations Coordinating Board to insert the theme of 'freedom' into American movies. On Friday 16 December 1955, a secret gathering was convened by the Joint Chiefs of Staff to discuss the how the idea of 'Militant Liberty' could be exploited by Hollywood. According to a top-secret report, 'Militant Liberty' was designed to 'explain the true conditions existing under Communism in simple terms and to explain the principles upon which the Free World way of life is based', and 'to awaken free peoples to an understanding of the magnitude of the danger confronting the Free World; and to generate a motivation to combat this threat'.[25] 'The idea was to create a slogan, a political catchword that most people would have the impression had arisen spontaneously but which in fact had been intentionally introduced into the culture,' explained cultural historian Christopher Simpson. 'It was a pretty sophisticated propaganda operation for its time.'[26] As the basis for a doctrinal campaign, Militant Liberty was approved at the highest levels. But it was not until the following year that the Pentagon finally found a concrete formula by which to deliver its message. In June and July 1956, representatives of the Joint Chiefs of Staff held several meetings in California with a posse of Hollywood figures dedicated to expunging Communism: John Ford, Merian Cooper, John Wayne and Ward Bond.

The meetings, which were held in the MGM office of John Ford, lasted up to six hours. According to a memo of 5 July 1956, 'Mr Wayne stated that in his pictures, produced by him (BacJac Productions), the [Militant Liberty] program would be inserted carefully.' To see how this might be done, Wayne invited everyone to his home at 4570 Louise Avenue, Encino, the following evening. 'After dinner, the movies *They Were Expendable* and *The Quiet Man* were shown and studied by Mr. Wayne and Mr. Ford for the manner in which favorable slants for the Navy and free-world cultural patterns had been introduced in the two films.'[27]

At another meeting, Merian Cooper pointed out that a series of films being made by Cornelius Vanderbilt Whitney, 'lacked a theme . . . and that he wished that he had had this (e.g. Militant Liberty) and further stated that he would put it in the others'.[28] It was arranged that Whitney would be briefed accordingly. A successful industrialist, Cornelius 'Sonny' Vanderbilt Whitney shared in the vast Whitney fortune which had fallen to his cousin, Jock, to manage. Like Jock, he was also close to the CIA (their cousin was Tracy Barnes), and more than ready to help it: as a trustee, Cornelius allowed the Whitney Trust to be used as a CIA conduit. He was also part of the team involved in formulating a psychological warfare initiative called the National Security Information Agency. Well known as a producer (in 1933, he went into business with David Selznick, and together they produced *A Star is Born*, *Rebecca*, and *Gone With the Wind*), in 1954 he set up C.V. Whitney Pictures Inc. and stated, 'I want to film what I would describe as an "American Series" to show our people their country and also to make certain that the rest of the world learns more about us.'[29] The first picture in the American Series was *The Searchers*, produced at a cost of $3 million, and directed by John Ford.

During the war, John Ford had been chief of the Field Photographic Branch of OSS. His job was to photograph the work of guerrillas, saboteurs and Resistance outfits in occupied Europe. Special assignments included producing top-secret films which were screened to government leaders. In 1946 he incorporated his own production company, Argosy Pictures. The principal investors, besides Ford and Merian Cooper, were all OSS veterans: William Donovan, Ole Doering (a member of Donovan's Wall Street law firm), David Bruce and William Vanderbilt. Ford was entirely in sympathy with the idea that the government's intelligence agencies should suggest themes for Hollywood audiences, and asked them to 'leave six copies of the Militant Liberty booklet with him and send him a dozen more so that he could pass them on to his script writers so that they can learn the nomenclature of the concept'. He further requested that a representative of the Joint Chiefs of Staff come to the Pensacola, Florida, location of the movie *Eagles Wings*, 'for assistance in putting Militant Liberty elements in the movie'.[30]

There, to help get the message across, was Merian Cooper, who had fought against Pancho Villa, and as an army flyer had been shot down over France by the Germans in 1918. Becoming a producer with RKO in the 1930s, he was responsible for teaming Fred Astaire with Ginger Rogers. Also on the set of *Eagles Wings* was Ward Bond, president of the Motion Picture Alliance for the Preservation of American Ideals, an organization dedicated to running Communists out of the industry, and to aiding the House Un-American Activities Committee (HUAC). Bond, said one acquaintance, 'would do anything that made him feel important, even at the expense of stomping on people'. Ford (who was himself disgusted by McCarthy's blacklists) used to say, 'Let's face it. Ward Bond is a shit. But he's our favourite shit.' Here was the Hollywood consortium at work, made up of a group of men who had known each other for decades, and who looked to one another for authorization and support.

Militant Liberty could only have happened in an America so conscious of a sense of imperial burden. Articulating the imperatives (and sacrifices) of the *pax Americana*, these films celebrated duty, the group, the response to command, the dominance of male derring-do. It was in this context that John Wayne, who went to extraordinary lengths to avoid military service in the Second World War, came to be regarded as the model of an American soldier, the personification of 'Americanism'. 'The Duke' was the frontier man, taming the world. In 1979, Congress struck a medal in his honour. The inscription read simply, 'JOHN WAYNE, AMERICA'. But his was the America of red-baiting and ethnic prejudice. As the eponymous hero in *Big Jim McLain* (1952), he starred in one of the crudest B-film expressions of Commie-hating (the film was made as a tribute to the House Un-American Activities Committee).

Movies, like propaganda, trade in fiction, but if this fiction is adroitly manufactured, it will be taken for reality. To perform this function well, Hollywood had long understood the need to cut its mythical patterns to suit the prevailing political and social mood. Thus it had switched from making anti-Bolshevik films in the 1920s and 1930s, to glorifying Russia as a wartime ally (in films such as *The North Star*, *Days of Glory*, *Song of Russia*, and the notorious *Mission to Moscow*, which had actually whitewashed the Moscow Trials and praised the Russians as defenders of democracy), to producing a rash of anti-Communist films in the 1950s – *The Red Nightmare*, *The Red Menace*, *Invasion USA*, *I Was A Communist for the FBI*, *Red Planet Mars*, *Iron Curtain*, *My Son John*, *Invasion of the Bodysnatchers*. *Walk East on Beacon Street*, which was scripted and financed by the FBI, was J. Edgar Hoover's personal favourite. Their titles as unconvincing as their plots, these films all revealed a neurotic obsession with the outsider, the unknown, 'the Other'. Just as Captain America had switched from battling Nazis to battling Communists, the attitude of American films towards Germany changed radically, the vanquished enemy now portrayed as heroic fighters and worthy opponents (*Rommel, The Desert Fox*, 1952; *The Sea Chase*, 1955; *The Enemy Below*, 1957). As Monday's enemies became Tuesday's friends, Hollywood showed how easily it could rip off the 'Good and Evil labels from one nation and [paste] them onto another'.[31]

Whilst such films played well to a domestic audience in thrall to exaggerated claims of the Communist menace – most Americans were now convinced that 'the Russians were coming and the bomb would soon fall in the night'[32] – in the international market they were poor performers. For a Europe still wounded by the memories of Fascism, the insensate hatred and verbal violence of Hollywood's anti-Communist offerings were unattractive in the extreme. Faring better were Disney's cartoons, and feel-good films such as *Roman Holiday* and *The Wizard of Oz*. But not all Europeans were seduced by these fictive paradises. Buried deep in the clauses of successive trade agreements (starting with the Blum–Byrnes accord of 1946) were provisions which guaranteed an increase in the quota of American films shown in countries such as France. Such agreements were met with indignant criticism in French intellectual circles and even, in 1948, led to violent street battles.

American strategists were surprisingly slow to respond to widespread resentment in Europe at the saturation levels of Hollywood imports. There was no diplomatic representation at the 1951 Cannes Film Festival, nor any formal delegation of American motion picture leaders, writers, technicians or artists. By contrast, the Russians had sent their Deputy Minister of Cinema, as well as the renowned director Poudovkine, who gave a brilliant resumé of Soviet achievements. After receiving reports that America had looked 'very silly' at Cannes, the US government resolved to give the motion picture industry more attention.

On 23 April 1953, after his appointment as special consultant to the government on cinema, Cecil B. DeMille strode into C. D. Jackson's office. Writing to Henry Luce two weeks later, C. D. said DeMille 'is very much on our side and . . . is quite rightly impressed with the power of American films abroad. He has a theory, to which I subscribe completely, that the most effective use of American films is not to design an entire picture to cope with a certain problem, but rather to see to it that in a "normal" picture the right line, aside, inflection, eyebrow movement, is introduced. He told me that any time I could give him a simple problem for a country or an area, he would find a way of dealing with it in a picture.'[33]

DeMille's acceptance of a consultancy with the Motion

Picture Service was a *coup* for government propagandists. Working through 135 United States Information Service posts in 87 countries, the MPS had a huge distribution network to hand. Awash with government funds, it was effectively a 'producer', with all the facilities available to a production company. It employed producer-directors who were given top-security clearance and assigned to films which articulated 'the objectives which the United States is interested in obtaining' and which could best reach 'the pre-determined audience that we as a motion picture medium must condition'.[34] It advised secret bodies like the Operations Coordinating Board on films suitable for international distribution. In June 1954, it listed thirty-seven films for showing behind the Iron Curtain, including: *Peter Pan*, *The Jolson Story*, *The Glenn Miller Story*, *The Boy from Oklahoma*, *Roman Holiday*, *Little Women*, *Showboat*, *The Caine Mutiny*, *Go, Man, Go* (a history of the Harlem Globetrotters), *Alice in Wonderland* and *Executive Suite*.

The MPS also regulated American participation in film festivals abroad, thus filling the embarrassing vacuum of the 1951 Cannes Festival. Naturally, it worked hard to exclude 'American motion picture producers and films which do not support American foreign policy, which in some cases are harmful'[35] from being shown at international festivals. Instead, it pushed films like *The Bob Mathias Story* (Allied Artists, 1954), 'an almost perfect portrayal of the best phase of American life – a small town boy with his family, his sweetheart, his career, his interest in sports – all building up to his two-time triumph as one of the outstanding athletes in the history of the Olympics . . . if it hasn't got the American values we want on the screen, then we have got to start looking for a new set of values to publicize.'[36]

In the search for allies in Hollywood who best understood 'the propaganda problems of the U.S.' and who were prepared 'to insert in their scripts and in their action the right ideas with the proper subtlety', C. D. Jackson, as usual, was embarrassed for choice. In January 1954, he set down a list of 'friends' who could be expected to help the government: Cecil B. DeMille, Spyros P. Skouras and Darryl Zanuck at Fox; Nicholas Schenk, president of MGM, and producer Dore Schary; Barney

Balaban, president of Paramount; Harry and Jack Warner; James R. Grainger, president of RKO; Universal's president, Milton Rackmil; Columbia Pictures president, Harry Cohn; Herbert Yates at Republic; Walt and Roy Disney; and Eric Johnston of the Motion Picture Association.

But C. D.'s most valuable asset in Hollywood was CIA agent Carleton Alsop. Working undercover at Paramount Studios, Alsop had been a producer and agent, working on the MGM lot in the mid-1930s, then with Judy Garland in the late 1940s and early 1950s, by which time he had already joined Frank Wisner's Psychological Warfare Workshop. In the early 1950s, he authored regular 'movie reports' for the CIA and the Psychological Strategy Board. These reports were compiled in response to a double need: first, to monitor Communists and fellow travellers in Hollywood; and second, to summarize the achievements and failures of a covert pressure group – headed up by Carleton Alsop – charged with introducing specific themes into Hollywood films.

Alsop's secret reports make extraordinary reading. They reveal just how far the CIA was able to extend its reach into the film industry, despite its claims that it sought no such influence. One report, dated 24 January 1953, concentrated on the problem of black stereotyping in Hollywood. Under the heading 'Negroes in pictures', Alsop reported that he had secured the agreement of several casting directors to plant 'well dressed negroes as a part of the American scene, without appearing too conspicuous or deliberate. "Sangaree" which is shooting doesn't permit this kind of planting, unfortunately, because the picture is period and laid in the South. It will consequently show Plantation negroes. However, this is being off-set to a certain degree, by planting a dignified negro butler in one of the principal's homes, and by giving him dialogue indicating he is a freed man and can work where he likes.'[37] Alsop also reported that 'some negroes will be planted in the crowd scenes' in the comedy film *Caddy* (starring Jerry Lewis). At a time when many 'negroes' had as much chance of getting into a golf club as they had of getting the vote, this seemed optimistic indeed.[38]

In the same report, Alsop referred to the film *Arrowhead*, which, for once, showed a readiness to question America's treatment of the Apaches. But this, said Alsop, 'presented a serious problem' in that 'the Commies could use [it] to their advantage'. Happily, a little tinkering on his part ensured that most of the offending scenes (the shipment of a whole tribe of Apaches by the army against their wishes to Florida, and the tagging of them like animals) had been removed or 'their impact significantly diluted'. Other changes were achieved by redubbing lines of dialogue after the picture had already closed. Presented 'on a commercial and patriotic basis', Alsop encountered no opposition from the movie's producer, Nat Holt.[39]

The Soviets never lost an opportunity to underline America's poor record in race relations. In 1946 James Byrnes, Truman's Secretary of State, found himself 'stumped and defeated' when he attempted to protest Soviet denial of voting rights in the Balkans, only to find the Soviets replying, rightly, that 'the Negroes of Mr. Byrnes' own state of South Carolina were denied the same right'.[40] Alsop's efforts in Hollywood were part of a broader campaign to discredit Soviet claims about American discrimination, low pay, unequal justice, and violence against African-Americans. For his part, C. D. Jackson wanted to confront the issue head on, and argued that 'It is time we stop explaining in terms of "this dreadful blot on our scutcheon" and look the whole world in the eye.'[41] To this end, psychological warfare experts on the Operations Coordinating Board (in close collaboration with the State Department) established a secret Cultural Presentation Committee whose chief activity was to plan and coordinate tours of black American artists. The appearance on the international stage of Leontyne Price, Dizzy Gillespie, Marian Anderson, William Warfield, the Martha Graham Dance Troupe, and a host of other multiracial and black American talent during this period was part of this covertly supervised 'export' programme. As was the extended tour of what one covert strategist described as the 'Great Negro folk opera', *Porgy and Bess*, which travelled through western Europe, South America and then the Soviet bloc for more than a decade, its cast of seventy African-Americans 'living demonstration of the American Negro as part of America's cultural life'.[42]

Curiously, the rise of this black American talent was in direct proportion to the demise of those writers who had first given voice to the poor status of blacks in American society. In 1955, the Russian magazine *Inostranaya Literatura* ('Foreign Literature') carried two short stories by Erskine Caldwell which caused American propagandists to choke on their breakfast. 'The first story is entitled "Crazy Money" (originally published in English as "The Windfall"), and it is innocuous,' wrote John Pauker of the United States Information Agency (USIA). 'The second story, however, is vicious: it is entitled MASSES OF MEN, and deals with corporate knavery, Negro poverty and the rape of a 10-year-old girl for 25¢.'[43] The USIA's concern was taken up by the American Committee for Cultural Freedom, which promised to pressurize Caldwell into publicly disclaiming the story. Echoing Sidney Hook's complaints of 1949 that Southern writers reinforced negative perceptions of America, with their 'novels of social protest and revolt' and 'American degeneracy and inanity',[44] the American Committee now resolved to 'steer clear of incestuous Southerners. Their work gives an exceedingly partial and psychologically colored account of our manners and morals.'[45] This was no isolated judgement, but one taken up by many cultural Cold Warriors, including Eric Johnston, who led the assault on the Southerners from his office in Hollywood: 'We'll have no more Grapes of Wrath, we'll have no more Tobacco Roads. We'll have no more films that show the seamy side of American life.'[46] Sales of books by Caldwell, Steinbeck, Faulkner and Richard Wright (the 'sepia Steinbeck') slumped in this period.

Back in Hollywood, Carleton Alsop was ever alert to portrayals of American seediness. In one report, he warned of a screenplay based on 'a novel called "Giant" by Edna Ferber'. This, he said, was 'one to watch', because it 'touches upon the following three problems: 1. Unflattering portrayal of rich, uncouth, ruthless Americans (Texans). 2. Racial denigration of Mexicans in Texas. 3. Implication wealth of Anglo-Texans built by exploiting Mexican labor.' Alsop's solution was simple: 'I'll see to it that it is killed each time someone tries to reactivate it at Paramount.'[47] He was only partially successful: Warner Brothers, not Paramount, made the film, James Dean's last, in 1956.

Alsop's reports continued to measure the political temperature in Hollywood, detailing the intricate job of nursing producers and studios into accepting what the CIA labelled its 'Hollywood formula'.[48] Out came the negative stereotypes, in came the characterizations which represented a healthy America. 'Have succeeded in removing American drunks, generally in prominent, if not principal roles, from the following pictures,' announced Alsop. 'Houdini. Drunken American reporter. Cut entirely. This may need a retake to correct. Legend of the Incas. Removed all heavy drinking on part of American lead from script. Elephant Walk. Keeping drunkenness to strict plot purposes only. Leininger and the Ants. All heavy drinking by American lead is being cut out of script.'[49]

On the subject of 'pictures striking at Religion' Alsop was especially sensitive: when one studio started developing the screenplay for d'Annunzio's *Daughter of Iorio*, in collaboration with Alberto Moravia, Alsop was convinced it would be '100% anti-clerical', and wondered 'How can we stop this one? I suppose the Vatican should do something about it. Don't think I'm taking too much of a pro-Catholic attitude which may be coloring my outlook. In this battle for the minds the first step the Commies must take is to debunk religion.'[50] Even more troubling was Roberto Rossellini's *Francesco, Giullare di Dio*, his treatment of the life of St Francis. 'This is really something,' Alsop wrote. 'You couldn't hope for a better picture debunking religion than this . . . St. Francis and his companions . . . are characterized in such an extreme oversimplified manner, that you get the feeling they are a bunch of nincompoops, not all there mentally and some of them perhaps homosexuals.'[51]

Alsop had joined Wisner's OPC at the same time as Finis Farr, a writer with Hollywood connections who had worked with John O'Hara. Recruited to the Psychological Warfare Workshop, Alsop and Farr were run by Howard Hunt, a former OSS-er whose taste for black propaganda (he later said he 'thought black') earned him a job running CIA training courses in political and psychological warfare.

Shortly after George Orwell's death in 1950, Howard Hunt had despatched Alsop and Farr to England to meet the author's widow, Sonia. They were not there to console her, but to invite her to sign over the film rights to *Animal Farm*. This she duly did, having first secured their promise that they would arrange for her to meet her hero Clark Gable. 'From this [visit],' wrote Howard Hunt, 'was to come the animated cartoon film of Orwell's *Animal Farm*, which the CIA financed and distributed throughout the world.'[52]

The rights having been acquired, Hunt set about securing a producer who could front for the CIA. He settled on Louis de Rochemont, who had employed Hunt when he made *The March of Time*, a series of monthly documentaries of which Time Inc. was the parent corporation.[53]

In liaison with Hunt, and using CIA funds injected by Alsop and Farr, de Rochemont began production of *Animal Farm* on 15 November 1951. Chosen to make the most ambitious animation film of its time (eighty cartoonists, 750 scenes, 300,000 drawings in colour) was the British firm of Halas and Batchelor Cartoon Films Ltd. Hungarian-born John Halas had come to England in 1936, and worked on *Music Man*, the first English cartoon in Technicolour. Teaming up with his wife, Joy Batchelor, he produced over a hundred government films for the British Central Office of Information, many of which helped publicize the Marshall Plan and NATO.

Animal Farm publisher Fredric Warburg took a keen interest in the Halas production, and kept his friends in the Congress for Cultural Freedom briefed on its progress. He visited the studio several times in 1952–3 to view sequences, and to add his suggestions for script changes (perhaps it was Warburg who suggested that the old Major, the prophet of the Revolution, should be given the voice and appearance of Winston Churchill?) At the same time, he was overseeing a new edition of *Animal Farm*, to be published by Secker and Warburg with stills from the Halas and Batchelor production.

The screenplay was also scrutinized by the Psychological Strategy Board. According to a memo of 23 January 1952, its officers were yet to be convinced by the script, finding its 'theme somewhat confusing and the impact of the story as expressed in cartoon sequence . . . somewhat nebulous. Although the symbolism is apparently plain, there is no great clarity of message.'[54] Curiously, the critique of America's intelligence bureaucrats echoed the earlier concerns of T. S.

Eliot and William Empson, both of whom had written to Orwell in 1944 to point out faults or inconsistencies in the central parable of *Animal Farm*.

The script problems were resolved by changing the ending. In the original text, Communist pigs and Capitalist man are indistinguishable, merging into a common pool of rottenness. In the film, such congruity was carefully elided (Pilkington and Frederick, central characters whom Orwell designated as the British and German governing classes, are barely noticeable) and, in the ending, simply eliminated. In the book, 'The creatures outside looked from pig to man, and from man to pig, and from pig to man again; but already it was impossible to say which was which.' Viewers of the film, however, saw an altogether different denouement, where it is the sight of the pigs which impels the other watching animals to mount a successful counter-revolution by storming the farmhouse. By removing the human farmers from the scene, to leave only the pigs revelling in the fruits of exploitation, the conflation of Communist corruption with capitalist decadence was reversed.

Even greater liberties were proposed when the CIA turned to Orwell's later work, *Nineteen Eighty-Four*. Orwell died before making over the film rights, but by 1954 they ended up in the hands of producer Peter Rathvon. Rathvon, a good friend of John Ford's, had been president of RKO until he was ousted by Howard Hughes in 1949. That year, he formed the Motion Picture Capital Corporation, which was engaged in motion picture production and financing. The corporation – and Rathvon himself – enjoyed a close relationship with the US government, financing films for the Motion Picture Service. According to Lawrence de Neufville, Howard Hunt solicited Rathvon's collaboration in the film version of Orwell's classic. Through Rathvon's corporation, government money was made available to start production on the film,[55] which appeared in 1956, starring Edmond O'Brien, Jan Sterling and Michael Redgrave.

Orwell's nightmare vision of the future in *Nineteen Eighty-Four* appealed to cultural strategists on a number of levels. CIA and Psychological Strategy Board officers (for whom the book was required reading) seized on its examination of the dangers of totalitarianism, ignoring the fact that Orwell was inveighing against the abuses that *all* controlling states, whether of the right or left, exercise over their citizens. Although its targets were complex, the overall message of the book was clear: it was a protest against *all* lies, against *all* tricks played by governments. But American propagandists were quick to designate it in terms of a specifically anti-Communist tract, leading one critic to argue that 'Whatever Orwell believed he was doing, he contributed to the Cold War one of its most potent myths . . . In the 1950s it was marvellous NATO Newspeak.'[56] On another level, *Nineteen Eighty-Four* was a book packed with distrust of mass culture and the dangers of universal slavery through bland ignorance (Winston's reaction to the popular song being trilled by the prole woman hanging out her washing perfectly encapsulates this fear of the 'mass-cult' and its easy soporific dullness). Again, its political target was less specific than universal: the abuse of language and logic – what Peter Vansittart called 'the squalid menace of Political Correctness' – was imputed to Us as well as Them. In the film version, this distinction was obscured.

The manipulation of Orwell's parable to suit the prejudices and assumptions of the film's makers was, of course, entirely consistent with the *parti pris* of the cultural Cold War. Helping to provide a structure for this partisan interpretation was none other than Sol Stein, Executive Director of the American Committee for Cultural Freedom, whom Rathvon consulted on several occasions for his advice on the screenplay. Stein had plenty to give. First, the script 'should have a great deal of relevance to the specifics of present day totalitarianism. For instance, the "Big Brother" posters ought to have the photograph of an actual human being, not a cartoon-like caricature of Stalin. In other words, the probability of Big Brother's real existence should not be diminished by linking him to the now dead Stalin.'[57] Nothing in the film should be caricature, Stein went on, 'but merely an extension of something we can directly witness today'. For instance, where 'members of the Anti-Sex League are supposed to wear sashes across their chests,' Stein worried that 'such sashes don't correspond to anything in totalitarian life as we know it but rather to the sashes worn by diplomats on ceremonial occasions.'[58] Stein therefore suggested that they wear armbands instead. Similarly, where Orwell had introduced trumpets in the novel, Stein wanted them 'eliminated' because for Americans, trumpets were 'associated with pageantry'.[59]

But it was the ending which most exercised Stein, who told Rathvon: 'The problem with the ending, as I understood it, is that it ends on a note of total despair: Winston Smith is robbed of his humanity and he has capitulated to the totalitarian state. I think we agreed that this presents a situation without hope when, in actuality, there is some hope . . . hope that human nature cannot be changed by totalitarianism and that both love and nature can survive even the horrendous encroachments of Big Brother.'[60] Stein proposed that Rathvon drop Orwell's ending in favour of the following resolution: 'Julia gets up and walks away from Winston. Couldn't Winston also leave the café, not go after Julia but in the opposite direction and as he walks despondently along the street, couldn't he see the children's faces, not the faces of the child who tattled on her father but the faces of children who have managed to maintain some of their natural innocence . . . He begins to walk faster, and the music comes up stronger until Winston is again near the secluded spot where he and Julia found refuge from the totalitarian world. Again we see the blades of grass, the wind in the trees, and even perhaps, through Winston's eyes, another couple nestling together. It is such things that for Winston, and for us, stand for the permanence that Big Brother cannot destroy. And as Winston walks away from this scene, we hear on the sound track his heart beating and he is breathless as he realizes what it is that Big Brother cannot take away from humanity, what will always be in contrast and in conflict with the world of 1984, and perhaps to clinch this point of view, we can see Winston looking at his hands: two fingers on his left hand, two fingers on his right hand, and he knows that two plus two make four. As he realizes this, we continue to hear his heart beating, and by extension, the human heart beating – louder, as the film ends.'[61]

The film actually concluded with two different endings, one for American audiences and one for British. Neither followed Stein's saccharine suggestions, though the British version was faithful to the idea of Stein's ending, with Winston gunned down after crying 'Down with Big Brother!', promptly followed by Julia. In the book, in direct contrast, Orwell explicitly denied the possibility of the human spirit rising above the pressures of Big Brother. Winston is entirely overcome, his spirit broken – 'The struggle was finished. He had won the victory over himself. He loved Big Brother.' Orwell's specific instructions that *Nineteen Eighty-Four* should not be altered in any way had been conveniently disregarded.

The films *Animal Farm* and *1984* were both ready for distribution in 1956. Sol Stein announced that they were 'of ideological interest to the American Committee for Cultural Freedom', and promised to see that they got as 'wide distribution as possible'.[62] Steps to encourage a favourable reception of the films were duly taken, including 'arranging for editorials in New York newspapers' and distribution of 'a very large quantity of discount coupons'.

It could be argued that 'forgeries' are inherent in all transitions from text to celluloid; that the making of a film is in itself – and not necessarily malignly – an act of translation or even re-invention. Isaac Deutscher, in 'The Mysticism of Cruelty', his essay on *Nineteen Eighty-Four*, claimed that Orwell 'borrowed the idea of *1984*, the plot, the chief characters, the symbols and the whole climate of his story from Evgeny Zamyatin's *We*'.[63] Deutscher's personal recollection of Orwell was that he 'dwelt on "conspiracies," and that his political reasoning struck me as a Freudian sublimation of persecution mania'. Worried by Orwell's 'lack of historical sense and of psychological insight into political life,' Deutscher cautioned: 'It would be dangerous to blind ourselves to the fact that in the West millions of people may be inclined, in their anguish and fear, to flee from their own responsibility for mankind's destiny and to vent their anger and despair on the giant Bogy-cum-Scapegoat which Orwell's *1984* has done so much to place before their eyes . . . Poor Orwell, could he ever imagine that his own book would become so prominent an item in the program of Hate Week?'[64]

But Orwell himself was not entirely innocent of such Cold War manipulations. He had, after all, handed over a list of suspected fellow travellers to the Information Research Department in 1949, a list which exposed thirty-five people as fellow travellers (or 'FT' in Orwell-speak), suspected front men, or 'sympathizers', amongst them Kingsley Martin, editor of the *New Statesman and Nation* ('Decayed liberal. Very dishonest'), Paul Robeson ('Very anti-white. Wallace supporter'), J. B. Priestley ('Strong sympathizer, possibly has some kind of organizational tie-up. Very anti-USA'), and Michael Redgrave (ironically, given his later appearance in the film *1984).*[65] Deeply suspicious of just about everybody, Orwell had been keeping a blue quarto notebook close to hand for several years. By 1949, it contained 125 names, and had become a kind of 'game' which Orwell liked to play with Koestler and Richard Rees, in which they would estimate 'to what lengths of treachery our favourite bêtes noires would go'.[66] The criteria for inclusion seem to have been pretty broad, as in the case of Stephen Spender, whose 'tendency towards homosexuality' Orwell thought worth noting (he also said he was 'very unreliable' and 'Easily influenced'). The American realist John Steinbeck was listed solely for being a 'Spurious writer, pseudo-naif', whilst Upton Sinclair earned the epithet 'Very silly'. George Padmore (the pseudonym of Malcolm Nurse), was described as 'Negro [perhaps of] African origin?', who was 'anti-white' and probably a lover of Nancy Cunard. Tom Driberg drew heavy fire, being all the things Orwell loved to fear: 'Homosexual', 'Commonly thought to be underground member', and 'English Jew'.[67]

But, from being a kind of game, what Orwell termed his 'little list' took on a new and sinister dimension when he volunteered it to the IRD, a secret arm (as Orwell knew) of the Foreign Office. Although the IRD's Adam Watson would later claim that 'Its immediate usefulness was that these were not people who should write for us', he also revealed that '*[their] connections with Soviet-backed organizations might have to be exposed at some later date*'.[68] In other words, once in the hands of a branch of government whose activities were not open to inspection, Orwell's list lost any innocence it may have had as a private document. It became a dossier with very real potential for damaging people's reputations and careers.

Fifty years later, Orwell's authorized biographer, Bernard Crick, stood firmly by Orwell's action, claiming it was 'no different from responsible citizens nowadays passing on information to the anti-terrorist squad about people in their midst whom they believe to be IRA bombers. These were seen as dangerous times in the late forties.'[69] This defence has been echoed by those determined to perpetuate the myth of an intellectual group bound by their ties to Moscow, and united in a seditious attempt to prepare the ground for Stalinism in Britain. There is no evidence that anybody on Orwell's list (as far as it has been made public) was involved in any illegal undertaking, and certainly nothing which would justify the comparison to Republican terrorists. 'Homosexual' was the only indictment which bore any risk of criminal conviction, though this does not seem to have deterred Orwell in his bestowal of the word. British law did not prohibit membership of the Communist Party, being Jewish, being sentimental or stupid. 'So far as the Right is concerned Orwell can do no wrong,' Peregrine Worsthorne has written. 'His judgement in these matters is trusted absolutely. So if he thought the Cold War made it justifiable for one writer to be positively eager to shop another, then that is that. End of argument. But it shouldn't be the end of argument. A dishonourable act does not become honourable just because it was committed by George Orwell.'[70]

This is not to say that Orwell was wrong to be concerned about what he called 'the poisonous effect of the Russian mythos on English intellectual life'.[71] He of all people knew the cost of ideology, and the distortions performed in its name by 'liberals who fear liberty and the intellectuals who want to do dirt on the intellect'.[72] But by his actions, he demonstrated that he had confused the role of the intellectual with that of the policeman. As an intellectual, Orwell could command an audience for his attacks on British Russomania, *openly*, by engaging his opponents in debate on the pages of *Tribune*, *Polemic*, and other magazines and papers. In what way was the cause of freedom advanced by answering (suspected) intellectual dishonesty with subterfuge?

'If I had to choose a text to justify myself, I should choose the line from Milton: "By the known rules of ancient liberty",' Orwell wrote in the preface to *Animal Farm*. The phrase, he explained, referred to his strong faith in the 'deep-rooted tradition' of 'intellectual freedom . . . without which our characteristic Western culture could only doubtfully exist'. He followed with a quote from Voltaire: 'I detest what you say; I will defend to the death your right to say it.'[73] Months before his own death, Orwell seemed to be saying, 'I detest what you say; I will defend to death your right to say it; but not under any circumstances.' Commenting on what she saw as Orwell's move to the right, Mary McCarthy remarked it was a blessing he died so young.

18

When Shrimps Learn to Whistle

> Freedom just became a series of clichés . . . the Cliché Uh-Huh: 'Not all societies that seem free are as free as they seem' . . . the Cliché Dubious: 'Freedom is Indivisible'.
>
> Dwight Macdonald, 1956

'Attention! Attention! Dear listeners, you will hear now the manifesto of the Federation of Hungarian Writers . . . This is the Federation of Hungarian Writers. To every writer in the world, to all scientists, to all writers' federations, to all scientific associations, to the intellectual elite of the world, we ask you all for your help and support. There is but little time. You know the facts. There is no need to give you a special report. Help Hungary. Help the Hungarian people. Help Hungarian writers, scientists, workers, peasants, and our intelligentsia. Help. Help. Help.'

Sunday, 4 November, 1956. At 8:07 a.m., minutes after broadcasting this message, Radio Budapest fell silent. Pouring into the capital under cover of night, the Soviet army had begun its brutal suppression of the October uprising. Over the next few months, 15,000 Hungarians would die, and 5,000 would be arrested without trial. As its tank divisions rolled down the central boulevards of Budapest, it was as if the Soviet Union was punishing the world for passing such bad judgement on her – Stalinism is dead? Long live Stalinism!

After a decade of plotting and analysing and collecting

intelligence and drawing up strategies for the liberation of the 'captive nations' of Europe, America now stood immobile and apparently aghast at this flexing of Soviet muscle. 'The Hungarian revolutionaries died, despairing of the free world which was willing to share their triumph but not their struggle,'[1] wrote a bitter Manès Sperber on 11 November. But with the simultaneous Anglo-French-Israeli invasion of Suez, Eisenhower found himself stuck in the moral mud, circumscribed by the cruelly obvious parallels of imperial aggression.

But it was not just Suez which paralysed America: whilst government strategists and intelligence supremos had spent years scheming for just such an event as the Hungarian uprising, it was as a chimera, an abstract game which turned out to be all but useless in the face of reality. 'Operation Focus', by which the CIA believed itself to be scrutinizing Hungarian affairs since the early 1950s, turned out to be hopelessly blurred. Lawrence de Neufville, who had been assigned to Radio Free Europe in 1954, remembered that in his first month there he had asked, 'What happens if a man in a raincoat comes here and says, "We've been listening to all this stuff and we're ready to start a revolution?" They discussed it in a special board meeting, and they didn't know what to do. It was a house of cards, and I told them so. They were all busy thinking they were doing good and nobody was doing any real plotting. And then events caught up on them.'[2]

During the October uprising, Radio Free Europe had repeatedly encouraged the insurrectionists. According to some claims, it even promised armed support, though this was – and still is – vigorously denied by the CIA. But according to de Neufville, the Agency was in no position to make such denials because, unbelievably, it had no idea what the Hungarian section was actually broadcasting. 'The whole thing was a sham and a delusion,' he explained. 'Radio Free Europe was regularly sending guidances to Washington and Munich about its broadcasts, but it was just all mud in your eye, because they simply ignored their own guidances. Moreover, the US government had an arrangement with the British for the monitoring and translating of broadcasts from Eastern Europe, but amazingly nobody ever translated Radio Free Europe broadcasts, so Washington simply didn't know what was going out on their radio. The CIA shouldn't have denied the Hungarian broadcasts, because they simply didn't know.'[3] The full transcripts of Radio Free Europe's Hungarian broadcasts in those crucial days of October 1956 have never been found.

As the realization hit that the October revolution had failed, thousands of Hungarians fled to Austria to escape Soviet reprisals. Pouring over the border, they made mostly for Vienna. Again, the Americans were completely unprepared. Writing to Shepard Stone at the Ford Foundation, Josselson warned that 'the situation involving the refugees seems to be reaching a state of intolerable chaos. Our own office in Vienna as well as all those who have returned from there in the last few days speak of an impending catastrophe unless some major steps are taken immediately.'[4] Also in Vienna was Frank Wisner, who had arrived from Washington just in time to witness the detritus of the failed revolution. Wisner became so emotionally distressed that he started to drink heavily. By the time he got to his next stop, Rome, the local CIA men there were struggling to get him through drink-sodden evenings. In Athens he ate some raw clams, from which came hepatitis, high fever, and delirium. Wisner's family and friends attributed his eventual decline as Allen Dulles's chief deputy to the emotional confusion of that autumn. Increasingly irritable and irrational, in 1958 he had a nervous breakdown and was replaced as Dulles's deputy.[5]

Melvin Lasky was also quickly on the scene, dashing back and forth from Vienna to the Hungarian border in a state of high excitement. Whilst Wisner found himself in a personal Gethsemane, Lasky was flushed with the satisfaction of a prophecy fulfilled. 'Hungary, well, that did for us,' he recalled brightly. 'I mean, you didn't have to pay a penny for it. It was the justification for the analysis, for our analysis, which said that totalitarianism is all a farce. And it placed freedom, bourgeois freedom, firmly on the agenda.'[6] Joining forces with Friedrich Torberg, whose *Forum* office became the impromptu headquarters for the Congress's Hungarian campaign, Lasky set up a register for refugee intellectuals and students, and worked to find them places in European universities (at a rate of fifteen a day). He also started compiling a dossier of documents (with help from his friends at Radio Free Europe and

Voice of America) *La Révolution Hongroise*, a White Book published in England by Secker and Warburg, and in the US by Praeger.

In Paris, the Congress came into its own, its offices at Boulevard Haussman heaving with people. 'It was a high point of tension and passion. It was incredibly exciting, like this was what we were there for,'[7] said John Hunt, who had arrived at the Congress only a few months earlier. Calling into play its extensive network of contacts and affiliates, the Paris office coordinated public protests from Santiago to Denmark, Lebanon to New York, Hamburg to Bombay. In Sweden, the local committee persuaded eight Nobel Prize winners to sign a cable of protest to Marshal Bulganin. The American Committee organized a mass meeting attended by Koestler and Silone (they wanted Hemingway, and cabled Josselson for help in locating him, but he replied 'Hemingway presumably in Europe whereabouts uncertain'). By January 1957 the Paris office was able to report that 'Never before have the actions of the various National Committees been so unified or strong.'[8]

Another outcome of the Hungarian crisis was the formation of the Philharmonica Hungarica, an orchestra assembled at Josselson's initiative under the musical direction of Antal Dorati with Zoltan Rozsnyay as conductor. Rozsnyay had escaped to Vienna along with a hundred members of the Budapest Philharmonic as soon as the Soviet tanks started shelling the Hungarian capital. With an initial grant of $70,000, the orchestra became a powerful focus for the *Kulturkampf*, and still tours today.

But perhaps the most exciting development for Josselson and his 'intellectual shock troops' was the news that Sartre had publicly repudiated the Communist Party, branding the Soviet leadership 'a group which today surpasses Stalinism after having denounced it'. Writing in *L'Express* on 9 November 1956, he denounced Soviet policy since the Second World War as 'twelve years of terror and stupidity', and 'wholeheartedly' condemned the intervention in Hungary. Reserving special invective for his own country's Communists, he declared: 'It is not, and never will be possible to resume relations with the men who are currently running the French Communist Party. Every one of their phrases, their every move, is the outgrowth of thirty years of lies and sclerosis. Their reactions are those of completely irresponsible persons.'[9] The Congress ran off thousands of copies of Sartre's statement, distributing it along with that of Camus, who threatened to lead a boycott of the United Nations if it failed to vote for 'the immediate withdrawal of Soviet troops' from Hungary, and to 'publicly denounce its bankruptcy and failure' if the UN fell short of this demand. 'There seems to be . . . a breakaway of the French intellectuals in a descending order of communists, fellow-travellers, progressists, anti-anti-communists, and now anti-communist-communists,'[10] Josselson remarked gleefully. Louis Aragon's Communist-backed Comité National des Ecrivains was, he said, 'virtually torpedoed . . . It is safe to say that the Communist "mystique" has been smashed.' But he also noted that 'The French Socialist party could have taken advantage of the situation were it not for the ill-fated intervention in Egypt.'[11]

A further truth about the Suez conflict now established itself in Josselson's mind. 'It is obvious that if Europe is not to succumb it has to become independent of its Middle Eastern oil sources,' he told one correspondent. 'A program of intensified scientific research for the replacement of oil by other sources of energy may be the answer.'[12] Specifically, Josselson meant nuclear energy. Attempts to gain acceptance for atomic power had long been an American foreign policy priority. In 1952, C. D. Jackson had noted in his log files that 'matters were progressing on LIFE on an article by Gordon Dean to remove the guilt complex from America on the use of the A-Bomb'.[13] C. D. Jackson was also closely involved in preparing Eisenhower's famous 'Atoms for Peace' address to the United Nations on 8 December 1953, in which the president proposed a unilateral reduction of atomic weapons, and outlined the means of diverting the military uses of nuclear power to civilian uses. Never one to miss a propaganda opportunity, C. D. Jackson submitted a memo to Frank Wisner in February 1954 in which he suggested extending the Eisenhower proposal to include 'the announcement of a plan to erect the first atomic power reactor in Berlin'. There were, said C. D., 'very practical as well as propaganda reasons for doing this. Every ounce of fuel, liquid or solid, used in Berlin has to be brought into the city across Soviet territory. In spite of the reserve stocks we have accumulated, a new blockade would be very serious.'[14] An atomic power plant, he reasoned, 'would be able to supply the basic [energy] needed to take care of the city under siege conditions'. The propaganda value, 'vis-a-vis the Germans and the Soviets', was 'obvious'. In fact, as propaganda, it would not even be necessary to take 'a final decision as to the actual erection of the power plant. The idea could be leaked simply as an idea. A survey group could wander around Berlin looking for a suitable site; a rubble area could be fenced off and put under guard with mysterious signs; and the project for the time being could be limited to the rumour stage, which from the standpoint of the Berliners and the Soviet observers is almost as good as actually getting on with the work.'[15]

Josselson possessed nothing close to this Machiavellian reasoning. He was genuinely taken by Eisenhower's idea of 'beating nuclear swords into ploughshares'.[16] His motives were sincere, if naïve: in a letter to Nabokov, he wrote that 'It is obviously the case that the exploitation of atomic energy will radically change the lot of mankind and society. I remain firmly convinced that it will also mark the swan song of Marxism, and provide a new philosophical and sociological basis for mankind, just as the industrial revolution provided the basis for Marx's theories.'[17] Welcoming the Eisenhower proposal to pool atomic energy resources for peaceful purposes as 'a stroke of genius', Josselson was keen to promote the idea through the Congress journals, but had run up against a wall of indifference. 'I have been desperately trying to have [Eisenhower's] proposal followed up with a series of articles in *Preuves*, from which they would have been picked up by other journals in Europe,' he told de Neufville in January 1954. 'Alas, the three non-communist leading scientists in France have declined under one pretext or another . . . It is the usual case of a good idea not being fully exploited because people are either too lazy or too busy or just don't give a damn.[18] Yet this is one idea that can instill new hope and confidence among some pretty desperate Europeans.' Josselson ended by saying, 'If you have any ideas, please don't keep them to yourself.'[19]

What happened next provides a rare insight into the workings of the clandestine bureaucracy behind the Congress for

Cultural Freedom. Josselson's letter was passed to C. D. Jackson at the White House. C. D. Jackson passed it on to Tracy Barnes at the CIA, with the suggestion that William Tyler be invited 'to ghost this piece for the appropriate big-name European scientist'. Tyler was public affairs officer at the American Embassy in Paris (though his many functions suggest that this was a cover). 'Besides writing impeccable Academie French,' said Jackson, 'Tyler has the added advantage of having been in on many of the . . . drafts of this speech, so that he has a complete grasp of the philosophy of the speech.' Jackson told Barnes to put this idea 'right back to Josselson' as a matter of urgency, as the next issue of *Preuves* was about to close.[20]

Whilst Josselson nurtured his plans for a nuclear-powered Europe united behind the concept of democratic freedom, Dwight Macdonald was in Egypt to witness western empires behaving badly, on assignment for *Encounter*, whose associate editor he had just become. Macdonald, who looked, said one friend, like a mad professor with a butterfly net, was at a high point in his career: he had just finished his lengthy profile of the Ford Foundation for *The New Yorker*, and relished the chance of working on a highbrow magazine like *Encounter*. So it was odd that his stint in Cairo should have failed to stimulate him into any good reportage. Indeed, when he heard a shell slamming into a building near his hotel, he upped and moved into the suburbs, where he hid for several days without contacting the *Encounter* office. Macdonald, who had described his arrest in 1940 for picketing the Soviet Consulate in New York as 'great fun', seemed now to have lost his taste for risk, never once venturing out of the city to see the war zone. 'We paid a couple of hundred pounds for his ticket and paid the hotel, so that Dwight could do a Suez post-mortem,' recalled Lasky, 'but what he wrote was absolutely unpublishable. He had writer's block out there, and then he came back and would sit around the office for months at a time and all there would be was this writer's block.'[21]

Macdonald's appointment to *Encounter* had been controversial from the start. Josselson had never been satisfied with Kristol's editorship, and the two had clashed over what the magazine should be from the very first issue. Josselson felt that

Kristol was too precious about Cold War issues, and demanded more emphasis on the political side of the magazine. 'We are not publishing cultural magazines with a capital C. I am disturbed about your failure to grasp this,'[22] Josselson lectured Kristol (in a remark which comes close to justifying one critic's comment that *Encounter* was a magazine of political propaganda with a cultural decor). Lasky, as ever, agreed with Josselson: 'We were concerned in the mid-fifties that *Encounter* wasn't paying enough attention to Soviet and Eastern bloc affairs. But Kristol didn't want to do this – he had a kind of nervous, compulsive fear of ideological discussion.'[23] Despite calling Kristol to heel at a series of meetings in Paris, by early 1955 Josselson was completely exasperated. 'You will remember that at our Executive Committee meeting everyone was in agreement that the period spent so far by *Encounter* in overcoming covert and overt resistance was time well spent,' Josselson wrote mysteriously, 'but that now it was time to go one step further.'[24] Kristol's response was hardly compliant. 'Basically,' he wrote, 'I have to do things my way . . . If my way turns out to be inadequate, there's always a "final solution."'[25]

Whilst Kristol referred idly to his own extinction, Josselson was already one step ahead, quietly instructing Nabokov and Lasky to do the rounds and ask for recommendations for a replacement editor. Isaiah Berlin, who was habitually consulted on such matters, suggested H. Stuart Hughes. Another suggestion was Philip Horton, a former OSS-er and the CIA's first station chief in Paris in 1947, who now worked for *The Reporter*. Spender, meanwhile, was busily engaged in undermining Kristol's position. 'I think it must be because he is so intensely competitive that he regards every decision as a kind of conflict in which he has to score a victory, either by keeping the decision to himself or by sabotaging it if it is made by his colleague,'[26] he told Josselson, leaving him in no doubt of the benefits of removing Kristol: 'If Irving goes we can then begin discussing things which could be decided immediately but which he turns into long drawn out battles.'[27] Nabokov, meanwhile, had another candidate in mind, and wrote to friend and confidant 'Arthuro' Schlesinger to ask if he could 'very, very tactfully' sound out Dwight Macdonald. Schlesinger was very enthusiastic. So was Malcolm

Muggeridge, whose comment that Kristol was a 'very nice fellow but perfectly useless and incapable of cutting any ice here' concealed what Lasky claimed was 'a biological hatred – he thought he was a barbarian'.[28]

Josselson agreed to discuss the possibility with Macdonald in New York, and went to meet him there in June 1955. The two got on well, but Josselson worried that Macdonald's gadfly temperament would not be easy to house within the Congress tent. He was, said Josselson, too 'lone wolf'. When Sidney Hook got wind of the meeting, he threatened to resign from the Executive Committee and said he would 'blow the Congress out of the water'[29] if Macdonald were appointed. Kristol, who had been kept in the dark throughout these negotiations, was incredulous when he finally learned that Macdonald was being considered as his replacement. 'It was ridiculous – he was an anarchist and a pacifist!'[30] he later exclaimed.

By the time of the Congress's Future of Freedom conference in Milan, September 1955, the matter was still unresolved. During that middle week of September 1955, the delegates' hotel steamed with intrigue. Stuart Hampshire remembered more of the boudoir politicking than of the debates themselves (which were, according to Hannah Arendt, 'deadly boring'). Whilst George Kennan was intoning on 'The Strategy of Freedom' (a typical Kennan theme – freedom, like foreign policy, needed to be strategically organized), Sidney Hook's bedroom became the focus of a cell opposed to Dwight's appointment. A quick shuffle down the corridor led to Arthur Schlesinger's bedroom, which was where the faction in support of Dwight's appointment gathered. 'Dwight was vetoed, principally by Sidney Hook,' Hampshire remembered. 'And I saw very strongly then that there was a central control – the apparat at work. Certainly, Dwight would have been a loose canon. You never knew what he might do or say next. And they weren't going to have it.'[31]

But Schlesinger dug his heels in: 'I supported him. So did the CIA, and they pressured Josselson to accept, which he did reluctantly.'[32] Eventually, a compromise was worked out whereby Macdonald would join *Encounter* for one year as a 'contributing editor', and Kristol would stay on. Writing to explain the arrangement to Muggeridge, Josselson said that he had given Kristol 'such a heavy dose of frank treatment bordering on brutality that a salutary change in his attitude can be expected'.[33] But within months, such expectations were dashed. The sniping continued, and Josselson found himself writing in exasperation to Kristol: 'I could not bite your head off if you would not stick your neck out. I don't know where you draw the line between editorial criticism and issues of principle.'[34] To Daniel Bell, Josselson privately confessed, 'I sometimes feel that Irving will change his ways when shrimps can learn to whistle.'[35]

Josselson had instinctively had misgivings about Macdonald. No sooner had his appointment (and a generous salary of $12,000 plus expenses) been confirmed, than Dwight submitted an article to *Encounter* called 'No Miracle in Milan'. His remarks on the luxurious accommodation enjoyed by the delegates, and their apparent lack of concentration at the conference debates, left Spender and Kristol in a spin. Contrary to what Macdonald had anticipated – before coming to London he wrote to Spender that he was 'Pleased as Punch' to hear about the Congress's attitude to *Encounter*; their 'hands-off policy . . . sounds positively idyllic'[36] – the article was discussed with Nabokov, Bondy, Lasky and Josselson before finally being passed back to Macdonald with a raft of suggested amendments. It was finally published in December 1955, a month after a far more respectful account by the conservative sociologist Edward Shils appeared. But this meddling was a taste of things to come.

In the wake of the tumultuous events of 1956, the Congress had struck its form. Although it did not think of itself 'exclusively as a militant organization for ideological combat and exposure of crimes, falsehoods, and inquisition',[37] this was precisely what it excelled at. More formal arrangements for this kind of activity were completed in October 1957, when Lasky presided over the formation of the Congress's Forum Service, which offered 'background information and analysis' to subscribers worldwide. In fact, Forum World Features (as it was renamed) was a classic CIA undercover operation, with John Hay Whitney once again acting as a front, registering the company under his name as a Delaware corporation with offices in London. By the 1960s, Forum World Features was the most widely circulated of the CIA-owned news services.

Nevertheless, under Josselson's careful stewardship, the Congress continued to be seen as the only independent international organization which consistently proclaimed the value of freedom. 'It was a matter of creating an area of cultural freedom itself, within which the great enterprises of literature, art, and thought could be pursued,' explained a Congress statement. 'In order to oppose a world in which everything serves a political purpose, which is for us unacceptable, it was necessary to create platforms from which culture could be expressed without regard to politics and without confusion with propaganda, where the direct concern would be for ideas and works of art in themselves.'[38] This was the criterion by which the Congress, ultimately, would stand or fall. Of course, the propaganda imperative was never relinquished by the Congress's secret angels. Josselson's job was to make sure that this imperative was carefully concealed, and for the moment at least, it seemed to be working: people were flocking to the Congress. If ever there were such a thing as anti-Communist chic, it was now.

Once again, the personal cost to Michael Josselson was high. In August 1957, he underwent a gruesome operation which involved stripping out and replacing arteries in his leg. As he recuperated, Melvin Lasky cheered him with news of the 'Battle of Brecht', in which the Congress ranged its artillery against Communist 'idolizers' of the 'Communist millionaire' at a conference held in Berlin, scoring another hit in 'German Kulturpolitik'. More cheering still was the news that the Ford Foundation had confirmed a new grant of £500,000 to the Congress, and that the Rockefeller Foundation was also renewing its largesse.

But the final say that year went to the Soviets, as they launched the world's first successful satellite into orbit on 4 October. Weighing less than 200 pounds, Sputnik 1 (the name meant 'fellow traveller') carried enormous weight in international affairs. As it bleeped across the globe, it instantly created an atmosphere of panic in the US government. 'I guess sputnik buries old Ike's reputation for all posterity . . . first in war, first in peace, first on the [golf] links – but second to the moon,'[39] Lasky told one correspondent. When, one month later, America's attempt to launch a much smaller satellite came crashing down to the ground in full view of the world's news cameras, the taste of defeat was bitter indeed.

19

Achilles' Heel

> Power was the first thing that went wrong with the CIA. There was too much of it, and it was too easy to bring to bear.
>
> Tom Braden

By the late 1950s, the CIA had come to see *Encounter* as its standard, agreeing with Josselson's assessment of the magazine as 'our greatest asset'. In Agency-speak, an 'asset' was 'any resource at the disposition of the agency for use in an operational or support role'.[1] The Agency's operational principle, as established by Tom Braden, dictated that organizations receiving its support should not be required 'to support every aspect of official American policy'.[2] This meant that a leftish agenda could survive in an organ like *Encounter*. But whilst it 'was left wing in the sense that it gave expression to some left wing views . . . it wasn't a free forum at all, which it purported to be',[3] according to British philosopher Richard Wollheim. 'I think the effect of it was to give the impression that it was the whole spectrum of opinion they were publishing. But invariably, they were cutting it off at a certain point, notably where it concerned areas of American foreign policy. It was skilfully done: there were opinions that were published in criticism of America, but it was never *really* critical.'[4] And this, according to Tom Braden, is how *Encounter* was expected to perform: 'It was propaganda in the sense that it did not often deviate from what the State Department would say US foreign policy was.'[5] When Braden offered a degree of laxity, he certainly didn't intend that *Encounter* should be free to *denounce* any or every aspect of official American policy. And this, in 1958, is precisely what it was set to do.

Early that year, Dwight Macdonald resurfaced in New York after his tenure at *Encounter*. To break the journey, he had stopped for two months in Tuscany, where he was overwhelmed with a sense of the fecundity of European tradition. Back in New York, where taxi drivers swore and public manners were 'atrocious', he suffered a serious case of culture shock. He sat down to write about his feelings of revulsion – at the violence, the tawdriness, the 'shapelessness' of America, a country without style, without a sense of past or present, bent on extracting the greatest amount of lucre. 'The national motto should be not "E Pluribus Unum," not "In God We Trust," but: "I got mine and screw you, Jack!"'[6] he asserted angrily.

What Macdonald wrote was a protracted lament for a country which he saw as already in decline. With so many intellectuals streaming across the threshold to embrace 'American' culture, Dwight the maverick rediscovered an urge to strike a posture 'against the American grain'. In January, he sent his thoughts to *Encounter* in an article entitled simply 'America! America!' Spender accepted it, without, he later claimed, reading it through properly. But Irving Kristol was appalled. He found it 'John Osborne-ish', unhealthily 'self-lacerating', poorly constructed. 'Dwight was a wonderful journalist but utterly unpredictable and sometimes capable of being quite silly,'[7] he said, adding that because Dwight came from a privileged background, he knew nothing about America, and the same impediment prevented him from understanding England, to which America was so disadvantageously compared in his piece. 'He knew nothing about England; he never went to a football game in England, he never went to a rugby game in England. His knowledge of England was from the various clubs in the St. James's area. He was a hick – he said "GROS-VENOR Square", for God's sake!'[8] This, from a man who had taken to wearing a bowler hat and carrying an umbrella on his way to work, was strong stuff. Lasky, too, thought it was 'a very poor article', and echoed Kristol's claim that Macdonald knew nothing about the real America because 'he was a Yale man and a Greenwich Village man, and that's about what he knew. And when he came over to England he had all the clichéd positions of an innocent Mark Twain American abroad. He loved everything British. He loved the pubs, and he loved the names of the streets and the squares and everything. We were embarrassed. Americans could be so naïve and at such a low level. It was a terrible article. I told Mike [Josselson] at the time that Dwight was the Achilles' Heel of the Congress, and I was right,'[9] Lasky concluded smugly.

But Macdonald's sin was far greater than his mispronunciation of Grosvenor Square. As a critique of contemporary America, the article certainly had its weaknesses. As the exclamatory nature of its title made clear, it was an instinctual, rather than a seriously argued rebuttal of American values. It compared America with England and Italy in a way which demonstrated a romantic weakness in Macdonald for idealizing foreign cultures. Yet it was also an extraordinarily apposite piece, exploiting a wealth of data and recent research, touching on just about every area of American life which was of concern to its publicists. As Macdonald set about knocking every sacred cow, it was uncanny, as if he had read somewhere a hit list of all the negative stereotypes which American covert operators were bent on eradicating. He denounced rampant materialism unmatched by any spiritual growth, violent crime, the unhindered advance of advertising billboards, the lack of discrimination amidst literary critics, the prevalence of racial discrimination. He attacked John Foster Dulles as 'the pious Artful Dodger', the perfect prototype of America's grossness and hypocrisy; Henry Luce as 'a Boy Scout acting like a gangster'; Vice-President Nixon for his gauche behaviour in Venezuela (for which he had been deservedly 'chronically mobbed'); President Eisenhower for being a gun-slinging reactionary; George Walker, vice-president of Ford Motors, for acting like 'an Eastern potentate'; the American labour unions for being more interested in public relations than the class struggle, and their leaders, David Dubinsky and Walter Reuther, for being 'so damned virtuous'.[10] On and on went this catalogue of contemporary American sins, Macdonald's animosity towards the decadent American imperium taking him to new depths of disgust: 'When one hears Europeans complaining about the Americanisation of Europe, one wishes they could spend a few weeks over here and get a load of the real thing . . . Even the Soviet Russians, for all their ruthlessness, barely covered by the fig of ideology, seem to speak a more common language with other peoples than we do.'[11]

Despite finding the piece 'utterly ridiculous', Kristol agreed to run it, claiming he had no choice given Stephen's acceptance. No sooner was it accepted than the Paris bureau got hold of a copy. Spender and Kristol were instantly urged not to run it, and warned that Junkie Fleischmann had said it would hurt the Congress and jeopardize its funding. 'I was easily moved not to run it, since I hadn't liked it in the first place,' Kristol later claimed. 'Stephen was a little more recalcitrant. But in the end we said [to the Paris office], if it's really going to make life that much more difficult for you, we can do without the article. And then Dwight published it elsewhere, complaining about censorship. Rejecting an article is not censorship. I've been an editor of magazines all my life, and I've rejected plenty of articles and I've never regarded that as a form of censorship.'[12]

It fell to Spender to tell Macdonald that they would not be able to run the piece without considerable alterations. Having reread the article, Spender said, he felt it was one-sided and too critical. He added that Nabokov had read the article and had 'become very upset'. Macdonald was furious to learn that 'General Secretary and Grand Master of International Decorum Nicolas Nabokov' had been providing the editors of *Encounter* with 'advice', and suggested to 'Stephenirvingnicholasmike or whoever's around and decides things' that from now on the editors simply 'consult the Paris office at once, on receipt of a "controversial" MS, so as to find out immediately what it thinks.'[13] As it happens, this was precisely what the editors were doing.

With Macdonald refusing to take on board any cuts, the piece was finally axed. It had been accepted, rejected, accepted, rejected. 'I feel badly about it,' said Spender in an interview shortly before his death. 'That's the only article that was not published in *Encounter* as a result of very strong pressure being brought on us by the Congress for Cultural Freedom. It's absolutely the only article. When there was trouble about it I thought it was a rather foolish kind of article, and I thought that probably if I had looked at it, I would either have wanted to alter it or I would have rejected it. Now looking back on it, this is the one thing that I regret very much, because I think even if having looked at the article I didn't like it, I still should've insisted, made a point on which one resigns: that we publish this article, because we had accepted it, and the only reason for rejecting it was its anti-Americanism.'[14]

But it wasn't just the Paris office that intervened. According to Diana Josselson (who thought that 'the whole [article] was very désabusé'), this was 'the one example of editorial intervention by the CIA, and Michael fought it very hard, but he didn't win'.[15] How did the Agency come by the article in the first place? If, as the orthodoxy upheld by those involved goes, Congress publications were not previewed by the Agency, how did news of the Macdonald piece reach them? Josselson was receiving advance copies of *Preuves*, and at least the table contents of *Encounter*. But surely it was not in his interests to pass this fiery piece on to his superiors in Washington? Josselson always preferred to deal with problems independently of the Agency, whose affiliation with the Congress he came increasingly to resent. There is no doubt, however, that 'America! America!' did the rounds in the corridors of Washington. Most probably, the article arrived there via the CIA's case officer in the Congress (who was, at that time, Lee Williams).

If the only thing wrong with the piece was its submission to cheap anti-Americanism, why did the Agency jeopardize the credibility of *Encounter*, its 'greatest asset', in an effort to suppress it? Surely, here was a great opportunity to demonstrate *Encounter*'s 'bona fides', to erode the view that it was uncritical of American failures, to re-balance the acoustics which, said some critics, had always sounded odd? More to the point, if the article was as ridiculous as everyone claimed, then what possible damage could it do to anyone other than its author?

Contrary to what Diana Josselson later remembered, Josselson was in fact against running the offending article from the beginning. He called it 'the most blatantly anti-American piece I have ever read', and said it belonged in 'Literaturnaya Gazeta'.[16] He knew that Macdonald 'will probably raise a stink and attack us publicly but I am ready to face it'. His fingerprints were all over the decision to axe it. Running it would have done considerable harm to *Encounter*'s reputation in Washington, and it would also have made Josselson look nothing short of a renegade. His own credibility was on the line.[17]

For those hardened clandestine operators who viewed the International Organizations Division as a bit of 'fluff on the side', who sneered at the idea of aiding and abetting people or organizations who were supposed to be 'friends' or have 'the same point of view', the Macdonald flap was a vindication. Richard Helms, Wisner's deputy, and later, CIA director, gave voice to this scepticism when he told a select committee that 'The clandestine operator . . . is trained to believe that you really can't count on the honesty of your agent to do exactly what you want or to report accurately unless you own him body and soul.'[18] That anybody in the employ of the CIA could have expected to domesticate the famously iconoclastic Macdonald seemed sheer folly.

All these arguments are distractions from the real reason for axing Macdonald's article. The anti-Americanism was one thing, but in and of itself, it might perhaps have been tolerated in a diluted form. But Macdonald's decision to conclude his attack with a *précis* of a lengthy article summarising a report on the behaviour of American servicemen captured during the Korean war, was a step too far. Extracted by Eugene Kinkead in *The New Yorker* the previous autumn, the report, commissioned by the US Army, was a damning indictment on the conduct of American prisoners: they 'often became unmanageable. They refused to obey orders, and they cursed and sometimes struck officers who tried to enforce orders . . . on winter nights, helpless men with dysentery were rolled outside the huts by their comrades and left to die in the cold.' The average American soldier seemed 'lost without a bottle of pills and a toilet that flushed'.[19] Most disturbingly, the report also indicated a high level of collaboration and indoctrination. Amazingly, the army had made its report public, thus creating a nightmare for government propagandists.[20]

The inclusion of this data in Macdonald's piece was the one good reason why publication in *Encounter* was guaranteed to be met with an official veto. It was precisely this last part which caused the trouble. And yet, years later, none of those directly involved in dropping Macdonald's piece was able to recall the Kinkead issue. 'I'm not aware that there was any collapse of morale among American soldiers at the end of the Korean war,' said Irving Kristol. 'And if there were, Dwight wouldn't know about it, since what did he know about the Korean war? He sat in New York writing for *The New Yorker*, he knew nothing about the Korean war, he'd never been to Korea. I don't think he had ever visited a regiment. About military dissatisfaction in the ranks, about that I had heard nothing. I don't remember its being in Dwight Macdonald's article at all.'[21]

Likewise, Melvin Lasky, when asked, could remember nothing of this. Nor could Stephen Spender. Nor could Diana Josselson. This can only be put down to a case of collective historical amnesia. Kristol's memory failure in particular is worth noting: writing to him in October 1958 (by which time the now infamous article had been printed in *Dissent*, a magazine to the left of *Partisan Review*, and Kristol had left London to work for *The Reporter* in New York), Josselson said, 'Now, as to his exhibitionist piece about America which you and Stephen were wrong in accepting in the first place, you may also recall that you asked him to re-write it and to leave out the whole section about Korea which had already appeared in *The New Yorker*. He did not do this.'[22] In 1959, Kristol was still embroiled in the Kinkead controversy, and attacked him in person in a televised debate.[23] For this he earned Josselson's (rare) approval, and a new and 'avid reader' of *The Reporter*.

By axing the Macdonald article (its belated appearance in *Tempo Presente*, when it had already been published elsewhere, was poor recompense), the credibility of the claim that CIA support came without strings attached was jeopardized. 'This was all about efforts to create vehicles which by definition were articulators of western values, of free and open debate,' claimed Congress case officer Lee Williams. 'We didn't tell them what to do, that would've been inconsistent with the American tradition. This doesn't mean there weren't themes we wanted to see discussed, but we didn't tell them what to do . . . We did not feed the line to anyone. We believed we should let the facts speak for themselves, let the dialogue go on, let the free voices have a place to express themselves. There was no "Thou shalt think in this way", "Thou shalt put out this line", "Thou shalt print this article". That was totally foreign to what we were doing.'[24] William Colby also vigorously challenged the claim that journals like *Encounter* were expected to perform as 'dollar megaphones' for the CIA. 'There was not a imposition of control from the CIA,' he said. 'We were supporting but not bossing, not telling what to do. You might sit down and as good friends you could argue about whether this particular line would make sense of that, but there was no sense of, This is it, bang! it comes from Washington, no answers. No. That goes for Moscow but it didn't go for Washington.'[25]

Both the Agency and the intellectuals it subsidized have done much to protect this altruistic myth. The Macdonald affair suggests a different reality. 'The CIA claimed that it was sponsoring freedom of expression. Of course that wasn't true,' said Jason Epstein. 'When Dwight Macdonald wrote his article for *Encounter*, the editors of the magazine, responding to what they knew to be the [Congress's] position, refused to publish it. That doesn't say much for promoting freedom of expression. [The CIA] was promoting a policy and a political line: that was what it was paying for and that's what it expected to get. Freedom of expression had nothing to do with it.'[26] Macdonald himself referred to Nabokov and Josselson as the 'front office Metternichs' of *Encounter*. 'You'd think USA was Venezuela, such touchy national pride,' he noted drily. 'Especially nice that the censorship is by a congress for cultural freedom!'[27] American sociologist Norman Birnbaum took up this point in an open letter to the Congress, arguing that the directive excluding the article from *Encounter* was 'an unmitigated insolence', and clearly showed that there was a gap between what the Congress preached and what it practised: 'The Congress for Cultural Freedom has for some years been lecturing the intelligentsia on the indivisibility of freedom. It's right: freedom is indivisible, it has to be fought for on issues large and small, and extended against a hundred dogmatisms and petty tyrannies – not least, apparently, those of its self-appointed champions.'[28] Birnbaum went further, accusing the Congress of submitting 'liberty' to the exigencies of American foreign policy: 'It seems to subscribe to something very like a Stalinist view of the truth: truth is, whatever serves the interests of the Party.'[29]

The charge that the Congress had dishonoured the cause it professed hit hard. Josselson smarted, convinced that the means justified the ends, but deeply troubled by the accusation that the Congress identified truth with the edicts of John Foster Dulles or Allen Welsh Dulles. He skirted the issue entirely when he wrote to explain the whole affair to Macdonald in April 1958, in a letter that was watery and unconvincing: 'You must understand that Irving and Stephen must eat, that you must be paid for your articles, that *Encounter* must be able to say the things that it is best qualified to say without jeopardizing its future'.[30] Macdonald's response was to say that 'Eliminating irreverent remarks about The American Way of Life from *Encounter* because some grey-flannel-suited Madison-Avenue philanthropoid might cut down on supplies is indeed a miserable business.'[31]

'The duty that no intellectual can shirk without degrading himself is the duty to expose fictions and to refuse to call "useful lies" truths,' Nicola Chiaromonte had announced in the second issue of *Encounter*. Whilst *Encounter* never shrank from exposing the useful lies by which Communist regimes supported themselves, it was never truly free itself of 'the bear-trap of ideology', of that pervasive Cold War psychology of 'lying for the truth'. By 'keeping silent on any hot controversial issues, by excessive diplomacy and hush hush attitude toward all the fakery and shoddiness that's for years been growing so in our whole intellectual atmosphere',[32] *Encounter* suspended that most precious of western philosophical concepts – the freedom to think and act independently – and trimmed its sails to suit the prevailing winds.

It has been said that 'a magazine article says what it says, and anyone can examine its arguments and disagree with it – it cannot be a covert performance'.[33] *Encounter*'s strange silences, its deliberate concealment of what lay below the bottom line, and its exclusion of material inconvenient to its secret backers, suggest that the contrary is true. As one historian put it, 'The pertinent question about *Encounter*'s independence was not whether there were instructions cabled to the editors from Washington, but who chose the editors in the first place, and who established the clear bounds of "responsible" opinion within which differences were uninhibitedly explored.'[34] Supporting this argument, Jason Epstein explained that 'It was not a matter of buying off and subverting individual writers and scholars, but of setting up an arbitrary and factitious system of values by which academic personnel were advanced, magazine editors appointed, and scholars subsidized and published, not necessarily on their merits – though these were sometimes considerable – but because of their allegiance.'[35]

Josselson had always been very hands-on with *Encounter*. He drew up the first mock covers, he reviewed and revised contents lists for the early editions, and continued to receive advance notice of its contents from the editors. He reprimanded them when standards dropped, and constantly cajoled them into considering articles or subjects for discussion. Sometimes he sounded as if he was issuing an order: enclosing a press release on the Congress's Asian conference to be held in Rangoon in January 1955, he told Kristol simply, 'It is essential that this Conference be written up in *Encounter*.'[36] Sometimes it was more teasing: 'I have a New Year's wish: a really first-rate discussion of the problem of co-existence in *Encounter*. Many of our friends, including Muggeridge and Irving Brown, have the same wish.'[37] Or urging Spender to open the literary pages to a new generation of American writers like Saul Bellow, J. D. Salinger, Truman Capote or Shirley Ann Grau. Or advising Kristol to publish a review of George Padmore's book *Pan-Africanism or Communism* ('I think it is quite important that this book be reviewed in *Encounter* by one of "our" people').[38] Josselson's approach to *Preuves* was the same, and frequently moved its editor François Bondy to resentment. In June 1952, Bondy had actually threatened to resign if the Executive Committee continued to discuss *Preuves* policy in his absence and to claim the right to issue editorial instructions.

Equally, Josselson did his utmost to protect the magazines from Agency interference. But the claim that the axing of Macdonald's piece was unique in the history of *Encounter* cannot be upheld. If this were true, then one might deduce that the contents of *Encounter* suited the exigencies of the Agency, which subsequently felt it had no need to exercise its veto. One critic described this process as 'the inevitable relations between employer and employee in which the wishes of the former become implicit in the acts of the latter'.[39] But according to Tom Braden, the Agency had meddled at least once before: 'We had some trouble with *Encounter* from time to time, and I used to say, "Let them publish what they want." But there was one time – it was over some question of foreign policy – and Larry [de Neufville] sent me a query about an article and we had to veto it. I think it had to do with US policy toward China. *Encounter* was to publish a piece that was critical of US policy, and we had a helluva fight back at the office. I remember going up and talking to Allen Dulles, and he refused to get involved. He just said, "You handle it." So we finally axed it, and I am sorry we axed it.'[40]

Monty Woodhouse, who was liaising with de Neufville at this time, was 'well aware that the Congress for Cultural Freedom was axing pieces. But I never knew of any formal guidelines for this which were precisely laid down anywhere.'[41] Woodhouse could not recall whether or not Leslie Fiedler's article on the Rosenbergs was seen by members of the intelligence community before publication, but it seems likely that such a controversial intervention in an area of critical importance to the US government would have commanded the CIA's attention.

The article to which Braden referred appeared on Josselson's desk on 28 July 1954, sent to him from London by Spender. The essay was by Emily Hahn, an eccentric contributor to *The New Yorker* and undisputed expert on China (she had lived in Hong Kong during the 1930s and 1940s, and had insisted on taking Joseph Alsop to an opium den when he visited in 1941. Both found themselves interned in the same Hong Kong camp after the Japanese invasion of 1942). Josselson wrote by return that he 'found it utterly shocking. It will certainly not make any new friends in England. I am passing it on to Nicolas and François and shall call you or Irving about it before this letter reaches you.'[42] Two days later, Nabokov wrote to Kristol and Spender: 'Before going into the matter of Miss Emily Hahn's piece, let me re-state some of the principles upon which we had all agreed in the course of the talks we had at the time of launching *Encounter*, as well as in our various subsequent meetings. *We agreed that all articles on controversial topics should be seen by us before they are shown to anybody outside*. We agreed that one of the fundamental policies of *Encounter* should be to work towards a better understanding between England and America and consequently, that all political issues should be discussed on the highest possible plane so that whenever controversy takes place, it should be stated in a manner as not to be offensive to national feelings on either side of the ocean. We have all read Miss Hahn's piece . . . all of us had the same negative reaction to this article. We feel that Miss Hahn gives an erroneous, superficial and slipshod statement of the American point of view on China. We feel that Miss Hahn's article is offensive in matters of style, temper and contents.'[43] Bondy concurred with Nabokov, saying the piece was full of 'hysterical abuse'.

After pointing out what this hysterical abuse was, Nabokov asked, 'Now, where do we go from here? . . . We would suggest that you should attempt to secure from Miss Hahn a re-write of her article, which would result in a *complete* change of tone eliminating its most abusive passages. In addition to Miss Hahn, you secure another article stating the American point of view on the Chinese problem but on a high and dignified level and in a more concise form. If this cannot be done, we think that Miss Hahn's article should be dropped and this crucial issue raised again at a later date with more responsible persons than Miss Hahn representing the American point of view.'[44]

In case this admonition wasn't enough, on 19 August, the newly installed Deputy Secretary of the Congress, CIA agent Warren Manshel, stepped forward with a raft of suggested amendments to the piece. 'We are all in agreement here that it would be unwise to publish the piece,' he wrote. 'If your commitments are irreversible, however, and the article has to appear, then the following sections will have to be changed as a minimum condition of its publication.'[45] There followed an exhaustive list of the sections in question, with detailed notes in Manshel's hand. But still he urged the editors to reconsider, warning them that 'the Hahn may well cook our goose'. The article never appeared. The reasons for its exclusion, which were withheld from *Encounter*'s readers and contributors, lend credence to the later charge that, in the magazine, where a truth was 'uncomfortable for the Soviet Union it is promulgated; where it is uncomfortable for the United States it is mitigated'.[46]

20

Cultural NATO

Mr Yermilov, turn in your grave: you have taken CIA money!

Nicolas Nabokov

Shortly after the Macdonald débâcle, Melvin Lasky was invited to succeed Irving Kristol at *Encounter*. Josselson, whose determination to replace Kristol had not waned, was delighted when Lasky agreed to take the London job. Kristol packed his bags. Josselson, at last, felt assured that the political side of the magazine was in the right hands. There would be no excuse – and no need – for the Agency to meddle from on high. No sooner had he settled into the editorial chair, Lasky received word from Fredric Warburg that Spender's salary was being paid by the British Society for Cultural Freedom, 'although the organization does not really exist'.[1] With *Encounter* serving the interests which the British Society had been created to advance, the Society itself had ceased to function. But it was a useful front for MI6's subsidies, for which Victor Rothschild had now become the principal conduit. Correspondence between Rothschild, Warburg and Muggeridge reveals how the money (£750 per quarter) was first passed to Rothschild's account at the Bury St Edmund's branch of the Westminster Bank, then to the Secker and Warburg Private Account, before being transferred to the Barclays Bank account of the British

Society, which then 'donated' the same amount to *Encounter*. In July 1960, Fredric Warburg suggested that 'this lunatic procedure of going through a non-existent society with two members, Malcolm Muggeridge and F. J. Warburg' be replaced by a 'direct payment made between the house of Rothschild and Panton House'[2] (*Encounter*'s address).

Amazingly, in all the years that Spender worked at *Encounter*, his salary was fixed at £2,500 per year. 'It never changed throughout his time there,' Natasha Spender remembered. 'That's why he had to take all those jobs in America.'

One effect of Spender's meagre salary was that he had to find other ways of boosting his income, chiefly by joining the international lecture circuit. This meant long absences from the *Encounter* office, which suited Lasky perfectly, giving him scope to sharpen the magazine's political edge undisturbed. Chiefly, Lasky's objective seems to have been to move the magazine closer to that group of Labour Party thinkers and politicians whom covert strategists had long since recognized as having 'at long last made the amazing discovery that there is probably more practical Socialism in the U.S. than there is in the Labour Party, *if* by Socialism one means individual welfare instead of doctrinaire class warfare, and that by and large the American worker is a darn sight better off than his British opposite number – and furthermore, is a much freer man. In other words, [they are] in the process of discovering American dynamic democratic capitalism.'[3]

The Labour Party's prestige had peaked at the end of the Second World War, bringing it a landslide victory in the general election of 1945 which ousted Churchill. But by the bitter winter of 1947, enthusiasm was on the wane, and the Cold War had driven a significant rift into the party. Those on the left divided into anti-Stalinists and those who looked to accommodate the Soviet Union, whilst those on the right were committed to defeating Communism. The latter group was organized around the journal *Socialist Commentary*, and counted amongst its most prominent members Denis Healey, Anthony Crosland, Rita Hinden and Hugh Gaitskell. It was this group – known as the 'revisionists' because of their commitment to modernizing the Labour Party, which included abolishing the famous Clause IV pledge to nationalization – which offered the CIA the hook it was seeking to harness British political thought to its designs for Europe. These were clearly drawn up in successive US policy documents as the consolidation of the Atlantic Alliance and the European Defense Community, and the creation of a Common Market, objectives which required the countries of Europe to sacrifice certain national rights in favour of collective security. But as Washington strategists well knew, England in particular, held fast to its habits of sovereignty. As one State Department report concluded gloomily, 'the United Kingdom can hardly be said to be gladly giving up certain sovereign rights in the interest of collective security [except those which it] has been forced by the logic of circumstances to make'.[4]

The principal pressure group for advancing the idea of a united Europe in partnership with America was the European Movement, an umbrella organization which covered a range of activities directed at political, military, economic and cultural integration. Guided by Winston Churchill, Averell Harriman and Paul-Henri Spaak, the Movement was closely supervised by American intelligence, and funded almost entirely by the CIA through a dummy front called the American Committee on United Europe, whose first Executive Secretary was Tom Braden. The cultural arm of the European Movement was the Centre Européen de la Culture, whose director was Denis de Rougemont. Additionally, a huge programme of grants to student and youth associations, including the European Youth Campaign (EYC), was inaugurated by Braden in 1950. Responding to CIA guidance, these organizations were at the cutting edge of a campaign of propaganda and penetration designed to draw the sting from left-wing political movements and generate acceptance of moderate socialism. As for those liberal internationalists interested in the idea of a Europe united around internal principles, and not according to American strategic interests, they were considered by Washington to be no better than the neutralists. The CIA and the Psychological Strategy Board were specifically instructed to 'guide media and programs toward destruction' of this particular heresy.

Central to the whole operation was Jay Lovestone, Irving Brown's boss, who from 1955 was run by James Jesus Angleton. Lovestone's task was to infiltrate European trade unions, weed out dubious elements, and promote the rise of leaders acceptable to Washington. During this period, Lovestone supplied Angleton with voluminous reports on trade union affairs in Britain, compiled with the assistance of his contacts in the TUC and the Labour Party. Angleton allowed his counterparts in British intelligence (those few whom he trusted) to share Lovestone's 'inside dope'. Essentially, it was the Lovestonites (even if they didn't think of themselves as such) within British Labour circles who found themselves in the ascendant by the late 1950s. To make fast its line into this group, the Agency deployed the Congress for Cultural Freedom, at whose expense Gaitskell undertook trips to New Delhi, Rhodes, Berlin and to the 1955 Future of Freedom conference in Milan (which also attracted Rita Hinden and Denis Healey). After losing his parliamentary seat in 1955, Anthony Crosland – whose influential book *The Future of Socialism* read 'like a blueprint for an Americanized Britain'[5] – was employed by Josselson to help plan the Congress's International Seminars under the directorship of Daniel Bell, who had been imported from America for this end. By the early 1960s, Crosland had worked his way onto the Congress's International Council. Rita Hinden, a South African academic based at the University of London, was described by Josselson as 'one of us', and in the mid-1960s was instrumental in securing a grant from Josselson to expand the Fabian Society's journal, *Venture*. The magazine's commitment to a strong united Europe became synonymous with Gaitskellite thinking. Denis Healey, whose Atlanticist credentials brought him into close contact with the American Non-Communist Left (he was London correspondent of the *New Leader*), became another staunch ally of the Congress, and *Encounter* in particular. Healey was also one of the recipients and recyclers of material produced by the Information Research Department. In turn, he supplied IRD with information on Labour Party members and trade unionists.[6]

Of these, Hugh Gaitskell, leader of the Labour Party, was the key figure, and no sooner had Lasky arrived in London, than he attached himself to the small group of intellectuals who gathered at Gaitskell's house in Frognal Gardens, Hampstead. Gaitskell, who had specialized in propaganda during his wartime work for the Special Operations Executive, and who was also close to IRD, could not have been ignorant of *Encounter*'s institutional ties. And so it was that when he launched his celebrated attack on the fellow-travelling left at the 1960 Labour Party conference in Scarborough, some people found themselves asking who he was travelling with. Writing after the conference to Michael Josselson, Lasky reported that Gaitskell had personally thanked him, Lasky, for *Encounter*'s support of his policies. Moreover, said Lasky, *Encounter* had been cited on the debating floor of the conference, evidence that the magazine was receiving 'much kudos'.[7] When Labour under Harold Wilson beat the Conservatives in the 1964 general election, Josselson wrote to Daniel Bell, 'We are all pleased to have so many of our friends in the new government'[8] (there were half a dozen regular *Encounter* writers in Wilson's new Cabinet). Lasky brought *Encounter* much closer to the political agenda of its hidden angels. The price, according to Richard Wollheim, was high. 'It represented a very serious invasion of British cultural life – and it bore responsibility for the complacency of many British intellectuals and the Labour Party over the Vietnam War.'[9]

It was the cultural side of the magazine (not to mention attractive fees) which continued to attract the best contributions, and for this the CIA still had Spender to thank. 'People wouldn't have written for *Encounter* at all if it wasn't for Stephen,' said Stuart Hampshire. 'All the good stuff – which Lasky used to call "Elizabeth Bowen and all that crap" – was commissioned by Stephen. He gave the magazine its respectability.'[10] Certainly, it did much to sustain the Congress's reputation as an organization dedicated primarily to culture, rather than politics.

But the Cold War constantly strained the idea that culture and politics could be kept separate. Indeed, the *Kulturkampf* was alive and well, as the Congress's celebration of the fiftieth anniversary of Tolstoy's death in the summer of 1960 demonstrated. American intelligence had long had an interest in Tolstoy as a symbol of 'the concept of individual freedom'. Its connection went back to OSS days, when Ilia Tolstoy, émigré grandson of the famous novelist, was an OSS officer. Other members of the Tolstoy family were in regular contact with the Psychological Strategy Board in the early 1950s, and received funds from the CIA for their Munich-based Tolstoy Foundation. In 1953, C. D. Jackson noted in his log file that he had promised one supplicant that he would telephone Frank Lindsay (Wisner's former deputy who had moved on to the Ford Foundation) regarding funds for the Tolstoy Foundation.

In December 1958, Cass Canfield told Nabokov that the Farfield Foundation was interested in supporting a 'western celebration of Tolstoy' to answer a Tolstoy festival planned by the Soviets, which he correctly predicted would appropriate the great writer as a precursor of Bolshevism. 'The contrast between the two presentations would be obvious to any independent thinker and this ought to make excellent propaganda for us,'[11] reasoned Canfield. It fell to Nabokov to devise 'a dignified answer to Communist propaganda', and this took the form of a lavish affair held on the Venetian island of San Giorgio in June and July 1960. Scores of prominent writers and scholars attended, including Alberto Moravia, Franco Venturi, Herbert Read, Iris Murdoch, George Kennan, Jayaprakash Narayan and John Dos Passos. Sixteen Soviet scholars were invited, but in their stead came four 'stooges'.

'In retrospect, it is very funny to remember, for instance, the silhouettes of two Russians, a thin, long one and a short, stocky one,' Nabokov later wrote. 'The thin one was the Secretary General of the Union of Soviet Writers, the short one an odious SOB called Yermilov, a nasty little party hack. They were standing, both of them, in line to receive their *per diem* and travel allowance from my secretary, or rather the administrative secretary of the Congress for Cultural Freedom. They had come, or rather had been sent, to attend a conference commemorating the 50th anniversary of the death of Tolstoy.' Nabokov closed the recollection on a jubilant note: 'Mr Yermilov, turn in your grave: *you have taken CIA money*!'[12]

'Expenses, the most beautiful word in modern English,' V. S. Pritchett once declared. 'If we sell our souls, we ought to sell them dear.' Those who did not queue up for *per diems* in Venice could stand in line for them at another Congress event taking place that June in Berlin, the 'Progress in Freedom' conference. Writing to Hannah Arendt, Mary McCarthy gave a wonderfully bitchy account of the personal rivalries and intellectual obfuscations which dominated the conclave: 'The main event, from the point of view of sheer scandal, was a series of furious clashes between Mr Shils and William [Phillips], on the subject of mass culture, naturally. I swear Shils is Dr Pangloss reborn and without Dr Pangloss's charm and innocence. I said so, in *almost* as many words, when I got into the fight myself. Another feature of the Congress was [Robert] Oppenheimer, who took me out to dinner and is, I discovered, completely and perhaps even dangerously mad. Paranoid megalomania and sense of divine mission . . . [Oppenheimer] turned to Nicholas Nabokoff [sic] . . . and said the Congress was being run "without love". After he had repeated this several times, I remarked that I thought the word "love" should be reserved for the relation between the sexes . . . George Kennan was there and gave a very good and stirring closing address (which ought to have crushed Mr. Shils and all his Luciferian camp forever) but the rumor was that he was crazy too, though only partly crazy.'[13] Aside from these and other such 'public idiocies', Mary McCarthy reported that 'the Congress was fun. I enjoyed the gathering-in of old friends and new ones, which had a sort of millennial character, including the separation of the sheep from the goats.'[14]

Also benefiting from CIA largesse that year was a group of journals invited to take advantage of the Congress's clearing house, which was set up as 'an effective and systematic means for placing before a broad international public much excellent material which now reaches a somewhat limited audience'.[15] As well as finding outlets for material produced by Congress-owned publications, the clearing house was intended to act as a distribution point for other cultural journals which were deemed worthy of membership of the Congress's 'world family of magazines'. These included *Partisan Review*, *Kenyon Review*, *Hudson Review*, *Sewanee Review*, *Poetry*, *The Journal of the History of Ideas* and *Daedalus* (the journal of the American Academy of Arts and Sciences), which under the umbrella of the Council of Literary Magazines also received Farfield Foundation grants to improve circulation abroad. Additionally, the Congress joined up with the Council of Literary Magazines to award an annual fellowship of $5,000 to an American writer. Who was appointed to manage the award? No less than Robie Macauley, who succeeded John

Crowe Ransom as editor of *Kenyon Review* in July 1959.[16] During the years the *Review* was tied to the Congress, Macauley was able to increase circulation from 2,000 to 6,000. It was his boast that he had 'found ways of making money that Mr. Ransom had never thought of'.[17] But in other ways, *Kenyon Review* suffered under Macauley's editorship. His long absences, a *sine qua non* of his employment with the CIA, and his high-handed manner (in 1963 he abruptly abolished the board of advisory editors) had a strong negative impact on the journal. The benefits to the Congress, by contrast, were considerable. By formalizing its relationship with these prestigious American journals, the Congress could now boast a publishing combine of unparalleled scope and influence, a kind of thinking man's Time-Life Inc.

'We were not selling a brand name, so we didn't always insist on the Congress imprimatur being used,'[18] explained John Hunt. So, many Congress journals were not readily recognizable as such. Amongst these was *Hiwar*, the Congress's Arabic magazine which appeared in October 1962, its first issue carrying an interview with T. S. Eliot and a plea by Silone for the independence of the writer and the autonomy of art. Attempts to conceal the Congress's ownership of the magazine were unsuccessful, and it was instantly attacked as a 'Trojan horse'. One Muslim newspaper claimed that the Congress was trying 'to propagate its evil theories by spreading money here and there, by establishing attractive magazines and by giving big receptions and conferences', and called for the Congress to be 'exposed and boycotted'.[19]

Other Congress journals launched in the 1960s included *Transition* in Uganda, which attracted writers like Paul Theroux and achieved a respectable circulation of 12,000 before its offices were raided and its editors imprisoned in 1968. In London, *Censorship* was launched in 1964 under Murray Mindlin, an eclectic figure who had translated Joyce's *Ulysses* into Hebrew. The advisory editors were Daniel Bell, Armand Gaspard of Switzerland, Anthony Hartley, Richard Hoggart and Ignazio Silone. It cost the Congress $35,000 a year, and ran at a substantial loss. When it folded in winter 1967, the *New Statesman* was moved to announce, 'This is bad news for writers, publishers and artists everywhere.'

Josselson, who never got on with Murray Mindlin, was less inclined to mourn (he said its 'relative success was due in part to subjects on sex which it featured from time to time'). *Censorship* was the model for *Index on Censorship*, founded in 1972 by Stephen Spender, with a substantial grant from the Ford Foundation.

But of all the magazines linked to the Congress, the case of *Partisan Review* is the most intriguing. 'The real riddle of *Partisan Review* has always seemed to me the question of how the mouthpiece of so small and special a group . . . has managed to become the best-known serious magazine in America, and certainly, of all American magazines with intellectual ambitions, the one most read in Europe,' pondered Leslie Fiedler in 1956.[20] Part of the answer to the riddle lay in the funding of the magazine, as Fiedler teasingly implied when he said that a 'detailed study of the economic ups-and-downs of *PR* would make [a] full-scale article'.[21] From 1937–43, the magazine was largely subsidized by the abstract painter, George Morris; after 1948, its chief source of financial support was Allan B. Dowling, who until 1951 'backed it single-handed, and has since then been president of and a chief contributor to the foundation which currently publishes the magazine'.[22] Fiedler made no mention of Henry Luce, whose generous donation of 1952 had been kept a secret. But he had noticed, along with others, that *Partisan Review* 'is referred to in such mass-circulation journals as *Life* and *Time*, with perfect confidence that it will stir the proper responses in their vast audience'.[23]

Certainly, no mention was made of the CIA, whose alleged involvement with America's most influential intellectual journal has long since puzzled historians. It is known that *Partisan Review* received Farfield Foundation dollars (via the American Committee) in early 1953, and this at Cord Meyer's instigation. It also received 'a grant for expenses' from the Farfield in the early 1960s.[24] But in the life of a magazine harried by financial crises, this hardly amounts to much. In 1957, the question of *PR*'s tax-exempt status had again been raised at the Internal Revenue Service: not only did the magazine stand to lose this status, but there was also talk of making all contributions to *PR* during and since 1954 retroactively taxable. 'This

I consider absolutely outrageous,' wrote C. D. Jackson to Cord Meyer.[25]

C. D. and Meyer rallied to *Partisan Review*'s cause. First they put in 'a good word' for the journal with the Tax Exemption Branch of the Internal Revenue. Subsequently, William Phillips reported to C. D. that he was encouraged by the Internal Revenue's initial response. Second, C. D. appealed directly to Allen Dulles. On 12 November 1957, C. D. sent Daniel Bell a confidential memo relaying the CIA's position on the matter: 'They have no direct monetary or operational interest in the *Partisan Review*. The present editor, however, is sympathetic to the Congress for Cultural Freedom, and is cooperating. Financial difficulties for *Partisan Review* might result in a change of management detrimental to [the CIA's] interest. Therefore, they have an indirect interest in seeing to it that favorable consideration is given to this request for tax exemption.'[26]

Partisan Review's problems had also been discussed at an Operations Coordinating Board (OCB) meeting in April 1956. Following up with a memo to the Policy and Planning Staff of United States Information Agency, the OCB called for action on a proposal to help boost *PR*'s revenue. Without identifying the author (most likely it was Sidney Hook, a member of *PR*'s Publications and Advisory Board, and 'official spokesman' for the magazine, according to Fiedler), the OCB representative quoted in full from this proposal, which began, 'As you know, for a long time I have complained about the fact that special foundation and other support is often arranged for *new* magazines, but that the old stand-bys and work horses in the anti-Communist field, such as the *New Leader* and *Partisan Review*, don't get helped, or helped as much as they should.'[27] After talks with William Phillips, continued the proposer, it seemed that the 'ideal situation [would be] if the American Committee for Cultural Freedom might be the means through which subscriptions, as gifts, to magazines like *Partisan Review* might be passed on to those foreign intellectuals most in need of them. I am thinking not only of those who are resolutely on our side . . . but also of that vast army of intellectuals who have not been sold on Communism but who think of America as an equally imperialistic, materialistic, culture-less and semi-barbaric country.'[28] 'I think there is major value in this type of proposal, especially if the concern of the U.S. government is not apparent, in reaching the targets indicated in the ideological approach,'[29] concluded the report. Within a month, *Partisan Review* was able to give Elizabeth Bishop a generous grant of $2,700. The money came from the Rockefeller Foundation, to the tune of $4,000 a year for three years, to be disposed of in literary fellowships. This may well have been a coincidence, but it is curious that, despite repeated requests for financial assistance, the Rockefeller Foundation had refused every single appeal from the magazine's editors for the past ten years.

In early 1958, William Phillips travelled to Paris, where he met with Michael Josselson to discuss 'the future of *PR*'. On 28 March 1958, Phillips wrote to ask whether Josselson had considered whether or not 'some of the things we talked about could be done'.[30] Within a few months, the American Committee for Cultural Freedom – moribund since its ignominious and *de facto* suspension in January 1957 – had been resuscitated for the sole purpose of standing as official publisher of *Partisan Review*, an arrangement which was to last for the next ten years. Commenting on this development, Hook told Josselson that there was 'no real desire to continue the Am. Com. except to accommodate *PR* . . . Phillips will go to any lengths to get help for *PR*'.[31] Josselson himself later recollected that 'The Committee would have disappeared entirely if at the last moment it had not decided to let the editors of *Partisan Review* take advantage of its tax exempt status, and since then the only "activity" of the Committee has consisted in posing as sponsors of *PR*.'[32] According to this account, the American Committee was not subsidizing *Partisan Review*, but providing it with a tax loophole.

But according to Daniel Bell, 'for several years, *PR* received some financial support from the Congress for Cultural Freedom, in the form of subscriptions bought for individuals overseas who received the magazine free. So far as I know, that funding was also kept secret.'[33] *Partisan Review*'s fortunes were now harnessed to the Congress, which from 1960 boosted the magazine's sales figures to the tune of 3,000 copies a year, which were distributed by the Congress outside of the

US. At the same time, the Congress extended similar help to the other high-level cultural magazines with which it had long been affiliated: *Kenyon Review* (1,500 copies), *Hudson Review* (1,500), *Sewanee Review* (1,000), *Poetry* (750), *Daedalus* (500) and *The Journal of the History of Ideas* (500). Purchase of these copies cost $20,000 per annum. Scheduled initially to run for a three-year period, the Congress's total commitment to these magazines came to $60,000, plus $5,000 for administrative costs. Fredric Warburg was contracted to distribute *Partisan Review* in England.[34] Warburg was also offered first refusal on a *Partisan Review* anthology, *Literature and Modernity* (edited by Phillips and Philip Rahv), whose contributors were nearly all connected at one time or another with the Congress for Cultural Freedom (including Koestler, Chiaromonte, Mary McCarthy and Alfred Kazin).

Partisan Review's fortunes continued to improve. 'I saw Will Phillips the other night,' Kristol wrote to Josselson in March 1960, 'and he remarked mysteriously that *Partisan Review*'s problems are now completely solved, though he wouldn't go into details . . . He even went so far as to say that they have *more* money than they thought they needed!'[35] But Phillips needed even more: 'I don't suppose the Congress could pay my fare on some grant basis for a trip to Europe this June on some necessary business?'[36] he asked Josselson a year later. Phillips made this request for a grant despite what he later described as his instinct 'to question [the Congress's] bureaucratic makeup and what was patently its secret control from the top'. In 1990, he wrote proudly of the fact that 'neither Rahv nor I was considered personally or politically reliable enough' to be invited to the 1950 launch of the Congress, whose personalities he described as 'breezy, rootless, freewheeling, cynically anti-Communist orgmen'.[37] Trading insults, Lasky later described Phillips as something of a freewheeler himself. 'He bluffed his way through everything. Why the hell was he sent over to Paris? He just sat around in the Deux Magots.'[38]

William Phillips later maintained that he owed no debt at all to the Congress. Whilst conceding he had been 'a fringe player in the global propaganda game', he wrote of this as a *de facto* consequence of his membership of the American Committee's Executive Board, to whose 'internal proceedings and calculations

[and] finances' he was not, he said, privy. Phillips also claimed to be 'shocked by – and perhaps envious of – the nouveau riche look of the whole operation, by the posh apartments of the Congress officials, the seemingly inexhaustible funds for travel, the big-time expense accounts, and all the other perks usually associated with the executives of large corporations. After all, *Partisan Review* was always trying to make ends meet, and my experience had led me to believe that poverty was the normal condition for serious political outfits and literary magazines. As for secret funding,' he continued, 'it seems to me to violate the very nature of a free intellectual enterprise, particularly when the financing is by a well-organized arm of the government, with its own political agenda.'[39]

Others, of course, had a different view of secret funding. Just as *Partisan Review* began to benefit from the deal with the American Committee for Cultural Freedom, so the *New Leader* received renewed munificence from its covert backers. In February 1956, C. D. Jackson wrote to Allen Dulles with a proposal to raise money for Sol Levitas's magazine. Time Inc. had been subsidizing the *New Leader* to the tune of $5,000 per annum since 1953, in exchange for 'information on worldwide Communist tactics and personalities, with particular reference to Communist activities within the labor movement'.[40] But this was a fraction of the money needed to keep the magazine afloat. By C. D. Jackson's calculation, nothing short of $50,000 would keep it solvent. 'If capitalistic enterprise can muster the wisdom to appreciate that the particular tone of voice with which Levitas speaks to a particular group of people here and abroad is unique and uniquely important, and is willing to back that hunch with quite a few thousand dollars,' he told Dulles, 'I hope that you will be able to go along with the current proposal. It seems to me to be the best formula I have yet seen for all of us to have our Levitas and let him eat, too.'[41] Dulles was easily persuaded, as he had been on previous occasions, that an Agency grant to the *New Leader* 'well justified the high payoff potential'. By the summer of 1956, the 'Save the New Leader' drive had earned the magazine the $50,000 it needed. The United States Information Agency pledged $10,000, as did the Ford Foundation, Mr H. J. Heinz, and Time Inc. The remaining $10,000 came in the form of a 'donation' of $5,000 from *Washington Post* publisher Philip Graham, and $5,000 which was listed simply as 'unforseeable manna'.[42]

As ever, the Congress for Cultural Freedom was folded into the new arrangements, both for *Partisan Review* and the *New Leader*. Collaboration with the Congress, in the form of joint publications, formal syndication agreements, and exchange of knowledge, brought both journals further material benefits. The prolific activity of the Congress in these years had made it a compelling feature of western cultural life. From the platforms of its conferences and seminars, and across the pages of its learned reviews, intellectuals, artists, writers, poets and historians acquired an audience for their views which no other organization – except for the Cominform – could deliver. The Paris office was a ferment, attracting visitors from all over the world, and even, in 1962, a bomb which exploded in the hallway (an event hailed by one member as 'a great and glorious and long expected, indeed well merited honour and a memorable date in the annals of the Congress').[43] For second and third generation would-be Hemingways, the Congress was now the repository of all those romantic myths of literary Paris, and they came to it in their droves.[44]

The Congress's high profile also attracted some unwelcome scrutiny. In 1962, it was the subject of a brilliantly perceptive parody by Kenneth Tynan and his BBC *That Was The Week That Was* team. 'And now, a hot flash from the Cold War in Culture,' began the sketch. 'This diagram is the Soviet cultural block. Every dot on the map represents a strategic cultural emplacement – theatre bases, centres of film production, companies of dancers churning out intercontinental balletic missiles, publishing houses issuing vast editions of the classics to millions of enslaved readers. However you look at it, a massive cultural build-up is going on. But what about us in the West? Do we have an effective strike-back capacity in the event of an all-out cultural war?' Yes, the sketch continued, there was the good old Congress for Cultural Freedom which, 'supported by American money, has set up a number of advanced bases in Europe and elsewhere to act as spearheads of cultural retaliation. These bases are disguised as magazines and bear codenames – Encounter, which is short for "Encounterforce

Strategy"'. A 'Congress spokesman' was then introduced, who boasted of a cluster of magazines which were a 'kind of cultural NATO', the aim of which was 'Cultural containment, or, as some of the boys like to put it, a ring around the pinkoes. In fact, I wouldn't say we had an aim. I'd say we had a historic mission. World readership . . . But whatever happens, we in the Congress feel it our duty to keep our bases on a round-the-clock, red-warning alert – always watching what the other fellow is doing, instead of wasting valuable time on scrutinizing ourselves.'[45]

The satire was biting and impeccably researched. Whilst the Congress 'spokesman' denounced the philistinism of the Soviet Minister of Culture, Tynan had him reveal, without a hint of irony, who the Congress's enlightened patrons were: the Miami District Fund, Cincinnati, the Hoblitzelle Foundation, Texas, and the Swiss Committee for Aid to Hungarian Patriots.

Such references to the Congress's financial suppliers, though they missed the ultimate target, caused Josselson sleepless nights, and confirmed his fear that the real Achilles' heel of the Congress was the CIA. Tensions between Josselson and his Agency bosses had been mounting ever since the collapse of the American Committee in early 1957. Josselson, temperamentally incapable of playing the monkey to anyone else's organ-grinder, now found himself increasingly at odds with Cord Meyer, who refused to let go his grip. Meyer had never recovered from his Kafkaesque treatment at the hands of the McCarthyites in 1953. Added to that was a string of personal tragedies which had made him increasingly gloomy and intractable. 'Waves of Darkness', Meyer's 1946 short story about his experience of war and near fatal injury on the beaches of Guam, also described the tragic motion of his future life. In 1956, his nine-year-old son Michael was killed by a speeding car. Less than a year after that, Cord separated from his wife, Mary Pinchot Meyer.[46]

Increasingly mulish and unreasonable, Meyer had become a relentless, implacable advocate for his own ideas, which seemed to gravitate around a paranoiac distrust of everyone who didn't agree with him. His tone was at best argumentative, at worst histrionic and even bellicose. 'Cord entered the Agency as a fresh idealist and left a wizened tool of Angleton,' said Tom Braden. 'Angleton was master of the black arts. He bugged everything in town, including me. Whatever Angleton thought, Cord thought.'[47] Arthur Schlesinger, an old friend of Meyer's, now found himself the victim of this idealist-turned-angry-intellectual-gendarme: 'He became so rigid, so unbending. I remember once he called me and suggested we meet for a drink. So I invited him over, and we sat upstairs in my house and talked. Years later, I asked CIA for my file, and the last document in the file was a report on me by Cord Meyer! In my own house, over a drink, and he wrote a report on me. I couldn't believe it.'[48] Just like James Stewart's character in Hitchcock's *Rear Window*, Meyer and Angleton ended up mirroring the deviance they tried to monitor.

In October 1960, Josselson met Cord Meyer and a group of IOD men in a room at a Washington hotel. A heated argument ensued, in which, according to one witness, Josselson was being 'taught to suck eggs' by his CIA colleagues. Josselson, who had what Diana described as 'this mind-body thing', felt his blood pressure soar and his temples thump before he crashed to the floor. 'He was demonstrative with his emotions,' said John Thompson. 'He'd get into arguments and faint and have heart attacks. He was very European.'[49] This heart attack was real enough. At two in the morning local time, Diana was awakened by Lou Latham, the Paris station chief (who was in Washington when it happened) to say that Michael had been rushed to hospital after collapsing. Diana boarded the first flight out of Paris that morning, with four-year-old Jennifer in tow. Stopping briefly at a hotel to leave Jennifer with her, Diana's, mother, Diana then made for the George Washington University Hospital. There, she found Michael lying in an oxygen tent. For the next few weeks, she kept constant vigil at his side. Slowly, he started to pull through. And in this prone state, he awoke once more to the urgency of his mission. 'All the time Michael was in hospital, he would "brief" me, and I would take notes,' remembered Diana. 'And then I'd go to the door of his room and "brief" Lee [Williams] and the other goons who turned up. It was fun to turn the tables on them.'[50]

Whilst Josselson was still under an oxygen mask, Bill Durkee, Meyer's deputy division chief, turned to Lee Williams while they were walking up a Washington street and said,

'Now we've got him where we want him.'[51] Reflecting on this years later, Diana concluded that whilst the Agency valued Michael for the job he was doing, 'he must have been at the same time a thorn in their side, going his own way, resisting them whenever they tried to assert control. Michael tried to keep them happy by telling them about was cooking on various stoves, and by force of personality kept them from being aware of their unimportance. He was friends with them, talked about their families and careers, and I had the idea – now shaken – that they admired him. Durkee, I'm now finally aware, was speaking for the lot of them. They must have been suspicious of all these intellectuals, foreigners to boot, and suffered from having all the money and American power, and not getting any credit for it . . . Besides, Michael was not a Yale man, he was practically a Russian and a Jew, and it was he who was hobnobbing with famous people, not they.'[52]

Still, it was clear that his health would not permit Josselson to expend so much energy on the Congress anymore. It was agreed that he should move permanently to Geneva, where he would continue to work for the Congress, but at one remove. John Hunt would take over responsibility for running the Paris office, including dealing with the Agency. When Hunt had arrived at the Congress in 1956, he spent the first two years, he later said, behaving like 'a cleaning boy, never saying anything, just watching and learning'.[53] Gradually, he had become what he described as 'Operations Officer' to Michael's 'Executive Officer'. Essentially, these roles remained unchanged for the life of the Congress. But with Josselson now working, with the aid of a secretary, from his home in Geneva, Hunt found himself in administrative control of the Paris headquarters.

21
Caesar of Argentina

> I never bade you go
> To Moscow or to Rome,
> Renounce that drudgery,
> Call the Muses home.
>
> W. B. Yeats, 'Those Images'

John Hunt took over the Paris office at a propitious time. The 'Eisenhower splurge' on the arts was followed by the Kennedy administration's announcement that it desired a 'productive relationship' with artists. Kennedy made the point when he invited 156 of the more famous of them (including Arthur Miller, Andrew Wyeth, Ernest Hemingway, Mies van der Rohe, Igor Stravinsky, Pierre Monteux, Paul Hindemith, Archibald MacLeish, Robert Lowell and Stuart Davis) to attend the inaugural festivities. 'The inauguration must have been fun,' Elizabeth Bishop wrote to Lowell. 'I see bits of it over and over in the newsreels. But I don't like that Roman Empire grandeur – the reviewing stand, for example, looks quite triumphal.'[1] But to many Cold Warriors, the imperial atmosphere was inspirational, as one admirer told Kennedy in early 1961: 'Just as in ancient times a Roman, wherever he went, could proudly proclaim "civis Romanus sum," now once again, similarly, wherever we go and with head erect and with pride, we can proclaim, "civis Americanus sum."'[2]

On 11 May 1962, Robert Lowell was again invited to the White House, this time for a dinner in honour of André

Malraux, then French Minister of Culture. Kennedy joked at the reception that the White House was becoming 'almost a café for intellectuals'. But Lowell was sceptical, and wrote after the White House dinner: 'Then the next morning you read that the Seventh Fleet had been sent somewhere in Asia and you had a funny feeling of how unimportant the artist really was, that this was sort of window dressing and that the real government was somewhere else, and that something much closer to the Pentagon was really running the country . . . I feel we intellectuals play a very pompous and frivolous role – we should be windows, not window-dressing.'[3]

Although rarely expressed openly, there was a growing inclination amongst some intellectuals to view the government's beneficence with suspicion. But the question of corruption did not unduly exercise the CIA, under whose auspices much of this bounty was being distributed. 'There are some times when you might as well be seduced,' said Donald Jameson. 'I think that almost everybody in a position of significance in the Congress [for Cultural Freedom] was aware that somehow or other the money came from some place, and if you looked around there was ultimately only one logical choice. And they made that decision. The main concern for most scholars and writers really is how you get paid for doing what you want to do. I think that, by and large, they would take money from whatever source they could get it. And so it was that the Congress and other similar organizations – both East and West – were looked upon as sort of large teats from which anybody could take a swig if they needed it and then go off and do their thing. That is one of the main reasons, really I think, for the success of the Congress: it made it possible to be a sensitive intellectual and eat. And the only other people who did that really were the Communists.'[4]

Whether they liked it or not, whether they knew it or not, scores of western intellectuals were now roped to the CIA by an 'umbilical cord of gold'. If Crossman could write in his introduction to *The God That Failed* that 'For the intellectual, material comforts are relatively unimportant; what he cares most about is spiritual freedom', it seemed now that many intellectuals were unable to resist a ride on the gravy-train. Some of the Congress's conferences 'were mainly show, and the attendees sometimes reminded one of the smart set commuting between St Tropez in summer and St Moritz or Gstaad in winter,' wrote the Sovietologist Walter Laqueur, himself a regular attendee at these conferences. 'There was a snobbism, particularly in Britain; the outward appearance of refinement, wit and sophistication combined with a lack of substance; college high-table talk and Café Royal gossip.'[5] 'These stylish and expensive excursions must have been a great pleasure for the people who took them at government expense. But it was more than pleasure, because they were tasting power,' said Jason Epstein. 'When visiting intellectuals came to New York, they were invited to great parties; there was very expensive food all around, and servants, and God knows what else, far more than these intellectuals themselves could have afforded. Who wouldn't like to be in such a situation where you're politically correct and at the same time well compensated for the position you've taken? And this was the occasion for the corruption that followed.'[6]

Those who were not receiving *per diems* in New York could take advantage of the Villa Serbelloni in Bellagio, northern Italy. Poised on a promontory between the northern lakes of Lecco and Como, the villa had been bequeathed to the Rockefeller Foundation by Principessa della Torre e Tasso (née Ella Walker). The foundation made the villa available to the Congress as an informal retreat for its more eminent members – a kind of officers' mess where frontliners in the *Kulturkampf* could recover their energy. Writers, artists and musicians on residency there would be met by a chauffeur in a blue uniform with the small insignia 'V. S.' on his lapel. Guests received no 'grant' as such, but accommodation was free, as were all travel expenses, meals, and the use of the tennis court and swimming pool. Writing on the villa's elegant stationery, Hannah Arendt told Mary McCarthy: 'You feel as though you are suddenly lodged in a kind of Versailles. The place has 53 servants, including the men who take care of the gardens . . . The staff is presided over by a kind of headwaiter who dates from the time of the "principessa" and has face and manner of a great gentleman of fifteenth-century Florence.'[7] McCarthy replied that she had discovered such luxurious surroundings were not conducive to hard work. The villa was also a congenial venue for the Congress's June 1965 seminar, 'Conditions of World Order', held in association with *Daedalus* and the American Academy of Arts and Sciences.

For a chosen few, there was also the possibility of joining Hansi Lambert (the millionairess friend of the Congress who also played host at her winter retreat in Gstaad), or Junkie Fleischmann, for Mediterranean cruises in their yachts. The Spenders were guests of both. When Stephen told Ernst Robert Curtius of his cruise from Corfu to Ischia in August 1955, the German said simply, 'You were a communist, and now you go on yachts in the Mediterranean, ja, ja.'[8] For those who preferred terra firma, the Congress arranged accommodation in Europe's more prestigous establishments. In London, there was the Connaught; in Rome, the Inghilterra; and at Cap Ferrat, the Grand. In Paris, Irving Brown continued to entertain at his home away from home, the Royal Suite at the Hotel Baltimore.

Despite his reservations about accepting government patronage, Robert Lowell was able to suppress them in favour of a first-class ticket to South America, offered by the Congress for Cultural Freedom in May 1962. For several years, his great friend Elizabeth Bishop, who was living in Rio de Janeiro, had been urging him to come; now, the offer of Congress funds prompted him into action. Bishop was delighted. The State Department people in Brazil 'behave so STUPIDLY and rudely', she wrote, and '[they] usually send very minor and dull novelists and professors'.[9] Lowell's visit promised to be much more interesting.

The Congress had been trying to increase its influence in South America for several years. Its journal there was *Cuadernos*, edited by Julian Gorkin. Gorkin had founded the Communist Party of Valencia in 1921, and worked in an underground network for the Comintern, learning, amongst other things, how to forge passports. Breaking with Moscow in 1929, he alleged that the Soviets had tried to persuade him to become an assassin. Towards the end of the Spanish Civil War he fled to Mexico, the traditional roost for Bolsheviks on the run, and there survived five attempts on his life, one of which left him with a hole in his skull. As editor of *Cuadernos*, his job was to try and penetrate the 'great distrust' in Latin America, where the only way to achieve significant impact, he joked, would be constantly to attack the US and sing the praises of Sartre or Pablo Neruda. Gorkin wasn't helped by the CIA-backed *coup* in Guatemala (1953) and Cuban Revolution of 1958. In the wake of American intervention in these areas, this was a period of 'euphoria for the Latin American Communists and their allies',[10] but Gorkin battled the odds, giving the Congress an important niche in a hostile environment.

Lowell arrived in Rio de Janeiro with his wife, Elizabeth Hardwick, and their five-year-old daughter Harriet, in the first week of June 1962. Nabokov was there to meet them at the airport, with Elizabeth Bishop. Things went fine until Lowell's family boarded the ship back to New York on 1 September, and he was left to continue the tour south to Paraguay and Argentina. Accompanying him was Keith Botsford, the Congress's 'permanent roving representative' in South America, who was 'plugged into the trip' by John Hunt in order to keep an eye on the poet (in CIA parlance, Botsford was Lowell's 'leash'). It was in Buenos Aires that the trouble started. Lowell threw away the pills prescribed for his manic depression, took a string of double martinis at a reception in the presidential palace, and announced that he was 'Caesar of Argentina', and Botsford his 'lieutenant'. After giving his Hitler speech, in which he extolled the Führer and the superman ideology,[11] Lowell stripped naked and mounted an equestrian statue in one of the city's main squares. After continuing in this vein for several days, Lowell was eventually overpowered, on Botsford's orders, wrestled into a straitjacket, and taken to the Clínica Bethlehem, where his legs and arms were bound with leather straps while he was injected with vast doses of Thorazine. Botsford's humiliation was completed when Lowell, from this position of Prometheus bound, ordered him to whistle 'Yankee Doodle Dandy' or 'The Battle Hymn of the Republic'.[12]

Later that month, Nabokov telephoned Mary McCarthy. His voice was tremulous and weary as he informed her that Lowell 'was in a mental ward in Buenos Aires and that Marilyn Monroe committed suicide because she had been having an affair with Bobby Kennedy and the White House had intervened'.[13] Sharing Nabokov's disgust, Mary McCarthy concluded: 'Our age begins to sound like some awful colossal movie about the late Roman Emperors and their Messalinas and Poppaeas. The Bobby Kennedy swimming pool being the bath with asses' milk.'[14]

The Lowell incident was an unmitigated disaster. Chosen by the Congress as 'as an outstanding American to counteract . . . Communist people like [Pablo] Neruda',[15] Lowell turned out to be an emissary for nothing beyond the powerful properties of Thorazine. He had badly let his side down (and in turn was badly let down by Botsford). Amazingly, neither Hunt nor Josselson dumped Botsford, but continued to use his services as their 'representative' in Latin America. More amazingly, less than a year later, they even considered sending Lowell to represent the Congress at a conference in Mexico. But Josselson stalled, afraid that Lowell would 'follow his psychiatrist's recommendations as little as he did the last time . . . there is no guarantee whatsoever that he will not again give some lunatic speeches in favour of Hitler'.[16] Botsford, who had no desire to repeat his previous experience, warned against sending Lowell, and it was agreed that Robert Penn Warren and Norman Podhoretz were more reliable candidates to send behind the Tortilla Curtain.

Although Josselson had his doubts about Botsford ('I am not even sure that he is capable of telling you straight facts'),[17] Hunt's protégé continued to flourish in the Congress.[18] He now told Hunt that Brazilian intellectuals regarded the Congress as a 'yanqui' front, and suggested that the Congress become more discreet, modest and 'invisible', supporting only projects that had strong local support. But Hunt rejected that approach, telling him that no area of the world should be neglected in the fight against Communism.[19] And in this mood, a campaign to undermine the poet Pablo Neruda was vigorously pursued by Hunt and Botsford.

In early 1963, Hunt received a tip-off that Pablo Neruda was a candidate to win the Nobel Prize for Literature for 1964. This kind of inside information was extremely rare, as deliberations of the Nobel committee are supposed to be conducted in hermetic secrecy. Yet by December 1963, a whispering campaign against Neruda had been launched. Careful to obscure the Congress's role, when Irving Kristol asked Hunt if it was true the Congress was 'spreading rumours' about Neruda, Hunt replied teasingly that it was inevitable that the poet's candidacy for the Nobel Prize would excite controversy.[20]

Actually, since February 1963, Hunt had been organizing the attack. Julian Gorkin had earlier written to 'a friend in Stockholm' about Neruda, and told Hunt that 'this man is ready to prepare a small book in Swedish on "Le cas Neruda"'.[21] But Hunt doubted the usefulness of such a book, and told Congress activist René Tavernier that a fully documented report written in French and English should be prepared for circulation to certain individuals.[22] Hunt stressed that there was no time to lose if the scandal of Neruda's winning the Nobel Prize was to be averted, and he asked Tavernier to organize the report in collaboration with Julian Gorkin and his Swedish 'friend'.[23]

Tavernier's report focused on the question of Neruda's political engagement, and argued that it was 'impossible to dissociate Neruda the artist from Neruda the political propagandist'.[24] It charged that Neruda, a member of the Central Committee of the Chilean Communist Party, used his poetry as 'an instrument' of a political engagement which was 'total and totalitarian'; this was the art of a man who was a 'militant and disciplined' Stalinist. Great use was made of the fact that Neruda had been awarded the 1953 Stalin Prize for his poem to Stalin, 'his master', which Tavernier labelled 'poetic servility'.[25]

Tavernier sent the proofs of the article to Hunt at the end of June. Hunt decided it needed pepping up and told its author to concentrate on the nature of Neruda's political engagement, and to focus on the anachronism of his Stalinist position, which bore little relation to the more tolerant mood of contemporary Russia. Hunt finished in professorial tone, telling Tavernier that he expected to see the revised report in a matter of days.[26]

'It's obvious they would've campaigned for Neruda not to get the Nobel Prize. It's a given,' said Diana Josselson.[27] Accordingly, Josselson had written to Salvador de Madariaga, the philosopher and honorary patron of the Congress to seek his intervention. But de Madariaga was sanguine, arguing that 'Stockholm aurait une réponse facile et impeccable: on a déjà couronné Nobel la poésie chilienne en la personne de Gabriela Mistral. Un point, c'est tout. Et la politique n'y a rien à faire.'[28] Politics, of course, had everything to do with it.

Pablo Neruda did not win the 1964 Nobel Prize for Literature. But there was no cause for celebration in the offices of the Congress when the winner was announced. It was Jean-Paul Sartre. He, famously, refused to accept the award. Neruda had to wait until 1971 before he was honoured by the Swedish Academy, by which time he was Chile's Ambassador to France, representing the democratically elected government of his friend Salvador Allende (who was then undemocratically unseated and murdered in 1973, with the help of the long arm of the CIA).

In 1962, just months after the construction of the Berlin Wall, Nicolas Nabokov was invited by Willy Brandt, the Mayor of West Berlin, to become Adviser on International Cultural Affairs to the Berlin Senate. This appointment solidified an old friendship, and it brought Nabokov back to the city which he felt closest to. 'Brandt and Nabokov got on very well,' remembered Stuart Hampshire. 'Brandt was financed by the Americans, and so was the Berlin cultural program. Brandt was perfectly at ease with this, it didn't worry him in the least. Nicky was highly sophisticated, he knew all the right people, so he was perfect for the job of organizing Berlin's cultural affairs.'[29] For Nabokov, West Berlin had lost some of its 'cosmopolitan glamour', and the time seemed ripe for its renewed investment in the 'cultural game'. According to John Hunt, Nabokov had 'never been ready to take on the world for his convictions', and he seemed now to have lost interest in the tired old paradigms of the Cold War. His plans and proposals for Berlin, which was now divided by a concrete wall, contained none of the old anti-Communist rhetoric. 'It was clear to me that in such a game one should try to gain the support and participation of scholars and artists from the Soviet Union and Socialist Bloc,'[30] he wrote, in a mood full of the warmth of *détente*. To this end, he befriended the Soviet Ambassador to East Berlin, Pyotr Andreyetvitch Abrassimov. The two spent hours together at the Soviet Embassy, Abrassimov eventually acceding to Nabokov's passionate requests to have Soviet artists represented at the Berlin Arts Festival, of which he was also director. For Abrassimov, this was a bold decision: Soviet intelligence was keeping a close eye on Nabokov. With a KGB spy planted on Brandt as an adviser, the Russians knew all about Nabokov's affiliations with the CIA-backed Congress.

Josselson wasn't entirely happy with Nabokov's new appointment, 'but he swallowed it', according to Diana. Nabokov, who was spending more and more time in Berlin, appeared to be wandering away from the Congress, but not from its expense account. Josselson, who had always urged restraint, could do little to limit Nicolas Nabokov's congenital extravagance. 'He had very expensive taste, and this had to be paid for,'[31] said Stuart Hampshire. But the link, which was formally agreed between the Congress and Brandt's office, did bring the Congress an opportunity to be represented at the Berliner Festwochen, and in 1964 it financed the appearance there of Günter Grass, W. H. Auden, Keith Botsford, Cleanth Brooks, Langston Hughes, Robie Macauley, Robert Penn Warren, James Merrill, John Thompson, Ted Hughes, Herbert Read, Peter Russell, Stephen Spender, Roger Caillois, Pierre Emmanuel, Derek Walcott, Jorge Luis Borges, and Wole Soyinka (John Hunt and François Bondy went as monitors).

But Josselson couldn't swallow his resentment at what he saw as Nabokov's desertion. 'He was jealous,' said Hampshire. 'He used to refer to "my group" of intellectuals. He flattered them, and he expected their loyalty. Nicky was part of his "group", and then he got interested in something else. Josselson was angry and hurt.'[32] By the end of 1964, Josselson's patience was wearing thin, and he wrote a caustic letter asking Nabokov why he had seen fit to claim expenses from the Congress for a trip to London which clearly originated in the interests of Berlin. With Nabokov currently receiving a generous salary from the Congress (Josselson had drawn nearly $30,000 from the Farfield to cover his activities there over a four-year period, of which $24,000 was set aside for his salary), why, Josselson asked, couldn't he draw such expenses out of the 50,000 Deutschmarks he was receiving from Berlin's taxpayers? Peeved that Nabokov had told him nothing of his visits to Abrassimov in the Soviet sector, or of Abrassimov's visit to Nabokov's house with Rostropovich,

Josselson ended angrily by telling Nabokov: 'I don't want to know anything more about what you are doing . . . Let's just suspend our official relationship until May 1 [when they were due to meet] and let's keep our fingers crossed that with your doings you will not unduly damage our friendship.'[33] Unable to resist one final slight, Josselson hoped that the Christmas holidays would give Nabokov 'an opportunity to reflect . . . and to compose some music instead of rushing around madly and rushing, who knows, towards a precipice'.[34]

A dark cloud was gathering over Nabokov's and Josselson's relationship. When Josselson learned that Nabokov was planning to undertake a trip to Moscow with Abrassimov to secure the participation of Soviet artists at the Berlin Festival, he wrote in urgent tones, urging him not to make the trip. Nabokov aborted the journey at the last moment, but demanded an explanation from Josselson. This was forthcoming, but cryptic in the extreme: 'I did not for one minute worry about your safety nor was I concerned about any consequences from your connection with the Congress. Believe me, I was only concerned about yourself and about a very embarrassing situation you could find yourself in, not immediately, but maybe a year or two from now. I don't want to write about this, but rest assured that what I have in mind is not something that I just picked up out of the air . . . Also, please bear in mind that you have many enemies in Berlin who are only waiting for an opportunity to knife you, and in your own interest, you would do well to cut the ground from under these people and their malicious gossip.'[35] There was more than just hurt behind Josselson's objections to his friend's new career move: Nabokov had become a security risk. 'You could become an unwitting instrument of Soviet policy in Germany,' he now warned him. 'You [have] already made a first step in that direction.'[36]

Shortly after this letter, in August 1964, a very worrying situation arose. In the course of a Congressional investigation into the tax-exempt status of private American foundations by Congressman Wright Patman, a leak occurred which identified a number of foundations (eight in all, known as 'The Patman Eight') as CIA fronts: the Gotham Foundation, the Michigan

Fund, the Price Fund, the Edsel Fund, the Andrew Hamilton Fund, the Borden Trust, the Beacon Fund and the Kentfield Fund. These foundations, it transpired, were 'mail-drops', often consisting of nothing more than an address, set up to receive CIA money which could then be transferred elsewhere with apparent legitimacy. After money was transferred to the mail-drop, the 'second pass' or 'pass-through' would occur: the front foundation would make a 'contribution' to a prominent foundation widely known for its legitimate activities. These contributions were duly listed as assets received by the foundations in their annual 990-A form filed with the Internal Revenue Service, which every tax-exempt non-profit organization was obliged to submit. This, of course, was where the system was most vulnerable. 'Maybe there wasn't really any other way to do it,' said Donald Jameson, 'but these foundations were required to file all kinds of tax documents and one thing and another, which they complied with to some extent. Which meant that when . . . people began exposing them, they could go to the tax records and link A to B to C to D directly through these things, and that was very unfortunate.'[37]

The 'third pass' occurred when the legitimate foundation made a contribution to the CIA-designated recipient organization. William Hobby, president of the *Houston Post* and trustee of the Hobby Foundation, explained how this worked: 'We were told that . . . we would receive certain funds from the CIA. Then we'd receive a letter, say from Organization XYZ, asking for funds. We granted the funds.' No questions asked. 'We believed that [the CIA] knew what they were doing.'[38]

The 990-A forms of four other foundations illustrated this pass-through operation: the M. D. Anderson Foundation of Houston, the Hoblitzelle Foundation of Dallas, the David, Josephine and Winfield Baird Foundation of New York, and the J. M. Kaplan Fund of New York. Each of these foundations were IOD 'assets'. From 1958 to 1964 the Anderson Foundation received $655,000 of CIA money through phoney foundations such as the Borden Trust and the Beacon Fund. It then disbursed the same amount to the CIA-supported American Fund for Free Jurists, Inc., a New York-based organization later known as the American Council for the International Commission of Jurists. The Baird Foundation received a total of $456,800 between 1961 and 1964 in 'pass-throughs', and piped the money on to CIA programmes in the Middle East and Africa. The Kaplan Fund – best known as the benefactor of New York's 'Shakespeare in the Park' season – gave almost a million dollars between 1961 and 1963 to the Institute of International Labor Research Inc. of New York. The Institute focused on CIA projects in Latin America, including a seed-bed for democratic political leaders called the Institute of Political Education, which was run by Norman Thomas and Jose Figueres in Costa Rica. The funding came from the CIA, channelled to the Kaplan Fund through designated pass-throughs: the Gotham, Michigan, Andrew Hamilton, Borden, Price and Kentfield funds – six of the Patman Eight. President and treasurer of the Kaplan Foundation was Jacob M. Kaplan who, it will be remembered, offered his services to Allen Dulles in 1956. The Hoblitzelle Foundation, between 1959 and 1965, received a similar amount from the CIA. The bulk of it ($430,700) was passed straight to the Congress for Cultural Freedom.

The Patman leak opened the hatch, however briefly, on the engine room of the CIA's covert funding. Combined with the information freely available for inspection at the Internal Revenue Service, it enabled a few imaginative journalists to piece together part of the jigsaw. In September 1964, the New York leftist weekly *The Nation* asked: 'Should the CIA be permitted to channel funds to magazines in London – and New York – which pose as "magazines of opinion" and are in competition with independent journals of opinion? Is it proper for CIA-supported magazines to offer large sums in payment of single poems by East European and Russian poets regarded as men of a character who might be encouraged to defect by what, in the context, could be regarded as a bribe? Is it a "legitimate" function of the CIA to finance, indirectly, variously congresses, conventions, assemblies and conferences devoted to "cultural freedom" and kindred topics?'[39]

Cord Meyer remembered that 'The story was carried on the back page of the *New York Times* and caused little stir at the time, although within the Agency it caused us anxiously to review and attempt to improve the security of [our] funding mechanisms.'[40] 'We used to have exercises at the Agency where we would ask ourselves what would happen if you took the back off the radio and started looking at where all those wires led,' said Lee Williams. 'You know, what if someone went down to IRS and looked at one foundation giving a grant and then seeing that the figures didn't tally? This was something which really worried us when the rumours were building up. We talked about it, and tried to find a way of protecting the people and organizations which were about to be exposed.'[41] But Hunt and Josselson, who were both in London when the story broke – Josselson at the Stafford Hotel, Hunt at Duke's Hotel – were suddenly very exposed. 'We're in trouble,' Josselson told Hunt bluntly on the telephone.

Josselson had been alert to the danger well before the Patman exposures. People were beginning to jabber at cocktail parties – 'half the problem was that people in Washington couldn't keep their mouths shut,' said Diana Josselson. Paul Goodman had hinted explosively at the truth as early as 1962, when he wrote in *Dissent* that 'Cultural Freedom and the Encounter of ideas are instruments of the CIA.' There can be little doubt that Josselson had been forewarned of Patman's findings two years later, thus accounting for his mysterious letter to Nabokov of June 1964.

Josselson had long fretted that the Congress's cover was insecure, and in 1961 he had persuaded Cord Meyer that they should find a crop of new 'sponsors'. 'In answer to Michael's and the CIA's apprehensions, they rather smartly thought they would diversify the source of funds, and so they did,'[42] recalled Diana Josselson. Nabokov went to New York in February 1961 to talk to foundation trustees. Curiously, none of the foundations he approached came through. It seems as though his trip was just a smokescreen, designed to make it look like the Congress was actively and openly seeking financial partners, whilst in fact the backroom deals were already being agreed between the CIA and other foundations. By 1963, the Congress's statement of receipts showed a brand new set of donors. These were the Colt, Florence, Lucius N. Littauer, Ronthelym Charitable Trust, Shelter Rock (whose 'donor' was Donald Stralem, a board member of the Farfield Foundation), Sonnabend, and Sunnen foundations.

As for the Farfield Foundation, its credibility as an

'independent' foundation had become increasingly stretched. 'It was meant to be a cover, but actually it was transparent. We all laughed about it, and called it the "Far-fetched Foundation",' said Lawrence de Neufville. 'Everybody knew who was behind it. It was ridiculous.'[43] Junkie Fleischmann's legendary personal meanness seemed to ensure the rumours now circulating at every Washington and New York party that he was not the real 'angel' of the Congress for Cultural Freedom. Nabokov later told Josselson that 'Junkie was the stingiest rich man I have ever known.'[44] Natasha Spender likewise recalled that 'Junkie was famously mean. At a dinner party in a Cincinnati restaurant with Junkie and others, I had to borrow a dime from him to make a telephone call. When we were going back in the taxi, Stephen said to me, "You must send that dime back tomorrow morning." And I thought he was joking, but he wasn't. So I sent the dime back.'[45]

It was now reasoned that if the Farfield Foundation were to disburse funds to American – as well as international – projects, then the CIA's interest, thus sandwiched, would become less conspicuous. 'The Farfield was engaged in other activities because it needed to cover for the foundation, in case anyone enquired what it was doing,'[46] explained Diana Josselson. The Farfield report for the period 1 January 1960 to 31 December 1963 lists some of the hundreds of grants made for that period. Recipients included the American Council of Learned Societies, the American Academy of Arts and Sciences, the Modern Language Association, the Dancers' Workshop, the Festival of Two Worlds at Spoleto, Italy (contributions towards general expenses and the participation of American students, and for the expenses of the poet Ted Hughes), the Institute for Advanced Studies in the Theatre Arts, the Living Theater of New York, the New York Pro Musica, the Association of Literary Magazines of America, *Partisan Review* ('a grant for expenses'), and the International Institute in Madrid (a grant to preserve the personal libraries of Lorca, Ortega and Fernando Almalgro). Under 'Travel and Study', the Farfield gave fellowships to scores of individuals, including Mary McCarthy ('to prepare an anthology of new European writing'), the Chilean painter Victor Sanchez Ogaz, the poet Derek Walcott ('for travel in the United States'), Patricia Blake,

Margerita Buber-Neumann, Lionel Trilling (for a trip to Poland, Rome, Athens, and Berlin), and Alfred Sherman, contributor to *The Spectator*, for a trip to Cuba.

Ironically, it was the sheer scale of the Farfield Foundation's endowments which made it especially vulnerable to discovery. In the wake of the Patman revelations, it wouldn't have taken a Conan Doyle to deduce who was the schemer behind the foundation. Astonishingly, not a single journalist thought to enquire any further. The CIA did take a 'hard look at this technique of funding', but, to the later amazement of a Select Committee enquiry into the matter, it did not 'reconsider the propriety of bringing the independence of America's foundations into question by using them as conduits for the funding of covert action projects'[47] – the very situation that had prompted Patman to leak his findings in the first place. 'The real lesson of the Patman Flap is not that we need to get out of the business of using foundation cover for funding, but that we need to get at it more professionally and extensively,'[48] reasoned the Chief of Covert Action's Staff Program and Evaluation Group.

This thinking was egregiously flawed, as later events would show. Josselson certainly did not subscribe to it. He knew that the current funding mechanisms were hopelessly vulnerable, and that he was sailing a leaky boat. 'The seas got rougher and rougher, and navigation got harder and harder, but still they were navigating, but in a state of constant alert,'[49] said Diana Josselson. From late 1964, Josselson tried frantically to steer the Congress for Cultural Freedom away from the pending revelations and the damage they would cause. He considered changing its name. He once again investigated cutting the financial link with CIA, to be replaced entirely by Ford Foundation funding. Above all, he attempted to direct the Congress away from its Cold War perspective and to minimize the plausibility of any suggestion that it was a tool of the US government in this Cold War. In October, he told the Executive Committee at its meeting in London: 'I frankly wouldn't like to see the Congress's *raison d'être* to be the Cold War. I somewhat get the feeling that this is its *raison d'être*, and, frankly, I don't like it.'[50]

22

Pen Friends

> . . . a new kind of man
> has come to his bliss
> to end the Cold War he has borne
> against his own kind flesh.
>
> Allen Ginsberg, 'Who Be Kind To'

The year 1964 was a bad one for Cold Warriors. The myths upon which they relied were being systematically exploded. First there was the publication of *The Spy Who Came in from the Cold*. Written in five months by a junior diplomat in the British Embassy in Bonn using the *nom de plume* John Le Carré, it sold 230,000 copies in America, and a further two million more in paperback in 1965, when Paramount released its film version. Le Carré traced the novel's origins to his own 'great and abiding bitterness about the East–West ideological deadlock'. Richard Helms, who was then in charge of CIA undercover operations, detested it. Le Carré was now ranked alongside Graham Greene (whose 1955 novel *The Quiet American* had appalled America's clandestine community) as authors the Agency liked to hate. They were 'dupes', said Frank Wisner, 'ill-wishing and grudge-bearing types'.

This was followed by Stanley Kubrick's film *Dr. Strangelove*, which satirized the madness of Cold War ideology. In a letter published in the *New York Times*, Lewis Mumford called it 'the first break in the catatonic cold war trance that has so long held our country in its rigid grip . . . what is sick is our supposedly moral, democratic country which allowed this policy to be formulated and implemented without even the pretense of public debate'.[1]

Then, on 18 September 1964, America's single most influential Cold Warrior, C. D. Jackson, died in a New York hospital. Days before, Eisenhower had flown down from Gettysburg, Pennsylvania, to see the critically ill C. D. The Boston Symphony Orchestra, which owed its global reputation largely to C. D.'s support, held a memorial concert for him, with the soloists Vitya Vronsky and Victor Babin playing Mozart. Later, the orchestra's summer school, Tanglewood, set up the C. D. Jackson Master Awards and Prizes in his memory. Sponsoring the prize were many alumni of that special school of Cold Warriorism over which C. D. had presided.

By 1964, these people were already walking anachronisms, members of a diminishing sect whose demise, though by no means complete, seemed ensured by a wave of revulsion and protest against the values they represented. They were like so many 'whifflebirds', the name one New York intellectual invented for a fabulous creature that 'flies backwards in ever decreasing circles until it flies up its own ass hole and becomes extinct'.[2] With the rise of the New Left and the Beats, the cultural outlaws who had existed on the margins of American society now entered the mainstream, bringing with them a contempt for what William Burroughs called a 'snivelling, mealy-mouthed tyranny of bureaucrats, social workers, psychiatrists and union officials'.[3] Joseph Heller in *Catch-22* suggested that what America deemed sanity was actually madness. Allen Ginsberg, who in his 1956 lament *Howl* had mourned the wasted years – 'I saw the best minds of my generation destroyed by madness' – now advocated the joys of open homosexuality and hallucinogenic 'Peyote solitudes'. Munching LSD, singing the body electric, reading poetry in the nude, navigating the world through a mist of benzedrine and dope, the Beats reclaimed Walt Whitman from stiffs like Norman Pearson Holmes, and sanctified him as the original hippy. They were scruffy rebels who sought to return chaos to order, in contrast to the obsession with formulae which characterized magazines like *Encounter*.

Exasperated by these developments, Sidney Hook wrote to Josselson on 20 April 1964: 'In Europe they have a theatre of the absurd, and in existentialism a philosophy of the absurd. In the U.S., the latest development among intellectuals is "a politics of the absurd" – whose slogans are "Down with U.S." "America stinks!" "Long Live Sex" etc. It is really very amusing – Mailer, Podhoretz etc. And they have a new and fervent disciple – Mr Jack Thompson whose discretion, I fear, is no better than his intelligence.'[4] Thompson had discretion enough to realize that it was the better part of valour, and stayed on as Executive Director of the Farfield.

Nineteen sixty-four also marked the first birthday of the *New York Review of Books*. Guided by Jason Epstein and Robert Silvers, the review's instant success clearly signalled that not all American intellectuals were happy to act as Cold War legitimists orbiting around the national security state. As the ruling consensus began to fragment, the review signalled the emergence of a newly critical intelligentsia, free to speak on those issues on which magazines like *Encounter*, bound, as it was, to a consensual discipline, were virtually mute. If the impression had been given that all New York intellectuals had, by some kind of reverse alchemy, transformed themselves from bright radicals to become just another base metal of the CIA and the rest of the Cold War establishment, here was evidence to the contrary. Far from being apologists for American power, these were thinkers who rallied to the review's readiness to denounce imperialism just as it denounced Communism. And, to the horror of the CIA, it became the flagship for intellectual opposition to the Vietnam war. 'We had a big problem with the yin and yang of the *New York Review* crowd, especially when it got so anti-Vietnam, and so left wing,'[5] remembered Lee Williams, who was less than forthcoming about what measures were taken to counteract the *Review*, limiting himself to saying that 'it wasn't a punch, counter-punch situation'.[6]

Michael Josselson himself was not impervious to the new spirit. Although he took pains to conceal his growing disillusionment with 'the American proposition', privately he conceded that he was appalled by the shape it had assumed. Years later, he was to write that 'the experience of working with and for the "outfit" [had become] truly traumatic . . . In the 1950s our motivation was buttressed by America's historic promises . . . in the second half of the 1960s our individual values and ideals [had] been eroded by our intervention in Vietnam and by other senseless U.S. policies.'[7] The claimed missile gap, the doomed U-2 flights, the Bay of Pigs, the Cuban missile crisis – all these imperial blunders had undermined Josselson's faith in the American Century, and in the government agencies which were charged with realizing it. Even Harry Truman, whose administration had founded the CIA in 1947, said he now saw 'something about the way the CIA has been functioning that is casting a shadow over historic positions, and I feel that we need to correct it'.[8] In an era which was beginning to embrace the idea of *détente*, Josselson now looked to move the Congress away from the habits of Cold War apartheid, and towards a dialogue with the East. Through its relationship with PEN, the Congress was ideally poised to do just that.

By the mid-1960s, International PEN had seventy-six centres in fifty-five countries, and was officially recognized by UNESCO as the organization most representative of all the writers of the world. Its task, fixed by statute, included a promise to avoid, in all circumstances, engagement 'in state or party politics'. It was this refusal to succumb to bias or *parti pris*, coupled with a robust defense of freedom of expression, which guaranteed the world-wide expansion of PEN during the Cold War years. But the truth is that the CIA made every effort to turn PEN into a vehicle for American government interests. And the Congress for Cultural Freedom was the designated tool.

The Congress had long taken an interest in PEN, despite Arthur Koestler's peroration that it was run by a bunch of 'arseholes' who worried that the campaign for cultural freedom 'meant fanning the Cold War'.[9] Initially, the Congress's efforts had been directed at keeping Eastern bloc delegates out of PEN, fearing that the Communists would attempt to infiltrate the organization and influence its debates. 'We are prepared to talk to Russian writers, Russian artists, Russian scientists,' Nabokov had written to Richard Crossman in 1956, 'but we do not want to meet and talk to Soviet bureaucrats or Soviet officials in their stead. Unfortunately . . . we are much too often confronted with precisely that type of subservient and police-minded Soviet bureaucrat (stony look, square shoulders, blue serge suit and baggy pants) whom we want to avoid.'[10] Rightly concerned to keep these impostors out, the Congress had liaised successfully with PEN's Secretary, David Carver. When news reached Josselson in 1956 that the Communists planned 'to make a big push' at the PEN conference in Japan the next year, he easily persuaded Carver that the Congress's 'top battery' (listed as 'Silone, Koestler, Spender, Milosz etc.') should be brought out in opposition.

John Hunt, himself a member of International PEN (he had joined in 1956 after publishing his first novel, *Generations of Men*), had a 'friendly relationship' with David Carver, who acted as an unofficial agent for *Encounter*, distributing copies of the magazine at PEN meetings. In 1964, Hunt decided that Carver was overworked and needed help. So, the Congress offered to provide help in the person of Keith Botsford, who had kicked his heels in South America for a while after the Lowell fiasco, before returning to the US to become co-editor with Saul Bellow of the literary magazine, *The Noble Savage*. Now, once again, he was conveniently on hand to help his friend Hunt, and duly appeared at the offices of International PEN in London in autumn 1964. 'It never occurred to me to wonder why Botsford suddenly turned up the way he did,' said a PEN activist. 'But now I think of it, it was a bit odd.'[11]

The French section of PEN was infuriated to learn of Botsford's appointment, and wrote angrily to Carver to demand an explanation. Defending the appointment, Carver said that he had been working with Botsford for some time 'in terms of complete harmony and close cooperation . . . [his] position is quite simple and uncomplicated. The English Executive Committee has appointed him my assistant and deputy and as I combine the offices of General Secretary of the English Centre and International Secretary, it follows that I naturally expect him to help me over the whole range of my work.'[12] The French had good reason to be worried. Suspicions about the nature of Botsford's links to the Congress for Cultural Freedom, and about that organization's links, in turn, to the US government, made them fear that the Americans were attempting to take over PEN. They were right.

It was Keith Botsford who telephoned Arthur Miller in 1965 and said he wanted to come and see him with David Carver.

Miller, who was in Paris at the time, knew Botsford vaguely from *The Noble Savage*, to which he had contributed two short stories. 'Now he was saying something about "PEN", of which I had only vaguely heard,' recalled Miller. The next day, Botsford arrived in Paris with David Carver, who invited Miller to become the next president of International PEN. 'The point now was that they had come to the end of the string,' Miller later wrote. 'The recent détente policy called for new attempts to tolerate East–West differences, which PEN had not yet gained the experience to do. A fresh start was needed now, and it was me.'[13] But, said Miller, 'I had a suspicion of being used and wondered suddenly whether our State Department or CIA or equivalent British hands might be stirring this particular stew. I decided to flush them out . . . PEN stood stuck in the concrete of what I would soon learn were its traditional Cold War anti-Soviet positions, but like the western governments at this point, it was now trying to bend and acknowledge Eastern Europe as a stable group of societies whose writers might well be permitted new contacts with the West.' Miller told one historian that 'it passed through my mind – that the government might have wanted me to become president of PEN because they couldn't otherwise penetrate the Soviet Union, and they figured that traveling behind me could be their own people. They wouldn't expect me to do it, I don't think. One of the early people who approached me about PEN – I can't remember his name now – but people later would say about him, "Why, that guy was an agent all the time." Now I have no evidence of that – it was gossip.'[14]

The Americans wanted an American President of PEN, and they were about to get one. Carver had in fact been 'going all out to get John Steinbeck' (winner of the 1962 Nobel Prize for Literature), but he never materialized, and Miller was the second choice. For the French, neither candidate was suitable. They wanted at all costs to keep the Americans out. As soon as they learned of Carver's intentions to find an American candidate, French PEN put forward one of their own in the person of Miguel Angel Asturias, the great Latin American novelist, and a member of PEN's French Centre. Josselson referred to him in disgusted tones as 'that old Nicaraguan fellow-travelling war-horse Asturias',[15] and wrote in urgent tones to

Manès Sperber, who was then living in Paris, urging him to appeal to André Malraux, de Gaulle's Minister of Culture, and a long-time friend of the Congress, to block the Asturias candidacy. Sperber was hesitant, writing back that the Ministry of Culture had nothing to do with PEN, an independent organization. But Josselson insisted, telling Sperber that nothing less than French prestige was at stake, and as such the government would surely take an interest. If Asturias was elected, Josselson claimed, 'it would be a catastrophe' as it would signal 'the end of our friend Carver'.[16]

Carver, with full backing from his American friends, continued to pursue his own candidate, writing an eight-page open letter to PEN members in April 1965, challenging the legitimacy of the French candidacy, accusing the French Centre of falsifying the facts, and dismissing Asturias as a man who lacked every qualification needed for the job of the international presidency. After receiving a copy of Carver's letter, veteran Cold Warrior Lewis Galantière, a member of the executive board of American PEN, warned his confrères that 'The French offensive is . . . designed not only to thwart the election of an American international president, but also to capture the International Secretariat . . . I consider the French move to be one more example of the over-weening hubris that has seized French officialdom (for I do not doubt that this has the approval of the Quai d'Orsay).'[17]

Members of the executive board of the American Center included several friends of the Congress, other than Galantière. One member in particular stands out on the letterhead: Robie Macauley. With Macauley, the CIA had a man with executive power in American PEN. This meant that when Cord Meyer decided to send him to London as the IOD's case officer for PEN, his interests in its activities there would appear to be perfectly natural. None the less, to make sure his cover was tight, Macauley was a Guggenheim Fellow and then a Fulbright Research Fellow for the two years he was in England. With Botsford and Macauley in London, and Carver a recipient of Congress funds (and, more directly, of Farfield funds), the CIA had achieved excellent penetration of PEN.

In the midst of the battle over the presidency, Carver and Botsford forged ahead with plans for the next big PEN

Congress, scheduled to take place at Bled in Yugoslavia in the first week of July 1965. John Hunt agreed to fund a group of writers to attend the meeting, and Kenneth Donaldson, the CIA's London-based 'Comptroller General', was instructed to organize payment to PEN out of the Congress's account. The list of proposed delegates was compiled by John Hunt, with the strict proviso that 'if any of these individuals cannot go, the PEN Club Secretariat must have the approval of the Congress in Paris to use the funds to send someone else'.[18] Hunt's list included David Rousset, Helmut Jaesrich (Lasky's successor as editor of *Der Monat*), Max Hayward, Spender, Chiaromonte and Silone. Under a separate grant from the Farfield Foundation, travel expenses were provided for Carlos Fuentes and Wole Soyinka.[19] Together with the other delegates, they elected Arthur Miller as PEN's new president.

Having scored a victory at the Bled Congress, John Hunt started preparing for the next PEN conclave, due to take place in New York the following June. This would be the first time in forty-two years that the American Center had played host to an International PEN Congress. With the stakes this high, the CIA decided to bring out the full battery of its covert arsenal. The Congress for Cultural Freedom, for one, was to play a significant role (it had already given £1,000 to Carver in June 1965 to start organizing the New York 'campaign', which was fine-tuned over lunch with Hunt at the Chanterelle restaurant on Brompton Road). The Ford Foundation made a timely intervention, awarding American PEN a 'substantial grant' ($75,000) in January 1966, and the Rockefeller Foundation coughed up an additional $25,000. The CIA also channelled money to American PEN through the Asia Foundation and the Free Europe Committee. With such investments at stake, John Hunt wrote to David Carver on 9 February 1966, telling him that he thought it wise to try and limit their liability.[20]

Hunt's proposed insurance was to place the Congress for Cultural Freedom's seminar organizer, Marion Bieber, either in Carver's office, or in New York for three weeks prior to and during the conference itself, at the Congress's expense. The multi-lingual Bieber, who was working for the Institute of Contemporary History in London, was a veteran of such campaigns from her work in the 1950s as Deputy Executive

Secretary of the Congress. With such a 'topflight' person placed in the heart of English or American PEN, Hunt could be assured that his interests would be protected.

At the same time, Hunt wrote to Lewis Galantière, now president of American PEN, to make a similar offer. Who better than Robie Macauley, recently returned to Washington, whose cover as editor of the prestigious *Kenyon Review* meant that he was above suspicion? Macauley was subsequently placed at the disposal of American PEN as a kind of fixer-factotum.[21] Additionally, Hunt agreed to pay travel expenses for prominent western intellectuals (of his choice) to attend the congress.

The 34th International PEN Congress took place between 12–18 June 1966. Its organizers – both overt and covert – congratulated themselves that the prestige of hosting the event meant that 'a blot on the U.S. record was thereby removed'. A report of the conference described euphorically how 'The pre-eminence of the U.S. as the pace-setter of contemporary civilization was triumphantly confirmed by the [fact] that the congress took place in New York City.' Organized around the theme of 'The Writer as Independent Spirit', the 'concentration on the writer's role in society and his concerns as artist was something which redounded to the credit of our country'.[22]

But not all observers came to the same conclusion. In a lecture delivered at New York University on the eve of the PEN conference, Conor Cruise O'Brien took a heavy sideswipe at the idea of intellectual independence. 'The Dr. Jekyll of the congress's general theme, "the writer as independent spirit", is . . . in danger of turning into Mr. Hyde, "the writer as public figure",' he said. Whereas writers in the past could be accused of being 'strangers to political passions' (Julien Benda), now they were 'liable to be distracted or debauched by them'.[23] O'Brien went on to summarize a recent article in *Encounter*, in which Denis Brogan had praised the magazine for its struggle against *la trahison des clercs*, the phrase Benda had used to attack writers of talent who made themselves spokesmen and propagandists for political causes. This, of a magazine which was so 'congenial to the prevailing power structures', struck O'Brien as misleading. Far from being politically quietist, O'Brien found that *Encounter* had consistently followed a political line, a key element of which 'was the inculcation of uniformly favorable attitudes in Britain towards American policies and practices'.[24]

The *New York Times* reported O'Brien's claims, which hung over the PEN meeting, and signalled the beginning of the end of the Congress for Cultural Freedom.

23

Literary Bay of Pigs

> Remember the figure of Marx – the bourgeois politicians of the 1840s, after '48 – who were clinging to the coattails of the one ahead, and trying to kick the one who was clinging to their own coattails? Well, a lot of coattails are going to be torn in the days to come . . . and I have grave fears that in the process of tearing coattails and kicking, there may be an injured testicle or two.
>
> James T. Farrell

Conor Cruise O'Brien's charge that intellectuals in the West were serving the 'power structure' hit hard at a time when American soldiers were dying in Vietnam. Something was rotten in the state of Denmark, and many of the professional anti-Communists grouped around the Congress for Cultural Freedom now found they could not 'escape the trap [their] deepest convictions had set for [them]'.[1] As custodians of the American Century, they believed, like the conservative columnist Joseph Alsop, that the Vietnam War was 'the logical and righteous extension of America's postwar vision and destiny'.[2] 'Come Vietnam, and our anti-Stalinism gets used to justify our own aggression,' Jason Epstein claimed. 'These people get into a real bind now. They're caught with their pants down: they *have* to defend Vietnam because they've toed the anti-Communist line for so long that otherwise they stand to lose everything. They did help make Vietnam possible; they did help make our policy with China possible; they did help make possible the brutal anti-Stalinism embodied in people like

McCarthy; they did contribute to the stagnation of intellectual culture in this country.'[3]

Arriving at the same conclusion, Robert Merry, biographer of the Alsop brothers, has written: 'Years later it would become fashionable to view the war as a policy aberration, a national tragedy that could have been avoided if America's leaders had simply seen clearly enough to avoid the commitment entirely. But this would ignore the central reality of U.S. involvement in Vietnam – that it was a natural, and hence probably inevitable, extension of the American global policy established at the dawn of the post-war era.'[4]

'There is literally a miasma of madness in the city. I am at a loss for words to describe the idiocy of what we are doing,'[5] wrote Senator William Fulbright, who had undertaken an extraordinary journey from Cold War ideologue to outspoken dissenter. Inveighing against the *pax Americana* and the hopeless illogicality of its foreign policy, Fulbright led the charge of the New Left – to which he never properly belonged – against what he saw as an uncritical acquiescence in the American imperium: 'Neither in the executive branch of our government nor in Congress were more than a few, isolated voices raised to suggest the possibility that Soviet policy in Europe might be motivated by morbid fears for the security of the Soviet Union rather than by a design for world conquest. Virtually no one in a position of power was receptive to the hypothesis that Soviet truculence reflected weakness rather than strength, intensified by the memories of 1919, when the western powers had intervened in an effort – however half-hearted – to strangle the Bolshevik "monster" in its cradle. Our own policy was formed without the benefit of constructive adversary proceedings.'[6]

With equal conviction, Norman Mailer argued that America's war in Vietnam was 'the culmination to a long sequence of events which had begun in some unrecorded fashion toward the end of World War II. A consensus of the most powerful middle-aged and elderly Wasps in America – statesmen, corporation executives, generals, admirals, newspaper editors, and legislators – had pledged an intellectual troth: they had sworn with a faith worthy of medieval knights that Communism was the deadly foe of Christian culture. If it were not resisted in the post-war world, Christianity itself would perish.'[7]

It was against this backdrop of critical dissent that the *New York Times* began to take an interest in what lay hidden in the dark recesses of the closet of American government. In April 1966, its readers were astonished by a splatter of revelations about the CIA. 'The ramifications of CIA activities at home and abroad seem endless,' read one article. 'Though satellites, electronics and gadgets have taken over much of the drudgery of espionage, there remains a deep involvement of human beings, who project the agency into awkward diplomatic situations, raising many issues of policy and ethics. That is why many persons are convinced that in the CIA a sort of Frankenstein's monster has been created that no one can fully control . . . Is the government of a proud and honorable people relying too much on the "black" operations, "dirty tricks", harsh and illicit acts in the "back alleys" of the world? Is there some point at which meeting fire with fire, force with force, subversion with subversion, crime with crime, becomes so prevalent and accepted that there no longer remains any distinction of honor and pride between grim and implacable adversaries? These questions are a proper and necessary concern for the people of the U.S.'[8]

One article, on 27 April 1966, reiterated Conor Cruise O'Brien's claims – which were now common knowledge – that *Encounter* magazine had been a recipient of CIA funds. There the matter might have rested but for Lasky's impetuous next move. He ran an article by Goronwy Rees, a man later described as a 'ridiculous and subsequently discredited fisher in Cold War waters',[9] which, rather than simply rebutting O'Brien's charges against *Encounter*, libelled him by questioning his conduct when he was a UN representative in the Congo a few years previously. O'Brien immediately issued a libel suit against *Encounter*. With Lasky absent (he had taken a trip to South America), and Spender in America, Frank Kermode, who had stepped in as co-editor of *Encounter* (and who had not been shown Rees's column before publication) was left to face the music.

In May of the previous year, Spender had written to Josselson with the news that he had been appointed Consultant Poet for the Library of Congress, the American equivalent of Poet Laureate (predecessors included Frost and Lowell, but

Spender was the first non-American ever to be offered the honour). Initially, Josselson was furious, writing to Muggeridge in June that Spender 'was unable to resist the call of a first siren'.[10] It was agreed that Spender should give up his *Encounter* salary for the year that he would be away, but Josselson, keen to maintain some kind of financial hold over Spender, arranged 'to continue to take care of him quite handsomely'.[11] This, he told Muggeridge, was 'strictly confidential'. Spender, meanwhile, had suggested that Frank Kermode would be a suitable replacement, at least for the time he was absent.

Lasky was delighted with this development. His relationship with Stephen (or 'Stee-fen', as he used to call him, perhaps, said Kermode, as 'a sort of quiet reproach to the poet for not spelling his name, American fashion, with a *v*') had always been strained, and was now at breaking point. 'As good as these [past] years have been, full of work and not a few successes, the worst part of them has been Stephen-in-the-next-office,' he complained to Josselson. 'How elated I have been at every prospect of his absence – and how calm things were then . . . I aways in the past (last year, five years ago) pooh-poohed the notion of getting a replacement. But I sometimes indulge in horrified speculation at what my life will be like with him around in the next years . . . To have to live with that kind of nagging, based on his own daily troubled guilty conscience, getting a maximum of glory for a minimum of work, doing only really his own books, plays, anthologies, articles, reviews, broadcasts . . . sinks me into despair. I don't mind doing it all – in fact, love it. I do mind being constantly harassed by his uneasy sense of cheating . . . Does he deserve it all? Must we always live under the cloud of his insincerity and characterlessness?'[12] Josselson eventually came round to Lasky's view, agreeing that 'the more time Spender spends in London, the more chances there are for clashes and for his going around bitching and gossiping to his outside friends'.[13]

But those closest to Josselson had their doubts about Kermode, too. Although no one came close to Philip Larkin's memorable description of him as a 'jumped up book drunk ponce' (Larkin also mocked him in verse: 'I turned round & showed/my bum to Kermode'), they damned him with faint praise. Edward Shils described him witheringly as an average little professor.[14] Robie Macauley told Josselson that he didn't like him as a person, though he enjoyed his writing. 'I am grateful for your remarks about Kermode,' Josselson told Macauley. 'I, too, like his writings, but haven't met him. From what you say about his personality, I can deduct that there is sure to be trouble ahead . . . At the same time, if Kermode proves to be strong enough, he can do a lot for the magazine, because it is the whole literary part, including the review section, that is so weak.'[15] In the same letter, Josselson made an extraordinary confession: 'I am having my problems with *Encounter*. I am beginning to get bored with it. I haven't confessed this to anyone else, except Diana who feels the same way. I find the *New York Review of Books* so much more exciting and get greater satisfaction even out of *Commentary*.'[16]

Despite the reservations of Josselson's inner circle, Kermode was officially invited to co-edit the magazine with Lasky in summer 1965. Kermode, who understood he was being asked to handle the literary side, with Lasky the uncontested boss, thought it odd that Lasky didn't choose someone better qualified, someone who at least lived in London (Kermode lived in Gloucestershire, and had a teaching job in Bristol). Actually, Kermode's distance from the daily running of the magazine made him a perfect candidate. 'What I took to be a handicap was in fact my chief qualification. Somewhere in my mind or heart, mixed in with mere vanity, and . . . my reluctance to disregard the wrong road, I knew I was being set up.'[17] Nevertheless, Kermode accepted the offer. He immediately discovered that 'the whole Encounter operation' was 'mysterious'. He could not discover the circulation of the journal, or how it was really financed. He was offered very little say in the make-up of the journal, and soon concluded that 'it would have made very little difference if I'd never turned up at all'.[18]

Kermode, like everybody else, had heard the rumours linking *Encounter* to the CIA. Spender told him that he too had been disconcerted by such allegations, but was satisfied that denials he had received from Josselson and the Farfield Foundation were proof to the contrary.[19]

In fact, by the time Kermode came on board, *Encounter* was no longer sponsored by the Congress for Cultural Freedom, but was being published by Cecil King's Daily

Mirror Group. Well, officially at least, that's how things stood. The King deal had been put together in response to a batch of critical reviews of *Encounter*, which had included a 1963 editorial in the *Sunday Telegraph* which referred to a secret and regular subvention to *Encounter* from 'the Foreign Office'. Such reports clearly threatened *Encounter*'s credibility, so the search for private angels began in early 1964. By July of that year, the editors were able to announce in *Encounter* that in future all financial and business affairs would be handled by Cecil King's International Publishing Corporation. As part of this deal, a controlling Trust was established consisting of Victor Rothschild, Michael Josselson and Arthur Schlesinger. Schlesinger's appointment was made in spite of Shils's warning that this would simply reduce the time in which Spender's twisted version of events would travel to Schlesinger, and thence from Schlesinger to the 'New York gang'.[20] Josselson took a more generous view, reasoning that as 'President Kennedy's premature death has left Arthur at somewhat loose ends . . . I thought it would be a nice gesture on our part to assure him at least one trip a year to Europe, which he could not afford on his own.'[21]

Of this new arrangement, Malcolm Muggeridge wrote disparagingly to Josselson, 'I now realize, that in fact, King's assumption of financial responsibility will alter nothing. He (or rather the Inland Revenue) will be out-of-pocket, instead of the Congress. Otherwise everything will be as it was . . . I was partly responsible for starting *Encounter*, and have subsequently tried in a desultory sort of way to help it along . . . [it's been successful, but] there are certain dangers, due to the circumstances in which it was founded – belated involvement in a phase of the Cold War which is over; too close and overt association with the Congress which, though a condition of its coming into existence in the first place, has now become inconvenient and unnecessary. I had hoped that the change in financial responsibility might provide an opportunity, to some extent at any rate, to circumvent these dangers. I now see that I was mistaken.'[22]

As Muggeridge well knew, the King deal kept *Encounter* very much in the intelligence fold. For a start, the Congress for Cultural Freedom did not, contrary to public claims, fully relinquish editorial or even financial control of the magazine, as Josselson later made clear in a letter: 'one aspect of the problem involved in making arrangements with publishers for some of our journals, viz. that we must find publishers who can be relied upon not to tamper with the contents or with the general line of the journals or not to replace the editors of our choice. We were fortunate in this respect to find a Cecil King in England and a Fischer Verlag in Germany [which took over *Der Monat*], but such people or publishers are rare.'[23] In fact, the deal with King specifically stated that 'the editorial salaries of the two senior co-editors and a partial remuneration for an assistant editor' would remain the responsibility of the Congress. 'These have in the past not been directly a part of *Encounter*'s expenses, and they will continue to be a separate expense,'[24] Josselson stated. The rest of *Encounter*'s regular subvention from the Congress – £15,000 annually – would, said Josselson, be redirected in the form of an outright grant to Encounter Books Ltd. The deal with Fischer Verlag assumed the same characteristics: ostensibly, the International Publications Company took over the publishing of *Der Monat*. In reality, the Congress was still the owner of the journal after it purchased 65 per cent of the shares in this company with a 'special grant of $10,000'. These shares were 'held in trust by [an intermediary] for the Congress'.[25] In both cases, the Congress for Cultural Freedom remained the editorial arbitrator, whilst concealing its influence and financial commitment.

Furthermore, with Victor Rothschild, Sir William Hayter and, by 1966, Andrew Schonfield on the board of trustees – a 'grisly trio', according to Muggeridge – *Encounter* found itself just as closely tied to British intelligence as it had always been. Before becoming Warden of New College, Hayter had been ambassador to Moscow and then Deputy Under Secretary of State at the Foreign Office. Prior to this, he had been head of the Services Liaison Department, and chairman of the UK Joint Intelligence Committee. As such he sat in with the Joint Planners under the Chiefs of Staff, dealing with all intelligence questions, and visiting various British intelligence posts overseas. Significantly, it was Hayter's draft proposal of December 1948 calling for a psychological warfare outfit 'to wage the

Cold War' which helped persuade Attlee's Cabinet to set up the Information Research Department, with which Hayter was subsequently closely involved. At Winchester, he had been a contemporary of Richard Crossman, and at New College, of Hugh Gaitskell. Like them, he was a social democrat, and broadly in sympathy with the Labour wing that *Encounter* under Lasky had cultivated so assiduously. Andrew Schonfield, director of the Royal Institute of International Affairs, was also well known to the intelligence community. Victor Rothschild, of course, was there in his capacity as a front for the Foreign Office. The members of this network all felt at home with Cecil King who, according to Peter Wright's *Spycatcher*, was himself a 'long-term contact' of MI5, an association which would have disposed him to be sympathetic to the covert cultural operations of the CIA.

But Josselson's efforts to remove the Congress's assets from damaging allegations were doomed to fail. There were now more holes than boat. If rumours had circulated on the cocktail circuits of London, Paris and New York for years, now they were beginning to harden into fact. Mary McCarthy later told her biographer, Carol Brightman, that Josselson intercepted a letter she had drafted to the *New York Times* around 1964 asserting the independence of the Congress's magazines, 'because he knew it wouldn't be true. He said, "Just lay off, dear. Forget it."' Why didn't the Agency fold its tent and leave the Congress, which was fully able to look after itself, to its own devices? What kind of hubris or vanity was it that inspired the ill-fated decision to cling to the Congress when Josselson himself was pleading for independence? 'They held on, I suppose, because it was one of their few successes. But they should've let go if they really cared about the integrity of the Congress,'[26] said Diana Josselson. But covert action has a bureaucratic momentum which is hard to break. For two decades, CIA officers had been conditioned by a project-based system which encouraged growth rather than leanness. By attaching undue significance to the elephantine *size* of its worldwide clandestine 'infrastructure', the Agency failed to note that the risk of exposure was exponentially increased. 'This is the only country in the world which doesn't recognize the fact that some things are better if they are small,'[27] Tom Braden later commented.

'Nobody, of course, was supposed to know who was financing the Congress for Cultural Freedom,' said Jason Epstein. 'But by the middle of the sixties anybody who didn't know it was a fool. *Everybody* knew. The director of the Farfield Foundation [Jack Thompson] at the time was a very good friend of mine and I would confront him with this and say, "Oh come on, Jack, what's the point of pretending?" And he would say, "Oh no, no, no. That's not true, that's not true at all. We're an independent outfit, nothing to do with the CIA."'[28] One day, whilst lunching with Spender, Epstein said, 'Stephen, I think this whole outfit is being paid for by the Central Intelligence Agency, and you haven't been told and you should find out right now what's going on.' And Spender replied, 'I will, I'm going to speak to Jack Thompson and find out right now whether what you tell me is true.' A while later Stephen called Epstein and said, 'Well, I did confront Jack and he told me it wasn't true, so I think it's not true.' 'And that's how it would go,' Epstein later remarked. 'Nobody wanted to admit what the sponsorship really was. But I think everybody knew and nobody wanted to say.'[29]

Spender had been investigating the rumour since 1964, at least. A letter from John Thompson to Spender, dated 25 May 1964 (three months before the Patman revelations), in which Thompson dismissed as ridiculous the claim that the Farfield Foundation was a front for the American government,[30] is proof of this. Two years later, Spender wrote to Junkie Fleischmann, raising the same query about funding. CIA agent and Farfield director Frank Platt had sent Spender's letter on to Josselson with a cover note saying: 'Sorry this letter to Junkie took so long a time getting over to you, but it has made the rounds.' Only after Spender's letter had been seen by the CIA did Fleischmann add his own strenuous denials, writing to Spender that 'Certainly as far as Farfield is concerned, we have never accepted any funds from any government agency.'[31] This was, of course, a gross deception.

According to a story told by Mary McCarthy, Spender had once been the object of an extraordinary confession by Nicolas Nabokov. McCarthy claimed to have been told by Spender that on an occasion when he was riding in a taxi with Nabokov suddenly Nabokov had turned to him and spilled the beans, then jumped out of the taxi just at that moment. 'This was a second-hand story, passed on by Mary to me,' conceded Carol Brightman, McCarthy's biographer. 'But you can imagine it happening. You can imagine that incidents like that happened dozens of times, over and over again. And it must have been a sort of a joke.'[32] 'I think Nabokov diddled Stephen from the very beginning,'[33] Natasha Spender later said. Certainly, Spender had been aware of the rumours from 1964, and before, as Wollheim's account shows.

Nonetheless, Spender had added his signature to that of Kristol and Lasky in a letter to the *New York Times*, dated 10 May 1966, which stated: 'We know of no "indirect" benefactions . . . we are our own masters and part of nobody's propaganda,' and defended the 'independent record of the Congress for Cultural Freedom in defending writers and artists in both East and West against misdemeanours of all governments including that of the US.'[34] Unofficially, Spender was not at all sure that this was the whole truth. 'I should be annoyed by all the echoes I hear from all sides of your conversations all around the world,' Josselson was later obliged to write. 'The *NY Times* seems to be your favorite subject these days and you seem to be bringing it up with every one you talk to, and what's more you seem to volunteer your agreement with the *NY Times* allegation [concerning the CIA's support of *Encounter*] without any shred of evidence.'[35]

A week before the Kristol–Lasky–Spender letter was published, John Hunt had flown to New York from Paris. He went straight to Princeton, where he met Robert Oppenheimer to discuss the *New York Times* allegations and to ask if there would be any way that he and certain others would agree to sign a letter testifying to the independence of the Congress. Oppenheimer was happy to oblige. Stuart Hampshire, who was in Princeton at the time, later recalled that 'Oppenheimer was amazed that I was amazed, and amazed that I was upset at the *New York Times* revelations. But I was upset, yes. There were people who were put in a terrible position. Oppenheimer wasn't amazed because he was half in it himself. He knew full well. He was part of the apparat. I don't think it bothered him morally. If you're imperially-minded, which the Americans were at the time, you don't think much about whether it's wrong or not. It's like the imperial British in the Nineteenth Century. You just do it.'[36]

The letter went off to the *New York Times* on 4 May, and was published on 9 May, just a day before the Spender–Lasky–Kristol letter. Signed by Kenneth Galbraith, George Kennan, Robert Oppenheimer and Arthur Schlesinger, it stated that 'the Congress . . . has been an entirely free body, responsive only to the wishes of its members and collaborators and the decisions of its Executive Committee'.[37] But it didn't explicitly deny the CIA link, leading Dwight Macdonald to comment that it 'was an evasion, not a lie, but not meeting the issue either'.[38] Schlesinger later claimed that the letter was his idea, and that he had contacted Oppenheimer and the others to ask for their cooperation. However, given the time scale, the text of the letter must have been agreed with Hunt *before* he left Oppenheimer.

A few people saw through the stratagem. Angus Cameron, Howard Fast's editor at Little, Brown (who had resigned in protest when the firm rejected *Spartacus* in 1949), commented: 'I think of liberals, generally speaking, as people who support the establishment by being niggling little side critics who can always be depended on to support the establishment when the chips are down. Arthur Schlesinger, Jr., is the classic example of that.'[39] Papers in Schlesinger's own archives testify to this. He was a source, a consultant (if not a paid one), a friend, a trusted colleague to Frank Wisner, Allen Dulles and Cord Meyer. He corresponded with all of them, over more than two decades, on subjects ranging from the American Committee for Cultural Freedom, *Encounter*, and the reception of Pasternak's *Doctor Zhivago*. He was even helping the CIA get coverage for themes it wanted aired, agreeing on one occasion to Cord Meyer's suggestion that he, Schlesinger, 'suggest to the editor' of an Italian journal 'that he run a series of articles on the problem of civil liberties inside the Soviet system as companion pieces to the articles on the status of civil liberties inside the US'.[40] And who was to doubt the probity of Schlesinger, a member of Kennedy's Kitchen Cabinet?

In the midst of all these manoeuvres, Frank Kermode had been to see a top London silk to take advice on O'Brien's libel action against *Encounter*. The solicitor recommended defending the action on the basis of an arcane legal defence called 'qualified privilege'. A friend of both Kermode and O'Brien urged Kermode not to defend the action. Kermode wavered. Then, invited to lunch at the Garrick with Josselson, he received solemn word that there was no truth whatsoever in O'Brien's allegations. 'I am old enough to be your father,' Josselson said, 'and I would no more lie to you than I would to my own son.' Josselson was, of course, lying. 'Michael was determined to protect the Congress from damaging revelations, and so was I,' Diana Josselson later said. 'I had no problem in lying about it. We sort of worked as a double act.'[41] 'Truth was reserved for the inside,' Tom Braden later wrote. 'To the outsider, CIA men learned to lie, to lie consciously and deliberately without the slightest tinge of the guilt that most men feel when they tell a deliberate lie.'[42]

Other than taking Kermode to lunch at the Garrick Club, what else did Michael Josselson do? A trial involving *Encounter* would result in exposure of evidence regarding its less-than-conventional funding and publishing arrangements, evidence which would have been especially embarrassing in the light of repeated official denials. And yet, curiously, Josselson failed to ensure that the whole thing was settled out of court, and instead allowed Kermode to go ahead. O'Brien had even offered to drop the action if an apology was printed. It was certainly within Josselson's power to stop the whole thing. But he didn't.

Conor Cruise O'Brien, meanwhile, had chosen to have the writ for libel served in a Dublin court. To Kermode's horror, he learned that the defence of qualified privilege was not recognized in Ireland. *Encounter*'s legal advisers now recommended they simply ignore the writ, as the magazine had no assets in Ireland. But before Kermode had time to consider this advice, he was overtaken by events which instantly made the *Encounter* defence redundant.

24

View from the Ramparts

> There was a girl in Norfolk, Virginia, who was suing a man for alleged rape. The judge said to her: 'When did this rape occur?' 'When did it occur, Judge?' said she. 'Why, hell, it was rape, rape, rape all summer long.'
>
> Michael Josselson

In early 1966, the CIA learned that the California-based magazine *Ramparts* was pursuing leads to the Agency's network of front organizations. Richard Helms, Deputy Director for Plans, immediately appointed a special assistant to pull together 'information on *Ramparts*, including any evidence of subversion [and] devising proposals for [CIA] counteraction'.[1] By May 1966, Helms was feeding the White House with the inside 'dope' on *Ramparts* as part of a campaign to smear the magazine, its editors and contributors. Much of the information supplied by Helms had been produced as the result of a trawl through Agency records, with additional dirt supplied courtesy of the the FBI.[2]

Helms, who was convinced that *Ramparts* was being used as a vehicle by the Soviets, ordered a full investigation of its financing, but failed to turn up any evidence of foreign involvement. After reading through the *Ramparts* file, presidential assistant Peter Jessup penned a memo with the memorable subject line 'A Right Cross to the Left Temple': 'In view of *Ramparts*' dedication to smearing the Administration and the murky background of its sponsorship, one might think that some agency of the government would be pursuing the threads involved here.'[3] A week later, the magazine *Human Events* ran a smear under the title 'The Inside Story of "Ramparts" Magazine'. Its journalists were dismissed as 'snoops', 'eccentrics', 'ventriloquists', and 'bearded New Leftniks' who had a 'get-out-of-Vietnam fixation'. Signed by one M. M. Morton, 'the pen name of an expert on internal security affairs', the article bore all the hallmarks of a CIA plant. As did a *News-Weekly* piece of the same week, 'Who Really Mans the Ramparts?', and an article in the *Washington Star*, both of which announced 'serious doubts about the bona fides' of *Ramparts*, which was described as 'not only a muckraker, but a muckraker with a malevolent motive'.

For more than a year the CIA did everything it could to sink *Ramparts*. 'I had all sorts of dirty tricks to hurt their circulation and financing,' Deputy Inspector General Edgar Applewhite later confessed. 'The people running *Ramparts* were vulnerable to blackmail. We had awful things in mind, some of which we carried off . . . We were not the least inhibited by the fact that the CIA had no internal security role in the United States.'[4]

Amazingly, given the awfulness of the CIA's intentions, *Ramparts* survived to tell the tale. Just as the CIA feared, *Ramparts* went ahead and published its investigation into CIA covert operations. The magazine's findings, published in April 1967, were swiftly picked up in national newspapers, and an 'orgy of disclosures' followed, leading one commentator to conclude that 'Before very long, every political society, philanthropic trust, college fraternity and baseball team in America will be identified as a front for the Central Intelligence Agency.'[5] It wasn't just domestic American fronts that were exposed, of course. As details of the CIA's sponsorship of the Congress for Cultural Freedom and its magazines emerged, everything O'Brien had said about *Encounter* appeared to be true. Spender, who was still in the States at the time the story broke, went into an instant spin. Desperate to contain him, Josselson and Lasky both appealed to Isaiah Berlin, who was known to have 'a moderating effect on Stephen's temperament', and who was teaching at the City University of New York at the time. 'Dear Isaai Mendelevich,' wrote Josselson on

8 April, 'what I wanted to discuss with you cannot very well be done over the phone. I am very seriously concerned about Stephen and *Encounter* ending up by being real victims of the present mess, if Stephen (like Natasha in London) keeps on pouring oil on the flames. I am genuinely fond of both of them, hence my concern, and I also know that if any one can influence Stephen, it is you. The situation is serious indeed, but surely *Encounter*'s future cannot be solved by making drastic moves under pressure.'[6]

'There is indeed a problem about Stephen and *Encounter*, and Arthur [Schlesinger] who has just informed Lasky that the issue is dead here and there is no need to have a meeting about all this in London is, I think, being somewhat optimistic,' wrote Berlin by return. 'Whatever may be the reactions here . . . the issue is likely to go boiling on in London, since both Stephen and Kermode are said to be troubled. It seems to me that whatever the future of *Encounter* . . . there will be *some* sense in publishing some kind of statement telling the readers that the editors of *Encounter* were not aware of the sources of funds to the Congress of [sic] Cultural Freedom; which will be true of at any rate most of them – how much Lasky did or didn't know I have, of course, no means of telling . . . At any rate I think you should probably recommend that a meeting of the relevant parties be held in London for the purpose of settling this issue. Transatlantic telephone calls to Stephen in Chicago, the others in London, Arthur in New York, yourself in Geneva, etc. etc. won't be enough. You will never see the situation as a whole unless there is some kind of meeting to settle the moral, intellectual, and organisational future of *Encounter*.'[7]

In London, meanwhile, Kermode's defence of the libel action was irretrievably lost. Furthermore, he was convinced that, although the new sponsorship of *Encounter* under Cecil King 'was perfectly licit', the magazine 'was still in rather devious ways under the control (however delicately channelled) of the CIA'. Kermode wrote to Lasky to detail his complaints and to tell him 'that in the absence of very persuasive explanations I couldn't go on working with him. He didn't answer the letter but came out to Gloucestershire to talk it over. As we walked, hour after hour, round the garden and paddock, he gave me the fullest account that could have been expected of his relation to the Congress and of the history of *Encounter*.'[8] This was the moment of Lasky's *soi-disant* confession: he admitted to Kermode that he had known of CIA support for some years now, but that he could not possibly say this publicly.

Soon after – and at Isaiah Berlin's urging – an emergency meeting of the *Encounter* trustees was convened, attended by Lasky, Kermode, Spender (who flew back from the States), Edward Shils, Andrew Schonfield and William Hayter. They met in a private room at Scott's restaurant on the Haymarket, just a few yards away from the *Encounter* office. Shils and Schonfield defended the CIA's actions, but Kermode and Spender announced their intention to resign. Lasky refused to resign, and inveighed against Spender, calling him a hypocrite. Then he dropped a bombshell. Spender should get off his high horse about CIA funding and consider this: his salary had for years been covered by a subvention from the Foreign Office. 'Spender became very agitated and announced that he was going off to look at some picture in the National Gallery to calm himself,'[9] Kermode remembered.

By the time Spender got home to St John's Wood, he was, said Natasha, 'in a shocked and angry state. Melvin had apparently said something to Stephen about his salary which Stephen said was completely incomprehensible.'[10] Spender decided to clear the matter up once and for all by speaking to Muggeridge. 'Malcolm had effectively been Stephen's employer throughout all this. As it happened, he spoke to Kitty, who said Malcolm couldn't speak to him as he was in Scotland. At that very moment, Malcolm was lying flat on his face in a chancel of a Scottish Cistercian monastery being filmed at prayer for a BBC television programme called *A Hard Bed to Lie On*. Anyway, an hour after, Malcolm called back. By this time, Stephen was absolutely fuming. I was on the other phone, so I could hear what was said. Stephen said, "Malcolm, you always told me my salary was coming from the *Daily Telegraph* and Alexander Korda." And Malcolm said, "So I did, dear boy, but you can't bet your bottom dollar where it really came from." You know that scene in *The Thirty-Nine Steps*, where he's looking for the man with the missing finger? There's a terrible moment when he realizes who the man is. That's the feeling we had when Muggeridge finally admitted it.'[11] Eric Bentley later told Spender that Lasky, too, had been in on the secret: 'Mel told me there was nothing in the rumors – which I have heard for years. When things started humming a year ago, I asked him to say "No" point blank to a clearly worded letter . . . Silence. At which point my attitude is: Mel can keep his Cold War.'[12] After his intemperate outburst against Spender, and his huge gaffe in revealing the source of his salary, Lasky was in a very precarious position.

Having secured the full backing of Cecil King (who rejected calls for his resignation, saying, 'It would surely be folly for us to lose the baby with the bath water'[13]), Lasky now turned to Isaiah Berlin, writing him an oily letter on 13 April. He hoped he was not burdening him, Lasky said, but 'you have been *so much* part of our history – our splendours and, alas, our miseries – that I feel you ought to be kept completely informed'.[14] Lasky said that it had been agreed 'that we should end the story by issuing a dignified statement, and also by settling the O'Brien affair . . . simply and quickly, if possible, on the basis of costs to O'Brien and the publication of the 10 lines of apology he wants. Why not? Emotions may rebel, but reason dictates.' Lasky ended by asking the great philosopher to 'drop me a word with your thoughts and advice. As you know, they mean much, and deeply, to me!'[15]

These were fulsome words for a man revered by many as 'The Prophet', but whom Lasky privately scorned as 'a mugwump' and 'a fence-sitter'.[16] The trouble with Berlin, said Lasky, was that 'He wasn't a crusader. There are some crusaders with temperament who say, devil take the hindmost, and there are those who are prudent. In the heat of the campaign you feel let down, you want to say, like Henry the Fourth, "Where *were* you?"'[17] But Berlin had always been there, the wise man to whom the Washington elite had turned all those years ago when it first came up with the idea of embracing the Non-Communist Left. Could he have managed *not* to know about the CIA's involvement in this? Anecdotal evidence suggests he was aware, though not actually willing to take an active part. Stuart Hampshire recalled that Berlin was repeatedly approached by members of the intelligence community: 'They were constantly making overtures to Berlin to be more involved. I remember they once approached him at Aspen, Colorado – that was CIA all over, they ran it – because they thought he was the ideal liberal to head up some organization or other. And he said he wasn't interested, but he suggested [somebody else].'[18] Another story has it that Berlin 'was once asked by one of the largest American foundations which wanted to "cut a swathe" in philosophy, "What can we do to help you? Pragmatism made a great contribution, but now is passé; how about existentialism?" Berlin had a momentary vision of subsidized CIA cafés in Paris, but replied that the only things he wanted were paper, a pen, and the occasional discussion.'[19]

In his letter to Berlin, Lasky enclosed the text of the editorial statement which had been drafted by the trustees, and which was due to be printed in the next issue of *Encounter*. 'In view of recent newspaper reports concerning the employment of CIA funds by some U.S. foundations to support cultural and educational organizations, we wish to make the following statement,' it read. 'We are distressed by the news that so much of world-wide American philanthropy from U.S. foundations should have been based on indirect and covert governmental subventions. This practise was unwise, unsound, and deplorable. We find it painful to learn that some of the grants which, in the past, came to us from the Congress for Cultural Freedom in Paris and which we accepted in good faith should have derived from such funds, whose real sources were so obscured. The leading writers and scholars who have been responsibly associated with the Congress in Paris have made it clear that there was never any interference in their policies or activities by any donor, known or unknown. ENCOUNTER in its turn has from the outset been independent and entirely free from any form of interference. The Editors alone have always been solely responsible for what they published, and the Congress never, in any way or on any occasion, had any say in editorial policy . . . ENCOUNTER continues to exercise its freedom to publish what it pleases.'[20] The statement was never published.[21]

Berlin, who at this point had no knowledge of Lasky's collusion in the secret behind *Encounter*, as confessed days before to Kermode, answered Lasky's letter on 18 April. He approved of the decision to settle with O'Brien out of court, and then, with great pragmatism, *schadenfreude* even, signposted the way out of the complicated web: 'You could perfectly well say that like other organizations in need of financial assistance you went to the Congress for Cultural Freedom; they went to other Foundations of a prima facie respectable kind; that recipient bodies are not in the habit of examining the sources of income of the prima facie respectable bodies which support them; but that since these revelations there is natural embarrassment and reluctance about accepting such sums. This is more or less what the Asia Foundation [another CIA front] said and it seems to me adequate . . . the proper role of *Encounter* is simply to say that they acted as they did in ignorance . . . and that now that you have been made an honest journal of the fact that you received grants indirectly from the CIA merely places you on an equality with a great many other organizations, who could not possibly have been expected to know what the ultimate sources of their funds were, or something of that kind. Men of sense and goodwill will understand this; those who lack it will continue to snipe anyway.'[22] If Berlin felt any moral repulsion at the complex deception he was here describing, he didn't show it. Rather, he borrowed from the rhetoric of the open society to defend what in reality was the attempted management of that society by a closed shop.

Publicly, however, Isaiah Berlin was soon to take a different tack. When the story of *Encounter*'s relationship with the CIA emerged, he spurned the magazine, and attacked Josselson and Lasky for having 'compromised decent people'. His biographer, Michael Ignatieff, asserts that Berlin was as shocked as anybody by this surreptitious relationship, and that 'he certainly had no official or unofficial relationship with either British intelligence or the CIA'.[23] Ridiculing this claim, Christopher Hitchens, reviewing Ignatieff's book, has written that 'The *Encounter* disavowal, taken literally, would mean that Berlin was abnormally incurious, or duller than we have been led to suppose, or had wasted his time in Washington.' Berlin's double stand on the whole issue emanated from his allegiance 'to the Anglo-American supranational "understanding"', which, says Hitchens, 'frequently bore the stamp of realpolitik and, well, calculation.'[24]

The trustees' meeting at Scott's restaurant having resolved nothing, a second emergency conference was called for the weekend of 21 April, for which Arthur Schlesinger now flew in from New York. According to Natasha Spender, it was decided at this meeting that Lasky should resign, and he agreed to do so. This would be announced in a statement of the trustees, to be published in *Encounter*. Lasky had opened by making a 'terrific personal attack on Stephen, saying that he must've known what was going on. All the other trustees told Lasky that this was totally out of order, and should be struck from the record,'[25] Natasha recalled. Edward Shils said he would find a position for Lasky in Chicago, and the next week Shils flew back with that aim in view. But the day after the meeting, Lasky had changed his mind, saying he had no intention of resigning, and he wasn't going to agree to the statement at all.

A few days before this meeting, Natasha took a telephone call from Michael Josselson in Geneva: 'And he told me not to rock the boat, and he went on and on about how he was trying to protect Stephen. And I think I said, "Whose boat? I don't think Stephen and Frank are in the same boat as Mel."'[26]

Having failed to calm either Natasha or Stephen by telephone, Josselson now tried a different tactic. In an attempt to remove them both from the fray, he hinted to Junkie Fleischmann that maybe the Spenders needed a holiday. But it didn't wash. 'I was absolutely furious with Junkie when, on top of everything that was going on, he sent us a telegram saying would we like to spend a week on his yacht,' fumed Natasha Spender. 'We sent him a stinker back, and that was that. We never saw him again.'[27]

The Junkie proposal came to nothing, so Josselson now wrote directly to Stephen. First, he said that Lasky's comments at the trustees' meeting about the Foreign Office subvention had been misinterpreted, the result of a confusion, and that he had only been referring to a rumour which had disturbed him deeply. 'I was afraid that if Mel was sufficiently nettled he would do just what he finally did at the Trustees' meeting. I had tried to prevent this as best I could and hence my plea to you and to Natasha not to rock the boat too much and my assurance that I was only trying to protect everybody. I got particularly alarmed after I heard from Brigitte Lasky that

Natasha had snubbed her at a recent party.' Josselson went on to say that Natasha Spender had been publicly and bitterly critical of Lasky. 'In view of what she's been through, I forgive Natasha everything,' wrote Josselson. 'But this conversation with her convinced me that it was not only a matter of her disliking Mel, but of her hating him – excuse the harsh word – pathologically.'[28] Josselson went on to apologize for Lasky's outburst against Spender – 'Mel has since told me how much he regrets having let himself get carried away' – and implored Spender not to resign. 'I still believe that *Encounter* is a truly magnificent achievement and I would hate to see it go under, and go under ignominiously, if the three of you – because obviously Mel would also resign – cannot view what has happened more dispassionately, more philosophically.'[29] Josselson offered a palliative: he hinted heavily that Lasky was due for a career change ('I think he should look for a situation in the academic world'), and that the tenth anniversary of his editorship of *Encounter*, due in 1968, would 'be psychologically a good time' for him to leave. Josselson also revealed that he had experienced 'recurring moments of despair' over the whole affair, but that this was given a perspective by 'a much greater problem . . . that of remaining an American citizen in the face of the war in Vietnam'. Finally, he said he had had no ulterior motives for keeping the funding secret: 'I was in a position to help hundreds of people all over the world do what they themselves wanted to to do, whether it was to write books, paint pictures, pursue certain studies, travel when and where they wanted to go, or edit magazines . . . All this I enjoyed doing, and if you think the CIA got anything out of it, believe me, the shoe was on the other foot!'[30]

On 8 May 1967, the *New York Times* ran a front page story under the headline 'Stephen Spender Quits Encounter'. Spender was quoted as saying he had heard rumours for several years that the magazine was being supported by CIA funds, 'but I was never able to confirm anything until a month ago. In view of the revelations that have been made and allegations which may still be made about past sources of *Encounter* funds, I feel that any editor who was knowingly or unknowingly involved in receiving these should resign. I have done so.'[31] So did Kermode, which left only Lasky at the helm. And there he clung, despite calls for his resignation, and to the consternation of Josselson, who knew the game was up. Later that afternoon, a statement was issued by Cecil King: 'We consider that *Encounter* without Mr Lasky would be as interesting as *Hamlet* without the prince.'

'When the whole thing blew, I was in Portofino with Isaiah and other friends,' Stuart Hampshire recalled. 'I remember that six of us cabled in defence of Stephen in London, but Mary McCarthy refused to sign, saying, "Oh, you're just turning on our little New York boy." Stephen was very upset, and Natasha even more so. And particularly with Lasky. But why were they surprised at his behaviour? Did they really expect him to resign? I mean, that's not what he would have done. Of course not.'[32] Writing to Spender some days later, Muggeridge said that he found it 'monstrous that in spite of everything Mel should remain in the chair'.[33]

Some days after Spender's resignation, Natasha, accompanied by a friend, went to collect his belongings from the *Encounter* office. To her horror, she found that Stephen's 'locked cupboard had been broken into, and [Lasky's secretary] said, "Oh well, we had a burglary here last week."'[34] Stuart Hampshire, who had begged Spender 'to keep a record of everything, to maintain a personal archive', was not surprised when he later learned of this. It was, he said, 'obvious'.[35]

25
That Sinking Feeling

You think you are
doing the pushing,
But it is you who are
being pushed.

Mephistopheles in Goethe's *Faust*

On 13 May, five days after Spender and Kermode resigned, Michael Josselson and John Hunt found themselves sitting in what had been Josselson's office on the second floor of the Boulevard Haussman. Josselson, accompanied by Diana and Jennifer, had arrived in Paris from Geneva, where from his sparsely elegant flat in the Plateau du Champel he had been battling tirelessly for the past weeks to contain the fall-out. In the streets below the Boulevard Haussman, cafés were opening to welcome the Saturday shoppers as they disgorged into the spring sunshine. Somewhere amongst them, Diana was taking Jennifer to buy a costume for her end-of-term ballet recital. But she was distracted, and moved through the crowd towards the Galeries Lafayette feeling strangely disengaged.

In a room adjoining the office where Josselson and Hunt sat, the General Assembly of the Congress for Cultural Freedom was locked in conference. Chaired by Minoo Masani (leader of the opposition party in India), the meeting consisted of Raymond Aron, Daniel Bell, Pierre Emmanuel, Louis Fischer, Anthony Hartley, K. A. B. Jones-Quartey, Ezekiel Mphahlele, Nicolas Nabokov, Hans Oprecht, Michael Polanyi, Denis de

Rougemont, Yoshihiko Seki, Edward Shils, Ignazio Silone and Manès Sperber. Flying in from all corners of the globe, their unenviable task was to pass judgement on Josselson and Hunt – whose letters of resignation lay on the table before them – and to decide the fate of the Congress. Sitting like philosopher-kings, they knew that their word would be final.

'Mike and I sat in his office most of the day right beside the meeting room,' remembered John Hunt. 'We sat there alone – what do you do at such a moment, with the jury across the hall?'[1] Michael sat in silence, his slender, well-manicured fingers drumming on the desk. He looked tired – tired of waiting here this morning, tired from the last two decades of relentless work. His hair was side-parted and combed across the dome of his head, revealing a high forehead and small eyes at the centre of which sat huge black pupils.

The 'jury', meanwhile, debated the evidence. For two decades, Michael Josselson had maintained an enormous lie, with John Hunt a secondary transgressor, having been involved in the deception for only half that time. The seriousness of this concealment had immediate implications for hundreds of people. Beyond that, it presented a moral dilemma that would never be easily resolved. Both men had made statements about their relationship with the CIA, and its relationship, in turn, to the Congress. Josselson had accepted full responsibility for what he still maintained had been a necessary lie. The General Assembly's opprobrium was by no means guaranteed. Sperber, Polanyi and Silone spoke up for Josselson and Hunt, and urged the Assembly to take 'a fighting position'. Sperber said something to the effect of 'To hell with all this, we don't care what the *New York Times* says! We helped set this up and run it for fifteen years, we've dealt with tougher things than this in our political life, so let's just go on as before, if there's support for it.'[2] But there wasn't. Aron and Emmanuel, especially, were bound to see things a little differently. As Frenchmen belonging to an organization based in Paris which was now tainted by associations with American intelligence, their reputations hung in the balance. 'They had a huge stake in this,' Hunt later said.[3] Aron, in fact, was so vexed by the matter before him that he withdrew stormily from the meeting, slamming the door as he left the room.

By lunchtime, no agreement had been reached, and at Masani's suggestion they took a break. Reconvening in the afternoon, the meeting dragged on until finally, at six o'clock, Nabokov and de Rougemont appeared before Josselson and Hunt, the draft statement of the Assembly in their hands. 'They read it out to Michael, me and Hunt,' said Diana, who had left Jennifer with a friend to admire her new tutu, and taken up position at her husband's side. 'It was shameful. There was no reference to Michael's and John's contribution. Michael and John went pale-faced, and walked out. Nicolas and Denis said to me, "What do you think?" I said, "I think it stinks." I think I was weeping.'[4] Why, asked Diana from behind bitter tears, was there no mention of Michael's devotion to the Congress, his unswerving dedication to the cause of cultural freedom? Why had they ignored the fact that without Michael, and indeed John, there would have been no Congress at all? Was this how intellectuals repaid the man to whom they were all indebted? Raising their skirts and fleeing at the first sign of trouble? Was no one prepared to stand and fight?

At this point, Nabokov, always a man of flamboyant gestures, clutched his chest and had – or faked – a heart episode. Somebody was despatched to get a glass of water and an aspirin. His confusion at this moment, if not the swooning fit, was genuine. What could Michael have expected? These were his friends, and he had misled them all these years. He had concealed the fact that he was a CIA employee, that the Congress for Cultural Freedom was the child of a covert CIA operation. What metal was he made of, that he now showed such indignant hurt? Did he really believe himself to be a man more sinned against than sinning? Suddenly, Nabokov, the man whose fortunes had been so deeply linked to Josselson's, began to see more clearly. This was Michael's life, his faith. It was all he had. There was nothing else.

Nabokov and de Rougemont, horrified at the idea they had behaved ungraciously, promised Diana that they would persuade the General Assembly to redraft the statement. Mollified, Diana went out to look for Michael and John. A while later, they listened as the revised communiqué was read out. The next day, it was released to the world's press.

'The General Assembly . . . expressed deep regret that the

information conveyed to it had confirmed reports that Central Intelligence Agency funds had been used . . . and that the Executive Director should have found it necessary to accept such aid without the knowledge of any of his colleagues. The Assembly affirmed its pride in the achievements of the Congress since its establishment in 1950. It wished to express its conviction that its activities had been entirely free of influence or pressure from any financial backers and its confidence in the independence and integrity of all those who had collaborated in its work. It condemned in the strongest terms the way in which the CIA had deceived those concerned and had caused their efforts to be called into question. The effect of such action, the Assembly stated, tends to poison the wells of intellectual discourse. The Assembly repudiated entirely the employment of such methods in the world of ideas . . . The Assembly took note of the resignations tendered by [Michael Josselson] and [John Hunt]. It expressed its renewed gratitude to them for the fact that despite the difficulties attendant on the mode of financing of Congress activities they maintained the complete independence and intellectual integrity of the organization and consequently requested them to continue to perform their duties.'[5]

The wording of the statement was, in many ways, disingenuous. Firstly, Josselson's resignation *was* accepted by the Assembly. This was later confirmed by both Diana Josselson and John Hunt, who said 'My distinct recollection was that Mike, whatever the minutes may say, was in effect told that he couldn't stay on. I was in a different category – in their minds – so this didn't apply to me.'[6] Secondly – and more importantly – it was simply inadequate to say that Josselson had accepted CIA aid 'without the knowledge of any of his colleagues'. 'I can tell you that several of the most important Congress people knew the truth because their governments had told them,' Hunt later revealed. 'Aron was told. Malraux *obviously* knew. And so did Muggeridge and Warburg, who were told by MI6 after the two agencies reached an agreement regarding *Encounter*.'[7]

'Who didn't know, I'd like to know? It was a pretty open secret,'[8] said Lawrence de Neufville. The list of those who knew – or thought they knew – is long enough: Stuart

Hampshire, Arthur Schlesinger, Edward Shils (who confessed to Natasha Spender that he had known since 1955), Denis de Rougemont, Daniel Bell, Louis Fischer, George Kennan, Arthur Koestler, Junkie Fleischmann, François Bondy, James Burnham, Willy Brandt, Sidney Hook, Melvin Lasky, Jason Epstein, Mary McCarthy, Pierre Emmanuel, Lionel Trilling, Diana Trilling, Sol Levitas, Robert Oppenheimer, Sol Stein, Dwight Macdonald. Not all of them were 'witting' in the sense that they were active participants in the deception. But they all *knew*, and had known for some time. And if they didn't, they were, said their critics, cultivatedly, and culpably, ignorant. 'Mike did try and tell some people, but they said they didn't want to know,' Hunt claimed. 'They knew, and they knew as much as they wanted to know, and if they knew any more, they knew they would have had to get out, so they refused to know.'[9] Attending the General Assembly meeting as an observer was the Australian poet James McAuley, founding editor of *Quadrant*. He noted that 'there was a contradiction between their wish to (1) support Mike in friendship – and in honesty because none of them had been *really* much deceived – and (2) take up a public position of outraged innocence.'[10] Hunt's wife, Chantal, who had worked for the French Ministry of Culture and, briefly, for the Congress, was dismissive of such moral fuzziness: 'Everyone in France, in my circle at least, knew the truth about who was behind the Congress,' she claimed. 'They all talked about it. They would say, "Why do you want to go and work there? It's CIA." Everyone knew except, apparently, those who worked for it. Isn't that odd? I always thought so.'[11] 'Mostly they all denied knowing anything about it,' said Diana Josselson, 'but they made crummy liars.'[12]

And what of Nicolas Nabokov, who had made every step of the journey from those early days in Berlin to this painful denouement in Paris alongside Josselson? Did he really believe his own angry rebuttal to charges of CIA involvement, in which he had said 'I deny everything. The Congress for Cultural Freedom . . . has never had any link, direct or indirect, with the CIA . . . the whole thing has been set up by the Soviets'?[13] Could anyone seriously believe that Nabokov, in all these years, had never been told – or figured out for himself –

that 'behind this stood the heavy guns of "the Virginian woods"' (his own words)? Mary McCarthy's story, in which Nabokov apparently revealed the truth to Spender in a London taxi, suggests otherwise. As does Chantal Hunt's recollection of Nabokov telling her 'in conspiratorial whispers over lunch one day' that he knew. Stuart Hampshire later noted with some irony that Nabokov 'wasn't particularly devastated at the revelations'.[14] As Nabokov stood before Josselson on that miserable day of 13 May, waving a resolution in his face which condemned him for deceiving his colleagues, the fact that he was eminently unsuited to pass judgement appeared not to drive a fume across his mind.

In his memoirs, Nabokov damned the 'abysmal and needless impropriety of the method of thinking (or absence of thinking) that preceded the decision to pass money through the CIA to cultural organizations'.[15] He added that this was 'especially glaring when one thinks that the Cold War was the toughest, most complex ideological war since the early Nineteenth Century, and that this impropriety occurred in a country that used to have a century-old tradition of what Camus called "moral forms of political thinking." It still hurts me to think of those "wanton bruises of immorality" and the fact that a marvellous structure built with love and care by brilliantly intelligent, dedicated, and profoundly incorruptible freethinking men and women was dragged into the mud and destroyed because of the oldest and most persistent hubris: unreasoned action.'[16] Privately, though, Nabokov showed nothing of this moral indignation: 'I do not feel that one should be apologetic about the funding of the Congress from the CIA,' he told one correspondent. 'Many of us suspected some sort of funding of this kind and it was the "talk of the town" in many capitals of Europe, Asia, Latin America and Africa. The point is not the funding, but what the Congress has done.'[17]

Feeling much like a contemporary Job – the 'perfect and upright' man harassed for his virtue – Josselson left Paris after first seeing his doctors, and then meeting McGeorge Bundy, presumably to discuss the implications for the CIA of the exposures (according to the *Washington Post*, McGeorge Bundy was the man who supervised the CIA's operations under Kennedy and Johnson). Back in Geneva, he had barely time to unpack before the volcano erupted. In the wake of the General Assembly's acknowledgement that the CIA had subsidized the Congress, newspapers across the world had a field day. Josselson collapsed, leaving Diana to answer a barrage of angry telephone calls. To the Spenders, she wrote that Josselson's 'day-and-night continuous battle under constant strain, trying to save what he can of the Congress' work in some form or another has me in a state of perpetual worry . . . The mess continues; it's like a Hydra.'[18] Utterly despondent, she declared, 'I want out, and a new life, and never to have anything to do with all these people ever again, except on a basis of friendship with those who are friends.'[19]

But the issue of friendship itself had now become hopelessly confused. 'My dear Mike,' wrote Natasha Spender, 'It's the HUMAN aspect which is so distressing. I can see, looking back in the light of present knowledge, that everybody has been a prisoner of this situation in different degrees and ways. It must have been awful for you to have to deceive your friends to whom you have always been so benevolent. But I'm sure it was wrong of the CIA to expect it, for the repercussions in personal torment and relationships are endless, and if one minds intensely, as one does, then one grieves over trusts broken which cannot be retrieved . . . So it really comes back to the fact that if a colleague withholds information, he is robbing his colleagues of their freedom and their honour, which in turn destroys the trust of *their* friends and ultimately too many people have suffered . . . I expect that you too, are relieved to be out of a false situation which robbed you of the right to be candid to your friends . . . What was really wrong about the silence imposed on you by the CIA is (from their point of view) that requiring you to treat your friends this way was forcing you to adopt the same ethics as the Communists and therefore making their methods of the West somehow on a par with those of the East in that respect.'[20]

The 'shit-storm', as Josselson would later refer to it, continued unabating. Incredibly, it was Tom Braden who now whipped it up to new furies when he penned an article for the *Saturday Evening Post*. Appearing under the headline 'I'm Glad the CIA is "Immoral"' in the 20 May edition, it was written, said Braden, to correct the 'concatenation of inane, misinformed twaddle' appearing in the newspapers. But Braden did more than correct inaccuracies: he volunteered hitherto secret information which would never have been uncovered by other means – solid proof to end all the ambiguities (and the possibility of any more denials). Explaining that those on the left in 1950s' Europe 'were the only people who gave a damn about fighting Communism',[21] he gave a detailed account of how the International Organizations Division had sought convergence with these people. He described the IOD's relationship with American Labor officials, and even accused Victor Reuther of spending CIA money 'with less than perfect wisdom'. He confirmed that money 'for the publication of *Encounter*' had been provided by the CIA, and then went on to claim that 'an agent became an editor of *Encounter*'. He added that CIA agents planted in this way 'could not only propose anti-Communist programs to the official leaders of the organizations, but they could also suggest ways and means to solve the inevitable budgetary problems. Why not see if the needed money could be obtained from "American foundations"? As the agents knew, the CIA-financed foundations were quite generous when it came to the national interest.'[22] Listing the battery of fronts deployed by the IOD, Braden said that 'By 1953 we were operating or influencing international organizations in every field.'[23] Operating? Influencing? Of course, had he wanted to, he could simply have written of 'support', 'friendly advice'. This was, after all, the official line which the Agency had always spun.

The effect of Braden's article was to sink the CIA's covert association with the Non-Communist Left once and for all. So what possessed him to write it? His own explanation was that his old friend Stewart Alsop rang him up in California and asked him to write a piece for the *Saturday Evening Post* to set the record straight. 'I think I regarded it as catching up with history,' Braden said. 'I was in on the beginning, and it was now twenty years later, and there were still things going on, and my thought was, it's become ridiculous, it's time to stop this pony show.'[24] Braden began drafting the article in early March. With a long lead of nearly three months, he had plenty of time to finesse it. He and Alsop conferred several times by telephone, and Braden sent several drafts in, each one becoming more and more revelatory.

Braden himself claimed he wanted 'to set the record straight', iron out the mistruths. But in his article, he deliberately disguised codenames, giving his own as Warren G. Haskins when it was Homer D. Hoskins. Why, in the midst of his incendiary revelations, did Braden bother to protect codenames? Was he thinking of the secrecy agreement which every CIA agent signed as part of the swearing-in process? When asked about this secrecy agreement, Braden gave an extraordinary answer: 'They could've reminded me of my secrecy agreement, but I had forgotten I'd even signed it. Cross my heart, I didn't know I had signed a secrecy agreement. I *had* signed it, but I didn't remember this. If I had remembered, I wouldn't have done it.'[25] 'If Tom was playing by the rules as a retiree, he would have had to get approval for what he wrote,' said Lawrence de Neufville. 'I don't think he was playing by the rules.'[26]

There is another scenario, one to which several CIA agents – and even Braden himself – later found themselves attracted. 'Tom was a company man, and he knew all about the secrecy agreement,' said John Hunt. 'This agreement had been invoked in the past, and Braden, if he was really acting independently, would have had much to fear. My belief is that he was an instrument down the line somewhere of those who wanted to get rid of the NCL [Non-Communist Left]. Don't look for a lone gunman – that's mad, just as it is with the Kennedy assassination. There were lots of interested parties. Braden is witting only up to a point. Maybe [Richard] Helms called him and said "I've got a job for you." I do believe there was an operational decision to blow the Congress and the other programs out of the water. I discussed Braden's piece with Mike, and we hypothesized that it was part of a coordinated, authorized operation to end the CIA's alliance with the NCL. But we never got to the bottom of it.'[27]

Jack Thompson also speculated along the same lines. 'An old device when you want to run down an operation is, you blow it. I have an imaginary scenario: President Johnson is sitting at his desk in the Oval office, and he's shuffling through some papers. He finds a copy of *Encounter* magazine. And he says, "Hey, what's this?" And someone says, "It's your magazine, Mr President." And he says, "My magazine? *My* magazine! These are guys who think *my* war is wrong, and they're writing in *my* magazine?" And that's it.'[28]

Thompson's fictional scenario is worth looking into. Lyndon Baines Johnson was a man of the 1930s, the poor Texas boy afloat in the world of eastern sophisticates, and he had no truck with all those intellectuals, no sense of the glamour which had surrounded Jack Kennedy's Athenian interlude. Johnson's idea of a cultural festival was limited to something that 'would please the ladies'. Two years before Braden's article appeared, on 14 June 1965, American intellectuals had turned a White House Festival of the Arts – originally conceived by the Johnson's advisers as 'a tool to quiet opposition to the war' – into an angry platform on Vietnam. Robert Lowell had refused his invitation (duly noted in his FBI file), as had Edmund Wilson, with a 'brusqueness' that stunned the festival's organizer, Eric Goldman. Dwight Macdonald did attend, but arrived bearing a petition supporting Lowell and denouncing American policy, which was signed by Hannah Arendt, Lillian Hellman, Alfred Kazin, Larry Rivers, Philip Roth, Mark Rothko, William Styron and Mary McCarthy (among the uninvited). Over dinner, Macdonald collected nine more signatures, almost coming to blows with Charlton Heston, who accused Macdonald of being short of 'elementary manners' and asked him, 'Are you really accustomed to signing petitions against your host in his home?'[29] Johnson was left with the feeling afterwards that the White House had been taken over by 'a gang of traitors'.[30]

The event was an unmitigated disaster, and 'President Johnson's reaction to it had added bricks to a wall between the President and these groups,' according to Eric Goldman. 'Mercifully, much of the story was unknown. But enough had become public to make the wall seem as impassable as the barbed concrete between East and West Berlin.'[31] Johnson was quoted as saying there was a conspiracy between 'these people' to insult him and his office, and 'to hurt their country at a time of crisis'.[32] They were 'sonsofbitches', 'fools', 'traitors' who had blown a minor event 'into a situation which could have anything but minor significance'. The President also told two of his aides, Richard Goodwin and Bill Moyers, that he was 'not going to have anything more to do with the liberals. They won't have anything to do with me. They all just follow the Communist line – liberals, intellectuals, Communists. They're all the same.'[33]

James Burnham, who had helped to harness the Congress for Cultural Freedom to the CIA in its earliest days, but who had done so in the interests of a very conservative kind of realpolitik, saw in the shambles proof of what he had long been warning was a 'fundamental flaw' in the CIA's thinking. 'The CIA mounted most of these activities in the perspective of "the non-Communist Left",' he wrote. 'The CIA estimated the NCL as a reliably anti-Communist force which in action would be, if not pro-Western and pro-American, at any rate not anti-Western and anti-American. This political estimate is mistaken. The NCL is not reliable. Under the pressure of critical events the NCL loosened. A large portion – in this country as in others – swung toward an anti-American position, and nearly all the NCL softened its attitude toward Communism and the Communist nations. Thus the organizational collapse is derivative from the political error. This political error is the doctrine that the global struggle against Communism must be based on the NCL – a doctrine fastened on CIA by Allen Dulles. Cuba, the Dominican Republic, and above all Vietnam have put the NCL doctrine and practice to a decisive test. A large part of the organizations and individuals nurtured by CIA under the NCL prescription end up undermining the nation's will and hampering or sabotaging the nation's security.'[34] The idea that Lyndon Johnson might have subsequently interested himself in the dissolution of the CIA's relationship with the Non-Communist Left is not hard to imagine.

The most interesting clue to what really happened lies in the question of Braden's secrecy agreement. At 2 p.m. on Wednesday, 19 April 1967, Walt Rostow, Johnson's Special Assistant, typed a 'secret memo' to the President which read simply: 'I assume you know of the forthcoming Braden article on the CIA in the *Saturday Evening Post*. Here is the story from Dick Helms.' Braden's piece appeared in the 20 May 1967 edition of the *Post*, fully a month after Rostow had notified the President of it. Richard Helms, who was now director of the CIA, was, according to Rostow's memo, aware of the article, and conceivably of its contents also. The CIA had ample time in which to invoke its secrecy agreement with Braden, and prevent him publishing the piece.

Rostow's memory on the matter was unsure. 'I knew Braden only socially as an amiable person to talk to. I don't remember the memorandum. I don't remember his piece,' he said. 'I assume Helms told me, and I assume I told the President. But it wasn't a big deal, it didn't impress me at the time.'[35] Why then, would Rostow have bothered to write a secret memo to the President about something which didn't impress him? 'Anything that would create a political item that would have an effect on the presidency, I would keep him informed,'[36] Rostow replied, somewhat contradictorily.

In fact, Rostow and Helms had plenty of occasion to keep the President informed. At Rostow's suggestion, Dick Helms had been invited to attend the Tuesday Lunch, the most important high-level national security meeting in the Johnson years, 'because I thought the President should have an intelligence man he could consult with'.[37] The subject of discussion at these weekly lunches by 1967 was almost exclusively Vietnam.

Another question: why was the CIA so concerned about the *Ramparts*' stories that they mounted a full-scale intelligence operation, and yet with Braden they made no attempt to stop him? 'I think it's quite probable that they were anxious to get rid of all these things,' Braden concluded. 'Stewart [Alsop] may have known this. I always assumed that by this time there would've been those in the Agency who wanted to get rid of things like this that were virtually blown already. Everyone knew – the cognoscenti, and people like Stew certainly knew that these things were all CIA fronts. I always had it in the back of my mind that they wanted it killed, but I can't prove it.'[38]

Stewart Alsop 'was a CIA agent', according to one high-level CIA official. Other sources said Alsop was particularly helpful to the Agency in discussions with officials of foreign governments – asking questions to which the CIA was seeking answers, planting misinformation advantageous to the US, and assessing opportunities for CIA recruitment of well-placed foreigners. Stewart's brother Joseph dismissed as 'absolute nonsense' the claim that Stewart was an 'agent', saying 'I was closer to the Agency than Stew was, though Stew was very close'.[39] But he went on: 'I dare say he did perform some tasks – he did the correct thing as an American . . . The Founding Fathers [of the CIA] were close personal friends of ours . . . It was a social thing. I have never received a dollar, I never signed a secrecy agreement. I didn't have to . . . I've done things for them when I thought they were the right thing to do. I call it doing my duty as a citizen . . . The CIA did not open itself at all to people it did not trust. Stew and I were trusted, and I'm proud of it.' Stewart Alsop referred to Dulles and his crowd as the 'brave easterners', and revelled in being part of that 'tight establishment, the *bruderbund*'.[40]

In one crucial respect, Braden's article did not have the expected outcome. His claim that the Agency had planted an agent at *Encounter* could only have been intended to expose that agent and precipitate his resignation. This man, Braden later elaborated, 'was one of our agents, a man of distinct intellectual achievement and writing ability, and we paid his salary'.[41] Irving Kristol, who was now co-editor with Daniel Bell of a journal called *The Public Interest* (which had been launched with the help of a generous grant of $10,000 from Josselson), was landed right in the soup. 'When Tom Braden published that article, saying that there had been a CIA agent at *Encounter*, I was furious, because I knew damn well that I had not been a CIA agent, and I certainly knew that Stephen Spender had not been a CIA agent,' he later said. 'What in God's name Mr Braden had in mind when he wrote that article I do not know.'[42] Spender, who was never in the frame, said: 'I just can't believe it was Kristol, I really can't. I know it wasn't me.'[43]

That left Lasky. Years later, he was, predictably, totally scornful of Braden's claim, calling him 'a doddery, foolish old man'. Dismissing the whole affair as so much James Bond melodrama, 'the syndrome of the spy-and-the-mole network', Lasky said, 'I've never edited a CIA magazine and I never have and never will.'[44] Who was the CIA agent? 'Was it you? Was it me? Was it who?' he replied. 'Listen, we did what we did. No, no, no, this was a fantasia, and not to be taken seriously, certainly not by historians.'[45] But Braden, thirty years later, was categorical. There was no fantasy.

The Josselsons were devastated by Braden's betrayal. 'I've always kept such nice memories of you at the six day bike races, etc. not to mention a high regard for your professional performance, so that I am all the more sad at the gratuitous betrayal of Mike and his friends in your article,' wrote Diana. 'Your totally false statement clearly implicating Irving K., whom you apparently forgot was completely unwitting . . . has created a situation of chaos and personal suffering which I believe you cannot imagine, though you may realize you have dealt a deathblow to a good magazine . . . As I know from lived experience through all these gruelling years, and as you must know in your heart, too, Tom: if ever there was a man who was a *free* agent, who answered only to the dictates of his own conscience, it was [Mike].'[46] Diana ended by imploring Braden to issue an apology, and retract his statement that Josselson was planted in Congress. Her letter was never answered.

Curiously, despite what would technically be known as a 'flap' in the Agency, there was apparently only 'a little bit of concern that this wasn't necessarily the happiest thing that ever happened'.[47] Tom Braden got off without any official censure. Furthermore, the careers of those agents who had been closely involved with the blown NCL programme were in no way prejudiced. Cord Meyer and his cohorts all moved swiftly on to bigger and better things (in Meyer's case, to become London station chief with responsibility for the entire CIA operation in Western Europe). Only those who had been recruited from the Non-Communist Left itself were now deemed dispensable. Robie Macauley got scuffed around a bit, and, according to Diana Josselson, 'eventually they squeezed him out'. He left the Agency – and *Kenyon Review* – for a job as fiction editor of *Playboy* magazine. John Thompson, who had begun flirting with the New Left in the mid-1960s, was also dropped from what he liked to call 'the Good Ship Lollipop'. Writing of America in 1968, he told the Josselsons that everything that wasn't Vietnam was going to be about the African–Americans (though the word he used to describe them was distinctly colonial).[48]

Josselson, despite the fact that he had resigned from the CIA some time before the General Assembly meeting of 13 May ('He left primarily to protect the Congress, so that if asked he could say he was no longer with the Agency,'[49] said Diana), was irretrievably compromised. His pension was derisory, and certainly no reflection of the enormous contribution he had made. In 1965, Josselson was 'employed' by the Farfield Foundation as its International Director for a period of two years at a salary of $21,000, which was paid in twelve instalments. Now, in principle at least, the CIA had no further financial obligations towards Josselson. But Frank Platt and John Thompson, conscious that he had been left high and dry, arranged a termination retirement plan for Josselson of $30,000 a year, payable from the capital reserve of the Farfield. According to Thompson, this reserve amounted to $1 million. Unable, for some reason, to return this fund to its donors, Thompson suggested that it be made immediately available.[50] Josselson's handshake, more brass than golden, accounted for a fraction of the 'termination fund' of the Farfield. How the rest was disbursed is not recorded.

Before even the *Ramparts*' exposures appeared, Senator Mike Mansfield demanded a wide-ranging congressional investigation of all clandestine financing by the CIA. President Johnson opted instead for a special three-man committee composed of Under Secretary of State Nicholas Katzenbach, Secretary of Health, Education and Welfare John Gardner, and CIA director Richard Helms. The Katzenbach Committee's final report, issued on 29 March 1967, concluded that 'It should be the policy of the U.S. government that no federal agency shall provide any covert financial assistance or support, direct or indirect, to any of the nation's educational or private voluntary organizations.'[51] The report set 31 December 1967 as the target date for the termination of all such covert agency funding. This was to allow the CIA opportunity to make a 'number of substantial terminal grants' – a technique known as 'surge funding' – to many of its operations (in the case of Radio Free Europe, this was enough to carry it over for a full two years of operations).

The Katzenbach report has been widely referred to as the instrument by which the government enjoined the CIA in future from this type of activity. But the CIA had a very different interpretation of what they could do in the post-Katzenbach era. According to the Select Committee Report on Government Intelligence Activities of 1976, Deputy Director of

Plans Desmond FitzGerald circulated the following guidance to all field offices after the report was published: 'a. Covert relations with commercial U.S. organizations are not, repeat, not barred. b. Covert funding overseas of foreign-based international organizations is permitted.'[52]

In other words, in the field of international covert operations, nothing at all had changed. Thus, when the CIA decided to continue funding Forum World Features (a Congress for Cultural Freedom spin-off) beyond 1967, it did so with no impediment. For although Johnson adopted the Katzenbach report as official government policy, it was not issued as an executive order or enacted as a statute. It had no firm legal status. Reading between the lines (and observing that there was no bottom line), an editorial in *The Nation* judged that the report was 'piously expedient', 'evasion by definition', and concluded, 'Mr Johnson's ringing slogan, The Great Society, begins to sound like one of the more cynical utterances of the Bourbon monarchs.'[53]

Ten years later, a government enquiry criticized the fact that 'Many of the restrictions developed by the CIA in response to the events of 1967 appear to be security measures aimed at preventing further public disclosures which could jeopardize sensitive CIA operations. They did not represent significant rethinking of where boundaries ought to be drawn in a free society.'[54]

26

A Bad Bargain

> In this vile world, everything is true or false according to the colour of the glass through which you view it.
>
> Calderon de la Barca

Throughout the rest of 1967, and well into 1968, Josselson found himself in a state of mental and physical exhaustion, daily reminded of the confusion and bitterness his actions had occasioned. 'It is inconceivable for me how any one who believed in freedom, in the open society, in the moral correspondence between means and ends, could have thought it proper to accept funds from an agency of international espionage,' wrote Jayaprakash Narayan, chairman of the Indian Congress for Cultural Freedom. 'It was not enough to assess that the Congress had always functioned with independence . . . The Agency was only doing what it must have considered useful for itself.'[1] Writing to announce he was quitting the Indian office, K. K. Sinha said, 'Had I any idea . . . that there was a time bomb concealed in the Paris headquarters, I would not have touched the Congress.'[2] For some, there were real explosives to be dealt with: in Japan, one Congress activist's house was fire-bombed, and he had to seek police protection. In Uganda, Rajat Neogy, the editor of *Transition*, had no sooner deduced that the damage to his magazine would be 'incalculable' than he was arrested and imprisoned.

'There were real victims,' said Diana Josselson, 'and Michael felt anguish, remorse and, at times, he questioned his judgement for going along with things at all. We wavered over the Jesuitical line of the ends justifying the means, but in the end we agreed it had been the right thing to do. But the real damage to people's reputations anguished him terribly.'[3] 'There were people in India, in the Lebanon, in Asia, in Africa – men and women who cast their lot in with the Congress on the strength of representations that I, Mike, and others made – who then found themselves caught in the hurricane,' said John Hunt. 'And I know many of them suffered deeply, and no amount of high strategy moralizing or discussion will make that fact go away. They put their honour and life on the line, and I haven't forgotten that. You can't override the moral dilemma by using phrases like "raison d'état" or "the cunning of history" or whatever. But I'd do it all over again if I had the chance. You can have regrets and still say it was all worthwhile.'[4]

In Europe and America, far from what K. K. Sinha called 'the din of the advancing threat', reactions were mixed. Michael Polanyi found the fuss around the CIA revelations 'contemptible', and said, 'I would have served the CIA (had I known of its existence) in the years following the war, with pleasure.'[5] Koestler described it merely as 'a storm in a teacup' which would blow over. Yehudi Menuhin thought 'much more of the CIA' for associating with 'people like us'.[6] George Kennan, predictably, issued a ringing defence, saying that 'The flap about CIA money was quite unwarranted, and caused far more anguish than it should have been permitted to cause. I never felt the slightest pangs of conscience about it. This country has no Ministry of Culture, and CIA was obliged to do what it could to try to fill the gap. It should be praised for having done so, and not criticized.'[7]

The idea that the CIA's involvement in the cultural life of the West could be rationalized as a necessary evil of democracy found increasingly few supporters. Writing of a 'deeper sense of moral disillusionment', Andrew Kopkind argued that 'The distance between the rhetoric of the open society and the reality of control was greater than anyone thought . . . Everyone who went abroad for an American organization was, in one way or another, a witness to the theory that the world was torn between communism and democracy, and anything in between was treason. The illusion of dissent was maintained: the CIA supported socialist cold warriors, fascist cold warriors, black and white cold warriors. The catholicity and flexibility of CIA operations were major advantages. But it was a sham pluralism, and it was utterly corrupting.'[8] This position, much repeated, was attractive for its moral simplicity. But it was too simple. The real point was not that the possibility of dissent had been irrevocably damaged (Kopkind's own arguments were witness to that), or that intellectuals had been coerced or corrupted (though that may have happened too), but that the natural procedures of intellectual enquiry had been interfered with. 'What most irritated us,' wrote Jason Epstein, 'was that the government seemed to be running an underground gravy train whose first-class compartments were not always occupied by first-class passengers: the CIA and the Ford Foundation, among other agencies, had set up and were financing an apparatus of intellectuals selected for their correct cold-war positions, as an alternative to what one might call a free intellectual market where ideology was presumed to count for less than individual talent and achievement, and where doubts about established orthodoxies were taken to be the beginning of all inquiry . . . It had at last become clear how bad a bargain the intellectuals had made, that it could never have been in the interest of art or literature, of serious speculation of any kind, or even of humanity itself, for them to serve the will of any nation.'[9]

'Do you think I would have gone on the *Encounter* payroll in 1956–7 had I known there was secret U.S. Government money behind it?' Dwight Macdonald angrily asked Josselson in March 1967. 'If you do, we are really out of contact. One would hesitate to work even for an openly Government-financed magazine . . . I think I've been played for a sucker.'[10] Suckers or hypocrites? Despite rubbing up against the 'front-office Metternichs' when they had axed his article in 1958, Macdonald had had no hesitation in asking Josselson in 1964 if he could employ his son, Nick, for the summer. This, at a time when anybody who was anybody had at least heard rumours connecting the Congress to the CIA. And what about Spender, who in the summer of 1967 broke down in tears at a party in Evanston, Chicago, when fellow guests responded ungenerously to his protestions of innocence? 'There they all were, like so many David Levine caricatures – Daniel Bell and his wife Pearl Kazin Bell, Richard Ellmann, Hannah Arendt, Stephen Spender, Tony Tanner, Saul Bellow, Harold Rosenberg, Mrs Polanyi,' recalled one of the less famous guests. 'They had all been involved with the Congress in some way or another. After the spaghetti, they all angrily engaged in calling each other "naïve" for not having known who their backers really were, and for not passing the information on to the rest. "I never trusted Irving," said Hannah Arendt. She said the same thing about Melvin Lasky. Daniel Bell busily defended both his friends. The argument became more and more fierce. Spender began to weep; he had been used, misled, knew nothing, never had. Some guests were heard to say Stephen was being "naïve". Others seemed to think he was just "faux naïf".'[11]

'Stephen was very upset,' said Stuart Hampshire. 'People have been very mean about Stephen, saying he must have known. I don't think he did. Maybe he didn't try too hard to find out, but he didn't really know anything about government or intelligence.'[12] Lawrence de Neufville, however, recalled things differently: 'I know people who knew he knew, but you can't blame him for denying it, because everything we did had to be plausibly denied, so he could very well plausibly deny it. Josselson knew that Spender had been told, and he told me so.'[13] 'My attitude on hearing of Spender and his wounded sensibilities after it all blew up – and maybe this is coloured by my sense of guilt – was that he *had* to have known,' said Tom Braden. 'And I think he did know.'[14] Natasha Spender, who always protested her husband's innocence, concluded mournfully that his was the role of Prince Mishkin in *The Idiot*.

Suckers or hypocrites? When Tom Braden was shown *Partisan Review*'s famous 'Statement on the CIA', drafted by William Phillips, and published in summer 1967, he laughed out loud. 'We would like to make public our opposition to the secret subsidization by the CIA of literary and intellectual publications and organizations, and our conviction that regular subsidization by the CIA can only discredit intellectually and morally such publications and organizations,' read the statement. 'We lack confidence in the magazines alleged to have been subsidized by the CIA, and we do not think they have responded appropriately to the questions that have been raised.'[15] Looking at the signatories – seventeen in all, including Hannah Arendt, Paul Goodman, Stuart Hampshire, Dwight Macdonald, William Phillips, Richard Poirier, Philip Rahv, William Styron, and Angus Wilson – Braden said simply, 'Of course they knew.'[16] Perhaps James Farrell had been right when he said that 'those *Partisan Review* people fear clarity as the devil does holy water.'[17]

From Geneva's Plateau du Champel, a residential square whose silence was broken once a week when the vegetable market arrived, Josselson could only watch bitterly as the Congress, now renamed the International Association for Cultural Freedom, moved on without him under its new director, Shepard Stone. For the first year, John Hunt was retained, at Shepard Stone's invitation, to 'help with the budget'. Initially, Josselson would call his former 'second lieutenant' every day. 'He would say, "Let's do this", or, "Let's do that",' Hunt remembered. 'And I would say, "Listen, Mike, Shep's in charge now." It was very sad. Mike was going on as if nothing had really changed.'[18] 'Josselson was a rather tragic character,' Stephen Spender said. 'I think that he was in the position of an ambassador who stays in a country too long, and instead of representing the people who've sent them there starts representing the people to whom he's sent, which is why ambassadors are never allowed to stay too long in countries because they tend to switch in this way. And I think that this kind of switch happened with Josselson. If you view the whole thing as a kind of operation, Josselson was the godfather and he really loved us all, and he was also an extremely cultivated man who cared greatly about literature and music and so on, but he also was a bullying and domineering person, who took his responsibilities frightfully seriously and was not at all frivolous about it. He was really broken, I think, when the whole thing was exposed.'[19]

Shepard Stone, the Ford Foundation executive who had brokered millions of dollars of philanthropic funds for the Congress, had been Josselson's candidate for his successor but, according to Diana, 'Michael soon realized it was a mistake. Michael was retained as a consultant, and the Congress being

Michael's life, he wrote many memos, but they were not answered. It was difficult for Shep, because he didn't want to be Michael's boy, his figurehead. But it wasn't done in a very elegant way. Michael disagreed with things that he did, such as peeling off the country and regional associations that weren't of interest to him – in other words, India, Australia, anything that wasn't European. Shep had no feeling for this at all – he hadn't been there, so those guys were just out. He revealed a profound lack of understanding of intellectuals. When presentations were made year after year to the Ford Foundation for funds, Shep would ask Michael to do it because he wasn't capable of doing it himself.'[20]

Now financed entirely by the Ford Foundation, the Congress had apparently achieved the independence which had eluded Josselson. Yet according to John Hunt, behind the scenes there was a bitter contest between the British, French and American secret services to secure leadership of the organization in that summer of 1967. 'The fear was always that one of these organizations in which there'd been an American involvement in the beginning would be taken over by a friendly service,' he explained. 'The thinking was that the callow, dumb, quiet Americans will go on putting up the money, and we [Europeans] will put up the brains, and we'll have a perfect, tidy operation, and we'll run it.'[21] In the end, everyone got a slice. The Americans got their candidate in as president and chief executive (Shepard Stone's entire career, from the High Commission in Germany to the Ford Foundation, and now the Congress, was littered with intelligence connections. In his memoirs, the East German spymaster Markus Wolf alleged that Stone was a CIA case officer); the French inserted their man Pierre Emmanuel – whose affiliations to the *Deuxième Bureau* had long been rumoured – as director; and the British, a while later, got their man in as co-director. He was Adam Watson, the SIS–CIA liaison in Washington in the early 1950s, the psychological warfare expert who had coordinated the Information Research Department's secret relationship with the Congress for Cultural Freedom. Everything had changed, but nothing had really changed.

Nothing, except for the rivalries and tensions which Josselson could rightly flatter himself he had contained for so many years. The bitchiness and friability of temperament inherent in all intellectual conclaves now came to dominate an organization which had lost the élan and sense of purpose which had made it so prominent at the height of the Cold War. From Geneva, Josselson could do nothing to stop the reconstituted Congress from sailing towards its own oblivion. Nabokov wrote occasionally with news, dismissing its new masters as 'Les compères'. Equally disparaging was Edward Shils, who broke with the organization in 1970. It was, he said, utterly discredited, a mere chatfest for complacent, overfed intellectuals.[22] In another letter to Josselson he wrote that he had no news of the Congress, though he had received an invitation to meet some 'leading goyim', to which his response was a flat refusal.[23] He shared with Sidney Hook an impression of Stone as a 'bumbling jackass' . . . 'a fool, enjoying a position and perquisites completely undeserved'.[24] The only thing Stone understood about world affairs, said Shils, was how to work an expense account. But the question that most troubled Shils, and which, he said, he would never be able to answer, was how the Communists, for all their evil deeds, had managed to command – and keep – the moral high ground.[25]

With the old *nomenklatura* no longer interested in its activities, and having lost the interest of its backers, the International Association for Cultural Freedom finally voted to dissolve itself in January 1979.

In 1959 George Kennan had written to Nabokov that he could think of 'no group of people who have done more to hold our world together in these last years than you and your colleagues. In this country in particular, few will ever understand the dimensions and the significance of your accomplishments.'[26] For decades, Kennan remained convinced that the articles of faith upon which he had helped design the *pax Americana* were the right ones. But in 1993, he renounced the monist credo upon which this had rested, saying 'I should make it clear that I'm wholly and emphatically rejecting any and all messianic concepts of America's role in the world, rejecting, that is, an image of ourselves as teachers and redeemers to the rest of humanity, rejecting the illusions of unique and superior virtue on our part, the prattle about Manifest Destiny or the "American Century".'[27]

It was upon this proposition – that it was America's destiny to assume responsibility for the century in place of a worn-out, discredited Europe – that the central myths of the Cold War had been built. And it was, in the end, a false construct. 'The cold war is a delusionary struggle between real interests,' Harold Rosenberg had written in 1962. 'The joke of the cold war is that each of the rivals is aware that the other's idea would be irresistible if it were actually put into practice . . . The West wants freedom to the extent that freedom is compatible with private ownership and with profits; the Soviets want socialism to the extent that socialism is compatible with the dictatorship of the Communist bureaucracy . . . [In fact] revolutions in the twentieth century are for freedom *and* socialism . . . a realistic politics is essential, a politics which would get rid once and for all of the fraud of freedom versus socialism.'[28] With these words, Rosenberg damned the Manichean dualism by which the two sides had locked themselves into a convulsive *pas de deux*, caught in the 'despotism of formulae'.

Milan Kundera once attacked 'the man of conviction', and asked: 'What is conviction? It is a thought that . . . has congealed . . . That is why a novelist must systematically desystemize his thought, kick at the barricade that he himself has erected around his ideas.' Only then, said Kundera, would 'the wisdom of uncertainty' emerge. The legacy of the 1967 revelations was a kind of uncertainty, but one which fell short of Kundera's 'wisdom'. It was an uncertainty cultivated to obscure what had happened, or to minimize its impact. Disgusted by what he saw as the lack of accountability amongst those intellectuals who had 'aided and abetted' the CIA's 'cultural manipulations', novelist Richard Elman detected a 'false blasé attitude [which] makes everything seem alike or, as one expects, a kind of *comme il faut* for venality and corruption, which perceives the world as essentially a paradigm for boredom . . . Nothing is quite worth discerning, and nobody can be truly honest.'[29] Renata Adler's *roman à clef*, *Speedboat*, captured the moral murkiness: 'Intelligent people, caught at anything, denied it. Faced with evidence of having denied it falsely, people said they had done it and had not lied about it, and didn't remember it, but if they had done it, or lied about it, they would have done it and misspoken themselves about it in an interest so much higher as to alter the nature of doing and lying altogether.'[30]

Primo Levi, in *The Drowned and the Saved*, offered a similar, though psychologically more sophisticated, insight: 'There are . . . those who lie consciously, coldly falsifying reality itself, but more numerous are those who weigh anchor, move off, momentarily or forever, from genuine memories, and fabricate for themselves a convenient reality . . . The silent transition from falsehood to sly deception is useful: anyone who lies in good faith is better off, he recites his part better, he is more easily believed.'[31]

If those who took part in the cultural Cold War really believed in what they were doing, then they can't be said to have been consciously deceiving anybody. If it was all a fiction, a fabricated reality, it was no less true for that. Someone once said that if a dog pisses on Notre-Dame, it doesn't mean there's anything wrong with the cathedral. But there's another proverb, one which Nicolas Nabokov was fond of quoting: 'You can't jump into the lake and come out dry.' The democratic process which western cultural Cold Warriors rushed to legitimize was undermined by its own lack of candour. The 'freedom' it purveyed was compromised, 'unfree', in the sense that it was anchored to the contradictory imperative of 'the necessary lie'. The context of the Cold War, as drawn up by the more militant intellectuals within the Congress for Cultural Freedom, was one where you operated under the sign of total fealty to an ideal. The ends justified the means, even if they included lying (directly, or by omission) to one's colleagues; ethics were subject to politics. They confused their role, pursuing their aims by acting on people's state of mind, choosing to slant things one way rather than another, in the hope of achieving a particular result. That should have been the job of politicians. The task of the intellectual should have been to expose the politician's economy with the truth, his parsimonious distribution of fact, his defence of the status quo.

Pursuing an absolutist idea of freedom, they ended up by offering another ideology, a 'freedomism', or a narcissism of freedom, which elevated doctrine over tolerance for heretical views. 'And of course "True Freedom" is actually a better name than freedom tout court,' says Anthony in *Eyeless in Gaza*. 'Truth – it's one of the magical words. Combine it with the magic of "freedom" and the effect's terrific . . . Curious people don't talk about true truth. I suppose it sounds too queer. True truth; true truth . . . No, it obviously won't do. It's like beri-beri, or Wagga-Wagga.'[32]

Epilogue

Some people's minds freeze.

David Bruce

After that disastrous summer of 1967, Nicolas Nabokov received a generous financial settlement of $34,500 from the Farfield Foundation, and moved to New York to lecture on 'The Arts in Their Social Environment' at City University, in a fellowship secured with Arthur Schlesinger's help. Nabokov and Stephen Spender exchanged bits of gossip about their former *confrères*, and joked about writing 'a funny Gogol like story about a man who, whatever he did, and whoever his employer, found he was always being paid for by the CIA'.[1] In 1972, they had a minor tiff. Isaiah Berlin advised Nabokov to let the matter drop. 'Let him be,' he said. Berlin also cautioned Nabokov not to go public with his memories of the Congress when, in 1976, the composer half joked, half threatened to write a book called 'Les Riches Heures du CIA'. 'If you [are] serious about this, let me earnestly advise you not to do this,' Berlin admonished. 'One's memory is not infallible; the subject is, to say the least, sensitive . . . I doubt if you can want to be for the rest of your life the centre of unending rows . . . So let me strongly advise you to leave that minefield alone.'[2]

Such reluctance to examine the past was shared by many. Spender, whose friendship with Nabokov had survived the tiff of 1972, recorded in his journals that in March 1976 he had attended a ceremony at the French Consulate in New York at which Nabokov was awarded the Légion d'Honneur: 'Atmosphere of comedy as the Consul made a speech, going through [Nabokov's] whole life, drawing throughout it a distinction between what he called "creation" and "career". Although the festivals he had organized were listed, the Congress for Cultural Freedom was skirted adroitly. The hollowness of French rhetoric on such occasions is so transparent that it acquires a kind of sincerity.'[3]

For his remaining years, Nabokov continued to teach and compose. His last major project was to score the music for Balanchine's *Don Quixote*, performed by the New York City Ballet. Reviewing it for *The New Yorker*, Andrew Porter wrote: 'There is nothing, alas, that can be done about Nicolas Nabokov's wretched score, which lays a deadening hand on the evening. It is short-breathed, repetitive, feeble in its little attempts to achieve vivacity by recourse to a trumpet solo or a gong stroke.'[4] Nabokov's motto, said one friend, could have been 'Go along, Get along.' Perhaps he had inherited this from his father. A young intelligence officer in post-war Berlin had once met Nabokov's ninety-year-old father at a party. 'The old man, like all the Nabokovs, had been a liberal in Imperial Russia. I observed him going over to some high-ranking Soviets and saying, "You know, I was always on the side of the people!" and then shuffling over to [his host] on the other side of the room with the same ingratiating smile, and saying, "I knew your grandfather, his Imperial Highness, Grand Duke Alexander Mikhailovich very well!" I wondered how anybody of ninety could feel the necessity for such hypocrisy!'[5]

Nabokov died in 1978. His funeral, according to John Hunt, 'was quite a scene. All the five wives were there. Patricia Blake was on crutches after a skiing accident, and she kept saying, "I feel like I'm still married to him." Marie-Claire took up the whole of the first pew, as if *she* was still married to him. Dominique, who was his wife when he died, said she was made to feel like she didn't exist; she was the only one who hung back. Another one draped herself over his coffin and tried to kiss him on the mouth.'[6] It was a fitting exit for a man who had lived by flamboyant gestures.

John Hunt left the International Association for Cultural Freedom, as planned, at the end of 1968. In a secret ceremony on a houseboat on the Seine, he was awarded a CIA medal for services rendered. He then turned up at the Salk Institute in California as its executive vice-president. He took a fuck-you-Ho-Chi-Minh stance on Vietnam, and watched bitterly as America, as he knew it, started to fall apart. He told Josselson that he felt like an alien in his own country.[7] After toying with the idea of working with Robie Macauley at *Playboy*, Hunt became executive vice-president of the University of Pennsylvania. In 1976, he wrote a play about Alger Hiss which was performed at the Kennedy Center. He later retired to the south of France.

Irving Kristol founded *The Public Interest* with Daniel Bell, and in 1969 became Henry R. Luce Professor of Urban Values at New York University. By then, he had already begun calling himself a 'neo-conservative', which he defined as 'a liberal who has been mugged by reality'. He attached himself to the American Enterprise Institute and the *Wall Street Journal*, gave lectures to corporate groups for huge fees, and was dubbed 'Patron Saint of the New Right'. His writing showed more and more how this young radical had aged into a morose reactionary at odds with the world around him, with its sexual licence, multiculturalism, welfare mothers and revolting students. He had become, like Lasky, like so many others, Arthur Koestler's 'Twentieth Century man', a 'political neurotic [who] carries his private Iron Curtain inside his skull'.[8] In 1981, he wrote an open 'Letter to the Pentagon' in which he deplored the fact that American soldiers failed to stand properly to attention during the national anthem. He called for the reinstitution of 'proper military parades' because 'There is nothing like a parade to elicit respect for the military from the populace.'[9] Looking back on the CIA's intervention in cultural politics, he remarked that 'Aside from the fact that the CIA, as a secret agency, seems to be staffed to an extraordinary extent by incorrigible blabbermouths, I have no more reason to despise it than, say, the Post Office.'[10] Of *Encounter*, he concluded: 'I think it's interesting that the only British magazine worth reading at the time was funded by the CIA, and the British should be damn grateful.'[11]

Melvin Lasky stayed on as editor of *Encounter* until it folded in 1990. By this time, few were ready to grant it a proper testimonial. In its last years, '*Encounter* often seemed something of a caricature of its former self, routinely given over as it became to cold war mongering, with many a dire warning against the perils of nuclear disarmament.'[12] The tory editor of the *Times Literary Supplement*, Ferdinand Mount, did write a valedictory on *Encounter*'s achievements, and acclaimed Melvin Lasky as a 'prophet uniquely without honour in his adopted homeland'.[13] But this isolated tribute cut little ice with those who believed that Lasky should perhaps have stayed at home.

After the withdrawal of CIA funds, *Encounter* swayed from one financial crisis to the next, and Lasky spent much of his time in these final years seeking backers. In 1976, Frank Platt (who stayed on in the CIA) wrote to Josselson of a 'Wonderful picture of . . . Mel talking with violent right wing (Makes old man Hunt look like Gus Hall) head of Coors beer empire in Denver while back. He wanted to take over mag, make it his own. Wore shoulder holster and Colt 45 throughout meeting! No thank you Master Coors.'[14] Whilst Lasky was 'out in the sticks looking for green', Platt did his bit to help by requesting money from the William Whitney Foundation. Later, when confronted with the issue of the CIA's support of *Encounter*, Lasky fired back, 'Well, who's gonna give the money? The little old lady wearing sneakers from Deduke, Iowa? Will she give you a million dollars? Well, I mean, pipe dreams! Where will the money come from?'[15]

Every English co-editor to work with Lasky had resigned (Spender, Kermode, Nigel Denis, D. J. Enright), except for the last, Anthony Hartley. Lasky did his best to keep what was left of the old gang together, organizing 'A Last Encounter' in Berlin in 1992, a celebration of the end of the Cold War over which Lasky presided, 'his beard sharp enough to stab any fellow-traveller'.[16] Gathered there were the veterans of the *Kulturkampf* – Irving Kristol and his wife the conservative historian Gertrude Himmelfarb, Edward Shils, François Bondy, Robert Conquest, Leo Labedz, Peter Coleman, men and women from Radio Liberty and Radio Free Europe, frail in form, some of them, but the fire still burning bright. This, said Bernard Levin, was 'the motley army which, without a shot fired, fought for the truth against lies, for reality against mirages, for steadfastness against capitulation, for civilization against barbarism, for the peaceful word against the brutal blow, for applauding courage against excusing cowardice, for put most simply, democracy against tyranny. And we were right: entirely, completely, provably, joyfully, patiently and truthfully right.'[17] The ranks of this 'army of the truth' had been thinned by death – Hook, Koestler, Aron, Malraux, Nabokov, Sperber. But they were also reduced by Lasky, who did not invite the longest-serving member of *Encounter*'s staff Margot Walmsley, or Diana Josselson, or the Spenders. Michael Josselson's name was not mentioned once.

Levin's 'motley army' did not shed tears when the Soviet system finally imploded. And yet, the radio propagandist George Urban spoke for them all when he said he felt 'a curious pang of loss. A sparring partner who had in some ways served me well had fallen by the wayside. A predictable foe beyond the hills, often heard but seldom seen, had paradoxically been a source of reassurance. Having a great enemy had been almost as good as having a great friend and – at times of disaffection within our own ranks – arguably better. A friend was a friend, but a good adversary was a vocation. Or was it, I sometimes wondered, that my long preoccupation with the "dialectic" had so thoroughly infected me that I could imagine no life beyond an adversarial one?'[18]

Shortly after the fall of the Berlin Wall, George Urban was approached by a former KGB officer who claimed to have run the Kremlin's propaganda school. 'And did you find our writings in *Encounter* useful as a clue to what the "enemy" was plotting?' asked Urban. 'Useful, useful – I found it so fascinating that gradually you and your colleagues weaned me away from my oath and my ideology and made me into a dissident,' came the answer. 'You see, the *Encounter* syllabus was too persuasive. It spawned doubt, then occasional insubordination, and finally open dissent in the mind of a master spy!'[19] Urban related the incident to Lasky, who was ecstatic to learn that the enemy had studied *Encounter*. 'It stunned me! What a compliment, the KGB were using this thing! We felt at the time that this ideological spearhead that we cold warriors thought up was hitting on target, and turns out we were right.'[20] 'People like Lasky thought in exactly the same way as the Russians did. It was all just a strategic game to them,' concluded Natasha Spender.[21]

Frank Platt stayed on at the Farfield Foundation, as its director, until 1969 (when its pre-1967 funds were still being disbursed). In September 1976, Platt acted as a 'clearing house' and 'liaison' for PEN's Writers in Prison Committee in London. Two months later, he told Josselson, 'I've been asked by Kurt [Vonnegut], Jack Mac [Michael Scammell], others if I'd consider overseeing/taking over PEN Writers in Prison work, keeping in touch with Scammell in London at *Index* [*on Censorship*] who is taking it on for International PEN. Coordinator more like it. Said yes, of course. Interesting work. Travel involved.'[22]

At the same time, Platt fed Josselson with regular nuggets of gossip about the CIA, which he liked to refer to as 'the chocolate factory'. After Cord Meyer was publicly exposed as the London station chief in 1975 (when thirty-four Labour MPs demanded his expulsion), Platt wrote teasingly: 'In the Land of The Blind the One Eyed Man saw the writing on the wall perhaps? Who knows. The [Agency] is in one hell of a mess is ALL I know. Tant pis.'[23] Meeting Meyer at a Georgetown party some time later, one journalist watched in horror as he harassed an elderly Canadian diplomat over the issue of Canadian secessionism. 'The diplomat, who had a serious heart ailment, was visibly distressed, but Meyer ploughed on, without wit, taste, or mercy,' wrote the journalist, unaware of the eerie resonance of the scene, following, more than a decade later, that in which Josselson had suffered a heart attack. As another observer put it, 'Meyer's generation and class never, in Cromwell's phrase, bethought themselves in the bowels of Christ that they might be mistaken.'[24]

On 23 February 1983, James Burnham received the Presidential Medal of Freedom from Ronald Reagan, whose career in politics had been launched under the banner of the Crusade for Freedom. The citation read: 'Since the 1930s, Mr Burnham has shaped the thinking of world leaders. His observations have changed society and his writings have become guiding lights in mankind's quest for truth. Freedom, reason and decency have had few greater champions in this century than James Burnham.'[25] A week later, Arthur Koestler committed suicide with an overdose of barbiturates and alcohol in his London flat. Dying with him was his third wife Cynthia Jeffries. He was seventy-seven, she was twenty years younger. In 1998, Koestler was literally taken off his pedestal when his bronze bust was removed from public display at Edinburgh University following revelations by biographer David Cesarani that he had been a violent rapist. 'Enmeshed in antique conflicts, unimpressive over-production and lifelong bad behaviour, [Koestler's] time is simply gone,' wrote one reviewer after reading Cesarani's book.[26] Burnham died in 1987, but his spirit lived on in William Buckley, whose *National Review* Burnham had edited. In 1990, Buckley declared that 'the United States' protracted opposition to Communism is one of our truly ennobling experiences'.[27]

Tom Braden went on to enjoy a successful career as a syndicated columnist and co-host of the CNN talkshow *Crossfire*. In 1975, whilst a government committee was preparing the fullest ever review of US intelligence activities, Braden penned a swingeing attack on a CIA subsumed by power, arrogance, and an obsession with lying. 'It's a shame what happened to the CIA,' he wrote. 'It could have consisted of a few hundred scholars to analyze intelligence, a few hundred spies in key positions, and a few hundred operators ready to carry out rare tasks of derring-do. Instead, it became a gargantuan monster, owning property all over the world, running airplanes and newspapers and radio stations and banks and armies and navies, offering temptation to successive Secretaries of State, and giving at least one President [Nixon] a brilliant idea: since the machinery for deceit existed, why not use it?'[28] Braden concluded by advocating the dissolution of the CIA, and the transfer of its remaining functions (those few which could still be justified) to other departments. 'I would turn the psychological warriors and propagandists over to the Voice of America. Psychological warriors and propagandists probably never did belong in a secret agency.'[29] He also wrote *Eight is Enough*, a happy series about an all-white American family, which was adapted for television, and was later the inspiration for *The Brady Bunch*.

He finally retired to Woodbridge, Virginia, to a house guarded by two enormous but soppy Alsatians.

Lawrence de Neufville left the CIA shortly after the Hungarian uprising of 1956. He took a variety of jobs, before becoming a stockbroker. He remained a loyal friend to Michael Josselson, whom he had recruited all those years ago in Berlin. Interviewed for this book from his home in West Hartford, Connecticut, he was amused at the thought that his cover would finally be blown. 'I guess the old boys here in my town will get a bit of a surprise,'[30] he joked. He died before he could witness their reaction.

William Colby went on to mastermind the Phoenix Program in Vietnam, which involved the torture and murder of over 20,000 Vietcong. As CIA director from 1973 to 1976, he was responsible for sacking James Jesus Angleton. Under him, the Agency stumbled from one public relations fiasco to the next. After his retirement, he continued to reap the benefits of his career in espionage by selling his services as consultant to the heads of East European intelligence services after the collapse of the Soviet Union. He died in April 1996, after falling headlong into the swirling waters of the Potomac River.

After resigning from *Encounter*, Stephen Spender attached himself to the New Left, and rediscovered his revolutionary fervour. Mary McCarthy came across him in June 1968 at a Sorbonne meeting convened by revolting students. 'Stephen Spender was very good throughout,' she told Hannah Arendt. 'I saw a great deal of him. I think he was expiating the CIA.[31] For him, amusingly, the moral problem turned on his house in Provence – a ruin they bought and have been slowly fixing up with the revenue, drearily earned, of his American lectures; he decided, in the first days, that he did not "own" that house and that if the revolution took it, OK. Whenever he would be talking to some especially *enragé* student, he would say to him, mentally, "Yes, yes, you can have my house!" He took money around to a group of American draft-resisters, whom he found in total isolation in a room in one of the Facultés and virtually, he thought, starving.'[32] In 1972, he founded *Index on Censorship* with a grant from the Ford Foundation. He was knighted in 1983, a grand old citizen of the republic of letters. In later years, Spender acknowledged that people had been telling him of *Encounter*'s links to the CIA for years, 'But it was as with the people who come and tell you that your wife is unfaithful to you. Then you ask her yourself, and if she denies it, you are satisfied with it.'[33] Spender never read or bought another issue of *Encounter*. When he died in 1995, one of the last links to the 1930s, that rubescent dawn which was to turn into the darkest of ages, was broken. His widow, Natasha Spender, recalled bitterly, 'All those wasted years, all the arguments, all the upsets,' of Stephen's association with the Congress for Cultural Freedom. 'It had a terrible effect on him,' she said. 'He was so tired, so weary from all the bickering, and he never seemed to have the time to write poetry, which is what he most wanted to do.'[34]

Michael Josselson died in January 1978. Despite strenuous efforts to find employment, he had been knocked back by virtually all his former collaborators. In 1972, he was refused a Fellowship by the American Council of Learned Societies. Shepard Stone wrote to Senator William Benton, owner and publisher of *Encyclopaedia Britannica*, to recommend Josselson, but no work was forthcoming. Even Gimbel-Saks, Josselson's old firm, could find nothing for him. Time Inc. told him they couldn't find him a place for him, despite his 'extraordinary credentials'. In March 1973 he was informed he had not been nominated for a Guggenheim Fellowship. He was also turned down by the Hoover Institution on War, Revolution and Peace.

Eight years before he died, and with Diana's collaboration, he sat down to write a biography of General Barclay de Tolly, who was replaced by Field Marshal Kutuzov in command of the Russian armies fighting Napoleon in 1812. The general's direct descendant, Major Nicholas de Tolly, had served with the US military government in Berlin. Perhaps Josselson had met him, and been impressed by the tale of a great Estonian commander unjustly humiliated, and of whom Pushkin had written:

In vain! Your rival reaped the triumph early planted
In your high mind; and you, forgotten, disenchanted,
The sponsor of the feast, drew your last breath,
Despising us, it may be, in the hour of death.

Josselson's funeral in January 1978 was a quiet affair. Writing of it to Hook, Lasky said: 'Had he died on that occasion when they repaired his heart some 14 years ago, the funeral would have been a European, a Western occasion – a thousand would have been there to bid him farewell.'[35] According to Diana, Lasky himself 'turned up at Michael's funeral and "stole the show"'.[36] Also present was a representative of the CIA, who chose the moment to present Diana with Michael's service medal. 'It was so ungermane – as if they were saying, you did this for the medal, and nothing could be further from the truth. I refused to accept it.'[37] Diana continued to live in the apartment at Plateau du Champel, surrounded by mementoes and photographs of those heady days when the Congress for Cultural Freedom had seemed to her like the French Revolution or the Oxford Movement or the first hundred days of the Kennedy administration. Michael, she said, had 'lived for the Congress, and in the end he died for it. But it was the best thing in my life. They were wonderful years.'[38]

And what of that *Bruderbund*, the 'inner club of men less mortal and more patriotic', that tiny minority who knew what everyone else should know but didn't, making their own secret judgements in the name of a new age of enlightenment? 'They wanted to have it both ways, to be walking with the devil in the shadows secretly, and to be walking in the sun,'[39] said one CIA veteran. For many, the contrast was too much. Proponents of the Cold War, they were also in some measure its victims, destroyed by the moral ambiguities of the Great Game.

In the later years of the Congress, Jack Thompson, the former protégé of John Crowe Ransom who had ended up holding the rudder of the 'SS *Farfield*' (a CIA nickname for the Farfield Foundation), became 'obsessed with saving Africans from the Russians, and he travelled there a lot,' according to Jason Epstein. 'He would offer fellowships to African scholars and intellectuals, and their governments would allow them to go on condition they never returned (they were glad to get rid of them). So what Jack was doing, without realizing it, was getting them exiled. You can expect to get into a mess if you take your country's claims literally.'[40] Frank Wisner took his own life in 1965, having never recovered from the nervous breakdown after the failed revolution in Hungary. Other suicides included Royall Tyler, one of Allen Dulles's most flamboyant early collaborators, who took his life in 1953; and James Forrestal, Secretary of Defense after the Second World War, one of the men who had helped design America's clandestine action arm, who killed himself in 1949. *Washington Post* publisher Philip Graham turned a shotgun on himself in 1963. 'He was all out for the most conventional sort of success. He achieved it on the largest scale. And then, somehow, it turned to dust and ashes in his mouth,'[41] Joseph Alsop told Isaiah Berlin, in what serves as an epitaph for them all.

Behind the 'unexamined nostalgia for the "Golden Days" of American intelligence' lay a much more devastating truth: the same people who read Dante and went to Yale and were educated in civic virtue recruited Nazis, manipulated the outcome of democratic elections, gave LSD to unwitting subjects, opened the mail of thousands of American citizens, overthrew governments, supported dictatorships, plotted assassinations, and engineered the Bay of Pigs disaster. 'In the name of what?' asked one critic. 'Not civic virtue, but empire.'[42]

Notes and Sources

The following archival collections were consulted:

AB/MoMA	Alfred H. Barr Papers, Museum of Modern Art, New York
ACCF/NYU	American Committee for Cultural Freedom Papers, Tamiment Library, New York University, NY
AWD/PU	Allen Welsh Dulles Papers, Seeley Mudd Manuscript Library, Princeton University
BC/FO924/PRO	British Council Records, Public Records Office, Kew, London
BCCB/FO924/PRO	British Control Commission, Berlin, Public Records Office, Kew, London
CCF/CHI	Congress for Cultural Freedom Papers, Joseph Regenstein Library, University of Chicago, Illinois
CDJ/DDE	C. D. Jackson Papers and Records, Dwight D. Eisenhower Library, Abilene, Kansas
CIA.HSC/RG263/NARA	CIA History Source Collection, National Archives & Records Administration, Washington, DC
DM/STER	Dwight Macdonald Papers, Sterling Memorial Library, Yale University

FA/COL	Frank Altschul Papers, Butler Library, Columbia University, New York
GG/DDE	Gordon Gray Papers, Dwight D. Eisenhower Library, Abilene, Kansas
GO/UCL	George Orwell Papers, University College, London
HL/COL	Herbert Lehman Papers, Butler Library, Columbia University, New York
IB/GMC	Irving Brown Papers, American Federation of Labor-Congress of Industrial Relations, George Meany Center, Washington, DC
IRD/FO1110/PRO	Information Research Department, Public Records Office, Kew, London
MJ/HRC	Michael Josselson Papers, Harry Ransom Humanities Research Center, Austin, Texas
MS/COL	Meyer Schapiro Papers, Butler Library, Columbia University, New York
NN/HRC	Nicolas Nabokov Papers, Harry Ransom Humanities Research Center, Austin, Texas
NSF/LBJ	National Security Files, Lyndon Baines Johnson Library, Austin, Texas
NSF/JFK	National Security Files, John F. Kennedy Library, Boston University
OCB/Cen/DDE	Operations Coordinating Board, Central File Series, Dwight D. Eisenhower Library, Abilene, Kansas
OMGUS/RG260/	Office of Military Government United States, National Archives & NARA Records Administration, Washington, DC
PEN/HRC	International PEN Papers, Harry Ransom Humanities Research Center, Austin, Texas
SD.PPW/RG59/NARA	State Department, Political and Psychological Warfare, National Archives & Records Administration, Washington, DC
PSB/DDE	Psychological Strategy Board Records, Dwight D. Eisenhower Library, Abilene, Kansas
PSB/HT	Psychological Strategy Board Records, Harry S. Truman Library, Independence, Missouri
RH/COL	Random House Papers, Butler Library, Columbia University, New York
SCHLES/JFK	Arthur M. Schlesinger, Jr., Papers, John F. Kennedy Library, Boston
SD.CA/RG59/	State Department, Cultural Affairs Office, National Archives & Records NARA Administration, Washington, DC
ENC/S&W/RU	Encounter Papers, Secker & Warburg, MS 1090, Reading University, Reading

WHO/DDE	White House Office, Office of the Staff Secretaries: Records 1952–1961/Cabinet Series, Dwight D. Eisenhower Library, Kansas
WHO/NSC/DDE	White House Office, National Security Council Staff Papers 1948–1961, Dwight D. Eisenhower Library, Kansas

All interviews, unless otherwise stated, were with the author

Introduction

1 Arthur Koestler, in Richard Crossman (ed.), *The God That Failed: Six Studies in Communism*, (London: Hamish Hamilton, 1950).
2 Saul Bellow, *Humboldt's Gift* (New York: Viking, 1975).
3 Arthur M. Schlesinger, Jr., *A Thousand Days: John F. Kennedy in the White House* (London: André Deutsch, 1965).
4 Ibid.
5 National Security Council Directive, 10 July 1950, quoted in *Final Report of the Select Committee to Study Governmental Operations with Respect to Intelligence Activities* (Washington: United States Government Printing Office, 1976).
6 Ibid. [My italics.]
7 Archibald MacLeish, *New York Times*, 21 January 1967.
8 Tzvetan Todorov, 'The Communist Archives', *Salmagundi*, Summer 1997.

1 Exquisite Corpse

1 Willy Brandt, quoted in 'The Big Chill', *Sunday Times*, 5 January 1997.
2 Clarissa Churchill, 'Berlin Letter', *Horizon*, vol.13/75, March 1946.
3 Susan Mary Alsop, *To Marietta from Paris 1945–1960* (New York: Doubleday, 1975). See also Antony Beevor and Artemis Cooper, *Paris After the Liberation, 1944–1949* (London: Hamish Hamilton, 1994).
4 Nicolas Nabokov, *Old Friends and New Music* (London: Hamish Hamilton, 1951).
5 James Burnham, quoted in Peter Coleman, *The Liberal Conspiracy: The Congress for Cultural Freedom and the Struggle for the Mind of Postwar Europe* (New York: The Free Press, 1989).
6 Michael Josselson, 'The Prelude to My Joining The "Outfit"' (MJ/HRC).
7 Ibid.
8 Stuart Hampshire, interview, Oxford, December 1997.
9 Michael Josselson, op.cit.
10 Nicolas Nabokov, *Bagázh: Memoirs of a Russian Cosmopolitan* (London: Secker & Warburg, 1975).
11 Benno D. Frank, Chief, Theater & Music Control, OMGUS Education & Cultural Relations Division, 30 June 1947, 'Cancellation of

Registration for German Artists' (OMGUS/RG260/NARA).
12 Nicolas Nabokov, *Old Friends and New Music.*
13 Ibid.
14 Melvin Lasky, interview, London, August 1997.
15 Michael Josselson, op.cit.
16 Nicolas Nabokov to Michael Josselson, 28 October 1977 (MJ/HRC).
17 At a meeting of the 'Referendary Commission at the Ministry for Education for Judging the Political Attitude of Artists, Singers, Musicians, Conductors, and Producers Performing Independently or Intended to be Employed in the Federal Theatres', Vienna, 25 March 1946, it was agreed that: 'The notorious shortage of first rate conductors makes it imperative that Karajan should work in Austrian musical life, especially at the 1946 Salzburg Festival, all the more so since invitations sent to four prominent conductors of world fame (Toscanini, Bruno Walter, Lord Beecham, Erich Kleiber) have, so far, been declined. There is no doubt, too, that Karajan must be classed as a first conductor of European competency.' (NN/HRC).
18 William Donovan, quoted in R. Harris Smith, *OSS: The Secret History of America's First Central Intelligence Agency* (Los Angeles: University of California Press, 1972).
19 Arthur Miller, *Timebends: A Life* (London: Methuen, 1987).
20 Gregory Bateson, Research & Analysis, OSS, to General Donovan, 18 August 1945 (CIA.HSC/RG263/NARA).
21 Richard Mayne, *Postwar: The Dawn of Today's Europe* (London: Thames & Hudson, 1983). Mayne's book is a vivid reconstruction of the physical and psychological conditions of post-Fascist Europe. I am indebted to his chapter on Berlin during the Allied occupation.
22 R. E. Colby, British Control Commission, Berlin, to Montague Pollock, 19 March 1947 (BCCB/FO924/PRO).
23 Alonzo Grace, Director, Education & Cultural Relations Division, 'Out of the Rubble: An Address on the Reorientation of the German People', Berchtesgaden, undated (OMGUS/ RG260/NARA).
24 W. G. Headrick, OMGUS Information Control Division, 'Facts About the US Information Centers in Germany', 19 August 1946 (OMGUS/RG260/NARA).
25 *Amerika-Haus Review*, July 1950 (OMGUS/RG260/NARA).
26 OMGUS Education & Cultural Relations Division, Theater & Music Section, 'Periodic Report', March 1947 (OMGUS/ RG260/NARA).
27 Lionel Royce, Theater & Music Section, OMGUS Education & Cultural Relations Division, to Hans Speier, Office of War Information, Washington, 12 May 1945 (OMGUS/RG260/ NARA).
28 Douglas Waples, Publications Section, OMGUS Information Control Division, 'Publications for Germany: Agenda for Pyschological Warfare Division and Office of War Information Conference', 14 April 1945 (OMGUS/RG260/NARA).
29 Ula Moeser, OMGUS Information Control Division, 'Political Education Program', undated (OMGUS/RG260/NARA).

30 Quoted in *Amerika-Haus Review*, July 1950 (OMGUS/RG260/NARA).
31 Ibid.
32 Ralph Burns, Chief, OMGUS Cultural Affairs Branch, 'Review of Activities', July 1949 (OMGUS/RG260/NARA).
33 Ibid.
34 George C. Marshall, Harvard Commencement Address, 5 June 1947, printed in *Foreign Relations of the United States*, vol.3, 1947 (Washington: United States Government Printing Office, 1947).
35 John Crowe Ransom, 'Address to the Scholars of New England' (Harvard Phi Beta Kappa Poem), 23 June 1939, *Selected Poems* (New York: Knopf, 1964).
36 Harry S. Truman, Address to Congress, 12 March 1947, printed in Harry S. Truman, *Memoirs: Year of Decisions* (New York: Doubleday, 1955).
37 Dean Acheson, quoted in Joseph Jones, *Fifteen Weeks* (New York: Viking, 1955).
38 Joseph Jones, ibid.
39 *Pravda*, 17 June 1947.
40 George Kennan, quoted in Walter L. Hixson, *George F. Kennan: Cold War Iconoclast* (New York: Columbia University Press, 1989).
41 Walter L. Hixson, ibid.
42 Dennis Fitzgerald, quoted in ibid.
43 Richard Bissell, *Reflections of a Cold Warrior: From Yalta to the Bay of Pigs* (New Haven: Yale University Press, 1996).
44 Quoted in Americans for Intellectual Freedom, 'Joint Statement on the Cultural and Scientific Conference for World Peace', March 1949 (ACCF/NYU).
45 Andrei Zhdanov, 'Report on the International Situation', *Politics and Ideology* (Moscow: 1949).
46 Ibid.
47 Melvin Lasky to Dwight Macdonald, 10 October 1947 (DM/STER).
48 Melvin Lasky, 'The Need for a New, Overt Publication', 7 December 1947 (OMGUS/RG260/NARA).
49 Ibid.
50 Ibid.
51 Melvin Lasky, 'Towards a Prospectus for the "American Review"', 9 December 1947 (OMGUS/RG260/NARA).
52 Jean Cocteau, quoted in Serge Guilbaut, 'Postwar Painting Games', *Reconstructing Modernism* (Cambridge: MIT Press, 1990).

2 Destiny's Elect

1 *Final Report of the Select Committee to Study Governmental Operations with Respect to Intelligence Activities* (Washington: United States Government Printing Office, 1976). Hereafter, this report is referred to as 'Final Report of the Church Committee, 1976', after its chairman, Senator Frank Church.

2 Norman Mailer, *Harlot's Ghost* (London: Michael Joseph, 1991).
3 Quoted in *New York Times*, 25 April 1966.
4 William Colby, *Honorable Men: My Life in the CIA* (New York: Simon & Schuster, 1978).
5 Drew Pearson, quoted in R. Harris Smith, *OSS*.
6 Tom Braden, interview, Virginia, July 1996.
7 Quoted in R. Harris Smith, op.cit.
8 Ibid.
9 Ibid.
10 Nicolas Nabokov, *Bagázh*.
11 George Kennan, quoted in Walter L. Hixson, *George F. Kennan*.
12 George Kennan (writing as 'X'), 'The Sources of Soviet Conduct', *Foreign Affairs*, vol.26, July 1947.
13 George Kennan, National War College Address, December 1947, quoted in *International Herald Tribune*, 28 May 1997.
14 Deborah Larson, *The Origins of Containment: A Psychological Explanation* (New Jersey: Princeton University Press, 1985).
15 National Security Council Directive 10/2, quoted in *Final Report of the Church Committee*, 1976.
16 Ibid.
17 Ibid.
18 Ibid.
19 Harry Rositzke, quoted in Evan Thomas, *The Very Best Men: The Early Years of the CIA* (New York: Touchstone, 1996).
20 Allen Dulles, quoted in Evan Thomas, ibid.
21 Tom Braden, interview, Virginia, August 1996.
22 Harrison E. Salisbury, *Without Fear or Favor: The New York Times and its Times* (New York: Ballantine, 1980).
23 Edgar Applewhite, quoted in Evan Thomas, op.cit.
24 *Final Report of the Church Committee*, 1976. 'The winners in Wisner's office were the managers who could produce the most projects. His model was a law firm: the more clients, the more cases, the more reward.' Evan Thomas, op.cit.
25 William Colby, op.cit.
26 Michael Josselson, 'The Prelude to My Joining The "Outfit"' (MJ/HRC).
27 Lawrence de Neufville, telephone interview, February 1997.
28 George Kennan to Nicolas Nabokov, 14 July 1948 (NN/HRC).

3 Marxists at the Waldorf

1 Arthur Miller, *Timebends*. For the Waldorf Astoria conference, see also Carol Brightman, *Writing Dangerously: Mary McCarthy and Her World* (New York: Lime Tree, 1993), and Nicolas Nabokov's colourful, though not entirely reliable, account in *Bagázh: Memoirs of a Russian Cosmopolitan*.
2 Lionel Abel, quoted in Leonard Wallock (ed.), *New York 1940–1965* (New York: Rizzoli, 1988).

3 Jason Epstein, interview, New York, June 1994.
4 Arthur Miller, op.cit.
5 Nicolas Nabokov, op.cit.
6 Arthur Miller, op.cit.
7 Dmitri Shostakovich, *Testimony: The Memoirs of Dmitri Shostakovich*, Solomon Volkov (ed.) (New York: Harper & Row, 1979). There remains some doubt as to the 'authenticity' of Shostakovich's memoirs. Published well before the era of *glasnost*, they are widely suspected of being used as propaganda by the Soviets. But propaganda or not, Shostakovich can be seen to represent a body of Eastern bloc artists who resented the simple-mindedness of some American anti-Communists.
8 Norman Mailer, quoted in Carol Brightman, op.cit.
9 Arthur Miller, op.cit.
10 It is unlikely, though not impossible, that Hoover had read the manuscript of *Spartacus*. In the FBI's campaign against American writers, questions of content were nearly always secondary to the status of the author. In Howard Fast's case, his record as a Communist Party member, and his appearance at the Waldorf conference were enough to secure Hoover's wrath. See Natalie Robins, *Alien Ink: The FBI's War on Freedom of Expression* (New York: William Morrow, 1992).
11 Peter Coleman, *The Liberal Conspiracy*.
12 Nicolas Nabokov, op.cit.
13 Melvin Lasky, interview, London, August 1997.
14 Nicola Chiaromonte, quoted in Carol Brightman, op.cit.
15 Arthur Miller, op.cit.
16 Donald Jameson, interview, Washington, June 1994.

4 Democracy's Deminform

1 Carol Brightman, *Writing Dangerously: Mary McCarthy and Her World* (New York: Lime Tree, 1993).
2 Ernest Bevin, 'Top Secret Cabinet Paper on Future Foreign Publicity Policy', 4 January 1948 (IRD/FO1110/PRO).
3 Robert Bruce Lockhart, *The Diaries of Robert Bruce Lockhart, 1939–1965*, Kenneth Young (ed.) (London: Macmillan, 1980).
4 Adam Watson, telephone interview, August 1998.
5 Sir Ralph Murray to Chief of Defence Staff, June 1948 (IRD/FO1110/PRO).
6 Adam Watson, telephone interview, August 1998.
7 Ernest Bevin, 'Top Secret Cabinet paper on Future Foreign Publicity', 4 January 1948 (IRD/FO1110/PRO).
8 Mamaine Koestler, *Living with Koestler: Mamaine Koestler's Letters 1945–1951*, Celia Goodman (ed.) (London: Weidenfeld & Nicolson, 1985).
9 As in George Babbitt, 'the eponymous anti-hero of Sinclair Lewis's brilliant 1922 novel who, in the midst of a mid-life crisis, is temporarily seduced from solid American values by the lure of Bohemian ways and

superficial radicalism', David Cesarani, *Arthur Koestler: The Homeless Mind* (London: William Heinemann, 1998). Cesarani's excellent biography gives a detailed account of Koestler's 1948 trip to the United States.

10 Arthur Koestler, quoted in Iain Hamilton, *Koestler: A Biography* (London: Secker & Warburg, 1982).

11 Jean-Paul Sartre, *Les Temps modernes*, October 1954.

12 Michael Warner, 'Origins of the Congress for Cultural Freedom', *Studies in Intelligence* vol.38/5, Summer 1995. An historian working for the CIA's History Staff, Warner has access to classified material unavailable to other scholars. As such, this article is invaluable. But it contains several errors and deliberate omissions, and should be read with that in mind.

13 Arthur M. Schlesinger, Jr., *The Vital Center: A Fighting Faith* (Cambridge: Riverside Press, 1949).

14 Arthur Schlesinger, interview, New York, August 1996.

15 Carol Brightman, interview, New York, June 1994.

16 Robert Bruce Lockhart, op.cit.

17 Ibid.

18 Richard Crossman to C. D. Jackson, 27 August 1948 (CDJ/DDE).

19 HICOG Frankfurt, 'Evaluation Report', 1950 (SD.CA/RG59/ NARA).

20 Richard Crossman (ed.), *The God That Failed.*

21 Ignazio Silone, *Emergency Exit* (London: Gollancz, 1969).

22 Lee Williams, interview, Washington, June 1994.

23 IRD, Top Secret Cypher, 24 March 1949 (IRD/FO1110/PRO).

24 Ibid.

25 Anthony Carew, 'The American Labor Movement in Fizzland: The Free Trade Union Committee and the CIA', *Labor History*, vol.39/1, February 1998.

26 Quoted in Michael Warner, op.cit.

27 Robert Bruce Lockhart, op.cit.

28 Sidney Hook, quoted in Peter Coleman, *The Liberal Conspiracy.*

29 Sidney Hook, 'Report on the International Day of Resistance to Dictatorship and War', *Partisan Review*, vol.16/7, Fall 1949.

30 Ibid.

31 Michael Warner, op.cit.

32 Sidney Hook, 'Report on the International Day . . .' op. cit. [Hook's italics.]

33 Arthur Miller, *Timebends.*

34 Frank Wisner, quoted in Michael Warner, op.cit.

35 Ruth Fischer, quoted in Michael Warner, op.cit.

36 Lawrence de Neufville, telephone interview, February 1997.

37 Michael Warner, op.cit.

38 Ibid.

39 Ibid.

5 Crusading's the Idea

1 Arthur Schlesinger, interview, New York, August 1996.
2 Sidney Hook, *Politics*, Winter 1949.
3 Sidney Hook, 'The Berlin Congress for Cultural Freedom', *Partisan Review*, vol.17/7, 1950.
4 Nicolas Nabokov, *Bagázh*.
5 Ignazio Silone, quoted in Celia Goodman (ed.), *Living with Koestler*.
6 Ignazio Silone, 3 April 1930, printed in *La Stampa*, 30 April 1996.
7 Ignazio Silone, quoted in Peter Coleman, *The Liberal Conspiracy*.
8 Arthur Koestler, quoted in Peter Coleman, op.cit.
9 Ernst Reuter, quoted in Congress for Cultural Freedom brochure, undated (CCF/CHI).
10 Lawrence de Neufville, telephone interview, February 1997.
11 Mamaine Koestler, in Celia Goodman (ed.), op.cit.
12 James Burnham, 'Rhetoric and Peace', *Partisan Review*, vol.17/8, 1950.
13 Sidney Hook, op.cit.
14 James Burnham, op.cit.
15 Hugh Trevor-Roper, interview, London, July 1994.
16 André Philip, 'Summary of Proceedings', Berlin 1950 (CCF/CHI).
17 Melvin Lasky, interview, London, July 1994.
18 Hugh Trevor-Roper, interview, London, July 1994.
19 Sidney Hook, op.cit.
20 Arthur Koestler, quoted in Iain Hamilton, *Koestler*.
21 Edward Barrett, *Truth is our Weapon* (New York: Funk & Wagnalls, 1953). Barrett's sentiments were shared by many others. Arthur Koestler was once confronted by an American journalist who told him that 'people who had once been Communists should shut up and retire to a monastery or a desert island, instead of going around "teaching other people lessons"'. Barrett's reference to the usefulness of ex-Communists as 'informers' or 'tipsters', however, is interesting, an indication that the US government's secret strategy of embracing the Non-Communist Left was quick to establish itself.
22 Melvin Lasky, quoted in *Boston Globe*, 24 June 1950.
23 Lawrence de Neufville, telephone interview, February 1997.
24 Hugh Trevor-Roper, interview, London, July 1994.
25 Tom Braden, interview, Virginia, June 1994.
26 Mamaine Koestler, in Celia Goodman, op.cit.
27 Manifesto of the Congress for Cultural Freedom, July 1950 (CCF/CHI).
28 Ibid.
29 Quoted in Michael Warner, 'Origins of the Congress for Cultural Freedom', *Studies in Intelligence* vol.38/5, Summer 1995.

6 'Operation Congress'

1 Frank Wisner, 'Berlin Congress for Cultural Freedom: Activities of

Melvin Lasky', in Michael Warner, 'Origins of the Congress for Cultural Freedom', *Studies in Intelligence* vol.38/5, Summer 1995.
2 Michael Warner, op.cit. See also Evan Thomas, *The Very Best Men: The Early Years of the CIA* (New York: Touchstone, 1996), footnote on page 263.
3 Edward Shils, 'Remembering the Congress for Cultural Freedom', 1990 (unpublished proofs).
4 Natasha Spender, interview, Maussane, July 1997.
5 Melvin Lasky, interview, London, August 1997.
6 'All CIA operations had cryptonyms preceded by a two-letter "diagraph" for signals security.' Evan Thomas, op.cit.
7 George Kennan to Robert Lovett, 30 June 1948 (SD.PPW/RG59/NARA).
8 Tom Braden, interview, Virginia, July 1996.
9 E. Howard Hunt, *Undercover: Memoirs of an American Secret Agent* (California: Berkeley Publishing Corporation, 1974).
10 Miles Copeland, *National Review*, 11 September 1987.
11 C. D. Jackson to Abbott Washburn, 2 February 1953 (CDJ/DDE).
12 James T. Farrell to Meyer Schapiro, 11 September 1941 (MS/COL).
13 Carol Brightman, interview, New York, June 1994.
14 Arthur Koestler, 'Immediate Tasks for the Transition Period', 4 July 1950 (IB/GMC).
15 Donald Jameson, interview, Washington, June 1994.
16 Manifesto of the Congress for Cultural Freedom, July 1950 (CCF/CHI).
17 Arthur Schlesinger to Irving Brown, 18 July 1950 (IB/GMC).
18 Arthur Schlesinger, interview, New York, August 1996.
19 Ibid.
20 Peter Vansittart, *In the Fifties* (London: John Murray, 1995).
21 Robert Bruce Lockhart, *The Diaries of Robert Bruce Lockhart, 1939–1965*.
22 James Simmons, 'The Ballad of Bertrand Russell', *Judy Garland and the Cold War* (Belfast: Blackstaff Press, 1976).
23 Giles Scott-Smith, *The Politics of Apolitical Culture: The Congress for Cultural Freedom and the Cultural Identity of Post-War American Hegemony 1945–1960* (unpublished Ph.D thesis, Lancaster University, 1998).
24 Lawrence de Neufville, telephone interview, February 1997.
25 Nicolas Nabokov, Address to the Congress for Cultural Freedom, Berlin, July 1950 (CCF/CHI).
26 C. D. Jackson to Tyler Port, 8 March 1950 (CDJ/DDE).
27 Nicolas Nabokov to Irving Brown, 6 December 1950 (IB/GMC).
28 Nicolas Nabokov to Irving Brown, 17 January 1951 (IB/GMC) Quite what the source of this extra remuneration was remains unclear. Soon, however, Nabokov's salary supplement was listed as an expense of the American Committee for Cultural Freedom, which in turn was supported by grants from the Farfield Foundation, a CIA front.

29 Tom Braden, 'I'm Glad the CIA is "Immoral"', *Saturday Evening Post*, 20 May 1967.
30 William Colby, interview, Washington, June 1994.
31 Tom Braden, op.cit.
32 Tom Braden, interview, Virginia, July 1996.
33 Ibid.
34 Ibid.
35 National Security Council Directive, March 1950, quoted in Scott Lucas, 'The Psychological Strategy Board', *International History Review*, vol.18/2, May 1996. See also, Trevor Barnes, 'The Secret Cold War: The CIA and American Foreign Policy in Europe 1946–56, part II', *The Historical Journal*, vol. 25/3, September 1982. Barnes reveals that the idea of a Kremlin masterplan for global domination was viewed with some suspicion by a group of CIA analysts. Project Jigsaw, a top-secret review of world Communism, set up in late 1949, concluded there was no such masterplan, even if the Kremlin did manipulate the Communist parties of other nations. Jigsaw was probably influenced by Kennan, who was rethinking his views about the USSR. But its conclusions were so unorthodox that they were smothered, even within the Agency itself.
36 Edward Barrett, *Truth is our Weapon*.
37 Tom Braden, interview, Virginia, June 1994. Braden used another phrase: 'the battle for Picasso's mind'. Taken literally, this would of course have been a Sisyphean task. When Cleve Gray, a young American painter serving in the US army, followed the pilgrimage trail to Picasso's studio after the liberation, he arrived late morning to find Picasso in his underpants, having just got out of bed. Picasso stood by the side of the bed holding a copy of the Communist newspaper *L'Humanité* in one hand while he held out the other for Jaime Sabartès, his factotum, to thread it through a shirt sleeve, then he transferred the newspaper to the other hand while Sabartès pulled on the other sleeve. Picasso was just about to join the Communist Party, telling the world 'one goes to the Communist Party as to a spring of fresh water'. The scene is described in Antony Beevor and Artemis Cooper, *Paris After the Liberation, 1944–1949*.
38 Tom Braden, 'I'm Glad the CIA is "Immoral"', *Saturday Evening Post*, 20 May 1967.
39 Arthur Koestler to Bertrand Russell, 1950, quoted in Peter Coleman, *The Liberal Conspiracy*.
40 Other Branch Chiefs were given responsibility for the IOD's burgeoning group of fronts, which Braden created in a punch for punch response to Soviet deviousness. He answered the Communist-backed International Association of Democratic Lawyers with the International Commission of Jurists; for the World Peace Council, there was the National Committee for a Free Europe; the Cominform-backed Women's International Democratic Federation was challenged by the International Committee of Women; the International Union of

Students by the CIA-infiltrated National Students' Association; the World Federation of Democratic Youth by the World Assembly of Youth; the International Organization of Journalists by the International Federation of Free Journalists; the World Federation of Trade Unions by the International Federation of Free Trade Unions.

41 Lawrence de Neufville, telephone interview, February 1997.
42 Nicolas Nabokov, *Bagázh*.
43 Nicolas Nabokov to James Burnham, 6 June 1951 (CCF/CHI).
44 Carol Brightman, interview, New York, June 1994.
45 Diana Josselson, interview, Geneva, March 1997.
46 Nicolas Nabokov to James Burnham, 27 June 1951 (CCF/CHI).
47 Peter Coleman, op.cit.
48 François Bondy and Georges Altman to Michael Josselson, October 1950 (IB/GMC).
49 Nicolas Nabokov to Irving Brown, 3 September 1951 (IB/GMC).
50 There were strong reasons for trying to silence the anti-clericalist clamour of the Italian outfit. At this time, Lawrence de Neufville was involved in highly sensitive talks with the Vatican, as part of a CIA initiative to deploy Catholic trade unions throughout Europe as a counterforce to Communist-dominated labour groups. The potential embarrassment to the CIA of one of its 'assets' publicly criticizing the Church was great.
51 Nicolas Nabokov to James Burnham, 6 June 1951 (CCF/CHI).
52 Ibid.

7 Candy

1 Tom Braden, interview, Virginia, July 1996.
2 Lawrence de Neufville, telephone interview, February 1997.
3 Richard Bissell, *Reflections of a Cold Warrior.*
4 Lawrence de Neufville, telephone interview, February 1997.
5 Donald Jameson, interview, Washington, June 1994.
6 Ibid.
7 Lawrence de Neufville, telephone interview, February 1997.
8 Tom Braden, interview, Virginia, June 1994.
9 John Hunt, interview, Uzés, July 1997.
10 Walter Laqueur, 'Anti-Communism Abroad: A Memoir of the Congress for Cultural Freedom', *Partisan Review*, Spring 1996.
11 Ben Sonnenberg, interview, New York, February 1997. After he had been appointed Secretary of the British Society for Cultural Freedom in late 1952, Jasper Ridley was summoned to Paris to explain why he had concealed the fact that he had once belonged to the Communist Party. According to Diana Josselson, her husband 'had to clear Congress employees with the CIA', and this oversight had made him look 'very stupid' in Washington. Ridley's account of the arraignment which followed is chilling: 'Nabokov questioned me, but his questions and my answers were interrupted by Josselson, who walked around the room, barking out questions and interjections . . . he could have been an actor

playing the part of a domineering, bullying Soviet apparatchik.' Jasper Ridley, telephone interview, August 1997.

12 Michael Goodwin to Nicolas Nabokov, 15 January 1952 (CCF/CHI).

13 Diana Josselson, interview, Geneva, March 1997.

14 Nicolas Nabokov to Michael Goodwin, 19 December 1951 (CCF/CHI).

15 Michael Goodwin to Nicolas Nabokov, 31 December 1951 (CCF/CHI).

16 Jasper Ridley recalled a Spender who was capable of outright hostility. Visiting him at his house around this time to discuss some matter relating to the British Society for Cultural Freedom, he found Spender in steely mood, and his wife Natasha Litvin 'even more hostile; she went on playing the piano without greeting me or turning round to look at me'. Jasper Ridley, telephone interview, August 1997.

17 John Clews to Nicolas Nabokov, 27 June 1952 (CCF/CHI).

18 Jasper Ridley, telephone interview, August 1997.

8 Cette Fête Américaine

1 Nicolas Nabokov to Irving Brown, undated, 1951 (IB/GMC).

2 Melvin Lasky, interview, London, August 1997.

3 Nicolas Nabokov to Irving Brown, undated, 1951 (CCF/CHI).

4 Tom Braden, interview, Virginia, July 1996.

5 Thomas Jennings, Public Affairs Officer, American Consulate, Marseilles, to State Department, 'Report on concerts of Smith College Chamber Singers in southern France', 11 August 1952 (SD.CA/RG59/NARA).

6 Tom Braden, interview, Virginia, July 1996.

7 Susan Sontag, 'Pilgrimage', *The New Yorker*, 21 December 1987.

8 Nicolas Nabokov to Irving Brown, undated, 1951 (IB/GMC).

9 Albert Donnelly, Jr., to Julius Fleischmann, 15 November 1951 (ACCF/NYU). America was disposed to let the right kind of African-Americans 'out', but evidently not those who threatened to damage the interests of the US. When the Reverend Adam Clayton Powell, celebrated congressman and ex-Harlem minister, announced he was going to attend the 1955 Bandung Conference, C. D. Jackson attempted to persuade Nelson Rockefeller to block his visa request, on the basis that 'There was a time not so long ago when [Powell's] Communist flirtations were pretty shocking.' C. D. Jackson to Nelson Rockefeller, 28 March 1955 (CDJ/DDE).

10 James Johnson Sweeney, press release, 18 April 1952 (ACCF/NYU).

11 Quoted in American Embassy, Paris, report to State Department, 'Local Press Reaction to Congress for Cultural Freedom', 9 May 1952 (SD.CA/RG59/NARA).

12 Janet Flanner, 'Letter from Paris', *The New Yorker*, 20 May 1952.

13 Janet Flanner, 'Festival of Free World Arts', *Freedom and Union*, September 1952.

14 Guy Dumur, *Combat*, quoted in American Embassy, Paris, report to

State Department, 'Local Press Reaction to Congress for Cultural Freedom', 9 May 1952.
15 *Combat*, ibid.
16 Serge Lifar, ibid.
17 *Franc-Tireur*, ibid.
18 *L'Humanité*, ibid.
19 C. D. Jackson to Klaus Dohrn, 16 August 1956 (CDJ/DDE).
20 Janet Flanner, 'Festival of Free World Arts', *Freedom and Union*, September 1952.
21 Lawrence de Neufville, telephone interview, February 1997.
22 Melvin Lasky, interview, London, August 1997.
23 Diana Josselson, interview, Geneva, May 1996.
24 C. D. Jackson to Francis Hatch, 5 September 1952 (CDJ/DDE).
25 Tom Braden, interview, Virginia, June 1994.
26 Farfield Foundation brochure (CCF/CHI).
27 Tom Braden, interview, Virginia, August 1996.
28 Tom Braden, telephone interview, October 1997.
29 Tom Braden, interview, Virginia, June 1994.
30 Diana Josselson, interview, Geneva, March 1997.
31 Ibid.
32 Nicolas Nabokov, *Bagázh*.
33 Graham Greene, *The Quiet American* (London: Bodley Head, 1955).

9 The Consortium

1 Certificate of Incorporation of Committee for Free Europe, Inc., 11 May 1949 (CJD/DDE).
2 Dean Acheson, quoted in G. J. A. O'Toole, *Honorable Treachery: A History of U. S. Intelligence, Espionage, and Covert Action from the American Revolution to the CIA* (New York: Atlantic Monthly Press, 1991).
3 Certificate of Incorporation of Committee for Free Europe, Inc., op.cit. According to the Committee's 'Confidential Report on Friendship Stations', one of its major objectives was 'to increase disintegrating psychological pressures on the Soviet power center' and 'to forge new psychological weapons for an offensive cold war'. The report also argued that 'propaganda divorced from action ultimately recoils upon the user', a timely warning in view of what was to unfold in Hungary in 1956 (see below, Chapter 18).
4 Blanche Wiesen Cook, *The Declassified Eisenhower: A Divided Legacy of Peace and Political Warfare* (New York: Doubleday, 1981).
5 Harrison E. Salisbury, *Without Fear or Favor.*
6 Donald Jameson, interview, Washington, June 1994.
7 National Committee for a Free Europe Inc., 'Report to Members', 5 Jan 1951 (CDJ/DDE).
8 Philip Barbour, Radio Free Europe Committee, to Frank Altschul, 'Report from Research Department', 23 March 1950 (FA/COL).

9 Henry Kissinger, *The White House Years* (London: Weidenfeld & Nicolson, 1979).
10 Janet Barnes, quoted in Evan Thomas, *The Very Best Men*. The CIA gave Thomas unprecedented access for his book, as did the families of 'the very best men' of his title. Both as an historical study and as a collective biography, therefore, it is the most definitive account to date, and as such I am indebted to it.
11 William Colby, interview, Washington, June 1994.
12 Lee Williams, interview, Washington, June 1994.
13 J. M. Kaplan to Allen Dulles, 10 August 1956 (CDJ/DDE).
14 *Final Report of the Cox Committee*, 1952, quoted in René Wormser, *Foundations: Their Power and Influence* (New York: Devin-Adair, 1958).
15 *Final Report of the Church Committee*, 1976.
16 Ibid.
17 Tom Braden, interview, Virginia, June 1994.
18 Cord Meyer, *Facing Reality: From World Federalism to the CIA* (Maryland: University Press of America, 1980).
19 Richard Bissell, *Reflections of a Cold Warrior.*
20 James Laughlin, quoted in Kathleen D. McCarthy, 'From Cold War to Cultural Development: The International Cultural Activities of the Ford Foundation 1950–1980', *Daedalus*, vol.116/1, Winter 1987.
21 Quoted in Kathleen D. McCarthy, ibid.
22 Irving Kristol to Stephen Spender, 25 March 1953 (CCF/CHI).
23 Kai Bird, interview, Washington, June 1994.
24 John Hunt, interview, Uzés, July 1997.
25 Tom Braden, interview, Virginia, August 1996.
26 Neil Berry, 'Encounter', *London Magazine*, February–March 1995.

10 The Truth Campaign

1 Walt Rostow, telephone interview, July 1997.
2 C. D. Jackson, 'Notes of meeting', 28 April 1952 (CDJ/DDE).
3 Dwight D. Eisenhower, quoted in Blanche Wiesen Cook, *The Declassified Eisenhower.*
4 Charles Burton Marshall to Walter J. Stoessel, 18 May 1953 (CDJ/DDE).
5 Ibid.
6 Ibid.
7 Donald Jameson, interview, Washington, June 1994. 'From the [CIA's] point of view this image is really of a dog being led on a very long leash. Central to its success with intellectuals, who were said to be committing themselves to freedom, and independence, was the Agency's calculation that some, if not most, should be permitted to remain "unwitting" because they were in basic agreement with Agency politics, or could be more cooperative and useful if permitted to act as if they were unwitting.' Richard Elman, *The Aesthetics of the CIA* (unpublished manuscript).

8 Raymond Allen, quoted in Scott Lucas, 'The Psychological Strategy Board', *International History Review*, vol.18/2, May 1996.
9 Psychological Strategy Board, 'US Doctrinal Program', 29 June 1953 (PSB/DDE).
10 Scott Lucas, op.cit.
11 C. D. Jackson, Log Files (CDJ/DDE).
12 Ibid.
13 C. D. Jackson to Henry Luce, 28 April 1958 (CDJ/DDE).
14 C. D. Jackson to Abbott Washburn, 2 February 1953 (CDJ/DDE).
15 Lawrence de Neufville, telephone interview, April 1997.
16 Diana Josselson, interview, Geneva, March 1997.
17 Ibid.
18 Ibid.
19 Ibid. Irving Brown's contacts were many and varied, and with such large cash sums at his disposal, he found himself dealing with some dangerous characters. Recently discovered documents reveal that the Federal Bureau of Narcotics was tailing Brown in the mid-1960s on suspicion of trafficking drugs (or money laundered from drugs' trafficking operations) to the US. The documents link Brown to notorious French crime bosses, and their Italian counterparts in the Mafia. Federal Bureau of Narcotics, memorandi, October 1965. I am grateful to Tony Carew for showing me these documents.
20 Tom Braden, interview, Virginia, July 1996.
21 Diana Josselson, interview, Geneva, March 1997.

11 The New Consensus

1 Jason Epstein, interview, New York, June 1994.
2 Irving Kristol, interview, Washington, July 1996.
3 John Hunt, interview, Uzés, July 1997.
4 Sidney Hook's contacts with the CIA and the Psychological Strategy Board are referred to in a letter from Gordon Gray to Hook, 4 October 1951 (GG/DDE). According to Lawrence de Neufville, Hook was 'a regular consultant to CIA on matters of mutual interest'. In 1955, Hook was directly involved in negotiations with Allen Dulles and Cord Meyer at the CIA to secure funding for the ailing American Committee for Cultural Freedom.
5 Sidney Hook, 'To Counter the Big Lie – A Basic Strategy', *New York Times Magazine*, 11 March 1951.
6 Elliot Cohen, quoted in Peter Coleman, *The Liberal Conspiracy*.
7 Norbert Muhlen, quoted in Peter Coleman, ibid.
8 'Our Country and Our Culture', *Partisan Review*, May–June 1952.
9 Norman Podhoretz, *Making It* (London: Jonathan Cape, 1968).
10 William Phillips, quoted in Leonard Wallock (ed.), *New York*.
11 Lionel Trilling, quoted in Leonard Wallock, ibid.
12 Carol Brightman, interview, New York, June 1994.
13 Quoted in Leonard Wallock, op.cit.
14 Dwight Macdonald, 'Politics Past', *Encounter*, March 1957.

15 Michael Wreszin, *A Rebel in Defense of Tradition: The Life and Politics of Dwight Macdonald* (New York: Basic Books, 1994).
16 Philip Rahv, quoted in Hugh Wilford, *The New York Intellectuals* (Manchester: Manchester University Press, 1995).
17 Daniel Bell to John Leonard, editor, *Sunday Times Book Review*, 16 October 1972 (MJ/HRC).
18 Jason Epstein, interview, New York, June 1994.
19 Sidney Hook to Irving Brown, 31 October 1951 (IB/GMC).
20 Tom Braden, interview, Virginia, August 1996.
21 C. D. Jackson to Abbott Washburn, 2 February 1953 (CDJ/DDE).
22 Richard Fletcher, 'How CIA Money Took the Teeth out of British Socialism', in Philip Agee and Louis Wolf, *Dirty Work: The CIA in Western Europe* (New York: Dorset Press, 1978).
23 Tom Braden, telephone interview, June 1998.

12 Magazine 'X'

1 Jasper Ridley, telephone interview, August 1997. 'I fully agree the *New Statesman* is an important target, and must be dealt with systematically,' Michael Goodwin told Nicolas Nabokov, 15 January 1952 (CCF/CHI). Goodwin's efforts were not enough to satisfy his secret sponsors. Washington's interest in destroying the influence of the *New Statesman* was later taken up by the American Committee for Cultural Freedom, which despised the journal's 'spirit of conciliation and moral lassitude vis-a-vis Communism', and proposed the 'publication of "An Inventory of the New Statesman and Nation", exposing its line of compromise with totalitarianism, for world-wide distribution to English-reading intellectuals.' American Committee for Cultural Freedom, Memorandum, 6 January 1955 (ACCF/NYU).
2 Malcolm Muggeridge, *Like It Was* (London: Collins, 1981).
3 Tosco Fyvel to Irving Brown, 4 August 1951 (IB/GMC).
4 C. D. Jackson to William Griffin, 11 May 1953 (CDJ/DDE).
5 Kim Philby, *My Silent War* (New York: Grove Press, 1968).
6 Ibid.
7 Christopher Montague Woodhouse, *Something Ventured* (London: Granada, 1982).
8 Ibid.
9 Kim Roosevelt left the CIA in 1958, and went on to become a partner in a Washington PR firm representing, among other international clients, the government of Iran.
10 Stephen Spender, 'My Parents', in *Collected Poems, 1928–1985* (London: Faber & Faber, 1985).
11 Stephen Spender, *Journals, 1939–1983* (London: Faber & Faber, 1985).
12 Anita Kermode, interview, Devon, July 1997.
13 Stephen Spender, 'We Can Win the Battle for the Mind of Europe', *New York Times Magazine*, 25 April 1948.
14 Ibid.

15 Raymond Aron, 'Does Europe Welcome American Leadership?', *Saturday Review*, 13 January 1951.
16 Stuart Hampshire, interview, Oxford, December 1997.
17 Natasha Spender, telephone interview, August 1997.
18 Irving Kristol to Frederic Warburg, 26 February 1953 (ACCF/NYU).
19 Michael Josselson to Stephen Spender, 27 May 1953 (CCF/CHI).
20 Christopher Montague Woodhouse, telephone interview, July 1997.
21 Lawrence de Neufville, telephone interview, April 1997.
22 Malcolm Muggeridge, 'An Anatomy of Neutralism', *Time*, 2 November 1953.
23 Malcolm Muggeridge, *Chronicles of Wasted Time: The Infernal Grove* (London: Collins, 1973).
24 Jasper Ridley, letter to the author, 31 October 1997.
25 Michael Josselson to Stephen Spender, 5 March 1953 (MJ/HRC).
26 Stephen Spender to Irving Kristol, undated (ACCF/NYU).
27 Irving Kristol to Stephen Spender, 26 March 1953 (ACCF/NYU).
28 Christopher Montague Woodhouse, telephone interview, July 1997.
29 Irving Kristol, interview, Washington, June 1994.
30 Stephen Spender, interview, London, July 1994.
31 Philip Larkin, in *Selected Letters of Philip Larkin, 1940–1985* (London: Faber & Faber, 1992).
32 John Thompson, telephone interview, August 1996.
33 Natasha Spender, interview, Maussane, July 1997.
34 Irving Kristol to Michael Josselson, 15 September 1953 (CCF/CHI).
35 Irving Kristol to Michael Josselson, 16 September 1953 (CCF/CHI).
36 Judge Irving Kaufman, quoted in *New York Times*, 5 April 1951.
37 Jean-Paul Sartre, quoted in Stephen J. Whitfield, *The Culture of the Cold War* (Baltimore: Johns Hopkins University Press, 1991).
38 Ben Bradlee, *A Good Life: Newspapering and Other Adventures* (London: Simon & Schuster, 1995).
39 Melvin Lasky, interview, London, August 1997.
40 Douglas Dillon to State Department, 15 May 1953 (CJD/DDE).
41 Bowen Evans, Office of Intelligence Research, to Jesse MacKnight, Psychological Strategy Board, 14 January 1953 (PSB/DDE).
42 Douglas Dillon to State Department, 15 May 1953 (CJD/DDE).
43 Charles Taquey to C. E. Johnson, Psychological Strategy Board, 29 March 1953 (CJD/DDE).
44 C. D. Jackson to Herbert Brownell, 23 February 1953 (CJD/DDE).
45 C. D. Jackson, 'Memo for the file', 27 May 1953 (CJD/DDE).
46 Handwritten notes of the Cabinet meeting, 19 June 1953 (WHO/DDE).
47 Ibid.
48 Ibid.
49 Diana Josselson, interview, Geneva, March 1997.
50 American Committee for Cultural Freedom to President Eisenhower, 13 June 1953 (CCF/CHI).
51 Diana Josselson, interview, Geneva, March 1997.

52 Quoted in Hugh Wilford, *The New York Intellectuals*.
53 Leslie Fiedler, 'A Postscript to the Rosenberg Case', *Encounter*, October 1953.
54 Alger Hiss was a promising diplomat who, in 1949, fell under suspicion of being a Soviet spy in the State Department. Indicted by a federal grand jury for perjury, his case filled the newspapers and consumed America's body politic. He was finally convicted of perjury – though not of espionage – and sentenced to prison in January 1950 for five years.
55 Leslie Fiedler, 'A Postscript to the Rosenberg Case', *Encounter*, October 1953.
56 James T. Farrell to Meyer Schapiro, 4 September 1940 (MS/COL).
57 Sidney Hook, quoted in Irving Kristol to Michael Josselson, 4 August 1953 (CCF/CHI).
58 E. M. Forster, quoted in Stephen Spender to Michael Josselson, 22 October 1953 (MS/COL).
59 Stephen Spender to Michael Josselson, ibid.
60 Ibid.
61 Natasha Spender, telephone interview, May 1997.
62 Christopher Montague Woodhouse, telephone interview, December 1997. Woodhouse was unable to recall where this scene had taken place. Woodhouse occasionally bumped into Spender at social gatherings. He was also a contributor to *Encounter*, though he was scrupulous in protecting his affiliations to MI6, both from its editors and, naturally, its readers.
63 Stephen Spender to Michael Josselson, 22 October 1953 (CCF/CHI).
64 Anthony Hartley, the *Spectator*, 9 October 1953. If Hartley had misgivings at this time, he must have persuaded himself that he was in error. In 1962, when he became foreign editor of the *Spectator*, half his salary was paid by *Encounter*, of which he eventually became co-editor, alongside Melvin Lasky. There was something of a pattern to this kind of conversion. Josselson tracked critics, whether of *Encounter* or the Congress generally, and devoted his energy to bringing them 'onside'. In 1955, only months after he had reported in the *New Statesman* that *Encounter* was 'viewed with suspicion, because it was so obviously subsidized and people wanted to know by whom, and who laid down its "line"', David Daiches featured as a contributor to *Encounter*, a small but significant gain in what Neil Berry describes as *Encounter*'s campaign 'to sap the *New Statesman*'s ideological hegemony'. Neil Berry, 'Encounter', *London Magazine*, February–March 1995.
65 Graham Hough, text of a broadcast for the Third Program, BBC Radio, May 1954 (CCF/CHI).
66 A. J. P. Taylor, *Listener*, 8 October 1953.
67 Mary McCarthy to Hannah Arendt, in Carol Brightman (ed.), *Between Friends: The Correspondence of Hannah Arendt and Mary McCarthy 1949–1975* (London: Secker & Warburg, 1995).

68 Richard Wollheim, telephone interview, December 1997.
69 Stephen Spender to Irving Kristol, 24 April 1954 (CCF/CHI).
70 Michael Josselson to Irving Kristol, 4 October 1954 (CCF/CHI).
71 Stephen Spender to Michael Josselson, 10 July 1955 (CCF/CHI).

13 The Holy Willies

1 Susan Mary Alsop, *To Marietta from Paris.*
2 Richard Rovere, quoted in Stephen Whitfield, *The Culture of the Cold War.*
3 Arthur Miller, *Timebends.*
4 William Colby, interview, Washington, June 1994.
5 Howard Fast, quoted in Natalie Robins, *Alien Ink.*
6 Quoted in Stephen Whitfield, op.cit.
7 Stephen Whitfield, op.cit.
8 Quoted in Taylor D. Littleton and Maltby Sykes, *Advancing American Art: Painting, Politics and Cultural Confrontation* (Alabama: University of Alabama Press, 1989).
9 State Department and USIA cables, April–July 1953 (SD.CA/RG59/NARA).
10 American Embassy, Paris, to State Department, 20 April 1953 (SD.CA/RG59/NARA).
11 Tom Braden remembered being 'very alarmed' by the news that Thomas Mann was preparing to 'defect' back to Europe. Mann did indeed return to Europe, for good, in 1952.
12 Stephen Whitfield, op.cit.
13 Natalie Robins, op.cit.
14 Ibid.
15 Arthur Miller, op.cit.
16 Murray Kempton, quoted in Natalie Robins, op.cit.
17 Handwritten notes of the Cabinet meeting, 10 July 1953 (WHO/DDE).
18 Robert W. Merry, *Taking on the World: Joseph and Stewart Alsop, Guardians of the American Century* (New York: Viking Penguin, 1996).
19 Lyman Kirkpatrick, *The Real CIA* (New York: Macmillan, 1968).
20 Ibid.
21 Roy Cohn, *McCarthy* (New York: New American Library, 1968).
22 Arthur Schlesinger, interview, New York, June 1994.
23 John Hunt, interview, Uzés, July 1997.
24 Kai Bird, interview, Washington, June 1994.
25 James T. Farrell, quoted in American Committee for Cultural Freedom, 'Minutes of Planning Conference', 1 March 1952 (IB/GMC).
26 Dwight Macdonald, ibid.
27 Bertram Wolfe, ibid.
28 Boris Shub, ibid.
29 Richard Rovere, ibid.
30 Mary McCarthy to Hannah Arendt, 14 March 1952, in Carol Brightman (ed.), *Between Friends.*

31 Ibid.
32 Ibid.
33 Max Eastman, 'Who Threatens Cultural Freedom in America?', 29 March 1952 (ACCF/NYU).
34 Ibid.
35 Richard Rovere, 'Communists in a Free Society', 29 March 1952 (ACCF/NYU).
36 Arthur Schlesinger, interview, New York, August 1996.
37 Frank Wisner, Deputy Director CIA, to Deputy Assistant Director for Policy Coordination, in Michael Warner (ed.) *Cold War Records: The CIA Under Harry Truman* (Washington: Center for the Study of Intelligence, CIA, 1994).
38 Ibid.
39 Arthur Schlesinger to Nicolas Nabokov, 18 June 1951 (NN/HRC).
40 According to the *Final Report of the Church Committee*, 1976, 'back-stopping' was the CIA term for 'providing appropriate verification and support of cover arrangements for an agent or asset in anticipation of enquiries or other actions which might test the credibility of his or its cover'.
41 Tom Braden, telephone interview, October 1997.
42 Jasper Ridley, letter to the author, 31 October 1997.
43 T. R. Fyvel, 'The Broken Dialogue', *Encounter*, April 1954.
44 Leslie Fiedler, 'McCarthy', *Encounter*, August 1954.
45 Peregrine Worsthorne, 'America – Conscience or Shield?', *Encounter*, November 1954.
46 This 'McCarthy-as-man-not-phenomenon' line echoes the CIA view of how to approach the subject. It seems reasonable to assume that Nabokov was repeating Wisner's official 'guidance' on this subject, as indeed was Leslie Fiedler in his *Encounter* essay (op.cit.), which focused on McCarthy as a living gargoyle, 'his palsied head trembling'.
47 Nicolas Nabokov to Arthur Schlesinger, 21 April 1952 (ACCF/NYU).
48 Lee Williams, interview, Washington, July 1996.
49 John Steinbeck, quoted in Peter Vansittart, *In the Fifties*.
50 John Henry Faulk, quoted in Peter Vansittart, ibid.
51 Joseph and Stewart Alsop, 'Why Has Washington Gone Crazy?', *Saturday Evening Post*, 29 July 1950.
52 Ibid.
53 Sidney Hook, 'To Counter the Big Lie – A Basic Strategy', *New York Times Magazine*, 11 March 1951.
54 Irving Kristol, letter to *New York Times*, 10 August 1952 (ACCF/NYU).
55 Stephen Spender to Czesław Milosz, 12 October 1953 (CCF/CHI).
56 Tom Braden, interview, Virginia, July 1996.
57 Melvin Lasky, interview, London, August 1997.
58 Michael Josselson to Shepard Stone, 12 January 1968 (MJ/HRC).
59 Mary McCarthy to Hannah Arendt, 2 December 1952, in Carol Brightman, (ed.) *Between Friends*.

60 Roy Cohn, op.cit.
61 Tom Braden, interview, Virginia, August 1996.
62 R. Harris Smith, *OSS*.
63 Ibid.
64 Cord Meyer, *Facing Reality*.
65 Ibid.
66 Dwight Macdonald, quoted in Michael Wreszin, *A Rebel in Defense of Tradition*.
67 Taylor D. Littleton and Maltby Sykes, *Advancing American Art*.
68 William Fulbright, 'In Thrall to Fear', *The New Yorker*, 8 January 1972.
69 Richard Bissell, *Reflections of a Cold Warrior*.
70 Tom Braden, 'What's Wrong with the CIA?' *Saturday Review*, 5 April 1975.

14 Music and Truth, *ma non troppo*

1 Josselson decided to close *Science and Freedom* down in 1961. Kingsley Martin alleged that this was done in a fit of Cold War pique because the Committee on Science and Freedom was planning a public symposium on nuclear politics. Josselson was a passionate advocate of atomic power, and he might well have been hesitant about Polanyi's intentions. But Polanyi himself was showing all the signs of mental illness at this time, perhaps a nervous breakdown, so it's hard to tell. Josselson decided to sponsor a new and more scholarly quarterly, *Minerva*, to be edited by Edward Shils.
2 Peter Coleman, *The Liberal Conspiracy*.
3 Ibid.
4 Michael Josselson to Walter Laqueur, 1 April 1955 (CCF/CHI).
5 Peter Coleman, op.cit.
6 James McAuley, 'Proposal for an Australian Quarterly Magazine', undated (IB/GMC). McAuley's successor was Peter Coleman, who in 1989 published *The Liberal Conspiracy*, which advertised itself as the full account of the Congress for Cultural Freedom. Yet Coleman also conceded that he had failed to acquire any 'significant news from official sources about the extent of the CIA's involvement'. In the absence of such information, he decided that 'the cloak-and-dagger questions of who paid whom, how, and for what' were insignificant enough to ignore altogether. As a former activist of the organization he writes about, Coleman is necessarily partisan, but his credentials as official historian of the Congress are impeccable, and *The Liberal Conspiracy* is an invaluable resource.
7 Peter Coleman, op.cit.
8 John Thompson, telephone interview, August 1996.
9 Diana Josselson, interview, Geneva, March 1997.
10 Melvin Lasky, 'Some Notes on Preuves, Encounter and Der Monat', April 1956 (CCF/CHI).
11 Ibid.

12 Ibid.
13 Robert Silvers, quoted in Carol Brightman, *Writing Dangerously.*
14 Al Alvarez, *New Statesman*, 29 December 1961.
15 Conor Cruise O'Brien, *New Statesman*, 20 December 1962.
16 Jason Epstein, interview, New York, June 1994.
17 Malcolm Muggeridge, *New Statesman*, 19 May 1967.
18 Malcolm Muggeridge, *Esquire*, January 1973.
19 Herbert Read, 'Masterpieces of the Twentieth Century' address, Paris, April 1952 (ACCF/NYU).
20 Nicolas Nabokov, *New York Herald Tribune*, 8 February 1953.
21 Nicolas Nabokov to Julius Fleischmann, 6 May 1953 (ACCF/NYU).
22 *Musical America*, May 1954.
23 Susan Sontag, 'Pilgrimage', *The New Yorker*, 21 December 1987.
24 Pierre Boulez to Nicolas Nabokov, undated, 1954 (CCF/CHI).
25 Nicolas Nabokov to Julius Fleischmann, 7 September 1954 (CCF/CHI).
26 Enesco had expressed his desire to be buried in his homeland, Romania. But according to Diana Josselson, when Enesco died in May 1955, Nabokov and Josselson were involved in a frantic bid to prevent his body from leaving France. They succeeded, and Enesco was buried in Paris, at the Père Lachaise cemetery.
27 C. D. Jackson to Cecil Morgan, 26 March 1957 (CDJ/DDE).
28 C. D. Jackson to Theodore Streibert, Director, USIA, 28 July 1955 (CDJ/DDE).
29 C. D. Jackson to Allen Dulles, 20 May 1953 (CDJ/DDE).
30 Julius Fleischmann to C. D. Jackson, 17 February 1953 (CDJ/DDE).
31 C. D. Jackson to George Sloan, 17 March 1953 (CDJ/DDE).
32 American Committee for Cultural Freedom to Al Manuti, American Federation of Musicians, 21 February 1951 (ACCF/NYU).
33 American Committee for Cultural Freedom, 'Statement of Principles', 1953 (IB/GMC).
34 George F. Kennan, 'International Exchange in the Arts', printed in *Perspectives*, Summer 1956.
35 When Lasky discovered in 1956 that his research assistant on his White Book on Hungary (*The Hungarian Revolution*) had been a much-reviled Nazi, his first reaction was one of pragmatism: 'Oh my God, now they're going to tear into the book, it'll be smeared by his association.' But Lasky thought it best to do nothing: 'I swallowed my anxieties and left him on the project.' Melvin Lasky, interview, London, August 1997.
36 Lee Williams, interview, Washington, June 1994.
37 James T. Farrell to Meyer Schapiro, 25 July 1942 (MS/COL).
38 Arthur Schlesinger to James T. Farrell, 16 March 1955 (ACCF/NYU).
39 Clinton Rossiter to Sol Stein, 10 November 1955 (ACCF/NYU).
40 Jason Epstein, interview, New York, August 1996.
41 Hannah Arendt once described ex-Communists as Communists 'turned upside down'. The point that she and George Urban make is

that the Cold War was an adversarial cause, and as such, appealed to the radical image many intellectuals held of themselves. 'The vocabulary of opposition remained intact, the sense of a militant critique was preserved, even if its target had been switched from capitalism to communism.' Andrew Ross, *No Respect: Intellectuals and Popular Culture* (London: Routledge, 1989).

42 George Urban, *Radio Free Europe and the Pursuit of Democracy: My War Within the Cold War* (New York: Yale University Press, 1997).

43 Michael Josselson to Sidney Hook, 23 November 1955 (CCF/CHI).

44 Sol Stein to Norman Thomas, 27 April 1955 (ACCF/NYU).

45 Norman Thomas to Sol Stein, 28 April 1955 (ACCF/NYU).

46 Cord Meyer to Arthur Schlesinger, 16 May 1955 (SCHLES/BU). Although Schlesinger recalled only a social relationship with his CIA friends during these years, his own papers, deposited at the John F. Kennedy Library in Boston, indicate a deeper involvement. Schlesinger appears to have acted as Cord Meyer's line into the American Committee for Cultural Freedom, sending him minutes of its Executive Meetings, and generally keeping him informed of internal developments. How formal this arrangement was is unclear, but in a memo to President Kennedy, Schlesinger later acknowledged serving 'as a periodic CIA consultant' in the years since the Second World War. Arthur Schlesinger, 'Subject: CIA Reorganization', 30 June 1961 (NSF/JFK).

47 Michael Josselson to Irving Kristol, 7 April 1956 (CCF/CHI). Russell was certainly not senile, but he was showing signs of his will to 'live till ninety so that I can say all the wrong things'. In Josselson's mind, Russell could no longer say anything right, and by 1963, he was wondering hopefully whether 'the s.o.b.' would 'do us the favour of dying'. Michael Josselson to Edward Shils, 10 April 1963 (MJ/HRC).

48 American Committee for Cultural Freedom, open letter to Bertrand Russell, *New York Times*, 6 April 1956 (ACCF/NYU).

49 Congress for Cultural Freedom Executive Committee to American Committee for Cultural Freedom, 24 April 1956 (IB/GMC).

50 James T. Farrell to Meyer Schapiro, 5 August 1941 (MS/COL).

51 James T. Farrell, letter of resignation, to Norman Jacobs, 28 August 1956 (MS/COL).

52 Michael Josselson to Norman Thomas, 27 September 1956 (ACCF/NYU).

15 Ransom's Boys

1 According to CIA mythology, 'retirement' is something of a misnomer. 'Once a CIA man, always a CIA man,' goes the mantra. The process by which people who left the Agency continued to remain faithful (and useful) to it was known as 'sheepdipping'. However, many would later allege that Braden did not fit this archetype; that he was, in fact, a whistleblower.

2 *Final Report of the Church Committee*, 1976.
3 Doolittle Study Group on Foreign Intelligence, quoted in Stephen Whitfield, *The Culture of the Cold War*.
4 Tom Braden, interview, Virginia, August 1996.
5 Lee Williams, interview, Washington, July 1996.
6 Diana Josselson, interview, Geneva, May 1996.
7 Diana Josselson, interview, Geneva, March 1997.
8 Donald Jameson, interview, Washington, June 1994.
9 Lawrence de Neufville, telephone interview, February 1997.
10 Lee Williams, interview, Washington, July 1996.
11 Cord Meyer, *Facing Reality*.
12 William Sloane Coffin, quoted in Jessica Mitford, *The Trial of Dr Spock, the Rev. William Sloane Coffin, Jr., Michael Ferber, Mitchell Goodman and Marcus Raskin* (London: Macdonald, 1969). Coffin later returned to his original calling, and became chaplain at Yale University.
13 William Corson, *The Armies of Ignorance: The Rise of the American Intelligence Empire* (New York: Dial Press, 1997).
14 Doug Henwood, 'Spooks in Blue', *Grand Street*, vol.7/3, Spring 1998.
15 Ibid.
16 Tom Mangold, *Cold Warrior: James Jesus Angleton, The CIA's Master Spy Hunter* (New York: Simon & Schuster, 1991).
17 Ibid.
18 Clare Booth Luce, quoted in Tom Mangold, ibid.
19 Ian Hamilton, *Robert Lowell: A Biography* (New York: Random House, 1982).
20 John Crowe Ransom to David McDowell, 11 August 1953 (RH/COL). Ransom's insouciance at the news of his protégé's job offer from the CIA suggests that he may well have been Meyer's official unofficial 'line of contact' at Kenyon.
21 Lee Williams, interview, Washington, July 1996.
22 Jason Epstein, interview, New York, June 1994.
23 John Thompson, quoted in Richard Elman, *The Aesthetics of the CIA* (unpublished manuscript).
24 Timothy Foote to Michael Josselson, 5 March 1956 (CCF/CHI).
25 Diana Josselson, interview, Geneva, March 1997.
26 Ibid.
27 Ibid.
28 Chief of Covert Action Staff, CIA, quoted in *Final Report of the Church Committee*, 1976.
29 Ibid.
30 *New York Times*, 25 December 1977.
31 E. Howard Hunt, *Undercover: Memoirs of an American Secret Agent*. *The New Class* was published in collaboration with the Congress for Cultural Freedom.
32 Eugene Fodor, quoted in *New York Times*, 25 December 1977.
33 Carol Brightman, interview, New York, June 1994.

34 Richard Elman, interview, New York, June 1994. Richard Elman also believed that 'the CIA's interest in imaginative literature and its creators and publishers has been depicted by some as misguided benevolence, or even a championing of Western values and human freedoms against the totalitarian mind, but it was also profoundly meant to be an Agency "dirty trick", the means of influencing consciousness, an attempt to "preempt", in Agency lingo.' Richard Elman, *The Aesthetics of the CIA*. See also Jason Epstein, 'The CIA and the Intellectuals', *New York Review of Books*, 20 April 1967, in which he claims that the CIA and its allies 'were not moved by a disinterested love of the intellect or by deep aesthetic convictions, they were interested in protecting and extending American power'.

35 Allen Ginsberg, 'T. S. Eliot Entered My Dreams', *City Lights Journal*, Spring 1978.

36 Irving Kristol, quoted in Peter Steinfels, *The Neoconservatives: The Men Who Are Changing American Politics* (New York: Simon & Schuster, 1979). As Christopher Lasch pointed out, the elitism of those intellectuals who had once been attracted to Leninism was in no way contradictory: 'even after they had dissociated themselves from [Leninism's] materialist content, they clung to the congenial view of intellectuals as the vanguard of history'. Christopher Lasch, 'The Cultural Cold War', *The Nation*, 11 September 1967.

37 Allen Tate, quoted in Marian Janssen, *The Kenyon Review 1939–1970* (Mijmegen: M. Janssen, 1987).

38 Dwight Macdonald, quoted in Andrew Ross, *No Respect*. Alexander Solzhenitsyn used a similar, if more graphic, metaphor when he described American popular culture as liquid manure seeping under the door.

39 Robert Lowell, Valedictory Address, Kenyon College, 1940, quoted in Ian Hamilton, op.cit.

40 Richard Elman, interview, New York, June 1994.

41 Bollingen judges, quoted in William Barrett, 'A Prize for Ezra Pound', *Partisan Review*, vol.16/4, 1949.

16 Yanqui Doodles

1 George Dondero, quoted in William Hauptman, 'The Suppression of Art in the McCarthy Decade', *Artforum*, October 1973. In 1957, George Dondero received a Gold Medal of Honor from the American Artists Professional League (AAPL), 'for his congressional exposure of Communism in art'. AAPL press release, 30 March 1957.

2 Harold Harby, quoted in William Hauptman, op.cit.

3 The Communist affiliations of these artists were carefully documented by the Committee on Un-American Activities, whose files were quoted in the Congressional Record of May 1947. The blacklist runs to over forty names, including William Baziotes, Stuart Davis, Arthur Dove, Adolph Gottlieb, Philip Guston and John Marin. House Congressional Record, 13 May 1947.

4 Frederic Taubes, *Encyclopaedia Britannica*, 1946.
5 Budd Hopkins, quoted in Frances Stonor Saunders, *Hidden Hands: A Different History of Modernism* (London: Channel 4 Television, 1995).
6 Clement Greenberg, 'The Decline of Cubism', *Partisan Review*, March 1948.
7 Robert Hughes, *American Visions: The Epic History of Art in America* (New York: Knopf, 1997).
8 Jason Epstein, interview, New York, June 1994.
9 Taylor D. Littleton and Maltby Sykes, *Advancing American Art*. 'It was within [a] broad context of cultural diplomacy that "Advancing American Art" was formed and projected as one element in an international definition of American reassurance, stability, and enlightenment.'
10 Alfred M. Frankfurter, quoted in Taylor D. Littleton and Maltby Sykes, ibid.
11 Quoted in Taylor D. Littleton and Maltby Sykes, ibid.
12 Senator Brown, House Congressional Record, 14 May 1947.
13 Jane De Hart Mathews, 'Art and Politics in Cold War America', *American Historical Review*, vol.81/4, October 1976.
14 Tom Braden, interview, Virginia, June 1994.
15 Clement Greenberg, 'Avant-Garde and Kitsch', *Partisan Review*, Fall 1939.
16 Tom Braden, interview, Virginia, June 1994.
17 Ibid.
18 Philip Dodd, interview, London, July 1994.
19 Donald Jameson, interview, Washington, June 1994.
20 Ibid.
21 E. J. Kahn, 'Man of Means', *The New Yorker*, 11 August 1951.
22 David Wise and Thomas B. Ross, *The Espionage Establishment* (New York: Random House, 1967).
23 Russell Lynes, *Good Old Modern: An Intimate Portrait of the Museum of Modern Art* (New York: Atheneum, 1973).
24 G. Hellman, 'The Imperturbable Noble', *The New Yorker*, 7 May 1960.
25 Ibid.
26 Quoted in Carl Bernstein, 'The CIA and the Media', *Rolling Stone*, 20 October 1977.
27 Eva Cockroft, 'Abstract Expressionism: Weapon of the Cold War', *Artforum*, vol.12/10, June 1974.
28 Ibid.
29 Lawrence de Neufville, telephone interview, April 1997.
30 Michael Kimmelman, 'Revisiting the Revisionists: the Modern, its Critics, and the Cold War', *Studies in Modern Art 4* (New York: Museum of Modern Art, 1994).
31 Museum of Modern Art, Report of the Trustees, 1945, in Alfred Barr, *Painting and Sculpture in the Museum of Modern Art 1929-1967: An Illustrated Catalogue and Chronicle* (New York: Museum of Modern Art, 1977).

32 Ibid.
33 Lincoln Kirstein, *Harper's Magazine*, October 1948.
34 Samuel Kootz, quoted in Lynn Zelevansky, 'Dorothy Miller's "Americans" 1942–1963, *Studies in Modern Art 4* (New York: Museum of Modern Art, 1994).
35 Dwight Macdonald, 'Action on West 53rd Street', *The New Yorker*, 12 and 19 December 1953.
36 Lynn Zelevansky, op.cit.
37 Reviewing the retrospective show of 1943, 'Romantic Painting in America' (which included Bingham, Burchfield, Eakins, Homer and Watkin), Greenberg dismissed it as representing 'a period in which dry bones are being re-clad with flesh, corpses resuscitated and illusions revived by our failing nerves in every field of endeavor.' Clement Greenberg, 'Art', *The Nation*, 1 January 1944.
38 Alfred Barr to Henry Luce, 24 March 1949 (AB/MoMA).
39 Alfred Barr, introduction to *The New American Painting* catalogue, 1958. Fully illustrated, the catalogue was produced thanks to 'two generous donations – one from a British donor, who wishes to remain anonymous, and one from the USIA'.
40 Russell Lynes, op.cit.
41 American Embassy, Paris, to State Department, 11 June 1953 (SD.CA/RG59/NARA).
42 Waldo Rasmussen, interview, New York, June 1994.
43 Ibid.
44 James Johnson Sweeney, press release, 18 April 1952 (ACCF/NYU).
45 Alfred Barr, 'Is Modern Art Communistic?', *New York Times Magazine*, 14 December 1952.
46 The twelve artists were Jackson Pollock, Arshile Gorky, John Kane, David Smith, Ben Shahn, Alexander Calder, John Marin, Morris Graves, Stuart Davis, Edward Hopper, Ivan Albright, and Theodore Roszak.
47 American Embassy, Paris, to State Department, 11 June 1953 (NA, RG59). Jean Cassou was a crucial link man between the art establishments in New York and Paris. A minor poet appointed to direct the Musée National d'Art Moderne as a reward for his activities in the Resistance, he was an *haut fonctionnaire* who knew less about art than how to attach himself to politically significant groups, not least the Congress for Cultural Freedom.
48 American Embassy, Paris, ibid.
49 Julius Fleischmann to Bob Thayer, 25 February 1960 (CCF/CHI).
50 Monroe Wheeler to Nicolas Nabokov, 9 April 1954 (CCF/CHI).
51 The Congress's magazines provided a useful base for critics favourable to the new art. Michael Josselson was fully appreciative of the political significance of abstraction, which he believed to be democracy's answer to socialist (read 'social') realism. After a public debate in early 1954 at which Alberto Moravia was reported to have rallied to the Communist point of view regarding socialist realism, Josselson was

furious. He wrote immediately to Nicolas Nabokov, who was then in Rome, instructing him to organise a meeting at which Moravia's statements would be discredited, and Moravia himself would be showed up as a 'hypocrite'. Michael Josselson to Nicolas Nabokov, 22 January 1954 (CCF/CHI). The following year, after reading an article by the *New Statesman*'s art critic John Berger, which criticized a London exhibition of Italian painters for excluding such realists as Renato Guttuso (whose work, wrote Berger, proved that 'it is neither necessary for a Western European artist to cut off his right hand and paint as though he were an old academician in Moscow, nor to cut off his left to feel at home in the Museum of Modern Art, New York'), Melvin Lasky wrote Josselson: 'If ever that devastating brochure on the *New Statesman and Nation* is ever [sic] done, it should include the credo of its art critic, party-liner John Berger, which is printed on p.180 of the issue of 5 February [1955]. Look at it – and tear your bloody hair out.' Melvin Lasky to Michael Josselson, 7 February 1955 (CCF/CHI).

52 Michael Josselson to Porter McCray, 8 October 1956 (CCF/CHI).
53 Press clipping (source unidentifiable), summer 1955 (ACCF/ NYU).
54 Dwight D. Eisenhower, 'Freedom in the Arts', MoMA 25th Anniversary Address, 19 October 1954, in *Museum of Modern Art Bulletin*, 1954.
55 August Heckscher, MoMA 25th Anniversary Address, ibid. Heckscher worked at the *New York Herald Tribune*, a Whitney-owned publication which consistently championed the Abstract Expressionists.
56 George Kennan, 'International Exchange in the Arts', Address to the Council of MoMA, 1955, printed in *Perspectives*, summer 1956.
57 Ibid.
58 Ibid. [my italics.]
59 Ruby D'Arschot to Julius Fleischmann, 28 October 1959 (CCF/CHI).
60 Quoted in Clifford Ross, *Abstract Expressionism: Creators and Critics* (New York: Abrams, 1990).
61 Quoted in Clifford Ross, ibid.
62 Adam Gopnik, 'The Power Critic', *The New Yorker*, 16 March 1998.
63 John Canaday, *New York Times*, 8 August 1976.
64 Ibid.
65 Jason Epstein, interview, New York, June 1994.
66 Dwight Macdonald, op.cit.
67 Paul Burlin, quoted in Serge Guilbaut, *How New York Stole the Idea of Modern Art* (Chicago: University of Chicago Press, 1983).
68 Alan Filreis, 'Beyond the Rhetorician's Touch: Stevens's Painterly Abstractions', *American Literary History*, spring 1992.
69 Barnett Newman, catalogue introduction to the *First Exhibition of Modern American Artists*, Riverside Museum, January 1943.
70 Willem de Kooning, quoted in Clifford Ross, op.cit.
71 Jackson Pollock, quoted in Clifford Ross, op.cit.
72 Robert Motherwell, quoted in Clifford Ross, op.cit.

73 Robert Motherwell to Patrick Heron, 2 September 1975. I am grateful to Patrick Heron for showing me this letter.
74 Ad Reinhardt, quoted in Annette Cox, *Art-as-Politics: The Abstract Expressionist Avant-Garde and Society* (UMI Research Press, 1982).
75 Giles Scott-Smith, *The Politics of Apolitical Culture: The Congress for Cultural Freedom and the Cultural Identity of Post-War American Hegemony, 1945–1960* (unpublished Ph.D thesis, Lancaster University, 1998).
76 Philip Dodd, interview, London, July 1994.
77 Saul Bellow, *Humboldt's Gift*.

17 The Guardian Furies

1 Dwight D. Eisenhower, quoted in Stephen Whitfield, *The Culture of the Cold War.* Whilst propagandists in the Eisenhower administration liked to talk of deploying spiritual weapons, the Department of Defense launched a programme of expenditure on a stockpile of nuclear and non-nuclear weapons amounting to $354 billion in less than six years.
2 Daniel Boorstin, quoted in Taylor D. Littleton and Maltby Sykes, *Advancing American Art*.
3 Paul Nitze, quoted in Evan Thomas, *The Very Best Men*.
4 Eisenhower's ancestors had been Mennonites, but when they settled in Texas there was no Mennonite church, so they read from the Bible.
5 John Kobler, *Henry Luce: His Time, Life and Fortune* (London: Macdonald, 1968).
6 Ibid.
7 Ibid.
8 Sidney Hook, 'The New Failure of Nerve', *Partisan Review*, January 1953. In December 1951, the director of the Psychological Strategy Board recommended to Tracy Barnes of the CIA that Niebuhr be approached as a possible 'consultant' to the PSB. Gordon Gray to Tracy Barnes, 21 December 1951 (GG/DDE). This, combined with Niebuhr's position as chairman of the Advisory Committee of the Policy Planning Staff (which oversaw the creation of the CIA), meant that the theologian was ideally placed to 'to make God an instrument of national policy'.
9 Whittaker Chambers, *Witness* (Chicago: Regnery, 1952).
10 Harry S. Truman, Address to Congress, 12 March 1947, printed in Harry S. Truman, *Memoirs: Year of Decisions*.
11 George Santayana, quoted in Gore Vidal, *Palimpsest* (London: André Deutsch, 1995).
12 Billy Graham, quoted in Stephen Whitfield, op.cit.
13 Norman Mailer, *Armies of the Night* (New York: New American Library, 1968).
14 Arthur Miller, *Timebends*.
15 Ibid.

16 Leslie Fiedler, quoted in Taylor D. Littleton and Maltby Sykes, op.cit.
17 Sol Stein to Aware, Inc., 28 January 1955 (ACCF/NYU).
18 Ibid.
19 Ibid.
20 Aware, Inc. to Sol Stein, 26 February 1955 (ACCF/NYU).
21 Sol Stein to Whittaker Chambers, 20 December 1954 (ACCF/NYU).
22 Whittaker Chambers, op.cit.
23 André Malraux, quoted in Stephen Whitfield, op.cit.
24 Arthur Miller, op.cit.
25 Joint Chiefs of Staff, 'Presentation of "Militant Liberty" to Chief of Naval Operations', 16 December 1955 (PSB/HT).
26 Christopher Simpson, interview, Washington, June 1994.
27 Joint Chiefs of Staff, 'Report of Conference in California in Connection with Cornelius Vanderbilt Whitney's "American Film Series" and "Militant Liberty"', 5 July 1956 (PSB/HT).
28 Ibid.
29 Cornelius Vanderbilt Whitney, quoted in ibid.
30 Joint Chiefs of Staff, ibid.
31 Arthur Miller, op.cit.
32 Gore Vidal, op.cit.
33 C. D. Jackson to Henry Luce, 19 May 1953 (CDJ/DDE).
34 Turner Shelton, Motion Picture Service, to Cecil B. DeMille, 11 May 1953 (CDJ/DDE).
35 Geoffrey Shurlock to Andrew Smith, Motion Picture Service, 28 September 1954 WHO/NSC/DDE.
36 Ibid.
37 Carleton Alsop, Hollywood Reports, 1953 (CDJ/DDE).
38 Ibid. Despite the stand taken by the National Association for the Advancement of Colored People against 'the stereotypical representation in films of Negroes as bumbling, comical characters', Hollywood made no positive advance in its treatment of African-Americans on screen. Indeed, between 1945 and 1957 the number of black movie performers declined from 500 to 125. In the 1953 film *Skirts Ahoy*, the black musician Billy Eckstein was forbidden to look at any white actress during his performance.
39 Ibid.
40 Walter L. Hixson, *Parting the Curtain: Propaganda, Culture and the Cold War, 1945–1961* (New York: Macmillan, 1997).
41 C. D. Jackson to Abbott Washburn, 30 January 1956 (CDJ/DDE).
42 C. D. Jackson to Nelson Rockefeller, 14 April 1955 (CDJ/DDE). In the same letter, C. D. Jackson warned his CIA colleagues not to get the 'smarty pants' idea of using these artists as intelligence sources – 'I don't think that these people are emotionally capable of playing a double role' – but he did agree that 'After they return they can of course be skillfully debriefed.'
43 John Pauker, USIA, to Sol Stein, 20 October 1955 (ACCF/NYU).
44 Sidney Hook, 'Report on the International Day Against Dictatorship

and War', *Partisan Review*, vol.16/7, Fall 1949.

45 T. S. Colahan to Sol Stein, October 1955 (ACCF/NYU).

46 Eric Johnston, quoted in Walter L. Hixson, op.cit. US government propagandists were uniformly wary of Steinbeck, and indeed that whole school of American literature deemed to carry loaded social data. In July 1955, a psychological warfare expert urged the government to withdraw its sponsorship of the Museum of Modern Art's photographic exhibition, *The Family of Man*, because it portrayed American society 'in a *Grapes of Wrath* type of display of an old or wealthy upper class', and left 'the impression that all US laborers are downtrodden or exploited', and as such was 'a Communist propagandist's dream'. P. J. Corso, Operations Coordinating Board, July 1955 (OCB.Cen/DDE). One critic detected in all this a 'paranoid quest for decontamination'. Tom Hayden, quoted in Andrew Ross, *No Respect*.

47 Carleton Alsop, op.cit.

48 Reference to the CIA's 'Hollywood Formula' is made in C. D. Jackson's log journal for 15 May 1953. Although heavily censored by government classification experts, the entry is the only known documentary evidence that the CIA had developed a formal strategy for penetrating the motion picture industry. According to the diary, C. D. met that day with Tracy Barnes's deputy John Baker (de Neufville's recruiter), to discuss the CIA's 'Hollywood Formula', which appears to have been the concern of Baker, Barnes and Wisner, with Alsop as their man on the West coast.

49 Carleton Alsop, op.cit.

50 Ibid.

51 Ibid.

52 E. Howard Hunt, *Undercover: Memoirs of an American Secret Agent* (California: Berkeley Publishing Corporation, 1974).

53 De Rochemont had won favour as an independent producer with *House on 92nd Street*, in which valiant FBI agents did combat with German spies. The film was praised for its realistic – de Rochemont called it 'non-fiction' – restaging of an actual case from J. Edgar Hoover's files. According to one historian, de Rochemont 'had a career-long obsession with spies', a useful credential for someone who was about to work with several of them. Lawrence de Neufville, who met him in England during the filming of *Animal Farm*, recalled de Rochemont's excitement at 'hanging around with guys from the Agency, like he was in one of his own films'. Lawrence de Neufville, telephone interview, April 1997.

54 Richard Hirsch, PSB, to Tracy Barnes, 'Comment on Animal Farm script', 23 January 1952 (PSB/HT).

55 Official financing for *1984* included a $100,000 subsidy from the United States Information Agency, to make what its chairman described as 'the most devastating anti-Communist film of all time'. Tony Shaw, *The British Cinema, Consensus and the Cold War 1917–1967* (unpublished manuscript).

56 Alan Sinfield, *Literature, Politics and Culture in Postwar Britain* (London: Athlone Press, 1997).
57 Sol Stein to Peter Rathvon, 30 January 1955 (ACCF/NYU).
58 Ibid.
59 Ibid.
60 Ibid.
61 Ibid.
62 Sol Stein, memo to the American Committee for Cultural Freedom, 11 January 1955 (ACCF/NYU).
63 Isaac Deutscher, 'The Mysticism of Cruelty', quoted in Alexander Cockburn, *Corruptions of Empire* (London: Verso, 1987).
64 Ibid.
65 George Orwell, in Peter Davison (ed.), *The Complete Works of George Orwell* (London: Secker & Warburg, 1998).
66 Richard Rees, quoted in Michael Sheldon, *Orwell: The Authorised Biography* (London: Heinemann, 1991).
67 George Orwell, in Peter Davison, op.cit. Orwell was fiercely anti-Zionist, believing that 'The Zionist Jews everywhere hate us and regard Britain as *the* enemy, more even than Germany.' For this reason, he advised IRD that it was 'bad policy to try to curry favour with your enemies', and warned them not to think that 'anti-anti-semitism is a strong card to play in anti-Russian propaganda'. George Orwell to Celia Kirwan, 6 April 1949 (IRD/FO1110/PRO).
68 Adam Watson, telephone interview, August 1998. [My italics.]
69 Bernard Crick, *Evening Standard*, 11 July 1996.
70 Peregrine Worsthorne, *The Spectator*, 29 July 1996.
71 George Orwell, 'The Prevention of Literature', *Polemic*, no. 2, 1945.
72 George Orwell, 'The Freedom of the Press', 1944, printed in *New Statesman*, 18 August 1995.
73 Ibid.

18 When Shrimps Learn to Whistle

1 Manès Sperber, 11 November 1956, quoted in Michael Josselson to Shepard Stone, undated (CCF/CHI).
2 Lawrence de Neufville, telephone interview, April 1997.
3 Ibid.
4 Michael Josselson to Shepard Stone, undated (CCF/CHI).
5 Evan Thomas, *The Very Best Men.*
6 Melvin Lasky, interview, London, August 1997.
7 John Hunt, interview, Uzés, July 1997.
8 Quoted in Peter Coleman, *The Liberal Conspiracy.*
9 Jean-Paul Sartre, *L'Express*, 9 November 1956.
10 Michael Josselson to Shepard Stone, undated (CCF/CHI).
11 Ibid.
12 Ibid.
13 C. D. Jackson, Log Files (CDJ/DDE).
14 C. D. Jackson to Frank Wisner, 27 February 1954 (CDJ/DDE).

15 Ibid.
16 Richard Crockatt, *The Fifty Years War: The United States and the Soviet Union in World Politics 1941–1991* (London: Routledge, 1995).
17 Michael Josselson to Nicolas Nabokov, 23 January 1954 (CCF/CHI).
18 Curiously, Eisenhower himself, who later observed that 'the proposals were revolutionary', offered scant follow-up to his address at the time. The proposals were rebuffed by the Soviets.
19 Michael Josselson to Lawrence de Neufville, undated (CDJ/DDE).
20 C. D. Jackson to Tracy Barnes, 5 January 1954 (CDJ/DDE).
21 Melvin Lasky, interview, London, August 1997.
22 Michael Josselson to Irving Kristol, 1 December 1955 (CCF/CHI).
23 Melvin Lasky, interview, London, August 1997.
24 Michael Josselson to Irving Kristol, quoted in Peter Coleman, *The Liberal Conspiracy.*
25 Irving Kristol to Michael Josselson, quoted in Peter Coleman, ibid.
26 Stephen Spender to Michael Josselson, 10 July 1955 (CCF/CHI).
27 Ibid.
28 Melvin Lasky, interview, London, August 1997.
29 Not surprisingly, Michael Josselson was appalled at Hook's threat to expose the Congress. But Josselson held his ground, and defended the decision to appoint Macdonald in Kristol's place on the grounds that he 'had very good reason to be dissatisfied with Irving after having made every effort to nurse him along over a period of more than two years'. Michael Josselson to Sidney Hook, 18 August 1955 (CCF/CHI).
30 Irving Kristol, interview, Washington, July 1996.
31 Stuart Hampshire, interview, Oxford, December 1997.
32 Arthur Schlesinger, interview, New York, February 1997.
33 Michael Josselson to Malcolm Muggeridge, 19 September 1955 (CCF/CHI).
34 Michael Josselson to Irving Kristol, 10 December 1955 (CCF/CHI).
35 Michael Josselson to Daniel Bell, 29 October 1955 (CCF/CHI). The expression was borrowed from Nikita Khrushchev, who once gloomily predicted that only when shrimps learned to whistle would the Cold War end.
36 Dwight Macdonald to Stephen Spender, 2 June 1955 (CCF/CHI).
37 Congress for Cultural Freedom brochure, undated (CCF/CHI).
38 Ibid.
39 Melvin Lasky to Boris Shub, 6 November 1957 (CCF/CHI).

19 Achilles' Heel

1 *Final Report of the Church Committee*, 1976.
2 Tom Braden, 'I'm Glad the CIA is "Immoral"', *Saturday Evening Post*, 20 May 1967.
3 Richard Wollheim, telephone interview, December 1997.
4 Ibid.
5 Tom Braden, interview, Virginia, June 1994.

6 Dwight Macdonald, 'America! America!', *Dissent*, Fall 1958.
7 Irving Kristol, interview, Washington, June 1994.
8 Ibid.
9 Melvin Lasky, interview, London, August 1997.
10 Macdonald's attacks on the American labour leadership dated back to the 1930s, when he had dismissed them as 'sit-down-strikers-turned-bourgeois-pragmatists', completely absorbed into the capitalist system and its consumer culture. In his own journal, *Politics*, he had ridiculed Walter Reuther as a 'boyscout labor fakir'.
11 Dwight Macdonald, 'America! America!', *Dissent*, Fall 1958.
12 Irving Kristol, interview, Washington, June 1994.
13 Dwight Macdonald to 'Stephenirvingnicholasmike', 16 April 1958 (DM/STER).
14 Stephen Spender, interview, London, July 1994.
15 Diana Josselson, interview, Geneva, March 1997.
16 Michael Josselson to John Hunt, 27 May 1958 (MJ/HRC).
17 Josselson, though he liked Macdonald as a person, was always wary of his gadfly tendencies. When, in 1956, Spender revealed plans to commission a piece by Macdonald on the European Coal and Steel Community, Josselson warned Spender to give the idea 'a little more thought. [It] would be very sound if there was not the danger of his coming up with a completely destructive piece.' Spender subsequently dropped the idea.
18 Richard Helms, quoted in *Final Report of the Church Committee*, 1976.
19 Dwight Macdonald, 'America! America!', *Dissent*, Fall 1958.
20 Government officials had long known of the deplorable behaviour of American POWs, but had worked fastidiously to conceal the facts from a wider audience. On 23 April 1953, C. D. Jackson noted in his log file: 'Big telephone hassle today on indoctrinated Korean prisoners being returned. Got agreement from Dulles and [Walter Bedell] Smith that [it] should be advised that it was imperative for the Pentagon to see to it that all indoctrinated POWs should be kept in one place and . . . to release a story on this rather than let these indoctrinated jokers jump the gun on us.' C. D. Jackson Log Files (CDJ/DDE).
21 Irving Kristol, interview, Washington, June 1994. Kristol had evidently forgotten his letter to Macdonald in which he wrote: 'I do wish you would reconsider the Korean episode.' Irving Kristol to Dwight Macdonald, 19 May 1958 (DM/STER).
22 Michael Josselson to Irving Kristol, 31 October 1958 (MJ/HRC).
23 Thirty years later, Kristol acknowledged that American soldiers stationed in Germany after the Second World War would have behaved appallingly but for the rule of military law. Asked if he would have expressed such doubts at the time, he replied, 'No. Out of loyalty, I wouldn't. I'm American, I'm a patriot.'
24 Lee Williams, interview, Washington, June 1994.
25 William Colby, interview, Washington, June 1994.

26 Jason Epstein, interview, New York, June 1994.
27 Dwight Macdonald, quoted in Hugh Wilford, *The New York Intellectuals*.
28 Norman Birnbaum, open letter to the Congress for Cultural Freedom, 3 November 1958, printed in *Universities and Left Review*, December 1958 (MJ/HRC).
29 Ibid. Birnbaum found it hard to believe 'that the defence of the west is in good hands when these consist of those New York Jews whose devotion to America is matched only by their conspicuous want of all the American virtues, aided by that section of the British intelligentsia – a large one, I fear – recruited from those boys who weren't good at rugby at boarding school.' Quoted in Hugh Wilford, op.cit.
30 Michael Josselson to Dwight Macdonald, 28 April 1958 (DM/STER).
31 Dwight Macdonald, letter to the editor, *Universities and Left Review*, 16 December 1958 (DM/STER).
32 Dwight Macdonald, quoted in Michael Wreszin, *A Rebel in Defense of Tradition.*
33 Derwent May, *The Times*, 2 July 1996.
34 Peter Steinfels, *The Neoconservatives.*
35 Jason Epstein, 'The CIA and the Intellectuals', *New York Review of Books*, 20 April 1967.
36 Michael Josselson to Irving Kristol, 6 December 1954 (CCF/CHI).
37 Michael Josselson to Irving Kristol, 23 December 1954 (CCF/CHI).
38 Michael Josselson to Irving Kristol, 9 August 1956 (CCF/CHI).
39 Jason Epstein, 'The CIA and the Intellectuals', *New York Review of Books*, 20 April 1967.
40 Tom Braden, interview, Virginia, July 1996.
41 Christopher Montague Woodhouse, telephone interview, December 1997.
42 Michael Josselson to Stephen Spender, 28 July 1954 (CCF/CHI).
43 Nicolas Nabokov to Irving Kristol and Stephen Spender, 30 July 1954 (CCF/CHI). [My italics.]
44 Ibid.
45 Warren D. Manshel to Irving Kristol, 19 August 1954 (CCF/CHI).
46 Conor Cruise O'Brien, 'Journal de Combat', *New Statesman*, 20 December 1963.

20 Cultural NATO

1 Fredric Warburg to Melvin Lasky, 8 October 1958 (ENC/S&W/RU).
2 The correspondence relating to the Rothschild 'donations' to *Encounter* runs from June 1958 to October 1960 (ENC/ S&W/RU).
3 C. D. Jackson to Nelson Rockefeller, 18 November 1954 (CDJ/DDE).
4 Herbert F. Propps, American Embassy, London, 'Lack of Published Material on United Kingdom Willingness to Modify Sovereignty in the Interest of Collective Security', to State Department, 9 December 1952 (SD.CA/RG59/NARA).
5 Neil Berry, 'Encounter', *London Magazine*, February–March 1995.

6 As head of the Labour Party's International Department in 1948, Denis Healey helped to distribute IRD papers. He also sent regular reports on Communist activities in the European trade union movement to the department. Later, he acted as an intermediary in introducing useful East European émigrés to IRD officers (IRD/FO1110/PRO).
7 Melvin Lasky to John Hunt, 11 October 1960 (CCF/CHI).
8 Michael Josselson to Daniel Bell, 28 October 1964 (MJ/HRC).
9 Richard Wollheim, quoted in Neil Berry, op.cit.
10 Stuart Hampshire, interview, Oxford, December 1997. Similarly, Isaiah Berlin described Spender's role as lending *Encounter* its 'certificate of respectability to the English intelligentsia'.
11 Cass Canfield to Nicolas Nabokov, 23 December 1958 (CCF/CHI). The Soviets and the Americans tussled over many revered cultural figures during these years. Responding to what it called the 'spiritual vandalism' of the Soviets when they attempted, in 1952, to exploit the memories of Victor Hugo and Leonardo da Vinci as 'partisans of the Soviet way of life', the American Committee for Cultural Freedom claimed Hugo and da Vinci as apostles of free culture to whom the Soviet model would have been 'repugnant'.
12 Nicolas Nabokov, *Bagázh*.
13 Mary McCarthy to Hannah Arendt, 20 June 1960, quoted in Carol Brightman (ed.), *Between Friends*.
14 Ibid.
15 Congress for Cultural Freedom press release, 1 July 1959 (CCF/CHI).
16 Macauley was at the time still a case officer for the Congress, and unable to take up his responsibilities at Kenyon. When he accepted Ransom's offer, he had just received the Kenyon Fellowship in Fiction, and 'had already made arrangements to spend that year abroad'. By autumn 1959, he still hadn't returned to Kenyon, leaving Ransom feeling 'mightily fagged out' and obliged to keep 'the home fires burning about seven weeks after my retirement waiting for Robie'. John Crowe Ransom, quoted in Marian Janssen, *The Kenyon Review*.
17 Robie Macauley, quoted in Marian Janssen, ibid.
18 John Hunt, interview, Uzés, July 1997.
19 Quoted in Peter Coleman, *The Liberal Conspiracy*.
20 Leslie Fiedler, 'Partisan Review: Phoenix or Dodo?', *Perspectives*, Spring 1956.
21 Ibid.
22 Ibid.
23 Ibid.
24 Farfield Foundation Annual Report 1962--1963 (CCF/CHI).
25 C. D. Jackson to Cord Meyer, 1 November 1957 (CDJ/DDE).
26 C. D. Jackson to Daniel Bell and Allen Grover, 12 November 1957 (CDJ/DDE).
27 Quoted in Edward Lilly, Operations Coordinating Board, to Arthur Vogel, United States Information Service, 9 April 1956 (WHO/NSC/DDE).

28 Ibid.
29 Ibid.
30 William Phillips to Michael Josselson, 28 March 1958 (CCF/CHI).
31 Sidney Hook to Michael Josselson, 8 December 1959 (MJ/HRC).
32 Michael Josselson to Shepard Stone, 12 January 1968 (MJ/HRC).
33 Daniel Bell to John Leonard, editor, *Sunday Times Book Review*, 16 October 1972 (MJ/HRC).
34 Warburg appears to have been less than energetic in his role as *Partisan Review*'s English distributor, leading the publisher Roger Straus, in his 'official' capacity as an 'adviser' to *Partisan Review*, to wonder 'what the hell you guys are doing about the distribution business that I discussed with your confreres'. Roger Straus to Fredric Warburg, 30 June 1959 (ENC/S&W/RU).
35 Irving Kristol to Michael Josselson, 9 March 1960 (CCF/CHI).
36 William Phillips to Michael Josselson, 10 May 1961 (MJ/HRC).
37 William Phillips, 'The Liberal Conspiracy', *Partisan Review*, Winter 1990.
38 Melvin Lasky, interview, London, August 1997.
39 William Phillips, 'The Liberal Conspiracy', *Partisan Review*, Winter 1990.
40 Time Inc.-New Leader contract, 14 May 1964 (CDJ/DDE). This contract followed the same template as the one drawn up in 1953.
41 C. D. Jackson to Allen Dulles, 21 February 1956 (CDJ/DDE).
42 William Furth to Henry Luce and C. D. Jackson, 'Confidential memo re. New Leader', 24 July 1956 (CDJ/DDE). Delegated to organize the drive was veteran Cold Warrior Frank Lindsay, formerly Deputy Chief of the CIA's Office of Policy Coordination, then a Ford Foundation executive and now a management consultant at McKinsey and Company.
43 Herbert Luthy to Michael Josselson, 19 February 1962 (MJ/HRC).
44 In some cases, the route was via the *Paris Review*, the journal founded by George Plimpton and CIA agent Peter Matthiessen in 1953. Nelson Aldrich worked as an editorial assistant there, before moving on to the Congress. Frances FitzGerald, daughter of the CIA division chief in charge of operations against Castro, worked at the *Paris Review* in the summer of 1962, then, after holidaying with the Wisners in Tangier, graduated to a job in the Congress. George Plimpton later stressed that 'the *Paris Review* never received any monetary aid from the Congress or any other agency of that sort and nor was there any evident political or sociological slant to anything Peter [Matthiessen] as an editor picked for the magazine. Frankly, I must say that I personally would have welcomed funds from the Congress to help keep us afloat. *Encounter*, *Preuves*, and other magazines supported by the Congress were superb publications – with no strings attached in terms of what was published that I could ever see. What a shame that these days it's all seen in such an ugly light . . . reputations tainted by association with the least of it. I guess we were lucky.' George Plimpton, letter to the

author, 27 August 1997.

45 Kenneth Tynan, 'Congress for Cultural Freedom', *That Was The Week That Was*, 1962.

46 Mary Pinchot Meyer was found dead on the towpath of a Washington canal in 1964, murdered in an apparently motiveless attack. She had been romantically linked to John F. Kennedy, and recorded her affair in a diary which CIA dirty trickster James Jesus Angleton stole from her house (after having picked the lock) the day after her death.

47 Tom Braden, interview, Virginia, July 1996.

48 Arthur Schlesinger, interview, New York, August 1996.

49 John Thompson, telephone interview, August 1996.

50 Diana Josselson, interview, Geneva, March 1997.

51 Lee Williams, interview, Washington, July 1996.

52 Diana Josselson, letter to the author, 4 April 1997.

53 John Hunt, interview, Uzés, July 1997.

21 Caesar of Argentina

1 Elizabeth Bishop to Robert Lowell, 1 March 1961, quoted in Ian Hamilton, *Robert Lowell: A Biography.*

2 Frank Altschul to John F. Kennedy, 30 January 1961 (FA/COL).

3 Robert Lowell to Edmund Wilson, 31 May 1962, quoted in Ian Hamilton, op.cit.

4 Donald Jameson, interview, Washington, June 1994.

5 Walter Laqueur, 'Anti-Communism Abroad: A Memoir of the Congress for Cultural Freedom', *Partisan Review*, Spring 1996.

6 Jason Epstein, interview, New York, June 1994.

7 Hannah Arendt to Mary McCarthy, 22 August 1972, in Carol Brightman (ed.), *Between Friends.*

8 Ernst Robert Curtius, quoted in Stephen Spender, *Journals.* Michael Josselson once complained that it was hard to get a meeting with Spender, who was always 'off on some cruise or lecturing somewhere else'.

9 Elizabeth Bishop to Marianne Moore, 17 August 1954, quoted in Ian Hamilton, op.cit.

10 John Mander, quoted in Peter Coleman, *The Liberal Conspiracy.*

11 Lowell had an obsessive and morbid interest in Hitler. Jonathan Miller, who stayed with him in New York in the late 1950s, remembered discovering that within the (suspiciously fat) covers of Lowell's copy of *Les Fleurs du Mal* was hidden a well-thumbed copy of *Mein Kampf*.

12 Ian Hamilton, op.cit.

13 Mary McCarthy to Hannah Arendt, 28 September 1962, quoted in Carol Brightman, op.cit.

14 Ibid.

15 Keith Botsford, quoted in Ian Hamilton, op.cit.

16 Michael Josselson to John Thompson, 4 September 1963 (MJ/HRC).

17 Michael Josselson to John Thompson, 10 July 1964 (MJ/HRC).

18 Botsford's variety of jobs for the Congress included keeping an eye on

an outfit called Colombianum, a Jesuit-run organization which cultivated left-wing intellectuals in Latin America, run by a priest called Padre Arpa, whom Josselson described as 'a Jesuit Communist homosexual dressed in Dior'.

19 John Hunt to Keith Botsford, 29 March 1963 (CCF/CHI).
20 John Hunt to Irving Kristol, 23 December 1963 (CCF/CHI).
21 René Tavernier to John Hunt, 28 February 1963 (CCF/CHI).
22 John Hunt to René Tavernier, 1 July 1963 (CCF/CHI).
23 Ibid.
24 René Tavernier, 'Pablo Neruda', June 1963 (CCF/CHI).
25 Ibid.
26 John Hunt to René Tavernier, 1 July 1963 (CCF/CHI).
27 Diana Josselson, interview, Geneva, March 1997. The year 1963 also saw the CIA spend $3 million in an effort to influence Chile's general election, the equivalent of a dollar per vote, twice as much per voter as Goldwater and Johnson spent in the 1964 US presidential campaign. See Evan Thomas, *The Very Best Men*.
28 Salvador de Madariaga to Michael Josselson, 1 January 1963 (MJ/HRC).
29 Stuart Hampshire, interview, Oxford, December 1997.
30 Nicolas Nabokov, *Bagázh*.
31 Stuart Hampshire, interview, Oxford, December 1997.
32 Ibid.
33 Michael Josselson to Nicolas Nabokov, 10 December 1964 (NN/HRC).
34 Ibid.
35 Michael Josselson to Nicolas Nabokov, 29 June 1964 (MJ/HRC).
36 Ibid.
37 Donald Jameson, interview, Washington, June 1994.
38 William Hobby, quoted in *Newsweek*, 6 March 1967.
39 Editorial, *The Nation*, 14 September 1964.
40 Cord Meyer, *Facing Reality*.
41 Lee Williams, interview, Washington, June 1994.
42 Diana Josselson, interview, Geneva, March 1997.
43 Lawrence de Neufville, telephone interview, February 1997.
44 Nicolas Nabokov to Michael Josselson, 19 March 1977 (NN/HRC).
45 Natasha Spender, telephone interview, May 1997.
46 Diana Josselson, interview, Geneva, March 1997.
47 *Final Report of the Church Committee*, 1976.
48 Quoted in ibid.
49 Diana Josselson, interview, Geneva, March 1997.
50 Michael Josselson, quoted in Congress for Cultural Freedom, 'Minutes of the Executive Committee Meeting', London, October 1964 (CCF/CHI).

22 Pen Friends

1 Lewis Mumford, quoted in Stephen Whitfield, *The Culture of the Cold*

War.
2 Gwynne Nettler, quoted in Michael Wreszin, *A Rebel in Defense of Tradition*.
3 William Burroughs, quoted in Taylor D. Littleton and Maltby Sykes, *Advancing American Art*.
4 Sidney Hook to Michael Josselson, 20 April 1964 (MJ/HRC). Hook was wrong, surely about Norman Podhoretz, who scorned the Beat rebellion as 'the revolt of the spiritually underprivileged and the crippled of soul'.
5 Lee Williams, interview, Washington, July 1996.
6 Ibid.
7 Michael Josselson, 'The Story Behind the Congress for Cultural Freedom', unpublished manuscript (MJ/HRC).
8 Harry S. Truman, 1963, quoted in *New York Times*, 25 April 1966.
9 Arthur Koestler to Michael Josselson, 24 July 1963 (MJ/HRC).
10 Nicolas Nabokov to Richard Crossman, November 1956 (CCF/CHI).
11 Elizabeth Paterson, interview, London, July 1997.
12 David Carver to Jean de Beer, Secretary General, French PEN, 10 March 1965 (PEN/HRC).
13 Arthur Miller, *Timebends*.
14 Arthur Miller, quoted in Natalie Robins, *Alien Ink*. Miller learned in 1986, when he finally managed to get his FBI dossier, that the reason he had been chosen was just as he had speculated: he was considered to be acceptable to both East and West, the perfect PEN president at a time when the organization's very existence was in grave question.
15 Asturias was in fact Guatemalan. He was an outspoken enemy of the Congress, and specifically of Botsford, whose 'games' in South America he heartily disapproved of.
16 Michael Josselson to Manès Sperber, 24 November 1964 (MJ/HRC).
17 Lewis Galantière to Members of the Executive Board, American PEN, 26 April 1965 (PEN/HRC).
18 Tim Foote to Kenneth Donaldson, 28 April 1965 (CCF/CHI).
19 According to PEN's own report of the Bled conference, the CIA's Free Europe Committee, of which Lewis Galantière was an active member, also provided money. Most likely, it was Allen Dulles who organized the grant. Dulles, although retired from the CIA, continued to play an active part in the Cold War machinery he had erected. Furthermore, he was himself a newly elected member of PEN.
20 John Hunt to David Carver, 9 February 1966 (CCF/CHI).
21 John Hunt to Lewis Galantière, 4 March 1966 (CCF/CHI).
22 PEN report, June 1966 (PEN/HRC).
23 Conor Cruise O'Brien, 'Politics and the Writer', 19 May 1966, printed in Donald H. Akenson (ed.), *Conor: A Biography of Conor Cruise O'Brien* (Montreal: McGill-Queen's University Press, 1994).
24 Ibid.

23 Literary Bay of Pigs

1 Robert W. Merry, *Taking on the World.*
2 Ibid.
3 Jason Epstein, interview, New York, June 1994.
4 Robert W. Merry, op.cit.
5 William Fulbright, 'In Thrall to Fear', *The New Yorker*, 8 January 1972.
6 Ibid.
7 Norman Mailer, *Armies of the Night.*
8 *New York Times*, 27 and 29 April 1966.
9 Karl Miller, *Dark Horses: An Experience of Literary Journalism* (London: Picador, 1998).
10 Michael Josselson to Malcolm Muggeridge, 25 June 1965 (MJ/HRC).
11 Ibid. Natasha Spender was later perplexed by Josselson's reference to such financial arrangements, which she said were never put in place.
12 Melvin Lasky to Michael Josselson, undated (MJ/HRC).
13 Michael Josselson, 'Memo for the Record: Talks with Muggeridge, London 25 and 28 February 1964', 3 March 1964 (MJ/HRC).
14 Edward Shils to Michael Josselson, 2 November 1967 (MJ/HRC).
15 Michael Josselson to Robie Macauley, 30 December 1965 (MJ/HRC).
16 Ibid.
17 Frank Kermode, *Not Entitled: A Memoir* (London: Harper Collins, 1996).
18 Ibid.
19 Richard Wollheim remembered confronting both Lasky and Spender with the rumour several years previously, when he had been asked to join the board of *Encounter*. 'We discussed it over dinner at some club, and I asked for assurance on the score of the rumours then circulating about the CIA. Lasky said, "Nothing easier. You can inspect the accounts, and see for yourself." And Stephen looked hugely relieved, and said, "See, there's no truth to it." But then Lasky added, "Of course, we're not going to do that. Because why should we open the books to every Tom, Dick and Harry who falls for some crazy rumour?"' At this, Stephen's jaw dropped. He was silent throughout the rest of the meal. Wollheim declined the offer to join the board. Richard Wollheim, telephone interview, December 1997.
20 Edward Shils to Michael Josselson, 28 February 1964 (MJ/HRC).
21 Michael Josselson to Malcolm Muggeridge, 27 April 1964 (MJ/HRC).
22 Malcolm Muggeridge to Michael Josselson, 9 June 1964 (MJ/HRC).
23 Michael Josselson to James Perkins, 20 July 1966 (MJ/HRC).
24 Michael Josselson to Cecil King, 10 May 1964 (MJ/HRC).
25 Michael Josselson to Ulrich Biel, 14 May 1964 (MJ/HRC).
26 Diana Josselson, interview, Geneva, May 1996.
27 Tom Braden, 'What's Wrong with the CIA?', *Saturday Review*, 5 April 1975.
28 Jason Epstein, interview, New York, June 1994.
29 Ibid.
30 John Thompson to Stephen Spender, 25 May 1964 (MJ/HRC).

31 Julius Fleischmann to Stephen Spender, 16 September 1966 (MJ/HRC).
32 Carol Brightman, interview, New York, June 1994.
33 Natasha Spender, interview, Maussane, July 1997.
34 Melvin Lasky, Irving Kristol, Stephen Spender, letter to *New York Times*, 10 May 1966.
35 Michael Josselson to Stephen Spender, 2 October 1966 (MJ/HRC).
36 Stuart Hampshire, interview, Oxford, December 1997.
37 Kenneth Galbraith, George Kennan, Robert Oppenheimer, Arthur Schlesinger, Jr., letter to *New York Times*, 9 May 1966.
38 Dwight Macdonald to Michael Josselson, 30 March 1967 (MJ/HRC).
39 Angus Cameron, quoted in Natalie Robins, *Alien Ink*.
40 Cord Meyer to Arthur Schlesinger, 1 February 1954 (SCHLES/JFK).
41 Diana Josselson, interview, Geneva, May 1996.
42 Tom Braden, 'What's Wrong with the CIA?', *Saturday Review*, 5 April 1975. Cord Meyer epitomized this sanguine attitude. In his memoirs he wrote: 'American assistance to democratic political parties and institutions seemed essential if a free and pluralistic society was to survive in Western Europe. The fact that our assistance had to be kept secret did not disturb me. The European political and cultural leaders who solicited our aid in their unequal struggle with the Soviet-subsidized apparatus made it a condition that there be no publicity, since the Communist propaganda machine could exploit any overt evidence of official American support as proof that they were puppets of the American imperialists. Discretion and secrecy were required if our assistance was not to be self-defeating.' Cord Meyer, *Facing Reality*.

24 View from the Ramparts

1 *Final Report of the Church Committee*, 1976.
2 *Ramparts*, like all other 'subversive' literature, found its most avid readers at FBI headquarters. A 25-page FBI memo analysed the 'topics and themes' of the magazine, presumably in order to make plans to harass it. A CIA report attached to the memo concluded that most of the writers listed in the *Ramparts* glossary had 'most frequently and most vehemently expressed major Communist themes in their published articles'.
3 Peter Jessup to Walt Rostow, 4 April 1967 (NSF/LBJ).
4 Edgar Applewhite, quoted in Evan Thomas, *The Very Best Men*.
5 Andrew Kopkind, 'CIA: The Great Corrupter', *New Statesman*, 24 February 1967.
6 Michael Josselson to Isaiah Berlin, 8 April 1967 (MJ/HRC).
7 Isaiah Berlin to Michael Josselson, 16 April 1967 (MJ/HRC).
8 Frank Kermode, *Not Entitled*.
9 Ibid.
10 Natasha Spender, telephone interview, May 1997.
11 Ibid.
12 Eric Bentley to Stephen Spender, undated. I am grateful to Natasha Spender for showing me this letter.

13 Cecil King to Michael Josselson, 28 April 1967 (CCF/CHI).
14 Melvin Lasky to Isaiah Berlin, 13 April 1967. I am grateful to Dr Henry Hardy for showing me this letter.
15 Ibid.
16 Melvin Lasky, interview, London, August 1997.
17 Ibid.
18 Stuart Hampshire, interview, Oxford, December 1997.
19 Ben Whitaker, *The Foundations: An Anatomy of Philanthropy and Society* (London: Eyre & Methuen, 1974). According to Christopher Hitchens, Isaiah Berlin 'may have been designed, by origins and by temperament and by life experience, to become one of those witty and accomplished *valets du pouvoir* who adorn, and even raise the tone of, the better class of court. But there was something in him that recognized this as an ignoble and insufficient aspiration, and impelled him to resist it where he dared.' Christopher Hitchens, 'Moderation or Death', *London Review of Books*, 26 November 1998.
20 Melvin Lasky to Isaiah Berlin, 13 April 1967.
21 In its place, buried on the back page of *Encounter*'s July 1967 issue, came an announcement of editorial changes at the magazine. Signed by the trustees, there was no mention of the CIA.
22 Isaiah Berlin to Melvin Lasky, 18 April 1967 (MJ/HRC).
23 Michael Ignatieff, *Isaiah Berlin: A Life* (London: Chatto, 1998).
24 Christopher Hitchens, 'Moderation or Death', *London Review of Books*, 26 November 1998. The exact nature of Isaiah Berlin's relationship with British and American intelligence will probably never be known. The British spy Robert Bruce Lockhart recorded several wartime meetings with the young Berlin, when he was working for the British government in Washington. Lockhart was under the impression that Berlin was working for the Psychological Warfare Executive, but Berlin's coterie have vigorously contested this. It has also been alleged that during the war, Berlin featured on the Secret Intelligence Service's (SIS) secret list, the Special Register, which meant he had rendered service to SIS in the past and had agreed to join it during wartime. Freya Stark, Graham and Hugh Greene, and Malcolm Muggeridge, were also said to be on the list. As for American intelligence, it can be said, at least, that Berlin enjoyed an informal relationship with the CIA, whose members were not shy of approaching the philosopher for his support, as recalled by Stuart Hampshire and Lawrence de Neufville, who said that Berlin was told of the Agency's involvement in the Congress for Cultural Freedom. None of this means that Berlin colluded with covert operators, but it does suggest a degree of proximity which, in and of itself, may reward further research.
25 Natasha Spender, telephone interview, May 1997.
26 Ibid.
27 Natasha Spender, telephone interview, May 1997.
28 Michael Josselson to Stephen Spender, 26 April 1967 (MJ/HRC).
29 Ibid.

30 Ibid.
31 Stephen Spender, quoted in *New York Times*, 8 May 1967.
32 Stuart Hampshire, interview, Oxford, December 1997.
33 Malcolm Muggeridge to Stephen Spender, 22 May 1967 (MJ/HRC).
34 Natasha Spender, telephone interview, August 1997.
35 Stuart Hampshire, interview, Oxford, December 1997.

25 That Sinking Feeling
1 John Hunt, interview, Uzés, July 1997.
2 Manès Sperber, quoted by John Hunt, ibid.
3 John Hunt, ibid.
4 Diana Josselson, interview, Geneva, March 1997.
5 General Assembly of the Congress for Cultural Freedom, Press Release, 13 May 1967 (CCF/CHI).
6 John Hunt, interview, Uzés, July 1997.
7 Ibid.
8 Lawrence de Neufville, telephone interview, February 1997.
9 John Hunt, interview, Uzés, July 1997.
10 James McAuley, quoted in Peter Coleman, *The Liberal Conspiracy.*
11 Chantal Hunt, interview, Uzés, July 1997.
12 Diana Josselson, interview, Geneva, May 1996.
13 Nicolas Nabokov, July 1966, unidentifiable clipping (CCF/CHI).
14 Stuart Hampshire, interview, Oxford, December 1997.
15 Nicolas Nabokov, *Bagázh*.
16 Ibid.
17 Nicolas Nabokov to J. E. Slater, 11 August 1971 (MJ/HRC).
18 Diana Josselson to the Spenders, 18 May 1967 (MJ/HRC).
19 Diana Josselson to Stephen Spender, 26 May 1967 (MJ/HRC).
20 Natasha Spender to Michael Josselson, undated (MJ/HRC).
21 Tom Braden, 'I'm Glad the CIA is "Immoral"', *Saturday Evening Post*, 20 May 1967.
22 Ibid.
23 Ibid.
24 Tom Braden, interview, Virginia, August 1996.
25 Tom Braden, telephone interview, October 1997.
26 Lawrence de Neufville, telephone interview, April 1997.
27 John Hunt, interview, Uzés, July 1997.
28 John Thompson, telephone interview, August 1996.
29 Charlton Heston, quoted in Ian Hamilton, *Robert Lowell: A Biography.*
30 Carol Brightman, *Writing Dangerously.*
31 Eric Goldman, quoted in Ian Hamilton, op.cit.
32 Ibid.
33 Lyndon B. Johnson, quoted in Stephen Whitfield, *The Culture of the Cold War*.
34 James Burnham, 'Notes on the CIA Shambles', *National Review*, 21 March 1967.

35 Walt Rostow, telephone interview, July 1997.
36 Ibid.
37 Ibid.
38 Tom Braden, telephone interview, October 1997.
39 Joseph Alsop, quoted in Carl Bernstein, 'The CIA and the Media', *Rolling Stone*, 20 October 1977.
40 Joseph Alsop, quoted in Carl Bernstein, ibid.
41 Tom Braden, 'I'm Glad the CIA is "Immoral"', *Saturday Evening Post*, 20 May 1967.
42 Irving Kristol, interview, Washington, June 1994.
43 Stephen Spender, interview, London, July 1994.
44 Melvin Lasky, interview, London, July 1994.
45 Ibid.
46 Diana Josselson to Tom Braden, 5 May 1967 (MJ/HRC).
47 Lee Williams, interview, Washington, June 1994.
48 John Thompson to Michael Josselson, 7 July 1968 (MJ/HRC).
49 Diana Josselson, interview, Geneva, March 1997.
50 John Thompson to Michael Josselson, 28 October 1967 (MJ/HRC).
51 *Final Report of the Katzenbach Committee*, quoted in White House press release, 29 March 1967 (NSF/LBJ).
52 Desmond FitzGerald, quoted in *Final Report of the Church Committee*, 1976.
53 Editorial, *The Nation*, 10 April 1967.
54 *Final Report of the Church Committee*, 1976.

26 A Bad Bargain

1 Jayaprakash Narayan to Raymond Aron, 22 June 1967 (CCF/CHI).
2 K. K. Sinha to John Hunt, 1 June 1967 (CCF/CHI).
3 Diana Josselson, interview, Geneva, March 1997.
4 John Hunt, interview, Uzés, July 1997.
5 Michael Polanyi, quoted in Peter Coleman, *The Liberal Conspiracy*.
6 Yehudi Menuhin to Nicolas Nabokov, 14 May 1966 (CCF/CHI).
7 George Kennan to Shepard Stone, 9 November 1967 (CCF/CHI).
8 Andrew Kopkind, 'CIA: The Great Corrupter', *New Statesman*, 24 February 1967.
9 Jason Epstein, 'The CIA and the Intellectuals', *New York Review of Books*, 20 April 1967. Epstein's point about second-class passengers travelling first-class had earlier been made by Conor Cruise O'Brien, who argued that the success of operations like *Encounter* lay in attracting writers of high principle to provide a kind of cover for 'writers of moderate talents and adequate ambition' who were, in effect, a Trojan horse, engaged in 'sustained and consistent political activity in the interests . . . of the power structure in Washington'. Conor Cruise O'Brien, 'Politics and the Writer', 19 May 1966, printed in Donald H. Akenson (ed.), *Conor: A Biography of Conor Cruise O'Brien*.
10 Dwight Macdonald to Michael Josselson, 30 March 1967 (CCF/CHI).

11 Richard Elman, interview, New York, June 1994.
12 Stuart Hampshire, interview, Oxford, December 1997.
13 Lawrence de Neufville, telephone interview, February 1997.
14 Tom Braden, interview, Virginia, July 1996.
15 'Statement on the CIA', *Partisan Review*, vol.34/3, Summer 1967.
16 Tom Braden, interview, Virginia, July 1996.
17 James T. Farrell to Meyer Schapiro, 27 July 1942 (MS/COL).
18 John Hunt, interview, Uzés, July 1997.
19 Stephen Spender, interview, London, July 1994.
20 Diana Josselson, interview, Geneva, March 1997.
21 John Hunt, interview, Uzés, July 1997.
22 Edward Shils to Michael Josselson, 11 November 1975 (MJ/HRC).
23 Edward Shils to Michael Josselson, 11 December 1975 (MJ/HRC)
24 Sidney Hook to Michael Josselson, 23 September 1973 and 2 November 1972 (MJ/HRC).
25 Edward Shils to Michael Josselson, 10 February 1976 (MJ/HRC).
26 George Kennan to Nicolas Nabokov, 19 June 1959, quoted in Peter Coleman, *The Liberal Conspiracy*.
27 George Kennan, *Around the Cragged Hill: A Personal and Political Philosophy* (New York: Norton, 1993).
28 Harold Rosenberg, 'The Cold War', in *Discovering the Present: Three Decades in Art, Culture and Politics* (Chicago: University of Chicago Press, 1973).
29 Richard Elman, *The Aesthetics of the CIA* (unpublished manuscript).
30 Ibid.
31 Primo Levi, *The Drowned and the Saved* (London: Michael Joseph, 1988).
32 Aldous Huxley, *Eyeless in Gaza* (London: Chatto & Windus, 1936).

Epilogue
1 Stephen Spender to Nicolas Nabokov, 26 August 1970 (NN/HRC).
2 Isaiah Berlin to Nicolas Nabokov, 18 December 1972, 21 December 1976 (NN/HRC).
3 Stephen Spender, *Journals*.
4 Andrew Porter, *The New Yorker*, 17 February 1973.
5 David Chavchavadze, *Crowns and Trenchcoats: A Russian Prince in the CIA* (New York: Atlantic International, 1990).
6 John Hunt, interview, Uzés, July 1997.
7 John Hunt to Michael Josselson, undated, 1969 (MJ/HRC).
8 Arthur Koestler, 'A Guide to Political Neuroses', *Encounter*, November 1953.
9 Irving Kristol, quoted in Hugh Wilford, *The New York Intellectuals*.
10 Irving Kristol, *Neo-Conservatism: The Autobiography of an Idea, Selected Essays 1949–1995* (New York: The Free Press, 1995).
11 Irving Kristol, interview, Washington, June 1994.
12 Neil Berry, 'Encounter', *London Magazine*, February–March 1995.
13 Ferdinand Mount, quoted in ibid.

14 Frank Platt to Michael Josselson, 13 October 1976 (MJ/HRC).
15 Melvin Lasky, interview, London, July 1994.
16 Bernard Levin, *The Times*, 15 October 1992.
17 Ibid.
18 George Urban, *Radio Free Europe*.
19 Ibid.
20 Melvin Lasky, interview, London, August 1997.
21 Natasha Spender, interview, Maussane, July 1997.
22 Frank Platt to Michael Josselson, 11 November 1976 (MJ/HRC).
23 Frank Platt to Michael Josselson, 15 December 1977 (MJ/HRC).
24 Godfrey Hodgson, 'Superspook', *Sunday Times Magazine*, 15 June 1975.
25 Unidentifiable clipping, 23 February 1983 (MJ/HRC).
26 Michael Hofmann, *Guardian*, 23 January 1998.
27 William Buckley, quoted in Gore Vidal, *Palimpsest*.
28 Tom Braden, 'What's Wrong with the CIA?', *Saturday Review*, 5 April 1975.
29 Ibid.
30 Lawrence de Neufville, telephone interview, April 1997.
31 Mary McCarthy came to much the same conclusion about Nicola Chiaromonte. On 22 May 1969 she wrote: 'It may be that he's been deeply scarred or crippled, poor man, by the CIA experience and that whatever he writes or thinks is in some way a *justification* of it, over and over.' Chiaromonte died in a lift after giving a broadcast on Italian radio on 18 January 1972.
32 Mary McCarthy to Hannah Arendt, 18 June 1968, in Carol Brightman (ed.), *Between Friends*.
33 Stephen Spender, interview, London, July 1994.
34 Natasha Spender, telephone interview, Maussane, August 1997.
35 Melvin Lasky to Sidney Hook, quoted in Peter Coleman, *The Liberal Conspiracy*.
36 Diana Josselson, interview, Geneva, May 1996.
37 Ibid.
38 Diana Josselson, interview, Geneva, March 1997.
39 Edgar Applewhite, quoted by Richard Elman, interview, New York, June 1994.
40 Jason Epstein, interview, New York, June 1994.
41 Joseph Alsop to Isaiah Berlin, quoted in Robert Merry, *Taking on the World*.
42 Doug Henwood, 'Spooks in Blue', *Grand Street*, vol.7/3, Spring 1998.

Select Bibliography

Abel, Lionel, *The Intellectual Follies: A Memoir of the Literary Venture in New York and Paris* (New York: Norton, 1984)

Acheson, Dean, *Present at the Creation* (New York: Norton, 1969)

Agee, Philip, and Wolf, Louis, *Dirty Work: The CIA in Western Europe* (New York: Dorset Press, 1978)

Alsop, Susan Mary, *To Marietta from Paris, 1945–1960* (New York: Doubleday, 1975)

Barrett, Edward, *Truth is our Weapon* (NewYork: Funk & Wagnalls, 1953)

Beevor, Antony, and Cooper, Artemis, *Paris After the Liberation, 1944–1949* (London: Hamish Hamilton, 1994)

Bell, Daniel, *The End of Ideology: The Exhaustion of Political Ideas in the Fifties* (New York: The Free Press, 1960)

Bellow, Saul, *Humboldt's Gift* (New York: Viking, 1975)

Bernstein, Barton J. (ed.), *Toward a New Past: Dissenting Essays in American History* (New York: Knopf, 1967)

Bissell, Richard, *Reflections of a Cold Warrior: From Yalta to the Bay of Pigs* (New York: Yale University Press, 1996)

Bradlee, Ben, *A Good Life: Newspapering and Other Adventures* (London: Simon & Schuster, 1995)

Brands, H. W., *The Devil We Knew: America and the Cold War* (Oxford: Oxford University Press, 1993)

Brightman, Carol, *Writing Dangerously: Mary McCarthy and Her World* (New York: Lime Tree, 1993)

Brightman, Carol, (ed.), *Between Friends: The Correspondence of Hannah Arendt and Mary McCarthy, 1949–1975* (London: Secker & Warburg, 1995)

Broadwater, Jeff, *Eisenhower and the Anti-Communist Crusade* (Carolina: University of North Carolina Press, 1992)
Cesarani, David, *Arthur Koestler: The Homeless Mind* (London: William Heinemann, 1998)
Chambers, Whittaker, *Witness* (Chicago: Regnery, 1952)
Chiaromonte, Nicola, *The Worm of Consciousness and Other Essays* (New York: Harcourt, 1976)
Church, Senator Frank, (chairman), *Final Report of the Select Committee to Study Governmental Operations with Respect to Intelligence Activities* (Washington: United States Government Printing Office, 1976)
Cline, Ray, *Secrets, Spies and Scholars* (Washington: Acropolis, 1976)
Cockburn, Alexander, *Corruptions of Empire* (London: Verso, 1987)
Cohn, Roy, *McCarthy* (New York: New American Library, 1968)
Colby, William, *Honorable Men: My Life in the CIA* (New York: Simon & Schuster, 1978)
Coleman, Peter, *The Liberal Conspiracy: The Congress for Cultural Freedom and the Struggle for the Mind of Postwar Europe* (New York: The Free Press, 1989)
Cook, Blanche Wiesen, *The Declassjfied Eisenhower: A Divided Legacy of Peace and Political Warfare* (New York: Doubleday, 1981)
Corson, William, *The Armies of Ignorance: The Rise of the American Intelligence Empire* (New York: Dial Press, 1997)
Crockatt, Richard, *The Fifty Years War: The United States and the Soviet Union in World Politics, 1941–1991* (London: Routledge, 1995)
Crossman, Richard (ed.), *The God That Failed: Six Studies in Communism* (London: Hamish Hamilton, 1950)
Diggins, John Patrick, *Up From Communism: Conservative Odysseys in American Intellectual History* (New York: Harper & Row, 1975)
Fromkin, David, *In the Time of the Americans* (New York: Vintage, 1995)
Goodman, Celia (ed.), *Living with Koestler: Mamaine Koestler's Letters, 1945–1951* (London: Weidenfeld & Nicolson, 1985)
Green, Fitzhugh, *American Propaganda Abroad* (New York: Hippocrene, 1988)
Gremion, Pierre, *L'Intelligence et L'Anticommunisme: Le Congrès pour la liberté de la culture à Paris, 1950–1975* (Paris: Fayard, 1995)
Grose, Peter, *Gentleman Spy: The Life of Allen Dulles* (London: André Deutsch, 1995)
Guilbaut, Serge, *How New York Stole the Idea of Modern Art: Abstract Expressionism, Freedom and the Cold War* (Chicago: University of Chicago Press, 1983)
Hamilton, Iain, *Koestler: A Biography* (London: Secker & Warburg, 1982)
Hamilton, Ian, *Robert Lowell: A Biography* (New York: Random House, 1982)
Hersh, Burton, *The Old Boys: The American Elite and the Origins of the CIA* (New York: Scribner's, 1992)

Hixson, Walter L., *George F. Kennan: Cold War Iconoclast* (New York: Columbia University Press, 1989)

Hixson, Walter L., *Parting the Curtain: Propaganda, Culture and the Cold War, 1945–1961* (New York: Macmillan, 1997)

Hofstadter, Richard, *The Paranoid Style in American Politics and Other Essays* (New York: Knopf, 1965)

Hook, Sidney, *Out of Step: An Unquiet Life in the Twentieth Century* (New York: Harper & Row, 1987)

Howe, Irving, *A Margin of Hope: An Intellectual Autobiography* (London: Secker & Warburg, 1983)

Hunt, E. Howard, *Undercover: Memoirs of an American Secret Agent* (California: Berkeley Publishing Corporation, 1974)

Kahn, E. J., *Jock: The Life And Times of John Hay Whitney* (New York: Doubleday, 1981)

Keller, William H., *The Liberals and J. Edgar Hoover: The Rise and Fall of a Domestic Intelligence State* (New Jersey: Princeton University Press, 1989)

Kennan, George F., *Around the Cragged Hill: A Personal and Political Philosophy* (New York: Norton, 1993)

Kermode, Frank, *Not Entitled: A Memoir* (London: Harper Collins, 1996)

Kirkpatrick, Lyman, *The Real CIA* (New York: Macmillan, 1968)

Kissinger, Henry, *The White House Years* (London: Weidenfeld & Nicolson, 1979)

Kobler, John, *Henry Luce: His Time, Life and Fortune* (London: Macdonald, 1968)

Koestler, Arthur, *The Stranger on the Square* (London: Hutchinson, 1984)

Kristol, Irving, *Neo-Conservatism: The Autobiography of an Idea, Selected Essays,* 1949–1995 (New York: The Free Press, 1995)

Larson, Deborah, *The Origins of Containment: A Psychological Explanation* (New Jersey: Princeton University Press, 1985)

Lasch, Christopher, *The Agony of the American Left* (New York: Vintage, 1969)

Littleton, Taylor D., and Sykes, Maltby, *Advancing American Art: Painting, Politics and Cultural Confrontation* (Alabama: University of Alabama Press, 1989)

Lottman, Herbert, *The Left Bank: Writers, Artists, and Politics from the Popular Front to the Cold War (*Boston: Houghton Mifflin, 1982)

Lynes, Russell, *Good Old Modern: An Intimate Portrait of the Museum of Modern Art* (New York: Atheneum, 1973)

McAuliffe, Mary S., *Crisis on the Left: Cold War Politics and American Liberals* (Amherst: University of Massachusetts Press, 1978)

Mailer, Norman, *Armies of the Night* (New York: New American Library, 1968)

Mailer, Norman, *Harlot's Ghost* (London: Michael Joseph, 1991)

Malraux, André, *Anti-Memoirs* (New York: Random House, 1968)

Mangold, Tom, *Cold Warrior: James Jesus Angleton, The CIA's Master Spy Hunter* (New York: Simon & Schuster, 1991)

Mayne, Richard, *Postwar: The Dawn of Today's Europe* (London: Thames & Hudson, 1983)

Merry, Robert W., *Taking on the World: Joseph and Stewart Alsop, Guardians of the American Century* (New York: Viking Penguin, 1996)

Meyer, Cord, *Facing Reality: From World Federalism to the CIA* (Maryland: University Press of America, 1980)

Michaud, Yves (ed.), *Voire, Ne Pas Voire, Faux Voire* (Nimes: Editions Jacqueline Chambon, 1993)

Miller, Arthur, *Timebends: A Life* (London: Methuen, 1987)

Miscamble, Wilson D., *George F. Kennan and the Making of American Foreign Policy* (New Jersey: Princeton University Press, 1992)

Muggeridge, Malcolm, *Chronicles of Wasted Time: The Infernal Grove* (London: Collins, 1973)

Muggeridge, Malcolm, *Like It Was* (London: Collins, 1981)

Nabokov, Nicolas, *Old Friends and New Music* (London: Hamish Hamilton, 1951)

Nabokov, Nicolas, *Bagázh: Memoirs of a Russian Cosmopolitan* (London: Secker & Warburg, 1975)

O'Toole, G. J. A., *Honorable Treachery: A History of U. S. Intelligence, Espionage, and Covert Action from the American Revolution to the CIA* (New York: Atlantic Monthly Press, 1991)

Pells, Richard H., *Not Like Us: How Europeans Have Loved, Hated, and Transformed American Culture Since World War II* (New York: Basic Books, 1997)

Philby, Kim, *My Silent War* (New York: Grove Press, 1968)

Phillips, William, *A Partisan View: Five Decades of the Literary Life* (New York: Stein, 1983)

Podhoretz, Norman, *Making It* (London: Jonathan Cape, 1968)

Podhoretz, Norman, *The Bloody Crossroads: Where Literature and Politics Meet* (New York: Simon & Schuster, 1986)

Ranelagh, John, *The Agency: The Rise and Decline of the CIA* (New York: Simon & Schuster, 1987)

Reich, Carey, *The Life of Nelson Rockefeller, 1908–1958* (New York: Doubleday, 1997)

Riebling, Mark, *Wedge: The Secret War Between the FBI and CIA* (New York: Knopf, 1994)

Robins, Natalie, *Alien Ink: The FBI's War on Freedom of Expression* (New York: William Morrow, 1992)

Ross, Andrew, *No Respect: Intellectuals and Popular Culture* (London: Routledge, 1989)

Ross, Thomas B., and Wise, David, *The Espionage Establishment* (New York: Random House, 1967)

Salisbury, Harrison E., *Without Fear or Favor: The New York Times and its Times* (New York: Ballantine, 1980)

Schlesinger, Arthur M. Jr., *The Vital Center: A Fighting Faith* (Cambridge: Riverside Press, 1949)

Schlesinger, Arthur M. Jr., *A Thousand Days: John F. Kennedy in the White House* (London: André Deutsch, 1965)
Silone, Ignazio, *Emergency Exit* (London: Gollancz, 1969)
Sinfield, Alan, *Literature, Politics and Culture in Postwar Britain* (London: Athlone Press, 1997)
Smith, R. Harris, *OSS: The Secret History of America's First Central Intelligence Agency* (Los Angeles: University of California Press, 1972)
Sonnenberg, Ben, *Lost Property: Confessions of a Bad Boy* (London: Faber & Faber, 1991)
Spender, Stephen, *Engaged in Writing* (New York: Farrar Straus, 1958)
Spender, Stephen, (ed. John Goldsmith) *Journals, 1939–1983* (London: Faber & Faber, 1985)
Steinfels, Peter, *The Neoconservatives: The Men Who Are Changing American Politics* (New York: Simon & Schuster, 1979)
Stone I. F., (ed. Neil Middleton) *The 'I. F. Stone's Weekly' Reader* (New York: Random House, 1973)
Thomas, Evan, *The Very Best Men: The Early Years of the CIA* (New York: Touchstone, 1996)
Truman, Harry S., *Memoirs: Year of Decisions* (New York: Doubleday, 1955)
Urban, George, *Radio Free Europe and the Pursuit of Democracy: My War Within the Cold War* (New York: Yale University Press, 1997)
Vansittart, Peter, *In the Fifties* (London: John Murray, 1995)
Vidal, Gore, *Palimpsest* (London: André Deutsch, 1995)
Walker, Martin, *The Cold War and the Making of the Modern World* (London: Fourth Estate, 1993)
Wallock, Leonard (ed.), *New York, 1940–1965* (New York: Rizzoli, 1988)
Warner, Michael (ed.), *Cold War Records: The CIA under Harry Truman* (Washington: Center for the Study of Intelligence, CIA, 1994)
Whitfield, Stephen J., *The Culture of the Cold War* (Baltimore: Johns Hopkins University Press, 1991)
Wilford, Hugh, *The New York Intellectuals* (Manchester: Manchester University Press, 1995)
Winks, Robin, *Cloak and Gown: Scholars in the Secret War, 1939–1961* (New York: William Morrow, 1987)
Woods, Randall B., *Fulbright: A Biography* (Cambridge: Cambridge University Press, 1995)
Woodhouse, Christopher Montague, *Something Ventured* (London: Granada, 1982)
Wreszin, Michael, *A Rebel in Defense of Tradition: The Life and Politics of Dwight Macdonald* (New York: Basic Books, 1994)
Young, Kenneth (ed.), *The Diaries of Robert Bruce Lockhart, 1939–1965* (London: Macmillan, 1980)

Index